SURVEY
OF
SOCIAL
SCIENCE

SURVEY
OF
SOCIAL
SCIENCE

PSYCHOLOGY SERIES

Volume 2
467-946

Career and Personal Testing—Emotion and Stress

Edited by

FRANK N. MAGILL

Consulting Editor

JACLYN RODRIGUEZ
OCCIDENTAL COLLEGE

SALEM PRESS

Pasadena, California   Englewood Cliffs, New Jersey

Library of Congress Cataloging-in-Publication Data
Survey of social science. Psychology series/edited by
Frank N. Magill; consulting editor, Jaclyn Rodriguez.
   p. cm.
   Includes bibliographical references and index.
   1. Psychology—Encyclopedias. I. Magill, Frank Nor-
then, 1907-   . II. Rodriguez, Jaclyn.
BF31.S79   1993   93-34708
150'.3—dc20   CIP
ISBN 0-89356-732-9 (set)
ISBN 0-89356-734-5 (volume 2)

Second Printing

PRINTED IN THE UNITED STATES OF AMERICA

CONTENTS

page

Career and Personnel Testing 467
Career Selection, Development, and Change 474
Case-Study Methodologies 481
Causal Attribution 487
Central and Peripheral Nervous Systems, The 494
Cerebral Cortex, The 500
Child Abuse 507
Circadian Rhythms 514
Clinical Depression 521
Clinical Interviewing, Testing, and Observation 527
Codependent Personality, The 534
Cognitive Ability: Gender Differences 540
Cognitive Behavior Therapy 546
Cognitive Development Theory: Piaget 553
Cognitive Dissonance Theory 560
Cognitive Maps 566
Cognitive Psychology: An Overview 572
Cognitive Social Learning: Walter Mischel 580
Cognitive Therapy 586
Collective Unconscious, The 592
College Entrance Examinations 598
Color Blindness 606
Color Vision 611
Community Psychology 618
Complex Experimental Designs: Interactions 625
Computer Models of Cognition 631
Concept Formation 637
Conditioning: Higher-Order 643
Conditioning: Pavlovian versus Instrumental 649
Consciousness, Functions of 656
Consciousness, Levels of 663
Consumer Psychology: Decisions 669
Contact Hypothesis, The 675
Conversion, Hypochondriasis, Somatization, and Somatoform Pain 682
Cooperation, Competition, and Negotiation 689
Cooperative Learning 695

PSYCHOLOGY

page

Coping: Social Support 700
Coping Strategies: An Overview 706
Coping with Cancer 711
Couples Therapy 718
Creativity: Assessing Special Talents 726
Creativity and Intelligence 731
Crowd Behavior 737
Crowding 744

Data Description: Descriptive Statistics 751
Data Description: Inferential Statistics 757
Death and Dying: Theoretical Perspectives 763
Decision Making as a Cognitive Process 769
Defense Reactions: Species-Specific 775
Dementia, Alzheimer's Disease, and Parkinson's Disease 783
Depression: Theoretical Explanations 789
Depth Perception 796
Development: Theoretical Issues 804
Development of Emotion 810
Developmental Methodologies 817
Dissolution 824
Dream Analysis 830
Dreams 836
Drive Theory 843
Dyslexia 849

Educational Psychology 855
Ego Defense Mechanisms 860
Ego Psychology: Erik Erikson 867
Electroconvulsive Therapy 874
Emotion: Cognitive and Physiological Interaction 881
Emotion: Cultural Variations 887
Emotion: Definition and Assessment 893
Emotion, Functions of 900
Emotion: Mind-Body Processes 907
Emotion: Neurophysiology and Neuroanatomy 914
Emotion and Attribution Theory 921
Emotion and Health 928
Emotion and Learning Theory 934
Emotion and Stress 941

Alphabetical List XXIII
Category List XXXI

SURVEY
OF
SOCIAL
SCIENCE

CAREER AND PERSONNEL TESTING

Type of psychology: Personality
Fields of study: Ability tests; intelligence assessment; personality assessment

The popularity of career and personnel testing reflects the trend toward the utilization of interest surveys, ability and aptitude tests, and personality tests for the systematic development of personal careers.

Principal terms

ABILITY: a person's capacity or potential to perform or achieve mentally

ACHIEVEMENT: a person's state of knowledge or skill, based on previous learning

INTELLIGENCE: a person's abilities in a wide range of areas, which are thought to reflect the person's learning potential

INTEREST INVENTORY: a type of test designed to determine areas of interest and enjoyment, often for the purpose of matching a person with a career

PSYCHOLOGICAL TEST: a device, instrument, or test assessing or measuring the characteristics of human beings

PSYCHOMETRICS: the field that seeks to measure mental abilities, usually via developing and evaluating tests for that purpose

Overview

Psychologists have developed more than thirty-five hundred testing devices for assessing human capabilities. The groups of tests which have been utilized most frequently for career and personnel purposes have been tests which measure interests, abilities and aptitudes, and personality.

Inventories that survey interest patterns are useful in providing indications of the areas in which individuals might work. Research by E. K. Strong, Jr., has shown that people in the same line of work also tend to have similar hobbies, like the same types of books and magazines, and prefer the same types of entertainment.

Further psychological research by J. L. Holland concluded that most occupations can be grouped into six general themes. He termed these the realistic, investigative, artistic, social, enterprising, and conventional interest themes. Holland's six vocational themes reflect certain employment preferences: "realistic," favoring technical and outdoor activities such as mechanical, agricultural, and nature jobs; "investigative," interested in the natural sciences, medicine, and the process of investigation; "artistic," favoring self-expression and dramatics such as the musical, literary, and graphic art occupations; "social," reflecting an interest in helping others, as in teaching and social service; "enterprising," interested in persuasion and political power, as in management, sales, politics, and other areas of leadership; and "conventional," including enjoyment of procedures and organization such as office practices, clerical, and quantitative interest areas.

Tests that measure ability include intelligence tests, achievement tests, and aptitude tests. Intelligence tests purport to measure objectively a person's potential to learn, independent of prior learning experiences. Attempting such objective measurement is a highly complex task; whether it can truly be achieved is open to debate. The very concept of "intelligence," in fact, has been controversial from its inception. The two most highly developed tests of individual intelligence are the fourth revision of the Stanford-Binet (1984), a scale originally developed in 1916, and the Wechsler Adult Intelligence Scale-Revised (1981), a version of a scale originally developed in 1939.

Achievement tests are designed to measure how much a person has learned of specific material to which he or she has been previously exposed. Aptitude tests measure a personal ability or quality (such as musical or mechanical aptitude) in order to predict some future performance. For example, the military would like to be able to predict the likelihood that a given candidate for pilot training will successfully complete the complicated and expensive course of training. Flying a plane requires good physical coordination and a good sense of mechanical matters, among other things. Therefore, candidates for flight training are given a battery of aptitude tests, which include tests of mechanical aptitude and eye-hand coordination, in order to estimate later performance in flight training. People who score poorly on such aptitude tests tend to fail pilot training.

Psychologists recognize that it is important to understand a person's interests and abilities—and their personality tendencies—if a thorough appraisal of career potentials is to be made. Personality tests measure dispositions, traits, or tendencies to behave in a typical manner. Personality tests are described as either objective (a structured test) or subjective (a projective personality test). Objective tests are structured by providing a statement and then requiring two or more alternative responses, such as in true-or-false questions (an example of such an approach is the Woodsworth Personal Data Sheet). In contrast, projective personality tests ask open-ended questions or provide ambiguous stimuli which require spontaneous responses (as in the Rorschach inkblot test). The two types of personality test evoke different information about the respondent.

The development of objective personality tests was greatly improved when studies showed that personality tests did not have to rely completely upon face validity, or the apparent accuracy of each test question. Through empirical research, the accuracy of a question can be tied to the likelihood of a question being associated with certain behavior. Consequently, it does not matter whether a person answers the question "I am not aggressive" as either "true" or "false." What does matter is whether that question is accurately associated with aggressive or nonaggressive behavior for a significant number of people who answer it in a particular way. This approach is referred to as criterion keying: The items in a test are accurately associated with certain types of behavior regardless of the face validity of each question.

Applications

In order for people to enter careers that will be satisfactory for them, it is desirable to make an effort to match their personal interests with the day-to-day activities of the careers they will eventually choose. Interest inventories are one method of helping people make career choices that compare their interest patterns with the activities of persons in the occupation they hope to enter. There are more than eighty interest inventories in use.

The Strong Vocational Interest Blank (SVIB) was developed by E. K. Strong, Jr., a psychologist. It matches the interests of a person to the interests and values of a criterion group of employed people who were happy in the careers they have chosen. This procedure is an example of criterion keying. Strong revised the SVIB in 1966, using 399 items to relate to fifty-four occupations for men and a separate form for thirty-two occupations for women. The reliability of this test to measure interests is quite good, and validity studies indicate that the SVIB is effective in predicting job satisfaction.

The Strong-Campbell Interest Inventory (SCII) was developed by psychologist D. T. Campbell as a revision of the SVIB. In this test, items for both the men's and women's forms were merged into a single scale, reducing the likelihood of sex bias, a complaint made about the SVIB. Campbell developed a theoretical explanation of why certain types of people like working in certain fields; he based it on Holland's theory of vocational choice. Holland postulated that interests are an expression of personality and that people can be classified into one or more of six categories according to their interests and personality. Campbell concluded that the six personality factors in Holland's theory were quite similar to the patterns of interest that had emerged from many years of research on the SVIB. Therefore, Holland's theory became incorporated into the SCII. The SCII places individuals into one of the six Holland categories, or groupings of occupations, with each group represented by a national sample. There are now dozens of occupational scales with both male and female normative comparisons.

The Kuder Occupational Interest Survey (KOIS) ranks second to the SCII in popularity; it was first developed in 1939. This survey also examines the similarity between the respondent's interests and the interests of people employed in different occupations. It can provide direction in the selection of a college major. Studies on the predictive validity of the KOIS indicate that about half of a selected group of adults who had been given an early version of the inventory when they were in high school were working in fields that the inventory suggested they enter. The continuing development of this measure suggests that it may be quite useful for guidance decisions for high school and college students.

The Minnesota Vocational Interest Inventory (MVII) is designed for men who are not oriented toward college and emphasizes skilled and semiskilled trades. It is modeled after the SVIB and has nine basic interest areas, including mechanical interests, electronics, and food service, as well as twenty-one specific occupational scales, including those of plumber, carpenter, and truck driver. The Career Assessment Inventory (CAI) was developed by Charles B. Johansson and is designed for the 80 percent of Americans who have fewer than four years of post-secondary education. It is written at the sixth-grade reading level. The CAI provides information similar to that yielded by the SCII, including the six occupational theme scales and basic interest areas, such as carpentry, business, and food service. Studies of this inventory suggest that it has desirable psychometric properties and that people who find employment in occupations for which they have expressed strong interests tend to remain at their jobs and find more satisfaction with work than do those who have low scores for those occupations.

Several ability and aptitude tests have been used in making decisions concerning employment, placement, and promotion. The Wonderlic Personnel Test (WPT) was based on the Otis Self-Administering Tests of Mental Ability. The WPT is a quick (twelve-minute) test of mental ability in adults. Normative data are available for more than fifty thousand adults between twenty and seventy-five years of age. The Revised Minnesota Paper Form Board Tests (RMPFBT) is a revision of a study in the measurement of mechanical ability. The RMPFBT is a twenty-minute speed test consisting of sixty-four two-dimensional diagrams cut into separate parts. The test seems to measure those aspects of mechanical ability requiring the capacity to visualize and manipulate objects in space. It appears to be related to general intelligence.

Personality tests were developed in an effort to gain greater understanding about how an individual is likely to behave. As tests have been improved, specific traits and characteristics have been associated with career development, traits such as leadership propensities or control of impulses. Several personality tests have been used in career and personality development. The Minnesota Multiphasic Personality Inventory II (MMPI-2) is the 1989 version of a scale developed in 1943 by S. R. Hathaway and J. C. McKinley. The test was designed to distinguish normal from abnormal behavior. It was derived from a pool of one thousand items selected from a wide variety of sources. It remains the premier objective personality test. The California Psychological Inventory (CPI) was developed by Harrison Gough in 1957 and was revised in 1987. Although about a third of the 462 items on the CPI are identical to items on the MMPI, it is regarded as a good measure for assessing normal individuals for interpersonal effectiveness and internal controls.

The 16 Personality Factor Questionnaire (16PF) was developed by Raymond Cattell in 1949 and was revised in 1970. Considerable effort has been expended to provide a psychometrically sound instrument to measure personality, and it remains an exemplary illustration of the factor-analytic approach to measuring personality traits. The Personality Research Form (PRF) was developed by Douglas Jackson in 1967. It was based on Henry Murray's theory of needs. The PRF includes two validity scales and twenty multidimensional scales of personality traits. It has been favorably reviewed for its psychometric rigor and is useful in relating personality tendencies to strengths and weaknesses in working within a corporate or employment setting.

Context

The previously described instruments are examples of tests that are frequently used for career and personnel assessment. The range of psychological assessment procedures includes not only standardized ability tests, interest surveys, personality inventories and projective instruments, and diagnostic and evaluative devices, but also performance tests, biographical data forms, scored application blanks, interviews, experience requirement summaries, appraisals of job performance, and estimates of advancement potential. All these devices are used, and they are explicitly intended to aid employers who make hiring decisions in order to choose, select, develop, evaluate, and promote personnel. Donald N. Bersoff notes that the critical element in the use of any psychological test for career and employment purposes is that employers must use psychometrically sound and job-relevant selection devices. Such tests must be scientifically reliable (appropriate, meaningful, or useful for the inferences drawn from them) and valid (they must measure what they claim to measure).

Each of the test procedures previously described would be used for different purposes. Ability tests can be used to determine whether a person has the potential ability to learn a certain job or specific skills. Ability tests are used for positions that do not have a minimum educational prerequisite (such as high school, college, or professional degree). They are also used to select already employed individuals for challenging new work assignments and for promotion to a more demanding employment level. The United States Supreme Court has held that the appropriate use of "professionally developed ability tests" is an acceptable employment practice; however, the employer must demonstrate a relationship between the relevance of the selection test procedure to job qualification. This requirement is to assure that the ability test provides a fair basis for selection and is nondiscriminatory. The goal of Title VII of the Civil Rights Act of 1964 was to eliminate discrimination in employment based on race, color, religion, sex, or national origin in all of its forms. The use of a selection procedure or test must meet this standard.

Interest tests have been developed to identify a relationship between the activities a person enjoys and the activities of a certain occupation. For example, a salesperson should enjoy meeting people and persuading others to accept his or her viewpoint. An interest inventory can validly link a person's preferences and interests with associated social activities and can thereby identify sales potential. Interest inventories are frequently given when an employer seeks more information that could lead to a good match between a prospective employee and a job's requirements. Interest inventories typically survey a person's interests in leisure or sports activities, types of friends, school subjects, and preferred reading material.

Personality, or behavior traits, can be identified by test inventories and related to requisite employment activities. Once again, these personality dimensions must be demonstrated to be job-related and must be assessed reliably from a performance appraisal of the specific position to be filled. For example, behavior traits such as "drive" or "dependability" could be validated for use in promoting individuals to supervisory bank teller positions if demonstrated to be job-related and assessed reliably from a performance appraisal.

The use of psychological tests has grown immensely since the mid-twentieth century. Increased public awareness, the proliferation of different tests, and the use of computer technology with tests indicate that continually improving career and personnel tests will emerge. Yet these developments should proceed only if testing can be conducted while protecting the human rights of consumers—including their right *not* to be tested and their right to know test scores, interpretation, and how test-based decisions will affect their lives. Psychological testing must also be nondiscriminatory and must protect the person's right to privacy. Psychologists are ethically and legally bound to maintain the confidentiality of their clients.

Making a selection among the many published psychological tests is a skill requiring experienced psychologists. In personnel selection, the psychologist must determine if the use of a psychological test will improve the selection process above what is referred to as the base rate, or the probability of an individual succeeding at a job without any selection procedure. Consequently, the use of a test must be based on its contributing something beyond chance alone. This requirement necessitates that a test be reasonably valid and reliable, in that it consistently tests what it was designed to test. Consequently, the use of a test is only justified when it can contribute to the greater likelihood of a successful decision than would be expected by existing base rates.

Existing theories of career selection have related career choices to personal preferences, developmental stages, and the type of relationship a person has had with his or her family during childhood. More extensive research will continue to assess other relationships between one's psychological makeup and successful career selection. This positive beginning should eventually result in more innovative, more objective, and more valid psychological tests that will greatly enhance future career and personnel selection.

Bibliography

American Psychological Association. "Ethical Principles of Psychologists." *American Psychologist* 36 (1981): 633-638. Documents psychologists' ethical responsibilities concerning human rights, particularly pertaining to the right of privacy.

Bersoff, Donald N., Laurel P. Malson, and Donald B. Verrilli. "In the Supreme Court of the United States: *Clara Watson v. Fort Worth Bank and Trust*." *American Psychologist* 43 (December, 1988): 1019-1028. This brief was submitted to inform the Supreme Court of the state of current scientific thought regarding validation of personnel assessment devices.

Buros, Oscar Krisen, ed. *Vocational Tests and Reviews*. Highland Park, N.J.: Gryphon Press, 1975. This source consists of the vocational sections selected from *The Seventh Mental Measurements Yearbook* and *Tests in Print II*, and it contains comprehensive reviews of testing materials and comments on the validity and reliability of vocational tests.

Campbell, D. T. *Manual for the Strong-Campbell Interest Inventory.* Stanford, Calif.: Stanford University Press, 1977. This manual describes the SCII instrument and its uses. It represents a progression in the use of interest inventories, because it is merged with Holland's vocational themes.

Committee to Develop Standards for Educational and Psychological Testing. *Standards for Educational and Psychological Testing.* Washington, D.C.: American Psychological Association, 1985. This document provides a framework for the evaluation and validation of testing and other assessment devices.

Darley, John M., Samuel Glucksberg, and Ronald A. Kinchia. *Psychology.* 5th ed. Englewood Cliffs, N.J.: Prentice-Hall, 1991. This introductory psychology text discusses the relationship between an aptitude test and the prediction of future performance, providing examples to aid in differentiating aptitude from achievement.

Holland, J. L. *Manual for the Vocational Preference Inventory.* Palo Alto, Calif.: Consulting Psychologists Press, 1975. Describes Holland's vocational classification system, including work activities, general training requirements, and occupational rewards. Holland's theory of vocational choice is basic to a number of tests used for career development.

Kaplan, Robert M., and Dennis P. Saccuzzo. *Psychological Testing: Principles, Applications, and Issues.* Pacific Grove, Calif.: Brooks/Cole, 1989. Reviews major issues in psychological testing in a broad range of psychological tests, including selection and personnel decision and tests for choosing careers.

Sweetland, R. C., and D. J. Keyser. *Tests: A Comprehensive Reference for Assessment in Psychology, Education, and Business.* Kansas City, Mo.: Test Corporation of America, 1983. A compendium describing more than thirty-five hundred psychological tests and their uses in psychology, education, and business.

Robert A. Hock

Cross-References

Ability Testing: Individual and Group, 1; Ability Tests: Uses and Misuses, 27; Career Selection, Development, and Change, 474; Interest Inventories, 1349; Testing: Historical Perspectives, 2540.

CAREER SELECTION, DEVELOPMENT, AND CHANGE

Type of psychology: Developmental psychology
Field of study: Adulthood

The world of work is changing at an increasingly rapid rate, and many working people find themselves forced to find new careers. By examining their personal interests and needs as well as the possibilities for financial rewards in a given field, those people selecting or changing careers can be more certain of career satisfaction and success.

> *Principal terms*
> CAREER: one's advancement or achievement in a particular lifework, vocation, or profession
> *DICTIONARY OF OCCUPATIONAL TITLES* (DOT): a job classification system developed by the U.S. Department of Labor
> DIFFERENTIAL APTITUDE TEST (DAT): a paper-and-pencil test of various aptitudes, such as reasoning and spatial ability
> GENERAL APTITUDE TEST BATTERY (GATB): a test of eleven aptitudes often given to workers, especially those taking a job for the first time
> *OCCUPATIONAL OUTLOOK HANDBOOK, THE* (OOH): a handbook, revised every two years by the U.S. Department of Labor, that provides current, accurate, detailed occupational information
> RE-CAREERING: the process of acquiring marketable skills and then changing careers in response to one's own needs or to the changing needs of society
> REDIRECTION: the process of repackaging one's own skills with little or no reeducation in order to change to an entirely different career

Overview

A review of theories prominent in the psychology of career development points to their profound preoccupation with the desire that adults have to work. The average adult spends more time working than any other waking activity. Satisfaction in one's career has been found empirically to have the potential for fulfilling the needs of productivity, competition, altruism, functioning as a team member, independence, and others. It is one's most important avenue for fulfilling one's dreams. These studies also reveal that both personality traits and career interest change over time.

The reasons behind these changes are varied. A major career theory early in the history of career development is summarized by Elizabeth B. Yost and M. Anne Corbishley in *Career Counseling* (1987). The trait factor model of the early 1900's matched personal traits to job characteristics. Its assumptions included the idea that people possess stable and persistent traits, among them interests, talents, and intelligence. A related assumption was that jobs could be differentiated in terms of their needs for differing skills and levels of ability. The person with certain traits could therefore be matched with certain job needs, and the individual would be satisfied forever. Psychological tests became prominently used to measure traits and to classify occupations. Later theorists found this theory to be too mechanistic. Today's world is less stable and more complex, and change is more dynamic. Mechanistic rigidity had to give way to flexibility and adaptability.

Another theory described by Yost and Corbishley is the three-stage developmental theory; the three stages are fantasy, tentative, and realistic. During the fantasy stage, which lasts to about age eleven, career interests are unrealistic. During the tentative stage, which takes over until about age seventeen, interests, capacity, values, and transition are developing. The realistic stage that follows is marked by exploration, crystallization, and specification.

An important contributor to the psychology of careers is Donald Super (1957), who states that career choice develops in five stages: growth (birth through age fourteen), exploration (ages fourteen through twenty-five), establishment (ages twenty-five through forty-five), maintenance (ages forty-five through sixty-five), and decline or disengagement (age sixty-six and older). He refers to this long-term developmental process as the "maxicycle." He emphasizes, however, that as a person matures and becomes more realistic, the possibility of career change may direct the individual into a new job or even an entirely new career. The maxicycle may then be repeated from the beginning in a very brief time frame, in "minicycle" form. In changing to the new position, the person experiences growth, exploration, establishment, and maintenance, but focused into days, weeks, or months rather than years.

Perhaps the most impressive and invasive work on the psychology of career development is that of John Holland, which he has revised several times since 1959. His highly respected and useful research resulted in the development of six categories of persons and jobs: realistic (R), investigative (I), artistic (A), social (S), enterprising (E), and conventional (C). Holland assumes that most people have a dominant type and one or two other types of some, but lesser, importance. To reflect this belief, he has arranged the typology in a clockwise order around a hexagon, as R, I, A, S, E, C. He argues empirically that some types are more compatible and some are less compatible. The closer they are on the hexagon, the more compatible. RS, AC, and IE would be examples of those, therefore, who would have lower job achievement and satisfaction and less stable choices and personalities.

Holland leaves room, however, for change to occur. His basic belief is that personality type stabilizes between ages eighteen and thirty, and is thereafter rather difficult to change. The more consistent a person's type is, the more he or she will find a satisfactory job environment. Consistent types, he says, will more often deal with job dissatisfaction by altering the work environment rather than by changing their own personalities. The need for a new repertoire of skills, new training, and new credentialing when making drastic career changes tends to reduce the amount of personality change people need to make. In other words, changing careers, even when this requires reeducation, may be preferred over major changes in personality.

This brief review of major psychological theories of career development points to their recognition of the possibility, and even probability, of change. The change may be in job choices within a particular career, a process of redirecting one's energies with a minimum of reschooling. The change may, however, involve more than re-direction and move into major re-careering. The reasons for this are especially important to psychologists who believe that career satisfaction invades all facets of psychological wholeness. They believe that adults work for more than a livelihood. Otherwise, the rich would cease working, and those who could work in high-paying jobs would not choose work that pays much less than their earnable income.

Super studied numerous lists of human motives, of reasons for working, and of reasons people like or dislike jobs. These lists emanated from the research of a variety of students of human nature. His comparison and reduction of these lists pointed to three major needs for which satisfaction is sought: human relations, the work itself, and livelihood. Human relations involve the recognition of the person, independence, fair treatment, and status. Work means that the activity is interesting, is an opportunity for self-expression, and has a satisfying physical work situation and conditions. Livelihood refers to adequate earnings and security. Although Super's work is a product of the 1950's, it is updated in *Career Development in Organizations*, by Douglas Hall (1986). During the long interim, Super's work had persisted in healthy fashion. He added self-realization to his motives for working. This is a common term used in humanistic psychology to emphasize the integration or wholeness that Carl Rogers believed achievable by the "fully functioning individual." Work has the potential for satisfying personal determinants that are psychological and biological, as well as satisfying situational determinants that are historical and socioeconomic.

From Super's lengthy and impressive research, the implications for change in careers are noteworthy. The frustration of any one or a combination of the three basic satisfactions sought in work (human relations, interesting work, and livelihood) that hinders one from achieving self-realization is sufficient motivation for change. To say it negatively, one may feel frustration in human relations because of lack of recognition, or feel frustration in work because it fails to maintain interest, or feel frustration in livelihood because of insufficient earnings and security.

Super's work dealing with change based on changing interests and circumstances includes the idea that new careers emerge with changing times. The worker today has literally hundreds of new careers to consider. S. Norman Feingold and Norma Reno Miller underscore this idea in their book *Emerging Careers: New Occupations for the Year 2000 and Beyond* (1983). Their finding was that scores of occupations are disappearing from the American scene and that scores of new jobs are being added that did not exist twenty-five years ago. Their research consisted of an intensive survey of the professional literature on new emerging careers. Computerized search techniques were used to gain information on emerging careers. Feingold and Miller also wrote to more than five hundred colleges and universities to learn what new courses were being offered related to emerging careers. Their text implies again that today's worker should be educated to respond to the possibility of re-careering and encouraged to keep options open.

Applications

The idea of changing careers, or re-careering, is a contemporary phenomenon. The 1980's produced hundreds of books centering on the topic. A valuable asset to the reader of such books is a strong statistical message: that people change jobs or careers several times during their tenure of work. Dick Goldberg suggests that the average rate of career change is three to four times in a lifetime, and that some 40 million out of 100 million people in the work force are in some stage of career transition at any given time. One example of such a change might be a bank employee who moves to another bank but fills an entirely new position, with new requirements and job description (redirection). The job has actually changed. Redirection does not refer to the person who works in a bank and then moves to another bank in an identical position but at a higher salary. Career change includes both redirection and re-careering. Another, more drastic example is of a social worker with a master's degree in social work. After nine years of listening to people's problems, she is burned out; she also finds the pay increments to be insufficient for her needs. She begins exploring the possibility of combining her interest in helping people with her developing interest in investment counseling (re-careering).

Goldberg's book *Careers Without Reschooling* (1985) recounts an interview with Richard Nelson Bolles, author of *What Color Is Your Parachute?* This book was published in 1971 and has been revised and published many times since. Bolles regularly emphasizes that career change and job hunting are repetitive activities for every working person in the United States. According to statistics, the average job in the United States, at least when people are new to the job market, lasts about 3.6 years. "The average person," says Bolles, "will have ten employers in his or her lifetime and three distinct careers." This concurs with the Goldberg findings. A very practical suggestion, then, emerges from his writing: "You must learn how to conduct the search, for you are surely going to have to do it again!"

Career change requires methodology. The hundreds of self-help books on career change provide valuable advice as to the methods of re-careering. They provide practical ideas on reassessing one's assets and liabilities, narrowing one's choices, determining one's career preferences, packaging or repackaging oneself, writing a résumé, and negotiating the career change. Such changes are often more easily executed within the same career. The individual, for example, who is in business marketing may, as he or she matures, decide that management rather than marketing would provide a greater challenge and better financial security. Such a career may not require reschooling as much as it does repackaging oneself as to interests, strengths, and desired goals. An actor who tires of acting may find new zest in the areas of directing and producing.

One example of career change (a true example) involves a man who began as a high school science teacher. He later became a high school principal. Still later, he changed to become a consultant for the Ohio State Board of Education. Finally, he took an administrative position at a liberal arts college. In his case, re-careering involved additional graduate work and the meeting of certain requirements. He took all the suggested steps of reassessment, determining preferences, repackaging himself, interviewing, and negotiating the change. The necessary further education and meeting of certification requirements along the way seemed to be well worth the effort to him. The result is a professional educator with an obviously renewed zest for life because of the challenges of attaining desired goals. He was very excited about his original job as high school science teacher, but as he changed, so did his interests and goals.

The literature, whether in the form of vocational guidance and career development, in the psychology of career counseling, or in the practical paperbacks that teach concrete steps to be taken, all carries the same theme: Career change is a skill that can be learned and applied with considerable success. Individuals are told in various ways, whether by noted theorists such as Super and Holland, or by practitioners such as Goldberg, Feingold, and others, to identify and communicate transferable skills or to acquire new job-related skills.

Ronald L. Krannich states that re-careering is a process that means repeatedly acquiring marketable skills and then changing careers in response to one's own interests, needs, and goals, as well as in response to the changing needs and opportunities of a technological society. The standard careering process of the 1960's, 1970's, and 1980's must be modified with three new careering emphases: acquiring new marketable skills through retraining on a regular basis, changing careers several times during a lifetime, and utilizing more efficient communication networks for finding employment. Sigmund Freud said very little about adulthood except that it is the time "to love and to work." A large segment of life's satisfaction derives from satisfaction in one's work, and will, no doubt, carry over to enhance the chances of one's ability to love.

Context

The psychology of careers has long made room for the need for redirection and re-careering. Yost and Corbishley report that Frank Parson's 1909 book entitled *Choosing a Vocation*, in which he outlined his theory of matching personal traits to job characteristics, was the inspiration for subsequent research. This early model continued to be reformulated until it spawned the U.S. Employment Service's *Dictionary of Occupational Titles* in 1972. The DOT is a compendium of tens of thousands of jobs, each one described and classified. It is continually being updated. Psychological testing also became a focus as the result of Parson's trait factor theory. Two exceptionally well-known aptitude tests were developed: the General Aptitude Test Battery (GATB) and the Differential Aptitude Test (DAT). They are still in substantial use.

It took until the 1950's, when the heyday of trait factor theory was over, for researchers to become involved in more sophisticated research methodology and more elaborate ways of viewing human behavior. This resulted in a greater complexity of career theory that allowed for the possibility, even probability, of development and growth in interests, abilities, personality traits, and sociological conditions. Emphasis began to be placed on the dynamic character of the psychological aspects of career development throughout the life span.

This theoretical emphasis on the complexity of human change had to be coupled with the societal phenomenon of dynamic technological change. More and greater changes are to come, as attested by the suggestions of researchers that future workers should be equipped with skills, flexibility, and the keen notion that their options should remain open throughout life. One cannot now fathom what new occupations will arise in the future. *The Occupational Outlook Handbook*, published by the U.S. Department of Labor, is unable to update itself fast enough. Newspapers are publishing career supplements in which advertisements appear for specialists in robot behavior, ocean hotel management, and subquarkian physics. The horizon, say Feingold and Miller, is filled with possibilities.

Bibliography

Feingold, S. Norman, and Norma Reno Miller. *Emerging Careers: New Occupations for the Year 2000 and Beyond.* Garret Park, Md.: Garret Park Press, 1983. The authors study the professional literature on new, emerging careers and survey more than five hundred colleges and universities as to new courses being offered related to emerging careers. Shows the astounding changes in career choices, with hundreds being eliminated and new ones being added. A futuristic view of emerging career fields and the need to adapt to them.

Goldberg, Dick. *Careers Without Reschooling.* New York: Continuum, 1985. Goldberg is a talk-show host on public radio and television whose consummate interests are business and psychology. At least fifty of these shows addressed the issues of careers and the job hunt. Some were interviews related to the job hunt, which make up the first seven chapters. The remaining fourteen are informational interviews on specific careers.

Hall, Douglas T. *Career Development in Organizations.* San Francisco: Jossey-Bass, 1986. Hall studies the ability of organizations to adjust to the times. He believes that with massive corporate restructuring, demographic changes, value and cultural changes, and turbulent external environments, organizations will find their own adaptabilities increasingly dependent upon the capacity of their employees to change and adapt.

Krannich, Ronald L. *Re-Careering in Turbulent Times: Skills and Strategies for Success in Today's Job Market.* Manassas, Va.: Impact Publications, 1983. Discusses the methodology of career development, redirection, and re-careering. Recognizes the need to prepare for an uncertain future by linking work skills to job-search skills. Outlines how one can re-career in the decades ahead.

Lewis, Adele Beatrice, and Bill Lewis, with Steve Radlaver. *How to Choose, Change, Advance Your Career.* Woodbury, N.Y.: Barron's Educational Series, 1983. A book about choosing, changing, and advancing one's career from the vantage point of professionals in the marketplace. The authors emphasize the importance of the career person's participation in the process. Their thirty years in the personnel business affords excellent help to the individual seeking a sense of direction.

Super, Donald Edwin. *The Psychology of Careers: An Introduction to Vocational Development.* New York: Harper, 1957. After Frank Parson's early text *Choosing a Vocation* (1909), this is possibly the next volume incorporating the results of significant research of psychologists, sociologists, and economists during the interim of almost fifty years. It served as a catalyst to launch the important work of researchers in recent decades. Super is still active in structuring his developmental theory to meet contemporary needs.

Yost, Elizabeth B., and M. Anne Corbishley. *Career Counseling.* San Francisco: Jossey-Bass, 1987. Takes a unique approach to clients' career problems by integrating traditional career counseling techniques with psychological methods of assessment and intervention. Has value for clinical psychologists, social workers, counselors, counseling psychologists, and career specialists such as service counselors, vocational counselors, and college placement counselors.

F. Wayne Reno

Cross-References

Ability Testing: Individual and Group, 1; Generativity in Adulthood: Erikson, 1075; Human Resource Training and Development, 1197; Interest Inventories, 1349; Midlife Crises, 1575; Self-Actualization, 2168.

CASE-STUDY METHODOLOGIES

Type of psychology: Psychological methodologies
Field of study: Descriptive methodologies

Case-study methodologies represent a number of techniques to study people, events, or other phenomena within their natural setting. Typically, case studies involve careful observations made over an extended period of time in situations where it is not possible to control the behaviors under observation. The results and interpretation of the data are recorded in narrative form.

Principal terms

EXTRANEOUS VARIABLE: a variable that has a detrimental effect on a research study, making it difficult to determine if the result is attributable to the variable under study or to some unknown variable not controlled for

INDEPENDENT VARIABLE: the variable in a study that is under the control of the experimenter

LABORATORY RESEARCH: a method in which phenomena are studied in an artificial setting with rigorous procedures in place to control for outside influences

NATURALISTIC OBSERVATION: a method in which, in contrast to laboratory research, subjects are studied in the environment in which they live, with little or no intervention on the part of the researcher

QUASI-EXPERIMENTS: experiments that do not allow subjects to be assigned randomly to treatment conditions

SYSTEMATIC INTERVIEWING TECHNIQUES: structured interviews that ask a series of questions that have been prepared in advance

Overview

According to social scientist Robert Yin, case-study research is one of the most frequently misunderstood methods used to study behaviors. Yin, in his book *Case Study Research: Design and Methods* (1984), points out that misconceptions have come about because of the limited coverage that case-study research receives in the average textbook on research methods. In addition, most texts typically confuse the case-study approach with either "qualitative" research methods or specific types of quasi-experimental designs.

Yin defines a case study as a method for studying contemporary phenomena within their natural setting, particularly when the behaviors under study cannot be manipulated or brought under the experimenter's control. Thus, unlike studies which are performed in the well-controlled—and sometimes rigidly sterile—confines of the laboratory, the case-study approach collects data where the behaviors occur in real-life contexts. Although behavior in natural settings can lead to a mother lode of data waiting to be mined, it also has its drawbacks. One who uses this approach needs to recognize that the lack of control over extraneous variables can compound the difficulty associated with trying to identify the underlying variables that are causing the behaviors. Despite this concern, case-study methods are seen as valuable research tools to help unlock the mysteries behind events and behaviors. The approach has been used by psychologists, sociologists, political scientists, anthropologists, historians, and economists, to name a few.

Yin suggests that case-study designs vary according to two distinct dimensions. One dimension accounts for the number of "cases" being studied: the presence of either single- or multiple-case designs. A second dimension allows for case studies to be either "holistic"—that is, studying the entire unit of analysis as a single global entity—or "embedded," which allows multiple units of analysis to be studied for the purpose of understanding their interworkings. According to Yin, this classification system leaves the researcher with a choice among four different design types: single-case (holistic) design, single-case (embedded) design, multiple-case (holistic) design, and multiple-case (embedded) design. Choosing among these designs involves the kinds of research questions the researcher is attempting to answer.

Case-study methods are initiated for a variety of reasons, one of which is to serve as a vehicle for exploratory research. As a new research area begins to develop, the initial uncharted territory is sometimes best studied (particularly when the research questions are ill-defined) using a case-study method to determine which direction should be first pursued. This method has therefore been commonly misperceived as being able to contribute only in a limited exploratory capacity; however, the case study can, and should, be used not only to help focus initial research questions but also to describe and explain behaviors. As Yin makes clear, both "how" and "why" questions can be answered by this approach.

A frequently asked question is "When should one choose to conduct a case study, rather than an experiment?" To answer this question, it is important to understand some basic differences between case-study methods and experimental designs. Experiments allow the researcher to manipulate the independent variables that are being studied. For example, in a study to determine the most effective treatment approach for severe depression, subjects could be randomly assigned to one of three different treatments. The "treatments" are under the control of the researcher in the sense that he or she determines who will get a particular treatment and exactly what it will be. On the other hand, case studies are used in situations where the variables cannot be manipulated. Experiments typically, although not exclusively, are performed in a laboratory setting; case studies, as previously described, occur in naturalistic settings. Experiments are characterized as having rigorous control over extraneous variables; case studies typically lack such control. Experiments place a heavy emphasis on data-analysis procedures that use numbers and statistical testing; case studies emphasize direct observation and systematic interviewing techniques, and they are communicated in a narrative form. Experiments are designed so that they can be repeated; case studies, by their very nature, can be quite difficult to repeat.

Applications

One of Yin's dimensions for classifying case studies involves single-case versus multiple-case studies. In some instances, only a single-case study is necessary or at times even possible; this is true when a unique "case" comes along that presents a valuable source of information. For example, a social scientist wanting to explore the emotional impact of a national tragedy on elementary school children might choose to study the *Challenger* space shuttle disaster, or perhaps the Chernobyl nuclear catastrophe, as a single-case study.

Eminent Russian psychologist Aleksandr Luria, in his book *The Mind of a Mnemonist: A Little Book About a Vast Memory* (1968), has, in a most engaging style, described a single-case (holistic) study. The case involved a man by the name of Shereshevskii (identified in the book as subject "S"), who possessed an extraordinary memory. Luria began to observe "S" systematically in the 1920's after "S" had asked him to test his memory. Luria was so astounded by the man's ability to study information for brief periods of time and then repeat it back to him without an error that he continued to observe and test "S" over the next thirty years. Luria was convinced that this man possessed one of the best memories ever studied.

Because of the nature of the phenomenon—an unusually vast memory—and the fact that this man was capable of performing memory feats never before witnessed, a single-case (holistic) study was begun. Studying rare phenomena, as in this instance, it is not possible to find the number of subjects typically required for an experiment; thus, the case-study approach presents the best alternative. Over the next thirty years, Luria carefully documented the results of literally hundreds of memory feats. In some instances, Luria presented "S" with a list of words to memorize and asked him to recall them immediately. At other times, without any forewarning, Luria asked "S" to recall words from lists given more than fifteen years before. In most of these instances, "S" recalled the list with only a few errors. Luria commented on much more than the results of these memory tests; he also carefully studied the personality of "S." Luria wanted to understand him as a whole person, not only as a person with a great memory. Closely involved with the subject, Luria personally gave the instructions and collected the data. Whereas the data from the memory tasks provided some degree of objectivity to the study, most of the information came from the subjective observations and judgments made by Luria himself. The study was reported in a book-length narrative.

A second example involves a case study that was part of a larger group of studies known as the Hawthorne studies, conducted at the Western Electric Company, near Chicago, in the 1920's. One particular study called the Bank Wiring Observation Room Study was initiated to study the informal social interactions that occur within a small group of employees in an industrial plant.

A group of fourteen men was moved to a self-contained work room which simulated the plant environment; a psychologist was assigned to observe the behavior of the group. No manipulation of any variables occurred; there was only passive observation of the employees' behavior. As might be expected, the presence of the observer discouraged many of the men from behaving as they normally would if someone was not present. The men were suspicious that the psychologist would "inform" their supervisor of any behaviors that were not allowed on the job. After a month passed, however, the men became accustomed to the observer and started to behave as they normally did inside the plant. (Notice the length of time needed to begin observing "normal" work behaviors; most experiments would have been terminated long before the natural behaviors surfaced.) The informal social interactions of this group were studied for a total of eight months.

This study was significant in that it exposed a number of interesting social phenomena that occur in a small division at work. One finding was that informal rules were inherent in the group and were strictly enforced by the group. For example, workers always reported that the same number of units were assembled for that day, regardless of how many were actually assembled. This unspoken rule came from a group that had considerable influence over the rate of production. Also, despite a company policy that forbade an employee to perform a job he was not trained to do, men frequently rotated job assignments to counteract the boredom that typically occurs in this kind of work.

This study was important because it systematically observed the naturally occurring relationships and informal social interactions that exist in an industrial setting. The case-study method proved to be very effective in bringing this information to light.

Context

Long before the scientific community began to formalize the procedures associated with conducting case studies, scientists, philosophers, and physicians were studying phenomena in their natural contexts by making direct observations and later systematically recording them. Although it is difficult to pinpoint how long this method has been used, there are a number of documented cases dating back to the second and third centuries. Galen, a leading physician in Rome in the second century, spent five years as a surgeon to the gladiators in the Roman Colosseum. During this time, Galen made painstaking observations correlating head injuries the gladiators received with the loss of intellectual abilities. In a sense, this was a prelude to the case study of today.

Psychology has been heavily influenced by the natural sciences. Since the natural sciences gave birth to the scientific method, with its emphasis on experiments, it is not surprising that psychology adopted a modified version of the scientific method that could be applied to the study of people and other organisms. It soon became apparent, however, that not all situations lend themselves to study by an experiment. Thus, it was important for alternative methodologies to be developed and used. The case study is an outgrowth of this quest to find alternative methods for studying complex phenomena.

Over the years, case-study methods have not received universal acceptance. This can even be seen in the limited exposure they receive in social science textbooks on methodology; it is not uncommon for a textbook to devote only a few paragraphs to this method. This is attributable in part to some of the criticisms raised about case-study designs. One criticism is that this technique lends itself to distortions or falsifications while the data are being collected. Since direct observation may rely on subjective criteria, in many instances based on general impressions, it is alleged that this data should not be trusted. A second criticism is that it is difficult to draw cause-and-effect conclusions because of the lack of control measures to rule out alternative rival hypotheses. Third, the issue of generalization is important after the data have been collected and interpreted. There will often be a question regarding the population to which the results can be applied.

During the second half of the twentieth century, there appears to have been a resurgence of the use of case-study methods. Part of the impetus for this change came from a reactionary movement against the more traditional methods that collect data in "artificial" settings. The case-study method plays a significant role in studying behavior in real-life situations, under a set of circumstances that would make it impossible to use any other alternative.

Bibliography

Baker, Therese L. *Doing Social Research.* New York: McGraw-Hill, 1988. Gives the reader a general introduction to field research, observational studies, data collection methods, survey research, and sampling techniques, as well as other topics which will help the reader evaluate "good" field experiments from those that are poorly constructed.

Berg, Bruce L. *Qualitative Research Methods for the Social Sciences.* Boston: Allyn & Bacon, 1989. Discusses a field strategy used by anthropologists and sociologists to study groups of people; in addition, discusses the ethical issues that arise while conducting research. Looks at the dangers of covert research and provides the guidelines established by the National Research Act.

Griffin, John H. *Black Like Me.* New York: American Library, 1962. This excellent book is a narrative of the author's experiences traveling around the United States observing how people react to him after he takes on the appearance of a black man. This monumental field study, which contributed to an understanding of social prejudice, provides the reader with an excellent example of the significance of and need for conducting field research.

Luria, Aleksandr R. *The Mind of a Mnemonist: A Little Book About a Vast Memory.* Pickering, Ontario: Basic Books, 1968. A fascinating case study written by the "father of neuropsychology," who was one of the most significant Russian psychologists. Directed toward a general (nonspecialist) audience. The case study focuses on his subject Shereshevskii (subject "S") and the extraordinary memory he possessed.

McCall, G. J., and J. L. Simmons. *Issues in Participant Observation: A Text and Reader.* Reading, Mass.: Addison-Wesley, 1969. This text provides an in-depth discussion on how to get inside a group as a participant observer and conduct observational field research. Also provides a number of examples from the literature to help understand how this research is conducted.

Singleton, Royce, Jr., et al. *Approaches to Social Research.* New York: Oxford University Press, 1988. This well-written text discusses various aspects of field experimentation such as how to select a research setting and gather information, how to get into the field, and when a field study should be adopted. The chapter on "experimentation" can be used to contrast "true" experiments with field studies.

Yin, Robert K. *Case Study Research: Design and Methods.* Beverly Hills, Calif.: Sage Publications, 1984. This rare volume is perhaps the finest single source on case-study methods in print. Yin shows the reader exactly how to design, conduct, analyze, and even write up a case study. Approximately forty examples of case studies are cited with brief explanations. The book is written for an audience that is not highly technical.

Bryan C. Auday

Cross-References

Archival Data, 293; Data Description: Descriptive Statistics, 751; Sources of Experimental Bias, 1006; Experimentation: Ethics and Subject Rights, 1013; Field Experimentation, 1031; Hypothesis Development and Testing, 1248; Observational Methods in Psychology, 1700; Survey Research: Questionnaires and Interviews, 2507.

CAUSAL ATTRIBUTION

Type of psychology: Social psychology
Field of study: Social perception and cognition

Causal attribution concerns the explanations people offer about the causes of their own or other people's behavior. It has contributed to an understanding of emotions as well as people's reactions to failures, and the reasons that they give for those failures.

Principal terms

CONSENSUS INFORMATION: information concerning other people's responses to an object

CONSISTENCY INFORMATION: information concerning a person's response to an object over time

DISTINCTIVENESS INFORMATION: information concerning a person's response to a series of objects

EXTERNAL CAUSES: causes that are within a person's environment or surroundings

INTERNAL CAUSES: causes that are within a person, such as personality traits and abilities

STABLE CAUSES: causes that do not change over time

UNSTABLE CAUSES: causes that fluctuate across time

Overview

When one hears about the behavior of a serial killer, sees a person shoplift, or is rejected by a friend, one may ask oneself why such behaviors or events occurred. Identifying the causes of behaviors may help people learn what kind of behaviors they can expect. People speculate about the causes of positive behaviors as well. For example, one may want to understand why a great athlete has set a number of records, why someone got a job promotion, or why one did well on a test.

The study of causal attribution focuses on the explanations people make about the causes of their own or other people's behavior. Researchers in this area have gone beyond identifying attributions to trying to understand why people make the attributions they do. Research on causal attribution has contributed to an understanding of many other aspects of people's behavior (attitude change, interpersonal attraction, and helping behavior).

Causal attributions are classified in a number of ways. One of the most important classifications is whether the attribution is made to an internal state or an external force. Internal attributions are made to causes internal to the person, such as individual personality characteristics, moods, abilities, and so on. For example, one may attribute the cause of a shoplifter's behavior to kleptomania, of a friend's rejection to one's own lack of social skills, and of an athlete's records to his or her ability. External attributions, on the other hand, are made to causes external to the person, characteristics of the environment. Thus, the shoplifter's behavior might be perceived to be caused by a broken home, a friend's rejection by some characteristic of the friend (for example, lack of loyalty), and the athlete's record to the efforts of the team.

Causal attributions are also classified according to their stability. Stable causes are relatively permanent and are consistent across time. Unstable causes fluctuate across time. Internal and external causes may be either stable or unstable. For example, a person's ability is usually considered internal and stable, whereas effort is internal and unstable. Laws are external and stable, whereas the weather is external and unstable. If shoplifting is attributed to kleptomania, the cause is internal and stable, whereas if shoplifting is attributed to a dare from someone, the cause is external and unstable.

Bernard Weiner includes a third classification for causal attributions, that of controllability/uncontrollability: Some causes are within a person's control, whereas other causes are beyond a person's control. In this approach, controllability can exist with any combination of the internal/external and stable/unstable dimensions. Thus, ability—an internal, stable cause—is largely perceived as an uncontrollable cause. For example, people have little control over whether they have the ability to distinguish green from red. On the other hand, effort—an internal, unstable cause—is perceived as controllable; a student can choose whether to study hard for a test.

Psychological research on causal attributions has gone beyond the classification of attributions. Psychologists have developed theories that help predict the circumstances under which people make various attributions. In this regard, Harold Kelley's theory has been extremely useful in making predictions about how people make internal and external attributions. From Kelley's perspective, attributions are made on the basis of three kinds of information: distinctiveness, consensus, and consistency.

Information about distinctiveness is derived from knowing the extent to which a person performs a certain behavior only in a certain situation. For example, the behavior of a person who only steals items from stores has higher distinctiveness than the behavior of a person who steals from stores, people's homes, and people on the street. According to Kelley, a behavior low in distinctiveness is likely to elicit an internal attribution. Thus, the behavior of a person who steals in a number of situations is more likely to be explained by an internal attribution (kleptomania) than by an external one.

Information about consensus is derived from knowing the way other people respond to the stimulus object. If the behavior is shared by a large number of people—if everyone steals items from stores, for example—the behavior has higher consensus than if few people steal from stores. A behavior high in consensus is likely to elicit an external attribution. If everyone steals from a store, there might be something about the store that elicits shoplifting.

Finally, information about consistency is derived from knowing the way the person responds over time. If the person shoplifts much of the time he or she shops, the behavior has higher consistency than if the person shoplifts occasionally. According to Kelley, behaviors high in consistency are likely to elicit internal attributions. Thus, the behavior of a person who shoplifts much of the time is likely to be explained by an internal attribution (kleptomania).

Kelley's theory has generated many more predictions than can be described here. His theory, along with those of other attribution researchers, assumes that people have a need to predict behavior. If behavior is predictable, the world becomes a more controllable place in which to live.

Applications

One of the earlier applications of the research on causal attributions by social psychologists was in understanding emotions. Stanley Schachter and Jerome Singer proposed that perceptions of emotions are influenced by the physiological arousal a person feels and by the cognitive label the person uses (for example, "I'm jealous" or "I'm angry"). They argued that the physiological arousal is the same for all emotions. For example, the rapid heart rate one feels because of intense love is the same as that one feels because of intense anger. According to Schachter and Singer, when someone feels physiologically aroused, the person looks to the situation to label his or her feelings. If someone is unaware of the true source of his or her arousal, it is possible for him or her to misattribute that arousal to a plausible cause.

An example will illustrate this approach. When "George" began drinking coffee as a teenager, he was unaware of the physiologically arousing effects of caffeine. He can recall drinking too much coffee one morning and getting in an argument about some issue. The caffeine created arousal; however, because George was in an argument, he labeled the arousal as caused by his being angry. As a result of that attribution, he acted in an angry manner. Thus, George misattributed the physiological arousal produced by the caffeine to a feeling of anger.

Psychological investigations of the emotions of love and crowding have used this attributional approach. In an experiment on romantic attraction by Gregory White, Sanford Fishbein, and Jeffrey Rutsein, male subjects ran in place for 120 seconds (high physiological arousal) or 15 seconds (low physiological arousal) and were presented with a picture of an unattractive or attractive woman. Subsequently, the subjects were asked to evaluate the woman in terms of romantic attractiveness. Male subjects with high physiological arousal indicated that they were more romantically attracted to the attractive woman than did the male subjects with less physiological arousal. Similarly, in an experiment on crowding by Stephen Worchel and Charles Teddie, subjects sat close (high physiological arousal) or far apart (low physiological arousal). For some of the subjects, there were pictures on the wall; for other subjects, there were no pictures on the wall. Subsequently, subjects were asked how crowded they felt. For the subjects with high physiological arousal, those with no pictures on the wall indicated that they felt more crowded than did those with pictures on the wall. Without pictures on the wall, the subjects could only attribute their arousal to other people. In each of these examples, the subjects used an external cue to label their internal state (emotion).

Causal attributions have also been used to understand the phenomenon of learned helplessness. Martin E. P. Seligman has demonstrated in a number of experiments that people take longer to solve soluble problems after they have tried and failed to solve a series of insoluble problems than if they had not been presented with the insoluble problems. Seligman initially proposed that people did not try harder on the soluble problems because they learned that their outcomes (failures on the insoluble problems) were independent of what they did. From an attributional perspective, however, the argument would be that people do not try harder on the soluble problems because it is less damaging to their self-esteem to attribute their failure on the insoluble problems to the lack of effort, an internal, unstable cause, rather than to an internal, stable cause, such as ability. People can then retain the belief that they can always do better next time if they try harder. Research favors the attributional interpretation of learned helplessness, as is indicated by the research of Arthur Frankel and Melvin Snyder.

An area in which causal attribution has played a crucial role is in excuse theory as proposed by C. R. Snyder. People make excuses to protect themselves from their failure experiences. Excuses help people feel that they are not totally responsible for their failures. Kelley's attribution theory has been influential in the development of Snyder's model of excuse making. Thus, people can excuse a poor performance by using consensus-raising excuses, consistency-lowering excuses, or distinctiveness-raising excuses.

When people employ distinctiveness-raising excuses, they claim that the poor performance is specific to one situation and not generalizable to others ("I performed poorly only in this class"). When people employ consistency-lowering excuses, they claim that they have a poor performance occasionally, not frequently ("This was the only time I performed poorly"). Finally, when people employ consensus-raising excuses, they claim that everyone performed as poorly as they did ("This test was so hard that everyone did poorly on it"). George Whitehead and Stephanie Smith have examined the impact of an audience on the use of consensus-raising excuses. They found that people are less likely to use consensus-raising excuses in public than in private. Thus, one is more likely to say, "This test was hard, and everyone did poorly on it," to oneself than to one's teacher, who knows how everyone else performed.

Context

The basic ideas for causal attribution were presented by Fritz Heider in his 1958 book *The Psychology of Interpersonal Relations.* From the richness of Heider's writings, a number of social psychologists have generated different attributional theories. One problem with this research area, as with other research areas in social psychology, is that there is no one theory that effectively encompasses all the different ideas proposed by causal attribution theorists. Nevertheless, causal attribution research has played an important role in the history of psychology because of its emphasis on cognition—how people think.

In the late 1950's, when Heider wrote his book, and in the early 1960's, when

Schachter and Singer did their experiment regarding emotion, psychology was heavily influenced by behaviorism, and had been for many years. From a behavioristic perspective, the study of thinking was in disrepute because it involved processes that were largely unobservable. Theorizing about causal attribution involved theorizing about the way people think about the causes of behavior. Today, as can be seen from the amount of research on causal attribution and other cognitive processes, psychology's interest in cognition has broadened.

Early research on causal attribution often tested the theories. Research generally supported the theories but often found they had limitations as well. For example, research on Kelley's attribution theory found that people do use information about distinctiveness, consensus, and consistency when making attributions. Kelley's theory further suggests that each type of information should be considered equally important in the attribution process. Subsequent research, however, indicated that consensus information may be underutilized in certain circumstances. Further theoretical research on causal attributions will be of continuing interest to psychologists.

Researchers in the future will want to know the influence of people's culture on the causal attributions they make. Much of the theorizing and empirical research on causal attribution has been done in the United States. It is important to know whether the phenomena psychologists have documented with people in the United States generalize to people from other cultures. Evidence from several sources has indicated that people from the United States attribute outcomes more to internal causes than do people from Third World nations. This finding is believed to reflect different cultural traditions, but more cross-cultural research on causal attribution is needed.

Finally, once the causal attributions that people make are understood, research can focus on the consequences of these attributions. For example, when people excuse a poor performance, they should feel better about themselves. Also, when people attribute their positive outcomes to internal factors, their feelings about themselves should be better than when they attribute their positive outcomes to external factors. This is one of many areas that is likely to receive more attention from social psychological researchers in the future.

Bibliography

Fiske, Susan T., and Shelley E. Taylor. *Social Cognition.* Reading, Mass.: Addison-Wesley, 1984. Reviews the various attribution theories and the research these theories have generated. Attribution theories are also presented within the broader context of social cognition.

Frankel, Arthur, and Melvin L. Snyder. "Poor Performance Following Unsolvable Problems: Learned Helplessness or Egotism?" *Journal of Personality and Social Psychology* 36, no. 12 (1978): 1415-1423. This experiment is typical of the research that tests the competing explanations for the performance deficit following failure. The article provides a review of each explanation and shows how attributions can protect people's positive image of themselves.

Heider, Fritz. *The Psychology of Interpersonal Relations.* New York: John Wiley & Sons, 1958. Included is the chapter that stimulated theorizing about causal attribution. Also presents ideas about social behavior that stimulated research on balance theory. The book is extremely thought provoking.

Schachter, Stanley, and Jerome Singer. "Cognitive, Social, and Physiological Determinants of Emotional State." *Psychological Review* 69, no. 5 (1962): 379-399. This experiment is considered a classic by some psychologists. It presents the paradigm that is so often utilized in research on the misattribution of arousal, as exemplified by Worchel and Teddie (1976) and White, Fishbein, and Rutsein (1981). Most general psychology textbooks include this experiment in their chapter on emotions.

Seligman, Martin E. P. *Helplessness: On Depression, Development, and Death.* San Francisco: W. H. Freeman, 1975. Defines helplessness, presents experiments on helplessness, and integrates them into a theory. The experiments utilize a diversity of subjects including dogs and people. Also compares helplessness to depression and proposes a therapeutic strategy for depression. Nicely illustrates how a theory is developed.

Snyder, C. R., Raymond L. Higgins, and Rita J. Stucky. *Excuses: Masquerades in Search of Grace.* New York: John Wiley & Sons, 1983. Presents a theory of excuse making and delineates different types of excuses. A number of research studies are also marshaled to support the theory. Highly readable; includes many examples of adaptive and maladaptive excuses.

White, Gregory L., Sanford Fishbein, and Jeffrey Rutsein. "Passionate Love and the Misattribution of Arousal." *Journal of Personality and Social Psychology* 41, no. 1 (1981): 56-62. This experiment nicely illustrates the misattribution-of-arousal paradigm and shows how a hypothesis about the development of passionate love can be tested empirically.

Whitehead, George I., III, and Stephanie Smith. "Competence and Excuse-Making as Self-Presentational Strategies." In *Public Self and Private Self,* edited by Roy F. Baumeister. New York: Springer-Verlag, 1986. Presents the authors' hypothesis and research regarding when and why particular excuses are utilized. This research follows from the excuse-making theory as proposed by Snyder, Higgins, and Stucky (1983).

Worchel, Stephen, and Charles Teddie. "The Experience of Crowding: A Two-Factor Theory." *Journal of Personality and Social Psychology* 34, no. 1 (1976): 30-40. This experiment nicely illustrates the misattribution-of-arousal paradigm. In addition, it was an important experiment in environmental psychology because it showed that population density and crowding are not necessarily the same.

George I. Whitehead III
Stephanie Smith

Cross-References

Abnormality: Cognitive Models, 46; Attributional Biases, 338; Cognitive Maps, 566; Emotion and Attribution Theory, 921; Learned Helplessness, 1425; Motivation: Cognitive Theories, 1606.

THE CENTRAL AND PERIPHERAL NERVOUS SYSTEMS

Type of psychology: Biological bases of behavior
Fields of study: Auditory, chemical, cutaneous, and body senses; nervous system; thought

The central nervous system (CNS) includes the brain and spinal cord; the peripheral nervous system (PNS) consists of nerve branches which connect the brain or spinal cord with other regions of the body, including fingers and toes. Signals from the PNS are processed within the brain, resulting in thought and senses.

Principal terms
ALZHEIMER'S DISEASE: a form of presenile dementia, characterized by disorientation, loss of memory, and speech disturbances
CEREBELLUM: the portion of the brain which controls voluntary muscle activity; located behind the brain stem
CEREBRUM: the largest and uppermost portion of the brain; the cerebrum performs sensory and motor functions and affects memory, speech, and emotional functions
GRAY MATTER: tissue within the brain or spinal cord; consists primarily of the cell bodies from neurons
MEDULLA OBLONGATA: the bulbous portion of the brain stem, which directly connects with the spinal cord; controls cardiac and respiratory activity
NEURON: the basic nerve cell of the nervous system, which consists of a cell body with one or more extensions called axons
PONS: the nerve connection between the cerebellum and the brain stem
WHITE MATTER: the tissue within the central nervous system, consisting primarily of nerve fibers

Overview

The nervous system in humans is anatomically divided into two sections: the central nervous system (CNS) and the peripheral nervous system (PNS). The CNS consists of the brain and spinal cord, while all nerve structures outside the CNS are considered part of the PNS. The peripheral nervous system, in turn, can be subdivided into a somatic division (monitoring senses and muscle movement) and an autonomic division (regulating involuntary functions, such as heart rate or blood pressure).

The dominant feature of the central nervous system is the brain. The average human brain weighs about 1.4 kilograms (or about 3 pounds) and consists primarily of two types of cells: neurons, or nerve cells, which carry out CNS activity, and glial cells, which provide support function.

The brain is generally divided into three regions: the forebrain, midbrain, and hindbrain. The midbrain and hindbrain are collectively called the brain stem. The forebrain is the largest and most obvious portion of the brain. It includes the cerebrum, with an outer layer of gray matter (nerve cells) and an underlying mass of nerve extensions (axons) called white matter. The cerebrum is divided into right and left hemispheres, each half consisting of gray and white matter. When one visualizes the brain, it is generally the cerebrum one pictures, with its convoluted and lobed regions. Lobes within the cerebrum perform so-called higher functions, such as processing senses (such as smell and touch and speech). The brain's electrical activity, which can be recorded on a machine called an electroencephalograph for identification of states of consciousness or for determination of brain dysfunction, originates within the cerebrum. Also found within the forebrain is the thalamus, an entry point of sensory nerves. It is this portion of the forebrain which integrates sensory information from various parts of the body, sending the signals to the appropriate regions of the cerebrum. For this reason, the thalamus has been called the brain's "relay station." The region below the thalamus is the hypothalamus; this is the portion of the brain which regulates metabolism in the body and influences human "drives" such as those for eating, thirst, and sex.

The midbrain connects the forebrain and hindbrain. Large numbers of nerve tracts pass through the midbrain into the forebrain, including those which receive stimuli from the eyes or ears. Response to sights or sounds is in part processed within this region, including the control of eye movements and dilation of the pupils in response to changes in light.

The hindbrain is found within the lowest portion of the brain, and it serves as the entry point for impulses from nerves in the spinal cord. This portion of the brain is divided into the cerebellum, the medulla oblongata, and the pons. The cerebellum is in the lower rear portion of the brain, in the back of the head. It has been described as having the shape and size of a walnut. Its function lies primarily in the coordination of movements, some of which are involuntary, reflexive types of motions. Sensory input from other parts of the body, including eyes and ears, is intricately involved in this function.

The medulla oblongata is the lowest portion of the brain and is the region through which spinal nerves enter the brain. It is within the medulla that breathing and heart rate are regulated. The pons is found just above the medulla, and it contains nerve tracts which link the cerebellum with the forebrain. The spinal cord exits the base of the brain and passes into the spine, extending as far as the lumbar region near the pelvis (approximately 0.5 meter, or 1.5 feet). It consists of nerve pathways which, like the brain, can be differentiated into white and gray matter. The cord is protected by the bones of the spine, or vertebrae. Emerging from spaces between individual vertebrae are spinal nerves, which eventually branch into the structure referred to as the peripheral nervous system.

The peripheral nervous system contains twelve pairs of cranial nerves, thirty-one pairs of spinal nerves, plus the branches from this system found in far reaches of the body. Sensory (called afferent) nerves transmit information from these regions of the body back to the central nervous system, while motor (or efferent) nerves transmit information from the CNS to organs or muscles. Both voluntary (somatic) movements and involuntary (autonomic) responses are controlled by elements of the PNS. For example, the rapid heartbeat which results from a sudden onset of fear (or from observing a person of interest of the opposite gender) is a function of the autonomic portion of the peripheral nervous system.

Though divided into specialized areas, the CNS and PNS clearly carry out closely related functions. The 160,000 or so kilometers of nerve fibers within the body provide an intricate system of interactions which reach and regulate activities throughout the organism, producing bodywide communication. All that one perceives and does—the essence of one's being—is a function of the nervous system.

Applications

A fuller understanding of the relationship of much of the central and peripheral nervous systems has come about through the study of pathologies in those systems. In fact, many of the so-called psychological disorders have their origins in nervous system disorders. These disorders can include dementias, "insanity," and even drug and alcohol addiction.

When most persons visualize the brain, they think of the region called the cerebrum. Certainly this area, with its large convoluted surface, is the most obvious portion of the central nervous system. The cerebrum is found in all vertebrate animals (those with backbones), but the development and function differ significantly when one compares one type of animal with another. For example, as Robert Wallace has pointed out, if the cerebrum is removed from a frog's brain, little change is seen in the animal's behavior. The frog is still capable of catching flies and still exhibits normal sexual behavior. A cat from which the cerebrum is removed can still meow and eat. Primates (humans, apes, and monkeys) which have suffered cerebral damage, however, become paralyzed and blind. As animals have become more highly evolved, more brain functions have become associated with the cerebrum, rather than occurring within other portions of the brain.

In humans, the cerebrum is divided into four lobes. In the frontal lobe, body movements and speech are regulated; in the occipital lobe, sight is regulated. The parietal lobe, containing sensory areas which respond to touching of the skin, also allows for the perception of spatial relationships of objects. The fourth lobe is the temporal lobe, in which the senses of hearing and smell are analyzed.

Though each of these cerebral areas is obviously of importance, the frontal lobe is arguably the region which makes humans most "human." (It should be pointed out, however, that the frontal lobes of chimpanzees and gorillas are equally well developed.) It is within the frontal lobe, for example, that sensory information is sorted out and is even integrated with emotional information derived from other regions.

Much of what is known of frontal lobe function has come about through two sources. In the mid-nineteenth century, a railway construction foreman was injured when, during an accidental explosion, a tamping iron was blown into his head. The damage to his frontal lobe resulted in significant behavioral changes. Literally overnight, he changed from a responsible, hardworking individual to a profane drifter unable to hold a job. Additional understanding of the role played by the frontal lobe has come through observation of individuals who have undergone frontal lobotomies—that is, the surgical removal of the frontal lobe—or through observations of persons suffering from frontal lobe tumors.

Certain changes in behavior seem to be common among these individuals. These persons frequently exhibit diminished levels of caring, even showing indifference to the outside world. In some tragic cases, the person assumes what is almost a vegetative state. In addition, the person's ability to plan or reason is often affected. He or she may exhibit a lack of ethics or show inappropriate behaviors, such as laughing or crying uncontrollably. On the other hand, damage to the frontal lobe generally has little effect on memory or intellect.

Within the central nervous system is a series of structures often called the limbic system. Though the system is at best ill-defined, it primarily includes the regions of the thalamus and hypothalamus, in addition to the hippocampus and amygdala (both regions being found within the temporal lobe). The limbic system is connected with other areas of the brain, linking the forebrain and midbrain, and is generally modulated by those regions. Regions of this system are associated with emotions or feelings, including anger, fear, sadness, and sexual arousal. If the amygdala, a group of cells within the temporal lobe, is electrically stimulated, fits of rage may result. Removal of the amygdala results in docility.

The hypothalamus has been described as the heart of the limbic system. Its primary function is to maintain homeostasis, a constancy of the internal environment. It consists primarily of densely packed neurons and secretory cells which respond to stimuli from the peripheral nervous system. In this manner, body temperature, appetite, and sleep are regulated. Tumors in the hypothalamus have been known to activate a "rage" center, causing the person to act uncontrollably.

The peripheral nervous system consists of nerve branches that connect the central nervous system to all regions of the body. As noted above, the PNS is divided into a somatic system, which regulates voluntary muscles, and an autonomic nervous system, which controls involuntary functions. The autonomic nervous system within the PNS primarily carries out a motor function. Nerve impulses are transmitted from the central nervous system for regulation of various organs. People are generally unaware of these functions, except in moments of stress. At these times, a reflex popularly known as the "fight-or-flight" response is activated. Many people can remember when, as children, they encountered a school bully. Suddenly one's heart rate accelerated, one began breathing more deeply, while one's mouth seemed to dry up. In an extreme case, bladder control might even be lost. If the bully then walked in the other direction, however, each of these responses was reversed. Both the induction of these activities and their later relaxation are under the control of the peripheral nervous system. It is critical to remember that neither the central nervous system nor the peripheral system functions in a vacuum. Each depends on the other, and each functions smoothly only in conjunction with the other.

Context

Modern knowledge of functions associated with the nervous system dates from the late nineteenth and early twentieth century work of Sir Charles Scott Sherrington. In 1884, in collaboration with John N. Langley, Sherrington demonstrated the localization of cerebral function through the experimental excision of the cerebral cortex of a dog. Over the following three decades, Sherrington published more than three hundred research papers in which he mapped areas of motor function in the cortex of the brain. Among those who were to advance this work was Edgar Douglas Adrian, a British neurophysiologist and major figure in the study of brain functions until the mid-twentieth century.

Langley was himself a pioneer in the study of the peripheral nervous system. In particular, he studied autonomic functions within that system. In fact, it was Langley who first applied, in 1898, the term "autonomic nervous system" to those portions of the PNS which innervate involuntary muscles and glands. His major work, *The Autonomic Nervous System*, was published in 1921.

It was clear from these works that the ability to monitor the outside world is a function of the nervous system. Input from the senses—taste, touch, smell, and so on—travels along the peripheral nerves to the spinal cord and brain, where it is processed, coordinated, and interpreted. Changes that result in the brain form the basis of thought and learning. Damage to those same areas results in loss of function and even loss of memory.

It is particularly in this area of loss of function that one may hope to see great advancements in the future. Since nerves, unlike most other cells in the body, do not regenerate, death or damage to regions of the nervous system often results in permanent loss of function. In the case of a stroke, damage is often extensive and catastrophic. The ability to replace or repair nervous tissue could significantly reverse this damage.

Tragically, the natural process of aging is often accompanied by dementia, the loss of cognitive function. The most common form of late-life dementia is Alzheimer's disease. First described by Alois Alzheimer in 1907, the disease is characterized by loss of memory, confusion, and speech disturbances. Often developing in the late middle years, Alzheimer's disease is associated with formation of fibrous plaques throughout much of the brain. In particular, cortical areas of the cerebral lobes are affected. This accounts for at least some of the symptoms typical of the disease. While no reversal of the disease is in sight, it is hoped that the course of the illness can at least be slowed.

The human nervous system is thus composed of two parts: a central nervous system, in which information is processed, and a peripheral system, which serves as a window to the world. All regions of the body are served, and in turn, each region has a part in the protection and function of the body.

Bibliography

Cotman, Carl W., and James L. McGaugh. *Behavioral Neuroscience: An Introduction.* New York: Academic Press, 1980. An excellent introduction to the area. Descriptions of nervous system function are basic and easily understood by nonexperts. Sections of the book cover material in great depth. Summaries and definitions are provided at the end of each topic.

Scientific American 241 (September, 1979). This entire issue of the journal deals with the topic of the brain. Articles are somewhat technical, but they are well written and nicely illustrated.

Selkoe, Dennis J. "Amyloid Protein and Alzheimer's Disease." *Scientific American* 265 (November, 1991): 68-78. A summary of the pathology and possible cause of the most common form of aging dementia. Written for the person with at least college-level knowledge of science, but well illustrated. Diagrams are at a basic level.

Stevens, Leonard A. *Explorers of the Brain.* New York: Alfred A. Knopf, 1971. A history of the explanation of brain function. Chapters are devoted to those researchers who mapped out the areas of the brain. A good overview to how research in the past was carried out, written at the level of the nonexpert.

Wallace, Robert A., Gerald P. Sanders, and Robert J. Ferl. *Biology: The Science of Life.* 3d ed. New York: HarperCollins 1991. Though a college text, the book contains several excellent chapters on the functions of the nervous system which should be easily understood by persons not in the field. Illustrations are plentiful and clear. Definitions and a summary are provided at the end of each chapter.

Richard Adler

Cross-References

The Autonomic Nervous System, 362; Brain Injuries: Concussions, Contusions, and Strokes, 448; Brain-Stem Structures, 461; The Cerebral Cortex, 500; Forebrain Structures, 1043; Hindbrain Structures, 1175; Neural and Hormonal Interaction, 1648; Neurons, 1661; Neurotransmitters, 1673.

THE CEREBRAL CORTEX

Type of psychology: Biological bases of behavior
Fields of study: Nervous system; thought; vision

The outer gray matter of the cerebrum, the cortex, contains sensory and motor regions and areas that integrate these functions. Intelligence, memory, language, personality, and other behavioral characteristics are controlled there.

Principal terms

BRAIN WAVES: electrical activity produced by the neurons of the cerebral cortex and recorded using an electroencephalograph; these produce distinct patterns related to healthy and diseased brain functions

CEREBRAL CORTEX: the outer covering of the cerebrum, consisting of gray matter that conducts most of the integrative aspects of higher brain functions

CEREBRAL HEMISPHERES: the right and left halves of the cerebrum, separated incompletely by the longitudinal fissure

FRONTAL LOBE: the anterior portion of each cerebral hemisphere, containing control of motor areas and most of the higher intellectual functions of the brain, including speech

GRAY MATTER: unmyelinated neurons that make up the cerebral cortex, so called because they lack the fatty covering (myelin) found on neurons of the white matter

INTEGRATION: the function of most of the neurons of the cerebral cortex, summarizing the incoming sensory information and producing a consensus as to what the nervous system will do next

OCCIPITAL LOBE: the posterior portion of each cerebral hemisphere, where visual stimuli are received and integrated

PARIETAL LOBE: the side and upper middle part of each cerebral hemisphere, site of sensory reception from skin, muscles, and other areas, and containing part of the general interpretive area

TEMPORAL LOBE: the lower side portion of each cerebral hemisphere, containing the sites of sensory interpretation, memory of visual and auditory patterns, and part of the general interpretive area

Overview

The cerebrum is the largest portion of the brain in higher vertebrates. In lower vertebrates, it develops from the front end of the embryonic nerve cord as the forebrain or prosencephalon and is specialized for smell and taste. This development progresses in higher vertebrates to a highly convoluted structure called the telencephalon, most of which becomes the cerebrum—the location of the highest levels of behavioral control. In humans, deep convolutions of the cerebrum produce a greatly increased surface area, the cerebral cortex, also called the neocortex because it is the newest development in the evolution of vertebrate brains. The cortex is the site of the integration of sensory nerve impulses and of the intellectual processes, such as memory and learning. It is also the site of the initiation of voluntary motor impulses to the skeletal muscles. One theory for the massive enlargement of the cerebral cortex in humans as compared to other mammals is that such growth resulted from the development of language in early social groups. This is thought to have increased the integrative or associative functions, producing the rise in intelligence and cortical surface that accompanied language development.

The cerebral cortex is the largest portion of the cerebrum by volume and generally consists of four to six layers of the cell bodies of neurons. This is called gray matter because the cells are not covered with a white fatty myelin coating, and they look darker than cells that are myelinated. The cortex overlies a region of white matter made of the myelinated axons that extend from the cell bodies of cortical neurons. The tissue of the cortex composes about 80 percent of the brain in a human; it varies in thickness from about 1.5 to 3 millimeters. The wrinkling of the convoluted tissue greatly increases the cortex area that can be contained within the small volume of the cranial cavity, with a surface area of about 2,500 square centimeters. The clefts and ridges of the convolutions are called sulci and gyri respectively (singular, sulcus and gyrus). A deeper cleft, called a fissure, is usually recognized as the boundary between different lobes of the cerebrum.

The cerebrum is divided into nearly symmetrical right and left halves, called the cerebral hemispheres, by the medial longitudinal fissure. Each hemisphere is further divided into four sections called the frontal, parietal, temporal, and occipital lobes. The gyri and sulci within each lobe may differ slightly between the two hemispheres of a single individual, and they can vary widely among different individual brains. The frontal lobes are the largest, extending backward in each hemisphere from the front of the brain to the central sulcus, and downward to the lateral fissure. Each parietal lobe begins just behind the central sulcus and extends downward to the lateral fissure. Below the lateral fissure of each hemisphere is the temporal lobe, under the frontal and parietal lobes on each side of the head, and separated from the occipital lobe by the parieto-occipital sulcus. The back portion of each hemisphere is occupied by the occipital lobe. Each of these lobes does not have a single recognizable function, but they are useful as anatomical markers for the location of many different activities that occur in each lobe. These activities may vary in their placement from one individual to another, so localizations are not exact.

Different regions of the cortex are connected by three kinds of projections of axons from neurons. Many short linkages connect neurons in adjacent gyri; longer connections join together one lobe and another from the same hemisphere; and commissures link the same points in opposite hemispheres. In addition to pathways from one part of the cortex to another, there are also links between cortical neurons and cells of other areas of the brain, such as the thalamus. This further complicates the task of determining the functions of parts of the brain, since a pathway may lead from an area of the cortex to the thalamus and then to another cortical area. Damage to such a linkage may produce the same kind of behavioral response as damage to the cortical area that actually controls the behavior.

Crossed pathways from one hemisphere to the other are of great importance in the perception of sensations and the origination of movements. Each hemisphere of the brain controls the activities of the contralateral (opposite) side of the body, so that an itchy sensation on the right arm will send the great majority of its sensory impulses to the cortex of the left side of the brain. Similarly, a motor impulse to the left hand to scratch the itch will originate from the cortex of the right side of the brain. A variation of this rule is seen in the visual system, where incoming sensory impulses from the two eyes are sent to both sides of the brain. Half the fibers of the optic nerve from each eye cross before reaching the visual cortex, and the information that arrives as an upside-down image is interpreted as if it were right-side up. This allows the production of a continuous image, which would not be possible if each eye sent its impulses to only one side of the brain, either the contralateral or ipsilateral (same) side.

Applications

Neuroanatomists and psychologists construct different kinds of topographical maps based on the various functions of the cerebral cortex that are being examined. Projection maps of the sensory and motor functions are built by tracing the pathways of sensory neurons from different areas of the body to the different parts of the brain, or the pathways of motor neurons from the brain to different action sites in the body. Functional maps are made from studies of the brain itself, either by directly stimulating different brain regions electrically and observing the resultant behavior, or by recording brain waves produced by particular areas of the brain during certain behaviors. Histological study of the kinds of neurons and accessory cells in different areas of the cortex is used in the development of cytoarchitecture maps.

Using a primary sensory projection map, one can link the visual system to the posterior occipital lobe, the auditory system to the temporal lobe, and the somatosensory system (carrying sensation from most of the body) to the postcentral gyrus of the parietal lobe. Most primary motor projections come from the precentral gyrus of the frontal lobe, immediately in front of the central sulcus that separates the frontal and parietal lobes. Nearby areas that receive information from primary sensory areas or that send information to primary motor areas of the cortex are called secondary projection areas. These regions in turn contain pathways leading to or from tertiary projection areas. The secondary and tertiary areas are parts of the association cortex, where integration of impulses takes place to interpret the various kinds of information. It is a major oversimplification, however, to consider the different lobes to have only the one function mentioned, since sensory, motor, and integrative activities occur in all parts of the cerebral cortex. The listed functions are simply most concentrated in the given areas.

The best-known functional map of the human cerebral cortex was described by

W. G. Penfield and his associates in the 1950's. It was developed through research done during brain surgery on conscious individuals. Patients were asked what sensations were perceived when certain specific regions of the postcentral gyrus (somatic sensory area) were electrically stimulated. The precentral gyrus (motor area) was also stimulated, and observations were made of what muscles responded by contracting. As a result of such work in numerous subjects, Penfield was able to draw a sensory homunculus and a motor homunculus—strangely distorted humans with enormous lips, tongues, and hands, and tiny bodies. The homunculi extend along the precentral and postcentral gyri, with each part drawn to correspond to its functional representation on the sensory or motor cortex. The lips and hands are large on the sensory homunculus because of the large number of sensory receptors located there. The hands are large on the motor homunculus because there are many nerves supplying the fine muscular control of the fingers. The bodies are small because of the relative lack of sensory reception and motor control there. The homunculi do not represent all the functions of the cerebral cortex, only those of the motor and sensory areas on either side of the dividing central fissure between the frontal and parietal lobes.

Early in the 1900's, histological studies produced a cytoarchitecture map that highlights the different kinds of cell combinations occurring in the six or so layers of neurons in the cerebral cortex. Later, similar maps have increased the level of detail and complexity. Brodmann's map and his regional numbering system are still widely used to differentiate anatomical regions of the cortex. The relationship between anatomical structure and function is quite striking, with distinct boundaries between cellular regions being reproduced in the limits of functional regions. Areas with indistinct cytoarchitectural boundaries seem to be most concerned with associative or integrative functions that are not strongly delineated.

Context

Studies of the location of neurological and behavioral functions have been undertaken for more than a hundred and fifty years. As early as the 1830's, it was recognized that aphasia, a loss of speech capability, was associated with brain lesions in an area of the left frontal lobe. Many subsequent studies involving damaged areas of the brain and electrical stimulation during surgery have shown the locations of numerous functions in different areas of the cerebral cortex. The ability to understand speech has been localized to a part of the temporal lobe, near the auditory cortex. Impulses from the retinas are known to stimulate the visual cortex in the posterior part of the occipital lobes, with associative visual areas located nearby. Sensory impulses from the skin and body surface are processed by the somatosensory regions of the parietal lobes. These sensory regions seem to be organized into columnar structures within the six layers of neurons in the cortex. Studies of these columns have been most thorough in the visual cortex, where it is known that adjacent columns of cells are stimulated by the opposite eyes. Association areas located near the sensory regions are usually involved in the integration of information brought to the brain through the sensory neurons.

Knowledge of the functions of various areas of the cerebral cortex is important in psychology and related disciplines because of the need to know where to look for a lesion or for damage that might cause a neurological or behavioral disorder. One way of looking for brain damage in a behaviorally disordered patient is through production of an electroencephalogram, or EEG. This noninvasive procedure involves the use of electrodes attached to the head in particular locations over the cortical areas to be examined for electrical current production. Very tiny currents are recognized from each area, with cycles of wavelengths that vary according to the level of activity and normality of function of the targeted area. Records are made of the brain waves produced from each hemisphere or lobe during periods of different kinds of activity. Alpha waves show a rhythm of about 8 to 13 cycles per second and moderate amplitude, and indicate resting or reduced use of a brain area. Reduced height and increased frequency of the waves (14 to 30 cycles per second) are characteristic of beta waves. Production of these from an area is indicative that the area is being more active than when waves of high amplitude are produced. Delta waves are much less frequent (1 to 5 cycles per second); in an awake adult, they indicate brain damage.

Studies of these electrical aspects of the working brain are still rather crude, but they can be used to show the relative use of the two hemispheres during different kinds of tasks. Information from these observations supports the concept that the right side of the brain is more involved with spatial, artistic, and musical processing, while the left side is concerned with logical, mathematical, and verbal activities. This lateralization of brain function is further supported by observations made on patients following the complete surgical separation of the two hemispheres of the brain. The hemispheres are normally connected by the corpus callosum, a set of fibers containing millions of cells that link the two sides of the brain. Split-brain procedures undertaken to relieve epilepsy, as well as accidental separation of the two hemispheres, produce individuals who literally fit the expression "the right hand doesn't know what the left hand is doing." In such individuals the right brain, controlling the left hand, can reproduce a drawing that the right hand (controlled by the left brain) is unable to copy. An unseen object placed in the left hand can be recognized by the right brain, but the left brain is unable to describe it verbally because the connection between the sides is lost. It is a mystery why such separation of function should occur, but the lateralization exists in normal individuals as well as in those with lesions. It is stronger in men than in women, one of several anatomical and functional differences in brain development between the sexes. If an injury occurs to one side of the brain, as in a stroke, often the other side can be trained to take over the functions of the damaged region, especially in children and younger individuals.

Higher associative functions such as personality, memory, and learning are also associated with the cerebral cortex, as well as with other parts of the brain. Memories are stored in certain specific areas of the cerebral cortex. Some neurons code for simple features of visual memory, for example, such as edges and the orientation of objects that are seen. Other neurons code for shape and color of objects, especially in the secondary visual areas of the occipital lobe. Information is sent from these neurons to the visual area of the temporal lobe, where they seem to be interpreted and remembered. Interpretation of sensory information and storage of the information in memory areas have been further localized to different areas for different kinds of information, such as faces, places, names, shapes, language, and motor functions. Further studies in humans, monkeys, and even rats will lead to greater understanding of the newest and most human portion of the brain, the cerebral cortex. The study of the cerebral cortex has been called the greatest frontier of research in neuroscience, and it is likely to remain so for a long time to come.

Bibliography

Chadwick, David, Niall Cartlidge, and David Bates. *Medical Neurology.* Edinburgh: Churchill Livingstone, 1989. This medical resource discusses disorders of the nervous system and problems associated with them. Chapter 6 includes disorders of awareness and mental function, often caused by damage to areas of the cerebral cortex. Chapter 19 covers functional and psychiatric disorders. Clinical features and the causes of these disorders, diagrams of affected brain areas, and numerous tables are included. References.

Kirshner, Howard S. *Behavioral Neurology: A Practical Approach.* New York: Churchill Livingstone, 1986. Discusses various disorders of behavior that have their source in dysfunction of the brain, particularly the cerebral cortex. Areas covered include language, reading and writing, learned movement, recognition, memory, dementias, and epilepsy. Specific disorders of the right cerebral hemisphere and the frontal lobes are also considered. References accompany each chapter.

Kolb, Bryan, and Ian Q. Whishaw. *Fundamentals of Human Neuropsychology.* 2d ed. New York: W. H. Freeman, 1985. Much of this undergraduate textbook addresses the functions and disorders of the cerebral cortex. Part 3 includes chapters on neocortical organization and the sensory and motor systems. Part 4 contains chapters on cerebral asymmetry and the individual cerebral lobes. Higher functions, development, and recovery are discussed in parts 5 and 6. An excellent resource with many references.

McCrone, John. *The Ape That Spoke: Language and the Evolution of the Human Mind.* New York: William Morrow, 1991. While not addressing the cerebral cortex directly, this book for general readers discusses the increased size of the cortex as being associated with the development of language. It gives an interesting outlook on how the mind functions by capturing and holding each thought for a short time only. Bibliographical notes include numerous references.

Montgomery, Geoffrey. "The Mind's Eye." *Discover* 12 (May, 1991): 50-56. This article is written for the nontechnical reader. Presents an excellent discussion of the formation of visual maps in the function of the visual cortex. Comparison is made among reptiles, primitive mammals, and primates in how they perceive visual stimuli.

Ornstein, Robert Evan, and Richard F. Thompson. *The Amazing Brain.* Boston: Houghton Mifflin, 1984. This is a clearly written and well-illustrated book for the nonscientist, presented as a tour of the brain. It discusses the architecture of the brain and how it receives sensory impulses, with emphasis on those for vision. Memory and the effects of separating the two cerebral hemispheres are also covered.

Romero-Sierra, C. *Neuroanatomy: A Conceptual Approach.* New York: Churchill Livingstone, 1986. Addresses the simple concepts of the nervous system components first, then their integration as a functioning whole. Several chapters cover material on the cerebral hemispheres and the functions of the cerebral cortex. A brain atlas is useful in finding structures, and a wide bibliography is included.

Springer, Sally P., and Georg Deutsch. *Left Brain, Right Brain.* 3d ed. New York: W. H. Freeman, 1989. Provides a thorough discussion of the differences between the right and left hemispheres. Techniques of measurement are considered, along with the physiological correlates of asymmetry. Normal brain and split-brain studies show variation between individuals and between the sexes. Numerous references.

Tortora, Gerard J., and Nicholas P. Anagnostakos. *Principles of Anatomy and Physiology.* 6th ed. New York: Harper & Row, 1990. Chapter 14 of this undergraduate college text covers the brain, and chapter 15 is about the sensory, motor, and integrative systems that are contained within the cerebral cortex. Numerous photographs and diagrams help the reader visualize the area under discussion. Excellent as introductory coverage of this material. Selected readings at the end of each chapter refer to easily accessible material.

Van De Graaff, Kent Marshall, and Stuart Ira Fox. *Concepts of Human Anatomy and Physiology.* 2d ed. Dubuque, Iowa: Wm. C. Brown, 1989. An undergraduate text that covers introductory information on the brain clearly and succinctly. The cerebrum is discussed in chapter 15, accompanied by numerous diagrams and tables. References are given at the end of the book.

Jean S. Helgeson

Cross-References

Brain Injuries: Concussions, Contusions, and Strokes, 448; Brain Specialization, 455; The Central and Peripheral Nervous Systems, 494; Forebrain Structures, 1043; Language and Cognition, 1401; Neural Anatomy and Cognition, 1640; Neural Damage and Plasticity, 1655; Neurons, 1661; Neurotransmitters, 1673; Split-Brain Studies, 2355.

CHILD ABUSE

Type of psychology: Developmental psychology
Fields of study: Adolescence; infancy and childhood

The experience of physical or psychological abuse in childhood can have a profound, long-term, deleterious effect upon a person's social development and emotional well-being. Child abuse places a youngster at increased risk to develop a variety of psychological problems, including low self-esteem, anxiety and depression, behavior disorders, educational difficulties, and distorted relationships with peers and adults.

Principal terms

NEGLECT: the repeated failure to meet minimal standards for satisfying a child's basic needs for food, clothing, shelter, medical care, and safety

PHYSICAL ABUSE: any nonaccidental injury caused by a parent or a person responsible for a child's care, including fractures, burns, bruises, welts, cuts, and internal injuries

PSYCHOLOGICAL ABUSE: acts by which children are rejected, terrorized, corrupted, isolated, ridiculed, or humiliated; parental behavior fails to meet the child's need for nurturance or penalizes the child for normal behavior

SEXUAL ABUSE: any contact between a child and an adult in which the child is being used for the sexual stimulation of the perpetrator or another person; includes exhibitionism, fondling, rape, and sodomy

Overview

It is difficult to imagine anything more frightening to a child than being rejected, threatened, beaten, or molested by an adult who is supposed to be his or her primary source of nurturance and protection. Yet throughout human history, children have been abandoned, incarcerated, battered, mutilated, and even murdered by their care givers. Although the problem of child maltreatment is an old one, both the systematic study of child abuse and the legally sanctioned mechanisms for child protection are relatively new and have gained their greatest momentum in the last half of the twentieth century.

In the United States, the Federal Child Abuse Prevention and Treatment Act of 1974 broadly defines child abuse as

the physical or mental injury, sexual abuse or exploitation, negligent treatment, or maltreatment of a child under the age of eighteen . . . by a person who is responsible for that child's welfare under circumstances which indicate that the child's health or welfare is harmed or threatened thereby.

When applied by legal and mental health professionals in real-world situations, however, the definition of abuse may vary according to the developmental age of the child victim, the frequency or intensity of the behaviors regarded as abusive, the degree of intentionality, and a consideration of extenuating circumstances. In general, however, child abuse includes any act or omission on the part of a parental figure that damages a child's physical or psychological well-being or development that is nonaccidental or the result of a habitual behavioral pattern. A broad spectrum of behaviors are considered to be abusive, ranging from the more easily recognizable physical abuse to the more subtle forms of maltreatment including neglect, sexual abuse, and emotional abuse.

Estimates of the extent of child abuse in the United States have ranged from two hundred thousand to four million cases per year. The most widely accepted incidence figure comes from the National Committee for the Prevention of Child Abuse, which estimates that more than a million children are "severely abused" each year, including more than two thousand abuse-related deaths annually. It is important, when considering the actual magnitude of the problem of child maltreatment, to remember that the estimates given most likely underestimate the true incidence of child abuse, both because of the large number of cases that go unreported and because of the lack of agreement as to precisely which behaviors constitute "abuse" or "neglect." In addition, abusive treatment of children is rarely limited to a single episode, and it frequently occurs within the context of other forms of family violence.

Certain forms of maltreatment seem to appear with greater regularity within certain age groups. Neglect is most often reported for infants and toddlers, with incidence declining with age. Reports of sexual abuse and emotional maltreatment are most common among older school-aged children and adolescents. Physical abuse seems to be reported equally among all age groups; however, children less than five years old and adolescents have the highest rates of actual physical injury.

Although research studies generally conclude that there is no "typical" child abuse case consisting of a typical abused child and a typical abusive parent or family type, there are certain characteristics that occur with greater regularity than others. For example, there is considerable evidence that premature infants, low-birth-weight infants, and children with problems such as hyperactivity, physical handicaps, and mental retardation are at particularly high risk for being abused by their care givers. Physical abuse and neglect are reported with approximately equal frequency for girls and boys, while sexual abuse against girls is reported four times more frequently than is sexual abuse against boys.

Contrary to the once-held stereotype of abusive parents, only a small proportion (5 to 10 percent) of abusive parents suffer from a severe psychiatric disorder. While female care givers are the perpetrators in approximately 60 percent of all reported cases of child maltreatment, male care givers are more likely to inflict actual physical injury, and they are the primary perpetrators in cases of sexual abuse of both male and female children. Although no one abusive personality type has been identified, research has revealed a number of areas of psychological functioning in which abusive parents often differ from nonabusive parents. Abusive parents tend to exhibit low frustration tolerance and express negative emotions (for example, anger or disappointment) inappropriately. They are more socially isolated than are nonabusive parents. Abusive parents also tend to have unrealistic expectations of their children, to misinterpret their children's motivations for misbehaving, to utilize inconsistent and inflexible parenting skills, and to view themselves as inadequate or incompetent as parents.

Research also indicates that marital conflict, unemployment, large and closely spaced families, overcrowded living conditions, and extreme household disorganization are common in abusive homes. Statistics regarding race, education level, and socioeconomic status of abusive families are somewhat controversial in that there exists the possibility of an under-reporting bias favoring the white, middle- to upperclass family; however, like several other negative outcomes in childhood (for example, underachievement, criminality, teen pregnancy), child abuse is associated with poverty, underemployment, insufficient education, and the increased experience of unmanageable stress and social isolation that coexists with these sociodemographic variables.

Applications

Abused children are believed to be at much greater risk of developing some form of pathology in childhood or in later life. When considered as a group and compared to nonabused youngsters, abused children exhibit a variety of psychological difficulties and behavioral problems. Yet there is no single emotional or behavioral reaction that is consistently found in all abused children. It is important, when investigating the impact of child abuse, to view the abuse within a developmental perspective. Given a child's different developmental needs and capabilities over the course of his or her development, one might expect that both the psychological experience and the impact of the abuse would be quite different for an infant than if the same maltreatment involved an eight-year-old child or an adolescent. One should also note that the abuse occurs within a particular psychological context, and that the experience of the abuse per se may not be the singular, most powerful predictor of the psychological difficulties found in abused children. Rather, the child's daily exposure to other, more pervasive aspects of the psychological environment associated with an abusive family situation (for example, general environmental deprivation, impoverished parent-child interactions, or chronic family disruption and disorganization) may prove to be more psychologically damaging. Finally, it is important not to view the range of symptoms associated with abused children solely as deficits or pathology. These "symptoms" represent an abused child's best attempt at coping with an extremely stressful family environment given the limited psychological resources and skills he or she has available at that particular time in his or her development.

From the home environment, and from parents in particular, children learn their earliest and perhaps most influential lessons about how to evaluate themselves as valuable, loveable, and competent human beings. They learn about controlling their own actions and about successfully mastering their environment. They learn something about the goodness of their world and how to relate to the people in it. Growing up in an abusive home distorts these early lessons, often resulting in serious interference with the most important dimensions of a child's development: the development of a healthy sense of self, the development of self-control and a sense of mastery, the capacity to form satisfying relationships, and the ability to utilize one's cognitive capacities to solve problems.

In general, research has shown that abused children often suffer from low self-esteem, poor impulse control, aggressive and antisocial behaviors, fearfulness and anxiety, depression, poor relationships with peers and adults, difficulties with school adjustment, delays in cognitive development, lowered academic achievement, and deficits in social and moral judgment. The way in which these difficulties are expressed will vary according to a child's stage of development.

In infancy, the earliest sign of abuse or neglect is an infant's failure to thrive. These infants show growth retardation (weight loss can be so severe so as to be life-threatening) with no obvious physical explanation. To the observer, these infants appear to have "given up" on interacting with the outside world. They become passive, socially apathetic, and exhibit little smiling, vocalization, and curiosity. Other abused infants appear to be quite irritable, exhibiting frequent crying, feeding difficulties, and irregular sleep patterns. In either case, the resulting parent-child attachment bond is often inadequate and mutually unsatisfying.

Abused toddlers and preschoolers seem to lack the infectious love of life, fantasy, and play that is characteristic of that stage of development. They are typically anxious, fearful, and hypervigilant. Their emotions are blunted, lacking the range, the spontaneity, and the vivacity typical of a child that age. Abused toddlers' and preschoolers' ability to play, particularly their ability to engage in imaginative play, may be impaired; it is either deficient or preoccupied with themes of aggression. Abused children at this age can either be passive and overcompliant or oppositional, aggressive, and hyperactive.

School-aged children and adolescents exhibit the more recognizable signs of low self-esteem and depression in the form of a self-deprecating attitude and self-destructive behaviors. They are lonely, withdrawn, and joyless. Behaviorally, some act in a compulsive, overcompliant, or pseudomature manner, while others are overly impulsive, oppositional, and aggressive. Problems with school adjustment and achievement are common. With the school-aged child's increased exposure to the larger social environment, deficits in social competence and interpersonal relationships become more apparent. Progressing through adolescence, the manifestations of low self-esteem, depression, and aggressive, acting-out behaviors may become more pronounced in the form of suicide attempts, delinquency, running away, promiscuity, and drug use.

These distortions in self-esteem, impulse control, and interpersonal relationships often persist into adulthood. There has been much concern expressed regarding the possibility of an intergenerational transmission of abuse—of the experience of abuse as a child predisposing a person to becoming an abusive parent. Research indicates that abused children are six times more likely to abuse their own children than the general population.

Context

Child maltreatment is a complex phenomenon that does not have a simple, discrete cause, nor does it affect each victim in a predictable or consistent manner. Since the "battered child syndrome" gained national attention in the early 1960's, theories attempting to explain child maltreatment have evolved from the simplistic psychiatric model focusing on the abuser as a "bad" parent suffering from some form of mental illness to a view of child abuse as a multidetermined problem, with anyone from any walk of life a potential abuser.

Perhaps the most comprehensive and widely accepted explanation of child abuse is the ecological model. This model views abuse as the final product of a set of interacting factors including child-mediated stressors (for example, temperamental difficulties, or a mental or physical handicap), parental predispositions (for example, history of abuse as a child, emotional immaturity), and situational stresses (for example, marital conflict, insufficient social support, or financial stress) occurring within a cultural context that inadvertently supports the mistreatment of children by its acceptance of corporal punishment and tolerance for violence, and its reluctance to interfere with family autonomy. Utilizing this ecological framework, one can imagine how an abusive situation can develop when, for example, an irritable, emotionally unresponsive infant is cared for by an inexperienced, socially isolated mother in a conflict-filled and financially strained household embedded within a larger cultural context in which the rights and privileges of childhood do not necessarily include freedom from violence.

Knowledge regarding the impact of child abuse has also changed over the years, from a view of maltreated children as almost doomed to develop some form of psychopathology to an acknowledgment that child abuse, like other major childhood stressors, can result in a broad spectrum of adaptive consequences, ranging from psychological health to severe psychiatric disorder. Some children actually "do well" in their development despite their experience with extreme stress and adversity. For example, while adults who were abused as children are more likely than nonabused individuals to become child abusers, nearly two-thirds of all abused children do not become abusive parents. The important questions to be answered are why and how this is so. Research on "stress-resistant" individuals such as these nonabusers has shifted the focus away from pathology to the identification of factors within the individual (for example, coping strategies) and within the environment (for example, social support) that appear to serve a protective function.

Finally, while the treatment of abused children and their abusive caregivers remains an important goal in the mental health field, a focus on the prevention of child abuse has also gained momentum. Many abused children and their families can be helped with proper treatment; however, the existing need for services far exceeds the mental health resources available. An increased understanding of the factors that protect families against engaging in abusive behaviors has resulted in the creation of successful preventive interventions. These prevention programs seek to reduce the incidence of new cases of child abuse by encouraging the development and strengthening of competencies, resources, and coping strategies that promote psychological well-being and positive development in parents, children, and families.

The problem of child abuse does not occur in isolation. It coexists with other abhorrent problems facing American children such as poverty, lack of guaranteed adequate medical care, insufficient quality daycare, and unequal educational resources. Child abuse, like these other problems, can be prevented and eradicated. People have come a long way in terms of their understanding of child maltreatment; yet until the needs of children truly become a national priority, child abuse will continue, brutally and unnecessarily, to rob children of their childhood.

Bibliography

Brassard, Marla R., Robert Germain, and Stuart N. Hart, eds. *Psychological Maltreatment of Children and Youth.* New York: Pergamon Press, 1987. An edited collection of articles that considers emotional maltreatment as the "core" component of all other forms of child abuse. Discusses issues of the definition, dynamics, consequences, and treatment of the psychological abuse of children.

Cicchetti, Dante, and Vicki Carlson, eds. *Child Maltreatment: Theory and Research on the Causes and Consequences of Child Abuse and Neglect.* New York: Cambridge University Press, 1989. Edited chapters by leading experts in the field providing a state-of-the-art evaluation of what is known about the causes and consequences of child maltreatment. Describes the history of child maltreatment and intervention strategies designed to prevent or remediate the negative consequences of abuse.

Clark, Robin E., and Judith Freeman Clark. *The Encyclopedia of Child Abuse.* New York: Facts on File, 1989. In encyclopedia form, provides comprehensive information regarding all forms of child maltreatment. Includes discussions of causation, consequences, treatment, and prevention. Entries reflect a range of disciplines including psychology, law, medicine, sociology, economics, history, and education. An extensive bibliography also included.

Finkelhor, David. *A Sourcebook on Child Sexual Abuse.* Beverly Hills, Calif.: Sage, 1986. Provides a comprehensive overview of the clinical and research knowledge base regarding child sexual abuse, including its causes, consequences, and treatment.

Garbarino, James, and Gwen Gilliam. *Understanding Abusive Families.* Lexington, Mass.: Lexington Books, 1980. Presents an ecological and developmental perspective on child abuse. Explores the interrelated contributions of child characteristics, parental characteristics, and the community context to the development of an abusive parent-child relationship. Considers the way in which the causes, dynamics, and consequences of abuse may change from infancy through adolescence.

Straus, Murray Arnold, Richard J. Gelles, and Suzanne K. Steinmetz. *Behind Closed*

Doors: Violence in the American Family. Newbury Park, Calif.: Sage, 1981. Reports the results of the first comprehensive national study of violence in the average American family in nontechnical language. The problem of child abuse is discussed within the larger context of other expressions of family violence.

Wolfe, David A. *Child Abuse: Implications for Child Development and Psychopathology.* Newbury Park, Calif.: Sage, 1987. Presents a thorough review of facts and issues regarding the abuse of children, emphasizing topics such as sociodemographic risk factors, variations in family socialization practices, factors associated with healthy versus abusive parent-child relationships, psychological characteristics of the abusive parent, and a developmental perspective on the abused child.

Judith Primavera

Cross-References

Aggression: Definitions and Theoretical Explanations, 162; Attachment and Bonding in Infancy and Childhood, 307; Ego Defense Mechanisms, 860; Gender-Identity Formation, 1062; Psychoanalytic Psychology and Personality: Sigmund Freud, 1912; Separation, Divorce, and Family Life: Children's Issues, 2227; Trust, Autonomy, Initiative, and Industry: Erikson, 2591.

CIRCADIAN RHYTHMS

Type of psychology: Consciousness
Fields of study: Depression; nervous system; sleep

Circadian rhythms underlie and regulate normal human physiology and psychology; the daily rhythms appear to originate within the organism and are usually synchronized with the external environment by factors such as light. The sleep-wake cycle, body temperature, and mental abilities all fluctuate in circadian rhythms. Sleep disorders, shift-work problems, jet lag, and seasonal affective disorders are often caused in part by alterations in circadian rhythms.

Principal terms

CIRCADIAN RHYTHM: a cyclical variation in a biological process or behavior that has a duration of about a day; in humans under constant environmental conditions, the rhythm usually reveals its true length as being slightly more than twenty-four hours

ENDOGENOUS: a term for rhythms that are expressions of internal processes within the body

FREE-RUNNING: a term describing a rhythm that is not synchronized by an environmental signal such as the light-dark cycle

JET LAG: the malaise, headache, fatigue, gastrointestinal disorders, and other symptoms that result from traveling across several time zones within a few hours

MELATONIN: a hormone produced by the pineal gland within the forebrain that is usually released into the blood during the night phase of the light-dark cycle

PERIOD: the length of one complete cycle of a rhythm

SEASONAL AFFECTIVE DISORDER (SAD): manic depression that undergoes a seasonal fluctuation resulting from various factors, including seasonal changes in the intensity and duration of sunlight

SUPRACHIASMATIC NUCLEI: a pair of clusters of nerve-cell bodies located in the hypothalamus of the forebrain that produce at least some circadian rhythms

ZEITGEBER: a German word meaning "time giver"; a factor that serves as a synchronizer or entraining agent, such as light, noise, or social cues

Overview

Circadian rhythms are a fundamental characteristic of life, and their study in humans is an essential part of human physiology as well as psychology. "Circadian" refers to rhythms that are about a day in length (from the Latin *circa*, "about," and *diem,* "day"); the term was coined by Franz Halberg. Although historically many of the early observations were made on plants and animals, the examples cited here will deal primarily with humans.

The most obvious rhythm of human activity is the sleep-wake cycle. Each day, humans are mostly active during the daylight hours, then sleep for much of the dark period. A species with this schedule is called "diurnal" (animals active during the dark period are termed "nocturnal"). This pattern is such a natural part of human lives that its role in human physiology has been overlooked, and relatively little is known about the function of sleep. People are essentially diurnal, but shift workers may adapt completely over a period of weeks to a nocturnal schedule of activity.

The sleep-wake cycle is not determined as rigidly as many other physiological rhythms. For example, one can choose not to sleep for several days and thereby temporarily abolish the pattern. A more fundamental and less easily modified rhythm is the circadian rhythm of body temperature. In this case, there is a daily fluctuation of slightly more than 1 degree centigrade over the course of twenty-four hours, with the lowest body temperature occurring around 4:00 A.M. to 5:00 A.M. Of importance is the fact that the temperature rhythm continues its fluctuation, although somewhat dampened, even if a person stays awake for several days. There are additional characteristics of circadian rhythms that are surprising.

For example, the rhythms behave as though they are endogenous—that is, oscillations are produced within the organism rather than originating from the outside. An area of the brain called the hypothalamus has a pair of clusters of nerve-cell bodies called the suprachiasmatic nuclei, which, if destroyed, will abolish various rhythms, including the temperature rhythm in some animals. Scientists disagree over whether all the body's circadian rhythms are regulated by this part of the brain. One additional source of evidence that circadian rhythms are basically endogenous is the fact that when living organisms, including humans, are kept in constant conditions, the rhythms free-run and show a period, or length, which is different from exactly twenty-four hours.

Free-running rhythms are observed in humans if the individual lives for many days or weeks in an isolated cave or bunker where possible time cues such as the light-dark cycle or other factors have been eliminated. The famous cave explorer Michel Siffre found that he had a sleep-wake cycle of twenty-four hours, thirty-one minutes when he lived alone in a cave without time cues for two months. Similar studies in more controlled environments—World War II bunkers—were carried out by the German scientist Jürgen Aschoff. In each case, it was found that the body's rhythms gradually drifted out of phase with the actual time of day when watches and the natural cycle of light changes were eliminated. Aschoff termed such factors *Zeitgebers,* or "time givers." Individual subjects were found to have their own unique period, or length, for their free-running rhythms—for example, 24.3, 24.5, 24.7, or 24.9 hours. Also, it has been well documented that various rhythms such as the sleep-wake cycle, body temperature, blood pressure, respiration rate, and urinary excretion of sodium, under constant conditions, will show slightly different period lengths and will therefore become desynchronized. Desynchronization, which may occur in the elderly under normal living conditions, is thought by some scientists to be a forerunner to various disease states. It is thought that, under normal conditions, the circadian rhythms are reset each day, perhaps at dawn or dusk, so that the greater-than-twenty-four-hour rhythms are synchronized with the twenty-four-hour day.

Various mental abilities in humans have been shown to be subject to circadian variations. Thus, one's mood generally changes during the day. One's ability to esti-mate time duration varies during the day inversely to the daily change in tempera-ture. The ability to memorize numbers is better in the morning than in the after-noon, and one's ability to add random numbers is better in the morning than in the afternoon. Eye-hand coordination changes with a circadian rhythm, with skills bet-ter during the day and performance reduced at night. The existence of these rhythms has many implications, and the further study of such rhythmic factors remains a vital common ground between physiology and psychology.

Applications

The sleep-wake cycle does not conform strictly to a circadian rhythm, inasmuch as a person willfully can avoid sleeping for many hours. The resultant fatigue, how-ever, does not increase uniformly, as can be attested by students who study late at night and feel better once they stay awake past the 3:00 A.M. to 4:00 A.M. period. Some researchers envision an underlying circadian rhythm of alertness and fatigue that enhances one's ability to awaken in the morning and to fall asleep in the late evening. In general, it is easier to awaken in the morning, when one's body tempera-ture is increasing, and it is easier to fall asleep in the late evening, when one's temperature is falling. So-called owls and larks do exist in the human population; persons who fall into these two groups show a marked difference in how soon their body temperature peaks during the day: The larks peak earlier.

The detailed makeup of sleep itself shows circadian influences. Thus, from mea-suring brain waves with electroencephalographs, it has been found that there is a circadian rhythm in the occurrence of rapid eye movement (REM) sleep, associated with dreaming, so that it occurs more frequently later during the sleep period. In subjects in isolation without time cues, the sleep pattern may change so that they sleep only eight hours every forty-eight hours, or even eight hours every twelve hours. The release of some hormones, such as growth hormone, occurs during the sleep phase, and there is evidence that some sleep disorders and endocrine disorders may be related. Most major cities now have sleep laboratories in which scientists monitor the sleep of patients and apply theories involving circadian rhythms to improve the type and timing of medications.

Shift work is required in circumstances in which around-the-clock services are either essential or economically beneficial. These include medical, police, military, utility, transportation, and other essential services, as well as in the chemical, steel, petroleum, and various other manufacturing industries. Work is done and days off are given according to many different schedules. Within the population, there are "owls" who do not mind working all night, and such persons can adapt to shift work without the fatigue, headaches, and gastrointestinal disorders experienced by their comrades. A number of catastrophic events, such as the Three Mile Island nuclear accident, the chemical explosion in Bhopal, India, and the Chernobyl nuclear accident happened during the late-evening or night shift, when fatigue of ill-adapted workers may have been a factor. It is known that physiological and behavioral rhythms will shift to a new schedule only if the schedule is kept the same every day for a period of weeks. The worker who works the night shift during the week but then enjoys family life during the day on weekends never does completely shift rhythms. Shift workers who stay on their schedule of night work and day sleep will quickly shift their sleep-wake cycle and eventually shift their various behavioral and more fundamental physiological rhythms such as body temperature. Because the body's circadian rhythms are more than twenty-four hours in length, it is easier to start work later on successive days than it is to start work earlier. In some ways, adapting to shift work is similar to overcoming jet lag.

What later became known as jet lag was first experienced by Wiley Post and Harold Gatty on their 1931 around-the-world airplane trip. By the 1950's, increasing numbers of tourists, diplomats, flight crews, and pilots were suffering from the general malaise, headaches, fatigue, disruptions of the sleep-wake cycle, and gastrointestinal disorders that can occur when people cross several time zones within a few hours. Again, as for shift work, there have been catastrophic accidents that may have been caused in part by the inability of workers to adjust rapidly to a new time frame. The effects are worse on eastward flights than on westward flights, perhaps because the circadian rhythms can undergo an adjustment to a lengthening in timing better than to a shortening. A night flight from New York to Paris results in a six-hour time shift, with breakfast coming six hours early according to one's nonshifted circadian rhythms. Within a few days, one's sleep-wake cycle adjusts, but deeper physiological rhythms may take two or more weeks to shift to the new time zone.

Various means have been used to reduce the effects of jet lag. Most experienced diplomats or business persons plan to arrive at the site of negotiations a few days early so that they will have a chance to adjust. It can also help to begin to shift one's activities and sleep pattern a few hours in the direction of the anticipated shift a day or two before one leaves home. Mild sedatives can be used effectively to induce sleep, but the efficacy of complicated diets and most other regimens recommended in the popular press has not been extensively demonstrated in studies performed on humans.

A relatively recent application of an understanding of biological rhythms is found in the study of seasonal affective disorder, or SAD. Persons suffering from this disorder undergo mild to drastic changes in mood and personality with the seasons of the year. Poets and writers have described such changes for ages, but medical science has only recently recognized the truth expressed by such nonscientists. Thus, there are "seasons of the mind": Winter may be full of melancholy and despair, offering little hope for the future, while spring brings happiness, joy, and the energy for new projects. Although as many as one in four persons may show slight seasonal effects, the full-blown disorder is more rare. Some highly creative individuals, such as the artist Vincent van Gogh, writers Edgar Allan Poe and Tennessee Williams, and President Abraham Lincoln, suffered from manic depression (bipolar disorder) and may possibly have had the specific type known as SAD.

Both seasonal and circadian rhythms are involved in SAD. The seasonal rhythm seems to be caused by seasonal changes in the intensity and duration of natural sunlight, an effect which is especially pronounced in the temperate regions of the world. As the days shorten in autumn, some individuals become progressively more blue and moody, unable to work, uninterested in food or sex, and, in extreme cases, suicidal. If such persons take a midwinter vacation to the sunny south, they usually recover their optimism and interest in life within three or four days. Alternatively, Alfred Lewy and other psychiatrists recommend the use of light therapy. For example, early in the morning, upon awaking, a person sits for two or three hours a day near a bright (1,500 lux or greater) light box that mimics the sunshine available during the summer. Light therapy for three to four days usually restores the person to normal mental health, and the use of the light box throughout the autumn and winter avoids the symptoms of SAD for most individuals.

Circadian rhythms are fundamentally involved in the underlying physiology of SAD and its successful treatment with light. The human brain contains a small organ about the size of a pea that is located in the midline underneath the large cerebral hemispheres. This organ, the pineal gland, produces a hormone called melatonin, which is normally released into the bloodstream during the night. The eyes detect light during the day and transmit that fact to the brain and pineal gland by specific nerve pathways. If light is present, or if light interrupts the normal dark period, then the synthesis and release of melatonin is inhibited. The use of bright-light therapy inhibits the release of melatonin and thereby seems to alter circadian rhythms in the brain. An understanding of the details of the functioning of the brain in SAD and the exact role of circadian rhythms awaits further research.

Context

The history of the development of the concept of circadian rhythms is brief. An early record by Androsthenes, written during the marches of Alexander the Great in the fourth century B.C., noted the daily movement of the leaves and flower petals of the tamarind tree, which open during the day but close at night. In 1729, a French astronomer, Jean Jacques d'Ortous de Mairan, reported his observations on the leaf movements of a "sensitive" heliotrope plant that continued to open and close its leaves approximately every twenty-four hours even when it was kept in continuous dark. This was the first demonstration of a free-running rhythm. Studies on humans included those by Sanctorius, who in the seventeenth century constructed a huge balance upon which he was seated in a chair. He found evidence for a circadian rhythm in body weight. Later researchers studied circadian rhythms in plants until about 1930, when some animal studies were begun. It was the 1950's before circadian rhythms were more widely studied and research on humans began to be more common.

In psychology, Nathaniel Kleitman and Eugene Aserinsky in the 1940's discovered rapid eye movement, or REM, sleep. The rhythmic patterns in REM sleep and their relation to the circadian sleep-wake cycle have remained an active area for research. The psychobiologist Curt Richter carried out work at The Johns Hopkins University on the activity rhythms in rats, which he caught in the alleys of Baltimore, and was the first researcher to use running wheels to record circadian locomotor activity. Richter also identified the general area in which the suprachiasmatic nuclei are found as a region of the hypothalamus important in controlling circadian rhythms. Simon Folkard and colleagues have studied various human performance tests and have found numerous circadian rhythms. They found that the circadian rhythms in memory tests peaked at different times, depending on the complexity of the number to be memorized.

There is a need for more research by psychologists who are aware of the importance of circadian rhythms. The existence of circadian rhythms is often not considered when experiments are designed. Always doing an experiment at the same time of the day is not a sufficient measure for removing the effect of circadian rhythms. Instead, it is necessary to study circadian rhythms in detail in an attempt to understand better the particular phenomenon that a psychologist is investigating.

Bibliography

Ahlgren, Andrew, and Franz Halberg. *Cycles of Nature: An Introduction to Biological Rhythms.* Washington, D.C.: National Science Teachers Association, 1990. An easy-to-read introduction to biological rhythms written expressly for the high school student. Contains simple experiments, some of which would make ideal science-fair projects or classroom demonstrations. Very nicely illustrated and well written, this booklet covers most of the fundamental characteristics of circadian rhythms. Highly recommended to students and teachers alike.

Coleman, Richard M. *Wide Awake at 3:00 A.M.: By Choice or by Chance?* New York: W. H. Freeman, 1990. A popular account of the applications of circadian rhythms to human physiology and psychology, written by a former director of the Stanford University Sleep Disorders Clinic. Coleman writes for the layperson and covers a variety of topics, including shift work, jet lag, sleep, and dreams. The appendix includes a questionnaire that helps readers determine whether they are owls or larks. The book explains terms as they are presented and has a glossary.

Halaris, Angelos. *Chronobiology and Psychiatric Disorders.* New York: Elsevier, 1987. A technical review of the diagnosis and treatment of depression and their relationship to circadian rhythms. Not recommended for light reading, but helpful for details when specific information is required. Many of the experts surveyed here present their theoretical models for depression in terms of altered brain chemistry of neurotransmitters.

Minors, D. S., and J. M. Waterhouse. *Circadian Rhythms and the Human.* Boston:

John Wright, 1981. A comprehensive textbook that reviews hundreds of research reports to give an outstanding overview of the field. Written for the college level and above. A classic.

Moore-Ede, Martin C., Frank M. Sulzman, and Charles A. Fuller. *The Clocks That Time Us.* Cambridge, Mass.: Harvard University Press, 1982. A general textbook on circadian rhythms that includes information on animals as well as humans. Some sections are too theoretical for all but the most dedicated of readers. Well illustrated, with an excellent list of references.

Rosenthal, Norman E. *Seasons of the Mind: Why You Get the Winter Blues and What You Can Do About It.* New York: Bantam Books, 1989. A fascinating, clearly written description of the symptoms and treatment of seasonal affective disorder. A must for anyone who wants a broad discussion of the topic. References to poets, artists, and writers who may have had (or have noted) SAD are especially enlightening. Includes a guide listing physicians experienced in treating patients with this type of depression.

Siffre, Michel. *Beyond Time.* New York: McGraw-Hill, 1964. An enthralling account of the adventures of a cave explorer who stays without a clock alone in caves for months at a time and carefully notes his physiological and psychological changes. Written for the general public, this book generated wide interest in such isolation experiments. Fascinating reading.

Winfree, Arthur T. *The Timing of Biological Clocks.* New York: Scientific American Library, 1987. A beautifully illustrated book that covers philosophical concepts of time and clocks as well as the nature of circadian and other biological rhythms. Some sections are rather mathematical, but these are well worth the effort to understand and appreciate. Recommended for the college-level or motivated high school student.

John T. Burns

Cross-References

Bipolar Disorder, 422; Dreams, 836; Ethology, 992; Health Psychology, 1139; Insomnia, 1303; Seasonal Affective Disorder, 2155; Sleep: Stages and Functions, 2277.

CLINICAL DEPRESSION

Type of psychology: Psychopathology
Field of study: Depression

Clinical depression is an emotional disorder characterized by extreme sadness and a loss of ability to experience pleasure. Its clinical features also include cognitive (for example, low self-worth), behavioral (for example, decreased activity level), and physical (for example, fatigue) symptoms. Depression is a frequently diagnosed disorder in both inpatient and outpatient mental health settings.

Principal terms

ANHEDONIA: a symptom of clinical depression; a loss of the capacity to experience pleasure

BECK DEPRESSION INVENTORY (BDI): a brief questionnaire used to measure the severity of depression; developed by Aaron Beck

CHILDREN'S DEPRESSION INVENTORY (CDI): a modified version of the BDI that was developed to measure the severity of depression in children; developed by Maria Kovacs

COGNITIVE THERAPY FOR DEPRESSION: a treatment that helps depressed clients think more accurately and effectively about their experiences; largely based on Aaron Beck's cognitive theory of depression

DYSPHORIA: a symptom of clinical depression; extreme sadness

DYSTHYMIC DISORDER: a form of depression in which mild to moderate levels of depressive symptoms persist chronically

HELPLESSNESS: the belief that one has little or no control over the events in one's life; viewed by Martin Seligman as an important cause of depression

MONOAMINE OXIDASE (MAO) INHIBITORS: a class of antidepressant drugs

TRICYCLICS: a class of antidepressant drugs

Overview

Clinical depression is a severe emotional disorder that is characterized by four classes of symptoms: emotional, cognitive, behavioral, and physical. The major emotional symptoms, at least one of which is necessary for the diagnosis of depression, are dysphoria (extreme sadness or depressed mood) and anhedonia (lack of capacity to experience pleasure). Other emotional symptoms, which may but do not necessarily occur in depression, are anxiety and anger. Depressed individuals also experience cognitive symptoms. They have negative or pessimistic thoughts about themselves, the world around them, and the future. They misinterpret their experiences so as to support these negative views. In some cases, the negative views of self and future are so extreme that the individual contemplates suicide. Behavioral symptoms of depression include decreased activity level and slowed rate of activity. Depressed individuals also experience several physical symptoms. They become easily fatigued, lose their appetites, and experience sleep disturbances (including insomnia, an inability to fall asleep; and morning waking, awakening in the early morning and being unable to return to sleep).

Depression is one of the more commonly experienced mental disorders. For example, in 1985, psychologists John Wing and Paul Bebbington examined research that used psychological tests to measure the prevalence of (or lifetime risk for) depression in the general population. They found that estimates of the prevalence of depression generally ranged from about 5 to 10 percent. Interestingly, all the studies examined by Wing and Bebbington agreed that depression was more common in women than in men. Estimates of the prevalence of depression ranged from 2.6 to 4.5 percent in men and from 5.9 to 9.0 percent in women.

Depression is also related to other characteristics. Risk for depression increases with age. The evidence is clear that depression is more common in adults and the elderly than in children or adolescents. Interest in childhood depression has increased since the early 1970's, however, and the number of children and adolescents who have been diagnosed as depressed has increased since that time. Depression is also related to socioeconomic status. In general, people who are unemployed and who are in lower income groups have higher risks for depression than others. This may be a result of the higher levels of stress experienced by individuals in lower-income groups. Finally, family history is related to depression. That is, clinical depression tends to run in families. This is consistent with both biological and psychological theories of depression.

Psychologists face several difficulties when attempting to determine the prevalence of depression. First, the symptoms of depression range in severity from mild to severe. It may not always be clear at which point these symptoms move from the mild nuisances associated with "normal" levels of sadness to significant symptoms associated with clinical depression. Since the early 1970's, clinical psychologists have devoted an increased amount of attention to depressions that occur at mild to moderate levels. Even though these milder depressions are not as debilitating as clinical depression, they produce significant distress for the individual and so warrant attention. In 1980, the term "dysthymic disorder" was introduced to describe depressions which, although mild to moderate, persist chronically.

Another complication in determining the prevalence of depression is that it may occur either as a primary or as a secondary problem. As a primary problem, depression is the initial or major disorder which should be the focus of clinical intervention. On the other hand, as a secondary problem, depression occurs in reaction to or as a consequence of another disorder. For example, many patients experience such discomfort or distress from medical or mental disorders that they eventually develop the symptoms of depression. In this case, the primary disorder and not depression is usually the focus of treatment.

There are several major approaches to the treatment of clinical depression, each focusing on one of the four classes of symptoms of depression. Psychoanalytic therapists believe that the cause of depression is emotional: underlying anger which stems from some childhood loss and which has been turned inward. Psychoanalysts therefore treat depression by helping the client to identify the cause of the underlying anger and to cope with it in a more effective manner.

Psychiatrist Aaron T. Beck views depression primarily as a cognitive disorder. He holds that depressives have negative views of self, world, and future, and that they interpret their experiences in a distorted fashion so as to support these pessimistic views. A related cognitive model of depression is that of Martin E. P. Seligman. He argues that depression results from the perception that one is helpless or has little or no control over the events in one's life. Seligman has shown that laboratory-induced helplessness produces many of the symptoms of depression. Cognitive therapy for depression, which Beck described in 1979, aims at helping depressed clients identify and then change their negative and inaccurate patterns of thinking.

Behavioral therapists view depression as the result of conditioning. Psychologist Peter Lewinsohn suggests that depression results from low amounts of reinforcement. His behavioral therapy for depression aims at increasing reinforcement levels, through scheduling pleasant activities and improving the client's social skills.

Biologically oriented therapies exist as well. Two classes of antidepressant medications, monoamine oxidase (MAO) inhibitors and tricyclics, are effective both in treating clinical depression and in preventing future episodes of depression. Electroconvulsive (shock) therapy (ECT) has also been found to be effective in treating severe depression. Although the reasons the biological treatments work have not been conclusively identified, it is thought that they are effective because they increase the activity or amount of norepinephrine and serotonin, two neurotransmitters which are important in the transmission of impulses in the nervous system.

Applications

In 1983, Eugene Levitt, Bernard Lubin, and James Brooks reported the results of the National Depression Survey, which attempted to determine the prevalence and correlates of depression in the general population. They interviewed more than three thousand people, including 622 teenagers, who were randomly selected to be a representative sample of the entire United States population. Subjects completed a brief self-report measure of depression and answered questions concerning their age, occupation, education, religion, and other variables.

Levitt, Lubin, and Brooks found that slightly more than 3 percent of the population was experiencing depression that was severe enough to warrant clinical intervention and so could be termed clinical depression. This figure is similar to that found by other investigators. In addition, Levitt, Lubin, and Brooks found that depression was related to sex, age, occupational status, and income. Depression was higher for subjects who were female, older, lower in occupational status, and either low or high in income (earning less than $6,000 or more than $25,000).

One of the most widely used measures of depression is the Beck Depression Inventory (BDI). Beck introduced this test in 1961 to assess the severity of depression in individuals who are known or suspected to have depression. The BDI has twenty-one items, each concerning a symptom of depression (for example, weight loss, suicidal thinking) which is rated for severity. The BDI can be self-administered or can be completed by an interviewer.

Since its introduction, the BDI has become one of the most widely used measures of depression for both research and clinical purposes. Many studies have shown that the BDI is an accurate and useful measure of depression. For example, BDI scores have been found to be related to both clinicians' ratings of the severity of a client's depression and clinical improvements during the course of treatment for depression, and to be able to discriminate between the diagnosis of clinical depression and other conditions.

Psychologist Maria Kovacs developed the Children's Depression Inventory (CDI) by modifying the BDI for use with children. Similar in format to the BDI, the CDI contains twenty-eight items, each of which concerns a symptom of depression that is rated for severity. Research has supported the utility of the CDI. CDI ratings have been found to be related to clinicians' ratings of childhood depression. CDI scores have also been found to discriminate children hospitalized for depression from children hospitalized for other disorders. The CDI (along with other recently developed measures of childhood depression) has contributed to psychology's recent research on and understanding of the causes and treatment of childhood depression.

Many research projects since the 1970's have examined the effectiveness of cognitive and behavioral treatments of depression. Beck and his colleagues have demonstrated that cognitive therapy of depression is superior to no treatment whatsoever and to placebos (inactive psychological or medical interventions which should have no real effect but which the client believes have therapeutic value). In addition, this research has shown that cognitive therapy is about as effective as both antidepressant medications and behavior therapy. Similarly, Lewinsohn and others have shown the effectiveness of behavior therapy on depression by demonstrating that it is superior to no treatment and to placebo conditions.

One of the most important studies of the treatment of depression is the Treatment of Depression Collaborative Research Program, begun by the National Institute of Mental Health (NIMH) in the mid-1980's. A group of 250 clinically depressed patients was randomly assigned to four treatment conditions: interpersonal psychotherapy, cognitive behavioral psychotherapy, tricyclic antidepressant medication, and placebo medication. Treatment was presented over sixteen to twenty sessions. Patients were assessed by both self-report and a clinical evaluator before treatment, after every fourth session, and at six-, twelve-, and eighteen-month follow-ups after the end of treatment.

This study found that patients in all four treatment conditions improved significantly over the course of therapy. In general, patients who received antidepressant medication improved the most, patients who received the placebo improved the least, and patients who received the two forms of psychotherapy improved to an intermediate degree (but were closer in improvement to those receiving antidepressant medication than to those receiving the placebo). This study also found that, for patients in general, there was no significant difference between the effectiveness rates of the antidepressant medication and the two forms of psychotherapy.

For severely depressed patients, however, antidepressant medication and interpersonal psychotherapy were found to be more effective than other treatments; for less severely depressed patients, there were no differences in effectiveness across the four treatment conditions.

Context

Clinical depression is one of the most prevalent psychological disorders. Because depression is associated with an increased risk for suicide, it is also one of the more severe disorders. For these reasons, psychologists have devoted much effort to determining the causes of depression and developing effective treatments.

Theories and treatments of depression can be classified into four groups: emotional, cognitive, behavioral, and physical. In the first half of the twentieth century, the psychoanalytic theory of depression, which emphasizes the role of the emotion of anger, dominated clinical psychology's thinking about the causes and treatment of depression. Following the discovery of the first antidepressant medications in the 1950's, psychologists increased their attention to physical theories and treatments of depression. Since the early 1970's, Beck's and Seligman's cognitive approaches and Lewinsohn's behavioral theory have received increased amounts of attention. By the 1990's, the biological, cognitive, and behavioral theories of depression had all surpassed the psychoanalytic theory of depression in terms of research support for their respective proposed causes and treatments.

Another shift in emphasis in psychology's thinking about depression concerns childhood depression. Prior to the 1970's, psychologists paid relatively little attention to depression in children; classical psychoanalytic theory suggested that children had not yet completed a crucial step of their psychological development that psychoanalysts believed was necessary for a person to become depressed. Thus, many psychologists believed that children did not experience depression or that, if they did become depressed, their depressions were not severe. Research in the 1970's demonstrated that children do experience depression and that, when depressed, children exhibit symptoms similar to those of depressed adults. Since the 1970's, psychologists have devoted much effort to understanding the cause and treatment of childhood depression. Much of this work has examined how the biological, cognitive, and behavioral models of depression, originally developed for and applied to adults, may generalize to children.

Another shift in psychology's thinking about depression concerns the attention paid to mild and moderate depressions. Since the 1960's, clinical psychology has been interested in the early detection and treatment of minor conditions in order to prevent the development of more severe disorders. This emphasis on prevention has influenced the field's thinking about depression. Since the early 1970's, psychologists have applied cognitive and behavioral models of depression to nonpatients who obtain high scores on measures of depression. Even though these individuals are not clinically depressed, they still experience significant distress and so may benefit from the attention of psychologists. By using cognitive or behavioral interventions with these individuals, psychologists may prevent the development of more severe depressions.

Bibliography

Beck, Aaron T., A. J. Rush, B. F. Shaw, and G. Emery. *Cognitive Therapy of Depression*. New York: Guilford Press, 1979. Summarizes the cognitive theory of depression and describes how this model can be applied in the treatment of depressed clients.

Beckham, Ernest Edward, and William R. Leber, eds. *Handbook of Depression: Treatment, Assessment, and Research*. Homewood, Ill.: Dorsey Press, 1985. Presents a comprehensive overview of depression. Presents the major approaches to explaining, diagnosing, and treating depression, along with the research evidence concerning each.

Levitt, Eugene E., Bernard Lubin, and James M. Brooks. *Depression: Concepts, Controversies, and Some New Facts*. 2d ed. Hillsdale, N.J.: Lawrence Erlbaum, 1983. Reviews the symptoms, theories, and epidemiology of depression. Also describes the results of a national survey of depression.

Lewinsohn, Peter M., R. F. Munoz, M. A. Youngren, and A. M. Zeiss. *Control Your Depression*. Englewood Cliffs, N.J.: Prentice-Hall, 1978. A self-help book written for a general audience. Describes Lewinsohn's behavioral therapy, which has been found to be an effective treatment for depression.

Rehm, Lynn P., ed. *Behavior Therapy for Depression: Present Status and Future Directions*. New York: Academic Press, 1981. An overview of behavioral and cognitive behavioral models of depression.

Rush, A. John, and Kenneth Z. Altshuler, eds. *Depression: Basic Mechanisms, Diagnosis, and Treatment*. New York: Guilford Press, 1986. Presents research concerning the biological models of the cause and treatment of depression.

Rutter, Michael, Carroll E. Izard, and Peter B. Read, eds. *Depression in Young People: Developmental and Clinical Perspectives*. New York: Guilford Press, 1986. Presents research on many aspects of the problem of depression in children, which had not received much attention from psychologists until the 1970's.

Seligman, Martin E. P. *Helplessness: On Depression, Development, and Death*. San Francisco: W. H. Freeman, 1987. Seligman explains the learned helplessness theory of depression, describing his early research and comparing the symptoms of laboratory-induced helplessness to those of clinical depression.

Michael Wierzbicki

Cross-References

Bipolar Disorder, 422; Cognitive Behavior Therapy, 546; Cognitive Therapy, 586; Depression: Theoretical Explanations, 789; Psychological Diagnosis and Classification: DSM-III-R, 1925; Seasonal Affective Disorder, 2155; Suicide, 2501.

CLINICAL INTERVIEWING, TESTING, AND OBSERVATION

Type of psychology: Psychopathology
Field of study: Personality assessment

Clinical interviewing, testing, and observation are the principal methods of psychological assessment; they are most often used by professionals in applied psychology in order to gather information that will help them make important decisions about others.

Principal terms
> ATTRIBUTES: a person's unique characteristics or traits
> CLINICAL PSYCHOLOGIST: a person specially trained to assess and treat mental disorders and behavior problems
> DIAGNOSIS: an attempt to distinguish one disorder from another
> INTELLIGENCE QUOTIENT (IQ): a person's mental ability in comparison with the rest of the population (with age taken into consideration)
> LEARNING DISABILITY: the inability to learn academic subjects such as reading or math in a normal manner despite having an average intelligence level
> NORMATIVE DATA: a representative sample of scores which are used as a standard when comparing test results
> PERSONALITY: an individual's unique collection of behavioral responses that are consistent across time and situations
> RELIABILITY: the consistency of test results across time
> VALIDITY: the extent to which tests measure what they are designed to measure

Overview

Psychological assessment uses a set of techniques to collect information about a person and to make various decisions based on that information. The goal of assessment is usually to describe, evaluate, or make predictions about a person. For example, a clinical psychologist may conduct an assessment on a depressed person in order to evaluate how severe the depression is and to predict whether the person might attempt suicide. This information can then be used in deciding whether the person needs to be hospitalized or in determining which treatment approach to use.

The first step in the assessment process is deciding which information needs to be collected. Sometimes this is obvious, as in a case in which someone is referred to a psychologist to answer a specific question; for example, a judge may want to know whether a person is mentally retarded. At other times, the situation is more open-ended. For example, a mother may want to know why her daughter is failing in school. In this case, it may be important to collect information about the girl's personality, mental ability, motivation level, emotional problems, or a number of other possible causes.

The second step of the assessment process is deciding how to obtain the information. In general, psychologists use three methods to collect assessment data: the clinical interview, testing, and observation. The interview is the most widely used method for collecting information in clinical psychology. It can be defined as a controlled conversation with a special purpose. The conversation is controlled by the interviewer, and the purpose is the collection of specific information. There are many types of interviews, and each has a particular objective. For example, the initial, or intake, interview is used to collect general information about the person and the problem that presents itself. A case history interview is used to collect information about the person's background, family history, or other personal information, such as educational and work experience. A third type is called the mental-status interview. Here the purpose is to help define the problem and come up with a diagnosis.

An interview can be structured or unstructured, but most types of interview fall somewhere in between. In a structured interview, the topics and questions are planned, and questions are usually given in a specific order. Structured interviews are often used to arrive at a diagnosis or collect specific types of information. In an unstructured interview, the topics and questions are not specifically planned and are frequently based on the responses given by the interviewee. The questions may be open-ended and may cover diverse topic areas. Regardless of whether the interview is structured, the first step in this process is to put the person at ease and make him or her feel comfortable. This is important because most people feel apprehensive about talking to strangers, especially about information that may be embarrassing or personal.

A second method for collecting information about a person is testing. Testing is a very broad concept covering many diverse areas, such as medical tests, subject matter tests given in school, and tests that only a trained psychologist can give. This discussion, however, will be limited to psychological testing, which is defined as collecting a sample of a person's behavior under standard conditions. This definition addresses several issues. First, there is an almost infinite amount of information that can be collected about a person. Usually, the intention is to collect a representative sample of a particular attribute in a short amount of time. In a sense, testing results in a behavioral "snapshot" of a person. Second, unlike physical characteristics such as height and weight, psychological features cannot be measured directly. They must be inferred from observable and measurable behavior. For example, a person's intelligence level is estimated from the overt responses given in a mental-ability test. Third, psychological tests need to be given with clearly defined administrative and scoring procedures in order to prevent bias and ensure that test results are obtained the same way for each person.

Psychological tests must have three qualities in order to be useful. First, they must be valid. This means that they must truly measure what they were designed to measure. Second, they must be consistent, or reliable; if the same person were to be tested more than once over a period of time, the results should be approximately the same each time (assuming that the attribute does not change). Finally, the test needs to have standards which can be used to interpret obtained results. These are usually called normative data, or norms. For example, if a person obtains a score of 70 on a test and the average of the normative data is 50, it can be seen that this person's score is above average.

The third method of gathering psychological information is observation. This allows a firsthand look at behaviors and is also a way of collecting information that may not be available otherwise. For example, a good way of evaluating the progress of a person who is being treated for shyness is to observe the individual at a social function. The process of observation first entails selecting the category of behaviors, situations, or time periods of interest: for example, observing a child in a classroom, a mental patient applying for a job, or the number of times a couple argue in an hour. Second, a decision is made whether to generate the behaviors or situations artificially or to wait until they occur naturally. Inducing the behaviors artificially may produce results that are different from naturally occurring behaviors, but often this is the only way observation can be done.

Sometimes structured behavior checklists are used to help record the behavior, or it may be audio- or videotaped. Usually, the subject is aware that he or she is being observed, but the observer may not always be visible (for example, observation may be conducted through a two-way mirror). The exact procedure is based on the goal of the assessment, the characteristics of the person being evaluated, and the setting in which the observation is conducted.

Observational data can be used in a number of ways, which vary greatly among psychologists. Some use such data only to supplement test results and interviews. Others, such as behaviorally oriented psychologists, use observational data as their primary form of information gathering. Behaviorists use observation in order to help define behaviors, to assess how the behaviors originated and how they are maintained, and to help design a program to change them. Although observation provides much useful information, its chief disadvantage is the time and effort involved in using the procedure.

These major assessment techniques are used in a wide variety of settings, such as schools, mental hospitals, industry, the military, and the community. Psychological tests are used to measure personality traits, mental ability, career interests, and other attributes; they are also used to predict future performance in college, graduate school, or in a profession.

Applications

An example will provide an illustration of how these techniques are used. A twelve-year-old boy was referred to a clinical psychologist because he was failing school and had started wetting the bed. The psychologist initially held a number of interviews: one with the boy alone, one with the parents alone, and a third with the parents and child together. In meeting with the boy alone, the psychologist wanted to establish a relationship with the child that would help ensure that he was honest and also serve as a starting point for the therapeutic process. In addition, he wanted to ask the child a number of questions that he might be reluctant to answer in front of his parents—for example, questions regarding the use of drugs or alcohol, or possible abuse of some kind, either by the parents or by someone else. Although he denied being abused or using drugs and alcohol, he did admit that his natural father and mother had been divorced and that he was upset when his mother had recently remarried.

The psychologist also conducted a mental-status examination to help him decide which psychological tests might be used and to help him arrive at a diagnosis. He found that the boy was not psychotic (which generally means he was in good contact with reality) and that there did not appear to be any serious mental illness. Although he was somewhat depressed over the recent divorce, he did not have any suicidal thoughts or plans.

The interview with the stepfather and mother revealed that the boy was failing math and science and was doing below-average work in English and other subjects. In the past, the boy had never been an exceptional student but had been able to get passing grades. The bed-wetting had started after the mother had remarried. The parents had had the boy examined by their family physician, who could find no medical reason for his wetting the bed. The boy was not really a behavioral problem at home. He had never run away and, as far as they knew, had never engaged in unlawful acts. The mother had divorced the boy's real father about two years earlier; since that time, he had seemed more withdrawn. The stepfather reported getting along well with the child in general, but they were not close. When the boy was asked to join his parents, the psychologist noticed that he was very quiet and passive. He sat next to his mother and did not volunteer any information. It appeared that he was hiding his thoughts and feelings from his parents.

The psychologist gave the boy intelligence and personality tests. The intelligence test showed that the boy's IQ was in the average range, but it suggested a possibility of a learning disability. Further tests supported this contention. The personality test did not indicate any serious mental illness but did imply that the boy was somewhat anxious and depressed. It also suggested "passive-aggressive" personality traits, which meant that the boy was likely to express his anger or hostility indirectly.

The last step of the assessment process was observation of the boy in the school setting. This was done by a school psychologist, who reported that the boy interacted well with teachers and other students. He was not a behavioral problem and seemed to put forth his best effort in the classroom. He completed all homework assignments and appeared to pay attention in class. Despite all this, he had great difficulty understanding much of the material that was presented, which is consistent with a learning disability.

After gathering all this information, the psychologist came to the following conclusions. The primary reason for the recent school failure appeared to be the learning disability, although the boy's depression may have contributed as well. He probably always had had this disability but had been able to compensate for it until the academic material became more difficult, in the seventh grade. The reason the disability was not detected sooner is that he did not exhibit disruptive behaviors such as the inability to sit still or pay attention, which often accompany learning disabilities and which may have made it more likely that the classroom teacher would have referred him for a psychological evaluation sooner.

The boy's bed-wetting was more difficult to diagnose. Since a physical problem was ruled out, the psychologist speculated that it was related to his parents' divorce and mother's remarriage. For example, the boy's passive-aggressive traits would suggest that the bed-wetting might be an indirect way of expressing his anger and hostility toward the mother for remarrying. This would also be consistent with the psychologist's observation that the boy had difficulty expressing his true feelings to his parents.

The treatment plan was designed so that the boy would receive special services at school to address his learning disability. Once these were initiated, his grades started to improve. The psychologist held individual treatment sessions with the boy in order to get him to become more assertive and to help him adjust to the divorce and new stepfather. He also held family sessions in order to teach the parents and child to communicate more effectively with one another and to show them how to resolve conflicts. Finally, a specific procedure was designed to deal directly with the bed-wetting.

Context

Modern assessment techniques began with the birth of psychology in the nineteenth century. Initially, the focus of this new science was the measurement of physiological responses such as the perception of touch or sound. It quickly moved, however, to the measurement of differences between individuals, which is the backbone of modern psychological assessment (if everyone had the same traits or attributes, it would make no sense to try to measure them).

It is perhaps legitimate to say that Francis Galton, a cousin of Charles Darwin, was the father of psychological assessment. His studies led to the development of statistical techniques which are an essential aspect of assessment. He also developed the first crude intelligence test. In 1905, Alfred Binet, who was working in France, developed the first modern intelligence test, which in some ways launched the field of psychological assessment. A revised English translation of this test is still widely used. Perhaps the biggest catalyst for the use of assessment instruments, however, was World War I, during which the United States was faced with the task of testing the intellectual and emotional states of thousands of recruits. This led to the development of group personality and intelligence tests and resulted in the training of a large number of psychologists to administer these tests. After the war, these new skills were used to develop new techniques and expand assessment services to many public and private settings. By the 1930's, there were thousands of tests in print, and psychological assessment was a firmly established field.

Psychological assessment also helped launch the field of clinical psychology; prior to War World II, clinical psychology and assessment were virtually synonymous. At the time, clinical psychologists spent most of their time assessing clients, and most treatment was done by psychiatrists (medical doctors specially trained to treat mental disorders). World War II resulted in a shortage of psychiatrists; therefore, clinical psychologists were trained to provide treatment as well as assessment services. When the war ended, these newly trained psychologists continued to offer these services in a variety of settings. Clinical psychologists now make up the single largest segment of the profession.

Either directly or indirectly, psychological assessment has affected the lives of everyone in this culture, and the field is continually expanding and changing. Computers are used to administer and score psychological tests, and some programs can tailor questions to fit the profile of an individual. Computers will continue to play a major role in future psychological assessments. The major breakthrough in the field, however, will occur when new methods are developed that will allow attributes such as intelligence and personality traits to be measured in a much more direct and therefore accurate fashion.

Bibliography

Cohen, R. J., P. Montague, L. S. Nathanson, and M. E. Swerdlik. *Psychological Testing: An Introduction to Tests and Measurement.* Mountain View, Calif.: Mayfield, 1988. A college-level textbook introducing the basic concepts of psychological testing and assessment. Twenty chapters cover all the broad aspects of this field, including historical background, use of statistics, major theories, and a review of personality and mental ability tests and assessments. Discusses computer-based assessment and includes a large list of test publishers. The lack of a glossary, however, makes this less useful for novice readers.

Gould, Stephen Jay. *The Mismeasure of Man.* New York: W. W. Norton, 1981. A historical description of the appraisal of intelligence, starting with the measurement of skulls and proceeding to modern theories of mental ability. By carefully examining and reevaluating original data, Gould concludes that many of these theories, with their contention that intelligence is hereditary, are biased and racist. A detailed and well-documented book for the advanced reader.

Matarazzo, J. D. "Psychological Assessment Versus Psychological Testing." *American Psychologist* 45 (1990): 999-1017. An important article written by one of the best-known specialists in psychological assessment. Provides a brief historical review of psychological assessment and details the differences between psychological testing and assessment. Outlines the framework of psychological assessment and its relevance to courtroom testimony. Written for professional psychologists but comprehensible, for the most part, to college-level readers.

Mischel, Walter. *Personality and Assessment.* New York: John Wiley & Sons, 1968. A somewhat dated but often-cited textbook which helped launch the controversy over whether the environment or personality "traits" are more important in shaping behavior. Does a good job of covering the basic factors involved in measuring psychological constructs. With some important exceptions, remains largely relevant; but should only be used in conjunction with more recent publications.

Nietzel, M. T., D. A. Berstein, and R. Milich. *Introduction to Clinical Psychology.* 3d ed. Englewood Cliffs, N.J.: Prentice-Hall, 1991. An introductory, relatively easy-to-read college-level textbook on clinical psychology. Includes three chapters on testing, interviewing, and observation, and one introductory chapter on psychological assessment. Covers the material well and includes a history of each of the three techniques and general procedures. Provides easy-to-follow examples and case studies.

Sweetland, R. C., and D. J. Keysor, eds. *Tests.* Kansas City, Mo.: Test Corporation of America, 1986. A reference book which covers a broad range of assessments in psychology, business, and education. Provides brief descriptions of more than four thousand tests, including age level, details of administration, purpose of test, scoring method, cost, and publisher. Easy to use; provides information in a simple, straightforward format.

Salvatore Cullari

Cross-References

Ability Tests: Individual and Group, 1; Behavioral Assessment and Personality Rating Scales, 387; Interest Inventories, 1349; Personality: Psychophysiological Measures, 1790; Personality Interviewing Strategies, 1797; Projective Personality Traits, 1885; Psychological Diagnosis and Classification: DSM-III-R, 1925; Testing: Historical Perspectives, 2540.

THE CODEPENDENT PERSONALITY

Type of psychology: Psychopathology
Fields of study: Personality theory; substance abuse

The codependent personality is characterized by a lack of a stable self-concept, which manifests itself in a troubled perception of self and disturbed relationships with others. By compulsively taking care of others and denying their own needs, often to the point of serious self-neglect, codependents seek an identity through achieving a favorable image in the eyes of others.

Principal terms
   ADDICTION: a progressive, out-of-control pursuit of a substance, object, or relationship that results in life-damaging consequences for the addicted person
   COMPULSION: a behavior or thought pattern in which the individual feels driven to engage, normally to ward off anxiety or other uncomfortable feelings
   IDENTITY DEVELOPMENT: the process of forming a separate self with distinct thoughts, needs, and feelings that differentiate the self from others
   SELF-CONCEPT: the individual's thoughts about the value of the self, particularly in relationship to others; it influences self-esteem, or feelings about the self
   SYSTEMS THEORY: the interconnection of individuals in family, work, and community systems so that change in one member in the system necesarily produces change in the other members as well

Overview

At the foundation of the codependent personality is a pervasive lack of identity development. Codependents look to others for thoughts, feelings, and values that would normally come out of a well-developed sense of self. For example, when asked to offer an opinion on the death penalty, a typical codependent reaction would be to wait for the group consensus and offer a "safe" response—one that would be most in keeping with the thoughts of the group. This is often done subconsciously and is in contrast to the healthy reaction of offering an honest personal viewpoint.

In truth, codependents do not withhold their feelings as much as they are unaware of what they feel, because of their incomplete development of a separate self: They cannot reveal what they literally do not know. Since their self-perceptions are composites of the reflections they have received from others, how they present themselves will vary, often markedly, depending on who is with them. Codependents have difficulty recognizing and articulating feelings, and they often hold back their feelings out of fear. Though they may not be aware of their feelings, their feelings do, nevertheless, influence them. Their needs remain unmet in their desire to please others, or at the very least to avoid disapproval. As a result, they accumulate anger and rage for which they have no healthy outlet. Depression is also common, particularly a low-grade, chronic depression that would be relieved if they could focus on their own needs.

Codependents have high, and often unrealistic, expectations for themselves, and they tend to be perfectionists. An exaggerated fear of failure drives them, as does a barely conscious sense of being defective or somehow incomplete as a person. As the result of this poor evaluation of themselves, codependents fear getting close to others because others may judge them as harshly as they judge themselves. To guard against being "found out," they keep emotionally distant, though their behaviors may appear to others as genuinely warm and intimate. In truth, their real selves are closely guarded and available to no one—including themselves.

They often channel this backlog of unmet emotional needs into addictive or compulsive behaviors. When the pressure builds, codependents may seek diversion in shopping, gambling, work, chemicals, overeating, or other addictions. Instead of experiencing the emotional development that occurs from facing and overcoming interpersonal problems, codependents retreat further from their feelings through the quick "fix" of indulging in addictive behaviors. The effect of their inattention to their needs is cumulative and progressive and interferes with interpersonal relationships. Codependents take care of others, both emotionally and physically, to feel needed as caretakers. Their focus is primarily external, so they pay close attention to how others are feeling and behaving, then adjust how they act to receive the approval they crave.

Since codependents cannot be sure they are interpreting others' wants and needs correctly, their efforts to achieve approval are often unsuccessful. They have unrealistic perceptions of their abilities to control the environment, and when faced with normal limitations, they may frantically increase their efforts in the aim for perfection. As with all their efforts, the goal is self-esteem through external approval. Even when the approval is forthcoming, ironically, the satisfaction is small, because the approval is for a false representation of self. This leaves them feeling that if others really knew them, they would not be accepted. Codependents typically channel this feeling, as they do most other feelings, into more controlling and caretaking behaviors in an attempt to bolster self-esteem.

Because codependents have not developed clear identities, the interdependence between two persons that is characteristic of healthy relationships is not possible. Getting close brings fears of losing what little identity they have. Typically codependents move closer to others to achieve intimacy, then retreat when they fear the closeness will overwhelm them. They fear abandonment as well, so when the emotional distance from others seems too great, they move closer to others and again face their fears of intimacy overwhelming them. This dance between intimacy and distance is ultimately not satisfying and leaves the codependent feeling even more alone.

Codependency originates in settings where individuals feel unwilling or unable to display their true identities. Most typically, codependency occurs in addictive family systems where the family members' needs are secondary to the needs of the addicted individual. Family members cope with and adapt to the addiction in an attempt to stabilize the family system. Individual members' needs are not met if they conflict with the central need of keeping the family in balance and denying the effects of the addiction. Children in these family systems fail to develop separate identities because so much of their energy goes to controlling the environment. The adults in the family also may have failed to develop identities as children, or they may have abandoned their identities as adults under the pressure of keeping the family stable. In other words, codependency can be the result of the failure of normal identity development or of the abandonment of an already developed identity under the pressure of a dysfunctional family system.

Applications

A look at identity development in a healthy family system provides a clearer picture of codependency. Theorist Erik Erikson proposed in 1963 that identity formation occurs through the resolution of crises throughout the life cycle. According to Erikson, as the individual masters the tasks of the various stages of development, he or she moves on to the next stage. Failure to work through the tasks of any stage results in incomplete development for the person. In a healthy family that meets a child's basic needs, he or she receives support and guidance to pass through the early stages of identity formation, as outlined by Erikson.

Stage one, trust versus mistrust, occurs from birth through the age of eighteen months; the second stage, autonomy versus shame and doubt, occurs between eighteen months and three years. Stage three, initiative versus guilt, lasts from the age of three to the age of six. Industry versus inferiority, the fourth stage, lasts from the age of six to age eighteen. The emerging identity is built upon the basic sense of trust the child develops in the early years of life. If experience teaches the child that others are not trustworthy, then the child's sense of self will be weak. Therefore, efforts to move through the later developmental stages will be hampered. In short, trust is essential to all the later developmental work.

In a family in which trust is not easily developed, such as in an addictive family system, the children direct most of their energy toward achieving a feeling of relative safety. The children learn to look to others to provide the sense of safety they could not develop internally. As they take care of other family members' needs, the family system remains stable, which provides a type of security, though the children's individual needs are not recognized and met. This external focus is adaptive in the short term, as the children are meeting some of their safety and security needs, but ultimately, mature identity development is thwarted. The more stable and emotionally healthy the parents are, the more likely it is that the child will successfully move through the later developmental stages. With the mastery of the developmental tasks, the child begins to feel like a competent individual in a stable and predictable environment. This emerging identity then forms the core of the self as a distinct individual.

Claudia Black (1981) identified roles that children adopt in alcoholic families in order to get some of their needs met. These roles have been found to be applicable to other dysfunctional family systems as well. The "responsible one," who is often the oldest child, functions as an adult by taking care of many basic needs of the family members, sometimes including the parents. The "adjuster" adapts to whatever the family system needs and avoids calling attention to himself or herself. The "placater" brings comfort and diversion to the family and takes on the responsibility for the family members' emotional stability. A final role is the "acting-out child," who keeps the family focused on his or her problem behaviors and receives punishment, criticism, and predominantly negative attention.

These roles can overlap so that the "responsible one" may alternate his or her overly mature behaviors with periods of acting out that direct the family's attention to the current problem and away from the fact that the whole family system is in trouble. The family can then console itself that without "the problem," it would be fine. The "placater" also might shift roles and take care of physical needs and responsibilities that would be more appropriately handled by the adults in the family. The "acting-out child" does not always act out; she or he can stop delinquent behaviors if they are not needed. The important issue for the development of codependency is not that children put the needs of the family ahead of their own but that they fill these roles to achieve safety emotionally and physically and fail to develop their own individual thoughts, needs, and feelings. Their development gets lost in their efforts to maintain the family balance.

This ability of codependents to adopt roles and cope despite how they feel is a major strength in certain settings, such as in an alcoholic or other unpredictable family setting. The adapting and responding to others becomes a problem when it is not a choice but is the only way that the codependent knows how to react. As adults, their behavioral repertoire is limited, as their response to demands is to adapt and take care of what everyone else needs first.

The picture is not as bleak as it may seem. Basic personality traits for such occupations as teaching, nursing, and counseling include empathy and the ability to "read" others, which are typically highly developed skills for codependents. On the whole, codependents are resourceful people who learned to survive in difficult circumstances by being acutely aware of the needs and viewpoints of others. The focus of treatment for these individuals is not to reconstruct their personalities but to help them expand their range of behavioral and emotional options.

Context

The term "codependency" originated in the 1970's in the alcohol-treatment field to describe individuals whose lives had become unmanageable because of their relationships with alcoholics. Prior to that time the term used was "co-alcoholic" or "para-alcoholic," which described a cluster of symptoms that the family members of the alcoholic displayed that included depression, anxiety, and interpersonal difficulties. The introduction of the term "codependency" helped to define the cluster of symptoms more clearly so that codependency became a legitimate focus for treatment. Families began receiving treatment targeted at their needs, at times completely independent of the alcoholic's treatment. Research showed that this focus on the family's needs resulted in longer-term sobriety for the alcoholic.

In the 1980's, clinicians became aware that while codependency most obviously arose from alcoholic families or relationships, it also occurred where other addictions or serious dysfunctions were present. Thus, the model for understanding codependency began to be applied by professionals to diverse problems such as eating disorders, gambling, and other addictions. Codependency as an issue began to gain the attention of professionals beyond the addictions field and in other treatment disciplines.

Many traditional clinicians and researchers have been slow to accept codependency as a legitimate treatment issue since the theory has not been grounded in the scholarly research considered necessary for establishing new trends in the field. Clinicians who treat clients for codependency issues maintain, however, that it is not necessary to wait for research to verify what has already been shown to be useful in clinical practice. Their position is that when a treatment modality helps people, it is ethical to continue the treatment concurrently with the research that should ultimately validate their work. Treatment for codependency has been multifaceted and is apparently most effective when it includes some combination of individual or group therapy, self-help groups, workshops, and educational resources. Through the various treatment strategies, codependents begin to recognize the positive aspects of their personalities, such as adaptiveness and the ability to intuit what others need. In time they can learn to extend to themselves the same attention and caretaking they previously gave only to others.

A common fear of codependents is that if they stop being "caretakers" of others they will become uncaring individuals. This fear is usually unfounded, since greater intimacy and depth of emotion are possible in relationships in which individuals give to others by choice rather than through the continuing sacrifice of their own needs. Codependent personalities develop out of dysfunctional family, community, or other systems; when left untreated, this situation results in a continued poor self-concept and in disturbed relationships with others. Treatment has apparently been effective in helping codependents make significant changes. Recognition of codependent traits can therefore be a springboard for personal growth and development rather than a cause for despair.

Bibliography

Ackerman, Robert J., ed. *Growing in the Shadow: Children of Alcoholics.* Pompano Beach, Fla.: Health Communications, 1986. A collection of brief essays by leaders in the adult children of alcoholics and codependency recovery movements. Includes an outline of the causes and treatments of codependency as well as cross-cultural and family treatment considerations. Valuable to the professional yet readily comprehensible by the lay reader.

Beattie, Melody. *Codependent No More.* New York: Harper/Hazelden, 1987. A comprehensive overview of codependency that is complete with clear examples. A bestseller for many months and probably the most frequently read book in the codependency recovery movement. The majority of the book is devoted to self-help principles for codependents.

Black, Claudia. *It Will Never Happen to Me!* Denver: M.A.C., 1981. A brief book designed to introduce family members to the dysfunctional rules and roles of the alcoholic family.

Cermak, Timmen L. *Diagnosing and Treating Co-Dependence.* Minneapolis: Johnson Institute Books, 1986. A proposal to have "codependency" declared a diagnostic category by the American Psychiatric Association. Aimed at a professional audience, but may be of interest to the lay reader.

Erikson, Erik H. *Identity, Youth, and Crisis.* New York: W. W. Norton, 1968. Erikson's theory on the development of identity throughout the stages of the life cycle. A highly theoretical work.

Friel, John. *Adult Children: Secrets of Dysfunctional Families.* Deerfield Beach, Fla.: Health Communications, 1988. A comprehensive overview of dysfunctional family systems and their predictable effects on family members. Clearly written, a valuable resource for both general and professional audiences.

Schaef, Anne Wilson. *Co-Dependence: Misunderstood-Mistreated.* San Francisco: Harper & Row, 1986. An integration of the principles of the chemical dependency and mental health fields. Covers the history and development of the concept of codependence. Mostly written for a general audience; some chapters are directed toward professionals.

Linda E. Meashey

Cross-References

Addictive Personality and Behaviors, 102; Alcoholism, 213; Identity Crises: Erikson, 1255; Personality Theory: Major Issues, 1804; Self-Esteem, 2188; Substance Abuse: An Overview, 2489; Trust, Autonomy, Initiative, and Industry: Erikson, 2591.

COGNITIVE ABILITY: GENDER DIFFERENCES

Type of psychology: Developmental psychology
Fields of study: Cognitive development; cognitive processes

Cognitive differences between men and women have been attributed to both biological and social learning differences. Most differences are quite small; others can be reduced by educational and social intervention. Furthermore, different cognitive styles may encourage diverse solutions to important problems.

Principal terms

COGNITIVE STYLE: the way in which a person prefers to solve a problem or decide whether something is true; includes logical and intuitive styles

GENDER: the behaviors and characteristics that society expects from people of one biological sex; social maleness and femaleness

INTUITIVE THOUGHT: the use of personal reactions and "hunches" to support the truth of something

LOGICAL THOUGHT: the use of external evidence and lack of contradiction to prove the truth of something

MATHEMATICAL ABILITY: the ability to understand and solve problems in higher mathematics, including algebra, geometry, and calculus

SEX: biological maleness or femaleness, determined by genetic endowment and hormones

SOCIAL EXPECTATIONS: the ideas about appropriate behavior held by most people in a society

SPATIAL ABILITY: the ability to manipulate objects and imagine how parts of objects fit together; useful in building and engineering

VERBAL ABILITY: the ability to use words and sentences fluently and effectively, in reading, writing, and speaking

Overview

The study of differences between men and women includes biological, emotional, social, and cognitive variables. Cognitive psychology studies the ways people solve problems as well as variations in different types of thinking abilities. A pioneer review of all the studies concerning gender differences by Eleanor Maccoby and Carol Jacklin, published in 1974, concluded that the two sexes are more alike than different. Published studies note that there is considerable overlap between men's and women's performance, no matter what is being measured. An individual male or female may be much better than most of the opposite sex on any characteristic that is studied. The term "gender differences" refers to differences between groups, rather than between particular individuals. The amount of difference necessary to call something significant does not have to be very large but the difference must show up reliably.

Cognitive abilities include verbal ability, or the ability to use and understand words and sentences; mathematical ability, or the ability to manipulate abstract symbols; and spatial ability, the ability to manipulate objects in space. Other aspects of thinking abilities include creativity, which is the talent for combining ideas or objects into a new and useful product, and interpersonal competence, which is the ability to solve problems between people. Cognitive abilities are frequently studied by testing students with standardized examinations on particular school subjects as well as on broader abilities. Students' grades may also be examined, or test subjects may be asked to solve specific problems.

It is important to specify which ability is being studied; it is also useful to try to establish the causes for any differences that are found. Because males and females are different biologically, those biological differences may be the cause for cognitive differences; however, this is not necessarily the case. Differences in thinking may be the result of social learning experiences that affect males and females differently. For example, women may come to believe that they cannot or should not do certain things; potential abilities may wither. It is often impossible to state that an ability difference is attributable solely to biology or to learning.

Infants and preschool children are typically tested and observed on a one-to-one basis in the areas of verbal development and spatial ability. Differences before age six are relatively minor, but girls do have a slight advantage in verbal development. Some people believe that this occurs because their central nervous systems mature somewhat earlier than boys' nervous systems. Other studies have found that adults talk to girls more than to boys, perhaps changing the environment for the two sexes and thus their developing abilities.

In grade school, girls typically outperform boys, although boys receive more attention from teachers. Girls do at least as well in mathematics, and usually better in verbal activities such as reading, writing, and spelling. Boys' relatively poorer performance has been attributed to the predominantly feminine atmosphere of the early school years and to their somewhat slower rate of neurological development. Boys also tend to perform more extremely than girls: They are more often found in classes for disabled learners, and they more often have extremely high scores on tests. It has been suggested that boys may be more vulnerable to physical problems that interfere with school learning, and thus they are more often placed in special-education classes.

In adolescence, gender differences are at their most extreme. Girls who did quite well in school before adolescence often show a drop in grades as well as standardized test performance. Boys do much better, particularly in the areas of mathematics and science. A few researchers have suggested that increased amounts of testosterone, a male sex hormone, may be related to the teenage boy performing better in mathematics and related studies. Others, such as Jacquelynne Eccles-Parsons, note that adolescent girls often feel that there are negative social consequences to their academic achievements. Many girls believe that popularity is more important than school success, and they stop working as hard. Educators often steer girls away from science and advanced mathematics courses, and their abilities remain hidden. In contrast, males are more strongly encouraged, and therefore achieve more. Girls' lesser performance may also be related to the availability of fewer women in mathematics and science professions who can act as models for them.

In adulthood, test-score differences tend to diminish. Janet Hyde has concluded that there are no verbal differences between the genders. Males, however, have traditionally accomplished more and have more often received social acknowledgments, such as the Nobel Prize. This seems to be a difference in performance rather than ability. It is caused by social expectations of appropriate gender roles—expectations of what is appropriate for each sex to do. Women have traditionally been expected to interrupt their careers for child care and have often been victims of sexism at work. Since World War II, many more women have become career-oriented, and consequently their records of accomplishments have also greatly increased.

Males and females do equally well on tests of creativity, but their accomplishments have differed. In adulthood, men are more often seen as creative, whether it is in invention and scientific theory or in art and music. This also seems a result of the different demands Western society places on the two sexes in terms of family obligations and career involvement. Similarly, differences in interpersonal style are related to differing expectations about male and female behavior.

Cognitive style, or the way in which people solve problems, represents another area of gender differences. Jean Piaget studied cognitive development in children and noted that adolescent boys used more formal operational thinking than did adolescent girls. In formal operational thinking, people approach problems in a precisely logical way. William Perry, studying college students, found that males used logic and debate as preferred styles. Mary Belenky, Blythe Clinchy, Nancy Goldberger, and Jill Tarule studied women's thinking styles. They found that while some women preferred the logical approach and others used an intuitive style, still others combined empirical evidence with their own personal, subjective knowledge. They concluded that these differences were caused by personal experiences and education, rather than by biological sex.

Applications

Male and female differences have been noted in achievement tests such as the Scholastic Aptitude Test (SAT) and the American College Test (ACT). The tests are designed not to benefit one sex more than the other, but gender differences are still found. Males are more likely to have extremely high scores and to do better in mathematics. For example, a study of mathematically precocious youth surveyed forty thousand seventh-graders who scored extremely well on the Scholastic Aptitude Test, a test usually taken by college-bound eleventh- and twelfth-graders. Of the 280 children who scored above 700, only twenty were female.

Females generally do better on verbal tests. The difference in verbal scores has decreased, but the mathematics score difference has not changed. Some educators have suggested that heavy reliance on these test scores may make it harder for girls to be accepted into very competitive colleges and less likely that they will be awarded scholarships.

Differences in mathematics ability have been used to explain why some occupations are male-dominated and some are mostly female. For example, there are many more male scientists and engineers than female scientists and engineers. These differences seem to be more a matter of training and encouragement than of innate biological characteristics. In recent years, the number of women scientists and engineers has dramatically increased, largely because of special efforts made to introduce girls to these occupations and to make the jobs seem relevant to a feminine role.

Differences in male and female abilities have interested educators as they try to maximize the potential of all their students. It is vitally important that both boys and girls receive encouragement to excel in all areas of thinking. In grade school, boys need male teachers to imitate. In later years, girls need to have contact with female scientists, engineers, and mathematicians. Counselors should be especially aware of the need to allow adolescents to explore fully different careers, and they should not limit children's options.

Training is an important factor in gender differences. Mathematics scores are directly related to the number of mathematics classes a person has taken. Gender differences on tests of spatial perception can also be eliminated by training. Paul Tobin used the embedded figures test, which requires people to pick out a drawing hidden within another drawing. He gave the test to teenage boys and girls, finding that boys performed better. After one practice session, however, the gender differences were eliminated.

Cognitive abilities are also related to social and family environment. In their study of women's cognitive styles, Belenky and associates did intensive interviews with women of various backgrounds and ages. They found that some women did not believe that they could think things out for themselves. One group of women were called "silent" and had typically been physically or emotionally abused. These "silent" women did not believe that they could understand anything. Another group believed that they could only repeat what an authority had said; often these women had been "silent" earlier in their lives. This research suggests that differences in cognitive abilities cannot be understood unless one also looks at family backgrounds.

There seem to be two times in a person's life when change is easiest to make: early adolescence and the college years. In early adolescence, young people are most sensitive to peer influence. It is also the time of greatest conformity. If adolescents can be exposed to a culture in which cognitive abilities are not seen by the society as being more appropriate for a particular gender, differences in cognitive development are likely to diminish greatly. A second time for change can be during the college years, but frequently people have been channeled into particular kinds of study by that time, and change is much harder to accomplish.

Context

Interest in gender differences is common to most societies, but only recently have scientists begun to ask about the origins of such differences. The scientific study of gender differences began in the United States at the beginnning of the twentieth century, as the school of functional psychology, pioneered by William James, concentrated on measuring individual differences. Biological explanations of differences were emphasized. Early studies supported the idea of greater male superiority and variability; they also supported the cultural beliefs of the time.

An increased demand for social justice that arose during the 1960's renewed interest in the question of gender differences. Eleanor Maccoby and Carol Jacklin surveyed every research report on male and female cognitive differences up to 1970 and concluded that the research supported very few real differences. Further studies have suggested that social influences are at least as important as biological influences, if not more so.

One reason women have been found to be inferior to men is that male behavior has traditionally been used as the standard. If women behave differently from men, it is concluded that they are inferior. In the area of personality, Sigmund Freud came to the conclusion that women are innately psychologically inferior. Karen Horney, however, looked at feminine psychology from a different perspective and showed how women's weaknesses are typically socially caused. Matina Horner studied achievement motivation and found that women often expressed fears about the consequences of success, especially in a male-dominated career; she suggested that such fears can prevent a woman from achieving her potential. In Lawrence Kohlberg's study of moral reasoning, women were found to use less advanced styles of reasoning; however, Kohlberg used male reasoning to form his theory. Carol Gilligan examined women's moral reasoning and decided that women use different standards from the typical male, relationship-oriented rather than justice-oriented standards. Women are different, not inferior.

The findings of science are that cognitive differences are small and that they emerge primarily under the pressures of adolescence. Common belief, however, is that gender differences are large; this affects expectations, treatment, and career development. Further research and education are needed to determine to what extent abilities can be modified by experience, and to what extent they are strictly caused by biology. The research suggests that environment and biology interact to create likely outcomes for individuals.

Bibliography

Belenky, Mary Field, et al. *Women's Ways of Knowing: The Development of Self, Voice, and Mind.* New York: Basic Books, 1986. Describes an intensive series of interviews with more than ninety women, and identifies five types of cognitive styles that were used by these women. Individual descriptions and quotations make the book interesting reading. A copy of the survey is included in the book.

Bleier, Ruth. *Science and Gender.* New York: Pergamon Press, 1984. Describes the reasons there are more men than women in science and engineering, and reports on other studies concerning male and female abilities.

Hare-Mursten, Rachel T., and Jeanne Marecek. "The Meaning of Difference: Gender Theory, Post-Modernism, and Psychology." *American Psychologist* 43 (June, 1988): 455-464. This article is serious reading, but it is not intended for specialists. Presents theories on gender differences developed in the 1980's.

Hyde, Janet Shibley. *Half the Human Experience.* 4th ed. Lexington, Mass.: Heath, 1991. This excellent book reviews research and theory pertaining to all aspects of gender differences. An accessible text for college students that many high school students also could use. Includes many references to other authors and researchers. Particularly valuable as it relates differences in cognitive development to social and biological factors.

Hyde, Janet Shibley, and Marcia C. Linn, eds. *The Psychology of Gender: Advances Through Meta-Analysis.* Baltimore: The Johns Hopkins University Press, 1986. A collection of scholarly articles that reanalyze many research efforts. Should be read by advanced undergraduates for their understanding of gender differences to be complete.

Jacklin, Carol. "Female and Male: Issues of Gender." *American Psychologist* 44 (February, 1989): 127-133. The coauthor of the pioneering work on sex differences (noted below) summarizes research between 1974 and 1989.

Maccoby, Eleanor E., and Carol Nagy Jacklin. *The Psychology of Sex Differences.* Stanford, Calif.: Stanford University Press, 1974. Reviews all research on gender differences to the early 1970's. This book is somewhat scholarly but is useful, as it presents the most comprehensive and balanced review of the research up to its publishing date.

Mary Moore Vandendorpe

Cross-References

Ability Testing: Individual and Group, 1; Bias in Ability Tests, 7; Achievement Motivation, 96; Cognitive Development Theory: Piaget, 553; College Entrance Examinations, 598; Gender-Identity Formation, 1062; Intelligence: Definition and Theoretical Models, 1328; Intelligence Tests, 1341; Psychology of Women: Karen Horney, 1950; Sexism, 2240.

COGNITIVE BEHAVIOR THERAPY

Type of psychology: Psychotherapy
Field of Study: Behavioral therapies

A number of approaches to therapy fall within the scope of cognitive behavior therapy. These approaches all share a theoretical perspective that assumes that internal cognitive processes, called thinking or cognition, affect behavior; that this cognitive activity may be monitored; and that desired behavior change may be effected through cognitive change.

Principal terms

BEHAVIOR THERAPY: a branch of psychotherapy narrowly conceived as the application of classical and operant conditioning to the alteration of clinical problems, but more broadly conceived as applied experimental psychology in a clinical context

COGNITION: private or internal processes such as imagery, symbolic representation of external events, and the verbal coding of experience

COGNITIVE RESTRUCTURING: any behavior therapy procedure that attempts to alter the manner in which clients think about life so that they change their overt behavior and emotions

COGNITIVE THERAPY: a therapeutic approach developed by Aaron T. Beck, the goal of which is for patients to discover for themselves the irrationality of their thoughts

DEPRESSION: strong feelings of sadness, dejection, and often apathy that last more than two weeks and pervade a person's thoughts

Overview

The cognitive behavior therapies are not a single therapeutic approach, but rather a loosely organized collection of therapeutic approaches that share a similar set of assumptions. At their core, cognitive behavior therapies share three fundamental propositions. Cognitive activity affects behavior, cognitive activity may be monitored and altered, and desired behavior change may be effected through cognitive change.

The first of the three fundamental propositions of cognitive behavior therapy suggests that it is not the external situation which determines feelings and behavior, but rather the person's view or perception of that external situation that determines feelings and behavior. For example, if one has failed the first examination of a course, one could appraise it as a temporary setback to be overcome or as a horrible loss. While the situation remains the same, the thinking about that situation is radically different in the two examples cited. Each of these views will lead to significantly different emotions and behaviors.

The third cognitive behavioral assumption suggests that desired behavior change may be effected through cognitive change. Thus, while cognitive behavior theorists do not reject the notion that rewards and punishment (reinforcement contingencies) can alter behavior, they are likely to emphasize that there are alternative methods for behavior change, one in particular being cognitive change. Many approaches to therapy fall within the scope of cognitive behavior therapy as it is defined above. While these approaches share the theoretical assumptions described above, a review of the major therapeutic procedures subsumed under the heading of cognitive behavior therapy reveals a diverse amalgam of principles and procedures, representing a variety of theoretical and philosophical perspectives.

Rational-emotive therapy, developed by psychologist Albert Ellis, is regarded by many as one of the premier examples of the cognitive behavioral approach; it was introduced in the early 1960's. Ellis proposed that many people are made unhappy by their faulty, irrational beliefs, which influence the way they interpret events. The therapist will interact with the patient or client, attempting to direct the patient to more positive and realistic views. Cognitive therapy, pioneered by Aaron T. Beck, has been applied to such problems as depression and stress. For stress reduction, ideas and thoughts that are producing stress in the patient will be questioned; the therapist will get the patient to examine the validity of these thoughts; thought processes can then be restructured so the situations seem less stressful. Cognitive therapy has been found to be quite effective in treating depression, as compared to other therapeutic methods. Beck held that depression is caused by certain types of negative thoughts, such as devaluing the self or viewing the future in a consistently pessimistic way.

Rational behavior therapy, developed by psychiatrist Maxie Maultsby, is a close relative of Ellis' rational-emotive therapy. In this approach, Maultsby combines several approaches to include rational-emotive therapy, neuropsychology, classical and operant conditioning, and psychosomatic research; however, Maultsby was primarily influenced by his association with Albert Ellis. In this approach, Maultsby attempts to couch his theory of emotional disturbance in terms of neuropsychophysiology and learning theory. Rational behavior therapy assumes that repeated pairings of a perception with evaluative thoughts lead to rational or irrational emotive and behavioral reactions. Maultsby suggests that self-talk, which originates in the left hemisphere of the brain, triggers corresponding right-hemisphere emotional equivalents. Thus, in order to maintain a state of psychological health, individuals must practice rational self-talk that will, in turn, cause the right brain to convert left-brain language into appropriate emotional and behavioral reactions.

Rational behavior therapy techniques are quite similar to those of rational-emotive therapy. Both therapies stress the importance of monitoring one's thoughts in order to become aware of the elements of the emotional disturbance. In addition, Maultsby advocates the use of rational-emotive imagery, behavioral practice, and relaxation methods in order to minimize emotional distress.

Self-instructional training was developed by psychologist Donald Meichenbaum in the early 1970's. In contrast to Ellis and Beck, whose prior training was in psychoanalysis, Meichenbaum's roots are in behaviorism and the behavioral therapies. Thus Meichenbaum's approach is heavily couched in behavioral terminology and procedures. Meichenbaum's work stems from his earlier research in training schizophrenic patients to emit "healthy speech." By chance, Meichenbaum observed that patients who engaged in spontaneous self-instruction were less distracted and demonstrated superior task performance on a variety of tasks. As a result, Meichenbaum emphasizes the critical role of "self-instructions"—simple instructions such as, "Relax. . . . Just attend to the task"—and their noticeable effect on subsequent behavior.

Meichenbaum developed self-instructional training to treat the deficits in self-instructions manifested in impulsive children. The ultimate goal of this program was to decrease impulsive behavior. The way to accomplish this goal, as hypothesized by Meichenbaum, was to train impulsive children to generate verbal self-commands, to respond to their verbal self-commands, and to encourage the children to self-reinforce their behavior appropriately.

The specific procedures employed in self-instructional training involve having the child observe a model performing a task. While the model is performing the task, he or she is talking aloud. The child then performs the same task while the model gives verbal instructions. Subsequently, the child performs the task while instructing himself or herself aloud, then while whispering the instructions. Finally, the child performs the task covertly. The self-instructions employed in the program included questions about the nature and demands of the task, answers to these questions in the form of cognitive rehearsal, self-instructions in the form of self-guidance while performing the task, and self-reinforcement. Meichenbaum and his associates have found that this self-instructional training program significantly improves the task performance of impulsive children across a number of measures.

Systematic rational restructuring is a cognitive behavioral procedure developed by psychologist Marvin Goldfried in the mid-1970's. This procedure is a variation on Ellis' rational-emotive therapy; however, it is more clearly structured than Ellis' method. In systematic rational restructuring, Goldfried suggests that early social learning experiences teach individuals to label situations in different ways. Further, Goldfried suggests that emotional reactions may be understood as responses to the way individuals label situations, as opposed to responses to the situations themselves. The goal of systematic rational restructuring is to train clients to perceive situational cues more accurately.

The process of systematic rational restructuring is similar to systematic desensitization, in which a subject is to imagine fearful scenes in a graduated order from the least fear-provoking to the more fear-provoking scenes. In systematic rational restructuring, the client is asked to imagine a hierarchy of anxiety-eliciting situations. At each step, the client is instructed to identify irrational thoughts associated with the specific situation, to dispute them, and to reevaluate the situation more rationally. In addition, clients are instructed to practice rational restructuring in specific real-life situations.

Stress inoculation training incorporates several of the specific therapies already described in this section. This procedure was developed by psychologist Donald Meichenbaum. Stress inoculation training is analogous to being inoculated against disease. That is, it prepares clients to deal with stress-inducing events by teaching them to use coping skills at low levels of the stressful situation, and then gradually to cope with more and more stressful situations. Stress inoculation training involves three phases: conceptualization, skill acquisition and rehearsal, and application and follow-through.

In the conceptualization phase of stress inoculation training, clients are given an adaptive way of viewing and understanding their negative reactions to stressful events. In the skills-acquisition and rehearsal phase, clients learn coping skills appropriate to the type of stress they are experiencing. With interpersonal anxiety, the client might develop skills that would make the feared situation less threatening (for example, learning to initiate and maintain conversations). The client might also learn deep muscle relaxation to lessen tension. In the case of anger, clients learn to view potential provocations as problems that require a solution rather than as threats that require an attack. Clients are also taught to rehearse alternative strategies for solving the problem at hand.

The application and follow-through phase of stress inoculation training involves the clients practicing and applying the coping skills. Initially, clients are exposed to low levels of stressful situations in imagery. They practice applying their coping skills to handle the stressful events, and they overtly role-play dealing with stressful events. Next, the client is given homework assignments that involve gradual exposure to actual stressful events in his or her everyday life. Stress inoculation training has been effectively applied to many types of problems. It has been used to help people cope with anger, anxiety, fear, pain, and health-related problems (for example, cancer, hypertension). It appears to be suitable for all age levels.

Problem-solving therapy, as developed by psychologists Thomas D'Zurilla and Marvin Goldfried, is also considered one of the cognitive behavioral approaches. In essence, problem-solving therapy is the application of problem-solving theory and research to the domain of personal and emotional problems. Indeed, the authors see the ability to solve problems as the necessary and sufficient condition for emotional and behavioral stability. Problem solving is, in one way or another, a part of all psychotherapies.

Applications

Cognitive behavior therapists have taught general problem-solving skills to clients with two specific aims: to alleviate the particular personal problems for which clients have sought therapy, and to provide clients with a general coping strategy for personal problems.

The actual steps of problem solving that a client is taught to carry out systematically are as follows. First, it is necessary to define the dilemma as a problem to be solved. Next, a goal must be selected which reflects the ultimate outcome the client desires.

The client then generates a list of many different possible solutions, without evaluating their potential merit (a kind of brainstorming). Now the client evaluates the pros and cons of each alternative in terms of the probability that it will meet the goal selected and its practicality, which involves considering the potential consequences to oneself and to others of each solution. The alternative solutions are ranked in terms of desirability and practicality, and the highest one is selected. Next, the client tries to implement the solution chosen. Finally, the client evaluates the therapy, assessing whether the solution alleviated the problem and met the goal, and, if not, what went wrong—in other words, which of the steps in problem solving needs to be redone.

Problem-solving therapies have been used to treat a variety of target behaviors with a wide range of clients. Examples include peer relationship difficulties among children and adolescents, examination and interpersonal anxiety among college students, relapse following a program to reduce smoking, harmony among family members, and the ability of chronic psychiatric patients to cope with interpersonal problems.

Self-control therapy for depression, developed by psychologist Lynn Rehm, is an approach to treating depression which combines the self-regulatory notions of behavior therapy and the cognitive focus of the cognitive behavioral approaches. Essentially, Rehm believes that depressed people show deficits in one or some combination of the following areas: monitoring (selectively attending to negative events), self-evaluation (setting unrealistically high goals), and self-reinforcement (emitting high rates of self-punishment and low rates of self-reward). These three components are further broken down into a total of six functional areas.

According to Rehm, the varied symptom picture in clinically depressed clients is a function of different subsets of these deficits. Over the course of therapy with a client, each of the six self-control deficits is described, with emphasis on how a particular deficit is causally related to depression, and on what can be done to remedy the deficit. A variety of clinical strategies are employed to teach clients self-control skills, including group discussion, overt and covert reinforcement, behavioral assignments, self-monitoring, and modeling.

Structural psychotherapy is a cognitive behavioral approach that derives from the work of two Italian mental health professionals, psychiatrist Vittorio Guidano and psychologist Gianni Liotti. These authors are strongly persuaded by cognitive psychology, social learning theory, evolutionary epistemology, psychodynamic theory, and cognitive therapy. Guidano and Liotti suggest that for an understanding of the full complexity of an emotional disorder, and subsequent development of an adequate model of psychotherapy, an appreciation of the development and the active role of an individual's knowledge of self and the world is critical. In short, in order to understand a patient, one must understand the structure of that person's world.

Guidano and Liotti's therapeutic process utilizes the empirical problem-solving approach of the scientist. Indeed, the authors suggest that therapists should assist clients in disengaging themselves from certain ingrained beliefs and judgments, and in considering them as hypotheses and theories subject to disproof, confirmation, and logical challenge. A variety of behavioral experiments and cognitive techniques are utilized to assist the patient in assessing and critically evaluating his or her beliefs.

As can be seen, the area of cognitive behavior therapy involves a wide collection of therapeutic approaches and techniques. The approaches described here are but a representative sample of possible cognitive behavioral approaches. Also included within this domain are anxiety management training, which comes from the work of psychologist Richard Suinn, and personal science, from the work of psychologist Michael Mahoney.

The cognitive behavioral approaches are derived from a variety of perspectives, including cognitive theory, classical and operant conditioning approaches, problem-solving theory, and developmental theory. All these approaches share the perspective that internal cognitive processes, called thinking or cognition, affect behavior, and that behavior change may be effected through cognitive change.

These approaches have several other similarities. One is that all the approaches see therapy as time-limited. This is in sharp distinction to the traditional psychoanalytic therapies, which are generally open-ended. The cognitive behavior therapies attempt to effect change rapidly, often with specific, preset lengths of therapeutic contact. Another similarity among the cognitive behavior therapies is that their target of change is also limited. For example, in the treatment of depression, the target of change is the symptoms of depression. Thus, in the cognitive behavioral approaches to treatment, one sees a time-limited focus and a limited target of change.

Context

Cognitive behavior therapy evolved from two lines of clinical and research activity: First, it derives from the work of the early cognitive therapists (Albert Ellis and Aaron Beck); second, it was strongly influenced by the careful empirical work of the early behaviorists.

Within the domain of behaviorism, cognitive processes were not always seen as a legitimate focus of attention. That is, in behavior therapy, there has always been a strong commitment to an applied science of clinical treatment. In the behavior therapy of the 1950's and 1960's, this emphasis on scientific methods and procedures meant that behavior therapists focused on events that were directly observable and measurable. Within this framework, behavior was seen as a function of external stimuli which determined or were reliably associated with observable responses. Also during this period, there was a deliberate avoidance of such "nebulous" concepts as thoughts, cognitions, or images. It was believed that these processes were by their very nature vague, and one could never be confident that one was reliably observing or measuring these processes.

It is important to note that by following scientific principles, researchers developed major new treatment approaches which in many ways revolutionized clinical practice (among them are systematic desensitization and the use of a token economy). Yet during the 1960's, several developments within behavior therapy had emphasized the limitations of a strict conditioning model to understanding human behavior.

In 1969, psychologist Albert Bandura published his influential volume *Principles of Behavior Modification*. In this volume, Bandura emphasized the role of internal or cognitive factors in the causation and maintenance of behavior. Following from the dissatisfaction of the radical behavioral approaches to understanding complex human behavior and the publication of Bandura's 1969 volume, behavior therapists began actively to seek and study the role of cognitive processes in human behavior.

Bibliography

D'Zurilla, Thomas J., and Arthur M. Nezu. "Social Problem-Solving in Adults." In *Advances in Cognitive-Behavioral Research and Therapy*, edited by Philip C. Kendall. Vol. 1. New York: Academic Press, 1982. An excellent summary of problem-solving therapy. As indicated by its title, the Kendall book in which this article appears also contains other informative articles dealing with cognitive behavior therapy.

Goldfried, Marvin R. "The Use of Relaxation and Cognitive Relabeling as Coping Skills." In *Behavioral Self-Management: Strategies, Techniques, and Outcomes*, edited by Richard B. Stuart. New York: Brunner/Mazel, 1977. A description of systematic rational restructuring by Marvin Goldfried, who developed the technique; reveals its similarities to and differences from rational-emotive therapy.

Maultsby, Maxie C., Jr. *Rational Behavior Therapy*. Englewood Cliffs, N.J.: Prentice-Hall, 1984. An excellent summary of rational behavior therapy, as developed by Maultsby; discusses self-talk and its emotional and behavioral consequences.

Meichenbaum, Donald. *Cognitive Behavior Modification*. New York: Plenum Press, 1977. A well-written introduction to Meichenbaum's approaches, with clear examples of the applications of self-instructional training to impulsive children and schizophrenic patients.

_____. *Stress Inoculation Training*. New York: Pergamon Press, 1985. This short training manual presents a clear, useful overview of stress inoculation training, along with a detailed account of the empirical research completed in testing the approach.

Donald G. Beal

Cross-References

Abnormality: Behavioral Models, 33; Abnormality: Cognitive Models, 46; Behavioral Family Therapy, 394; Cognitive Social Learning: Walter Mischel, 580; Cognitive Therapy, 586; Existential Analysis and Therapy, 999; Rational-Emotive Therapy, 2052; Transactional Analysis, 2584.

COGNITIVE DEVELOPMENT THEORY: PIAGET

Type of psychology: Development psychology
Field of study: Cognitive development

Jean Piaget, in one of the twentieth century's most influential development theories, proposed a sequence of maturational changes in thinking. From the sensorimotor responses of infancy, the child acquires symbols. Later, the child begins relating these symbols in such logical operations as categorizing and quantifying. In adolescence, abstract and hypothetical mental manipulations become possible.

Principal terms

ACCOMMODATION: adjusting the interpretation (schema) of an object or event when the old interpretation does not fit a new instance

ASSIMILATION: the interpretation of a new instance of an object or event in terms of one's preexisting schema (or understanding); the fit, never perfect, is close enough

CONCRETE OPERATIONS STAGE: a cognitive stage characterized by a mental capacity to manipulate relationships of equivalence (quantitative rearrangements, categorization) that can be visualized

CONSERVATION: the comprehension of the essential equivalence when a given quantity (number, length, mass, volume) is rearranged; a basic concrete-operational skill

EGOCENTRIC THOUGHT: the assumption that everyone shares one's own perspective and the cognitive inability to understand the different perspective of another

FORMAL OPERATIONS STAGE: a cognitive stage in which reasoning can be speculative and include abstract ideals, hypothetical cases, and unobserved logical possibilities

OPERATIONS: mental transformations that can be reversed; for example, the concept that one gallon put into four quart bottles could also be put back into the gallon container

PREOPERATIONAL STAGE: a transitional stage of the preschool child, after mental representations (symbols) are acquired but before these can be logically manipulated

SCHEMA (*pl.* schemata): any process of interpreting an object or event, including habitual responses, symbols, or mental manipulations

SENSORIMOTOR STAGE: the stage (infancy) in which objects become familiar and are interpreted by appropriate habitual reactions

Overview

Jean Piaget (1896-1980), a Swiss psychologist, generated the twentieth century's most influential and comprehensive theory of cognitive development. Piaget's theory describes how the maturing child's interactions with the environment result in predictable sequences of changes in certain crucial understandings of the world about him or her. Such changes occur in the child's comprehension of time and space, quantitative relationships, cause and effect, and even right and wrong. The child is always treated as an actor in his or her own development. Advances result from the active desire to develop concepts or schemata which are sufficiently similar to the real world that this real world can be fitted or assimilated into these schemata. When a schema ("Cats smell nice") is sufficiently discrepant from reality ("That cat stinks"), the schema itself must be accommodated or altered ("That catlike creature is a skunk"). For children everywhere, neurologically based advances in mental capacity introduce new perceptions that make the old ways of construing reality unsatisfactory and compel a fundamentally new construction of reality—a new stage of development. Piaget conceptualizes four such stages: sensorimotor (in infancy), preoperational (the preschool child), concrete operational (the school-age child), and formal operational (adolescence and adulthood).

In the sensorimotor stage, the infant orients himself or herself to objects in the world by consistent physical (motor) movements to those sensory stimuli that represent the same object (for example, the sight of a face, the sound of footsteps, or a voice all represent "mother"). The relationship between motor responses and reappearing objects becomes progressively more complex and varied in the normal course of development. First, reflexes such as sucking become more efficient; then sequences of learned actions that bring pleasure are repeated (circular reactions). These learned reactions are directed first toward the infant's own body (thumb sucking), then toward objects in the environment (the infant's stuffed toy).

The baby seems to lack an awareness that objects continue to exist when they are outside the range of his or her senses. When the familiar toy of an infant is hidden, he or she does not search for it; it is as if it has disappeared from reality. As the sensorimotor infant matures, the infant becomes convinced of the continuing existence of objects that disappear in less obvious ways for longer intervals of time. By eighteen months of age, most toddlers have achieved such a conviction of continuing existence, or object permanence.

In the preoperational stage, the preschool child begins to represent these permanent objects by internal processes or mental representations. Now the development of mental representations of useful objects proceeds at an astounding pace. In symbolic play, blocks may represent cars and trains. Capable of deferred imitation, the child may pretend to be a cowboy according to his memory image of a motion-picture cowboy. The most important of all representations are the hundreds of new words the child learns to speak.

As one might infer from the word "preoperational," this period, lasting from about age two through ages six or seven, is transitional. The preschool child still lacks the attention, memory capacity, and mental flexibility to employ his or her increasing supply of symbolic representations in logical reasoning (operations). It is as if the child remains so focused upon the individual frames of a motion picture that he or she fails to comprehend the underlying plot. Piaget calls this narrow focusing on a single object or salient dimension "centration." The child may say, for example, that a quart of milk he or she has just seen transferred into two pint containers is now "less milk" because the child focuses upon the smaller size of the new containers. Fido is seen as a dog, not as an animal or a mammal. The child uncritically assumes that other people, regardless of their situation, share his or her own tastes and perspectives. A two-year-old closes his eyes and says, "Now you don't see me, Daddy." Piaget calls this egocentricism.

The concrete operations stage begins at age six or seven, when the school-age child becomes capable of keeping in mind and logically manipulating several concrete objects at the same time. The child is no longer the prisoner of the momentary appearance of things. In no case is the change more evident than in the sort of problem in which a number of objects (such as twelve black checkers) are spread out into four groups of three. While the four-year-old, preoperational child would be likely to say that now there are more checkers because they take up a larger area, to the eight-year-old, it is obvious that this transformation could easily be reversed by regrouping the checkers. Piaget describes the capacity to visualize the reversibility of such transformations as "conservation." This understanding is fundamental to the comprehension of simple arithmetical manipulations. It is also fundamental to a second operational skill: categorization. To the concrete-operational child, it seems obvious that while Rover the dog can for other purposes be classified as a household pet, an animal, or a living organism, he will still be a "dog" and still be "Rover." A related skill is seriation: keeping in mind that an entire series of objects can be arranged along a single dimension, such as size (from smallest to largest). The child now is also capable of role-taking, of understanding the different perspective of a parent or teacher. No longer egocentric, the child becomes able to see himself as others see him and to temper the harshness of absolute rules with a comprehension of the viewpoints of others.

The formal operations stage begins in early adolescence. In childhood, logical operations are concrete ones, limited to objects that can be visualized, touched, or directly experienced. The advance of the early adolescent into formal operational thinking involves the capacity to deal with possibilities that are purely speculative. This permits coping with new classes of problems: those involving relationships that are purely abstract or hypothetical, or that involve the higher-level analysis of a problem by the systematic consideration of every logical (sometimes fanciful) possibility. The logical adequacy of an argument can be examined apart from the truth or falsity of its conclusions.

Concepts such as "forces," "infinity," or "justice," nowhere directly experienced, can now be comprehended. Formal operational thought permits the mid-adolescent or adult to hold abstract ideals and to initiate scientific investigations.

Applications

Piaget was particularly clever in the invention of problems which illustrate the underlying premises of the child's thought. The crucial capability that signals the end of the sensorimotor period is object permanence, the child's conviction of the continuing existence of objects that are outside the range of his senses. Piaget established the gradual emergence of object permanence by hiding from the child familiar toys for longer periods of time, with the act of hiding progressively less obvious to the child. Full object permanence is not considered achieved until the child will search for a familiar missing object even when he or she could not have observed its being hidden.

The fundamental test of concrete operational thought is conservation. In a typical conservation task, the child is shown two identical balls of putty. The child generally affirms their obvious equivalence. Then one of the balls of putty is reworked into an elongated, wormlike shape while the child watches. The child is again asked about their relative size. Younger children are likely to say that the wormlike shape is smaller, but the child who has attained conservation of mass will state that the size must still be the same. Inquiries concerning whether the weights of the differently shaped material (conservation of weight) are the same, and whether they would displace the same amount of water (conservation of volume) are more difficult questions, generally answerable at older ages.

Since Piaget's original demonstrations, further progress has necessitated the standardization of these problems with materials, questions, procedures, and scoring so clearly specified that examiners can replicate one another's results. Such standardization permits the explanation of the general applicability of Piaget's concepts. Standardized tests have been developed for measuring object permanence, egocentricity, and role-taking skills. The "Concept Assessment Kit: Conservation," for example, provides six standard conservation tasks for which comparison data (norms) are available for children in several widely diverse cultures. The relative conceptual attainments of an individual child (or culture) can be measured. It is encouraging that those who attain such basic skills as conservation early have been shown to be advanced in many other educational and cognitive achievements.

Piaget's views of cognitive development have broad implications for educational institutions charged with fostering such development. The child is viewed as an active seeker of knowledge. This pursuit is advanced by his or her experimental engagement with problems which are slightly more complex than those problems successfully worked through in the past. The teacher is a facilitator of the opportunities for such cognitive growth, not a lecturer or a drillmaster. The teacher provides physical materials that can be experimentally manipulated. Such materials can be simple: Blocks, stones, bottle caps, and plastic containers all can be classified, immersed in water, thrown into fire, dropped, thrown, or balanced. Facilitating peer relationships and cooperation in playing games is also helpful in encouraging social role-taking and moral development.

Since each student pursues knowledge at his or her own pace, and in his or her own idiom, great freedom and variety may be permitted in an essentially open classroom. The teacher may nudge the student toward cognitive advancement by presenting a problem slightly more complex than that already comprehended by the student. A student who understands conservation of number may be ready for problems involving the conservation of length, for example. Yet the teacher does not reinforce correct answers or criticize incorrect ones. Sequencing is crucial. The presentation of knowledge or skill before the child is ready can result in superficial, uncomprehended verbalisms. Piaget does not totally reject the necessity of the inculcation of social and cultural niceties (social-arbitrary knowledge), the focus of traditional education. He would maintain, however, that an experimentally based understanding of physical and social relationships is crucial for a creative, thoughtful society.

Context

Piaget hypothesized sequences of age-related changes in ways of dealing with reality. His conclusions were based on the careful observation of a few selected cases. The voluminous research since Piaget's time overwhelmingly supports the sequence he outlined. The process almost never reverses. Once a child understands the conservation of substance, for example, his or her former conclusion that "Now there is more" seems to the child not simply wrong but absurd. Even within a stage, there is a sequence. Conservation of mass, for example, precedes conservation of volume.

Post-Piagetian research has nevertheless led to a fine-tuning of some of his conclusions and a modification of others. Piaget believed that transitions to more advanced cognitive levels awaited neurological maturation and the child's spontaneous discoveries. Several researchers have found that specific training in simplified and graded conservation and categorization tasks can lead to an early ripening of these skills. Other research has called into question Piaget's timetable. The fact that, within a few months of birth, infants show subtle differences in their reaction to familiar versus unfamiliar objects suggests that recognition memory for objects may begin earlier than Piaget's age for object permanence. If conservation tasks are simplified—if all distraction is avoided, and simple language and familiar materials are used—it can be shown that concrete operations also may begin earlier than Piaget thought. Formal operations, on the other hand, may not begin as early or be applied as universally in adult problem solving as suggested by Piaget's thesis. A significant percentage of older adolescents and adults fail tests for formal operations, particularly in new problem areas.

More basic than readjustments of his developmental scheduling is the reinterpretation of Piaget's stages. The stage concept implies not only an invariant sequence of age-related changes but also developmental discontinuities involving global and fairly abrupt shifts in an entire pattern or structure. Yet the prolonged development and domain-specific nature of many operational skills, cited above, suggest a process that is neither abrupt nor global. An alternative view is that Piaget's sequences can also be understood as the results of continuous improvements in attention, concentration, and memory. Stages represent only transition points on this continuous dimension. They are more like the points of a scale on a thermometer than the stages of the metamorphosis of a caterpillar into a moth.

Even with the caveat that his stages may reflect, at a more fundamental level, an underlying continuum, Piaget's contributions can be seen as a great leap forward in approximate answers to one of humankind's oldest questions: how human beings know their world. The eighteenth century philosopher Immanuel Kant described certain core assumptions, such as quantity, quality, and cause and effect, which he called "categories of the understanding." Human beings make these assumptions when they relate specific objects and events to one another—when they reason. Piaget's work became known to a 1960's-era American psychology that was dominated by B. F. Skinner's behavioral view of a passive child whose plastic nature was simply molded by the rewards and punishments of parents and culture. The impact of Piaget's work shifted psychology's focus back to a Kantian perspective of the child as an active reasoner who selectively responds to aspects of culture he or she finds relevant. Piaget himself outlined the sequence, the pace, and some of the dynamics of the maturing child's development of major Kantian categories. Such subsequent contributions as Lawrence Kohlberg's work on moral development and Robert Selman's work on role-taking can be viewed as an elaboration and extension of Piaget's unfinished work. Piaget, like Sigmund Freud, was one of psychology's pivotal thinkers. Without him, the entire field of developmental psychology would be radically different.

Bibliography

Ault, Ruth L. *Children's Cognitive Development: Piaget's Theory and the Process Approach.* New York: Oxford University Press, 1977. This short work both describes and illustrates Piaget's concepts and illuminates the implications of the theory by contrasting them with the non-Piagetian approach of experimental child psychology. Lucid, nontechnical, but thought-provoking.

Gelman, Rochel, and R. Baillargeon. "A Review of Some Piagetian Concepts." In *Handbook of Child Psychology*, edited by Paul H. Mussen. 4th ed. Vol. 3. New York: John Wiley & Sons, 1983. A thorough review, concept by concept, of the developmental research on the various types of conservation and classification problems. These authors conclude that the hypothesis of domain-specific changes fits the experimental research better than the idea of global stages does.

Phillips, John L. *The Origins of Intellect: Piaget's Theory.* 2d ed. San Francisco: W. H. Freeman, 1975. This thorough, clearly written text explains Piaget's concepts by providing many examples. An excellent source for the introductory-level student who seeks a comprehensive understanding of Piaget's ideas. Available in paperback.

Piaget, Jean. *The Essential Piaget.* Edited by Howard E. Gruber and J. Jacques Vonèche. New York: Basic Books, 1977. Contains English translations of most of Piaget's writings, from his earliest work (1909), which was heavily biological. Many of these earlier writings were unknown to Americans until translated from the French in the 1950's. Since reading Piaget himself is more difficult than most general works about his theory, the student might consult Piaget's papers selectively on topics of particular interest.

Sigel, Irving E., and Rodney R. Cocking. *Cognitive Development from Childhood to Adolescence: A Constructivist Perspective.* New York: Holt, Rinehart and Winston, 1977. A readable, condensed version of Piaget's theory. Can be used as an alternative to the Phillips summary if the reader finds this book easier to obtain. A good place for the introductory-level reader to begin.

Thomas E. DeWolfe

Cross-References

Adolescence: Cognitive Skills, 118; Cognitive Ability: Gender Differences, 540; Cognitive Psychology: An Overview, 572; Development: Theoretical Issues, 804; Language: The Developmental Sequence, 1387; Moral Development, 1594.

COGNITIVE DISSONANCE THEORY

Type of psychology: Social psychology
Field of study: Attitudes and behavior

Cognitive dissonance theory examines the effects of inconsistencies between attitudes and behaviors. It has evolved into an important theory of attitude change and has offered insights into diverse topics such as the effects of rewards, punishment, and choice on attitudes.

Principal terms
ATTITUDE: positive or negative evaluations of a person, place, or thing
COGNITION: knowledge one has about one's attitudes, beliefs, and behaviors
CONSONANCE: the psychological state in which cognitions are not in conflict
DISSONANCE: an unpleasant psychological and physiological state caused by an inconsistency between cognitions
EXTERNAL JUSTIFICATION: an environmental factor that can account for an inconsistency between cognitions

Overview

Cognitive dissonance theory, developed by social psychologist Leon Festinger, suggests that there is a basic human tendency to strive for consistency between and among cognitions. Cognitions are defined as what people know about their attitudes and behaviors. If an inconsistency does arise—for example, if an individual does something that is discrepant with his or her attitudes—cognitive dissonance is said to occur. Dissonance is an uncomfortable state of physiological and psychological tension. It is so uncomfortable, in fact, that when individuals are in such a state, they become motivated to rid themselves of the feeling. This can be done by restoring consistency to the cognitions in some way.

What exactly does dissonance feel like? Although it is very difficult to describe any kind of internal state, the reactions one has when one hurts the feelings of a loved one or when one breaks something belonging to someone else are probably what Festinger meant by dissonance.

When in a state of dissonance, there are three ways a person can restore consistency or (in the language of the theory) consonance. One is to reduce the importance of the conflicting cognitions. The theory states that the amount of dissonance experienced is a direct function of the importance of the conflicting cognitions. Consider, for example, a man who actively pursues a suntan. The potential for dissonance exists with such behavior, because the cognition "I am doing something that is increasing my chances for skin cancer" may be in conflict with the cognition "I would like to remain healthy and live a long life." To reduce dissonance, this person may convince himself that he would rather live a shorter life filled with doing enjoyable and exciting things than live a longer, but perhaps not so exciting, life. The inconsistency still exists, but the importance of the inconsistency has been reduced.

A second way to reduce dissonance is to add numerous consonant cognitions, thus making the discrepancy seem less great. The suntanner may begin to believe he needs to be tan to be socially accepted because all of his friends have tans. The tanner may also begin to believe that suntanning makes him look more attractive and healthier and, indeed, may come to believe that suntanning does promote health.

The last way that Festinger proposed that people could reduce dissonance is the simplest, but it is the one that caught the attention of many social psychologists. It is simply to change one of the discrepant cognitions. The suntanner could either stop suntanning or convince himself that suntanning is not associated with an increased risk of skin cancer. In either case, the inconsistency would be eliminated.

This latter possibility intrigued social psychologists because it offered the possibility that people's behaviors could influence their attitudes. In particular, it suggested that if someone does something that is inconsistent with his or her attitudes, those attitudes may change to become more consistent with the behavior. For example, imagine that a woman wanted a friend to favor a particular candidate in an upcoming election, and the friend favored the opposing candidate. What would happen if this woman convinced the friend to accompany her to a rally for the candidate the friend did not support? According to the theory, the friend should experience some degree of dissonance, as the behavior of attending a rally for candidate X is inconsistent with the attitude "I do not favor candidate X." To resolve the inconsistency, the friend may very well begin to convince herself that candidate X is not so bad and actually has some good points. Thus, in an effort to restore consonance, the friend's attitudes have changed to be more consistent with behavior.

Changes in behavior cannot always be expected to lead to changes in attitudes. Dissonance-induced attitude change—that is, attitudes that change in an effort to be consistent with a behavior—is likely to happen only under certain conditions. For one, there must not be any external justification for the behavior. An external justification is an environmental cause that might explain the inconsistency. If the friend was paid a hundred dollars to attend the rally for the candidate or was promised a dinner at a fancy restaurant, she most likely would not have experienced dissonance, because she had a sufficient external justification. Dissonance is most likely to occur when no external justification is present for a behavior.

Second, dissonance is most likely to occur when individuals believe that the behavior was done of their own free will—that is, when they feel some sort of personal responsibility for the behavior. If the friend had been simply told that she was being taken out for an exciting evening and was not told that she was going to this candidate's rally until she got there, she most likely would not have experienced dissonance.

Third, dissonance is more likely to occur when the behavior has some sort of foreseeable negative consequences. If the friend knew that when attending the rally, each person was required to pay a donation or was required to hand out pamphlets for the candidate, and she still elected to go, she would probably have experienced considerable dissonance; now she is not only attending a rally for a candidate she opposes but also actively campaigning against her preferred candidate.

Applications

Perhaps the most-researched application of dissonance theory concerns the effects on attitudes of rewarding people for doing things in which they do not believe. In one study, Festinger and J. M. Carlsmith had students perform a boring screw-turning task for one hour. They then asked the students to tell another student waiting to do the same task that the task was very interesting. In other words, they asked the students to lie. Half the students were offered twenty dollars to do this; the other half were offered one dollar. After the students told the waiting student that the task was enjoyable, the researchers asked them what they really thought about the screw-turning task. The students who were paid twenty dollars said they thought the screw-turning task was quite boring. The students who were paid only one dollar, however, said that they thought the task was interesting and enjoyable.

Although surprising, these findings are precisely what dissonance theory predicts. When a student informed a waiting student that the task was enjoyable, the possibility for dissonance arose. The cognition "This task was really boring" is inconsistent with the cognition "I just told someone that this task was quite enjoyable." The students paid twenty dollars, however, had a sufficient external justification for the inconsistency. Hence, there was no dissonance and no need to resolve any inconsistency. The students paid one dollar, however, did not have the same external justification; most people would not consider a dollar to be sufficient justification for telling a lie, so these students were in a real state of dissonance. To resolve the inconsistency, they changed their attitudes about the task and convinced themselves that the task was indeed enjoyable, thereby achieving consonance between attitudes and behavior. Thus, the *less* people are rewarded for doing things they might not like, the more likely it is that they will begin to like them.

Dissonance theory makes equally interesting predictions about the effects of punishment. In a study by Elliot Aronson and Carlsmith, a researcher asked preschool children to rate the attractiveness of toys. The researcher then left the room, but, before leaving, he instructed the children not to play with one of the toys they had rated highly attractive. This became the "forbidden" toy. The researcher varied the severity of the punishment with which he threatened the children if they played with the forbidden toy. For some children, the threat was relatively mild. The researcher said he would be upset. For others, the threat was more severe. The researcher said that he would be angry, would pack up the toys and leave, and would consider the child a baby.

Both threats of punishment seemed to work, as no children played with the forbidden toy. When the researcher asked the children later to re-rate the attractiveness of the toys, however, it was apparent that the severity of the threat did make a difference. For children who were severely threatened, the forbidden toy was still rated as quite attractive. For the mildly threatened children, however, the forbidden toy was rated as much less attractive.

By not playing with the forbidden toy, children were potentially in a state of dissonance. The cognition "I think this is an attractive toy" is inconsistent with the cognition "I am not playing with the toy." Those in the severe threat condition had a sufficient external justification for the discrepancy. Hence, there was no dissonance and no motivation to resolve the inconsistency. Those in the mild threat condition had no such external justification for the inconsistency, so they most likely felt dissonance, and they resolved it by convincing themselves that the toy was not so attractive. Thus, perhaps surprisingly, the more mild the threats used to get children not to do something, the more likely it is that they will come to believe that it is not something they even want to do.

A last type of everyday behavior for which dissonance theory has implications is decision making. According to the theory, many times when one makes a decision, particularly between attractive alternatives, dissonance is likely to occur. Before making a decision, there are probably some features of each alternative that are attractive and some that are not so attractive. When the decision is made, two sets of dissonant cognitions result: "I chose something that has unattractive qualities" and "I did not choose something that has attractive qualities." To resolve this dissonance, people tend to convince themselves that the chosen alternative is clearly superior to the unchosen alternative. So, although before the decision was made, each alternative was seen as equally attractive, after the decision, the chosen alternative is seen as much more attractive. For example, Robert Knox and James Inkster went to a racetrack and asked a sample of people who were waiting in line to place their bets how confident they were that their horse was going to win. They then asked a sample of people who were leaving the betting window the same question.

As might have been predicted by now, bettors were much more confident about their horse's chances after having placed the bet. Before placing a bet, there is no dissonance. After actually placing money on the horse, the potential for dissonance ("I placed money on a horse that might lose and I didn't bet on a horse that might win") arises. To avoid or resolve this dissonance, bettors become much more confident that their horse will win and, by default, more confident that other horses will not.

Context

Cognitive dissonance theory was introduced in 1957, at a time when interest in the motives underlying people's attitudes and behaviors was at a peak in social psychology. Although dissonance theory has emerged as perhaps the best-known and most-researched theory in social psychology, when it was first developed it was one of a handful of theories, now collectively known as cognitive consistency theories, that proposed that people are motivated to seek consistency among and between thoughts, feelings, and behaviors.

There are numerous explanations as to why cognitive dissonance theory has become as important as it has, but two seem particularly intriguing. One concerns the intellectual climate in psychology during the time the theory was introduced. At the time, research in most fields of psychology, including social psychological research on attitude change, was influenced by learning theory. Learning theory suggests that behavior is a function of its consequences: People do those things for which they are rewarded and do not do those things for which they are not rewarded or for which they are punished. Therefore, according to this perspective, to change significantly any form of behavior, from overt actions to attitudes and beliefs, some kind of reward or incentive needs to be offered. The bigger the incentive, the more change can be expected (similarly, the stronger the punishment, the more change can be expected). Research on attitude change, therefore, also focused on the role of rewards and punishment. What made dissonance theory stand out was its prediction that sometimes *less* reward or incentive will lead to more change. This counterintuitive prediction, standing in stark contrast to the generally accepted ideas about the roles of rewards and punishment, brought immediate attention to dissonance theory not only from the social psychological community but also from the psychological community in general; it quickly vaulted the theory to a position of prominence.

A second reason dissonance has become such an important theory was its particular influence on the field of social psychology. Before the theory was introduced, social psychology was identified with the study of groups and intergroup relations. Dissonance theory was one of the first social psychological theories to emphasize the cognitive processes occurring within the individual as an important area of inquiry. As a result, interest in the individual waxed in social psychology, and interest in groups waned. Indeed, the study of groups and intergroup relations began, in part, to be considered the province of sociologists, and the study of the individual in social settings began to define social psychology. Thus, dissonance theory can be credited with significantly changing the focus of research and theory in social psychology.

Bibliography

Aronson, Elliot. "The Theory of Cognitive Dissonance." In *Advances in Experimental Social Psychology.* Vol. 4, edited by Leonard Berkowitz. New York: Academic Press, 1969. This chapter by one of the leading dissonance researchers critically examines the original theory and offers a revised version of the theory based on empirical findings. Clearly written and easily accessible to nonpsychologists.

Brehm, Jack Williams, and Arthur R. Cohen. *Explorations in Cognitive Dissonance.* New York: John Wiley & Sons, 1962. The sixteen chapters in this volume examine, among other things, the implications of dissonance for decision making, the role of personality factors in the experience of dissonance, and possible physiological factors underlying dissonance. In addition, practical applications of the theory are discussed.

Festinger, Leon. *A Theory of Cognitive Dissonance.* Stanford, Calif.: Stanford University Press, 1957. Festinger's seminal work represents the formal introduction of the theory. Theory and data on decision making, attitude change, and exposure to attitude-discrepant information are addressed. It is interesting to compare this original work with later versions of the theory, such as Aronson's chapter.

Kiesler, Charles A., Barry E. Collins, and Norman Miller. *Attitude Change.* New York: John Wiley & Sons, 1969. Offers a critical analysis of dissonance theory. Also compares and contrasts dissonance theory with other prominent theories of attitude change and persuasion. An excellent general introduction to theory and research on attitude change.

Wicklund, Robert A., and Jack Williams Brehm. *Perspectives on Cognitive Dissonance.* Hillsdale, N.J.: Lawrence Erlbaum, 1976. Contains seventeen chapters that not only review the evidence for the basic tenets of the theory but also explore implications of the theory for areas such as politics, marketing, and clinical psychology. In addition, alternative explanations for dissonance phenomena are entertained.

Kenneth G. DeBono

Cross-References

Attitude-Behavior Consistency, 320; Attitude Formation and Change, 326; Causal Attribution, 487; Motivation: Cognitive Theories, 1606; Motivational Constructs, 1616; Self-Perception Theory, 2193.

COGNITIVE MAPS

Type of psychology: Learning
Field of study: Cognitive learning

Cognitive maps are mental images of the social, cultural, and physical environment that people within a cultural system use in making sense of their world; people who live in different social environments also inhabit different cultural worlds.

Principal terms

COGNITION: the manner in which people understand, grasp, and structure their behavior in response to their psychological, social, and cultural environment

COMPETENCE: the ability to speak a language appropriately and grammatically

CONTEXT: the total circumstances in which behavior occurs, including time, place, action, and audience

CULTURE: the rules underlying behavior that both shape behavior and are negotiated through behavior

EXPECTANCY: anticipation of sequencing of events

LATENT LEARNING: learning that is not immediately reflected in performance but that can be elicited in appropriate contexts

PERFORMANCE: the appropriate and grammatical application of language or other cultural symbol systems in concrete situations

Overview

Edward C. Tolman first identified what he later named cognitive maps as a result of a series of experiments conducted in the 1920's and 1930's. In these experiments, Tolman sought to discover whether learning occurred that might not be immediately reflected in performance—what he came to term "latent learning."

In a typical experiment, Tolman constructed an intricate maze. Three groups of hungry rats ran the maze once a day for twelve days. The first group, the rewarded control group, received food for successfully completing the maze. The second group, the nonrewarded control group, received no food; its members investigated the maze. The third group, the experimental group, also received no food for the first ten days of the experiment, and its members simply surveyed the maze. On the eleventh day, the experimental group was provided with food; on the twelfth day, this group performed as well as the rewarded control group.

The conclusion was that latent learning had taken place and that under the appropriate conditions, the experimental group reflected this learning through its performance—the successful completion of the maze. Tolman asserted that the rats had formed "cognitive maps" that enabled them to solve the maze.

Learning (defined here as the construction of cognitive maps), therefore, is not the same as performance. Although learning is reflected in performance, Tolman's work strongly suggests that the appropriate context is necessary to elicit that performance. In the case of the experimental group, it was the food the experimenters provided on the eleventh day of a twelve-day experiment. The rats, Tolman inferred, anticipated that successful completion of the maze on the next attempt would result in their receiving the desired food.

Research has supported Tolman's pioneering work. Emil W. Menzel (1978), for example, used chimpanzees to illustrate the spatial dimensions of cognitive maps. He hid food in a field and then carried a chimpanzee around the field with him. He did not allow the ape either to eat or approach the food, preventing both instrumental conditioning and primary reinforcement from taking place. Later, the chimpanzee that had been shown the food's hiding places and five experimental chimpanzees that had not seen them were released in the field. Invariably, the first chimpanzee went directly to the food. The experimental animals found their food through scrutinizing the area near the chimpanzee that had been shown the hidden supply of food or begging food from this chimpanzee.

David S. Olton and Robert J. Samuelson (1978) demonstrated spatial memory (cognitive maps) in rats through employment of a radial maze. Each arm of the maze had food at the end of it. Through a series of manipulations, the experimenters demonstrated that the rats remembered which arms they had explored and at which arms they had been fed. They eliminated the possibility that the animals used smell to locate the food through altering the animals' sense of smell. Furthermore, other researchers moved the maze to note whether other factors, such as tactile clues, influenced the rats. In each variation of the experiment, the rats behaved as if they were responding to spatial location and not tactile clues. The implication of the studies goes beyond rats. William Roberts and Nelly Van Veldhuizen (1985) have demonstrated that pigeons, as well as rats, can work the radial maze.

Applications

Cognitive theories in learning have gained in popularity. Tolman's pacesetting work established the concepts of cognitive map, internal spatial memories of the animal's relevant environment, and expectancy, an animal's anticipation of a sequence of events in time. Tolman's work, supported and developed through additional research, further established the distinction between learning and performance. Linguists such as Noam Chomsky express this distinction as one between competence and performance.

Cognitive anthropologists, influenced by Tolman's work, have applied his concept to the learning of individuals within sociocultural systems. Cognitive maps, in their view, provide guides to cultural behavior through organizing the psychological, social, and cultural landscape in terms of its relevant characteristics for members of any given society. There have been two famous covers of *The New Yorker* magazine, for example, that illustrate the point. One cover is a New Yorker's view of the West. In that view, the entire center of the United States comprises an area smaller than

Midtown Manhattan. The view to the East is little better: The Atlantic Ocean becomes a puddle, and the geography of Europe is greatly distorted. The point is not that New Yorkers are more ethnocentric than other people; it is that all people exaggerate those aspects of their landscapes or environments that are most important to them, and they neglect those features that they consider unimportant.

A number of factors enter into perceptions of what is most relevant and what is not. Some of these are personal, such as age, gender, likes, and dislikes; others are social—class, ethnic group, occupation. All factors, however, fit into a cultural context and take on meanings within that context. Anyone attempting to understand the manner in which people learn and demonstrate that learning through adequate and appropriate performance must take into account these factors and how they help shape an individual's cognitive map.

In education, the "prior learning" approach has sought to come to grips with these issues and to apply them to instructional ends. Essentially, this perspective maintains that it cannot be assumed that learning has not taken place merely because a student does not demonstrate the desired performance. William Labov (1966) demonstrated, for example, that the presumed inarticulateness of African-American street youths was a function of the setting in which people had tested them. In more natural settings, Labov determined that they were, in fact, highly articulate.

Tolman's insight that rats in a maze will demonstrate latent learning through performance when an appropriate stimulus is present has influenced cognitive therapy. This therapy is based on the hypothesis that people base their behavior on cognitive maps and expectancies. These internal representations of spatial relationships and anticipated sequences of events, based on past experiences—psychological, social, and cultural—form individuals' perceptions of reality even though these stimuli are not materially present.

Cognitive motivation theory is a "pull theory" of motivation. It is based on the hypothesis that people's expectancies provide incentives for behavior. There are positive-incentive and negative-incentive motivations. Working for a promotion along paths anticipated to achieve that desired goal is an example of positive-incentive motivation. In contrast, a youngster who is developing his martial arts skills in order to deal with bullies who beat him each time he encounters them provides an example of negative-incentive motivation.

Values enter intimately into cognitive motivation theory. In order to motivate people, incentives must be valued. If people do not value an incentive, such as a promotion, they are less likely to perform the actions they associate with receiving that incentive. If they receive the goal without performing the behavior (for example, if someone receives a promotion undeservedly), they are less likely to value the goal. In sum, there is an intrinsic relationship between expectancies and value.

Moreover, relief and frustration enter the picture. Relief refers to not receiving an expected negative result (a person does not fail a test for which he or she did not study). Frustration involves failure to attain a goal for which a person has prepared. Failure to receive a promotion to which a person is entitled is an example of frustration. Relief is an example of positive-incentive motivation, and frustration is an example of negative-incentive motivation.

Albert Bandura and others have advocated cognitive behavior therapy based on the application of positive and negative incentives. Such therapy seeks to alter the expectancies and relational maps of clients. Thus, clients can relearn their environment through redrawing cognitive maps and altering their expectancies. There are many techniques employed to bring about these changes in spatial and event expectations.

Therapists who employ Albert Ellis' rational-emotive therapy, for example, believe that the therapist should take a strong interventionist role in the therapy, aggressively confronting the client whenever he or she exhibits examples of irrational thought. These confrontations seek to force the client to learn new, more rational ways of thinking and, therefore, behaving.

Cognitive behavioral therapists seek to change a person's inappropriate thoughts to more effective ones. They first learn what their clients are thinking and then relate these thoughts to inappropriate behavior. They seek to help their clients learn new thoughts that will result in more appropriate behavior. Patients are taught to "talk to themselves," substituting good thoughts for bad. Rather than dwelling on failure, patients concentrate on success or positive aspects of their lives. A student taking an examination, for example, would stop thoughts of failure and remind himself or herself about how well test preparation had gone. Self-encouragement would replace self-disparagement.

Each of these applications is based on the theory that people's behavior is based on internal representations of the world. Each person's representations differ in some way from that of others. These representations influence both the way in which one learns about the world and the manner in which one represents that world. The application of Tolman's work on cognitive maps and their related internal representations, or expectancies, has led to a deeper understanding of learning.

Context

Edward C. Tolman's concept of the cognitive map grew out of a growing recognition that internal representations of reality influence behavior. Moreover, learning is not indistinguishable from performance—the two processes are analytically distinct. An organism may have learned behavior without demonstrating that behavior through performance. This latent learning can be elicited through the presentation of adequate incentives.

Tolman's work in the 1920's and 1930's did much to advance the field of cognitive psychology at a time when behavioral psychology dominated the schools. It provided an additional dimension to learning, advancing the position of internal representations of reality. The empirical evidence offered to support cognitive theory has been impressive, and the cognitive position has advanced accordingly in psychology; it is often combined with behavioral concepts, as in the work of Albert Bandura.

That combination has enabled educators and therapists to bring about behavioral changes based on changes in the manner in which students and patients perceive their worlds. New internal representations of the external environment can be brought about through changes in cognitive maps and expectancies. In turn, these changes alter the bases of decisions that influence an individual's future behavior.

Tolman's work has influenced linguistics, anthropology, sociology, and other social and behavioral sciences. Scholars in these areas have applied the concept of the cognitive map cross-culturally and within cultures to members of subgroups. Future work will apply it to the manner in which each individual negotiates his or her way within cultural and social systems. Continuing work in anthropology and sociology in the negotiated nature of sociocultural systems draws heavily on cognitive maps. Prior learning theory is based on the idea of latent learning, and proceeding work will continue to extract applications of significant value to education.

Future advances will likely occur in studies that investigate field dependence and independence in cognition as related to other aspects of culture, such as child-rearing patterns and subsistence practices. The continuing interest in the relationship between language and cultural organization of reality holds promise for further advances in understanding and applying cognitive maps. The role of choice in the individual's construction of these maps is also an area of intensive investigation.

Bibliography

Bandura, Albert. *Social Foundations of Thought and Action: A Social-Cognitive Theory.* Englewood Cliffs, N.J.: Prentice-Hall, 1986. Presents a clear and concise exposition of Bandura's combination of behavioral and cognitive perspectives in psychology. Advocates an approach that sees behavior resulting from cognitive maps and expectancies.

Chomsky, Noam. *Language and Mind.* New York: Harcourt Brace Jovanovich, 1972. The influential inventor of transformational grammar presents his views on the relationship of language and mind, as well as presenting another extension of Edward C. Tolman's concepts.

Fromkin, Victoria, and Robert Rodman. *An Introduction to Language.* New York: Holt, Rinehart and Winston, 1988. An introductory book that discusses the field of linguistics, including theoretical developments. Demonstrates the manner in which cognitive concepts are being developed in linguistics.

Labov, William. *The Social Stratification of English in New York City.* Washington, D.C.: Center for Applied Linguistics, 1982. Persuasive argument that in appropriate circumstances, the assumed inarticulateness of young African-American men disappears. Example of latent learning forming the basis for adequate performance in a setting that elicits appropriate behavior.

Menzel, Emil W. "Cognitive Mapping in Chimpanzees." In *Cognitive Processes in Animal Behavior,* edited by Stewart H. Hulse, Harry Fowler, and Werner K. Honig. Hillsdale, N.J.: Lawrence Erlbaum, 1978. Adds significantly to the research on cognitive mapping through reporting on Menzel's carefully controlled experiment with chimpanzees and hidden food.

Olton, David S., and Robert J. Samuelson. "Remembrance of Places Passed: Spatial Memory in Rats." *Journal of Experimental Psychology: Animal Behavior Process* 2, no. 2 (1976): 97-116. Research that reports on rats in a radial maze, further establishing the validity of cognitive maps and strengthening their place in learning theory.

Roberts, William A., and Nelly Van Veldhuizen. "Spatial Memory in Rats on the Radial Maze." *Journal of Experimental Psychology: Animal Behavior Processes* 11, no. 2 (1985): 241-260. Extends earlier findings of cognitive maps in rats on the radial maze to pigeons. Careful attention to method, allowing psychologists to extend their findings beyond confines of the research, should be noted.

Tolman, Edward Chace. "Cognitive Maps in Rats and Men." *Psychological Review* 55 (1948): 189-209. Summarizes Tolman's earlier experiments with rats in a clear and comprehensive manner. Applies the theory of cognitive maps to humans and suggests applications of the theory.

—————————. *Purposive Behavior in Animals and Men.* New York: Century, 1932. The first book to report Tolman's finding regarding cognitive maps. Serves as the initial source for understanding cognitive maps.

Frank A. Salamone

Cross-References

Cognitive Psychology: An Overview, 572; Cognitive Social Learning: Walter Mischel, 580; Cognitive Therapy, 586; Concept Formation, 637; Decision Making as a Cognitive Process, 769; Incentive Motivation, 1269; Learning: Concept, Expectancy, and Insight, 1431; Motivation: Cognitive Theories, 1606; Psycholinguistics, 1918.

COGNITIVE PSYCHOLOGY: AN OVERVIEW

Type of psychology: Cognition
Fields of study: Cognitive processes; thought

*Cognitive psychology is concerned with the scientific study of human mental ac-
tivities involved in the acquisition, storage, retrieval, and utilization of information.
Among its wide concerns are perception, memory, reasoning, problem solving, intelligence, language, and creativity; research in these areas has widespread practical
applications.*

Principal terms
ARTIFICIAL INTELLIGENCE: a branch of computer science whose goal is
to create a computer capable of mimicking human intelligence
AVAILABILITY HEURISTIC: a decision-making heuristic whereby a person
estimates the probability of some occurrence or event depending on
how easily examples of that event can be remembered
COGNITIVE SCIENCE: a multidisciplinary approach to the study of
cognition from the perspectives of psychology, computer science,
neuroscience, philosophy, and linguistics
EXPERT SYSTEMS: computer programs built to simulate human expertise
in particular domains
HEURISTIC: a shortcut or rule of thumb used for decision making or
problem solving that often leads to, but does not guarantee, a correct
response
INFORMATION-PROCESSING MODEL: the approach of most modern cognitive
psychologists; it interprets cognition as the flow of information
through interrelated stages, in much the same way that information
is processed by a computer
INTROSPECTION: the self-report of one's own sensations, experiences,
and thoughts

Overview
Cognitive psychology is that branch of psychology concerned with human mental
activities. A staggering array of topics fit under such a general heading. In fact, it
sometimes seems that there is no clear place to end the catalog of cognitive topics,
as mental operations intrude into virtually all human endeavors. As a general guideline, one might consider the subject matter of cognitive psychology as those mental
processes involved in the acquisition, storage, retrieval, and utilization of information.

Among the more specific concerns of cognitive psychologists are perception, attention, memory, and imagery. Studies of perception and attention might be concerned with how much of people's vast sensory experience they can further process

and make sense of, and how they recognize incoming information as forming familiar patterns. Questions regarding the quality of memory include how much information can be maintained, for how long, and under what conditions; how information is organized in memory and how is it retrieved or lost; and how accurate the memory is, as well as what can be done to facilitate a person's recall skills. Cognitive researchers concerned with imagery are interested in people's ability to "see" in their minds a picture or image of an object, person, or scene that is not physically present; cognitive researchers are interested in the properties of such images and how they can be manipulated.

In addition to these concerns, there is great interest in the higher-order processes of planning, reasoning, problem solving, intelligence, language, and creativity. Cognitive psychologists want to know, for example, what steps are involved in planning a route to a destination or a solution to a problem, and what factors influence people's more abstract ability to reason. They seek to understand the importance of prior knowledge or experience, to discover which strategies are effective, and to see what obstacles typically impede a person's thinking. They are interested in the relationships between language and thought, and between creativity and intelligence.

The following exchange is useful in illustrating some of the topics important to cognitive psychologists. Imagine that "Jacob" and "Janet" are two children on a busy playground:

JACOB: Do you want to play some football?

JANET: Sure! Tell me where the ball is and I'll go get it.

JACOB: The football's in my locker in the equipment room. Go back in the building. Go past our classroom, turn right at the water fountain, and it's the second door on your left. My locker is number 12, and the combination is 6-21-13.

JANET: Okay, it'll just take me a couple of minutes. [As she runs to get the ball, Janet repeats over and over to herself, "12; 6, 21, 13. . . ."]

JACOB: [*shouting*] The football field's being watered; meet me in the gym.

Even such a simple encounter involves and depends upon a rich assortment of cognitive skills. At a basic level, Jacob and Janet have to be aware of each other. Their sensory systems allow the detection of one another, and their brains work on the raw data (information) from the senses in order to perceive or interpret the incoming information. In this case, the data are recognized as the familiar patterns labeled "Jacob" and "Janet." During the course of the brief conversation, the children must also attend to (concentrate on) one another, and in doing so they may be less attentive to other detectable sights and sounds of their environment.

This scenario illustrates the use of more than one type of memory. Janet stores the locker number and combination in short-term memory (STM), and she maintains the information by rehearsing it. After Janet retrieves the ball and redirects her attention to choosing teams for the football game, she will probably quickly forget this information. Long-term memory (LTM) is also being displayed by the children. Jacob does not need to rehearse his combination continually to maintain it; rather, his frequent use of his combination and the meaningfulness of this information have helped him to store it in LTM. The language comprehension of the children also illustrates LTM. When Janet hears the words "football," "water fountain," and "locker," she effortlessly retrieves their meanings from LTM. Furthermore, metamemory, an understanding of the attributes of one's own memories, is demonstrated. Janet knows to rehearse the combination to prevent forgetting it.

Jacob probably employed mental imagery and relied on a cognitive map in order to direct Janet to the equipment room. From his substantial mental representation of the school environment, Jacob retrieved a specific route, guided by a particular sequence of meaningful landmarks. Seemingly without thought, both children communicate through the highly abstract symbol system of language. Not only do they have ample vocabularies, but also they know the relationships between words and how to arrange the words meaningfully; they have sophisticated knowledge of syntax and grammar.

In addition to their language capabilities and their abilities to form and follow routes, a number of other higher-level mental processes suggest something of the intelligence of these children. They appear to be following a plan that will result in a football game. Simple problem solving is demonstrated by Janet's calculation of how long it will take to retrieve the football and in Jacob's decision to use the gym floor as a substitute for the football field.

To understand cognitive psychology, one must be familiar not only with the relevant questions—the topic matter of the discipline—but also with the approach taken to answer these questions. Cognitive psychologists typically employ an information-processing model to help them better understand mental events. An assumption of this model is that mental activities (the processing of information) can be broken down into a series of interrelated stages and scientifically studied. A general comparison can be made between the information processing of a human and a computer. For example, both have data input into the system, humans through their sense organs and computers via the keyboard. Both systems then translate and encode (store) the data. The computer translates the keyboard input into electromagnetic signals for storage on a disk. People oftentimes translate the raw data from their senses to a linguistic code which is retained in some unique human storage device (for example, a piercing, rising-and-falling pitch may be stored in memory as "baby's cry"). Both humans and computers can manipulate the stored information in virtually limitless ways, and both can later retrieve information from storage for output. Although there are many dissimilarities between how computers and humans function, this comparison accurately imparts the flavor of the information-processing model.

Finally, it should be emphasized that cognitive psychologists employ a scientific approach. While the workings of the mind cannot be directly seen, one can objectively record the data input into the system and the ensuing response. One can also objectively measure the accuracy of, and the time required for, the response. Based upon this information, one can draw logical inferences as to the mental steps involved in generating that response. One of the continuing challenges of cognitive psychology is the construction of experiments in which observable behaviors accurately reveal mental processes.

Applications

For many psychologists, the desire to "know about knowing" is sufficient reason to study human cognition; however, there are more tangible benefits. Examples of these widespread practical applications may be found in the fields of artificial intelligence and law, and in the everyday world of decision making.

Artificial intelligence (AI) is a branch of computer science that strives to create a computer capable of reasoning, processing language, and, in short, mimicking human intelligence. While this goal has yet to be obtained in full, research in this area has made important contributions. The search for AI has improved the understanding of human cognition; it has also produced applied benefits such as expert systems. Expert systems are computer programs that simulate human expertise in specific domains. Such programs have been painstakingly developed by computer scientists who have essentially extracted knowledge in a subject area from a human expert and built it into a computer system designed to apply that knowledge. Expert systems do not qualify as true artificial intelligence, because, while they can think, they can only do so very narrowly, on one particular topic.

A familiar expert system is the "chess computer." A computerized chess game is driven by a program that has a vast storehouse of chess knowledge and the capability of interacting with a human player, "thinking" about each game in which it is involved. Expert systems are also employed to solve problems in law, computer programming, and various facets of industry. A medical expert system has even been developed to consult interactively with patients and to diagnose and recommend a course of treatment for infectious diseases.

There are legal implications for the cognitive research of Elizabeth Loftus and her colleagues at the University of Washington. Some of their experiments demonstrate the shortcomings of human long-term memory, research relevant to the interpretation of eyewitness testimony in the courtroom. In one study, Loftus and John Palmer showed their subjects films of automobile accidents and asked them to estimate the speeds of the cars involved. The critical variable was the verb used in the question to the subjects. That is, they were asked how fast the cars were going when they "smashed," "collided," "bumped," "hit," or "contacted" each other. Interestingly, the stronger the verb, the greater was the speed estimated. One interpretation of these findings is that the nature of the "leading question" biased the answers of subjects who were not really positive of the cars' speeds. Hence, if the question employed the verb "smashed," the subject was led to estimate that the cars were going fast. Any astute attorney would have no trouble capitalizing on this phenomenon when questioning witnesses to a crime or accident.

In a second experiment, Loftus and Palmer considered a different explanation for their findings. Again, subjects saw filmed car accidents and were questioned as to the speeds of the cars, with the key verb being varied as previously described. As before, those exposed to the verb "smashed" estimated the fastest speeds. In the second part of the experiment, conducted a week later, the subjects were asked additional questions about the accident, including, "Did you see any broken glass?" Twenty percent of the subjects reported seeing broken glass, though none was in the film. Of particular interest was that the majority of those who made this error were in the group which had been exposed to the strongest verb, "smashed."

Loftus and Palmer reasoned that the subjects were melding actual information that they had witnessed with information from another source encountered after the fact (the verb "smashed" presented by the questioner). The result was a mental representation of an event that was partly truth and partly fiction. This interpretation also has implications for the evaluation of eyewitness testimony. Before testifying in court, a witness will likely have been questioned numerous times (and received many suggestions as to what may have taken place) and may even have "compared notes" with other witnesses. This process is likely to distort the originally experienced information.

Consider next the topic of decision making, an area of research in cognitive psychology loaded with practical implications. Everyone makes scores of decisions on a daily basis, from choosing clothing to match the weather, to selecting a college or a career objective. Psychologists Amos Tversky and Daniel Kahneman are well known for their research on decision making and, in particular, on the use of heuristics. Heuristics are shortcuts or rules of thumb that are likely, but not guaranteed, to produce a correct decision. It would seem beneficial for everyone to appreciate the limitations of such strategies. For example, the availability heuristic oftentimes leads people astray when their decisions involve the estimating of probabilities, as when faced with questions such as, Which produces more fatalities, breast cancer or diabetes? Which are more numerous in the English language, words that begin with *k* or words that have *k* as the third letter? Experimental subjects typically, and incorrectly, choose the first alternative in the above questions. Kahneman and Tversky's research indicates that people rely heavily on examples that come most easily to mind—that is, the information most available in memory. Hence, people overestimate the incidence of breast-cancer fatalities because such tragedies get more media attention relative to diabetes, a more prolific but less exotic killer. In a similar vein, words that begin with *k* come to mind more easily (probably because people are more likely to organize their vocabularies by the initial sounds of the words) than words with *k* as the third letter, although the latter in fact outnumber the former. One's decision making will doubtless be improved if one is aware of the potential drawbacks associated with the availability heuristic and if one is able to resist the tendency to estimate probabilities based upon the most easily imagined examples.

Context

The workings of the human mind have been pondered throughout recorded history. The science of psychology, however, only dates back to 1879, when Wilhelm Wundt established the first laboratory for the study of psychology in Leipzig, Germany. Although the term was not yet popular, Wundt's primary interest was clearly in cognition. His students laboriously practiced the technique of introspection (the careful attention to, and the objective report of, one's own sensations, experiences, and thoughts), as Wundt hoped to identify through this method the basic elements of human thought. Wundt's interests remained fairly popular until around 1920. At that time, John B. Watson, a noted American psychologist and behaviorist, spearheaded a campaign to redefine the agenda of psychology. Watson was convinced that the workings of the mind could not be objectively studied through introspection and hence mandated that the proper subject matter for psychologists should be overt, observable behaviors exclusively. In this way, dissatisfaction with a method of research (introspection) led to the abandonment of an important psychological topic (mental activity).

In the 1950's, a number of forces came into play that led to the reemergence of cognitive psychology in America. First, during World War II, considerable research had been devoted to human-factors issues such as human skills and performance within, for example, the confines of a tank or cockpit. After the war, researchers showed continued interest in human attention, perception, decision making, and so on, and they were influenced by a branch of communication science, known as information theory, that dealt abstractly with questions of information processing. The integration of these two topics resulted eventually in the modern information-processing model, mentioned above.

Second, explosive gains were made in the field of computer science. Of particular interest to psychology were advances in the area of artificial intelligence. It was a natural progression for psychologists to begin comparing computer and brain processes, and this analogy served to facilitate cognitive research.

Third, there was growing dissatisfaction with behavioral psychology as defined by Watson, and with its seeming inability to explain complex psychological phenomena. In particular, Noam Chomsky, a well-known linguist, proposed that the structure of language was too complicated to be acquired via the principles of behaviorism. It became apparent to many psychologists that to understand truly the diversity of human behavior, internal mental processes would have to be accepted and scientifically studied.

Cognitive psychology is now a vibrant subdiscipline that has attracted some of the finest scientific minds. It is a standard component in most undergraduate and graduate psychology programs. More than half a dozen academic journals are devoted to its research, and it continues to pursue answers to questions that are important to psychology and other disciplines as well. The cognitive perspective has heavily influenced other subfields of psychology. For example, many social psychologists are interested in social cognition, the reasoning underlying such phenomena as prejudice, altruism, and persuasion. Some clinical psychologists are interested in understanding the abnormal thought processes underlying problems such as depression and anorexia nervosa, and cognitive developmentalists research the way people's thought processes change across the life span.

The burgeoning field of cognitive science represents a contemporary union of cognitive psychology, neuroscience, computer science, linguistics, and philosophy. Cognitive scientists are concerned with mental processes but are particularly interested in establishing general, fundamental principles of information processing as they may be applied by humans or machines. Their research is often heavily dependent on complex computer models rather than experimentation with humans. With fast-paced advances in computer technology, and the exciting potential of expertise shared in an interdisciplinary fashion, the field of cognitive science holds considerable promise for answering questions about human cognition.

Bibliography

Ashcraft, Mark H. *Human Memory and Cognition.* Glenview, Ill.: Scott, Foresman, 1989. A fine textbook, geared for college students who have had some background in psychology but accessible to the inquisitive layperson. Ashcraft writes informally and provides chapter outlines and summaries, a glossary of key terms, and suggested supplemental readings. Perception and attention, memory, language, reasoning, decision making, and problem solving are all well covered.

Baddeley, Alan D. "The Cognitive Psychology of Everyday Life." *British Journal of Psychology* 72, no. 2 (1981): 257-269. An interesting journal article in which Baddeley describes his research conducted outside the laboratory environment. Considers such practical topics as absentmindedness, alcohol effects, and the effectiveness of saturation advertising. A must for those who question the ecological validity (the real-life applicability) of cognitive research.

Berger, Dale E., Kathy Pezdek, and William P. Banks, eds. *Applications of Cognitive Psychology.* Hillsdale, N.J.: Lawrence Erlbaum, 1987. Five chapters each on three topics: educational applications, teaching of thinking and problem solving, and human-computer interactions. The chapters range in sophistication and accessibility, so this book should appeal to readers of diverse backgrounds. There are helpful name and subject indexes.

Kahneman, Daniel, Paul Slovic, and Amos Tversky, eds. *Judgment Under Uncertainty: Heuristics and Biases.* Cambridge, England: Cambridge University Press, 1982. A comprehensive source on heuristics and decision making with an easy-to-understand introductory chapter by the editors. A four-chapter section is devoted to the availability heuristic, and there is an interesting chapter on probabilistic reasoning in clinical medicine.

Kendler, Howard H. *Historical Foundations of Modern Psychology.* Chicago: Dorsey Press, 1987. A well-written account of the emergence of cognitive psychology and the contributions of other disciplines such as linguistics, engineering, and computer science. Approachable for the layperson; provides a fine historical backdrop. It is of limited use, beyond review, for the upper-level college student.

Wells, Gary L., and Elizabeth F. Loftus, eds. *Eyewitness Testimony: Psychological*

Perspectives. Cambridge, England: Cambridge University Press, 1984. A fourteen-chapter source with heavy consideration of laboratory research, but with references to courtroom cases as well. There is nice coverage of research on children as witnesses, as well as on "earwitness" testimony and the use of hypnosis as a memory aid.

Mark B. Alcorn

Cross-References

Artificial Intelligence, 299; Attention, 313; Computer Models of Cognition, 631; Decision Making as a Cognitive Process, 769; Language and Cognition, 1401; Logic and Reasoning, 1471; Neural Anatomy and Cognition, 1640; Pattern Recognition as a Cognitive Process, 1747.

COGNITIVE SOCIAL LEARNING: WALTER MISCHEL

Type of psychology: Personality
Fields of study: Behavioral and cognitive models; personality theory

Mischel's social learning theory presents a cognitive-social alternative to traditional personality theories. He posits that behavior is determined by a complex interaction of situational and cognitive variables and cannot be predicted from a few widely generalized traits. Consistent features in behavior result from cognitive person variables, defined as acquired and relatively stable modes of information processing.

Principal terms
CONSTRUCTION COMPETENCIES: behavioral skills and cognitive abilities acquired from experience; those things which a person is capable of doing
ENCODING STRATEGY: a specific form of cognitively processing information
EXPECTANCIES: expectations; for example, the expectation that a given behavior will lead to a certain outcome
PERSON VARIABLE: an acquired, relatively enduring cognitive attribute that affects how someone perceives the world
PERSONAL CONSTRUCT: an idiosyncratic or personalized way of cognitively elaborating experiences
PERSONALITY TRAIT: a stable disposition to behave in a given way over time and across situations
PROTOTYPE: the "best" or "typical" example of a concept
STIMULUS VALUE: the subjective value or worth that a person attributes to an object or event

Overview

Psychologist Walter Mischel developed a cognitive social-learning approach to personality that presents a serious challenge to traditional theories and their central tenet that behavior can be predicted from a few widely generalized traits. In his influential book *Personality and Assessment* (1968), Mischel reviewed the literature on personality traits. Although he found impressive consistencies for some attributes such as intelligence, the vast majority of behavior patterns were not consistent, even in highly similar situations. Mischel concluded that behavior is largely determined by situational variables that interact in complex ways with individual modes of information processing. Stable features in behavior result from acquired cognitive person variables (relatively stable individual differences that influence how people interact with their world).

Cognitive and behavioral construction competencies represent the first of the person variables. Mischel terms them "competencies" to emphasize that they represent potentials—that is, what people *can* do, rather than what they do. Referring to their "constructive" quality implies that people do not passively store but actively construct their experiences by transforming and synthesizing incoming information in novel ways. Another of these person variables involves encoding strategies and personal constructs. People encode information and classify events in personalized ways. For different individuals, traitlike constructs such as intelligence or honesty may therefore have some overlapping features but may also have many idiosyncratic ones. This explains why two people can witness and process the same event but interpret it differently. Both people only attend to stimuli consistent with their own personal construct systems and ignore discrepant information.

Mischel maintains that besides knowing people's potentials and how they construct events, to predict behavior people must also know their expectations. One type, termed stimulus-outcome expectancies, develops when people form associations between two events and begin to expect the second event as soon as the first occurs. For example, if a child learns to associate parental frowning with being scolded or spanked, any angry face alone may soon instill anxiety.

A second type, termed response-outcome expectancies, refers to learned "if-then rules," in which specific actions will result in certain outcomes. Outcome expectancies can have a significant influence on what people do. When expectations are inconsistent with reality, they can lead to dysfunctional behavior. Expecting relief from alcohol, when drinking actually leads to multiple problems, illustrates this point.

Subjective stimulus values are another type of person variable. In spite of holding identical outcome expectancies, people may behave differently if they do not attribute equal value to this outcome. For example, many believe that practice makes perfect, but not everyone values achievement. Furthermore, the worth of a given outcome often depends on its context. Even an avid skier might cancel a ski trip on an icy, stormy winter day.

Self-regulatory systems and plans are yet another kind of person variable. Besides being affected by external rewards and punishments, people are capable of regulating their own behavior. They set goals and mediate self-imposed consequences, depending on whether they meet their own standards. These self-regulatory processes produce individual differences in behavior independently from the effects of extrinsically imposed conditions.

More recently, Mischel and his colleagues have proposed that people also classify events based on cognitive prototypes. These are analogous to templates, and they contain only the best or most typical features of a concept. Although prototypes facilitate the classification of input information, they carry with them the danger of stereotyping. Anyone who, for example, has mistaken a female business executive for the secretary can appreciate the problem resulting from inaccurate classification.

In summary, with the concept of person variables, Mischel can explain behavioral consistency and at the same time take into account the environment as an important determinant of human actions. In psychologically strong situations, person variables play a minimal role (at a church service, for example, all people behave similarly). In psychologically weak situations (such as a cocktail party), however, individual differences are pronounced, because there are no consistent cues to signal what behaviors are deemed appropriate. Therefore, whether and how much cognitive dispositions influence behavior varies with the specific situation.

Applications

Despite a widespread tendency among people to describe themselves and others in traitlike terms (intelligent, friendly, aggressive, domineering, and so forth), research has shown that a person's behavior cannot be predicted from a few broadly generalized personality traits. This does not mean that behavior is totally inconsistent, but that dispositions alone are insufficient to explain consistency and that dispositional, as well as situational, variables need to be taken into account for a complete analysis.

To separate the effects of person and situation variables on behavior, Mischel and his colleagues conducted a series of experiments. In one study, the experimenters assessed adolescents' dispositions toward success or failure. Weeks later they had them solve skill-related tasks and, regardless of their actual performance, gave one group success, a second group failure, and a third group no feedback on their performance. Then the adolescents had to choose between a less desirable reward, one for which attainment was independent of performance on similar tasks, and a preferred reward, for which attainment was performance-dependent. In both bogus feedback conditions, the situational variables had a powerful effect and completely overrode preexisting dispositions toward success or failure. Adolescents who believed they had failed the tasks more often selected the noncontingent reward, while those who believed they had succeeded chose the contingent reward. For subjects in the no-feedback condition, however, the preexisting expectancy scores were highly accurate predictors of their reward choices. This study illustrates how dispositions emerge under weak situational cues but play a trivial role when the setting provides strong cues for behavior. Therefore, Mischel (1973) considers it more meaningful to analyze "behavior-contingency units" that link specific behavior patterns to those conditions in which they are likely to occur, rather than looking only at behavior. In other words, instead of labeling people "aggressive," it would be more useful to specify under what conditions these people display aggressive behaviors. Such precise specifications would guard against an oversimplified trait approach and highlight the complexities and idiosyncrasies of behavior as well as its interdependence with specific stimulus conditions.

Mischel and his colleagues also have conducted extensive research on self-control. Their work has been summarized in an article published in 1989 in the journal *Science*. In several experiments, the researchers attempted to clarify why some people are capable of self-regulation, at least in some areas of their lives, while others fail in such attempts. They found enduring differences in self-control as early as the preschool years. In one study, for example, they showed young children pairs of treats, one less and one more desirable (for example, two versus five cookies or one versus two marshmallows). The children were told that the experimenter would leave the room and that they could obtain the more valuable treat if they waited until he or she returned. They could also ring the bell to bring the experimenter back sooner, but then they would receive the lesser treat. During the waiting period, which lasted a maximum of fifteen minutes, the children were unobtrusively observed. Later, the children's strategies to bridge the waiting period were analyzed. It became apparent that self-control increased when the children used behavioral or cognitive strategies to bridge the delay, such as avoiding looking at the rewards, distracting themselves with singing, playing with their fingers, or cognitively transforming the rewards (for example, thinking of marshmallows as clouds). Interestingly, a follow-up study more than ten years later revealed that those preschool children who had displayed more self-control early were socially and academically more competent, more attentive, more verbal, and better able to cope with stress than their peers as adolescents. In a related study, the length of delay time in preschool proved to be correlated with the adolescents' Scholastic Aptitude Test (SAT) scores, suggesting that greater self-control is related to superior academic achievement.

These studies provide an excellent illustration of how cognitive person variables sometimes can have very stable and generalized effects on behavior. The early acquisition of effective cognitive and behavioral strategies to delay gratification had a positive influence on the children's long-term adjustment. Thus, self-control fulfills the requirements of a "personality disposition" in Mischel's sense, because it constitutes an important mediating mechanism for adaptive social behavior throughout the life cycle.

Although the examples presented above lend support to Mischel's theory, one might argue that children's behavior under the constraints of a research setting is artificial and may not reflect what they normally do in their natural environment. While this argument is plausible, it was not supported in a later study with six- to twelve-year-old children in a summer residential treatment facility. Observing children under naturalistic circumstances in this facility led to comparable results. Children who spontaneously used effective cognitive-attentional strategies for self-regulation showed greater self-control in delay situations and were better adjusted than their peers.

An unanswered question is how best to teach children effective information-processing skills. If these skills acquire dispositional character and influence overall adjustment, their attainment would indeed be of vital importance to healthy development.

Context

Until the late 1960's, the field of personality psychology was dominated by trait and state theories. Their central assumption, that people have traits that produce enduring consistencies in their behavior, went unchallenged for many years. The widespread appeal of these trait assumptions notwithstanding, since the late 1960's personality and social psychologists have been entangled in the "person-situation debate," a controversy over whether the presumed stability in behavior might be based more on illusion than reality. While doubts about the existence of traits were already raised more than forty years ago, the work of Walter Mischel was instrumental in bringing the controversy into the forefront of academic psychology. In reviewing a voluminous body of literature, Mischel showed in 1968 that virtually all so-called trait measures, except intelligence, change substantially over time and even more dramatically across situations. Traits such as honesty, assertiveness, or attitudes toward authority typically showed reliability across situations of .20 to .30. This means that if the correlation of behavior presumably reflecting a trait in two different situations is .30, less than one-tenth ($.30 \times .30 = .09$, or 9 percent) of the variability in the behavior can be attributed to the trait. Mischel therefore concluded that perceptions of behavioral stability, while not arbitrary, are often only weakly related to the phenomenon in question.

There is consensus, however, that human actions show at least some degree of consistency, which is evidenced most strongly by the sense of continuity people experience in their own selves. How can people reconcile the inconsistency between their own impressions and the empirical data? Mischel's cognitive social learning perspective presents one possible solution to this dilemma. Rather than trying to explain behavior by a few generalized traits, Mischel has shifted the emphasis to a thorough examination of the relationship between molar behavior patterns and the context in which they occur, as the following example illustrates. Assume that parents are complaining about their child's demanding behavior and the child's many tantrums. After observing this behavior in various situations, a traditional personality theorist might conclude that it manifests an underlying "aggressive drive." In contrast, a social learning theorist might seek to identify the specific conditions under which the tantrums occur and then change these conditions to see if the tantrums increase or decrease. This technique, termed "functional analysis" (as described in Mischel in 1968), systematically introduces and withdraws stimuli in the situation to examine how the behavior of interest changes as a function of situational constraints.

The controversy sparked by Mischel's work has not been completely resolved. Few psychologists today, however, would assume an extreme position and either argue that human actions are completely determined by traits or advocate a total situation-specificity of behavior. As with so many controversies, the truth probably lies somewhere in the middle.

Bibliography

Lieber, Robert M., and Michael D. Spiegler. *Personality: Strategies and Issues.* 5th ed. Chicago: Dorsey Press, 1987. Chapter 21 presents a readable synopsis of Mischel's cognitive social-learning theory and reviews the concept of person variables, Mischel's work on delay of gratification, and his position on the interaction of emotion and cognition. Highly recommended as an easy introduction to Mischel's work.

Mischel, Harriet N., and Walter Mischel, eds. *Readings in Personality.* New York: Holt, Rinehart and Winston, 1973. Presents a collection of papers by different authors on some of the central topics and viewpoints in personality psychology. Provides in-depth analyses of various trait, state, and social theories of personality. Several chapters by Walter Mischel present his views on social learning, personality, and his empirical work on self-control.

Mischel, Walter. *Personality and Assessment.* New York: John Wiley & Sons, 1968. Classic exposition of Mischel's early work, containing a compelling critique of traditional trait and state approaches to personality. Discusses issues relevant to the assessment and modification of maladaptive social behavior. Should be available in many public and all university libraries.

——————. "Toward a Cognitive Social Learning Reconceptualization of Personality." *Psychological Review* 80, no. 4 (1973): 252-283. Written in response to the many reactions Mischel's 1968 book provoked in the research community. Clarifies several common misunderstandings of Mischel's position (for example, the situation-specificity issue) and gives a thorough presentation of his five personality variables. No specialized knowledge in psychology or personality theory is necessary for the reader to be able to follow the author's main arguments.

Mischel, Walter, Yuichi Shoda, and Monica L. Rodriguez. "Delay of Gratification in Children." *Science* 244, no. 4907 (1989): 933-938. Presents an excellent, brief summary of Mischel's work on self-control and delay of gratification spanning almost two decades. Discusses a number of stable individual differences in information-processing and strategic behaviors used by preschool children that were predictive of adult social adjustment.

Edelgard Wulfert

Cross-References

Cognitive Behavior Therapy, 546; Cognitive Psychology: An Overview, 572; Cognitive Therapy, 586; Learning: Concept, Expectancy, and Insight, 1431; Personal Constructs: George A. Kelly, 1784; Social Learning: Albert Bandura, 2304.

COGNITIVE THERAPY

Type of psychology: Psychotherapy
Field of study: Cognitive therapies

Cognitive therapy holds that emotional disorders are largely determined by cognition or thinking, that cognitive activity can take the form of language or images, and that emotional disorders can be treated by helping patients modify their cognitive distortions. Treatment programs based on this model have been highly successful with depression, panic disorder, generalized anxiety disorder, and other emotional problems.

Principal terms

ARBITRARY INFERENCE: the process of drawing a conclusion from an experience where there is no evidence to support such a conclusion

AUTOMATIC THOUGHTS: thoughts experienced by individuals of which they are dimly aware and that seem believable, but that can be highly unrealistic and maladaptive

COGNITIVE SPECIFICITY HYPOTHESIS: the idea that each of the emotional disorders is characterized by its own patterns of thinking or cognitive distortions

COGNITIVE TRIAD: seen as the core of depression; consists of a negative view of the self, one's experiences, and the future

SCHEMATA: fundamental beliefs people hold about themselves or the world; these beliefs appear to be the rules by which one lives

SELECTIVE ABSTRACTION: focusing on something taken out of context and conceptualizing the experience on the basis of this particular element

Overview

Cognitive therapy, originally developed by Aaron T. Beck, is based on the view that cognition (the process of acquiring knowledge and forming beliefs) is a primary determinant of mood and behavior. Beck developed his theory while treating depressed patients. He noticed that these patients tended to distort whatever happened to them in the direction of self-blame and catastrophes. Thus an event interpreted by a normal person as irritating and inconvenient (for example, the malfunctioning of an automobile) would be interpreted by the depressed patient as another example of the utter hopelessness of life. Beck's central point is that depressives draw illogical conclusions and come to evaluate negatively themselves, their immediate world, and their future. They see only personal failings, present misfortunes, and overwhelming difficulties ahead. It is from these cognitions that all the other symptoms of depression derive.

It was from Beck's early work with depressed patients that cognitive therapy was developed. Shortly thereafter, the concepts and procedures were applied to other psychological problems, with notable success.

Two concepts of particular relevance to cognitive therapy are the concepts of automatic thoughts and schemata (schemata is the plural of schema). Automatic thoughts are thoughts that appear to be going on all the time. These thoughts are quite brief—only the essential words in a sentence seem to occur, as in a telegraphic style. Further, they seem to be autonomous, in that the person made no effort to initiate them, and they seem plausible or reasonable to the person (although they may seem far-fetched to somebody else). Thus, as a depressed person is giving a talk to a group of business colleagues, he or she will have a variety of thoughts. There will be thoughts about the content of the material. There is also a second stream of thoughts occurring. In this second channel, the person may experience such thoughts as: "This is a waste of time," or "They think I'm dumb." These are automatic thoughts.

Beck has suggested that although automatic thoughts are occurring all the time, the person is likely to overlook these thoughts when asked what he or she is thinking. Thus it is necessary to train the person to attend to these automatic thoughts. Beck pointed out that when people are depressed, these automatic thoughts are filled with negative thoughts of the self, the world, and the future. Further, these automatic thoughts are quite distorted, and finally, when these thoughts are carefully examined and modified to be more in keeping with reality, the depression subsides.

The concept of schemata, or core beliefs, becomes critical in understanding why some people are prone to having emotional difficulties and others are not. The schema appears to be the root from which the automatic thoughts derive. Beck suggests that people develop a propensity to think crookedly as a result of early life experiences. He theorizes that in early life, an individual forms concepts—realistic as well as unrealistic—from experiences. Of particular importance are individuals' attitudes toward themselves, their environment, and their future. These deeply held core beliefs about oneself are seen by Beck as critical in the causation of emotional disorders. According to cognitive theory, the reason these early beliefs are so critical is that once they are formed, the person has a tendency to distort or view subsequent experiences to be consistent with these core beliefs. Thus, an individual who, as a child, was subjected to severe, unprovoked punishment from a disturbed parent may conclude, "I am weak" or "I am inferior." Once this conclusion has been formulated, it would appear to be strongly reinforced over years and years of experiences at the hands of the parent. Thus, when this individual becomes an adult, he or she tends to interpret even normal frustrations as more proof of the original belief: "See, I really am inferior." Examples of these negative schemata or core beliefs are: "I am weak," "I am inferior," "I am unlovable," and "I cannot do anything right." People holding such core beliefs about themselves would differ strongly in their views of a frustrating experience from those people who hold a core belief such as "I am capable."

Another major contribution of cognitive therapy is Beck's cognitive specificity hypothesis. Specifically, Beck has suggested that each of the emotional disorders is characterized by its own patterns of thinking. In the case of depression, the thought content is concerned with ideas of personal deficiency, impossible environmental demands and obstacles, and nihilistic expectations. For example, a depressed patient might interpret a frustrating situation, such as a malfunctioning automobile, as evidence of his or her own inadequacy: "If I were really competent, I would have anticipated this problem and been able to avoid it." Additionally, the depressed patient might react to the malfunctioning automobile with: "This is too much, I cannot take it anymore." To the depressed patient, this would simply be another example of the utter hopelessness of life.

While the cognitive content of depression emphasizes the negative view of the self, the world, and the future, anxiety disorders are characterized by fears of physical and psychological danger. The anxious patient's thoughts are filled with themes of danger. These people anticipate detrimental occurrences to themselves, their family, their property, their status, and other intangibles that they value.

In phobias, as in anxiety, there is the cognitive theme of danger; however, the "danger" is confined to definable situations. As long as phobic sufferers are able to avoid these situations, then they do not feel threatened and may be relatively calm. The cognitive content of panic disorder is characterized by a catastrophic interpretation of bodily or mental experiences. Thus patients with panic disorder are prone to regard any unexplained symptom or sensation as a sign of some impending catastrophe. As a result, their cognitive processing system focuses their attention on bodily or psychological experience. For example, one patient saw discomfort in the chest as evidence of an impending heart attack.

The cognitive feature of the paranoid reaction is the misinterpretation of experience in terms of mistreatment, abuse, or persecution. The cognitive theme of the conversion disorder (a disorder characterized by physical complaints such as paralysis or blindness, where no underlying physical basis can be determined) is the conviction that one has a physical disorder. As a result of this belief, the patient experiences sensory and/or motor abnormalities that are consistent with the patient's faulty conception of organic pathology.

Applications

The goal of cognitive therapy is to assist the patient to evaluate his or her thought processes carefully, to identify cognitive errors, and to substitute more adaptive, realistic cognitions. This goal is accomplished by therapists helping patients to see their thinking about themselves (or their situation) as similar to the activity of a scientist—that they are engaged in the activity of developing hypotheses (or theories) about their world. Like a scientist, the patient needs to "test" his or her theory carefully. Thus patients who have concluded that they are "worthless" people would be encouraged to test their "theories" rigorously to determine if this is indeed accurate. Further, in the event that the theories are not accurate, patients would be encouraged to change their theories to make them more consistent with reality (what they find in their experience).

A slightly different intervention developed by Beck and his colleagues is to help the patient identify common cognitive distortions. Beck originally identified four cognitive distortions frequently found in emotional disorders: arbitrary inference, selective abstraction, overgeneralization, and magnification or minimization. These were later expanded to ten or more by Beck's colleagues and students.

Arbitrary inference is defined as the process of drawing a conclusion from a situation, event, or experience when there is no evidence to support the conclusion or when the conclusion is contrary to the evidence. For example, a depressed patient on a shopping trip had the thought, "The salesclerk thinks I am a nobody." The patient then felt sad. On being questioned by the psychologist, the patient realized that there was no factual basis for this thought. Selective abstraction refers to the process of focusing on a detail taken out of context, ignoring other, more salient features of the situation, and conceptualizing the whole experience on the basis of this element. For example, a patient was praised by friends about the patient's child-care activities. Through an oversight, however, the patient failed to have her child vaccinated during the appropriate week. Her immediate thought was, "I am a failure as a mother." This idea became paramount despite all the other evidence of her competence.

Overgeneralization refers to patients' patterns of drawing a general conclusion about their ability, their performance, or their worth on the basis of a single incident. For example, a student regards his poor performance on the first examination of the semester as final proof that he "will never make it in college." Magnification and minimization refer to gross errors in evaluation. For example, a person, believing that he has completely ruined his car (magnification) when he sees that there is a slight scratch on the rear fender, regards himself as "good for nothing." In contrast, minimization refers to minimizing one's achievements, protesting that these achievements do not mean anything. For example, a highly successful businesswoman who was depressed concluded that her many prior successes "were nothing . . . simply luck." Using the cognitive distortions, people are taught to examine their thoughts, to identify any distortions, and then to modify their thoughts in order to eliminate the distortions.

In terms of the therapeutic process, the focus is initially on the automatic thoughts of patients. Once patients are relatively adept at identifying and modifying their maladaptive automatic thoughts, the therapy begins to focus on the maladaptive underlying beliefs or schemata. As previously noted, these beliefs are fundamental beliefs that people hold about themselves. These beliefs are not as easy to identify as the automatic thoughts. Rather, they are identified in an inferential process. Common patterns are observed; for example, the person may seem to be operating by the rule: "If I am not the best ———, then I am a failure," or "If I am not loved by my spouse or mate, then I am worthless." As in the case of the earlier cognitive work with automatic thoughts, these beliefs are carefully evaluated for their adaptability or rationality. Maladaptive beliefs are then modified to more adaptive, realistic beliefs.

A variety of techniques have been developed by cognitive therapists for modifying maladaptive cognitions. One example of these techniques is self-monitoring. This involves the patient's keeping a careful hour-by-hour record of his or her activities, associated moods, or other pertinent phenomena. One useful variant is to have the patient record his or her mood on a simple zero-to-one-hundred scale, where zero represents the worst he or she has ever felt and one hundred represents the best. In addition, the patient can record the degree of mastery or pleasure associated with each recorded activity.

A number of hypotheses can be tested using self-monitoring, such as: "It does not do any good for me to get out of bed," "I am always miserable; it never lets up," and "My schedule is too full for me to accomplish what I must." By simply checking the self-monitoring log, one can easily determine if one's miserable mood ever ceases. A careful examination of the completed record is a far better basis for judging such hypotheses than is the patient's memory of recent events, because his or her recollections are almost always tainted by the depression.

As therapy progresses and patients begin to experience more elevated moods, the focus of treatment becomes more cognitive. Patients are instructed to observe and record automatic thoughts, perhaps at a specific time each evening, as well as recording when they become aware of increased dysphoria. Typically, the thoughts are negative self-referents ("I am worthless"; "I will never amount to anything"), and initially, the therapist points out their unreasonable and self-defeating nature. With practice, patients learn "distancing," that is, dealing with such thoughts objectively and evaluating them rather than blindly accepting them. Homework assignments can facilitate distancing: The patient records an automatic thought, and next to it he or she writes down a thought that counters the automatic thought, as the therapist might have done. According to Beck, certain basic themes soon emerge, such as being abandoned, as well as stylistic patterns of thinking, such as overgeneralization. The themes reflect the aforementioned rules, and the ultimate goal of therapy is to assist the patient to modify them.

Finally, cognitive therapy has been applied to a variety of psychological disorders with striking success. For example, studies from seven independent centers have compared the efficacy of cognitive therapy to antidepressant medication, a treatment of established efficacy. Comparisons of cognitive therapy to drugs have found cognitive therapy to be superior or equal to antidepressant medication. Further, follow-up studies indicate that cognitive therapy has greater long-term effects than drug therapy. Of special significance is the evidence of greater sustained improvement over time with cognitive therapy.

Cognitive therapy has been successfully applied to panic disorder, resulting in practically complete reduction of panic attacks after twelve to sixteen weeks of treatment. Additionally, cognitive therapy has been successfully applied to generalized anxiety disorder, eating disorders, and inpatient depression.

Context

Cognitive theory and cognitive therapy originated in Aaron T. Beck's observation and treatment of depressed patients. Originally trained in psychoanalysis, Beck observed that his patients experienced specific types of thoughts, of which they were only dimly aware, that they did not report during their free associations. Beck noticed that these thoughts were frequently followed by an unpleasant affect. Further, he noted that as the patients examined and modified their thoughts, their mood began to improve.

At the time of the emergence of the cognitive model, the treatment world was dominated primarily by the psychoanalytic model (with its heavy emphasis on the unconscious processes) and to a lesser extent by the behavioral model (with its emphasis on the behavioral processes, to the exclusion of thought). The psychoanalytic model was under attack, primarily because of a lack of careful empirical support. In contrast, behavior therapists were actively demonstrating the efficacy of their approaches in carefully designed studies. Beck and his students began to develop and test cognitive procedures systematically, and they have developed an impressive body of research support for the approach.

Bibliography

Beck, Aaron T. *Cognitive Therapy and the Emotional Disorders.* New York: International Universities Press, 1976. An easy-to-read book that presents a general overview of the cognitive model and illustrates the cognitive model of different psychological disorders.

Beck, Aaron T., and Gary Emery. *Anxiety Disorders and Phobias: A Cognitive Perspective.* New York: Basic Books, 1985. Presents the cognitive theory and model of anxiety disorders, as well as the clinical techniques used with anxious patients.

Beck, Aaron T., A. J. Rush, B. F. Shaw, and Gary Emery. *Cognitive Therapy of Depression.* New York: Guilford Press, 1979. Presents the cognitive theory of depression and actual techniques used with depressed patients. Both makes a theoretical contribution and serves as a clinical handbook on depression.

Burns, David D. *Feeling Good: The New Mood Therapy.* New York: William Morrow, 1980. Readable introduction to the major concepts and techniques of cognitive therapy; written by one of Beck's students.

Emery, Gary, Steven D. Hollom, and Richard C. Bedrosian, eds. *New Directions in Cognitive Therapy: A Casebook.* New York: Guilford Press, 1981. Contains cases presented by major cognitive therapists. Focuses on the application of cognitive therapy to a wide range of presenting problems (such as loneliness and agoraphobia), as well as diverse populations (such as adolescents, the elderly, and the psychologically naïve).

Donald G. Beal

Cross-References

Abnormality: Cognitive Models, 46; Cognitive Behavior Therapy, 546; Cognitive Social Learning: Walter Mischel, 580; Personal Constructs: George A. Kelly, 1784; Rational-Emotive Therapy, 2052; Reality Therapy, 2059; Transactional Analysis, 2584.

THE COLLECTIVE UNCONSCIOUS

Type of psychology: Personality
Fields of study: Personality theory; psychodynamic and neoanalytic models

The collective unconscious is Carl G. Jung's concept of a vast realm of unconscious influences, primarily archetypes, shared by all human beings.

Principal terms

ARCHETYPES: universal, inherited themes that exercise an influence on virtually all human beings, such as the motif of the "great mother"

COLLECTIVE UNCONSCIOUS: unconscious influences potentially experienced by all human beings, principally archetypes

INDIVIDUATION: the process of becoming a unique individual, often undertaken at midlife

PERSONAL UNCONSCIOUS: unconscious material that is unique to the individual

PRIMARY REPRESSION: in psychoanalytic terms, the repression of material that was never experienced by consciousness

REPRESSION: the forcing of material such as memories or impulses from consciousness because of its threatening nature

SYNCHRONICITY: Jung's term for meaningful coincidences

UNUS MUNDUS: "one world"; the term Jung used to refer to a deep unity of mind and matter

Overview

Unlike Sigmund Freud, who theorized the existence only of a personal or biographical unconscious composed of material from an individual's own personal history, Carl G. Jung proposed the existence of a much larger field of unconscious dynamics that he termed the collective unconscious.

Freud's basic structure of the mind, or psyche, included a relatively small region of consciousness associated mostly with the ego and a much larger domain of unconscious processes. The contents of this process, the unconscious mind, were either biological impulses never experienced directly by consciousness because they were too morally threatening (the fact that they had never been experienced led them to be termed primary repressions) or memories of personal events too painful to remain in consciousness and repressed sometime after they were first registered. An example of the first instance would be an incestuous impulse toward the parent of the opposite sex. An example of the second type would be a terrifying experience, such as a beating sustained as a child and later forced out of memory or repressed. Thus the Freudian, or psychoanalytic, picture of the personality contains two parts: a relatively small conscious region and a much larger unconscious one. Freud was famous for the iceberg analogy in which it is pointed out that four-fifths of the personality, like four-fifths of an iceberg, is beneath the surface.

Jung's structure of the psyche is much larger yet. It includes the conscious ego, the personal unconscious (essentially similar to Freud's entire unconsciousness), and a virtually limitless collective unconsciousness. The term "personal" refers to the individual biographical nature of this aspect of the unconscious, while the term "collective" suggests a larger field shared by many if not all human beings. While Jung agreed with Freud that repressed personal memories and desires play a significant role in the psychology of the individual, in contrast to Freud he tended to stress the importance of the collective unconscious.

The latter does not contain individual memories but rather the collective experiences or memories of the human species. Thus, it represents a kind of collective species memory. The contents of the collective unconsciousness are not passive but are made of dynamic images and themes, or "archetypes," that express themselves in dreams, mythology, art, literature, and the visions of psychotics, as well as in the fantasies and aspirations of all human beings. Much of Jung's understanding of archetypes came, for example, from the study of ancient myths and fairy tales from throughout the world. Indeed, there is no better source for understanding archetypes than the study of mythology. Greek myths seem particularly rich in this regard. The mythic tales of King Arthur and the knights of the Round Table are another frequently celebrated source. Archetypes, such as that of the hero, exert themselves not only in myth and literature but also directly in people's lives when they picture others in the role of the archetype or unconsciously act it out themselves. Two very important archetypes in Jungian psychology are the anima, the image of the feminine carried in the psyche of every man, and the animus, the image of the masculine carried in the psyche of every woman. When understood in Jungian terms, these lead to a whole psychology of the sexes in which each gender yearns to complete itself in a romantic relationship with the other. The central guiding archetype of the personality is the self, which asserts itself especially at midlife, moving the individual in the direction of becoming a unique and whole individual.

In Jung's view, the collective unconscious represents a cumulative expression of the experience of the species over its entire evolutionary history; it is considered to differ slightly with different nationalities and races. While most of its archetypal contents are common to all human beings, the collective experience of a Chinese, African, aboriginal Australian, or Native American person differs somewhat from that of the European person, as expressed, for example, in their different mythologies. For most purposes, such differences are not considered important, but they can represent an important starting point in understanding differences in the psychology of people from different regions of the world.

From the largest perspective, the collective unconscious would seem at first to be no more than a collection of archetypes; however, there is an even deeper level at which it is unified. At that level, the psyche and the physical merge in a common underlying reality beyond, or beneath, the ordinary experience of time and space. Jung used the Latin term for this unity, calling it the *unus mundus*, or "one world."

The connection of the psychic aspect of reality with the physical aspect presents a partial explanation for the uncanny phenomenon that Jung labeled synchronicity, referring to the seemingly chance coincidence of events that may carry a dramatic psychological meaning. Jung believed that synchronistic coincidences are triggered when an archetype becomes highly charged in the collective unconscious, ordinary consciousness is lowered, and events in the psychic and material world move into alignment outside the ordinary constraints of time, space, and causality.

From the largest perspective, the collective unconscious represents a vast realm of psychic activity in which consciousness or the ego occupies a small position near the center. Representing its activity at one extreme are the biological instincts associated with matter, while at the other end are the archetypes associated with the spirit.

Jung's ideas concerning the collective unconscious have long been criticized on the grounds that they are mystical and not verifiable by direct observation. This criticism, however, puts Jung in no worse position than Freud or any of the other so-called depth psychologists. The real problem, beyond this, is that there seems to be no conceivable scientific basis for the universal aspect of his archetypes—or indeed, for the notion of the collective unconscious. In his early writings, Jung seems to have believed that the archetypes were, in fact, expressions of genetically inherited brain structures. Late in his life, however, he came to think of them as fundamental aspects of the cosmos itself, as seen in the concept of the *unus mundus.* Interestingly, Jung's later and seemingly more mystical understanding of the collective unconscious is now receiving increasing attention by scientists who believe it may one day achieve a firm scientific footing in the nonmechanistic science of quantum physics. In particular, it may be that nonlocal quantum events—that is to say, quantum-level events not restricted by ordinary rules of space and time causality—might encode, or carry, the types of information needed, for example, for the more or less universal expression of archetypes.

Applications

The collective unconscious represents a vast backdrop against which the conscious mental life takes place. Against this backdrop, Carl Jung emphasized the importance of the ego as the active agent of consciousness. A healthy individual has a strong and resilient ego, one that does not isolate itself from the influences of the collective unconscious but is responsive to them. For example, an executive who was in therapy with Jung dreamed that he was on a mountain-climbing expedition. As he ascended the heights of a mountain, the air became thin, and he found it hard to breathe. This dream can be taken as a message from the unconscious reflecting the man's isolation as he successfully climbed the corporate ladder. Eventually, his isolation began to cut him off from the source of life itself, which one can imagine represented all those things, and especially those relationships, that he was forced to sacrifice for his successful but stressful life-style.

Jung is well known for being one of the first theorists to consider seriously the conflicts and transformations of midlife. He believed that the first half of life is spent primarily in collective activities, that is, living out the common life-style of one's culture. For most people, this means activities such as rearing a family and struggling for professional success. All of this lets one participate in the common, or collective, expectations of society. At midlife, however, these goals have been met, and there is a tendency to enter a new phase of life that is less ego-dominated and more highly directed by the influence of the collective unconscious. The onset of this second phase of life is often heralded by powerful forces from the collective unconscious that challenge the previous supremacy of the ego.

A graceful transition at this point in life means giving up the arbitrary power of the ego and its individual life goals, such as success or dominance in business, in favor of following one's heart and intuition. Modern society prepares people poorly for the midlife transition. Men, with their heroic ego goals of the first half of life, find it especially troublesome and can become very distraught and unpredictable. Even if one is well prepared, this is likely to be a difficult time in one's life.

There is often a sense of destiny about the midlife transition, a feeling that one's life purpose lies elsewhere, perhaps in a different profession, in creative activities such as painting or writing, or in the service to others. If one succeeds in achieving (or at least pursuing) this calling, one grows old with grace, beauty, and purpose. Jung used the term "individuation" to refer to the process of following one's unique personal destiny, as opposed to the collective ego-directed behavior of the first half of life. Jung was known to have said that people spend the first half of their lives strengthening the ego and the second half giving up its control. The ego, however, is never to be dissolved but to become a servant of the larger process of individuation that is directed by the collective unconscious.

Jung first came to the idea of the collective unconscious during his early work with psychotic patients. He observed that, whereas the content of a neurosis (a disorder usually associated with feelings such as anxiety and guilt) seems to derive from the individual's own history, in psychoses (a more severe disorder that impairs one's contact with reality), especially of the paranoid type, the content of the delusions often seems to have a more universal quality. He likened these delusions to the types of dreams that in primary cultures are sometimes called "big dreams," which are highly impressive and frequently make use of universal mythic themes. Such themes Jung was to term "archetypes."

In an early and dramatic instance of this type, Jung reported a psychotic patient who pointed out that the sun has a phallus connected to it that is the origin of the wind. Whichever way it points determines the direction of the wind. He told Jung this in 1906. In 1910, Jung came into possession of a rare manuscript, recently translated from the Greek, that described an ancient pre-Christian mystery religion in which it was said that a tube hangs from the sun, and whichever way it points determines the direction of the wind. The translation suggested that the wind blows through the tube from the sun itself. Jung later observed a number of medieval paintings in which a sort of hose-pipe is seen reaching down toward Earth from under the robe of Mary. He noted further that the Holy Ghost was originally represented as a wind and that the spirit was sometimes thought to descend from the disk of the sun. All this suggests a commonality of themes from diverse cultural and historical origins that were manifested, all without his knowledge, in Jung's psychotic patient.

Jung was later to find a vast array of such themes, or archetypes, in dreams, art, literature, and mythology from throughout the world. Their universal aspect caused him to think of them as arising from a collective rather than an individual unconscious.

Context

Jung's concept of the collective unconscious is unique in psychology. Both its seemingly mystical dimensions and its inaccessibility to direct experimental measurement have set it in contrast to the tradition of empirical science found especially in Britain, the United States, and France. At the same time, it participates in a larger social heritage. In a very real sense, the idea of the collective unconscious is a rediscovery in psychological terms of ancient concepts of a "world soul," or guiding life principle that stands above and organizes the life of the world. The stoics of the late Roman Empire, for example, spoke of such a soul, attributing to it the notion of *logos*, or order. In other words, the world soul brought order into existence in its domain. Similar ideas are to be found in the Gnostic and Neoplatonic philosophies of that period.

In a more modern vein, Jung's concept of archetypes is related to the "elementary ideas," *Elementargedanken*, originally proposed by the great German anthropologist Adolf Bastian (1826-1905). These are common ideas or beliefs universally found in human cultures from throughout the world. They include, for example, a belief in malevolent and protective spirits or of life beyond death. Such ideas are expressed differently in various cultures. Bastian used the term *Völkergedanken*, or "folk ideas," to refer to their particular parochial expression in each culture. Similarly, archetypes are of a very general form, if thought of in the abstract, but take on a particular shape in the context of an individual experience in a particular culture. Visions of the Great or Divine Mother, for example, differ in India and in the West, as do images of demons. Along with this, the collective unconscious itself can be thought of as existing in levels, or layers, one corresponding to universal human experience, another to the unique regional or national experience, and so on.

In recent years, Jungian psychology has grown enormously in popularity and general interest, and with this growth there has been increasing interest in the notion of the collective unconscious. The latter is being reconsidered in the context of a less materialistic science than that which dominated the scientific world at the time it was conceived.

Bibliography

Combs, Allen L., and Mark Holland. *Synchronicity: Science, Myth, and the Trickster.* New York: Paragon House, 1990. Presents a readable discussion not only of synchronicity but also of the deep structure of the collective unconscious, including archetypes and the concept of the *unus mundus.*

Jung, Carl Gustav. *The Archetypes and the Collective Unconscious.* Translated by R. F. C. Hull. New York: Pantheon Books, 1959. This is volume 9, part 1, of Jung's *Collected Works.* A collection of essays, it contains Jung's original material about archetypes and the collective unconscious. Some find Jung's writing difficult, but it is the primary source for descriptions of his complex theory.

––––––––––––. *The Essential Jung.* Edited by Anthony Storr. Princeton, N.J.: Princeton University Press, 1983. An excellent collection of Jung's most essential and central ideas; it is organized by topic and includes a readable, high-quality commentary by Storr.

––––––––––––. *The Structure and Dynamics of the Psyche.* Translated by R. F. C. Hull. New York: Pantheon Books, 1960. This is volume 8 of Jung's *Collected Works.* Another source for writing by Jung concerning archetypes and the collective unconscious.

Von Franz, Marie-Luise. *Projection and Re-Collection in Jungian Psychology: Reflections of the Soul.* Translated by William H. Kennedy. La Salle, Ill.: Open Court, 1980. A set of very readable essays by a leading authority on Jung; contains a rare detailed discussion of the origins of the idea of the collective unconscious.

Whitmont, Edward C. *The Symbolic Quest: Basic Concepts of Analytic Psychology.* Princeton, N.J.: Princeton University Press, 1978. Whitman provides a good general introduction to Jung's theories. A good place for the reader to become more informed about Jung before tackling Jung's own writings.

Allen L. Combs

Cross-References

Analytical Psychology: Carl G. Jung, 240; Analytical Psychotherapy, 246; Archetypes: Origins and Nature, 286; Levels of Consciousness, 663; Dream Analysis, 830; Dreams, 836; Psychoanalytic Psychology: An Overview, 1905.

COLLEGE ENTRANCE EXAMINATIONS

Type of psychology: Intelligence and intelligence testing
Fields of study: Ability tests; intelligence assessment; methodological issues

College entrance examinations are one of several measures used by American colleges and universities to select candidates for admission. The examinations purport to measure aptitude for college work, and they are widely used. College entrance examinations have been strongly criticized, however, and these criticisms raise crucial methodological and ethical issues regarding the use of standardized tests for admission selection.

> *Principal terms*
>
> APTITUDE: the inborn or acquired ability to reason, learn, and perform certain skills or tasks
> "BOGIE" SCORE: an estimate of a college student's first-year grades based on Scholastic Aptitude Test scores and high school grades
> COGNATES: words in different languages that are spelled similarly but may have different meanings
> HOMOGRAPHS: words within a language that are spelled the same but have different meanings
> INFORMED CONSENT: consent given by human subjects to participate in experiments after being adequately informed about the nature of the experiments and the possible risks involved
> PERCENTILE: one of one hundred equally divided points on a frequency distribution that indicate the percentage of total cases that fall below that point
> RAW SCORE: a numerical test score that has not been standardized and is not comparable with scores from other tests
> VALIDITY: a measure of whether a test or other instrument measures what it purports to measure

Overview

American colleges and universities consider a variety of factors when selecting students for admission. These factors may include, but are not necessarily limited to, high school grades, class rank, difficulty of courses taken, personal interviews, letters of reference, and samples of students' written works. In addition, most colleges and universities require students to submit test scores from one or more of several nationally administered standardized tests. Known collectively as college entrance examinations, the most commonly used tests in the United States are the American College Test (the ACT) and the Scholastic Aptitude Test (the SAT). Some students also may take Achievement Tests (ATs), the Preliminary Scholastic Aptitude Test/National Merit Scholarship Qualifying Test (the PSAT/NMSQT), and Advanced Placement examinations (APs). Advanced Placement examinations are not used in admission decisions but are given to students who wish to receive college credit for classes taken in high school.

The American College Test is created and administered by the American College Testing Assessment Program (ACTAP). According to the ACTAP, the ACT is not content-specific. That is, students are not asked to recall specific information learned in high school. Rather, the ACT asks students to demonstrate their reasoning ability in four fields: English, mathematics, reading, and scientific reasoning. In each of these fields, students are required to think, reason, solve problems, and make inferences.

Each section of the ACT is timed. The complete test contains 215 multiple-choice questions, and students are given two hours and fifty-five minutes to complete these items. Students receive scores on a scale of 1 (low) to 36 (high) for each of the four skill areas, and a composite score. In addition, students receive scores on a scale of 1 (low) to 18 (high) for each of the seven subsections of the test. Student scores are also presented as percentiles.

The English test of the ACT asks students to read five prose passages and answer seventy-five questions based on the readings. Students are given forty-five minutes to complete the English test. The English test is designed to measure grammar, punctuation, sentence structure, style, organization, and writing strategy. Performance is reported as a total score and as two subscores: usage/mechanics and rhetorical skills. The mathematics test consists of sixty questions and is designed to measure skills in basic mathematics, algebra, geometry, and trigonometry. Students are allowed sixty minutes to complete the mathematics test. Performance is reported as a total score and as three subscores: pre-algebra/elementary algebra; intermediate algebra/coordinate geometry; plane geometry/trigonometry.

The reading test requires students to read a passage and answer ten questions for each of four fields of study within a thirty-five-minute period. The four fields of study are prose fiction, humanities, social science, and natural science. Besides a total score, student performance is presented as two subscores: art/literature and social studies/sciences. Students are allowed thirty-five minutes to complete the forty-question scientific reasoning test. Questions are drawn from all natural science disciplines (biology, chemistry, physics, earth science, astronomy, and meteorology). Students are presented materials in one of three formats (data representation, research summaries, and conflicting viewpoints) and are asked to evaluate conclusions or make predictions based on the material presented.

The Scholastic Aptitude Test, created and developed by Educational Testing Service (ETS), is administered in cooperation with the College Entrance Examination Board (CEEB). Like the ACT, the SAT is designed to measure skills necessary for college-level work. The SAT tests two basic skill areas, verbal ability and mathematical reasoning, using a multiple-choice format.

In the version of the SAT in use until the mid-1990's, the SAT was designed with two verbal sections. Section I contains forty-five questions, and section II contains forty questions. Students are allowed thirty minutes per section. Both verbal ability sections contain questions involving antonyms, analogies, sentence completion, and reading comprehension. The SAT also has two mathematical reasoning sections, containing thirty-five and twenty-five questions respectively. Students are allowed thirty minutes per section to complete these items. Both mathematical reasoning sections contain questions involving problem solving and quantitative comparisons. Each of these skill areas (verbal ability and mathematical reasoning) is scored on a scale of 200 (low) to 800 (high). Composite and percentile scores are provided.

This version of the SAT also contains a fifty-question test of standard written English and a series of "experimental" questions. The test of standard written English is used to measure writing ability and is designed to aid colleges and universities in determining an incoming student's course assignment for freshman English. The experimental questions, which may involve either verbal abilities or mathematical reasoning, are not included in the student's score but are used in the development of future test questions.

Some colleges and universities allow students to substitute scores from three to five Achievement Tests (ATs) for SAT scores. Alternatively, some colleges and universities may require students to take the SAT and one or more ATs. Administered by the College Board, Achievement Tests are one-hour multiple-choice examinations based on specific knowledge. ATs are discipline-specific and are available for a variety of fields: American history, European history, French, German, Hebrew, Latin, Spanish, mathematics, biology, chemistry, physics, English composition, and English literature.

In the 1990's, Educational Testing Service developed new tests, the SAT I and SAT II, intended to replace the SAT in the mid-1990's. Like the SAT, the SAT I tests two basic skill areas: verbal and mathematical reasoning. Unlike the SAT, the SAT I verbal reasoning section does not include questions on antonyms, nor does it include the test of standard written English. Instead, test items focus on analogies, sentence completion, and critical reasoning. The new critical reading section focuses on four skills: vocabulary in context, analysis and synthesis, interpretation, and evaluation. The mathematical reasoning section for the first time allows the use of electronic calculators, and a proportion of examination questions require "student-produced answers"; that is, students must enter the answer they calculate rather than being able to choose from a multiple-choice selection.

The SAT II was designed to replace the Achievement Tests and the test of standard written English. Content areas are expanded to include Japanese, Chinese, higher-level mathematics, and English and math placement tests. On the SAT II, the test of standard written English is combined with the English composition test (an Achievement Test). The new writing test of the SAT II contains a series of multiple-choice questions testing grammar and usage, as well as an essay section.

In addition to the ACT, SAT, and ATs, some students may take the Preliminary Scholastic Aptitude Test/National Merit Scholarship Qualifying Test. Administered primarily during the junior year in high school, the PSAT/NMSQT contains two sections testing verbal skills and mathematical reasoning in a multiple-choice format. Students are allowed fifty minutes per section to complete the PSAT/NMSQT. Test scores are used to award National Merit Scholarships, National Achievement Scholarships, and Achievement Scholarships.

Applications

As noted, college entrance examination scores are only one factor used by American colleges and universities in selecting potential students. While approximately fifty colleges and universities do not require ACT or SAT scores, relying on other measures for determining a student's eligibility for admission, most institutions do require submission of college entrance examination scores as part of the admissions process. In addition, almost three hundred American colleges and universities have minumum score requirements for admission to their institutions.

Despite their importance and wide use, college entrance examinations are not without their flaws or their critics. The two main organizations that create college entrance examinations, Educational Testing Service and the American College Testing Assessment Program, work to maintain and improve the validity and reliability of the tests and to avoid bias. Nevertheless, the tests have been subjected to some serious criticisms, and it is because of the tests' very importance that such criticism must be considered. Criticisms focus on six basic issues of testing: the existence of bias and flawed questions, testing procedures, and accusations of lack of due process, violation of privacy, and misuse of test results.

Critics have argued that standardized college entrance examinations are biased against women, the poor, minorities, students from rural areas, and students for whom English is not their first or primary language. Bias charges are serious because they call into question the validity of the tests and, if true, mean that some students may be unfairly denied admission to the college of their choice.

Other things being equal, high test scorers should perform better in college than low test scorers. National SAT test score averages have consistently showed that men perform better on the test than women. The gender gap in test scores varies by year but is generally 50 to 60 points. Gender differences on the SAT are greater on the mathematical reasoning section than on the verbal ability section. A similar pattern exists regarding PSAT/NMSQT scores. Men also score higher on the mathematics, reading, and scientific reasoning sections of the ACT. Women score, on average, 1.0 unit higher than men on the English test of the ACT but average 6.0 units lower than men on the composite score. If standardized college entrance examinations accurately predict future academic success, men should have higher average grades in college than women. Yet, at least during the first year, the reverse is true: Women have higher average grades during their freshman year than men.

Educational Testing Service states that women's scores are lower because greater numbers of women have been taking the test since 1970 than took it in previous decades. Consequently, the test pool for women is increasingly less selective and includes a greater number of low scorers, reducing the overall average. Ruth Ekstrom, Marilane Lockheed, and Thomas Donlon, however, have found that the structure of test questions influences gender performance. Women are less likely to answer a test item correctly if the question contains only, or refers primarily to, male characters. A survey of the reading comprehension passages contained in SAT examinations showed that 93 percent of the characters to which the passages refer are male. Gender differences in test performance may be, in part, a consequence of test structure. In addition, evidence indicates that college entrance examinations place more emphasis on subject areas in which men have traditionally outperformed women (science and mathematics). Accordingly, test content selection may account for some of the gender differences in test scores.

Phyllis Rosser notes that compared to men, women answer fewer questions on the SAT, are less likely to guess at questions, and answer a higher percentage of questions correctly. The SAT awards one raw point score for every correct answer but deducts only one-quarter point for an incorrect answer. On average, it is better to make educated guesses on the SAT than it is not to answer a question. Consequently, women's lower test scores may be the result of gender differences regarding test-taking strategies. The ACT does not penalize students for guessing. Scores are determined on the basis of correct answers. Other factors, not yet clearly identified, must account for gender differences regarding test scores on the ACT.

There is strong evidence that test performance on college entrance examinations is influenced by socioeconomic status. In the case of the SAT, students whose family income is more than $70,000 a year have test-score averages of 996. Students whose family income is under $10,000 a year have test-score averages of 780. As family income increases, test scores increase. ACT scores for students whose family incomes were more than $60,000 a year have test-score averages of 20.7. ACT scores for students whose family incomes were under $11,999 a year have test score averages of 16.0. Again, test scores increase with increases in family income. These patterns may stem from differences in educational opportunities rather than differences in aptitude. Additionally, less affluent students may be unable to afford test preparation courses, which can significantly increase scores on college entrance examinations.

Minority students score lower on college entrance examinations than whites. Differences vary by group and over time. For example, 1989 SAT scores show that average combined test scores for African Americans were 200 points lower than those of whites. Of all minority groups, Asian Americans performed the best. The 1989 SAT average combined score for Asian Americans was 934, compared to 937 for whites. ACT average composite scores indicate similar patterns. The average 1989 ACT composite score for African Americans was 5.8 units lower than that of whites. Asian Americans scored 0.5 unit higher than whites. These differences would be of less significance if college entrance examinations truly measured differences in aptitude. According to the National Center for Fair and Open Testing in 1989, however, there are still large gender and race gaps in SAT scores, even when they are matched for academic preparation. The center noted the findings of a federal court which reviewed ETS's arguments (which "removed the effect of variables such as ethnicity, parental education, high school classes and proposed major"). The court found that "under the most conservative studies presented in evidence, even after removing the effect of these factors," there was at least a "30 point combined differential [between males and females, out of approximately 60 points]" that remained unexplained.

There is also evidence that college entrance examinations may contain bias against students from rural areas and students for whom English is not their first or primary language. James Loewen found that incoming University of Vermont students from rural areas have SAT scores that average 100 points lower than those of students from urban areas; however, the actual academic performance of the two groups is similar. Alicia Schmitt found that Hispanic students who take the SAT are much more likely to answer incorrectly questions which contain cognates and/or homographs. Consequently, differences in test scores between Hispanics and whites may be partially the result of language differences, not differences in aptitude for college work.

In addition to bias, critics have charged that college entrance examinations contain flawed questions (questions that have more than one meaning or more than one answer), which may unfairly penalize test takers. For example, in 1981, Daniel Lowen successfully challenged an answer to a PSAT/NMSQT question. That same year, Michael Galligan successfully challenged an answer to an SAT question and forced ETS to raise the test scores of thousands of students. More than forty additional students received New York State Regents Scholarships because of this change.

Critics have also charged ETS with using unethical testing procedures, lack of due process protection, and invasion of privacy. John Weiss, Barbara Beckwith, and Bob Schaeffer claim the experimental questions on the SAT are fundamentally unfair because they violate the principle of informed consent and are flawed. In addition, no due process protection exists for students who are accused of cheating on the examination. Students may appeal to ETS, but ETS has sole discretion in determining guilt or innocence in cases of suspected cheating. Finally, Weiss et al. argue that the confidentiality of personal information on test takers collected by ETS is not protected under the current system, and say that ETS should be required to obtain consent before the release of any such data.

Finally, college entrance examinations have been criticized for being misused by scholarship agencies and colleges and universities. Many scholarships are awarded primarily on the basis of PSAT/NMSQT, SAT, or ACT scores, though college entrance examinations are not specifically designed for this purpose. The National Merit Scholarships, awarded by the National Merit Scholarship Corporation, are given on the basis of PSAT/NMSQT scores. Roughly 62 percent of National Merit Scholarships are awarded to men. Critics claim that gender, economic, racial, geographic, and language biases in the PSAT/NMSQT place women, the poor, minorities, rural Americans, and individuals for whom English is not their first or primary language at a competitive disadvantage for these awards. Furthermore, roughly 40 percent of American colleges and universities reject applicants on the basis of SAT or ACT test scores, although evidence suggests that college entrance examinations are unreliable predictors of academic achievement in college. According to ETS, students who retake the SAT have only a 66 percent chance of scoring within a 60-point range of their previous score. ETS also acknowledges that high school grades are a better predictor of college success than SAT scores.

Context

Until the creation of standardized college entrance examinations, many American colleges and universities used their own tests to assess the merits of potential students. These tests varied in quality. Scoring was frequently subjective, and because each institution used a different test, test scores from one school could not be used to apply for admission to another. Recognizing the need for uniformity in admission testing, the "committee of ten," a group of prominent American educators, created the College Entrance Examination Board in 1900. The board's function was to establish a centralized organizational structure for admission evaluation and to bring some degree of uniformity and objectivity to the selection process. The board quickly developed the College Board Examination, and it was first administered in 1901.

In the 1920's, as colleges and universities became more selective in their admission standards, use of the College Board Examination increased. Realizing the need for further refinement, the College Board appointed Carl Brigham chair of a committee to review and evaluate the board's test instruments and testing procedures. A former student of Robert Yerkes, a pioneer in the development of American intelligence testing, Brigham had long been interested in the standardization and mass application of testing procedures. In his *A Study of American Intelligence* (1923), for example, Brigham advocated the application of psychometrics to national immigration policy. Under Brigham's direction, a new college entrance examination was developed. Completed in 1926, the new test was called the Scholastic Aptitude Test.

While on the faculty of Princeton University, Brigham helped develop a formula through which SAT scores and high school grades could be used to produce a "bogie grade"—an estimate of the grade average of a potential applicant after one year at Princeton. The formula was gradually adopted by other institutions and became an important component in the admission decision process. Variations of this formula are still widely used today. With the success of the SAT, Brigham established a psychometric laboratory at Princeton. Development of the Achievement Tests was proposed in 1936. Under a plan presented by the president of Harvard, the College Board and other testing organizations were consolidated into the Educational Testing Service in 1947. Today, Educational Testing Service and its chief competitor, the American College Testing Assessment Program, dominate the creation and production of standardized college entrance examinations.

Standardized testing has become an established feature of American life. More than 100 million standardized tests are administered each year. Despite their flaws, college entrance examinations provide a systematic and relatively objective means to select candidates for admission. For schools that receive large numbers of applications for admission each year, test scores provide a relatively inexpensive and time-effective way to screen candidates. Realizing the flaws in standardized testing and the danger of overreliance on test scores, some institutions have developed alternatives to the traditional selection process. Some, such as Bowdoin College, have made submission of test scores optional. Other schools, such as Bates College, allow students to select, from a series of options, which test scores they will submit. Evidence indicates that these alternatives to the traditional admission selection process work well and deserve consideration for adoption by other institutions.

Bibliography

Crouse, James, and Dale Trusheim. *The Case Against the SAT.* Chicago: University of Chicago Press, 1988. Argues that the SAT is not useful in the admission selection process and is biased against minorities and lower-income individuals. Proposes alternative method of admission selection and the development of new achievement tests.

Daves, Charles W., ed. *The Uses and Misuses of Tests.* San Francisco: Jossey-Bass, 1984. Good discussion of critical issues regarding the use of standardized tests. Topics include the development of standards for test applications, the value of standardized tests for educational decision making, the misuse of standardized tests, and legal issues regarding test use.

Hoffmann, Banesh. *The Tyranny of Testing.* New York: Crowell-Collier, 1962. Dated but still relevant critique of standardized tests and their use in admission selection. Examines the problem of defective or ambiguous test questions and looks at issues regarding the validity and reliability of standardized tests.

Nairn, Allan. *The Reign of ETS: The Corporation That Makes Up Minds.* Washington, D.C.: The Ralph Nader Report on the Educational Testing Service, 1980. Presents an excellent discussion of the history of the Educational Testing Service and the development of standardized tests in America. Also provides a detailed critique of the Scholastic Aptitude Test and its use.

Rosser, Phyllis. *Sex Bias in College Admissions Tests: Why Women Lose Out.* 3d ed. Cambridge, Mass.: The Center, 1989. Charges that standardized college entrance examinations are biased against women. Discusses the impact of testing bias on admission selection and scholarship allocation.

Weiss, John G., Barbara Beckwith, and Bob Schaeffer. *Standing Up to the SAT.* New York: Arco, 1989. Describes the structure of the Scholastic Aptitude Test and presents relevant criticisms of the test and its testing procedures. Also discusses alternatives to standardized college entrance examinations.

Charles V. Smedley

Cross-References

Ability Testing: Individual and Group, 1; Bias in Ability Tests, 7; Ability Tests: Reliability, Validity, and Standardization, 21; Ability Tests: Uses and Misuses, 27; Cognitive Ability: Gender Differences, 540; Intelligence Tests, 1341; Testing: Historical Perspectives, 2540.

COLOR BLINDNESS

Type of psychology: Sensation and perception
Field of study: Vision

Color blindness is a hereditary trait that affects the pigments in the retina of the eye; it affects a person's ability to perceive and distinguish certain colors.

Principal terms

ALLELE: one of the many forms of a gene; it may be dominant (needing only one copy for the trait to appear) or recessive (needing two copies)

AUTOSOME: any chromosome other than a sex chromosome

CHROMOSOME: a segment of DNA that carries genetic information for physical traits; humans have forty-six chromosomes (two sets of twenty-three)

CONES: one type of visual receptor found in the retina of the eye; primarily for color vision

DEOXYRIBONUCLEIC ACID (DNA): an organic chemical that makes up the chromosome

GENE: a segment of DNA found on a chromosome that contains the information for a particular hereditary trait

PIGMENT: a chemical molecule that absorbs certain wavelengths of light

RETINA: the area in the back of the eye that contains rods and cones

RODS: photoreceptors in the retina that detect light without detecting color

SEX CHROMOSOME: the chromosomes that determine the sex of a child; in humans, the X and Y chromosomes

SEX LINKAGE: any gene that is found on the sex chromosome; usually found on the X chromosome

Overview

The ability to see colors is not unique to humans; color vision is also found in fish, reptiles, insects, and birds. Among the mammals, monkeys, apes, and humans can distinguish colors; dogs may be able to see certain colors. Bulls cannot see colors, so the red cape in a bullfight, in fact, is only a prop. The ability to see colors differs in different organisms; insects, for example, see colors that humans do not. Bees cannot readily distinguish red colors but can see in the ultraviolet region (pictures of flowers, under ultraviolet light, show guides for the bees to find the nectar that are not visible to the human eye). Understanding why some humans are color-blind requires knowledge of how humans perceive colors.

White light can be broken up by a prism, showing that white light is actually composed of different colors. A prism works by bending white light: Those colors with the shortest wavelength bend first, while the long wavelengths bend last. The shortest wavelength is violet, then blue, green, yellow, and orange; red is the longest wavelength of visible light.

The perception of these different colors occurs in the eye. Light passes through the structures of the eye and falls on the retina. It is there that the color receptors are located. The eye contains two types of receptors, rods and cones. The rods are the most abundant (120-140 million per eye) and are used at night or in dim light. The cones are the color vision receptors (6-7 million per eye) and are concentrated in a region of the eye called the fovea. Research has found three different types of cones, called blue, green, and red cones (though the red cone is actually more sensitive to yellow-green light). These cones allow humans to distinguish more than 7 million different colors.

This fits in well with the trichromatic (three-color) theory of color vision. The mixing of different wavelengths of light will cause the different cones to respond to various degrees, allowing a person to perceive different colors. This theory does not, however, explain how people see negative afterimages or why color-blind people usually are unable to see pairs of colors instead of only one color.

The other theory of color vision is the opponent process theory of color vision. In this theory, pairs of receptor cells are linked together: blue-yellow, red-green, and black-white receptor cells. They work in opposition to each other. Thus, when one stares at a picture that contains more blue than yellow, the blue receptor is stimulated; simultaneously, the firing of the yellow receptor cell is inhibited. If one stares at a blue picture, then a sheet of white paper, the negative afterimage will occur because the yellow receptor (in the above example) has not been stimulated, while the blue receptor is fatigued and cannot respond to the white light stimulus. Most psychologists agree that both theories are needed to explain color vision.

Most people take the ability to see colors for granted, but estimates indicate that up to 8 percent of males and 1 percent of females cannot distinguish at least certain colors. The total lack of any color vision is a very rare phenomenon (about one in 10 million); it results in the ability to distinguish brightness but not color.

The most common form of color blindness is the inability to distinguish between red and green, which are both seen as yellow. When color-blind drivers reach a stoplight, therefore, they must look for the brightness and location of the color. There are two types of this color blindness. One is the protan type; the other is the deutan type, which is the most common form of color blindness—making up perhaps 75 percent of all the cases. The main difference between the two types corresponds to the sensitivity to the longer wavelengths of light (green and red). The protan type is unable to detect long wavelengths of light at all, and the reds and greens appear yellowish in hue. The deutan type can detect longer wavelengths, but they still appear to be yellow. Another, rarer, type is yellow-blue color blindness, in which the individual cannot distinguish between yellow and blue colors.

There are rare cases in which a person is color-blind in one eye and has normal color vision in the other eye. This makes it possible for researchers to question the individual about the experiences of both types of vision. In one test, reds and greens were all seen as yellowish hues, while the shorter wavelengths of light appeared blue. There was also a narrow band of wavelengths that were a neutral gray in color.

The question can then be asked whether a chemical or a nervous-system factor accounts for the different types of color blindness. Much effort has gone into answering this question; the evidence points to a deficiency in cone pigments. The protan type lacks a red-sensitive pigment, while the deutan type lacks the green-sensitive pigment.

Applications

Color blindness is a relatively rare trait, with the added peculiarity that more males than females are color-blind. This is attributable to the way color blindness is usually inherited. A typical human has forty-six chromosomes: forty-four autosomes (twenty-two pairs of chromosomes) and two sex chromosomes. A male has forty-four autosomes and an X and Y sex chromosome, while a female has forty-four autosomes and two X chromosomes. Genes that are found on the sex chromosomes are said to be sex-linked. The X chromosome has a number of genes located on it; the Y chromosome has very few genes.

Red-green color blindness was recognized as early as the eighteenth century to be inherited and passed on to one's offspring. It was not until the twentieth century, however, that the mechanism of inheritance was understood. It was found to be located on the X chromosome and determined to be sex-linked.

Red-green color blindness is a recessive trait which is usually masked by the dominant form of the color-blindness allele. Thus, most people have the dominant form of the gene and can see color, whereas color-blind people have the recessive form of the gene. Sex-linked genes represent a more complex situation, however, because males have only one X chromosome.

Genes on the X chromosome show an interesting pattern of inheritance called crisscross inheritance. The gene for color blindness is found only on the X chromosome, not on the Y chromosome. Thus, males get only one copy of the color-blind gene, while females, having two copies of the X chromosome, get two copies of the color-blind gene. This is why more males are color blind than females and why color blindness can skip generations.

To illustrate this, imagine a color-blind male, represented by X_aY (a = color blind, A = normal color vision). The man marries a completely normal female (X_AX_A). When they have children, the mother will donate an X chromosome to either a boy or girl, while the father can donate an X or Y chromosome, depending on the sex of the child. Thus, all the sons will receive an X_A from their mother and a Y chromosome from their father and have normal color vision. The daughters will receive one X_A from their mother and an X_a from their father, and will also have normal color vision. The daughters will have the trait, but it will be masked by the normal color vision gene (X_A). These daughters are called carriers. The results show that no offspring will be color-blind.

Now imagine that one of the daughters (X_AX_a) marries a normal male (X_AY) and they have children. The father will donate an X_A chromosome. The mother can donate either X chromosome (X_A or X_a). All the daughters will still have normal color vision, because they all have one copy of the normal color-vision gene. On the other hand, the sons will receive a Y chromosome from their father and either X chromosome from their mother. If a son receives X_A, he will have normal color vision, but if he receives X_a from his mother, he will be color-blind like his grandfather (his mother's father).

Thus, red-green color blindness has all the characteristics of a sex-linked trait. It appears predominantly in males. It skips generations and appears in the grandsons, because the daughters are carriers of the color-blind trait even though they have normal color vision.

Research has confirmed the location of the red and green genes on the X chromosome. The blue gene has been found on chromosome 7, an autosomal chromosome. The genes have been isolated and their deoxyribonucleic acid (DNA) has been sequenced by Jeremy Nathans and coworkers. With this information, researchers might be able to learn why some people are color-blind by finding differences in the DNA sequence of people with normal color vision and those who are color-blind. This information may eventually lead to the discovery of why people cannot see different colors and could lead to a cure. There is still little information, however, on the blue gene and the total color-blindness gene.

Context

The understanding of color blindness began with the demonstration in 1802 by Thomas Young, an English physicist and physician, that all the colors in the visible spectrum could be produced by combinations of red, yellow, and blue. Young then hypothesized that the human eye has three color receptors, which respond to various colors, and that the brain processes the information to provide all the colors of the spectrum. This theory was modified by the German physiologist Hermann von Helmholtz; it became known as the Young-Helmholtz trichromatic theory of color vision.

At the time of the Young-Helmholtz theory, little was known about photoreceptors in the retina of the eye. It was not until 1964 that the existence of three different types of cones, which respond to certain parts of the color spectrum, were identified. This established the physiological basis for the trichromatic theory.

At the time of the Young-Helmholtz theory, a German physiologist named Ewald Hering proposed the opponent process theory of color vision (in 1872). Hering thought that people saw six basic colors (red, green, yellow, blue, black, and white) as pairs of colors, such as red and green. He believed that they worked in opposition to each other and helped to explain negative afterimages and color blindness. The physical basis for this theory was found in 1965. Most vision experts believe that both theories are at least partially correct in helping explain color vision.

These two theories provided a physiological basis for color blindness, but the way color blindness was inherited was not established until 1911. This had to wait until the chromosome theory of inheritance established that genes were located on chromosomes; it was first shown in fruit flies. Later, evidence showed the association of color blindness with the X chromosomes in humans. Other traits found on the X chromosome include hemophilia, retinitis pigmentosa, and muscular dystrophy. The knowledge that certain genes are located on the X chromosome has helped geneticists find the order of the genes on the chromosome. Color blindness has been one trait used quite extensively for this process, because it is an easily recognizable trait and can be followed through family trees.

Geneticists look for traits or diseases that are inherited together, such as color blindness and a sugar disorder. If they are almost always inherited together, then one can say that they are on the same chromosome. Occasionally such traits are not inherited together; when this happens, scientists are able to establish how far apart the two genes are on the chromosome. This provides what is called a genetic map of the chromosome, information that was invaluable in identifying and isolating the genes for color blindness in 1986.

Bibliography

Campbell, Neil A. *Biology.* 2d ed. Redwood City, Calif.: Benjamin/Cummings, 1990. A very easy-to-read college text which gives the basics of vision. Has two good chapters on genetics and human genetics with worked examples.

Crooks, Robert L., and Jean Stein. "Sensation and Perception." In *Psychology.* New York: Holt, Rinehart and Winston, 1988. A good review of the structure of the eye and the visual process. Has helpful pictures and examples of color blindness.

Feldman, Robert S. "Sensation." In *Understanding Psychology.* 2d ed. New York: McGraw-Hill, 1990. This chapter gives a brief review of vision and color vision; however, it lacks a more detailed account of color blindness. Easily accessible to the high school student.

Levinthal, Charles F. "Visual Perception." In *Introduction to Physiological Psychology.* 3d ed. Englewood Cliffs, N.J.: Prentice-Hall, 1990. A very good chapter on visual perception; extremely detailed. Nice detail on color vision and the different types of color blindness.

Maxson, Linda, and Charles Daugherty. *Genetics: A Human Perspective.* 2d ed. Dubuque, Iowa: Wm. C. Brown, 1988. An excellent book on human genetics. It explains inheritance very well and describes how color blindness is passed on. Very easy to read, and suitable for the high school student.

Stine, Gerald James. *The New Human Genetics.* Dubuque, Iowa: Wm. C. Brown, 1988. An advanced textbook on human genetics; it has a small section on color blindness that is easy to read. It also covers the basics of genetics.

Lonnie J. Guralnick

Cross-References

Color Vision, 611; Vision: Brightness and Contrast, 2610; Visual Development, 2616; The Visual Spectrum, 2635; Visual System Anatomy, 2640.

COLOR VISION

Type of psychology: Sensation and perception
Field of study: Vision

Color vision depends on three types of photoreceptors in the retina of the eye. Each photoreceptor type absorbs light maximally at a wavelength corresponding to one of the three primary colors. The colors perceived in the brain result from integration of the degree to which each photoreceptor type is stimulated by light at given wavelengths.

Principal terms

CHLOROLABE: a pigment of cones that absorbs light maximally at 535 nanometers (green light)

CONE: a photoreceptor of the retina specialized for discrimination of color

CYANOLABE: a pigment of cones that absorbs light maximally at 445 nanometers (blue light)

DARK ADAPTATION: an increase in the sensitivity of rods and cones to light through an increase in the concentration of light-absorbing pigments

DEUTERANOPE: an individual who has cones deficient in the chlorolabe pigment and is red-green color-blind

ERYTHROLABE: a pigment of cones that absorbs light maximally at 570 nanometers (yellow-orange light)

PHOTORECEPTOR: a sensory cell of the retina that absorbs light energy and converts it into the electrical energy of nerve impulses

PROTANOPE: an individual who has cones deficient in the erythrolabe pigment and is red-green color-blind

ROD: a photoreceptor of the retina specialized for the detection of light without discrimination of color

TRITANOPE: an individual who has cones deficient in the cyanolabe pigment and is blue-green color-blind

Overview

Light is a form of radiant energy that is absorbed by sensory cells in the retina of the eye. The absorbing cells, the photoreceptors, convert light into the electrical energy of nerve impulses. The impulses generated by photoreceptors travel along the optic nerves to the optic lobes of the brain, where they are integrated into perception of a visual image.

The energy of light follows a wave path through space. The distance from crest to crest in a wave path is called the wavelength; the wavelengths of light that are visible to humans fall between about 400 nanometers (seen as blue light) and 750 nanometers (seen as red light). Wavelengths outside this range are invisible to humans because human photoreceptors are not "tuned" to receive and convert them to electrical energy.

The cornea and lens of the eye, acting together, focus light rays reflected from objects in the environment into a picturelike image that falls on the retina of the eye. The retina contains the photoreceptors of the eye, called rods and cones because of their elongated shapes. The cones, which are shorter in length than rods and conically shaped at their outer tips, are the photoreceptor type responsible for color vision. The retina contains about 110 to 120 million rods and 6 million cones. More than half the cones are concentrated in the fovea, where rods are completely absent.

There are three types of cones in the retina. Each type absorbs light maximally at a different wavelength. One absorbs maximally at 445 nanometers (blue light), one at 535 nanometers (green light), and one at 570 nanometers (yellow light near the border of the spectrum with orange). The absorption maxima at these wavelengths depend on three types of pigment molecules that absorb light in the cones. One pigment, cyanolabe, absorbs maximally at blue wavelengths; the second, chlorolabe, absorbs maximally at green wavelengths; and the third, erythrolabe, absorbs maximally at yellow wavelengths.

Each type of cone cell contains only one of the three pigments. As a result, there is one population of cones in the retina that absorbs blue light maximally, one population absorbing green, and one absorbing yellow. The three types of cones are mixed intimately in the fovea, the region of clearest vision in the retina.

The 445-, 535-, and 570-nanometer wavelengths are the colors absorbed most efficiently by each type of cone; however, each photoreceptor type also absorbs other wavelengths near their absorption maxima, although less efficiently. For example, the cone type absorbing maximally at yellow wavelengths actually absorbs wavelengths beginning at about 460 nanometers and extending to nearly 700. As wavelengths are encountered farther from the absorption maximum, light absorption becomes progressively less efficient. The pattern produces a smooth absorption curve that starts near zero on either side and peaks at the 570-nanometer wavelength.

The total ranges absorbed by the three cone types overlap, so that light at any wavelength in the visible range is likely to be absorbed by, and stimulate, at least two of the three photoreceptor types. For example, orange light at 580 nanometers is absorbed by and stimulates both the green and yellow cone types, but not the blue photoreceptors. The green and yellow photoreceptor types, however, are stimulated to a different extent: At 580 nanometers, the yellow photoreceptors would be stimulated almost maximally, but the green photoreceptors would be stimulated to only about 40 percent of their maximum.

This difference in the absorption and stimulation of cones by light of a given wavelength is considered to underlie human perception of color. For example, when light stimulates the yellow photoreceptors at 99 percent, the green photoreceptors at 40 percent, and the blue photoreceptors at 0 percent, the color is perceived as orange. A wavelength stimulating the blue and green photoreceptors at 50 percent of their maxima, and yellow photoreceptors at 5 percent, is perceived as a blue-green color.

Light at wavelengths above about 620 nanometers stimulates only the yellow photoreceptors at or below 70 percent of their maximum; these wavelengths are perceived as red colors. For this reason, the photoreceptors absorbing maximally in the yellow wavelengths are often identified as red rather than yellow cones. Similarly, light at about 420 nanometers stimulates only the blue photoreceptors and is perceived as a deep blue. Light stimulating all three cone types equally is perceived as white. White is strictly a perceived color; there is no wavelength of light corresponding to white.

In response to absorbing light at various levels nearer or farther from their maxima, the photoreceptors generate nerve impulses. When absorbing at its maximum, a photoreceptor generates impulses at the highest frequency; at levels farther from the maximum, the frequency of impulses is proportionately reduced. The impulses sent by the three types of cones at various frequencies are partially integrated into color perception in the complex nerve circuitry of the retina, which may be considered as an extension of the brain into the eye, and partly in the optic lobes at the rear of the cerebral cortex. When objects are viewed in bright light, the total integration reconstructs the image focused in the fovea of the retina as a full-color perception of the scene viewed.

Each cone in the fovea has essentially a straight-line connection through neurons to the optic lobes. As a result, each detail of light, shade, and color in the image is likely to register as differences in stimulation between neighboring cones in the fovea, and to be registered and transmitted separately to the visual area of the brain. This arrangement specializes the cones in the fovea for the detection of minute details in full color.

Applications

Color reception by the cones is most efficient in bright light. As light intensity falls during and after sunset, stimulation of the cones drops off rapidly. (The cones have relatively little ability to adapt to dark as compared to the rods of the retina.) The yellow photoreceptors drop out first, so that colors in the yellow, orange, and red wavelengths fade and, in deep twilight, appear gray or black. The blue and green photoreceptors still retain some sensitivity at twilight, so that blues and greens can still be perceived. In deepest twilight, only the blue photoreceptors are stimulated, so that if any color can be perceived at all, the scene appears blue-black. The shift in color sensitivity toward the greens and blues in reduced light also explains why green fields and trees look so rich in color, and reds and yellows seem dull, on overcast or rainy days.

Adaptation to darkness occurs through an increase in the amount of pigment molecules in both the cone and rod photoreceptors. The ability of the cone cells to increase their quantities of pigment molecules is limited as compared to the rods, which can greatly increase their pigment quantities and their sensitivity to light. As a result, as light intensity decreases, visual perception shifts from the cones to the rods, which detect light but are not stimulated differentially by different wavelengths. This produces the perception of images of grays and blacks rather than color in light that is too dim to stimulate the cones. Because the rods are outside the region of sharp vision in the fovea, objects are perceived only as relatively unfocused, fuzzy images in light of very low intensity.

The rods are completely insensitive to red light. Therefore, it is possible to become completely dark-adapted even if relatively bright red light is used as a source of illumination. For this reason, persons who must work under conditions of reduced light, such as pilots flying at night, commonly use red light for required illumination.

Individuals who are color-blind carry gene mutations that reduce or inhibit the synthesis of one or more of the three color-absorbing pigments of the cones in the retina. A protanope, an individual who carries a mutation inhibiting synthesis of the erythrolabe, or yellow-absorbing pigment, is insensitive to red, orange, and yellow wavelengths and perceives all these colors as the same gray or greenish hue. Typically, such individuals cannot distinguish between green and red. A deuteranope, a person lacking the chlorolabe, or green-absorbing pigment, is also unable to distinguish between red, orange, yellow, and green. Since their inability to distinguish between red, orange, yellow, and green is similar, both protanopes and deuteranopes are classified as red-green color-blind. A tritanope, an individual deficient in the cyanolabe, or blue-absorbing pigment, cannot distinguish between blue and green. Persons deficient in all three pigments cannot perceive color and see the world only in shades of gray. Mutations affecting synthesis of the chlorolabe and erythrolabe pigments, producing green and red color blindness, are most common. About 2 percent of men are deficient in the erythrolabe pigment, and about 6 percent of men are deficient in the chlorolabe pigment, giving a total of about 8 percent of men who are red-green color-blind. The total red-green color blindness among women is about 2 percent. Blue color blindness is relatively rare in the human population; only about one in as many as 65,000 people is deficient in the blue-absorbing pigment.

Color blindness affects males more often than females—about twenty times more frequently—because it is a sex-linked, recessive trait. A color-blind father cannot pass the trait to any of his sons. A color-blind mother married to a man with normal vision will pass the trait to all of her sons. Her daughters will have normal vision but will be carriers of the trait. The sons of a female carrier of the trait married to a man with normal vision have a 50 percent chance of being color-blind; all the daughters are expected to have normal vision. Half of the daughters, however, will be carriers of the trait. Deficiencies in color vision are presently uncorrectable.

Context

The beginnings of an understanding of color vision go back to 1801, when the English physicist Thomas Young proposed that the human eye has only three different kinds of receptors for color. According to Young, an ability to sense the hundreds of different colors that humans can recognize depends on an interaction between the three receptor types. Young based his idea on the fact that painters can mix any color by starting from only three: the red, blue, and yellow primary colors. Orange, for example, can be mixed from equal quantities of red and yellow. Young's highly perceptive explanation for this was that wavelengths in the orange range are not actually produced when light is reflected from mixed red and yellow pigments. Instead, he proposed that the mixture of red and yellow stimulates red and yellow receptors in the eye equally. This equal stimulation is summed and interpreted in the brain as the color orange. Young proposed that the sensation of white, which can be mixed from pigments by adding equal quantities of red, yellow, and blue, is produced through equal stimulation of all three receptors. Young's proposals, which turned out to be essentially correct, were later expanded by the German physicist and physiologist Hermann von Helmholtz into what is now known as the Young-Helmholtz trichromatic theory of color vision.

Two lines of more contemporary research revealed that there are only three types of color photoreceptors in the eye, as Young and Helmholtz proposed. One series of experiments, carried out in the 1960's by Paul K. Brown and George Wald at Harvard University, and Edward F. MacNichol, William H. Dobelle, and William B. Marks at The Johns Hopkins University, measured the wavelengths of light stimulating individual cones to generate nerve impulses. This work revealed that there are actually only three different types of cones, each absorbing light maximally at either the blue (445-nanometer), green (535-nanometer), or yellow-orange (570-nanometer) wavelength. These colors differ to some extent from the red, blue, and yellow photoreceptors proposed by Young and Helmholtz, whose ideas were derived primarily from the results obtained by mixing painter's pigments; however, they are exactly the colors used if colored lights rather than painter's pigments are used to mix additional colors from three primary colors.

The second line of major supporting evidence came from experiments carried out by George Wald, William A. H. Rushton, and others, identifying and isolating the pigments responsible for light absorption in the eye. Some of these experiments were done by the simple but elegant technique of shining a white or colored light into the eye and then analyzing the light reflected from the retina. The reflected light was missing the colors absorbed by the pigments in the eye; the colors absorbed in the eye were those absorbed by the pigments in rod cells. Only three different pigments were detected in the cones—the cyanolabe, chlorolabe, and erythrolabe pigments—by these experiments, as predicted by Young and Helmholtz so many years ago.

Bibliography

Berne, Robert M., and Matthew N. Levy, eds. *Physiology.* 2d ed. St. Louis: C. V. Mosby, 1988. Chapter 8, "The Visual System," in this standard college physiology text outlines the anatomy and physiology of the human organ systems integrated in the detection and perception of vision, including the eye and the optic lobes of the brain, and the nerve tracts connecting them. Intended for students at the college level, but written clearly enough so that it should be accessible to high school readers.

Masland, Richard H. "The Functional Architecture of the Retina." *Scientific American* 255 (December, 1986): 102-111. This clearly written article describes the types of cells in the retina and how they are arranged and organized into a system functioning in light absorption and the transmission of nerve impulses. Outlines the author's research in tracing the shapes of individual retinal nerve cells, and shows how his and other techniques will eventually lead to a complete three-dimensional reconstruction of the organization of the retina. Many diagrams and photos, including both light and electron microscope pictures, illustrate the text.

Nathans, Jeremy. "The Genes for Color Vision." *Scientific American* 260 (February, 1989): 42-49. A description of the research of the author and his colleagues in isolating the genes encoding the light-absorbing pigments of cones. Also describes the basics of color vision and discusses the implications of the author's work for color blindness and the evolution of color vision. Clearly written, and profusely illustrated with full-color illustrations that amplify and expand the text.

Neisser, Ulric. "The Process of Vision." *Scientific American* 259 (September, 1988): 204-214. Analyzes the interaction between the retinal image and the brain in the perception of visual images, including factors that affect visual perception such as memory and attention. Clearly and simply written; includes interesting illustrative examples. Demonstrates that what is perceived in vision is vastly more complex than the initial image projected on the retina.

Rushton, William A. H. "Visual Pigments and Color Blindness." *Scientific American* 232 (March, 1975): 64-74. Lucidly outlines the visual pigments, the basic theory of color vision, and characteristics of the color blindness produced by defects in the visual pigments. Includes a description of the experiments first establishing that three pigments determine color vision, including the author's own work with light reflected from the retina.

Schnapf, Julie L., and Denis A. Baylor. "How Photoreceptor Cells Respond to Light." *Scientific American* 256 (April, 1987): 40-47. Explains the techniques used to detect and record the responses to stimulation by single rods and cones in the retina, and the patterns in which the photoreceptors respond to light absorption. Describes the differences between rods and cones, and outlines the roles of cones in color vision. Clearly and simply written, with a wealth of illustrations, some in full color.

Stryer, Lubert. "The Molecules of Visual Excitation." *Scientific American* 257 (July, 1987): 42-50. Describes the chemical and molecular steps involved in the series of reactions leading from absorption of light to generation of a nerve impulse by a photoreceptor. Although the article concentrates on rods, the principles established apply in general terms to the cones of the retina as well. The topic is technical and molecular, but the description is lucid and should be easily understood by a nontechnical reader.

Stephen L. Wolfe

Cross-References

The Cerebral Cortex, 500; Color Blindness, 606; Sensation and Perception Defined, 2207; Vision: Brightness and Contrast, 2610; Visual Neural Processing, 2629; The Visual Spectrum, 2635; Visual System Anatomy, 2640.

COMMUNITY PSYCHOLOGY

Type of psychology: Social psychology
Fields of study: Attitudes and behavior; social perception and cognition

Community psychology is dedicated to the development of a knowledge base that can be used to implement and evaluate culturally congruent human-services programs. Community psychology is associated with the community mental health movement, and community psychologists have a particular interest in research and services that focus on prevention.

Principal terms

ACTION-ORIENTED RESEARCH: the study of real-world problems using ecologically valid methods; findings should be translated into a policy context and recommendations implemented

CULTURALLY CONGRUENT SERVICES: interventions that take into account the history, aspirations, belief systems, and environmental circumstances of the service recipient

ECOLOGY: the unique interactions of species and a specific environmental milieu

EPIDEMIOLOGY: the study of the rates and distributions of disorders as these data pertain to causes and prevention

INCIDENCE: the number of new cases of a disorder that occur in a given population over a specific time period

PERSON-ENVIRONMENT FIT: a concept related to the fact that adaptation requires compatibility between an individual's behavior and the demands of the environmental setting

PREVALENCE: the number of cases of a disorder in a given population

PRIMARY PREVENTION: interventions designed to eradicate the causes of disorders and/or the development of interventions that can be initiated before pathology develops

SECONDARY PREVENTION: interventions designed to reduce the prevalence of disorders by means of early identification and timely intervention

TERTIARY PREVENTION: interventions in which the underlying disorder is not directly treated or eliminated; instead, the focus is on mitigating the consequences of the disorder

Overview

Community psychology is founded on the following precepts: an emphasis on the competence of persons and communities; an appreciation of personal and cultural diversity; an orientation that promotes prevention; a preference for organizational, community- and/or systems-level intervention; and a belief in the need for an ecologically valid data base with which to determine the appropriateness and value of human-service interventions.

Community psychology emphasizes social, environmental, and cultural factors as significant elements influencing the development and expression of behaviors commonly identified as signs of maladjustment. Community psychology demands a respect for human diversity—people have a right to be different. Requiring that people fit into a particular mold or conform to a particular standard increases the probability that some will be considered failures or maladjusted individuals. Instead of focusing on how to motivate "deviant" people to adjust, the community psychologist attempts to increase behavioral options, expand cultural and environmental choices, redistribute resources, and foster the acceptance of variability.

From a community-psychology perspective, it is not the weakness of the individual that causes psychopathology but a lack of person-environment fit. The concept of person-environment fit is founded in ecology. Ecology posits that each organism is in constant interaction with all aspects of its environment, including all things animate and inanimate. From the ecological perspective, it is the unique interaction of species and the environmental milieu that dictates survival. In relation to people, ecology requires not only an appreciation for the ambient environment but also social, psychological, personal, and cultural factors that interact and influence an individual's adjustment and survival.

Community psychologists use their knowledge of ecological principles to create culturally congruent interventions that maximize service effectiveness. To develop services that are culturally congruent requires an appreciation for the history, aspirations, belief systems, and environmental circumstances of the community or group with which one is to work. Knowing that it is interactions and the fit between persons and environments that are of primary importance, community psychologists work to promote changes at a systems level rather than only working to change the individual. Community psychologists know, however, that even systems-level changes will be of little value—and will perhaps even lead to harm—if they are not personally and culturally relevant to the persons they are designed to help.

There is considerable diversity in the training and orientation of community psychologists. Still, as a general rule, community psychologists can be expected to have knowledge and expertise in the following areas: program development, resource utilization, community organization, consultation, community mental health programming, preventive interventions, program evaluation, grant writing, needs assessment, advocacy, crisis intervention, direct service delivery, manpower training, systems analysis, and the political ramifications of social change. Community psychologists use their knowledge of the preceding areas as they work within the framework of one of the following models: clinical/community, community/clinical, community activist, academic/research, prevention, social ecology, evaluation/policy analysis, or consultation.

Psychologists trained in the clinical/community model have expertise in individual assessment and psychotherapy. They are likely to work within community mental health centers or other human-services programs as direct service providers. They differ from traditionally trained clinical psychologists in having an orientation that is directed toward crisis intervention, public health, and prevention.

The community/clinical model leads to a primary emphasis of working with community groups to enable the development, implementation, and administration of human-services initiatives. This model is very similar to the community-activist model; persons with a community/clinical orientation, however, are more likely to work within the system than outside it.

Persons following the community-activist model draw on their training in psychology to enable them to confront social injustice and misallocation of resources. These individuals are versed in grass-roots community organization, the realities of social confrontation, and advocacy.

The academic/research model of community psychology is founded on the principles of action-oriented research. Here the researcher is directed to work on real-world problems using ecologically valid methods. Furthermore, action-oriented research requires that recommendations that follow from the researcher's findings be implemented.

Psychologists who advocate the prevention model use epidemiological data—information concerning the rates and distribution of disorders—to enable the development of programs designed to prevent mental health problems. Primary prevention programs—undertakings that attempt to keep problems from forming—are the preferred initiatives.

Persons trained in the social-ecology model participate in the development of research and interventions based on an ecological perspective. Here an appreciation of the complexities and the myriad interactions of communities and social organizations is paramount.

The evaluation/policy-analysis model requires that adherents be versed in program evaluation methods—techniques related to the assessment of the quality, efficiency, and effectiveness of service initiatives. This model dictates that information obtained from program evaluation be fed back into the system in the form of policy recommendations.

The consultation model provides a framework for the dissemination of knowledge. To be an effective consultant, the community psychologist must be cognizant of various consultation methods. Furthermore, she or he must have specialized expertise founded in one of the preceding models.

Regardless of the model followed, community psychology demands a commitment to the community, group, or individual served. The job of the community psychologist is to foster competence and independence. The ideal client, whether the client is an individual or a community, is the client who no longer needs the psychologist.

Applications

Community psychology has played a major role in sensitizing human-services professionals to the need for services oriented toward prevention. Many of the assumptions and principles of prevention are taken from the field of public health medicine. Public health officials know that disease cannot be eradicated by treatment alone. Furthermore, the significant gains in life expectancy that have occurred over the last one hundred years are not primarily the result of wonder drugs, transplants, or other marvels of modern medicine. Instead, improved sanitation, immunizations, and access to an adequate food supply have been the key factors in conquering diseases and increasing the human life span.

In order to design and implement effective prevention-oriented programs, one must have an understanding of epidemiology, incidence, and prevalence. Epidemiology is the study of the rates and distributions of disorders as these data pertain to causes and prevention. Incidence is the number of new cases of a disorder that occur in a given population in a specific period. Prevalence is either the total number of cases of a disorder in a given population at a specific point in time or the average number of cases during a specific period. By combining information concerning epidemiology, incidence, and prevalence, it is possible to arrive at insights into the causes of a disorder, likely methods of transmission, prognosis, and intervention methods that may prove fruitful.

Community psychologists identify prevention activities as falling into one of three classifications: primary prevention, secondary prevention, and tertiary prevention. Although some have argued that only primary prevention activities should be recognized as prevention, all three classifications have a place.

In tertiary prevention, the underlying disorder is not directly treated or eliminated; instead, tertiary prevention focuses on mitigating the consequences of a disorder. Tertiary prevention has no effect on incidence rates and little or no effect on prevalence rates. Reducing the stigma associated with the label "mental illness," increasing the self-help skills of persons who have mental retardation, promoting the independence of persons with chronic mental disorders, and developing programs to provide cognitive retraining for persons who have suffered head injuries are examples of tertiary-prevention activities.

An example of a tertiary-prevention program is the community lodge program developed by George Fairweather, which has come to be known as the Fairweather Lodge Program. The program was begun as an attempt to solve a problem that arose in an experiment in giving psychiatric patients the power to direct their treatment by means of self-governing groups. Although it was quite effective, the program suffered because many of its gains did not carry over after patients were discharged. The community lodge program was developed to deal with this problem. During their hospital stays, patients were encouraged to form small support groups. Prior to discharge, members of these support groups would be introduced to the lodge concept. The lodge concept called for former patients to live together, pool their resources, and work as a team in a lodge-owned enterprise. This program, which began in the early 1960's, has been replicated on numerous occasions. Data show that patients discharged to a community lodge are more likely to maintain gainful employment and are less likely to be readmitted to the hospital than are patients discharged to a traditional community mental health program.

Secondary prevention has its basis in the belief that prevalence rates can be reduced if disorders are identified and treated as early as possible. Diversion programs for youths who manifest predelinquent behavior, acute care for persons with mental disorders, employee assistance programs, and psychological screenings for schoolchildren are examples of secondary prevention.

An example of a secondary-prevention program is the Primary Mental Health Project (PMHP) developed by Emory Cowen in the late 1950's. The PMHP was founded on the basis of the idea that maladjustment in early school grades is associated with the development of behavioral and emotional problems later in life. The program was designed to provide early detection so that interventions could be introduced before significant dysfunction had an opportunity to develop. Furthermore, consultation and competency building—rather than traditional therapeutic techniques—were viewed as the most effective interventions. Although the PMHP has not had a demonstrated effect in reducing later psychiatric disorders, the program has been shown to have other beneficial effects.

Primary prevention is aimed at the eradication of the causes of disorders and/or the development of interventions that can be initiated before pathology develops. Primary prevention results in a lowering of both incidence and prevalence rates. Psychological services for disaster victims, genetic screening, parenting classes, reducing exposure to toxins, immunization for rubella, and maternal nutrition programs are examples of primary-prevention activities. Another example of primary prevention is community education programs designed to teach safe sex and/or to reduce the sharing of contaminated needles. To the extent that these programs reduce the spread of acquired immune deficiency syndrome (AIDS), they will also decrease the incidence of AIDS dementia complex.

Community psychologists are involved in many service activities besides prevention-oriented enterprises. These initiatives include the training and utilization of paraprofessionals, the promotion of self-help groups and natural helping networks, advocacy, community consultation, program evaluation, the planning and implementation of new human-services programs, crisis intervention, and mental health education.

Context

Community psychology had its origins in the 1960's, a time of radical ideas, antiestablishment attitudes, and a belief in the perfectibility of humankind. In 1965 in Swampscott, Massachusetts, a meeting was called to ascertain how psychology could most effectively contribute to the emerging community mental health movement.

A transformation in treatment focus was taking place at the time of the Swampscott meeting. This change had been provided with a blueprint for its development in a report by the Joint Commission on Mental Illness and Health written in 1961. The Joint Commission report, *Action for Mental Health*, called for a shift from treating psychiatric patients in large state mental hospitals to the provision of care through outpatient community mental health clinics and smaller inpatient units located in general hospitals. Additionally, the report included the following recommendations: increasing support for research, developing "aftercare," providing partial hospitalization and rehabilitation services, and expanding mental health education to ensure that the public became more aware of mental disorders and to reduce the stigmatization associated with mental illness.

On February 5, 1963, President John F. Kennedy became the first president of the United States to address Congress regarding the needs of the mentally ill and the mentally retarded. President Kennedy called for a "bold new approach" that would include funding for prevention; expanding the knowledge base regarding causes of disorders and treatment alternatives; and creating a new type of treatment facility that, independent of the ability to pay, would provide high-quality comprehensive care in the local community—the creation of community mental health centers.

In October of 1963, President Kennedy signed into law the Community Mental Health Centers Act. The law required that programs funded through the act provide five essential services: inpatient care, outpatient treatment, emergency services, partial hospitalization, and consultation and education.

Although the initial purpose for convening the Swampscott meeting had been to determine how psychology could contribute to the staffing needs of community mental health centers, the conferees took a broader perspective and chose to view the community mental health movement as addressing a limited aspect of a larger set of social problems. As a consequence, the meeting failed to address adequately the training needs of psychologists who would be working in the new community mental health centers; instead, the most significant result of the meeting was the birth of community psychology.

In the ensuing years, community psychology and community psychology training programs have varied in the degree to which they involve the educational needs of psychologists employed by community mental health centers. Still, there is no doubt that the research and service initiatives that community psychologists have developed in regard to crisis intervention, consultation, prevention, empowerment, the use of paraprofessionals, program planning, resource development, and program evaluation serve as valuable models and contribute to the successful operation of community mental health programs and a variety of other human-services activities.

Bibliography

Bloom, Bernard L. *Community Mental Health: A General Introduction.* 2d ed. Monterey, Calif.: Brooks/Cole, 1984. Although Bloom focuses primarily on community mental health, he provides much information that is relevant to community psychology. The discussion of direct service interventions is something that most books on community psychology lack.

Caplan, Gerald. *Principles of Preventive Psychiatry.* New York: Basic Books, 1964. Caplan was a key figure in directing attention to the need to be informed concerning biological, psychological, and sociocultural factors as they influence psychopathology. Furthermore, Caplan's call for an emphasis on primary prevention antedated the origin of community psychology.

Felner, Robert David, et al., eds. *Preventive Psychology: Theory, Research, and Practice.* New York: Pergamon Press, 1983. While its origins may be in community psychology, preventive psychology is presented as a broader enterprise. This volume attempts to provide an integrating framework for preventive psychology with the goal of stimulating applications.

Heller, Kenneth, et al. *Psychology and Community Change: Challenges of the Future.* 2d ed. Homewood, Ill.: Dorsey Press, 1984. Describes how knowledge of groups, organizations, and communities can be applied in addressing social problems. Ecological approaches and prevention-oriented interventions are the primary substance of the text.

Levine, Murray, and David V. Perkins. *Principles of Community Psychology: Perspectives and Applications.* New York: Oxford University Press, 1987. The authors provide an extended discussion of social problems, the conceptual foundations of community psychology, and the application of community-psychology principles to promote effective change. Substantial portions of the text are devoted to labeling theory and the effects of crises.

Mann, Philip A. *Community Psychology: Concepts and Applications.* New York: Free Press, 1978. The origins of community psychology and the relevance of the concept of community are described. Additionally, the assumptions and implications of four models are detailed: the mental health model, organizational model, social-action model, and ecological model.

Nietzel, Michael T., et al. *Behavioral Approaches to Community Psychology.* New York: Pergamon Press, 1977. The authors describe how behavior-modification techniques can be used to solve community problems. Behavior modification is presented as providing both a means to initiate change and a method for evaluating the results.

Rappaport, Julian. *Community Psychology: Values, Research, and Action.* New York: Holt, Rinehart and Winston, 1977. Rappaport provides a comprehensive survey of the paradigms, principles, and practice of community psychology. The book focuses attention on the social roots of pathology and the need for systems-level interventions that are culturally congruent.

Bruce E. Bailey

Cross-References

Abnormality: Sociocultural Models, 82; Aging: Institutional Care, 186; Environmental Psychology, 978; Human Resource Training and Development, 1197; Juvenile Delinquency, 1375; Mental Health Practitioners, 1569; Psychology: Fields of Specialization, 1939; Testing: Historical Perspectives, 2540.

COMPLEX EXPERIMENTAL DESIGNS: INTERACTIONS

Type of psychology: Psychological methodologies
Field of study: Experimental methodologies

Complex experimental designs in psychology research investigate the effects of two or more variables on an individual's behavior; when the effects of these variables combine to predict the behavior, rather than acting independently, this is called an interaction. Knowledge of interactions contributes to an ability to understand research observations.

Principal terms

ANALYSIS OF VARIANCE: a statistical technique, commonly abbreviated as ANOVA, used in inferential statistics to determine which behaviors that are measured are related to differences in other variables

BEHAVIOR: the actions of humans or other animals, including movements, choices, and physiological changes such as sweating

EXPERIMENTAL VARIABLE: a change made by an experimenter so that its effect on behavior can be determined

MAIN EFFECT: a statistically significant difference in behavior related to different levels of a variable and not affected by any other variable

STATISTICAL SIGNIFICANCE: differences in behavior large enough that they are probably related to the subject variables or manipulated variables—they are too large to be caused by chance alone

SUBJECT VARIABLE: any characteristic of an individual measured by the experimenter; also called an organismic variable

Overview

Psychology seeks to predict and understand the behavior of individuals, whether humans or other animals. To produce general rules about individual behavior, its research methods usually involve making large numbers of observations of behavior of different individuals or of the same individual at different times.

At the simple level of design, psychological research measures a single behavior repeatedly and summarizes these observations—for example, describing the mean amount of practice needed to learn a task, the percentage of people who express a particular attitude, or the mean reaction time to answer a question. Such research can show what typically happens, but it does not predict when this behavior will occur, suggest how it can be altered, or explain what causes it.

At an intermediate level of design, research in psychology is concerned with how one measured characteristic or experience of an individual human or animal relates to some behavior of that same individual which the researcher is trying to predict or understand. In a post facto intermediate research design, the predictor variable is some quality or characteristic of the individual which already exists, called a subject variable. In an experimental intermediate research design, the predictor variable is some recent experience or current stimulus, called a manipulated variable, which the psychologist performing the research has selected and administered.

Behavior is called a variable because it can differ (or vary) among individuals or in the same individual at different times. Subject variables, such as gender, self-consciousness, age, and birth order, also differ among individuals and, in some cases, within the same individual over time. Manipulated variables include psychoactive drugs, persuasive arguments, sensory isolation, and psychotherapy. They vary in the sense that the researcher exposes different individuals, or the same individual at different times, to different levels or amounts of that treatment.

Complex (or factorial) research designs investigate how two or more predictor variables are related to the individual's behavior. An example would be studying how a number of subject variables, such as age, ethnicity, religion, gender, and intelligence test scores, all combine to predict political attitudes. In this case, one has a post facto complex research design. If the predictor variables are all manipulated by the experimenter—the amount of an administered drug varied, differing anxiety-inducing instructions given, and tasks of contrasting difficulties presented—then this is an experimental complex research design. The most common approach combines the measurement of subject variables with the manipulation of variables for the purpose of learning whether the effects of the manipulation have the same effects on all kinds of individuals. This is the mixed complex research design. An example of the latter design would be the measurement of gender and age followed by the manipulation of the kind of message used to persuade individuals about the importance of recycling waste; later, the individuals' recycling behavior would be observed.

In this last example, the three factors being measured to see if they are related to recycling behavior may yield between zero and seven statistically significant results from an analysis of variance of the data. Of these, three may be main effects, meaning that the differences in observed behavior occur for any of the variables when averaged across all levels of the other variables. Any effects which are not main effects are interactions, meaning that the effect on behavior of one or more variables may be affected by a change in another variable.

In other words, if one message was found to be more effective than the other for boys but not for girls, an interaction would be said to exist. The effect of the message on recycling behavior would not be the same for all people, but rather would depend on the gender of the listener. When such an interaction occurs, it can be said that the effect of one variable on the measured behavior depends on the level of the other variable.

In this three-factor example, there are four possible interactions. One of them is the three-way interaction, since there is a possibility that the behavior for each combination of the factors cannot be predicted merely by adding the independent main effects for each factor. This means that the three factors contribute to behavior in some manner such that they interact, so that they are not independent of one another. An example would be if one of the messages is less appealing to older girls than it is to younger girls, or to boys of any age. The other three possible interactions in this experiment are all possible pairings of the variables: gender and age, gender and message, and age and message.

Applications

Imagine the example given above concerning recycling first as a simple research design. In this case, measurement (in some carefully defined and described manner) of behavior alone might find that 15 percent of all people practice recycling. To learn more about the causes of recycling, one might shift to an experimental intermediate research design. By measuring the effects of varying the message about recycling, one might find the results shown in the left panel of the figure. This shows that message B produced more recycling (24 percent) than did message A (17 percent).

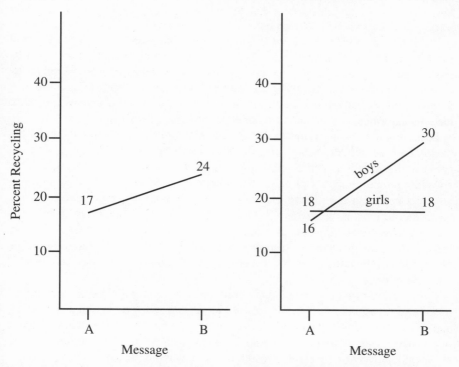

One should be wary of such a conclusion, however, whether it is found in published research or in one's own investigations. The mixed complex research design can make further measurements on subject variables to see whether these findings are the same for all individuals, or whether there is some personal characteristic which predicts the effect of the manipulated variable.

The right panel of the figure shows what might be found if gender were measured as well. Because equal numbers of boys and girls were assigned to each group, the mean recycling for each message remains the same (24 percent for message B, and 17 percent for message A), but it can be seen that the effect of each message was very different depending on the gender of the individual. Here an interaction, which was not evident in the simple or intermediate research designs, can be seen. It is an important interaction because it shows that the effect of the messages on recycling behavior is different depending on whether the listener is a boy or a girl.

Now imagine that another subject variable, age, was also measured. The children were grouped into two categories, ages six to ten and ages eleven to fourteen. Thus, there were four groups, differentiated by gender and age: younger girls, older girls, younger boys, and older boys. Keeping the numbers in each group equal, it might be found that there are no effects of age on which message influences recycling behavior except in the girls who heard message B. In this group, young girls showed 23 percent recycling, and older girls 13 percent. Thus, there would be a three-way interaction, in which both gender and age were dependent on each other to determine the effect of the message on behavior.

Psychological researchers want to know about such interaction effects for both practical and theoretical purposes. An example of a practical application might be environmentalists reading this research to learn how best to improve recycling by children. Whether through television commercials broadcast during programs with a known audience, or through messages in the schools, environmentalists can tailor the message which will be the most effective for a given audience.

Basic researchers are trying to develop theories to understand more general behavior, such as attitude change or motivational processes. These theories may become sophisticated enough to make predictions for practical purposes such as the recycling program mentioned here, changing people's behavior in therapy, or many other purposes. In the present example, the interactions observed may cause the researcher to look at the content of message B to attempt to understand why it was more effective for all boys and for younger girls but was rejected by older girls. If the researcher noted that the message used a popular cartoon action figure as a role model for recycling, then possibly it is only boys and younger girls who identify with that action figure.

From further reading in the field of developmental psychology, the researcher may hypothesize that older girls would identify more with romantic fictional characters, and so design a recycling message which would have more appeal to them. The test of this new message would be an example of how complex research designs work to build cumulatively on previous research to produce more precise practical applications and also to improve theories about the sources of individual behavior.

Context

Complex experimental designs were developed to answer detailed questions about individual behavior. Simple and intermediate research designs provide some information, but the experience of psychological researchers is that behavior is not simple. Behavior has multiple causes, which do not always act independently of one another. Thus there is the necessity for complex research designs, advanced statistical techniques, and sophisticated theories.

These methods are used in a great many areas of research in psychology. Therefore, the individual who wishes to know about the behavior of humans and other animals at a professional level must be able to understand the reports of the psychologists who do this research. Others can learn about psychology at a more general level by relying on secondary accounts written for a broader audience. Much of this research depends on the statistical technique of analysis of variance. This is often performed by using a computer software package designed for this purpose. These statistical software packages are great labor savers; at the same time, however, they can mislead a researcher into incorrect conclusions about behavior if he or she is not familiar with experimental methodology.

It is especially important when drawing conclusions to discriminate between subject variables and manipulated variables. The reason is causality. Subject variables are measured after the fact (post facto) and consist of characteristics which the individual already possesses. Logically, subject variables cannot be assured to be part of a cause-and-effect connection with the behavior of interest. They may possibly be the cause—for example, a measured trait of anxiety may affect reactions to stress—but characteristics such as age and gender may instead be contributors to socialization, experiences, hormonal changes, or peer pressures. Other subject variables such as education or social class may be a result of behavior rather than its cause. When subject variables are found in research to be related to behavior, they may be a cause of that behavior, but the research does not provide evidence to justify that conclusion. Only manipulated variables, in a careful controlled experiment, may be assumed to cause the behavior which they precede.

It is also important that the researcher remember that the variables selected only represent a few of the possible influences on behavior. In some cases, the subject variables are only related to more powerful variables yet to be discovered. For the example used here, it was suggested that gender and age were predictors of the most effective persuasive message. Perhaps what was most important was that these were approximate predictors of which individuals prefer action figures over romantic figures. An analysis of how the persuasive messages are working may find that the answer to a question such as "Which figures do you prefer for playing?" would be a much more accurate predictor of the behavior in this situation than the mere assumption that boys and girls separate along lines of gender in every preference and psychological process. Awareness of these and similar research refinements come with experience and training.

Bibliography

Edwards, Allen Louis. *Experimental Design in Psychological Research*. 4th ed. New York: Holt, Rinehart and Winston, 1972. Presents discussions of interactions and complex experimental designs through the use of concrete examples. More than most other statistics books, Edwards' is concerned with presenting the probabilistic basis for the concepts discussed, especially the probabilities of finding differences between groups as a result of accident or chance.

Martin, David W. *Doing Psychology Experiments.* 3d ed. Pacific Grove, Calif.: Brooks/ Cole, 1990. An important book about the design, execution, interpretation, and reporting of psychological research, written in a clear and engaging manner. Does not provide instructions for making statistical calculations; more for helping the reader or consumer of psychological research understand what was done and what it means. Exceptional sections on theory and on research ethics.

Myers, Jerome L. *Fundamentals of Experimental Design.* 2d ed. Boston: Allyn & Bacon, 1972. Provides excellent examples of graphing higher-order interactions and of calculational methods. Contains discussions of designing an experiment and interpreting statistics. Has an important section on the further data analyses for simple main effects which should be performed after an interaction has been found.

Sprinthall, Richard C. *Basic Statistical Analysis.* 3d ed. Englewood Cliffs, N.J.: Prentice-Hall, 1990. Offers a comprehensive introduction to a wide variety of experimental and statistical procedures at the beginning university level. Notable for its discussions of cause and effect, nonparametrics, and computers in research. Better than average for its treatment of drawing and evaluating graphical representations of data.

Winer, B. J. *Statistical Principles in Experimental Design.* 2d ed. New York: McGraw-Hill, 1971. A widely recognized standard in the field of experimental design and statistical analysis. May be overly technical in spots for some readers, but also has very readable explanations of the meaning of interactions and how they can be understood. May be useful for understanding some of the methods and conclusions of research articles.

Roger A. Drake

Cross-References

Data Description: Descriptive Statistics, 751; Data Description: Inferential Statistics, 757; Field Experimentation, 1031; Psychological Experimentation: Independent, Dependent, and Control Variables, 1932; Quasi-Experimental Designs, 2024; Survey Research: Questionnaires and Interviews, 2507; Within-Subject Experimental Designs, 2647.

COMPUTER MODELS OF COGNITION

Type of psychology: Cognition
Fields of study: Cognitive processes; nervous system

The nervous system is the basis for all cognitive and mental activity. The nervous system can be viewed as processing information received from the environment. Computer models of cognition based on the actual structure of the human nervous system show great promise in understanding the relationship between cognition and the nervous system.

Principal terms

ARCHITECTURE: the particular structure of a neural network; that is, the way the processing elements are connected to one another

NATURAL INTELLIGENCE: a computer model of cognition based on the actual structure of the nervous system; differentiated from artificial intelligence

NETWARE: the software that represents the structure of the neural network and thus its ability to solve specific problems

NEURAL NETWORK: a computing system composed of a number of interconnected processing elements that process information

NEUROCOMPUTER: a specially designed digital computer that can perform the operations that characterize a neural network

PARALLEL DISTRIBUTED PROCESSING: describes the operation of a neural network; all the processing elements operate simultaneously or in parallel, as opposed to serial processing

PROCESSING ELEMENTS: the basic element or unit of a neural network; corresponds to the neuron, the unit of the human nervous system

TRAINING LAW: the particular data that specify how the neural network will react to input it receives; describes how the network is trained

TRANSFER FUNCTION: a mathematical description of the relationship of the input-output functions in a neural network

WEIGHTS: a mathematical description of the strength of an impulse that is received by a particular processing element

Overview

Human cognition depends upon the operation of the neural anatomy that forms the nervous system. Essentially, the brain is composed of some 100 billion neurons. Roger Penrose has divided the brain into three areas: primary, secondary, and tertiary. Each of these three areas has a sensory and motor component. The primary areas are the visual, olfactory, somatosensory, and motor areas. These areas handle the input and output functions of the brain. The secondary areas lay near the primary regions and process the input received by the primary areas. Plans of action are developed in the secondary areas, and these actions are translated into movements of the muscular system by the primary cortex. The tertiary area makes up the rest of the brain. The most complex, abstract, sophisticated, and subtle activity of the brain occurs here. Information from the different sensory areas is received, collected, integrated, and analyzed. As Penrose says, "memories are laid down, pictures of the outside world are constructed, general plans are conceived and executed, and speech is understood or formulated." Thus, information or stimulation from the environment is received or inputted at the primary sensory areas. This information is then processed in increasingly complex and sophisticated ways in the secondary and tertiary sensory areas. The processed sensory information is sent to the tertiary motor area in the form of a grand plan of action, and it is then refined into plans for specific actions at the secondary and primary motor regions.

The question for psychologists to solve is how to represent or model this complex activity that is the basis for human thought and action in the three regions of the brain. The theory of information processing contends that human cognition can be successfully modeled by viewing the operation of the brain as analogous to the operation of a computer. Penrose observed that the brain presents itself as "a superb computing device." More specifically, Robert J. Baron stated:

> The fundamental assumption is that the brain is a computer. It is comprised of some 100 billion computational cells called neurons, which interact in a variety of ways. Neurons are organized into well defined and highly structured computational networks called neural networks. Neural networks are the principal computational systems of the brain.

A field known as neurocomputing or computational neuroscience holds great promise for providing such a computer-based model. The particular kind of computer to be used is a neurocomputer, which is modeled on the actual structure or architecture of the brain. The unit of the neurocomputer is the processing element, or neurode, which corresponds to a biological neuron. The neurocomputer is constructed of many neurodes that are interconnected to each other to form a neural network. Each neurode can receive a number of inputs, either externally or from other neurodes, and each input has a weight or strength given to it. These weights are all summed, and a single output results. This output can then act as an input to other neurodes to which it is interconnected. If the output is excitatory, it will encourage firing of the interconnected neurodes; if the output is inhibitory, it will discourage firing of the interconnected neurodes. The neurocomputer processes all the inputs and outputs in a parallel manner (that is, all of the neurodes can potentially operate simultaneously). The software that runs the neurocomputer is called netware. The netware provides the interconnections between neurodes, how the neural network will react to the input it receives (training law), and how the input and output are related to each other (transfer function). Neurocomputers are drastically different from any other kind of computer because their architecture and operation are modeled after the human brain. Thus, neurocomputers can perform human functions, such as being taught to learn new behaviors. Maureen Caudill refers to these computers as being "naturally intelligent," as opposed to the serial computer used with "artificial intelligence."

Applications

Because neurocomputers are constructed as analogues of the human nervous system, they are particularly adept and useful for solving the kinds of problems that the human brain can solve. Conventional computers would have great difficulty solving these problems because they are constructed to perform certain kinds of tasks very quickly and efficiently (for example, processing large amounts of numbers very rapidly), tasks which the human brain cannot do nearly as well. The following two applications of neurocomputers and neural networks are discussed in a book by Maureen Caudill and Charles Butler called *Naturally Intelligent Systems* (1990).

A machine called the vectorcardiograph was found, in tests, to be able to detect heart problems better than cardiologists were. The usual electrocardiograph records signals received from up to twelve leads placed on different parts of the body. Each recording is made separately and in a particular sequential order. In contrast, the vectorcardiograph records signals from only three locations (front-back, head-foot, right-left), and it records all three sources of data simultaneously. This parallel processing of the information suits the vectorcardiograph very nicely to neural networks.

Essentially, the vectorcardiograph was trained in three stages to differentiate between normal and abnormal electrocardiograms, much as a human is trained to discriminate or distinguish between two stimuli. In the first stage, the system was trained to recognize all the normal cases presented to it and a portion of the abnormal cases presented to it. The input weights were then set at the appropriate values and training continued. In the second stage, the neural network was trained to also recognize all normal cases and a portion of the remaining abnormal cases. Again, the input weights were set at their appropriate values. The third stage of training commenced, and training continued until the system could recognize the remaining abnormal cases. The training set consisted of vectorcardiographs from 107 people, half of whom were judged to be normal and the other half of whom were judged to be abnormal. When the vectorcardiograph was presented with sixty-three new cases never before presented, it correctly diagnosed 97 percent of the normal and 90 percent of the abnormal cases. Trained clinicians were able to identify, respectively, 95 percent and 53 percent of the cases. The diagnostic capabilities of the vectorcardiograph demonstrate the capabilities and potentials of neural networks.

A neural network known as the Multiple Neural Network Learning System (MNNLS) can be trained to make decisions to accept or reject a mortgage application. The system uses twenty-five areas of information that are divided into four categories: cultural (credit rating, number of children, employment history); financial (income, debts); mortgage (amount, interest rate, duration); and property (age, appraised value, type).

The MNNLS is a system of nine separate neural networks that are divided into three different layers, with three networks in each area. Each layer is analogous to a panel of three experts. One expert in each of the three layers concerns itself only with financial information, the second only with cultural and mortgage information, and the third with all four categories. When presented with a mortgage application, the first layer attempts to arrive at a decision. If the three "experts" all agree, the mortgage is accepted or rejected; however, if one of the experts disagrees with another, then the application goes to the second layer of experts, and the same process is repeated. The MNNLS is useful because it is very efficient and accurate. It is efficient because it is able to process a wide variety of problems, since the neural networks correspond to different experts. The first layer effectively handles simple decisions, whereas the second and third layers can handle increasingly difficult decisions. When compared to decisions made by humans, MNNLS agreed about 82 percent of the time. In those cases where the MNNLS disagreed with the human decision, the MNNLS was in fact nearly always correct. This happens because the MNNLS is a neural network that insists upon consensus of a panel of experts (that is, consensus between separate neural networks). It would be economically unfeasible to have a panel of humans evaluate mortgages; however, a single person evaluating applications is more likely to make a mistake than a panel of evaluators.

Context
Stephen J. Hanson and David J. Burr astutely observed that "the computer metaphor has had a profound and lasting effect on psychological modeling." The influence of the computer can be seen especially in its use in artificial intelligence and in computer metaphors of learning and memory, in which information is processed, encoded, stored, and retrieved from three distinct memory stores (sensory, short-term, and long-term memory). The particular computer that has been used as the metaphor of the human mind and cognition has been the digital or serial computer.

It eventually became apparent to cognitive scientists, however, that the digital computer is actually a poor analogy for the human mind, because this computer operates in a decidedly nonhuman way. For example, the digital computer operates much too fast—much faster than the human mind can process information. It also processes much more data than the human mind can process. If the software is sound, the digital computer is perfect and operates error-free. Human problem solving, on the other hand, is characterized by making mistakes. The digital computer is not capable of autonomous learning. It does only what it is told to do by the program; it cannot teach itself new things, as can a human. The digital computer is very poor at pattern recognition tasks, such as identifying a human face, something an infant can do very rapidly. The digital computer provides no information about the underlying structure (the nervous system) that makes human cognition and information processing possible.

A number of cognitive scientists have argued that the fields of artificial intelligence and traditional cognitive science have reached dead ends because of their reliance on the digital computer analogy of the mind, which is limited and largely inaccurate. Cognitive science and neurophysiology are now striking out in a promising new direction by using neural networks and neurocomputers as the analogue of the human mind. The human mind is closely related to the human brain; many would argue that the mind is equivalent to the brain. Therefore, in order to study the mind and cognition, one must build a computer that is modeled on the architecture of the brain. The neurocomputer is modeled on the human brain, and the digital computer is not.

Regarding the above six points about the limitations of digital computers, neurocomputers operate in a manner consistent with the operation of the human nervous system and human cognition. Neurocomputers provide a potentially promising way to understand cognition, as well as providing a productive connection and interrelationship with neurophysiology.

Bibliography

AI Expert. This computer-oriented magazine, established in 1986, is published monthly by Miller Freeman in San Francisco. Most issues contain one or two informative articles on developments in neural networks.

Allman, William F. *Apprentices of Wonder: Inside the Neural Network Revolution.* New York: Bantam Books, 1989. Readable, nontechnical discussion of neural networks that presents their various aspects and features interviews with several key researchers in this field.

Baron, Robert J. *The Cerebral Computer: An Introduction to the Computational Structure of the Human Brain.* Hillsdale, N.J.: Lawrence Erlbaum, 1987. Compelling argument for viewing the human nervous system as a computer. The first chapters provide a good discussion of the relationship between neurophysiology and computers.

Caudill, Maureen, and Charles Butler. *Naturally Intelligent Systems.* Cambridge, Mass.: MIT Press, 1990. Provides a thorough introduction to neural networks—the different types and their uses. Among the applications discussed are those for the vectorcardiograph and for the Multiple Neural Network Learning System.

Hanson, Stephen J., and David J. Burr. "What Connectionist Models Learn: Learning and Representation in Connectionist Networks." *Behavioral and Brain Sciences* 13, no. 3 (1990): 471-518. The first several pages provide good background on cognitive psychology's use of computer analogues of the mind and their relationship to neural networks.

Penrose, Roger. *The Emperor's New Mind: Concerning Computers, Minds, and the Laws of Physics.* New York: Oxford University Press, 1989. Presents a somewhat different slant on the relationship between the brain and cognition, and the human mind as a computer; the author is a physicist.

Schneider, Walter. "Connectionism: Is It a Paradigm Shift for Psychology?" *Be-*

havior, Research Methods, Instruments, and Computers 19, no. 2 (1987): 73-83. Schneider's presidential address to the Psychonomic Society. Presents a good introduction to neural networks and the impact they can expect to have on cognitive psychology.

Stillings, Neil A., et al. *Cognitive Science: An Introduction.* Cambridge, Mass.: MIT Press, 1987. A standard textbook on cognitive psychology, with emphasis on neurophysiology. Also features one of the first presentations on neural networks and cognition to appear in a textbook.

Laurence Miller

Cross-References

Artificial Intelligence, 299; The Cerebral Cortex, 500; Cognitive Psychology: An Overview, 572; Neural Anatomy and Cognition, 1640; Neurons, 1661; Neuropsychology, 1667; Synaptic Transmission, 2514.

CONCEPT FORMATION

Type of psychology: Cognition
Fields of study: Cognitive processes; thought

In order to think and communicate about the endless objects, living things, and events in the world, a person simplifies those things by mentally grouping them and organizing them based on relationships and features they have in common. The process of constructing rules about how things go together is called concept formation, and it is a powerful mental tool.

Principal terms

ARTIFICIAL CONCEPTS: geometric patterns that are not usually experienced in daily life but are constructed so as to vary systematically along predetermined dimensions

CONCEPT: an abstract idea based on grouping objects or events according to their common properties

CONCEPT FORMATION: the process of distinguishing among the properties common to a class of objects or ideas

FUZZY BORDERS: conceptual borders that appear ill defined and shift according to the context in which the category member occurs

NATURAL CONCEPTS: unlike the concepts used in artificial-concept tasks, natural, everyday categories are ill defined and have fuzzy borders

PROTOTYPE: a pattern that best represents a category

STIMULUS MATERIALS: anything presented to a subject during the course of an experiment that requires that subject to make a response

Overview

Humans are faced with the task of making sense of a world that contains a seemingly endless array of unique objects and living things. In order to reduce this endless uniqueness to something that is mentally manageable, people form concepts. These concepts guide their thoughts and behaviors, so it is important to understand both the nature of those concepts and how people construct them.

In daily life, the term "concept" is used in a way that is different from the way in which psychologists use it. Whereas psychologists say that a concept exists when two or more things are grouped on the basis of a common feature or property of each, everyday language uses the term "concept" to refer to abstract ideas, such as the concept of "integrity," or to a mental picture in one's mind; for example, "I have a concept of how I want my room to look." The term is used here as psychologists use it. Psychologists also frequently use the word "category" as a synonym for "concept."

Psychologists have had to be very innovative when designing experiments to study concept formation, because there is no way to observe the way in which people think or form concepts directly. The techniques vary from study to study, but subjects are typically asked to choose which of several items fits a particular concept.

The early researchers in the area, including Jerome Bruner, Jacqueline Goodnow, and George Austin, used materials in their experiments that have since been referred to as "artificial" stimuli, because they used geometric figures, such as circles and squares of various sizes and shapes, that were deliberately devised to have only a certain number of alterable characteristics or features. Years later, researchers such as Eleanor Rosch became interested in "natural" concepts, based on complex real-world objects, in which partial membership in a category is a possible alternative.

In a typical study on artificial-concept formation, a psychologist would construct visual patterns that would not normally be encountered in daily life. The patterns would be printed on cards to create the stimulus materials. These visual patterns would vary in terms of size, shape, number, or color, for example, and would be referred to as dimensions. Basically, a dimension is any changeable characteristic of the stimulus. A dimension can have two or more values, and the value is determined by the number of sizes, shapes, numbers, or colors being utilized. In this example, pretend that each dimension can have three values. In other words, there would be objects of small, medium, and large size; circular, triangular, and square shapes; one, two, or three items; and purple, red, and green colors. Varying those dimensions and values, the particular stimulus patterns presented to the subject would be things such as two large green squares, three small red triangles, or perhaps one medium purple circle. The concept to be learned is selected by the researcher beforehand and is kept secret from the subject, because the subject must discover the concept. The concept might be something such as purple triangles of any size and any number. Thus, in this case, the specific concept to be learned would be "purple and a triangle."

In a concept-formation task, the stimuli are usually presented to the subjects in one of two ways: the reception method or the selection method. Using the reception technique, the subject is shown a single card and asked to state whether that card displays the concept that the experimenter had in mind. The experimenter then tells the subject whether the response is correct or incorrect. The subject is then shown another card. In comparison, using the selection technique, the entire set of cards is simultaneously displayed to the subject in one large array. The number of cards in the entire set is determined by the combination of all possible dimensions and values. Using the selection technique, the subject selects a particular card from the array, stating whether it displays the concept to be learned. Following each selection and judgment, the experimenter informs the subject about correctness.

Some tasks require subjects to discover the values, the rule, or both. A rule tells how the values must be combined. The two most common kinds of rules are called conjunction and disjunction. The conjunction rule uses the word "and," as in "all figures that are both purple and triangles." Thus, a subject learning a concept involving the conjunction rule would learn to respond yes to all purple triangles and no to all other figures. The disjunction rule uses the word "or," as in all figures that are purple or a triangle or both.

An important development in research on concepts involves natural concepts or real-life categories. Rosch pointed out that the artificial-concept learning tasks used materials unlike those encountered in the everyday world. Most concepts in the everyday world do not fall into neatly defined categories. Many have fuzzy borders that involve some uncertainty. For example, is a tomato a fruit or a vegetable? Rosch theorized that people decide whether an item belongs to a particular category by comparing that item with a prototype or best example for that category. An apple is highly prototypical of the fruit category, whereas a coconut is a less typical example.

Applications

If a person understands the concept of sunglasses, he or she can recognize something as a pair of sunglasses even though they may look different from all the other sunglasses the person has seen before. A new pair of sunglasses with iridium-coated lenses can be included within the concept because the pair has qualities that are common to the entire class of objects that people refer to as sunglasses. They have earpieces, they block out the sun to some degree, and they cover the eyes. Sunglasses belong to the even larger conceptual category of eyewear. Concepts such as eyewear, cookware, furniture, and vehicles are very useful. It would be impossible to think intelligently without the ability to form concepts. Without that ability, every time a person encountered something that was slightly different from other things, it would be necessary to learn about that object as if it were completely new.

A person would then primarily function instinctually because, according to Michael Eysenck, it would be impossible to relate prior learning to new situations. By applying concepts, a person can develop an immediate understanding of new objects or ideas, because they can be related to a general class of similar objects and ideas that are familiar. A person knows what to expect from an object, even when it is encountered for the first time. In this way, thinking beings save an amazing amount of work. Concepts reduce the complexity of the environment and eliminate the need to learn constantly.

The development and refinement of some concepts take place over a long period of time. A person can have general concepts about some things, precise concepts about others, and also be in the process of refining vague concepts. In the course of life, a person's understanding of a particular concept develops and expands with additional experience, advanced training, and new information. Understanding this has ramifications for formal education.

Much teaching is directed toward the development of concepts. In fact, it would be almost impossible to use the vast amount of mental information that is available to human beings to solve problems, make decisions, understand language, and communicate without the ability to simplify the world by means of conceptualization. One of the principal objectives of formal education is to allow students to formulate a hypothesis, or tentative guess, about how some attribute contributes to a concept. Students are then encouraged to test the hypothesis. If it is wrong, they can adopt a new hypothesis that incorporates different attributes or the same attributes but with different rules, based on feedback they receive from an instructor.

Researchers have identified a number of factors involved in concept learning that apply to the process of education. One factor is the number of attributes. It is easier to learn a concept if there are only one or two relevant attributes, rather than several. Another factor is salience. It is easier to learn a concept if the relevant attributes are salient, or obvious. A third factor is positive examples. People tend to make better use of positive examples, although it is sometimes helpful and even necessary to give some negative examples. For example, imagine teaching a young child the concept of "housecat" by using examples that are all positive. One shows the child pictures of a Persian, a Siamese, and a Russian Blue. From the viewpoint of a teacher, it is desirable to highlight or emphasize the relevant features of the concepts to make them salient, such as mentioning that the creatures in all the pictures have fur. The child learns to say "cat" to each picture. A teacher cannot, however, be certain which aspects of the pictures determine the child's response. For all the teacher knows, the child considers a picture of a cat to be another example of a "dog." For this reason, it is important to include relevant negative examples. In general, negative examples tend to be more useful in later stages of training.

As science fiction becomes fact, it is becoming desirable to be able to "teach" computers how to form concepts. This type of investigation is conducted in the field of artificial intelligence. In order to develop artificial ways of duplicating human thought and intelligence, it is important to know how the thought process is accomplished by humans. Imagine a task in which a computer is asked to identify whether something is a triangle. A computer could be programmed to learn the concept, but it would take a very sophisticated program. In comparison, it is easy for humans to recognize immediately what constitutes a triangle, based on vast experience with other triangular objects. Concept formation in computers provides the foundation for the ability to recognize handwriting, fingerprints, speech, and many other things electronically.

One of the problems for computers is that, although some concepts are well-defined, most are not: This is Rosch's point. In addition, human experience and context play an important role in concept formation, which poses difficulties for computers. Even more troublesome for a computer is the fact that many conceptual categories are based on human imagination. Because people have knowledge about the world and how it operates, they adjust their conceptual categories to fit reality. Unless computers have human knowledge and experience, their concepts will not be exactly like those of humans.

Context

Throughout the history of the scientific study of concept formation, three main types of theories have become apparent. They are association theory, hypothesis-testing theory, and information-processing theory. In the associationistic view, the organism passively receives information from the environment. Each example of the concept that has yet to be learned provides the organism with an additional piece of information. In this way, relevant features are reinforced, whereas irrelevant features disappear. This approach requires nothing from the organism except a memory of previous examples. This approach was in vogue in the first half of the twentieth century. According to associationistic views, stimuli gradually become associated with some response by means of a complex form of discrimination learning. By means of discrimination learning, discriminable aspects of stimulus patterns are detected and labeled. Later modifications of association theory introduced the idea of mediation, assuming that concepts are formed because of an intervening step in the mind of the learner, which connects the stimuli with the response.

A second line of theory development, hypothesis testing, views the subject as an active participant in the process of concept learning. According to this line of thought, the organism always has some hypothesis regarding the unknown concept. Incoming information is used to check the current hypothesis and is used as the basis for modifying that hypothesis if it is incompatible with existing evidence. Eventually, the organism hits on the correct hypothesis and forms the concept. The research of Bruner, Goodnow, and Austin, which was first published in 1956, adhered to the view of the organism as an active hypothesis tester.

Finally, theories were developed that emphasized the information-processing nature of concept formation. These theories view the process in terms of a sequence of decisions made by the learner. The learner is seen as accepting external information, or stimuli, processing the information in a variety of ways, and producing some final response. One of the earliest attempts to produce an information-processing model for the learning of concepts was made by Earl Hunt in 1962.

Although the reader may have the impression that only humans (and sometimes computers) are capable of concept formation, animals of all types have the ability to form concepts. Animals form concepts at a much more fundamental level than humans, but they have been shown to differentiate among various colors and various geometric patterns, for example. Throughout its long history, research on concept formation has used animals, such as pigeons and rats, as well as human subjects.

Bibliography

Bourne, Lyle E., Jr. *Human Conceptual Behavior.* Boston, Mass.: Allyn & Bacon, 1966. A short book of definite historical importance that summarizes the work on concept formation up to 1966. The writing style is enjoyable, and the book is clearly written, although the ideas it expresses are complex.

Bourne, Lyle E., Jr., Roger L. Dominowski, and Elizabeth Loftus. *Cognitive Processes.* 2d ed. Englewood Cliffs, N.J.: Prentice-Hall, 1986. A thorough textbook on the psychology of thinking. The chapter on concept formation is insightful and clear. The reading level is appropriate for psychologists and nonpsychologists alike.

Bruner, Jerome S., Jacqueline J. Goodnow, and George A. Austin. *A Study of Thinking.* New York: John Wiley & Sons, 1956. This book is a classic. The first three chapters provide an insightful introduction to concepts and concept formation in general. The latter chapters describe research and provide a methodological analysis of performance, beginning a tradition in concept formation that has now been discarded as a result of new findings and updated theoretical views. A pioneering book in the area of concept formation.

Eysenck, Michael W. *A Handbook of Cognitive Psychology.* Hillsdale, N.J.: Lawrence Erlbaum, 1984. Provides a readable introduction to the entire area of thinking, of which concept formation is one part. The section on categorization provides an overall perspective and succinctly summarizes the research.

Hunt, Earl B. *Concept Learning: An Information Processing Problem.* New York: John Wiley & Sons, 1962. Another historically relevant book that emphasizes the mathematical and probabilistic process of concept acquisition. Hunt's view of concept formation provided a theoretical breakthrough at the time. A substantial section of the book discusses concept acquisition as it relates to the area of artificial intelligence, which was a very new field of inquiry when the book was written.

Rosch, Eleanor H. "Classification of Real-World Objects: Origins and Representation in Cognition." In *Thinking: Readings in Cognitive Science*, edited by P. N. Johnson-Laird and P. C. Wason. Cambridge, England: Cambridge University Press, 1975. The chapter by Eleanor Rosch is important reading; she was one of the first people to break away from research using artificial concepts and begin to explore natural ones. The chapter is quite understandable.

Deborah R. McDonald

Cross-References

Cognitive Psychology: An Overview, 572; Decision Making as a Cognitive Process, 769; Learning Defined, 1443; Logic and Reasoning, 1471; Pattern Recognition as a Cognitive Process, 1747; Thought: Inferential, 2552; Thought Structures, 2565.

CONDITIONING: HIGHER-ORDER

Type of psychology: Learning
Field of study: Pavlovian conditioning

Higher-order conditioning is a procedure whereby the conditioned stimulus of the first order is used to condition a response to a new neutral stimulus. This is done in the absence of the original unconditioned stimulus, and it is generally a subtle effect that can be used to explain secondary reinforcers.

Principal terms
CHAINING: the process by which several neutral stimuli are presented in a series; they eventually assume reinforcing qualities by being ultimately paired with an innate reinforcer
COGNITIVE LEARNING: learning that results from associations being made between stimuli
CONDITIONED STIMULUS: a neutral stimulus that comes to yield a conditioned response similar to the unconditioned response after being paired with the unconditioned stimulus
PRIMARY REINFORCEMENT: a stimulus that acts as a reinforcer without there having been prior experience
SECONDARY REINFORCEMENT: a learned reinforcer that has acquired reinforcing qualities by being paired with other reinforcers
STIMULUS-RESPONSE LEARNING: learning that results from associations being made between stimuli and responses
UNCONDITIONED STIMULUS: a stimulus that at the outset yields a given unconditioned response reflexively

Overview

In the early 1900's, Ivan Pavlov and his Russian researchers stumbled upon the phenomenon of classical conditioning while investigating the digestive system in a dog. Since this serendipitous discovery, the field of psychology, and learning theory in particular, changed dramatically. It has been observed repeatedly that by contiguously pairing a once-neutral stimulus with a stimulus that regularly and consistently elicits a given response, the neutral stimulus can begin to drive a similar response. This has come to be known as classical or Pavlovian conditioning. A number of variations of the original paradigm were discovered and subsequently investigated. One of these, which has raised more questions than it has answered, has come to be known as higher-order conditioning.

A typical experimental situation that might be used to establish higher-order conditioning would be set up as follows. First, classical conditioning of (for example) a salivary response in a dog would be established by pairing a neutral stimulus, such as a bell, with food. The food reflexively elicits salivation, but after several pairings of the bell followed by food, the bell alone would come to elicit a similar, though not as strong, salivation response. Now that the bell produces salivation, the pairing of yet another neutral stimulus, such as a light, with the bell will eventually allow the light to elicit the salivation response as well. The response to the light will be much reduced when compared to that of the bell, because, while establishing the response to the light, the bell was repeatedly presented without the food. This in turn weakened its strength through the process known as extinction.

This particular form of higher-order conditioning is known as second-order conditioning. By using the conditioned stimulus of the second order (the light in the above example), one could then pair yet another neutral stimulus with it and arrive at third-order conditioning. The response would be weaker still. In fact, very few examples of successful third-order conditioning have been reported, and of those that have, most have employed the use of a noxious stimulus as the original unconditioned stimulus. No fourth-order classical conditioning research has been reported.

One of the basic questions that cuts across the entire field of learning theory is whether a cognitive or stimulus-response model best explains the phenomenon. In higher-order conditioning, the question may be interpreted this way. If the cognitive approach is correct, the second-order conditioned stimulus (the light, in this example) should yield the conditioned response through a cognitive association with the original conditioned stimulus (the bell, in this example). If one assumes that the second-order conditioned stimulus elicits its response through the representation of the first stimulus, then altering the strength of this first stimulus by weakening it via the extinction process (presenting the conditioned stimulus without the unconditioned stimulus) should also weaken the response to the second-order stimulus.

If the second-order stimulus comes to elicit the conditioned response via its own path, however, the response would not be affected by any alteration of the strength of the original conditioned stimulus. There is evidence to support both arguments. It is possible that both approaches may be correct, depending upon which stimuli are utilized and what type of conditioning paradigm is used.

To this point, the discussion has focused on higher-order conditioning in the Pavlovian paradigm. The phenomenon of secondary reinforcement in instrumental conditioning is an analogous situation. In Gregory A. Kimble's revision of Ernest Ropiequet Hilgard's *Hilgard and Marquis' Conditioning and Learning* (1961), the author points out that secondary reinforcement and higher-order conditioning represent one of the important similarities between the two types of conditioning. (It should also be noted that some psychologists believe that the two types of conditioning do not represent two distinct types of learning.)

Secondary reinforcers are typically established by pairing a neutral stimulus, such as a token, with a primary reinforcer, such as food. This aspect of the problem has been studied in depth and has been applied to the human predicament in a wide range of situations, as will be discussed. A typical paradigm to establish a secondary reinforcer would be arranged as follows. A rat may be taught to run to the black (as opposed to the white) arm of a T-maze, regardless of what side of the maze the black arm is placed, in order to get food. After the response has been established, the black (previously neutral) stimulus acquires reinforcing qualities because it has repeatedly been paired with the primary reinforcer, the food. In addition, the animal will begin to run to the black stimulus in other situations, even in the absence of food, because of the reinforcement associated with it. As in the Pavlovian paradigm, unless the black stimulus is paired with the food periodically, it will eventually have its reinforcing power extinguished. Long chains of secondary reinforcers can be established to maintain behavior over long periods of time with only periodic presentation of the primary reinforcer.

Applications

Higher-order conditioning and, to an even greater degree, its instrumental conditioning counterpart, secondary reinforcement, have been used to explain a wide variety of behaviors in both animal and human learning. The pairing of a neutral stimulus with a primary reinforcer can be used to explain how and why people work at various tasks for long periods of time seemingly in the absence of tangible rewards. The following are a chain of stimuli with which people are very familiar and a hypothetical mechanism by which the neutral stimuli have acquired valence by ultimately being associated with a primary reinforcer.

If one thinks of a loaf of bread as an unlearned reinforcer (similar to the food powder on the dog's tongue in Pavlov's experiment), the presentation of a gold nugget would acquire the food. This neutral stimulus—a piece of metal—has acquired reinforcing qualities because of its consistent contiguous pairings with primary reinforcers. In addition, a dollar bill has been paired with the gold; it has also become a reinforcer. The chain can become very long and complicated. The dollar bill could be paired with a check, which in turn could be paired with an IOU, which could ultimately be paired with someone's verbal promise. Notice that as the stimuli are located farther and farther away from the primary reinforcer, food, they become weaker and weaker.

It is also important to realize that often the primary reinforcer cannot be delivered at the appropriate time because of an environmental constraint or because of unavailability. In training pets to do various tricks, for example, if verbal praise or tactile stimulation is paired with the treat during training, it will become sufficient to maintain the desired behavior for extended periods of time in the absence of the treat. The phrase "Good dog" or a pat on the head will serve to maintain the behavior. The phrase "Good work" or an enthusiastic handshake can accomplish similar results with people.

The previously neutral stimuli are reinforcing trans-situationally; that is, the higher-order stimulus will be reinforcing in situations other than the one in which it was originally used. For example, "Good dog" will be reinforcing in virtually any situation, once its reinforcing properties have been established, but food or water will be effective only if the animal is hungry or thirsty. The strength of the higher-order stimuli is also affected by other parameters. The more often the pairings are accomplished, the stronger the higher-order stimuli will become. In addition, the greater the quality and/or quantity of the original unconditioned stimulus or primary reinforcer, the greater the strength of the higher-order stimulus as well.

Michael Cook and Susan Mineka performed an interesting second-order conditioning experiment with some ingenious alterations to the typical paradigm. In the first order, rhesus monkeys acquired a fear of snakes by observation. Following this procedure, the second-order stimulus, a black-striped box, was paired with the snake, the first-order conditioned stimulus. The results of the experiment indicated that a small but significant amount of the fear response did become conditioned to the box. This example illustrates the establishment of second-order conditioning with a noxious unconditioned stimulus in an observational milieu.

Graham Davey and Imelda McKenna conducted research studying second-order conditioning of the skin conductance response. This is a response whereby the electrical conductivity of the skin can be measured as the subject participates in the task. Electrical conductivity is positively correlated with anxiety and is often considered the best operational definition of anxiety; it is used as part of the analysis in a polygraph (lie detector) report. Davey and McKenna paired a neutral stimulus with a loud tone to establish the electrodermal response to the first-order stimulus. A second-order stimulus was subsequently paired with the first-order stimulus, and the skin conductance response was elicited. It was found that verbal instructions specifying the absence of the unconditioned stimulus erased the conditioned response. These results tend to support the cognitive interpretation of higher-order conditioning. Robert Rescorla believes that cognitive interpretations might explain the higher-order conditioning phenomenon best when the associated stimuli are in the same modality (category of sensation).

Context

The study of higher-order conditioning developed as a natural extension of the early work of Pavlov and his Russian associates. It was Pavlov and his associates who first reported the existence of the phenomenon in the early 1900's. It was not until the 1930's and 1940's, however, that the analogous effect of secondary reinforcement was investigated in detail. Much more interest has centered on the secondary reinforcement issue. There are probably several reasons for this. First, classical conditioning originated outside the United States. Although it was embraced readily because of the desire to operationalize psychology, it soon began to lose favor. Classical conditioning seemed to apply only to involuntary, autonomic nervous system responses such as salivation, eye blinks, and so on. Instrumental conditioning, with its study of voluntary behaviors, seemed to hold more promise for the understanding of complex human behavior. It was easier to apply to human situations, so the study of secondary reinforcement and chaining (the analogues to higher-order conditioning) took precedence. In addition, instrumental conditioning was an American endeavor, pioneered by American psychologists.

Understanding exactly how higher-order conditioning works and what parameters affect its strength will undoubtedly lead psychologists to a greater appreciation of how organisms acquire learned responses. The experiments that are aimed at determining the relative importance of cognitive processes in learning versus stimulus-response associations in acquisition seem to lend themselves quite easily to the field of higher-order conditioning. The different procedures used to weaken the strength of the unconditioned stimulus in order to observe the effects on the conditioned stimuli seem to point to promising results and interesting conclusions. As the nature of higher-order conditioning and secondary reinforcement becomes more clear, psychologists will also become more informed about how behavior, human and animal, can be maintained for long periods of time in the absence of primary reinforcers. A greater understanding of how various stimuli affect one another will also be a consequence of further research into higher-order conditioning. It is already known that certain combinations of stimuli seem to yield higher-order conditioning more easily than others; why this is so is still a question to be answered. Finally, Pavlovian conditioning seems to work with autonomic nervous system emotional responses. Gaining a greater understanding of higher-order conditioning will surely provide insight into the nature of the complex emotional responses of human beings.

Bibliography

Davey, G. C., and I. McKenna. "The Effects of Postconditioning Revaluation of CS_1 and UCS Following Pavlovian Second-Order Electrodermal Conditioning in Humans." *Quarterly Journal of Experimental Comparative and Physiological Psychology* 35B (May, 1983): 125-133. A very interesting study dealing with higher-order conditioning with human subjects. Using two different strategies, the study illustrates possible cognitive influences in the phenomenon.

Domjan, Michael, and Barbara Burkhard. *The Principles of Learning and Behavior.* Monterey, Calif.: Brooks/Cole, 1986. An excellent contemporary learning-theory text that deals with both Pavlovian and operant-conditioning issues. The discussions of higher-order conditioning and secondary reinforcement contain excellent studies that illustrate the topics.

Frolov, Y. P. *Pavlov and His School.* New York: Oxford University Press, 1937. Published just after Pavlov's death, this book contains a touching personal foreword about him. The reader comes to see how Pavlov was influenced by his predecessors, such as René Descartes and Charles Darwin, and how he came to his ideas about higher nervous system activity.

Hilgard, Ernest Ropiequet. *Hilgard and Marquis' Conditioning and Learning.* Revised by Gregory A. Kimble. 2d ed. New York: Appleton-Century-Crofts, 1961. Considered one of the classics in the field of learning theory. Excellent discussions of higher-order conditioning and secondary reinforcement in the context of demonstrating an important similarity between Pavlovian and operant conditioning.

Pavlov, Ivan P. *Lectures on Conditioned Reflexes.* Translated by W. Horsley Gantt. New York: International Publishers, 1928. An important historical treatise providing an excellent survey of the many experiments, with the actual data, that Pavlov and his associates conducted on conditioned reflexes. Photographs and a biographical sketch are also included.

Jonathan Kahane

Cross-References

Conditioning: Pavlovian versus Instrumental, 649; Instrumental Conditioning: Acquisition and Extinction, 1315; Pavlovian Conditioning: Acquisition, Extinction, and Inhibition, 1757; Pavlovian Conditioning: Theoretical Foundations, 1764; Reinforcement Schedules, 2077; Reinforcers and Reinforcement, 2084.

CONDITIONING: PAVLOVIAN VERSUS INSTRUMENTAL

Type of psychology: Learning
Fields of study: Instrumental conditioning; Pavlovian conditioning

Both Pavlovian and instrumental conditioning offer environmentally based approaches to learning. Pavlovian (classical) conditioning is considered a passive, involuntary mode in which a subject learns appropriate reactions to stimuli. Instrumental (operative) conditioning forces a choice between alternatives through interaction with the environment and is considered voluntary, or purposeful, learning.

Principal terms

ACQUISITION: the basic process that is presumed to take place when learning occurs; acquisition and learning are used interchangeably to describe a change in behavior because of experience

CONDITIONED RESPONSE: the response to a previously neutral stimulus that has been identified with an unconditioned stimulus

CONDITIONED STIMULUS: the coupling of an ordinarily unconnected, or neutral, stimulus with an unconditioned stimulus

DISINHIBITION: a renewed response to a stimulus because of resumed reinforcement; the result is the resumption of previously learned but forgotten behavior

EXTINCTION: the repeated presentation of a conditioned stimulus without reinforcement by the unconditioned stimulus; the result is the loss of learning

HIGHER-ORDER CONDITIONING: the linking of successive conditioned stimuli, the last of which elicits the conditioned response; higher-order associations are easily broken

IRRADIATION: in Pavlovian theory, a wave of nervous excitement generated by an unconditioned stimulus that spreads from one part of the brain to surrounding areas

SKINNER BOX: a cage in which an experimental subject has to press a lever in order to obtain food

UNCONDITIONED REFLEX: an animal's inborn neural capacity to respond to events necessary for survival

UNCONDITIONED STIMULUS: a specific example of a category of events necessary to the survival of an animal

Overview

Pavlovian, or classical, conditioning is a behavioral procedure and a type of learning. It rests upon three major premises: that physiochemical processes underlie experience-related changes in behavior; that animals have an inborn neural capacity (the unconditioned response, or UR) to react to circumstances necessary for survival (the unconditioned stimulus, or US); and that insights gleaned from the behavior of lower animals can be applied to humans. Pavlovian conditioning also relies on a specific definition of association—that events acquire shared meaning if they are closely connected in time and if one event reliably predicts the onset of its successor.

In the classic example, food presented to a hungry dog serves as the unconditioned stimulus; its appearance alone excites the unconditioned response of salivation. Salivation remains an appropriate reflex so long as the dog is allowed to eat the food shown to it, for that act maintains (reinforces) the association between the unconditioned stimulus and the unconditioned response. The associations between unconditioned responses and unconditioned stimuli represent an original relationship built into the architecture of the nervous system.

That initial relationship is, however, continually altered by experience. A dog repeatedly shown withheld food ceases to salivate, while the resumption of feeding restores salivation. In the first case, the unconditioned response undergoes extinction through inhibition, the opposite of reinforcement; in the second, lapsed neural associations are revived (disinhibited) through the resumption of reinforcement. A dog can also learn to discriminate between similar types of reinforced and unreinforced food—for example, salivating at brown bread that it is allowed to eat, while ignoring forbidden white bread. Moreover, connections can be redirected, for the repeated coupling of an unrelated stimulus such as a bell tone with the appearance of food can provoke salivation. The linkage of a conditioned stimulus (CS), the bell tone, with an unconditioned stimulus, the sight of food, establishes a conditioned response (CR). An extension of this process, called higher-order conditioning, links conditioned stimuli in order to explore an animal's ability to associate events and recognize similarities.

In Pavlovian theory, conditioned responses are formed (acquired) through the sensory association of stimuli that appear close together in time and are maintained through reinforcement. This happens because of the way the nervous system works. While it transfers sensations, it also forges neural pathways through the spread of nervous excitation from one part of the cerebral cortex into other areas. This process, called irradiation, is caused by the impact of the unconditioned stimulus on the cerebral cortex. When a wave generated by an unconditioned stimulus encounters the lesser wave produced by a conditioned one, a neural pathway appears. Reinforcement maintains the linkage, while lack of reinforcement produces a wave of inhibition that dissolves it.

Pavlovians believe that both unconditioned and conditioned responses reveal the workings of higher nervous activity. The speed of reflexes and the flow rate of involuntary secretions are windows into the workings of the cerebral cortex, indicating how organisms change behavior to match experience. Conditioned responses allow the anticipation of future events based on the most recent developments in an ever-changing environment.

Since classical conditioning theory asserts that subjects respond to, rather than act upon, their surroundings, many psychologists consider it an involuntary and rather simple form of learning. Because it is so passive, non-Pavlovians often conclude that it acts upon the autonomic nervous system rather than the cerebral cortex.

Pavlovian conditioning is traditionally contrasted with instrumental conditioning, which behaviorists generally view as an active, voluntary, purposeful kind of learning that relies on investigative interactions with the environment and reflects cortical activity. In the standard examples of instrumental conditioning, an animal discovers and manipulates an instrument such as a lever in order to gain a desired end, such as escape from confinement or access to food.

Five major methods of instrumental conditioning have been developed. The best known is reward training, which makes use of a maze or Skinner box to supply a satisfier of some kind after a conditioned response. The mirror image of reward training is escape training, where the conditioned response terminates an unpleasant stimulus such as an electric shock. A somewhat similar method is avoidance training, in which the conditioned response prevents the unpleasant stimulus from occurring. Omission training is a method by which undesirable behavior is halted by the withholding of satisfiers, and punishment training ends undesirable behavior by following it with a disagreeable stimulus.

Terminology in instrumental conditioning can differ from that of classical conditioning. For example, in instrumental conditioning, reinforcement is a reward for correct behavior rather than the presentation of the unconditioned stimulus, and it is related to the law of effect, which holds that those responses that are most quickly rewarded are most likely to recur. As in classical conditioning, however, association and extinction are essential concepts, and the relationship and timing of conditioned stimuli, responses to them, and reinforcement determine the shape of the learning curve.

While the distinction between Pavlovian and instrumental conditioning is useful, the assumption that they constitute different forms of learning has been challenged by the American psychologist B. F. Skinner. In a telling argument striking at the artificiality of classical and instrumental testing environments, Skinner maintained that investigators cannot detect all stimuli to which their subjects respond, and that all behavior, whether measured by Pavlovian or instrumental methods, is a response to stimuli. Therefore, the two methods may represent different aspects of a single learning process.

Applications

The significance of Pavlovian conditioning was immediately recognized in its country of origin, where it became involved in a broad-based oppositionalist movement against the undemocratic nature of czarism. Late Imperial Russia was an anomaly among the European powers, attempting rapid economic modernization while preserving aristocratic privilege and adhering to an autocratic mode of governance. One of its traditional means of control, a close association of throne and altar gained through subordination of the Russian Orthodox church to the state, provoked antireligious (and, therefore, antispiritual and antimentalist) reactions among important segments of the educated classes. The materialist assumptions of Pavlovian conditioning, combined with its undeniable successes in linking environment, physiochemical reactions, and nervous functions to the learning process, placed a new weapon in their hands.

Although his conditioning theory became part of a general ideological assault against the czarist regime, Ivan Petrovich Pavlov successfully deflected the adverse political repercussions arising from the nature of his work. While he was required to notify the St. Petersburg police of his personal and professional activities and was denied government funding for further research, he was able to expand his investigations into conditioning through large private donations. By 1914, he headed an extremely influential school of experimental physiology and had access to some of the best-equipped research laboratories in the world.

Classical conditioning concepts also found their way into pre-revolutionary Russian literature and literary theory, for they provided new perspectives on the way in which symbols acquired meaning. Through the theoretical writings of Andrey Bely (the pseudonym of Boris Bugayev), the Symbolist novelists and poets of the Merezhkovsky circle were introduced to modified interpretations of irradiation and higher-level conditioning. As a result, Symbolists such as Bely, Aleksandr Blok, and Gippius (Zinaida Merezhkovsky) increasingly incorporated rhythmic sound into their artistic quest to express the inexpressible.

The Bolshevik seizure of power in Russia established Pavlovian conditioning as the dominant learning theory, underpinning experimental biology, psychology, educational theory and practice, and cognitive theory. The new regime did so for several reasons: Pavlovian mechanical reductionism was compatible with Marxist materialism, Marxism and Pavlovian conditioning placed identical stress on the primacy of environmental factors in learning, and the scientific achievements of the Pavlovian school had propaganda value for the new socialist state.

That favoritism had untoward consequences; lavish state aid allowed Pavlov and his successors to conduct extensive research projects on complex aspects of conditioning, but the exclusion of rival approaches led to a relative methodological impoverishment. Psychiatry could not be practiced, and psychology had very few recourses with which to face behavioral problems. For example, if a fearful patient associated darkness with menacing shadowy figures, a Soviet psychologist was reduced to higher-order conditioning in hopes that, somewhere along the line, the negative conditioned response would drop out of the pattern. Even the Soviet space program, decades later, bore the imprint of Pavlovian conditioning. Rather than selecting a close relative of humans for the first unmanned test flights, Soviet scientists chose a dog, the classic symbol of Pavlovian experimentation.

While the effect of Pavlovian conditioning has been marginal in Western Europe, it has had a significant impact in the United States, where it has combined and recombined with native behaviorism. Since it also shares many features with instrumental conditioning (especially the goal of discovering the laws of behavior through precise, replicable methods), a certain merging of concepts has taken place in that area as well. For example, Skinner adopted the Pavlovian definition of the reflex as his fundamental physical unit of analysis and, as noted previously, raised the question as to whether instrumental and Pavlovian conditioning really differ at the most basic level.

Instrumental conditioning, with its emphasis on voluntary, exploratory behavior, has found direct application in fields ranging from animal learning to educational practice and behavior modification. The widespread use of stickers and decals in lower grades to recognize the accomplishment of educational tasks is one practical consequence of operant reward training studies; another example is the pacing of assigned work, so that students do not suffer the negative effects of overstimulation. In the first case, lessons regarding the effectiveness of rewards are drawn directly from experiments on the effects of various satisfiers; in the second case, conclusions are drawn from the shape of the learning curve after prolonged trial sessions.

Lessons drawn from omission training studies have frequently been used to change unwanted behavior in children. In one commonly encountered situation, privileges or other reinforcers are withdrawn from children who insist on undressing in inappropriate places or at inappropriate times. The loss of satisfiers has generally proved to be an effective way to terminate such unwanted behavior.

Instrumental conditioning studies also offer new insights into the impediments to revitalizing a culture's institutions. Organizational cultures can be analyzed in terms of patterns in reward training (learning what to do to gain recognition or influence) and avoidance training (learning what is not rewarded in a particular organizational culture), and these learned responses can pose real obstacles to change. In such cases, necessary culture shifts can be realized through the initiation of small periodic changes combined with response-extinguishing conditioning techniques.

Context

Pavlovian and instrumental conditioning techniques reflect materialistic trends in science dating back to the works of the seventeenth century philosopher and mathematician, René Descartes. Descartes's determination to exclude spiritual factors from an analysis of the physical world by postulating a separate arena for their existence, and his definition of life as highly organized matter in motion were further developed in the eighteenth century by materialists such as Joseph Priestley and Julien Offroy de la Mettrie. In the nineteenth century, the materialistic view was bolstered by the investigations of Charles Darwin, whose theory of evolution described a process by which both minds and bodies were transformed through the interactions of material organisms with their environments.

Pavlovian conditioning theory was further influenced by a particularly Russian materialistic current which included the nineteenth century radical journalist Nikolay Chernyshevsky, his nihilistic supporter, Dmitry Pisarev, and the noted physiologist Ivan Mikhaylovich Sechenov. Chernyshevsky and Pisarev rejected subjectivism because of its connection with czarist oppression, and Pavlov was particularly affected by their passionate, politically motivated, materialistic outlooks. His methodology was most influenced by Sechenov's reductionist views and speculations about the workings of the reflex arc.

Instrumental conditioning had a simpler lineage as an offshoot of functionalism, a current in psychology which expressed a Darwinian interest in adaptive mental processes. While preliminary work had been done in maze learning at the end of the nineteenth century, the most important early instrumental conditioning studies were conducted by Edward L. Thorndike, an American psychologist. Thorndike's experiments, published in 1911, involved cats that escaped puzzle boxes to reach food by pulling a string, raising a latch, or operating some other instrument. Instrumental conditioning theory developed rapidly and was quickly incorporated into the emerging behaviorist movement.

While Pavlovian and instrumental conditioning arose from an acute need to provide objective, precise, and replicable data on behavior, they also reflected a procedural shift from observations of specimens in artificial situations to observations of unrestricted animals in their normal surroundings. Neither technique represents the completion of that shift, however; while each uses healthy subjects, both techniques place animals in highly unnatural situations and invite charges that their conclusions are unreliable because their methods distort normal behavior.

Pavlovian conditioning has limited application when compared to instrumental conditioning, but the future of both methods is apparently secure. Pavlovian conditioning theory is unchallenged in Russia despite the weakening of authoritarianism, and it remains a vital part of American behaviorist currents. In the United States, elements of Pavlovian conditioning are often combined with instrumental conditioning theory, and both continue to affect developments in fields such as aversion theory, abnormal behavior, animal learning, language formation, and information processing.

The nature-nurture debate is far from ended, and both environmentally based learning methods face a strong challenge from a revived sociobiological movement. Nevertheless, their history of experimental successes, their valuable applications, and their usefulness to the dominant nurture-oriented ideologies in the United States and Russia should assure their continued importance.

Bibliography

Angermeier, Wilhelm F. *The Evolution of Operant Learning and Memory: A Comparative Etho-Psychology.* New York: Karger, 1984. A critical evaluation of instrumental conditioning by a prominent European psychologist. Provides insight into the general European suspicion of reductionist approaches. Includes tables, graphs, a bibliography, and an index.

Brush, F. Robert, and J. Bruce Overmier, eds. *Affect, Conditioning, and Cognition: Essays on the Determinants of Behavior.* Hillsdale, N.J.: Lawrence Erlbaum, 1985. A valuable collection of articles that point out recent directions taken by operant and classical conditioning research. Includes graphs, tables, illustrations, bibliographies, and subject and author indexes.

Graham, Loren R. *Science, Philosophy, and Human Behavior in the Soviet Union.* New York: Columbia University Press, 1987. An excellent treatment of Pavlov's contributions to Russian physiology and psychology. Includes chapters on the nature-nurture debate, biology and human beings, and cybernetics and computers. Notes, an extensive bibliography, and an index.

Kimble, Gregory A. "Conditioning and Learning." In *Topics in the History of Psychology*, edited by Gregory A. Kimble and Kurt Schlesinger. Vol. 1. Hillsdale, N.J.: Lawrence Erlbaum, 1985. An excellent orientation article that surveys Pavlovian and operant conditioning from their origins to the behaviorism of B. F. Skinner. With tables, illustrations, graphs, and a bibliography.

Klein, Stephen B., and Robert R. Mowrer, eds. *Contemporary Learning Theories: Pavlovian Conditioning and the Status of Traditional Learning Theory.* Hillsdale, N.J.: Lawrence Erlbaum, 1989. An extremely useful set of articles indicating applications of Pavlovian conditioning to learning problems. Tables, graphs, bibliographies, and subject and author indexes.

Schlesinger, Kurt. "A Brief Introduction to a History of Psychology." In *Topics in the History of Psychology*, edited by Gregory A. Kimble and Kurt Schlesinger. Vol. 1. Hillsdale, N.J.: Lawrence Erlbaum, 1985. A well-written article placing Pavlov and the behaviorists in a wide-ranging historical context; suffers somewhat, however, from a tendency toward hero worship. Contains a bibliography.

Skinner, B. F. "Operant Behavior." In *Operant Behavior: Areas of Research and Application*, edited by Werner K. Honig. Englewood Cliffs, N.J.: Prentice-Hall, 1966. A clearly written treatment by the foremost behaviorist of recent times. Surveys the theoretical foundations of instrumental conditioning and points out major pitfalls in analyzing experimental results. Includes a bibliography.

Michael J. Fontenot

Cross-References

Avoidance Learning, 375; Conditioning: Higher-Order, 643; Escape Conditioning, 985; Instrumental Conditioning: Acquisition and Extinction, 1315; Neural Anatomy and Cognition, 1640; Pavlovian Conditioning: Acquisition, Extinction, and Inhibition, 1757; Punishment, 2016; Reinforcement Schedules, 2077; Reinforcers and Reinforcement, 2084.

FUNCTIONS OF CONSCIOUSNESS

Type of psychology: Consciousness
Field of study: Cognitive processes

Although the functions of consciousness are debated by psychologists, most believe that consciousness serves to help people adapt to novel situations. Consciousness occurs as aspects of the environment are selected, attended to, and interpreted.

Principal terms

BEHAVIORISM: the theoretical approach which argues that the proper subject matter of psychology is observable behavior, not internal mental processes

CONSCIOUSNESS: a stream of awareness forming the subjective character of experience, including awareness of the external world and of one's own mental states

EPIPHENOMENON: a secondary by-product of a phenomenon, not essential for an understanding of the phenomenon

FUNCTIONALISM: the early school of psychology that emphasized the means by which organisms adapt to their environments

MINDLESSNESS: interacting with the world in an automatic fashion, following habitual scripts

SCRIPT: a temporally organized frame of knowledge; an internal representation of a sequence of events

STRUCTURALISM: a school of psychology which emphasized the studying of the mind by conscious introspection in an attempt to find the elementary units of conscious experience

Overview

The nature, origin, and functions of consciousness are some of the great mysteries of human existence. Although the nature of consciousness was explored by the first psychologists, contemporary psychology has been relatively silent about normal, everyday consciousness. Psychologists have studied altered states of consciousness such as those produced by drugs, dreams, and hypnosis. The importance of everyday consciousness is attested by the study of altered states of consciousness, in that one must have at least an intuitive sense of normal consciousness in order to identify a deviation from that normal state. The importance of normal, everyday consciousness is also attested when psychologists use people's reports of their own intentions, observations, attitudes, and evaluations as research evidence.

Some psychologists equate consciousness with the totality of mental life, whereas others equate it with all of adaptive behavior; however, each of these classifications seems too broad. A better definition equates consciousness with awareness, acknowledging that many aspects of mental life and adaptive behavior occur without conscious awareness. For example, when one drives one's car on a familiar route, one can execute very complex behaviors, adapting to a variety of environmental conditions such as traffic and weather, yet do so without conscious awareness of driving. Similarly, one may be consciously aware of the answer to an arithmetic problem—for example, know that two plus three equals five—but have no awareness of the cognitive processes that actually do the addition.

Clearly, people are not aware of everything, so their consciousness is the result of selection and construction. The mind selects stimuli to which to attend and places meaning on those stimuli. In this way, consciousness forms the subjective, personal character of human experience. Awareness of the world and awareness of one's own self are two components of consciousness. Human consciousness might be defined, then, as a stream of awareness, including the perception of the external world and an awareness of one's own mental state. Given that consciousness is not always present when one solves problems or engages in complex behaviors, the functions of consciousness have been debated. Some have argued that consciousness serves no function at all. From this point of view, it is an epiphenomenon—simply a by-product of brain activity, as exhaust is a by-product of a car engine. From this point of view, consciousness does not *do* anything; it does not cause thoughts or actions.

The epiphenomenalist position has been criticized on several grounds. First, it contradicts everyday experiences. People feel that they have conscious intentions or plans which they follow through in behavior, and conscious attention does seem to aid learning and problem solving in many cases; however, intuitions and common sense are sometimes wrong. A stronger argument against epiphenomenalism can be made by considering an evolutionary perspective. From an evolutionary perspective, characteristics are continued in a species because they give the species a reproductive advantage. That is, members who have the characteristic are more likely to reproduce, or to have more offspring, than others. From this point of view, consciousness must have arisen because it functions, in some way, to sustain life.

Most psychologists adopt the functionalist position described above. From this position, consciousness is viewed as functioning to facilitate humans' adaptations to novel situations. Conscious awareness requires cognitive effort; it seems to accompany the allocation of a certain amount of cognitive capacity or energy. As such, consciousness may be viewed as an aspect of mental activity rather than a mechanism per se. According to psychologist Robert Ornstein, the readiness to respond to novel stimuli *is* consciousness. Incoming stimuli are selected for one's conscious awareness when they are perceived as dissimilar to previous stimuli—when a well-learned automatic behavior may not be appropriate to the situation. An interpretation of the situation may then be sought with conscious awareness, and a response decided upon. For example, while automaticity may be the rule when one drives a car on a familiar route, consciousness generally intervenes when the road situation becomes hazardous. Consciousness, then, functions as a control mechanism, selecting stimuli and constructing interpretations and responses to those stimuli. This aids human survival, and those who survive longer have more opportunities to have off-spring.

A related, but radical, analysis of consciousness has been suggested by Julian Jaynes. According to Jaynes, consciousness involves the left hemisphere of the brain, the part of the brain that in most people is responsible for language. Jaynes suggests that, prehistorically, people were not conscious, but rather experienced their mental "voices" as the voices of the gods. As societies became complex, experienced stress, and encountered other societies with different organizations and beliefs, the voices became internalized and people became conscious. Jaynes's theorizing is controversial, but his argument concerning the functions of consciousness is compatible with the evolutionary perspective mentioned above. Instead of addressing the functional adaptation of individuals, however, Jaynes argues that consciousness arose in order to help societies adapt to novel situations.

Applications

Although references to consciousness are not widely found in psychological research, the topic has fascinated some individuals from a variety of subdisciplines in psychology. Ellen Langer, a social psychologist interested in interpersonal interactions, began studying conscious awareness in the 1970's in her research on "mindlessness." Some physiological psychologists have also pondered the implications for consciousness of their research on the structure of the brain.

Langer argues that much of human adult social interaction is "mindless." That is, she says that people follow social scripts that they have learned over their lifetimes and thus do not consciously attend to their social world. In one study, Langer, Arthur Blank, and Benzion Chanowitz had individuals approach a person who was using a copying machine and make one of three requests: "May I use the copy machine?"; "May I use the copy machine because I have to make copies?"; or "May I use the copy machine because I'm in a rush?" Subjects were more likely to respond positively to the request when it was phrased in either of the latter two ways than when the requester simply asked to use the machine. Although addition of the comment "because I have to make copies" adds no information to the simple request to use the machine, it is responded to as if a meaningful reason for the request were being given.

Langer argues that the subjects in this study were using a script which says that when a request, in addition to a reason, is given, one should comply; they were not really paying conscious attention to what was said. Many interactions may have this scripted quality. While the use of scripts may free cognitive energy for conscious attention to more important tasks, Langer argues that all too often people simply fall into mindless habits. If people can be taught to be mindful, to attend consciously to their world, they will, in Langer's view, be more likely to think creatively, consider alternative solutions for problems, and live more rational and productive lives. In one particular study, Langer, Chanowitz, and Richard Bashner trained people to be mindful. The subjects were shown slides of individuals with physical handicaps and were told to attend to the unique characteristics of these people. The researchers found that when people were thus trained to be mindful, they were less likely than untrained, "mindless" people to think stereotypically about others who have handicaps. Thus, consciousness may help people think more clearly about other people.

In another area of psychology, physiological psychologists have pondered the implications for consciousness of their theories about the structure of the mind. Although people experience their conscious mental lives as a unified whole, some psychologists argue that in fact there may be subcomponents to the mind; the mind may have a modular structure. If so, might consciousness itself have several discrete components?

This question is of particular interest when individuals who have undergone split-brain operations are considered. In split-brain operations, the corpus callosum, the fibers connecting the right and left hemispheres of the brain, are severed. The operation is done in order to improve severe conditions of epilepsy that have not responded to less extreme treatments. When the two hemispheres of the brain cannot communicate, do two separate consciousnesses arise? Does one become twice as intelligent; does one's ability to adapt to the environment double?

People who have undergone split-brain operations do not double their intelligence quotient (IQ) scores, and, over time, no obvious differences from normal people can be seen in their behavior. It can be argued, however, that the split-brain operation produces two different spheres of awareness. In controlled research, information can be directed to one hemisphere of the brain of the split-brain patient or the other. Information that is directed to the left hemisphere (the one where specialized language centers are usually located) can be responded to verbally. Thus it seems that the left hemisphere possesses conscious awareness. The right hemisphere is mute, and at first it may not seem to have consciousness. Yet when stimuli are directed to the right hemisphere, it too can respond—not verbally, but by pointing to a correct answer. For example, if a picture of a cat were presented to the left hemisphere of a person who had undergone a split-brain operation, the person could say "I saw a cat," thus demonstrating conscious awareness. If the same picture were shown to only the right hemisphere, the person would not be able to say what was seen. The person would, however, be able to point to the picture if it were presented along with several alternatives. Thus, the right hemisphere also seems to have a type of consciousness. Such research raises the interesting possibility that consciousness may be multifaceted in all people. Verbal consciousness may simply function as an interpreter for the brain's various subcomponents of awareness.

Context

Consciousness played an important role in the early history of psychology. The earliest experimental psychologists believed that conscious experience was the proper subject matter of psychology. The school of psychology called structuralism, which flourished in the late 1800's, used introspection in order to identify the basic units of consciousness. Their approach was criticized both because it reduced complex experience to elemental units and because introspection is inherently subjective.

The functions of consciousness were emphasized by the American school of psychology termed functionalism, which also flourished in the late 1800's. Functionalists such as William James were influenced by the evolutionary theory of Charles Darwin, and they thus explained consciousness in terms of its adaptive significance. James's writings on consciousness are particularly significant and continue to be meaningful to contemporary psychology.

In the United States, with the advent of behaviorism in the twentieth century, interest in consciousness waned. Behaviorists such as John B. Watson argued that observable behaviors, not inferred characteristics of the mind such as consciousness, are the proper subject matter of psychology. Until the 1950's, the behaviorist approach dominated psychology, particularly in the United States. Consciousness itself was not a common topic of psychology, although unconscious processes were studied by Freudian theorists and altered states of consciousness were a topic of some investigations.

With the cognitive revolution of the 1950's, and with the advancement of research in physiological psychology, normal, everyday consciousness again became a topic of study for at least a few psychologists. The computer revolution of the 1950's gave psychologists a new model of how the mind might work, the information-processing model. With this development, the mind in general, and consciousness in particular, again found a place in psychology. The information-processing approach often equates consciousness with attention or short-term memory, perhaps neglecting its broader implications. The focus on cognition has, however, opened the door for consciousness to be studied by a wide range of psychologists interested in personality, social interaction, and development.

Physiological research has also inspired some discussion of consciousness. With the study of the separate functions of the two hemispheres of the brain, researchers have speculated about the localization, function, and essence of consciousness. Some equate consciousness with the left hemisphere's ability to use language, but it is clear that the right hemisphere, too, possesses awareness. It is this research which in part inspired the speculative theorizing of Julian Jaynes, who argues that the consciousness which people experience is a relatively new development of the human mind. On the whole, consciousness remains a mystery, but contemporary psychology has found it to be a topic worthy of study. There is reason to hope that parts of the mystery will be solved as psychologists focus more energy on this topic.

Bibliography

Flanagan, Owen J., Jr. "Naturalizing the Mind: The Philosophical Psychology of William James." In *The Science of the Mind.* Cambridge, Mass.: MIT Press, 1984. A readable introduction, written by a philosopher, to the central philosophical and psychological issues of consciousness. Discusses criteria and functions for conscious mental life. A good introduction to reading William James. Further information relevant to consciousness may be found in the chapter in the same volume entitled "Cognitive Psychology and Artificial Intelligence: Philosophical Assumptions and Implications."

Gazzaniga, Michael S. *The Social Brain*. New York: Basic Books, 1985. A readable, interesting account of Gazzaniga's development as a physiological psychologist. Written for a general audience. Describes research on the brain, including research with split-brain patients. Discusses Gazzaniga's own speculative theory about the modular organization of the mind, which argues for the central role of language in consciousness.

James, William. "Consciousness." In *Psychology: The Briefer Course*. 1892. Reprint. New York: Harper & Row, 1961. Describes the nature and functions of consciousness from the perspective of the historically important functionalist school of psychology. Significant historically, but also relevant to contemporary psychology. Delightfully written for a relatively sophisticated audience. A fuller treatment of the topic of consciousness may be found in James's *The Principles of Psychology* (1890).

Jaynes, Julian. *The Origins of Consciousness in the Breakdown of the Bicameral Mind*. Harmondsworth, Middlesex, England: Pelican Books, 1976. A fascinating but highly speculative account of the origins of consciousness; not widely accepted by psychologists. Initial chapters provide a good review of the nature and functions of consciousness. Later chapters synthesize information from anthropology, history, and physiological and abnormal psychology into Jaynes's own unique theory.

Klein, David B. "The Functions of Consciousness." In *The Concept of Consciousness: A Survey*. Lincoln: University of Nebraska Press, 1884. A thorough and readable account of consciousness, excellent for getting an overview on the topic. The cited chapter provides an overview of the functions of consciousness, as considered historically in psychology, and discusses contemporary biological and psychological evidence. Written for a college audience.

Langer, Ellen J. *Mindfulness*. Reading, Mass.: Addison-Wesley, 1990. Reviews research showing the lack of consciousness, termed "mindlessness," in everyday life and argues for the importance of becoming more conscious ("mindful") for a healthy and adaptive life. Offers suggestions on how to increase mindfulness. Written for a general audience. A somewhat speculative presentation of the implications of Langer's social psychological research.

Ornstein, Robert E. *The Psychology of Consciousness*. 2d rev. ed. New York: Penguin Books, 1986. A readable account of consciousness by one of the first contemporary psychologists to address the issue. Contrasts the everyday consciousness of the Western world with the states of consciousness induced by meditation that are more common in the philosophies of the Eastern world. Argues for a unification of these two forms of consciousness.

Susan E. Beers

Cross-References

Altered States of Consciousness, 220; Attention, 313; Automaticity, 356; Cognitive Psychology: An Overview, 572; Levels of Consciousness, 663; Dreams, 836; Functionalism, 1055; Memory: Sensory, 1531; Short-Term Memory, 2265; Split-Brain Studies, 2355; Structuralism, 2477.

LEVELS OF CONSCIOUSNESS

Type of psychology: Consciousness
Fields of study: Cognitive processes; personality theory

Consciousness or awareness can be divided into three levels: unconscious, pre-conscious, and conscious. Given that one cannot be aware of everything that is going on around one all the time, the kind of processes that occur at each of these levels has profound implications for thought, behavior, and personality.

Principal terms

CONSCIOUSNESS: a level of experience that includes those things of which individuals are aware at any given moment, such as current ideas, thoughts, accessed memories, and feelings

EGO: the conscious aspect of personality postulated by Sigmund Freud that serves as a watchdog and helps to satisfy the desires of the id safely

ID: one of the unconscious aspects of personality postulated by Freud, the sole purpose of which is to satisfy animalistic urges and desires

PRECONSCIOUS: the transition level from those things occurring in one's mind of which one is unaware (unconscious) and those of which one is aware (conscious)

SUPEREGO: the third aspect of personality, according to Freud, which incorporates the moral values of parents and society, helping one to know right from wrong

UNCONSCIOUS: the deep-rooted aspects of the mind; Freud claimed that it includes negative instincts and urges that are too disturbing for people to become aware of consciously

Overview

Theories concerning levels of consciousness have painted elaborate pictures of the human mind and psyche. It is easy to take for granted the myriad complicated processes that must occur automatically every day in order for one to make sense of the world, make the hundreds of decisions that each day demands, and still have time and mental energy left over to concentrate on work, study, or play. Theories about levels of consciousness attempt to explain how it is that one can perform so many demanding tasks simultaneously and still do most of them well.

It is obvious that many bodily functions occur at a level that is below awareness. For example, if a man had to concentrate on breathing, regulating heart rate, and worrying about digesting the tacos he ate at lunch, there would be little attention left to give to the tasks required by a job or school. Human bodies are perfectly capable of performing many of these functions automatically without having constantly to get permission from a higher authority. The mind is divided in much the same way. If the individual had to concentrate on keeping each eye in focus, turning the ears on and off, keeping memories stored, and so on, trying to study for an examination or solve a crossword puzzle would be extremely difficult at best.

Contemporary psychologists tend to agree that the functions of the mind can be studied at three levels. These levels correspond roughly to the degree to which one is aware of what resides in, or is going on at, each level. The common analogy for this division of consciousness is an iceberg. Sigmund Freud was the first to use this analogy, and it easily demonstrates the varying levels of conscious awareness. Imagine an iceberg floating in the ocean. A person looks out of a ship and sees the tip. The part of the iceberg that floats above the surface of the water corresponds to "consciousness." Consciousness includes all those things of which a person is aware at any given moment. A woman may be aware of the words she is reading and of their meaning; she may also be aware of her stomach growling or of music playing in the background. Like the tip of the iceberg that can be seen above the water level, consciousness includes everything about people that they can "see" if their attention is focused on the self.

There is much more to an iceberg, however, than what meets the eye. As the passengers and crew of the *Titanic* quickly came to realize, the real power of the iceberg lies hidden below the surface. It is the same with levels of consciousness. Below the surface of consciousness lies a transition level, known as the "preconscious." The preconscious represents everything that is accessible to a person at any given time but is currently out of consciousness. This can include one's reservoir of memories and habits. Things can be drawn from the preconscious into consciousness. A person may not be aware at this moment of the name of his or her first-grade teacher, but this information can be pulled from the preconscious into consciousness with a bit of mental effort. Once something is no longer needed mentally or is no longer being given conscious attention, it will drop back into the preconscious, where it will reside until it is needed and pulled temporarily back into consciousness.

The largest piece of the iceberg lies deep below the surface of the water. This buried, "unconscious" aspect of the mind is a reservoir of things that are beyond awareness but that nevertheless exert a constant and powerful effect on behavior. This level of consciousness may include the tendency to be aggressive, needs or drives, and personality traits that may influence behavior without one being aware. People are not aware of what goes on at the unconscious level, but the level is very important in helping people handle day-to-day life. Unconscious processes include the filtering of incoming stimuli—organizing information as it is taken in from the environment and sending important bits of information to consciousness for further attention and processing. Without this level of consciousness, it would be impossible to process more than a few pieces of information at any time. Thus, one's mental capacity is greatly enhanced by this three-part division of consciousness. The unconscious contains those processes that can occur automatically to free conscious awareness for the moment-to-moment changes in one's environment. The preconscious allows a person to keep things in a sort of permanent file, where they can be called forth and refiled as many times as necessary. Consciousness provides a person with the unique powers of higher reasoning (for example, problem solving, self-contemplation, and free choice), which many consider to be the main thing separating humans from other animals.

Applications

Ideas concerning levels of consciousness have had a profound impact on psychological theory and methods since the early 1900's. At that time, Sigmund Freud developed a comprehensive theory of human personality in order to understand how and why humans behave the way they do. In this theory, which came to be called psychoanalytic theory, Freud proposed a tripartite division of personality that is intricately linked with levels of consciousness. Each of the three levels of consciousness is responsible for different mental functions and aspects of personality. Though Freud's theory was created to help explain the abnormal behavior of many of his patients, he believed that the theory worked to explain the normal everyday functioning of the mind as well. Freud argued that various aspects of personality reside at different levels of consciousness and that, in order to understand human behavior (because it is driven by personality), one must understand how personality and levels of consciousness tie together.

According to Freud, people are born with only one aspect of consciousness or personality, called the id. The id is a reservoir of psychic energy, which Freud called libido. The id is primarily driven by the need to be satisfied, and it will constantly push for libido energy to be used to carry out its wishes. For the most part, the id seeks gratification of sexual and aggressive urges that are buried deep in the unconscious, away from one's awareness. The problem with the id is that it seeks immediate gratification of its desires without any thought given to potential consequences of actions. According to Freud, this quickly leads to conflict in which the reality of the world clashes with the id's impulsive wishes.

To help the id deal with these conflicts, the second aspect of personality develops. This aspect of personality resides at the conscious level and is called the ego. The ego's function is to help the id by finding safe ways for the id's urges to be satisfied. Rather than walking into a bank during broad daylight and demanding all the money, for example, the ego may scheme and design a method by which the money can be stolen without the fear and danger of being caught. It must be remembered that the ego does not pass judgment on the id's desires. The ego's goal is to help the id get what it wants safely, regardless of how society and others feel about those actions.

Freud believed that human beings would quickly destroy one another in their rapid desire to satisfy urges if only the id and ego were at work. For this reason, Freud postulated a third aspect of personality that resides at the preconscious level. This is called the superego, and its job is to keep both the id and ego in check by making a person feel guilty for bad deeds and moral for good deeds; this can also be called the conscience.

The most widespread use of the levels of consciousness has been the application of Freud's psychoanalytic theory. Psychologists and psychiatrists alike have used this theory of the connection between levels of consciousness and aspects of personality to understand and explain both normal and abnormal behaviors. There have been increasing uses of the concept of levels of consciousness to help understand self-concept development and information processing. If a patient has been experiencing terrible dreams that keep him or her awake nights and cause general anxiety during the day, the psychiatrist's ability to help the patient may depend on the patient's ability to find the unconscious conflict that is serving as the energizing force for the dream.

Psychoanalytic theory claims that human behavior is driven by these unconscious forces and conflicts. If an abnormal behavior is to be eliminated, the therapist must help the client dig into the unconscious and expose the hidden cause. When the cause is uncovered, the problem often will disappear. In this way, levels of consciousness have been used comprehensively in the treatment of behavioral disorders.

Behaviorists have made many attempts to use the principles of reinforcement and punishment to eliminate unwanted behaviors and increase desired behaviors. Although most behaviorists would disagree with the terminology, the real goal is to alter behavior at an unconscious level. By consistently rewarding desired behaviors, it is possible for children to incorporate such behavior into their normal behavioral pattern. In this way, children can learn new, more acceptable behaviors without ever being consciously aware of the fact that it was external reward that caused them to engage in the behavior in the first place. Regardless of what motivated the behavior, once it is internalized, it becomes a significant influence on future behavior. In this way, unconscious ideas and feelings can alter the outward behavior.

Context

Though Sigmund Freud created the most comprehensive theory of levels of consciousness and their effects on human behavior, he was not the first to argue that there are different levels of consciousness. In ancient Greece, Plato argued for a three-part theory of the soul. He believed that the soul had three components: reason, feeling, and appetite. (Although Plato discussed these in terms of the concept of "soul," it is important to note that the meaning of "soul" in ancient times differed considerably from what the term means today.) These terms seem very similar to the functions of id, ego, and superego discussed by Freud. This historical precedent is critical because of the influence of philosophy on the birth of psychology as a science. Plato is often cited as a founding father in the science of psychology, and his historical influence on the unborn science deserves mention.

In the late 1600's, more than two hundred years before the writings of Freud, Gottfried Wilhelm Leibniz suggested that there can be varying levels of consciousness. This was a very early suggestion that processes which are below the threshold of conscious awareness can influence human behavior. The historical importance of levels of consciousness continues to grow as psychoanalytic theory is further refined. As already mentioned, the idea of levels of consciousness has gained importance in areas besides psychotherapy and the explanation and treatment of abnormal behavior. The field of psychology has become so dependent on these constructs and the belief in this three-part division in awareness and consciousness that it is often taken for granted. When a person says, "I did it without thinking," other people have no trouble understanding what this person means. This kind of understanding would be impossible if people did not have some intuitive understanding that they are not always aware of everything they do or the reasons they have for doing these things.

As society becomes more complicated and the demands on one's time become more urgent, certain tasks must be relegated to the unconscious. Driving a car, for example, would be impossible if every aspect of the task had to be consciously processed. There are too many small tasks to complete, too many instantaneous decisions to be made, and too many cars on the road for a driver to function if he or she had to concentrate to remember each time what a red light means or to recall which pedal is the brake. Psychology has been shaped so strongly by this three-part view of consciousness that it is difficult to imagine what the science of psychology would be like without it.

Bibliography

Eccles, John Carew, and Daniel N. Robinson. *The Wonder of Being Human.* New York: Free Press, 1984. An interesting short book that explains the connection between language, thought, and the brain. Discusses processes that range from unconscious to conscious levels. Although the book is somewhat technical, introductory psychology students will find it interesting and helpful.

Ornstein, Robert Evan, ed. *The Nature of Human Consciousness.* New York: Viking Press, 1973. A scholarly and useful book that presents original writings by some of the pioneer thinkers in levels of consciousness. Covers a wide range of topics from understanding humans to altered states of consciousness. The writing is technical and geared for a fairly advanced college audience.

_____. *The Psychology of Consciousness.* San Francisco: W. H. Freeman, 1972. Designed to help the general audience gain an understanding of consciousness and how to put consciousness to work effectively. Includes scientific research as well as self-help suggestions.

Pelletier, Kenneth R. *Toward a Science of Consciousness.* New York: Delacorte, 1978. Covers theories of consciousness from metaphysical, scientific, and self-help perspectives. Appropriate for high school or college students, or a general audience. Although some of the chapters are not quite mainstream, the overall effect is successful.

Smith, Barry D., and Harold J. Vetter. *Theories of Personality.* 2d ed. Englewood Cliffs, N.J.: Prentice-Hall, 1990. Although this is a college-level textbook, the writing is straightforward and easy to understand. Presents perhaps the best explanation of Sigmund Freud's iceberg analogy and his views of the connection between personality structures and levels of consciousness. High school and college students will find the book interesting.

Randall E. Osborne

Cross-References

Altered States of Consciousness, 220; Automaticity, 356; The Collective Unconscious, 592; Functions of Consciousness, 656; Dreams, 836; Psychoanalytic Psychology and Personality: Sigmund Freud, 1912.

CONSUMER PSYCHOLOGY: DECISIONS

Type of psychology: Cognition
Fields of study: Attitudes and behavior; cognitive processes; thought

Psychologists have investigated many aspects of consumer behavior; the ultimate goal of nearly all research on consumers is to understand how consumers obtain and process information and why they choose some goods and services and not others.

Principal terms

ATTITUDE: the degree of feeling, or affect, in favor of or against an object

BEHAVIORAL INTENTION: a personal plan or decision to engage in a specified behavior, such as the purchase of an object or service

BELIEF: a judgment of the extent to which an object has certain attributes

COMPENSATORY RULES: decision strategies that rest on overall evaluations of products, so that high values on one dimension can offset a low one on another

SUBJECTIVE NORM: the perceived belief of significant others regarding a specified behavior

Overview

The decision-making approach to understanding consumer behavior follows from the assumption that the consumer is someone who seeks and takes in information from numerous sources, processes it, and then makes a selection from a set of alternatives. A major proponent of this view is James R. Bettman. The essence of his theory, presented in *An Information Processing Theory of Consumer Choice* (1979), is an explanation of how consumers react to information—from advertisers, friends, family, salespeople, and so on. The theory integrates six components of information processing: limitations in the human capacity to process information; the motivation to move from some initial state to a desired state; attention to and perceptual encoding of information; the search for information from memory and the external environment, and the evaluation of this information; decision processes; and the effects of consumption and learning. All these components are related through the construct of choice. Put another way, one becomes motivated, pays attention, obtains and evaluates information, learns, and compares alternatives in order to reach a goal. Because of its comprehensive nature, Bettman's theory of consumer choice has been highly influential in the academic and marketing communities.

The information-processing and decision-making perspectives on consumer purchases stand in sharp contrast to an alternative view, called behavioral influence, which presumes that consumers respond directly to pressures of the environment and give little or no conscious thought to their purchases. There is some evidence that consumer purchase decisions can be influenced by factors (such as music) of which they are unaware. Hence, consumers can be influenced by factors that they cannot evaluate and weigh in a decision process. This raises special concerns about methods of protecting consumers.

Perhaps the most useful and enduring theory to explain consumer behavior is Martin Fishbein and Icek Azjen's theory of reasoned action. This theory states that behavior results from an intention. For example, the purchasing of a product is a consequence of an intention to purchase that product. Thus, what is important to understand is how people form intentions. Consumers form intentions by taking into account two types of information. One is their overall evaluation of the product. The other is the subjective norms supporting purchase of the product. According to this theory, people plan to purchase a product if they evaluate it positively and believe that their purchase of it would be approved by those who are important to them. Because this theory emphasizes attitudes concerning a behavior toward an object and not only the object itself, it has successfully predicted many behaviors that attitudes alone could not.

In reality, the extent to which information is sought, evaluated, and weighed in a decision process on the part of a consumer depends greatly on the extent to which the consumer is involved in the process. The complexity of the decision process varies with consumer involvement. If the consumer is relatively uninvolved, the search for information is likely to be limited, with little evaluation of alternatives. With such routine decision making, there is little opportunity for the formation of attitudes toward the product—until after purchase or consumption. Involvement is thought to be a result of the personality of the consumer, the nature of the product, and characteristics of the situation. Consumers who are more self-confident, younger, educated, or less experienced with the product category tend to engage in a more extensive information search. Consumers show greater information search for products with higher perceived financial, performance, social, or physical risk. Situational factors such as amount of time, quantity of product, or store alternatives also help determine the extent of information search.

The consumer's decision to buy involves two major components: what brand to buy and where to purchase it. The decision process used to purchase a product can be classified as either compensatory or noncompensatory. With a compensatory rule, only the overall evaluation is important. This means that high evaluations on one dimension can compensate for low ones on another. In contrast, a noncompensatory rule results in a product being eliminated if it falls below an acceptable level on one dimension, regardless of its standing on other dimensions.

The decision process has been monitored by a variety of techniques to learn whether compensatory or noncompensatory rules are being used. Another objective of studying the consumer-choice process is to learn how information is selected and used. Researchers have used eye-movement monitors, computerized information displays, and information boards to track the order and extent of information search.

Research by cognitive psychologists has shown that people tend to compare products on a single attribute rather than forming overall evaluations of each product and then making comparisons. This points to the value of information displays such as unit pricing or tables of nutritional requirements met by a product, which facilitate comparisons across products.

Applications

The prediction of behavior on the basis of attitudes has always been very complex. While it is true that people who have a positive attitude toward a product buy more of it than those who do not, other hypothesized links between attitudes and behavior simply do not hold. For example, life-style surveys have shown an increasing trend toward the belief that meal preparation should take as little time as possible. Yet during the same time period in which the study was conducted, sales of frozen pizza remained constant, and sales of frozen dinners fell.

Along similar lines, attitudes toward advertisements do not necessarily correlate with attitudes toward the product being advertised, let alone with purchase of the product. Even a specific attitude may fail to predict behavior toward an object. To demonstrate this, one might ask a friend to describe his or her attitude toward a Mercedes (or Porsche) and toward a Ford Pinto. The attitude of many people toward the former is far more favorable, but in reality they are less likely to purchase their preferred make of automobile.

One reason the theory of reasoned action has been successful is that it does not attempt to link attitudes to behaviors in general. Because of this, the prediction of specific behaviors toward "attitude objects" can be achieved. This theory can also be applied to changing specific behaviors. For example, if a person does not intend to engage in a safety practice, a traditional attitude-change approach would attempt to persuade the person of the value of the practice. Fishbein and Azjen's theory, however, suggests an alternative: persuading the person of the existence of subjective norms supporting the safety practice. This approach is not suggested by any other theoretical perspective on consumer behavior.

The debates about information and consumer decision making have had an impact on public policy and regulatory activities. illiam Wilkie identifies three concerns in the policy arena, all of them relating to the type, amount, and form of information that should be provided to consumers. First is the goal of providing consumers with complete information. Only by being fully informed can people spend their time, money, and effort in their best interest. Yet complete information may be impossible, and, even if it is available, the consumer may be unwilling or unable to process it all in decision making.

The second objective of public policy is to provide information that is "choice-neutral." Since the marketing community presents information that will favor particular brands, public policy provides balance with an emphasis on objective information. The last, and most difficult, public policy application concerns trade-offs between the freedom of marketers to control information dissemination and the costs and benefits of information to consumers. This is likely to remain a politically controversial matter.

An understanding of the decision rules used by consumers can be applied effectively in marketing. The use of noncompensatory rules is encouraged by product ratings of critical factors such as safety. It is easy to eliminate those brands that do not possess a certain rating or "seal of approval" from further consideration. Another application of this principle can be seen in attempts to create the belief that consideration of a particular attribute should dominate the choice process. By stressing price and only price, the marketer is in effect telling the consumer that no other attributes are relevant. No matter how competing brands may be evaluated on other attributes, they cannot compensate for inferior positions on the price dimension.

A good illustration of strategies to promote noncompensatory decision rules can be seen in the environmental movement. By focusing consumers on the environmental impact of their purchases, marketers prevent other attributes from being taken into consideration. Sometimes this can lead to the purchase of one product over another, as in the case of cloth rather than disposable diapers; or one brand of the product may be chosen over alternatives, as in the case of nonchlorine rather than chlorine bleach or a high- rather than a low-energy-efficient appliance. In the most extreme cases, noncompensatory rules in decision making can lead to "negative purchases": If all brands of tuna fish are obtained through techniques that kill dolphins, no brand is bought. Similarly, consumption of products with possible health hazards falls if a single dimension dominates information search and noncompensatory rules are used by consumers. No price reduction or rebate will induce one to purchase any brand if the product itself is judged unacceptable along the health dimension. One way of inhibiting such negative purchase decisions is to create ambiguity about the actual health hazards of the product or about information on product risks. With an overload of information that is difficult to process effectively, the consumer may become more reluctant to deem a product below the threshold necessary for purchase.

Context

There have historically been three independent forces stimulating research on consumer behavior. One arises from the desire to influence consumers. Consumer decision-making research combines with advertising and marketing to create desires for products, preferences for brands, and patterns of consumption. An opposing force encouraging consumer behavior research is the desire to protect consumers; organizations committed to consumer rights have identified their own agendas for research on the decision-making processes of consumers. The third group interested in consumer behavior consists of scientists with a fundamental interest in human behavior as it occurs in the marketplace. The field on the whole is neutral with respect to the interests of consumers or those who wish to influence them.

The strong emphasis on decision making in the field of consumer psychology has, as in many areas in psychology, been encouraged by the cognitive revolution. Although researchers continue to recognize that people respond to affective and emotional appeals, they have become more attuned to consumers' conscious processing of information. This trend can be expected to continue. The need to gather and evaluate information will grow as products and services become more diverse and complex. Another reason that consumer psychology will continue to place an emphasis on decision making is consumers' demand for more complete and accurate information about goods and services.

One of the limitations of the cognitive theories of consumer decision making is that they typically fail to take into account differences between individuals and groups of people. Consumer psychology is likely to become increasingly concerned with market segmentation as the ability to understand the diverse needs of various groups develops. Further specialization of research on the aged and children as consumers is also predictable. Among emerging global trends is an increased interest in marketing to women around the world.

Bibliography

Bettman, James R. *An Information Processing Theory of Consumer Choice.* Reading, Mass.: Addison-Wesley, 1979. A scholarly presentation of an integrated theory of consumer choice from an information-processing perspective. Numerous propositions are formulated, with frequent reference to empirical research.

Fenwick, Ian, and John A. Quelch, eds. *Consumer Behavior for Marketing Managers.* Boston: Allyn & Bacon, 1984. Reviews of the consumer-behavior research literature on issues concerning current applications. Of special interest is chapter 3, on the consumer decision-making process. Topics covered are the information overload controversy, low-involvement consumer information processing, and the view that consumer behavior involves the making of decisions.

Jacoby, Jacob, and Jerry C. Olson, eds. *Perceived Quality: How Consumers View Stores and Merchandise.* Lexington, Mass.: Lexington Books, 1985. A set of articles contributed by various specialists in perceptions of quality. Presents the views of retailers, manufacturers, and consumers; discusses regulatory and economic perspectives on quality.

McNeal, James U. *Children as Consumers.* Lexington, Mass.: Lexington Books, 1986. A multifaceted approach to the entire arena of children and consumption. Addresses issues of education and public policy. Reports interviews with children as well as summaries of data from research studies on children. Informative, thoughtful, and readable.

Wilkie, William L. *Consumer Behavior.* New York: John Wiley & Sons, 1986. A textbook stressing concepts, findings, and applications in the broad area of consumer psychology. Balanced and informative treatment of research, theory, and practice. Good coverage of the cognitive aspects of consumer behavior, including learning, information processing, perception, and decision making.

Janet A. Sniezek

Cross-References

Attitude-Behavior Consistency, 320; Attitude Formation and Change, 326; Cognitive Maps, 566; Field Experimentation, 1031; Group Decision Making, 1114; Motivation: Cognitive Theories, 1606; Survey Research: Questionnaires and Interviews, 2507.

THE CONTACT HYPOTHESIS

Type of psychology: Social psychology
Fields of study: Interpersonal relations; prejudice and discrimination; social
    perception and cognition

According to the contact hypothesis, intergroup bias (prejudice, stereotypes, and discrimination) arises, in part, from ignorance and misinformation; favorable face-to-face contact between members of different groups will foster more accurate perceptions, greater intergroup attraction, and less bias directed at one another.

Principal terms

DISCRIMINATION: behavior (usually unfavorable) toward persons that is
    based on their group membership rather than on their individual
    personalities
IN-GROUP: a social group to which a person belongs or with which
    a person identifies, thereby forming part of the self-concept
INTERGROUP BIAS: unfavorable reactions to members of another group
    that can occur as any combination of discrimination, prejudice, or
    stereotypes
OUT-GROUP: a social group to which a person does not belong and with
    which he or she does not identify
PREJUDICE: liking or disliking of persons based on their category or
    group membership rather than on their individual personalities
STEREOTYPE: a belief about members of a social group that applies
    to all or most members of that category
SUPERORDINATE GOAL: an outcome desired by members of different
    groups that can be attained only through cooperation between the
    groups

Overview

Intergroup bias manifests itself in three interrelated yet distinctive manners: feelings and attitudes (prejudice), generalized beliefs (stereotypes), and behaviors that favor one group over another (discrimination). In general, persons who are biased against members of another social group dislike those persons (prejudice), believe that they possess unpleasant or negative characteristics (stereotypes), and actively avoid or denigrate them (discrimination). Social psychologists have studied how intergroup bias arises and what tactics may be employed to ameliorate bias. They have observed that persons generally feel a sense of self-investment and identification with groups to which they belong (in-groups) rather than with groups to which they do not belong (out-groups). Consequently, they may associate with fellow in-group members more so than with out-group members and obtain a more accurate and complete knowledge of the in-group than of the out-group.

Ignorance of the out-group may contribute to intergroup bias, as persons are motivated to maintain a positive view of themselves by assuming the best about their in-groups and the worst about out-groups. Accurate information about an out-group that disconfirms negative expectations (prejudice and stereotypes) should improve intergroup relations, and accurate information may be obtained through face-to-face contact with members of the disliked out-group.

The contact hypothesis refers to the proposition that bias between groups can be reduced by bringing members of different groups together for face-to-face interaction. The contact hypothesis rests on two assumptions. First, intergroup bias is frequently based on ignorance or misinformation. Contact between group members provides the opportunity to disconfirm their erroneous beliefs and feelings about the groups. Second, the contact experience(s) will be sufficiently positive or pleasant to preclude exacerbation of existing bias.

Gordon Allport, in *The Nature of Prejudice* (1954), most clearly articulated the contact hypothesis when he argued that bringing members of disliked groups together can have a beneficial impact on intergroup relations, provided that the contact occurred under what have been termed favorable conditions. These include cooperative interaction, common goals, support from authorities or institutions outside the groups, and some degree of personal (as opposed to formal or superficial) contact. Research has generally supported these criteria as important in fostering contact that reduces bias between groups. Cooperation between groups produces more pleasant intergroup experiences than competition in which one group's gain comes at the expense of the other. Pursuit of a common goal, in particular a superordinate goal, encourages cooperation. Support for the contact from authorities and institutions helps to maintain it. Personal contact between members of the different groups can foster interpersonal attachments and reveal similarities and common interests between members of the different groups. Following Allport, the most influential voices in the area of the contact hypothesis have been Stuart Cook, Thomas Pettigrew, and Yehudi Amir.

Much of Stuart Cook's influential research has focused on the benefits of intimate contact with out-group members. Using laboratory groups engaged in cooperative tasks, Cook has found that contact is most effective in disconfirming stereotypes when it has "acquaintance potential." In other words, contact is most helpful when the different groups interact individually and get to know one another as unique persons, rather than as representatives of their groups. Unfortunately, Cook's research also indicates that while intergroup contact can improve relations among those involved in the contact experience, generalization of the positive experience to the out-group as a whole or to specific out-group members not present during the contact experience is often problematic.

Thomas Pettigrew has argued that to be successful, favorable contact with an out-group member must be interpreted positively by the parties. The attributions that group members make about the contact experience will determine the success of the experience. Thus, favorable contact with an out-group member may be ineffective if that experience is discounted as an atypical event, one that does not reflect the true intentions or dispositions of the out-group members. For the experience to be most effective, out-group members who behave positively in a contact setting must be seen as having behaved voluntarily (not forced to act pleasantly) and as being typical of others in their group (not exceptions to the rule). Laboratory research has found support for this conclusion. For example, in an experiment reported by David Wilder, subjects had a favorable contact experience with a member of a disliked out-group. The contact person was presented as either a typical or atypical member of the out-group. Results showed that the contact experience was effective in reducing intergroup bias when the contact person was seen as typical or representative of the out-group.

Proponents of social identity theory have raised some criticisms of the contact hypothesis. Factors that maximize the success of intergroup contact in promoting positive relations among persons in the contact setting may yield the least generalization to the out-group as a whole. As already mentioned, contact that involves positive, intimate experiences with out-group members is likely to create friendship bonds and reveal interindividual similarities that cut across the different group memberships, thereby diminishing the importance of the group categories for one's self-identity in that setting. Yet the contact person(s) may be perceived to be less representative of others in their group, with the result that generalization of the favorable contact experience to the out-group as a whole should suffer. For contact to be most effective, therefore, the contact persons must be judged to be very typical of their respective groups while behaving in an unexpectedly positive manner.

A related difficulty with the contact hypothesis is the assumption that contact will be effective to the extent that it reduces assumed differences between the groups. Yet reducing differences between groups may threaten each group's sense of uniqueness and identity. Social identity researchers argue that contact will be most successful if it focuses on diminishing negative beliefs and feelings between the groups, yet still perpetuates some distinctive differences between the groups. Ideally, then, the contact experience should not strive to eliminate all differences between the groups, but rather should reduce unfavorable and inaccurate beliefs while preserving those differences that cast both groups in a positive light.

Finally, the success of contact depends in part on the measurements used to assess its impact. While contact may foster a change in beliefs or feelings about an out-group, it may not always yield a change in behavior. For example, one may feel more positively toward a group following a favorable contact experience but may be reluctant to act differently toward members of that group because of social pressure from prejudiced members of one's own group. On the other hand, one may feel obligated to behave positively toward members of an out-group who have treated one well but may still harbor prejudice and unfavorable stereotypes of the out-group as a whole. For contact to be effective in producing the broadest change in intergroup bias, it not only must be favorable (involve cooperation in pursuit of common goals) but also should occur frequently across many situations and with many members of the out-group.

The contact hypothesis is best considered as a working hypothesis based largely on consistency and reward theories of social interaction. People prefer rewarding experiences and strive to maintain consistency among their beliefs and behaviors. To the extent that biased beliefs and attitudes are based on misconceptions or ignorance, favorable contact with members of the disliked out-group will generate positive feelings and will disconfirm negative stereotypes. The inconsistency between the favorable contact experience and prior beliefs about the out-groups should weaken those beliefs, provided that the contact experience cannot be dismissed as an "exception to the rule."

Applications

Several good examples of the contact hypothesis can be found in a variety of settings, ranging from small-scale experiments conducted by social psychologists to social policies implemented at the national level. Two examples will be discussed in some detail, because they reflect the strengths and weaknesses of the contact hypothesis in both research and naturalistic settings.

In a classic set of field experiments, Muzafer Sherif and his colleagues created hostility between groups of boys at summer camps and then employed intergroup contact as a means of reducing the hostility. In their experiments, the boys were divided into groups at the beginning of the camp session. The boys mainly associated with their fellow in-group members (they ate, played, and slept with one another). Initially, intergroup contact was designed to encourage intergroup hostility. For example, groups played against one another in competitive games. The researchers added fuel to the fire by staging pranks and other inconveniences for which each group blamed the others. After the groups had developed a severe dislike of one another, the experimenters, posing as camp counselors, attempted to reduce the intergroup hostility. They found that merely bringing the groups together to engage in pleasant activities, such as a party, was insufficient, as the group members hurled insults at one another upon sight. Sherif and his colleagues reported that intergroup contact was effective only when the groups interacted in pursuit of a "superordinate goal"— an objective desired by all groups but unattainable without mutual cooperation. After a series of cooperative encounters in pursuit of superordinate goals, they reported that intergroup barriers weakened and the boys were as likely to choose members of other groups as friends as members of their own group. The contact experiences were effective because they served both to create pleasant events (attainment of shared goals) and to dispel unpleasant assumptions about out-group members.

On a larger scale, the contact hypothesis has served as an argument for school and residential racial desegregation within the United States. The argument has been that part of the prejudice between blacks and whites can be attributed to the ignorance and misinformation that is the legacy of segregation. In American society, interracial contact experiences have usually been characterized by unequal status, with whites occupying a superior role (employer or landowner). Consequently, much of the contact has not met the equal-status, cooperative, and intimate conditions that maximize the probability that contact will dispel negative stereotypes and modify prejudice. Following the 1954 United States Supreme Court ruling that outlawed racial segregation in public schools, researchers have looked at the schools as a testing ground for the contact hypothesis.

Evidence indicates that contact is effective only under the limited conditions already discussed. Merely throwing black and white students together in classrooms is not sufficient to reduce intergroup bias. Indeed, forced contact can exacerbate bias when community and institutional support is absent. Moreover, contact situations may fail because persons feel uncomfortable in the unfamiliar position of interacting with the out-group, preferring to seek out fellow in-group members. At many integrated American colleges, a visitor can see how blacks mainly interact with blacks and whites with whites.

Interracial contact in the classroom appears to work best when it is patterned after the techniques advocated by Allport and used by Sherif in his summer-camp studies. Elliot Aronson has created a "jigsaw" procedure for classroom contact that consists of forming black and white children into integrated work groups. In these groups, all members are peers with equal status. The groups are given tasks to solve as a team so that cooperation is reinforced, rather than the interpersonal competition that characterizes many traditional classrooms. Under these circumstances, where contact is of equal status, is cooperative in pursuit of a common goal, and is sanctioned by authorities (a teacher), the contact experience produces a marked improvement in interracial relations.

Context

In social psychology, the contact hypothesis most clearly dates from the writings of Gordon Allport. Along with other social psychologists who had conducted research during World War II, he was struck both by the extent to which prejudice was based on ignorance and misinformation and by the lack of direct contact between social groups. Combining these observations, it seemed reasonable to infer that intergroup bias might be reduced by encouraging face-to-face contact between members of the groups. Intellectually, then, the contact hypothesis has grown from the assumption that ignorance and secondhand information encourage erroneous inferences, while direct experience with objects (in this case, members of an out-group) generates more accurate beliefs and attitudes about them. Furthermore, it has been implicitly assumed that the contact experiences will generate more positive than negative experiences and reveal more similarities and common values than dissimilarities. A large body of social psychological research has shown that similarity promotes attraction. People like those who share their beliefs and values, unless they are in a competitive, winner-take-all relationship with them.

In addition, the contact hypothesis can be related to another fundamental psychological principle, that of affective association or conditioning. Pleasant experiences with out-group members should generate positive affect, which becomes associated with those out-group members. After multiple favorable interactions, the presence

of out-group members should elicit a favorable response to them. By stimulus generalization, that positive response should spread to other members of the out-group as
well.

The prediction that favorable contact with members of an out-group will generalize to the out-group as a whole can also be derived from work on the principle of
cognitive consistency among cognitions. The argument goes as follows: If one likes
X, and X is associated with Y, then one should like Y as well. Balance or consistency among one's cognitions (thoughts, beliefs, and attitudes) is satisfying inasmuch as it provides greater certainty in one's dealings with the world. When one
detects inconsistency, one strives to restore consistency either by changing one or
more of the inconsistent cognitions or by generating an explanation that resolves the
contradiction. Therefore, if contact with members of an out-group causes one to like
them, then one should also feel more positively toward others with whom those
persons are associated, including other members of that out-group.

Bibliography

Allport, Gordon Willard. *The Nature of Prejudice.* Cambridge, Mass.: Addison-
Wesley, 1954. The classic social psychological study of prejudice. While the examples and terminology are dated, the theoretical insights and engaging writing are
as fresh as ever. Reviews early conceptualization and research on the contact hypothesis as well as theories of how prejudice develops and what techniques can be
used to reduce it. Accessible to the novice and expert alike.

Amir, Yehudi. "The Role of Intergroup Contact in Change of Prejudice and Ethnic
Relations." In *Towards the Elimination of Racism*, edited by Phyllis A. Katz. New
York: Pergamon Press, 1976. Comprehensive review of empirical studies examining the contact hypothesis along with a complete bibliography. Covers research
from the 1940's through the early 1970's.

Aronson, Elliot, et al. *The Jigsaw Classroom.* Beverly Hills, Calif.: Sage Publications, 1978. Presents the rationale of and reviews the findings from a research
program designed to create favorable interethnic contact in classroom settings.
Students are assigned to equal-status mixed racial groups to work cooperatively
on projects.

Hewstone, Miles, and Rupert Brown, eds. *Contact and Conflict in Intergroup Encounters.* Oxford, England: Basil Blackwell, 1986. A collection of chapters by leading researchers in the field of intergroup relations. Several chapters examine the
success of the contact hypothesis with the following conflicts: Arabs/Jews, blacks/
whites in U.S. schools, Catholics/Protestants in Northern Ireland, English speakers/
French speakers in Quebec, and blacks/whites in South Africa. Other chapters
evaluate the success of the contact hypothesis as well as its limitations.

Miller, Norman, and Marilynn B. Brewer, eds. *Groups in Contact: The Psychology
of Desegregation.* Orlando, Fla.: Academic Press, 1984. Chapters assess the consequences of intergroup contact in a variety of settings. Several chapters look at
issues of multiethnic relations in the United States such as the impact of school

desegregation as a means of fostering favorable interracial contact. Like the Hewstone and Brown book, this consists of contributions by active researchers discussing their areas of expertise.

Sherif, Muzafer. *Group Conflict and Cooperation.* London: Routledge & Kegan Paul, 1967. Well-written analysis of how intergroup conflict arises and the role of cooperation in reducing conflict. Includes a good description of his classic field experiments using children at summer camps in which intergroup conflict is created and resolved through contact in pursuit of superordinate goals.

David A. Wilder

Cross-References

Attitude-Behavior Consistency, 320; Attitude Formation and Change, 326; Attraction Theories, 332; Cooperative Learning, 695; Theories of Intergroup Relations, 1356; Effects of Prejudice, 1848; Reduction of Prejudice, 1855; Racism, 2037; Social Identity Theory, 2297; Social Perception: Others, 2311.

CONVERSION, HYPOCHONDRIASIS, SOMATIZATION, AND SOMATOFORM PAIN

Type of psychology: Psychopathology
Fields of study: Anxiety disorders; models of abnormality

Conversion, hypochondriasis, somatization, and somatoform pain are a group of mental disorders that are typically referred to as the somatoform disorders. The primary feature of these disorders, as their name suggests, is that psychological conflicts take on a somatic, or physical, form.

Principal terms
> CATHARTIC METHOD: a therapeutic procedure in which the patient recalls an earlier emotional trauma in order to express the accompanying tension and unhappiness in a useful manner
> CONVERSION DISORDER: the loss or impairment of some motor or sensory function when no organic illness is present
> HYPOCHONDRIASIS: a mental disorder in which the person is unrealistically preoccupied with the fear of disease and worries excessively about his or her health
> SOMATIZATION DISORDER: a mental syndrome in which the person chronically has a number of vague but dramatic medical complaints, which apparently have no physical cause
> SOMATOFORM DISORDERS: a group of mental disorders in which the person has physical complaints or symptoms that appear to be caused by psychological rather than physical factors
> SOMATOFORM PAIN: the experience of sensory pain which appears to be caused by psychological rather than physical factors

Overview

Conversion, hypochondriasis, somatization, and somatoform pain are thought by most mental health professionals, such as psychiatrists and clinical psychologists, to be the four major types of somatoform disorders. These disorders are typically studied together because they have an important similarity. With each of these disorders, a psychological conflict is expressed through a somatic, or physical, complaint.

The manifestation of a psychological conflict through a physical complaint is perhaps most apparent with conversion disorders. When an individual suffers from a conversion disorder, the psychological conflict results in some type of disability. While conversion disorders vary widely, some of the most common involve blindness, deafness, paralysis, and anesthesia (loss of sensation). In all these cases, medical examinations reveal that there is nothing wrong physiologically with the individual. The handicap stems from a psychological or emotional problem.

In many instances, the handicap is thought to develop because it gives the person an unconscious way of resolving his or her conflict. For example, an adult who is feeling powerful yet morally unacceptable feelings of anger and rage may wish to strike his or her young child. Rather than carry out this dreadful action, this person will suddenly develop a paralyzed arm. The unacceptable emotion impulse is then "converted" (thus the term "conversion") into a physical symptom. When this happens, individuals will sometimes seem strangely unconcerned about their new physical disabilities. They will have what is known by the French term *la belle indifference* (or "beautiful indifference"). While most people would be quite upset if they suddenly became blind or paralyzed, conversion patients will often be rather calm or nonchalant about their disability, because their symptom unconsciously protects them from their desire to act on an unacceptable impulse.

The situation is somewhat different for individuals with hypochondriasis or somatization disorder, since individuals with these syndromes generally do not experience a dramatic physical disability. Individuals with hypochondriasis or somatization disorder are troubled instead either by fear of illness or by complaints about being sick.

With hypochondriasis, the afflicted individual, who is typically referred to as a hypochondriac, often misinterprets ordinary physical symptoms as a sign of some extremely serious illness. For example, the hypochondriac with mild indigestion may think that he or she is having a heart attack. In a similar fashion, a mild headache may be interpreted as a brain tumor. Hypochondriacs are usually quite interested in medical information and will keep a wide array of medical specialists at their disposal. After a visit to the physician, the typical hypochondriac is relieved to learn that he or she does not suffer from some dreaded disease. When this person again experiences an everyday ache or pain, such as muscle soreness or indigestion, however, he or she will again mistakenly believe that he or she has come down with some terrible illness.

While the hypochondriac is typically afraid of having one particular disease, the individual with a somatization disorder will often have numerous medical complaints with no apparent physical cause. Somatization disorder is also sometimes known as Briquet syndrome, because a physician by that name described it in detail in 1859. The individual who develops a somatization disorder, or Briquet syndrome, is known as a somatizer. This person is not bothered by the fear of disease, but rather by the actual symptoms that he or she reports. This individual will generally describe numerous aches and pains in a vague and exaggerated manner. Like the hypochondriac, the somatizer will often seek out frequent, unnecessary medical treatment. The somatizer, however, will be a particularly difficult patient for the physician to handle. The somatizer will often present his or her physician with a long, vague, and confusing list of complaints. At times, it may seem as if the somatizer is actually developing new symptoms as he or she talks to the physician. The dramatic and disorganized manner in which these patients describe their problems, and their tendency to switch from one doctor to the next with great frequency, make somatizers some of the most frustrating patients that medical professionals are likely to encounter.

It will also be difficult for even the most capable of medical professionals to work effectively with an individual who is suffering from somatoform pain. The concept of somatoform pain is a relatively new diagnostic category, in which the individual experiences physical pain that is thought to be caused by emotional factors. Somatoform pain is similar to conversion disorder, except that the individual experiences pain rather than some type of disability or anesthesia. Since pain is a subjective sensory experience rather than an observable symptom, it is often quite difficult for physicians to determine whether pain is caused by psychological or physical factors. It is therefore very hard to diagnose somatoform pain with any certainty.

Applications

The somatoform disorders, like all psychiatric diagnoses, are worth studying only when they can contribute to an understanding of the experience of a troubled individual. In particular, the somatoform disorders are useful when they help show that while an individual may genuinely feel sick, or believe he or she has some physical illness, this is not always the case. There are times when a psychological conflict can manifest itself in a somatic form.

A classic example of this situation is a famous case of conversion disorder that was reported by Josef Breuer and Sigmund Freud in 1895. This case involved "Anna O.," a well-educated and extremely intelligent young Viennese woman who had rapidly become bedridden with a number of mysterious physical symptoms. By the time that Anna O. sought the assistance of Breuer, a prominent Austrian physician, her medical condition was quite serious. Both Anna O.'s right arm and her right leg were paralyzed, her sight and hearing were impaired, and she often had difficulty speaking. She also sometimes went into a rather dreamlike state, which she referred to as an "absence." During these periods of absence, Anna O. would mumble to herself and appear quite preoccupied with disturbing thoughts.

Anna O.'s symptoms were quite troubling to Breuer, since she did not appear to suffer from any particular physical ailment. To understand this young woman's condition, Breuer encouraged her to discuss her symptoms at length, and used hypnosis to explore the history of her illness. Over time, Breuer began to get Anna O. to talk more freely, until she eventually discussed some troubling past events. Breuer noticed that as she started to recall and discuss more details from her emotionally disturbing history, her physical symptoms began to go away.

Eventually, under hypnosis, Anna O. described what Breuer thought was the original trauma that had precipitated her conversion reaction. She indicated that she had been spending a considerable amount of time caring for her seriously ill father. After many days of patiently waiting at her father's bedside, Anna naturally grew somewhat resentful of the great burden that his illness had placed upon her. These feelings of resentment were morally unacceptable to Anna O., who also experienced genuine feelings of love and concern for her father. One day, she was feeling particularly tired as she sat at her father's bedside. She dropped off into what Breuer describes as a waking dream, with her right arm over the back of a chair. After she fell into this trancelike state, Anna O. saw a large black snake emerge from the wall and slither toward her sick father to bite him. She tried to push the snake away, but her right arm had gone to sleep. When Anna O. looked at her right hand, she found that her fingers had turned into little snakes with death's heads.

The next day, when Anna O. was walking outside, she saw a bent branch. This branch reminded her of her hallucination of the snake, and at once her right arm became rigidly extended. Over time, the paralysis in Anna O.'s right arm extended to her entire right side; other symptoms began to develop as well. Recalling her hallucination of the snake and the emotions that accompanied it seemed to produce a great improvement in her condition. Breuer hypothesized that Anna O. had converted her original trauma into a physical symptom, and was unable to recover until this traumatic memory was properly expressed and discussed. The way in which Breuer treated Anna O. eventually became known as the cathartic method.

Anna O.'s case and the development of the cathartic method eventually led to widespread interest in conversion disorders, as well as in the other types of somatoform disorders. Many mental health professionals began to suspect that all the somatoform disorders involved patients who were unconsciously converting unpleasant or unacceptable emotions into somatic complaints. The manner in which somatoform patients could misinterpret or misperceive their bodily sensations, however, remained rather mysterious. For example, how can an individual who has normal vision truly believe that he or she is blind? Research conducted by the team of Harold Sackheim, Johanna Nordlie, and Ruben Gur has suggested a possible answer to this question.

Sackheim and his colleagues studied conversion patients who believed they were blind. This form of blindness, known as hysterical blindness, can be quite debilitating. Patients who develop hysterical blindness are generally unable to perform their usual functions, and often report total loss of vision. But when the vision of these patients was tested in an empirical fashion, an interesting pattern of results emerged. On each trial of a special visual test there were two time intervals, each of which was bounded by the sounding of a buzzer. During each trial, a bright visual target was illuminated during one of the intervals. Hysterically blind subjects were asked to report whether the visual target was illuminated during the first or the second interval. If truly blind subjects were to attempt this task, they should be correct by chance approximately 50 percent of the time. Most hysterically blind subjects were correct only 20 to 30 percent of the time, as if they were deliberately trying to demonstrate poor vision. A smaller number of hysterically blind subjects were correct on almost every trial, suggesting that they were actually able to see the visual stimuli before them.

Sackheim and his colleagues have suggested that a two-state defensive reaction can explain these conflicting findings. First, the perceptual representations of visual stimuli are blocked from conscious awareness, so that subjects report that they are blind. Then, in the second part of the process, subjects continue to gain information from the perceptual representations of what they have seen. The performance of subjects on a visual task will then depend on whether the subjects feel they must deny access to the information that was gained during the second part of the visual process. If subjects believe that they must deny access to visual information, they will perform more poorly on a visual task than would be expected by chance. If subjects believe that they do not need to deny access to visual information, then they will perform like a normal subject on a visual task. In other words, according to Sackheim and his colleagues, hysterically blind patients base their responses on the consequences of their behavior.

The way in which hysterically blind patients can manipulate their ability to see has led many scholars to question whether these patients are being truthful. Sackheim, Nordlie, and Gur, however, report that there are patients with lesions in the visual cortex (a part of the brain which processes visual information) who report that they are blind. These patients believe that they cannot see, even though they have normal eyes and can respond accurately to visual stimuli. They believe they are blind because they have trouble processing visual information. It is thus possible that an individual can have normal eyesight, and still believe that he or she is blind. It may thus be the case that many somatoform patients truly and honestly believe that they have a physical symptom, even though they are actually quite healthy.

Context

The study of somatoform disorders is an important area of concern for both medical professionals and social scientists. The somatoform disorders are relatively common, and their great prevalence poses a serious problem for the medical establishment. A tremendous amount of professional energy and financial resources is expended in the needless medical treatment of somatoform patients, who really suffer from emotional rather than physical difficulties. For example, when Robert Woodruff, Donald Goodwin, and Samuel Guze compared fifty somatization patients with fifty normal control subjects in 1974, they found that the somatization patients had undergone major surgical procedures three times more frequently than had the normal controls. Since an effort was made to match the somatizing and control patients on the basis of their actual medical condition, one can assume that much of the surgery performed on the somatization patients was unnecessary.

On the other hand, there is also a considerable amount of evidence to indicate that many people who are genuinely ill are misdiagnosed with somatoform disorders. Charles Watson and Cheryl Buranen published a follow-up study of somatization patients in 1979 which found that 25 percent of the patients actually suffered from real physical disorders. It seems physicians who are unable to explain a patient's puzzling medical problems may be tempted to label the patient prematurely with a somatoform disorder. The diagnosis of a somatoform disorder needs to be made with great caution, to ensure that a genuine medical condition will not be overlooked. There is also a need for further research into the causes and nature of the somatoform disorders, so that they can be diagnosed in a more definitive fashion.

One hopes that further research will also shed light on the ways in which somatoform disorders can be treated. Most somatoform patients are truly in need of assistance, for while their physical illness may be imaginary, their pain and suffering are real. Unfortunately, at this time, it is often difficult for mental health professionals to treat somatoform patients effectively since these individuals tend to focus on their physical complaints rather than on their emotional problems. More research is needed on the treatment of somatoform patients so that they can overcome the psychological difficulties that plague them.

Bibliography

Bootzin, Richard R., and Joan Ross Acocella. *Abnormal Psychology: Current Perspectives.* 5th ed. New York: Random House, 1988. This textbook contains an excellent chapter on the somatoform disorders which describes relevant case studies and explains how different psychological theorists view the somatoform diagnoses. Discussion of hypochondriasis and conversion disorder is particularly informative. Clear, easy to read, and comprehensible to the high school or college student.

Breuer, Josef, and Sigmund Freud. *Studies in Hysteria.* Translated and edited by James Strachey, with the collaboration of Anna Freud. New York: Basic Books, 1982. In many ways, this landmark book, first published in 1895, was the genesis of contemporary psychotherapy. Describes the famous case of Anna O., as well as the histories of a number of other conversion patients. A challenging book, useful to the college student who has a serious interest in either conversion disorders or the history of psychology.

Jacob, Rolf G., and Samuel M. Turner. "Somatoform Disorders." In *Adult Psychopathology and Diagnosis*, edited by Samuel M. Turner and Michel Hersen. New York: John Wiley & Sons, 1984. Provides the reader with a scholarly overview of somatoform disorders. Relevant diagnostic issues are discussed, in conjunction with a thorough review of the major research studies that have been conducted on somatization disorder, hypochondriasis, and conversion disorder. This chapter is recommended for the college student who seeks a detailed and challenging discussion of somatoform disorders.

Sackheim, Harold A., Johanna W. Nordlie, and Ruben C. Gur. "A Model of Hysterical and Hypnotic Blindness: Cognition, Motivation, and Awareness." In *Journal of Abnormal Psychology* 88 (October, 1979): 474-489. Recommended for the college student or serious adult reader who is interested in learning about contemporary research on conversion disorders. In particular, research on hysterical blindness is described in a complete and detailed fashion. The authors attempt to explain why hysterically blind patients believe they have lost their vision, when in reality they are able to see.

Sarason, Irwin G., and Barbara R. Sarason. *Abnormal Psychology: The Problem of Maladaptive Behavior.* 5th ed. Englewood Cliffs, N.J.: Prentice-Hall, 1987. Includes a very readable chapter on the psychological factors which can produce physical symptoms. A well-organized overview of somatization disorders is enhanced with a number of lively examples. Recommended for the high school student, college student, or casual reader.

Waldinger, Robert J. *Psychiatry for Medical Students.* Washington, D.C.: American Psychiatric Press, 1984. An introductory clinical textbook designed for individuals (such as medical students) who are having their first encounters with emotionally disturbed patients. Contains a concise and informative section on the somatoform disorders which explains how to look for and recognize these syndromes.

Steven C. Abell

Cross-References

Abnormality: Psychodynamic Models, 74; Anxiety Disorders: Theoretical Explanations, 272; Health Psychology, 1139; Pain Management, 1734; Psychoanalytic Psychology and Personality: Sigmund Freud, 1912; Psychosomatic Disorders, 1975; Stress-Related Diseases, 2464.

COOPERATION, COMPETITION, AND NEGOTIATION

Type of psychology: Social psychology
Fields of study: Group processes; interpersonal relations

Cooperation, competition, and negotiation are social processes central to the functioning of a group. They influence the effectiveness of a group in making decisions, completing tasks, and resolving differences, and they have a major impact on interpersonal relationships among group members.

Principal terms

COMPETITIVE SOCIAL SITUATIONS: situations in which goal achievement by one group member hinders goal achievement by other group members

CONTRIENTLY INTERDEPENDENT GOALS: situations in which goal achievement by one group member facilitates goal achievement by other group members

PRINCIPLED NEGOTIATION: an alternative negotiation strategy identifying four basic elements to successful negotiation

PRISONER'S DILEMMA: a laboratory game used by psychologists to study the comparative strategies of cooperation and competition

SOCIAL TRAP: a situation in which, by mutually not cooperating, conflicting parties end up worse off than if they had cooperated

STRATEGIC NEGOTIATION: a reciprocal communication process where parties with conflicting interests can examine specific issues and make offers and counteroffers

Overview

The terms cooperation, competition, and negotiation are fairly common words used to describe frequent interpersonal experiences. Virtually everyone can immediately draw to mind experiences of each type. This discussion will focus primarily on dynamics within a group setting. Since a group is commonly defined by social scientists as two or more people exerting influence on one another, discussion of each term can be understood as describing a process among informal groups, such as friends, spouses, business partners, coworkers, and classmates, as well as more formally established groups, such as appointed or elected committees, boards of directors, faculty, and members of an organization.

When people cooperate with one another, it is assumed that members of the group have similar goals; when they compete with each other, it is assumed they have different (and often conflicting) goals. This distinction is illustrated in definitions offered by Morton Deutsch, a leading researcher in group processes. Deutsch suggested that in cooperative situations, goals are "contriently interdependent," which means simply that goal achievement by one group member facilitates goal achievement by other members. In competitive situations, goal achievement by one group member hinders goal achievement by other members. It is often under conditions of competition that the process of negotiation enters in. Cooperation and competition (with resulting negotiation) are central factors influencing group characteristics such as cohesiveness, effectiveness, and interpersonal relationships.

Researchers have been interested in studying behavior when long-term interests are served by cooperation but short-term interests are served by looking out for oneself. In fact, these dilemmas are frequently involved with issues threatening the future of society, such as waste recycling, pollution control, and the depletion of natural resources. The question left to answer is how one reconciles self-interest (for example, not spending money to fix the damaged pollution-control device on one's automobile) with societal well-being (the necessity of reducing pollutants).

Psychologists have used laboratory games to study such social dilemmas. Perhaps the most frequently used game is called the "prisoner's dilemma." In this game, a subject (here named John) is one of two criminal suspects who have been working in tandem. The two subjects are being questioned separately by a district attorney about a crime that has been committed; both are guilty. The DA, however, has only enough evidence to convict both of a lesser crime. The DA offers each suspect a chance to confess. If John confesses and his cohort does not, John will be granted immunity, and the DA will have enough evidence to convict his partner of the more serious offense. This is the best scenario for John but the worst for his partner. If the partner confesses and John does not, the partner is granted immunity and John receives the heavier sentence. This is the worst scenario for John but the best for his cohort. If neither confesses, each will receive a light sentence for the lesser crime; this is the second-best scenario for each individual but the best scenario for the overall partnership. Finally, if both confess, each will receive a moderate sentence for the lesser offense. This is the third-best scenario for each individual and is a bad option for the partnership.

It has been found that, in the prisoner's dilemma, most people will confess, although *not* confessing is the most cooperative approach with one's partner; confession is considering self-interest first, even at the expense of one's partner. If John adopts only an individualistic perspective and does not worry about the collective good, confessing is the better strategy; after all, if his partner does not confess, then he is free. If the partner does confess, John will get a moderate sentence rather than risking a severe sentence by not confessing.

There is, however, a catch in this situation: Both prisoners will think the same way; hence, both will receive a moderate sentence. If both had not confessed and, in a sense, cooperated with each other, both would receive a light sentence. By looking out for self-interest, both partners lose.

Variations of this dilemma have been developed around themes more relevant to the typical citizen, especially the college student (such as negotiation for bonus points in a course). Each variant of the game is structured so that each party is better off individually by not cooperating. Yet by *mutually* not cooperating, both parties end up worse off than if they had cooperated.

There are ways for persons or groups to avoid such "social traps." One approach is to employ strategic negotiation, a reciprocal communication process in which parties with conflicting interests can examine specific issues and make, as well as consider, offers and counteroffers. Negotiation involves the ability to communicate, which may not always be available in situations of conflict (including some of the laboratory games employed by psychologists).

Sometimes negotiation is viewed solely as a process of protecting self-interests. Some people, often called "hard bargainers," talk tough, even employing threatening tactics. The person who threatens to sue or claims that there is nothing to be negotiated would be an example of a hard bargainer. "Soft bargainers," on the other hand, are willing to bend, even to the point of sacrificing self-interests. Such individuals often believe that their "good faith" approach is a model for the other negotiator, thereby promoting reconciliation while still hoping for important concessions. In group settings, soft bargainers may be concerned about group cohesion and make concessions contrary to self-interest. The extent to which hard versus soft bargaining is effective is a complex matter, depending on many factors present in the negotiation process. Thus, it is neither easy nor necessarily accurate to claim one technique better than another.

Applications

Despite the hard-bargaining tone of the title *Getting to Yes: Negotiating Agreement Without Giving In* (1981), the authors, Roger Fisher and William Ury, drawing on research as part of the Harvard Negotiation Project (a project dealing with all levels of conflict resolution, ranging from marital relationships to global disputes), promote what they call "principled negotiation." Their approach identifies four basic elements to effective negotiation and problem solving. First, they recommend that negotiators separate the people from the problem. By focusing on the problem rather than the intentions or motives of the people involved, participants are more likely to see themselves as working together, attacking the problem rather than each other. Second, the authors recommend that negotiators focus on interests by identifying underlying issues rather than by negotiating specific positions. They claim that position-taking often obscures what the participants really want. Third, before trying to reach agreement, the negotiators should individually and collectively generate a variety of options, especially identifying options that may produce mutual gain. By adopting this strategy, the negotiation is transformed into a group problem-solving process. Finally, negotiators should insist that the eventual resolution be based on some objective criteria considered fair by both parties. The principled negotiator is thus neither necessarily hard nor soft, but is able to reach agreement without, as the title of the book says, giving in.

One of the key elements of Fisher and Ury's approach is the process of getting people to attack problems rather than each other, thus fostering a sense of cooperative teamwork. What is implied is that working cooperatively makes the task at hand more manageable and the negotiating process more enjoyable, with a more effective outcome resulting.

A series of studies conducted by Deutsch during the 1940's and 1950's generally supports these assertions. Small groups of five people met over a five-week period, some working in cooperative situations, others in competitive situations. Members of the cooperative groups, where all group members would be equally rewarded for a combined effort, indicated that they liked their group and individual members better, reacted more favorably to other members' contributions, and generally rated the overall experience higher than did members of competitive groups (in which group members were told that the amount and quality of their individual contributions to the task at hand would be rank-ordered).

More recent studies provide additional support demonstrating the superiority of cooperation. In one study, members of cooperative groups found the atmosphere more relaxing and felt greater freedom to contribute to the group process than did members of competitive groups. In general, it can be said without equivocation that interpersonal relationships are more positive in cooperative versus competitive group situations.

One might ask, however, whether cooperative groups are more effective in achieving goals or in making good decisions than are competitive groups. Results of several studies generally support, as expected, the notion that when group members coordinate their efforts, the outcome is more successful than when group members compete with one another. One study compared two groups of interviewers in a public employment agency. Interviewers in a cooperative atmosphere, in which interviewers worked together to place applicants in job settings, were more successful than interviewers in a more competitive atmosphere.

Is competition ever healthy in a group setting? Most of the research that stresses the advantages of a cooperative atmosphere has involved highly interdependent tasks. That is, in order to reach a goal, group members must rely on one another for success. Thus, it should not be surprising that teams in a sport that require considerable teamwork (for example, basketball or volleyball) should perform better when players get along with one another. For sports in which teamwork is less important (for example, cross-country track or skiing), however, a sense of harmony among team members may be less beneficial, especially if recognition is provided on an individual basis. Thus, although research has rarely documented advantages of a competitive atmosphere, there appear to be some conditions where a sense of competition among group members is not particularly disruptive. The key is whether the task requires a highly interdependent effort among group members.

Some surprising sex differences have been found with regard to individual cooperation and competition, especially in laboratory studies involving games such as the prisoner's dilemma. While the traditional sex-role stereotype for women is to be cooperative and accommodating in an attempt to maintain harmony, research seems to indicate that women sometimes demonstrate a more competitive nature than men. One explanation of this surprising finding is that women are more likely to make choices that are consistent with the interpersonal setting. If the interpersonal setting suggests competition (as it does in the prisoner's dilemma game), women compete at least as hard as men; if it suggests cooperation, women cooperate at least as much as men.

Context

Much of the work on cooperation and competition must be credited to Morton Deutsch, with his classic studies during the 1940's and 1950's. Deutsch's mentor was the respected social psychologist Kurt Lewin at the Massachusetts Institute of Technology. The relationship between Lewin and Deutsch was more than that of teacher and student. Lewin later founded the Commission on Community Interrelations. As a member of that commission, Deutsch was one of the first researchers to employ scientific methodology in studying societal effects of racially integrated housing. Undoubtedly, Lewin's work on leadership had a major impact on Deutsch. Just as Lewin's research suggested that leaders who facilitate a cooperative climate among group members in decision-making processes maximize group productivity and member satisfaction, Deutsch's research clearly stresses the superiority of a cooperative versus competitive intragroup atmosphere.

In the late 1950's, Muzafer Sherif also studied the comparative processes of competition and cooperation by creating such conditions in real-life settings. Sherif discovered that the social dynamics of preadolescent boys in a camp setting are very similar to patterns of group behavior among adults. Groups functioned well in a cooperative atmosphere, especially under conditions of intergroup competition. The most striking finding in Sherif's research was how the conflicting groups could overcome their differences when presented superordinate goals—that is, goals that were compelling for both groups but that could not be attained without the help of the other group.

Cooperation is not always easily attained. Much of the research discussed, particularly regarding negotiation, suggests that the unbridled pursuit of self-interest is detrimental to the collective good. This may help explain why history is replete with examples of military escalations between opposing countries and why mutual disarmament is so difficult. One-sided disarmament, of course, leaves that side vulnerable to exploitation, which, from that side's perspective, is the worst predicament in which to be.

Research conducted on group processes, including research on cooperation, competition, and negotiation, may help people further understand such important real-life issues as how a board of directors can most efficiently run a corporation or what atmosphere is most conducive to good decision-making—whether that decision is about a family vacation, a neighborhood plan to fight crime, or an international dispute. In an age of international tensions, interracial conflicts, labor-management disputes, and domestic friction, the study of group processes is crucial.

Bibliography

Duffy, Karen Grover, James W. Grosch, and Paul V. Olczak, eds. *Community Mediation: A Handbook for Practitioners and Researchers.* New York: Guilford, 1991.

Takes much relevant research and applies it to the topic of community mediation. As the title implies, it is meant for a wide audience, and it is scholarly but not overly technical. Easily readable by the college undergraduate.

Fisher, Roger, and William Ury. *Getting to Yes: Negotiating Agreement Without Giving In.* Boston: Houghton Mifflin, 1981. A very practical, short (160-page) paperback. This was a national bestseller for a good reason. The authors translate some high-powered research and communicate it in very understandable language; they make a reasonable case for "principled negotiation," though some of their suggestions and examples seem a bit unrealistic.

Jandt, Fred Edmund. *Win-Win Negotiating: Turning Conflict into Agreement.* New York: John Wiley & Sons, 1985. A very readable book designed for anyone involved in negotiation. Typical of popular books in that many bold claims are unsubstantiated, but the author has considerable experience as a consultant and seminar leader in conflict management and is a good writer. Highly readable at the high school level.

Pruitt, Dean G., and Jeffrey Z. Rubin. *Social Conflict: Escalation, Stalemate, and Settlement.* New York: Random House, 1986. Blends good scholarship with practical considerations, though the emphasis is much more on the former. Though not a lengthy book, the authors do a good job of reviewing the literature on conflict.

Rubin, Jeffrey Z., and Bert R. Brown. *The Social Psychology of Bargaining and Negotiation.* New York: Academic Press, 1975. As the title suggests, this book investigates social-psychological issues involved in the negotiation process. Designed for researchers, the book is nevertheless free of unnecessary jargon. The book's biggest drawback is its age, as much research has been conducted since the mid-1970's.

Peter C. Hill

Cross-References

Affiliation and Friendship, 142; Altruism, Cooperation, and Empathy, 228; Cooperative Learning, 695; Group Decision Making, 1114; Groups: Nature and Function, 1125; Theories of Intergroup Relations, 1356; Leadership, 1419; Parenting Styles, 1740; Social Identity Theory, 2297; Social Perception: Others, 2311.

COOPERATIVE LEARNING

Type of psychology: Social psychology
Fields of study: Group processes; prejudice and discrimination

Cooperative learning refers to a variety of ways that individuals work together to produce or obtain some defined goal. Research supports the effectiveness of cooperative learning strategies in the areas of achievement, positive interactions with others, and development of self-esteem.

Principal terms
DYAD: a pair of persons working together on a task
GROUP INVESTIGATION: a cooperative technique in which students do research to prepare a group presentation
LEARNING TOGETHER: a cooperative technique that emphasizes the development of social skills
STUDENT TEAMS-ACHIEVEMENT DIVISIONS (STAD): a cooperative technique that uses heterogeneous groups and group rewards
TASK SPECIALIZATION: the dividing up of responsibility among group members for separate aspects of the group activity
TEAMS-GAMES-TOURNAMENT (TGT): a cooperative technique that includes elements of competition

Overview

Cooperative learning involves working in small groups toward some desired end. Groups, in and of themselves, do not have to be cooperative. Group members may compete for benefits, or an individual group member may assume all the responsibility for a group task. Neither of these group situations is cooperative. In cooperative learning, individuals depend on one another to receive benefits. Cooperative learning methods can be contrasted with competitive methods, which have individuals work against one another to reach a goal, and individualistic methods, which encourage each person to work toward a goal without regard for the performance or behaviors of others.

Informal group activities such as sitting down and sharing ideas can be considered cooperative learning. Some psychologists believe that even simple cooperative interactions between individuals can be associated with enhanced cognitive and social development. Most of the research on cooperative learning, however, reflects a more formal, structured approach.

One of the first structured cooperative learning techniques, "jigsaw," was developed by social psychologist Elliot Aronson and his colleagues. Aronson envisioned an academic environment in which a heterogeneous mix of students could achieve success and learn to appreciate one another through equal-status contact. In jigsaw, students are placed in small groups that mix characteristics such as race, gender, and ability. The teacher assigns a common task, such as learning about Christopher Columbus, to the entire class. The assignment is broken down into subtopics. For example, the assignment on Columbus might include a review of Columbus' early life, information on his voyages, a description of life in and around America when Columbus set sail, and a review of Columbus' later life. Each student in a group assumes responsibility for one of the subtopics of the assignment. Students then meet with members from other groups who share the same subtopic. At this point, students have formed new, specialized groups in which individuals with the same information can help one another master the subtopic. Afterward, the members of the specialized groups return to their original groups to teach the material they have mastered and to learn the information on the other subtopics from other group members. Achievement is measured by testing students individually on all the information for the assignment. Jigsaw also includes extensive team-building and communication-training activities.

Although Aronson and his colleagues had high expectations for the cognitive and social benefits of jigsaw, reviews of the effects have been mixed. Cooperative learning methods that have emphasized group rewards over the individual rewards associated with jigsaw have shown more consistent benefits for learners. For example, Robert Slavin and his colleagues at The Johns Hopkins University have developed several successful group-reward cooperative learning methods including STAD, student teams-achievement divisions, and TGT, teams-games-tournament. In STAD, the teacher presents a lesson, and students study worksheets in small, heterogeneous groups. Afterward, students take individual quizzes. Group scores are computed based on how much each group member improves over previous performance; group scores are reported in a class newsletter. TGT differs by having group members compete against members of other teams with similar records of past performance; group scores are based on the competition.

Two techniques developed by other research teams, learning together and group investigation, also use group rewards. Learning together emphasizes the development of social skills such as trust, conflict resolution, and accurate communication. Students work together to complete a single piece of work and are rewarded for working cooperatively and for task performance. In group investigation, small groups of students choose topics from a unit the class is studying. Group members then choose a subtopic for each member to investigate. Like jigsaw, group investigation uses task specialization. Unlike jigsaw, in group investigation, group members work together to prepare a presentation on their work for the entire class and are rewarded for group work.

Taken together, the various cooperative learning methods illustrate that there are benefits to cooperative learning methods over traditional competitive or individualistic approaches to instruction. Cooperative learning is also credited with increasing positive social interactions. Researchers report greater interaction between members of different racial or ethnic groups, greater acceptance of mainstreamed students, and greater friendship among students. Teachers and students in cooperative classrooms report more positive attitudes toward school. Finally, students in cooperative learning studies often show increased levels of self-esteem.

Applications

Because of the clear relevance of cooperative learning techniques for the education of children, cooperative strategies have been investigated in a number of long-term school projects. A good example is the Riverside Cooperative Learning Project. One part of the project involved training student teachers in cooperative learning techniques and evaluating the effects of the training on their students. Elementary school student teachers were randomly assigned to either a traditional classroom structure, a STAD-structured classroom, or a TGT-structured classroom. STAD was considered the purest example of cooperative learning in the study because TGT contains a competitive element; in that group, members compete against members of other groups in order to gain points for their own group (team). Thus, TGT is more like a combination of cooperation and competition. TGT is still considered to be more of a cooperative method than the traditional classroom, which is oriented toward competitive and individualistic activities.

The gains that students made academically under the three classroom structures varied in the Riverside project based on the race of the students. African-American students made the greatest gains in the STAD classroom, the classroom considered to be the clearest example of cooperative learning. Students of European descent did best in the TGT (cooperative-competitive) structured classroom. Mexican-American students made the most gains in the traditional classroom. These results are important because they add support to the belief that some of the racial differences that occur in performance in schools may be related to culturally different preferences for one type of classroom structure over another.

In this study, the authors were surprised that the Mexican-American students did not do better in the cooperative classrooms, since studies on ethnic differences suggested that Mexican-American culture is oriented toward cooperation over competition. The Mexican-American children in the Riverside project, however, were third-generation Americans with little knowledge of Spanish. Before the study began, they tested like the European-American students in terms of cooperation; the African-American students, on the other hand, tested higher than the Mexican-American and the European-American students on cooperation. Knowing which classroom structure will be best for a student, then, is not as simple as determining the student's racial or ethnic heritage.

Classroom climate was more positive in the cooperative classrooms than in the traditional classroom, particularly for the Mexican-American and African-American students. Cooperativeness was higher among students in cooperative classrooms, and students in cooperative classes were more democratic in choosing friends. Schools that want to emphasize social change, then, might prefer cooperative learning methods. Yet while cooperative techniques seemed better overall, the Riverside project also demonstrated that a variety of classroom structures may be necessary in schools to optimize performance for a majority of students.

Cooperative learning methods have also been investigated in laboratory studies with adult learners. Such studies are important for understanding the extent of the effects of cooperative learning methods and for evaluating whether they might be useful with older students and with materials that might be found in work environments. If the effects of cooperative methods on achievement transfer to work environments, employers might begin to train people differently and increase job performance. If the effects of cooperative methods on social interactions transfer, employers might improve organizational climates and also enhance job performance. Since the work force is becoming more diversified, information on reactions to cooperative learning methods by different groups of people should be beneficial. A diversified environment also puts increased pressure on organizations to determine the best ways to get people to work together for increased productivity.

Preliminary studies on adults suggest that cooperative learning benefits can be obtained with dyads; individual accountability and external rewards may not be as critical as they are in the school setting, and personality differences and the type of material being learned may be more important.

Context

The topic of cooperation has been an important one for psychologists almost since the origins of psychology as a science in the late nineteenth century. John Dewey, a philosopher and educator who discussed the importance of cooperation in education, and Kurt Lewin, the psychologist who influenced the study of group dynamics in the 1940's, are both seminal figures in the study of cooperation. Most of the current research on structured cooperative methods, however, can be traced to studies in the 1970's. Some of those early researchers were particularly concerned with the changing demographic patterns in schools that made schools seem more heterogeneous than had been the case in the past. Civil rights legislation ordering desegregation contributed to changes in the makeup of some schools. Mainstreaming also added variety to the composition of classrooms. Around the same time, there was an increase in research on ethnicity that seemed to indicate that cultural differences between groups that considered themselves to be disenfranchised (for example, African Americans and Mexican Americans) and the European-American majority culture were not going to disappear. If anything, the nation was becoming more diverse, and the probability of intergroup conflict seemed even more likely if people did not learn to work together.

Some theoreticians also speculated that differences in achievement between different racial and ethnic groups might be related to clashes between cultural values and classroom structures. In essence, classroom structure might serve as a tool for discriminating against some potentially capable students. The traditional classroom atmosphere in the United States continues to be highly competitive and individualistic. Students compete for higher grades, often at the expense of others. Cooperation is for the most part discouraged, because teachers are asked to evaluate the work of the individual for grades. Yet the increasing ethnic diversity of the United States means that better understanding of ethnic groups and procedures that enhance learning for as many students as possible are important considerations for educators and employers. Since researchers and theoreticians of cooperative learning methods have addressed the cognitive, social, and personal effects of cooperative methods, they will be increasingly influential in a number of settings.

Bibliography

Aronson, Elliot, et al. *The Jigsaw Classroom.* Beverly Hills, Calif.: Sage, 1978. A classic in the field. Discusses the rationale for developing this cooperative learning method, explains the jigsaw technique in detail, and presents the research findings.

Johnson, David W., and Roger T. Johnson. *Learning Together and Alone.* Englewood Cliffs, N.J.: Prentice-Hall, 1987. Aimed primarily at teachers. Contrasts cooperative, competitive, and individualistic learning methods, and their appropriate uses.

Kagan, S., et al. "Classroom Structural Bias: Impact of Cooperative and Competitive Classroom Structures on Cooperative and Competitive Individuals and Groups." In *Learning to Cooperate, Cooperating to Learn*, edited by Robert E. Slavin et al. New York: Plenum Press, 1985. Only for those who want more information about the Riverside project. The project is described, and graphs are interpreted for the reader.

Slavin, Robert E. *Cooperative Learning: Theory and Research.* Englewood Cliffs, N.J.: Prentice-Hall, 1990. Reviews various cooperative learning methods, some in detail, and the cognitive, social, and personal benefits associated with cooperative learning.

_____. "Research on Cooperative Learning: Consensus and Controversy." *Educational Leadership* 47, no. 4 (1989/1990): 52-54. A very readable discussion of areas of agreement and disagreement in the field. Only one among a variety of articles in this issue by major theoreticians and teachers of cooperative learning methods.

Judith L. Gay

Cross-References

The Contact Hypothesis, 675; Cooperation, Competition, and Negotiation, 689; Educational Psychology, 855; Theories of Intergroup Relations, 1356; Learning: Concept, Expectancy, and Insight, 1431; Reduction of Prejudice, 1855.

COPING: SOCIAL SUPPORT

Type of psychology: Stress
Fields of study: Coping; group processes; stress and illness

Stress is a problem of modern society that everyone experiences at one time or another; people must develop ways to deal with stressful events, or they risk being overwhelmed by them. Social support, which means turning to other people for support in times of personal crises, is one of the most-often-used coping strategies.

Principal terms

COPING: action taken when faced with a stressful event in order to lessen the threat to oneself

RESOURCES: the internal (such as knowledge) and external (such as money or friends) things that a person can utilize to cope with a stressful event

SOCIAL COMPARISON: comparing attitudes, skills, and feelings with those of similar people in order to determine relative standing in a group

SOCIAL SUPPORT: resources provided by other people to enhance one's self-esteem and assist in coping with stress

STRESS: a state of tension felt in the presence of an object or a task that is perceived as presenting a challenge to one's safety or self-esteem

Overview

When there is a perceived discrepancy between environmental demands and one's ability to meet those demands, an individual is likely to feel stress. Stress has both psychological and physiological causes and effects. In order to continue to function in an adaptive way, everyone must learn to cope with stress. There are many ways to cope, varying from avoiding stress or denial of stress at one extreme to seeking and confronting the source of stress in an attempt to overcome it at the other extreme. One of the most-often-used approaches in coping with stress is social support, which can be used on its own or combined with other coping strategies.

Social support has many meanings. Sometimes it is defined simply as information that one receives from others. This information could come from a variety of sources—from family, friends, coworkers, or even the family's faithful dog. For social scientists, social support is sometimes defined as the possibility of human interactions, and it can be measured by indicators such as marital status. In that case, it may be assumed that an individual who is married receives more social support than does one who is not married. This is often incorrect, however; there are many supportive relationships outside marriage—the parent-child relationship, for example.

Sidney Cobb in 1976 indicated that social support should be viewed as the receipt of information that one is cared for, is valued, and belongs to a mutually supportive social network. Parent-child, and many other, relationships would thus be possible sources of social support. This multidimensional view of social support has gained acceptance. Research in the area of social support has found common themes related to the perception of outcomes of interactions between people. In this view, there are five major outcomes constituting social support: the perception of a positive emotion toward oneself from another; having another person agree with one's beliefs or feelings; encouragement by another person to express one's beliefs or feelings in a non-threatening environment; the receipt of needed goods or services; and confirmation that one does not have to face events alone, that others will be there when needed. Viewing social support in terms of the subjective perception of an interaction rather than as the opportunity to interact with another is a useful way to conceptualize social support.

The perception of social support serves an important function in maintaining a positive sense of well-being by enabling one to cope with and adapt to stress. It has been shown to have a positive effect on physical as well as on mental health. For example, the prognosis for an individual recovering from a heart attack or with a diagnosis of cancer is better for those with a good network of sources of social support.

There are different theories regarding the relationship between social support and stress. Some psychologists believe that social support has a buffering effect, while others believe that social support has a direct effect on stress. According to the buffering-effect model, social support is important when one is faced with a stressor because it comes between the individual and the source of stress, and thus it protects the individual from the negative effects of the stressor. In this case, social support acts as a safety net in much the same way as a safety net protects the trapeze artist from injury during a fall; unless there is a fall, the net does not serve any function. In contrast, the direct-effect model contends that social support is important regardless of the presence of a stressor. In this case, social support is seen as providing a generally positive effect on the individual which would incidentally provide the individual with resources that can be called into play when one is faced with stress. For example, experiencing positive interactions can boost one's self-esteem in general. The high self-esteem is incorporated into the individual's self-concept regardless of stress; however, when faced with stress, the self-esteem would then provide the individual with the confidence to engage in problem-solving techniques to overcome the stressor. There is evidence to support both suggested mechanisms for social support, and it is likely that social support has both a buffering and a direct effect.

Despite the evidence indicating that social support helps people cope with stress, some studies show a negative effect. It seems that there are different types of social support, and it is important to match the type of support provided to the type of support needed. Tangible support is the providing of material aid in the form of goods and services. This is often needed, but rarely given. One of the few instances in which it is offered is following a death in the family when friends and neighbors bring over casseroles so that the grieving family can eat nutritious meals. Long-term tangible support is more likely to come either from impersonal sources, such as community-supported welfare programs, or from the most intimate source, the immediate family. The intermediate social network, consisting of friends and neighbors, is not likely to provide long-term tangible support.

Informational support is offered more freely by sources at all levels. This form of support serves an educational function, providing information relevant to how to cope with a problem. An example of this would be telling people whom to call when they have no heat in their apartments. The third form of social support is emotional support, which comes from the more intimate sources, one's family and close friends. This form of support involves expressing positive feelings toward an individual, acknowledging that person's worth, and accepting his or her expressions of beliefs and feelings.

Applications

Social support is applied in a variety of settings, both informal and formal. Informal settings for social support include the sharing of one's problems with friends and family. For example, an advertising executive may be under pressure to put together a campaign for the company's biggest client, who is considering changing firms. Informational support may come from the executive's coworkers over lunch. She might explain to her coworkers the problems she is facing designing the program. The coworkers might have faced similar problems, and they could tell the executive what they did to cope with the problems when they were experiencing them. The coworkers might provide tangible support by volunteering their time to work together on the campaign. Emotional support is more likely to come from the executive's family when she describes her day over dinner. The family members need to convey their love and respect to the executive. In this case, they need to indicate that their regard for the person is not dependent on the success of any advertising account. It might be counterproductive for the spouse to express confidence in the executive's ability to develop a successful campaign; the executive may then feel under more pressure, because now she not only has to worry about keeping the account but also may worry about disillusioning the spouse and losing that important source of support. Members of social networks need to be careful that they provide the correct form of social support, because providing support which does not match the needs of the recipient may be harmful.

Social support is important not only in a work setting but in a personal setting as well. For example, a man who is trying to lose weight would benefit from emotional support from his family and friends who let him know that they care about him and support his decision to lose weight. Sometimes when dieting gets difficult, loved ones might be tempted to tell the dieter that they think he is fine just the way he is. That is not supportive of his decision to lose weight, however, and it works against his success. Informational support can be provided by giving the dieter information about ingredients and methods of preparation of meals. This kind of support can be provided by a variety of people; waiters are generally quite willing to discuss this subject with restaurant patrons to give the needed information for a wise choice from the menu. This kind of support is requested so often, in fact, that many restaurants now include such information on the menus themselves—an example of social support that is community based. Tangible support for weight loss can come from a diet or exercise buddy who embarks on a weight-loss program with the dieter; another example would be providing low-calorie meals for the dieter.

Both of the above examples of situations in which people need social support can also be used to illustrate support in a formal setting. The executive who is undergoing stress might seek professional help from a counselor. A counseling situation takes place in a supportive environment and is generally focused on emotional support; however, some therapy situations can also provide informational and tangible support. Behavior therapy can be a source of informational support, such as when the executive is given homework assignments to identify what specific behaviors or thoughts are triggers for her stress. A clear identification of the trigger will aid in setting up a program to combat the stress. Sometimes people take part in group therapy settings, where a counselor works with several clients at the same time. Participants in the session become a tight social network that provides emotional, informational, and sometimes even tangible support. In this case, the executive might practice her presentation for the group, and the other members' critique might include new ideas or techniques which can be used to solve her problem. Constructive criticism of a presentation is a service that could be considered a form of tangible support, as well as informational and emotional support.

A dieter can get support in a formal setting by joining an organized group such as Weight Watchers or Overeaters Anonymous. Losing weight alone is a difficult task, and many people find success only in a group setting. Emotional support comes from the fellow dieters who understand exactly what the dieter is experiencing and accept him as he is. In this case, everyone has the same problem, so the dieter does not feel that he does not fit into society. Informational support comes from the group leader, who helps set goals and explains what behaviors need to be modified to achieve those goals. It also comes from other group members, who share recipes and advice on how to combat challenges. Tangible support comes in the form of the low-calorie meals provided by some weight-control programs or by forming a bond with a group member who can become an exercise buddy. Social support from groups of people with a common problem has been found to be so helpful that the number of such support, or self-help, groups is growing enormously. These groups are being founded for people with a wide range of problems: rape victims, people with alcohol dependency, spouses of military personnel stationed in a war zone, parents of sudden infant death syndrome babies, and single parents. Formal social support groups, in a sense, act as the extended family that is so often absent in mobile modern society.

Context
Social support is best understood in the context of social comparison theory, first

presented by Leon Festinger in 1954. People have a need to be "correct," to do the right thing, and to behave in a socially appropriate manner. It is not always easy to determine the correct position to hold in different situations. For example, how does someone decide what to wear to a party? Often an individual will call a friend who is also going to the party and ask what the friend is planning to wear. A person tends to make decisions in ambiguous situations by looking around to see what other people are doing. In general, one feels comfortable when one is behaving, dressing, or thinking in a manner which is similar to those around one. A woman is likely to feel uncomfortable and "underdressed" if she wears a skirt and blouse to a party if everyone else is in a formal gown. A skirt and blouse are perfectly acceptable articles of clothing for a woman and are no less functional at a party than a formal gown would be. She may have worn that outfit to a social gathering previously and felt perfectly comfortable. When everyone else is dressed differently, however, she feels that she "sticks out like a sore thumb" and therefore is not dressed correctly. Correctness is determined by majority standards. People learn by the process of socialization to conform to those around them. Social comparison is the process by which people learn norms, or social expectations, in different settings.

In the process of learning norms, one also learns the social benefits of conformity: acceptance by others. When an individual expresses an idea or behavior which is consistent with the ideas or behaviors of others, then the social group is comfortable around that person and permits that person to join the group. If that person deviates from the group norm, then that person may be ostracized by the group. This is the basis of peer pressure, which people learn to apply at a young age.

When people turn to others for informational social support, they often are looking for guidance to help fit in with a social norm—to "do" or "think" the right thing. Emotional social support tells one that one is like others and that one is valued and accepted by others. Tangible social support tells one that one's needs are acceptable and that other people will perform behaviors similar to one's own behavior in order to meet those needs. The goal of both social comparison and social support is to validate oneself by ensuring that one does not deviate from social expectations.

In an interesting experiment designed to test the role of social comparison in emotional reactions, subjects were asked to wait until it was their turn to participate in an experiment; the experiment was explained to some subjects in a way designed to create apprehension. They were given the opportunity either to wait alone or to wait with others. Subjects who were made fearful tended to want to wait with others more than did subjects who were not made fearful. This demonstrated that fear creates a desire to affiliate. More important, however, subjects showed a preference to wait with others only if they were told that the others were waiting for the same experiment. Thus the saying "Misery loves company" can be revised to a more accurate depiction: "Misery loves miserable company." In this context, it is easy to understand the growth of support groups for specific problems. When facing a stressful situation, people need to be around others who can really understand what they are going through—in other words, other people with the same problem. There is strength in numbers.

Bibliography

Sarason, Barbara R., Irwin G. Sarason, and Gregory R. Pierce, eds. *Social Support: An Interactional View.* New York: John Wiley & Sons, 1990. The authors present a well-written, extensive reference tool examining social support from the perspective of personality processes. Results of research looking at individual differences in the impact of social interaction on stress are discussed.

Schaefer, C., J. C. Coyne, and R. S. Lazarus. "The Health-Related Functions of Social Support." *Journal of Behavioral Medicine* 4 (1981): 381-406. Describes the tangible, informational, and emotional categories of social support and the health-protective benefits to be reaped from their use. Useful in helping one understand the different forms of social support available.

Silver, R., and C. Wortman. "Coping with Undesirable Life Events." In *Human Helplessness,* edited by Judy Garber and Martin E. P. Seligman. New York: Academic Press, 1980. This chapter focuses on coping with stress and the resources available through interacting with other people. Social support is shown to be a multidimensional construct which is both productive and counterproductive in helping individuals cope with life events.

Suls, Jerry. "Social Support, Interpersonal Relations, and Health: Benefits and Liabilities." In *Social Psychology of Health and Illness,* edited by Glenn S. Sanders and Jerry Suls. Hillsdale, N.J.: Lawrence Erlbaum, 1982. An informative chapter that stresses the need to clarify what is meant by "social support" and suggests a more meaningful approach to understanding the concept. Presents research demonstrating both the benefits and problems arising from various forms of social support.

Vaux, Alan. *Social Support: Theory, Research, and Intervention.* New York: Praeger, 1988. This comprehensive book begins by helping the reader to conceptualize social support, then takes the reader from the theoretical level to the more practical levels of measurement, application, and outcomes. Despite limitations discussed in the book, this work shows the achievements to be made through the utilization of formal and informal social support networks.

Barbara A. Bremer

Cross-References

Coping Strategies: An Overview, 706; Coping with Cancer, 711; Health Psychology, 1139; Social Perception: Others, 2311; Adaptation to Stress, 2390; Stress: Cognitive Appraisals, 2404; The Concept of Stress, 2411; Effects of Stress, 2417; Stress-Related Diseases, 2464.

COPING STRATEGIES: AN OVERVIEW

Type of psychology: Stress
Field of study: Coping

When people are exposed to a stressful demand, they respond by coping; coping attempts either to reduce the demand, to reduce its effect, or to help one change the way one thinks about the demand. Coping can either help one in stressful situations or increase the kind and number of problems created by the demand.

Principal terms

COGNITIVE: any activity that involves thought, such as remembering, thinking, or problem solving
COPING: responses which are directed to dealing with demands upon an organism; these responses may either improve or reduce long-term functioning
PROGRESSIVE RELAXATION: a stress-management technique which involves intentionally tensing and relaxing each of the major muscles in the body until complete relaxation is achieved
STRESS RESPONSE: the body's response to a demand
STRESSOR: anything that produces a demand on an organism

Overview

Coping includes all the possible responses to stressors in one's environment. As a stressor makes demands on an organism and initiates a stress response, the organism initiates behaviors and thoughts which attempt to remove the stressor or to reinterpret its effects. Coping often reduces the negative effects of the stressor, but sometimes coping creates new and different problems.

Coping strategies may emphasize the physical, social, or psychological components of stress and the stress response. Coping strategies may attempt to eliminate or moderate the initial source of the stress reaction (stimulus-directed coping), reduce the magnitude of the stress response (response-directed coping), or change the way the stressor is perceived (cognitive coping).

The coping strategies directed toward the stressor itself in stimulus-directed coping may eliminate the cause of the problem. The physical changes which occur in response to stress are very much like pain in that they warn that something in the environment is unusual and is a potential threat. Taking action to eliminate the threat not only removes the present demand but also reduces the possibility of continued stress.

Several stress-management techniques are directed toward reducing the influence of the stressor itself. Improving problem-solving skills and knowledge about the problem increases understanding and improves access to solutions. Time-management techniques can also reduce stress by eliminating its source. Solving the most important problems first and improving the quality of time spent on tasks reduces stress by eliminating the problem sooner. Changes in the work environment can also reduce stress. Eliminating sources of stress in the workplace, improving communication between workers and management, allowing workers to have control over their jobs, using workers who are capable of doing the job, and rewarding workers for good job performance can all reduce job-related stress. Sometimes stress reduction involves changing jobs or eliminating the stress-producing activity or relationship. Even with good stimulus-directed coping skills, it is not always possible to eliminate the stressor itself.

Many of the techniques of stress management are directed toward reducing the stress response. The pattern of physiological arousal in a stress response feels uncomfortable to most people; moreover, the related physiological changes can increase one's chances of illness or injury. The stress response is often treated as a physical illness. Prescribed medication, such as tranquilizing drugs, may be provided to reduce the unpleasant symptoms of the stress response such as anxiety, muscle tension, and pain. Sometimes people medicate themselves, choosing alcohol or other nonprescription drugs to reduce the symptoms of the stress response. All these medications do reduce the effects of stress over the short term, but they also tend to create problems of their own. Medications can be habit forming and may continue to be used after the stressful situation is gone. They may promote an artificial contentment and limit the possibility of finding a permanent solution to the problem creating the stress. Tranquilizing medications also tend to produce sleepiness, slowed reaction time, poor coordination, and inhibitions in judgment. These effects may hinder work productivity and safety.

One physical approach to coping with stress involves increasing the level of exercise. Regular strenuous exercise has a wide range of benefits. It reduces tension in muscles, improves cardiac fitness, and improves the functioning of the central nervous system. Muscles, particularly those in the neck and back, tend to react to stress by becoming tight and rigid. This tightness then results in symptoms such as tension headaches and backaches. Exercise promotes cardiac fitness, which improves the strength of the heart and circulatory system and improves the resistance of the circulatory system to the demands of stressful events. Exercise also improves the ability to think clearly, as it improves circulation to the brain. Many traditional athletic activities can help reduce stress (although highly competitive events may add stressors of their own). Athletic activities can also have a psychological impact, as they provide social support and distraction from stressful situations.

The importance of social factors in coping with stress was first proposed by John Cassel in 1974. Friends and family can make it possible to cope more effectively with stressful situations. The freedom to express feelings and to gain insight from hearing the problem described from another perspective can improve understanding of the stressor. The opportunity to gain useful information about problem solving and access to economic or material support makes coping with stressful events and circumstances possible. The impact of social support is reflected in research which suggests that a woman with even one relationship with someone in whom she could confide is 90 percent less likely to suffer from depression than a woman with no close relationships. Family gatherings, recreation, and community activities help to form a social support network which is then available to provide listeners when one needs to talk, advice when one needs to listen, and the tools needed to accomplish the task of coping with stress.

Psychological coping strategies include techniques that change the way one thinks about the stressor or the stress response. Much of the stress response results from one's emotional reaction to events. Cognitive reappraisal and restructuring can help one to think of a stressful event as a positive challenge and can eliminate much of the arousal associated with stress. Imaging techniques are used to help the stressed individual see herself or himself as healthy and as successfully coping with the sources of stress.

Coping can also involve denying that the stressor exists or that it is a problem. Becoming emotionally detached can reduce the harmful effects of stress as physical arousal levels are prevented from increasing in the stressful situation, but this denial can also be harmful if it lasts for a long period of time or if it replaces an attempt to deal with the stressor. Denial of stressful events is seen by many theorists as a major contributor to mental and physical illness.

When considering the many possible approaches to coping with stress, it is important to remember that different individuals and different stressors can make one strategy more effective than another. Each individual will need to explore the options to find the most effective coping strategy.

Applications

Just as the stress response involves a general reaction of the body to a demand, many of the techniques used to cope with stress have an element in common. This common thread can be described as control. If one feels that one is in control of a situation, one is less likely to interpret it as threatening, and therefore stressful. If one learns to control one's thoughts about a stressor or to control one's physical reactions to the stressor, one is more likely to be successful at coping with stress.

Research on the effects of control has included animals and humans and has focused on many different types of control. For example, from what is known about stress, job stress should be related to physical illness, but this is not always found in the research literature. What has been found is that people with both high job demand and a lack of control over their work are more likely to have coronary heart disease.

Some of the earliest research on stress placed monkeys in a problem-solving situation. One monkey could prevent electric shocks from occurring by learning to solve a problem. A second monkey received a shock every time the first monkey did, but could do nothing to prevent the shocks from occurring. At autopsy, the second monkey, with less control over the situation, had more indications of stress-related physiological arousal.

One approach to stress that can give people a feeling of control is to teach them relaxation techniques; these range from meditation to progressive relaxation to bio-feedback techniques. One benefit of such techniques is that they reduce or eliminate the temptation to use medication to reduce stress responses. Progressive relaxation, one form of this training, involves tensing specific muscle groups for a brief period and then allowing that group of muscles to relax before continuing to the next. The tension both focuses attention on the muscle to be relaxed and fatigues the tensed muscle, making relaxation easier.

Biofeedback has been used successfully to reduce the physical tensions and result-ing pain often associated with the stress response. Biofeedback uses electronic in-struments to make physical changes more observable. Instrumentation which mea-sures physical changes in skin temperature, sweating, muscle tension, and blood pressure has been used to make people more aware of their bodies' functions. With training, the individual can learn to reduce the muscle tension which has been pro-ducing headaches or to regulate problems causing gastrointestinal activity.

Context

Stress has been recognized as contributing to mental and physical health and ill-ness, job satisfaction and dissatisfaction, and the ability to perform well in any set-ting. From Hans Selye's contributions concerning understanding the general nature of the physiological response to stressors to the research connecting the stress re-sponse to illness, stress has become a factor to be considered in a wide variety of life situations.

There have been two major approaches to the problem of coping with stress. One has involved the attempt to describe and define stress responses in the hope of deter-mining the causes and controlling factors. The second approach focuses on the con-trol the symptoms presented to doctors and therapists. Defining stress and the stress response includes not only Selye's physiological definition of the stress response but also cognitive factors such as locus of control. Julian Rotter proposed that behavior in and understanding of situations are determined by the perceived source of events. A person with an internal locus of control will feel that he or she is the determining factor in success or failure in life. The person with an external locus of control is more likely to place the responsibility on fate or luck and to feel that his or her action will not make much difference. These two interpretations of events have a number of implications for coping, as the coping strategy chosen may lead to a more effective or less effective solution to the stressful situation.

An external locus of control may lead to less active participation in coping and to more negative outcomes. An internal locus of control has been related to successful therapy and lower levels of depression, suggesting the use of effective coping strat-egies. Albert Bandura proposed a similar concept: self-efficacy. Individuals who are high in self-efficacy believe that they can change things by taking action. They are more likely to choose coping strategies which attempt to remove or reduce the influ-ence of the stressor rather than withdrawing or denying that the stressor exists and thereby failing to remove its influence.

Bibliography

Charlesworth, Edward A., and Ronald G. Nathan. *Stress Management: A Comprehensive Guide to Wellness.* New York: Atheneum, 1985. This book is easy to understand and provides a description of the stress response; it outlines many of the methods used to cope more successfully. Includes questionnaires to help one to assess one's current functioning as well as excellent and easy-to-follow instructions on relaxation. Cognitive techniques for stress reduction are also described. Sources for tapes and related materials are listed.

Goldberg, Philip. *Executive Health: How to Recognize Health Danger Signals and Manage Stress Successfully.* New York: Business Week, McGraw-Hill, 1978. This book puts stress management into a business context, both for the employee and for management. It provides a good general outline of the problem and suggests possible routes leading to solutions.

Goliszek, Andrew G. *Breaking the Stress Habit: A Modern Guide to One-Minute Stress Management.* Winston-Salem, N.C.: Carolina Press, 1987. This small but impressive book includes a detailed description of the stress response. Questionnaires are included which allow one to examine one's own problems; a wide variety of suggestions for the reduction of stress-related problems is included. Topics include job burnout, stress and aging, and time management, as well as tension-reduction techniques.

Powell, Trevor J., and Simon J. Enright. *Anxiety and Stress Management.* New York: Routledge, 1990. This book was written for therapists who must help people deal with anxiety and stress. It is clearly written and can be understood by the layperson. Includes an excellent description of anxiety as a response to stressors and gives the reader an idea of what a therapist might do to help someone suffering from severe problems with stress. Self-help techniques are also explained.

Shaffer, Martin. *Life After Stress.* New York: Plenum Press, 1982. This book is less detailed in its discussion of the stress response and self-assessment of stress levels. It provides relaxation instructions (including photographs) and suggestions for time management, managing work stress, nutrition, exercise, and improving communication and reducing stress in family relationships.

Susan J. Shapiro

Cross-References

Biofeedback and Relaxation, 416; Coping: Social Support, 700; Coping with Cancer, 711; Adaptation to Stress, 2390; Effects of Stress, 2417; Stress and Reappraisal, 2438; Stress Prediction and Control, 2458.

COPING WITH CANCER

Type of psychology: Stress
Fields of study: Coping; stress and illness

Cancer is many diseases, not one. Earlier diagnosis and improved treatment have changed the prognosis of many cancers from a death sentence to a chronic illness. Coping with cancer involves dealing with diagnosis, treatment, and survival. Positive attitudes, self-care, and the support of family, friends, and colleagues can make major differences in survival time and quality of life.

Principal terms

CANCER: a malignant new growth anywhere in the body in which the cells multiply out of the body's control

CHEMOTHERAPY: treatment involving pills or injections

CHRONIC ILLNESS: a long-term, as opposed to acute (or sudden), illness

METASTASIS: the transfer of disease from one part of the body to an unrelated part, often through the bloodstream or lymphatic system

RADIATION: treatment with X rays

RECURRENCE: the return of symptoms, after a period without overt illness

Overview

Cancer is the name given to a number of diseases; they vary in terms of location in the body, extent, duration, and severity. According to Susan Sontag, most people still react to cancer with more dread than nearly all other illnesses. Obituaries talk of "long illnesses," often shunning the word; problems such as drug abuse are metaphorically described as "cancers" of society. Learning that one has a disease that is too awful to mention or that is considered a synonym for social evils adds to the emotional burden of those patients newly diagnosed. Since most people only hear of cancer when there are serious problems, the old myth equating cancer with death is hard to dispel. Yet, with earlier diagnosis and greatly improved treatment, the majority of people with cancer survive for long periods. It is believed that there are now 6 million cancer survivors in the United States.

Coping with cancer involves living with the diagnosis, treatment, and survival. One of the most difficult tasks is sustaining a balance between continued awareness of the illness and being able to live each day as normally and fully as possible. All people, no matter what the state of their health, must learn both to live for the moment and to plan for the future—to hope for the best and a good, long life while planning for the worst, in terms of financial security and untimely death.

The initial response when someone learns of cancer is a combination of disbelief, anger, and despair: "Why me? Why now?" Some people become resigned to their fate and delay or resist treatment, virtually guaranteeing a bad outcome. In contrast, the majority of survivors concentrate on how to make the best of their lives, despite the illness. The process of adjusting and learning to cope is gradual, with shifts in mood as life circumstances change. Many people adjust by modifying their life priorities. Senator Paul Tsongas wrote a moving book about his decision to return to less demanding and stressful work when he was diagnosed with a lymphoma. After several years of remission, however, he declared his candidacy for the presidency.

Individual responses to cancer vary greatly, depending on personality and social environment. Some people share the burden of the diagnosis by joining support groups or seeking psychotherapy. Others feel more comfortable confiding in a few trusted people and keeping a journal. Most find techniques of stress reduction beneficial. For some, becoming an activist serves useful social and personal needs. People who fear they would lose their job if a cancer diagnosis were known, jeopardizing medical and life insurance, have no choice but to keep silent. Similarly, people diagnosed as having acquired immune deficiency syndrome (AIDS), which is not contagious under most circumstances, or mental illness, face even stronger social disapproval than people with cancer and often need to hide their condition.

Bernie Siegel and Carl and Stephanie Simonton are professionals who have emphasized the importance of a positive attitude and the reduction of stress in addition to nutrition, rest, and exercise. There are no guarantees for the person with cancer, however, and a positive attitude may not be enough to stem the course of illness. The person who thinks positively should not be blamed or feel personally responsible if complications develop or the illness worsens. It is critical not to be discouraged by setbacks and relapses. Coping with treatment involves dealing with many unknowns, including the fact that many interventions are still experimental. Several treatments (surgery, chemotherapy, and radiation therapy) may be used, often in combination. Many people believe that it is important to learn as much as possible about treatment options so that they can participate in decisions about their care. The National Cancer Institute has a toll-free number—1-800-4-CANCER—that provides up-to-date information.

Treatment may bring about side effects, such as nausea during chemotherapy or hair loss. Becoming sterile as a result of the illness or treatment can place serious strain upon a marriage. Some patients must deal with the psychological and physical impacts of loss of a body part. Prostheses, such as breast implants or artificial limbs, can aid in the adjustment. Great dependency on professional health care workers may develop. In a setting that is compassionate, during and after treatment, people can feel comforted and reassured. In cases when there is limited medical follow-up and there are few, if any, support programs, depression and a feeling of isolation frequently result. People with cancer must be conscientious about seeking regular check-ups. They must learn to walk a delicate line between becoming hypochondriacs and being very aware of changes in the body's functioning which may signal the activation of illness. An added complication is the possibility of decreased resistance to infection. If a fever develops, it is imperative to seek medical attention immediately.

Although five years is often given as a measure of assessing therapeutic success, the patient cannot use this measure as a sole standard for judging the outcome. Individuals who have survived five years or more past their diagnosis will have a sense of relief, but they should remember that having one cancer increases the risk for developing another and that metastases may arise years later. The layperson should discard the concept of "cure," which is not applied to other chronic conditions, such as diabetes, and concentrate instead on recovery and on maximizing the quality of long-term survival.

Applications

Available figures on cancer survival may frighten people, but they can be misleading. They list the average longevity without considering how early the diagnosis was made, how old the person was, or how other illnesses might complicate the picture. Statistics about an illness do not define any one individual's prognosis. Professor and author Stephen Jay Gould, diagnosed with a rare type of cancer, learned that the median survival time for his condition was eight months. He was determined to be among the 50 percent who lived longer, and he was.

Many people with cancer face prejudice and discrimination. Some people find that they are avoided because of anxiety that cancer is contagious. Many employers fire or do not promote employees with cancer, believing that they have a short life expectancy, do not perform well, or take too many sick days. Data indicate that, except for periods of hospitalization and active treatment, people with cancer do not miss more days of work than other employees. In addition, since medical and life insurance are typically denied to people with a history of cancer, young people and their families are often faced with the possibility of economic ruin. Fortunately, people over age sixty-five, who are eligible for Medicare, are saved from some of the catastrophic expenses.

Becoming ill with cancer unleashes strong emotions in the sick person and the person's relatives. While responses vary from person to person, nearly everyone experiences rage, jealousy, wishing others were afflicted instead, and brooding about the fact that bad things can happen to good people. Counterbalancing these thoughts are altruistic ones, in which an effort is made to leave a special mark upon the family or community, and an increasing love and tenderness toward others. Parents often wish they could change places with their sick child. There are times when the family or the sick person fails to live up to their self-imposed standards of enhancing the quality of life; at these moments, it is necessary to be compassionate.

A good support system is essential in handling the emotional and physical pain that may be associated with cancer. Coping involves not only the individual with cancer, but also his or her family and close friends, colleagues, and caregivers. They can be immeasurably helpful in relieving the isolation and sense of loss so typically experienced by people who recognize that their life expectancy is shorter than they would like. Family and friends go through parallel periods of denial and anger, often mourning in advance. Each deeply involved person must focus upon daily activities while having marginal thoughts of anxiety and grief. While it is important to recognize the centrality of the patient's needs, other people who are close also need emotional and financial support. A number of support groups have been formed to help those involved come to terms with the difficult times.

Family and friends must learn to tolerate the fatigue and lack of zest which become part of the life of some cancer patients. Friends and relatives sometimes become angry at the demands made of them to assume additional burdens or to listen compassionately at inconvenient moments. Extra energy may be demanded for hospital visits. After a lengthy hospital stay, readjustments in the household routine must be made to permit the ill person to resume an active role. All involved need to recognize how draining these periods are. Individual and group therapy, dream groups, meditation, and relaxation are among the techniques that have been used to relieve stress and help the cancer patient regain needed perspective. Some evidence indicates that people who seek psychological sustenance and engage in stress reduction have a better prognosis.

For work colleagues, there may also be special issues, caused in part by management's reluctance to think beyond the bottom line. Although it can safely be predicted that a certain number of people will miss workdays, most companies are ill prepared to provide coverage, especially when there is need for prolonged absence. Even where coworkers are well-disposed and would wish similar consideration if they were ill or had a family emergency, the lack of planning requires doing extra work, without compensation. This eventually leads to resentment. Insurance policies frequently force hospitalization because they do not reimburse fully for outpatient laboratory or X-ray tests. People of limited means have no choice but to be hospitalized and therefore away from work more than is medically necessary.

While there may be prolonged remissions or spontaneous cures, more often the outcome of cancer is death. Considerable attention has been paid to psychological preparation since Elisabeth Kubler-Ross wrote *On Death and Dying* (1969). For some, psychological help is beneficial; for others, religion or developing faith in reincarnation provides emotional sustenance. Hospices are preferred by some, while others choose to die at home. The concept of suicide or euthanasia to spare oneself and one's relatives from terminal pain is gaining adherents.

Many survivors have commented on the extent to which the diagnosis has led to a rearrangement of life priorities and to emotional and personal gain from having the opportunity to redirect their lives in constructive ways. Often this means reevaluating the balance between work and family and examining the way one wants to spend the time that is left. When every minute counts, it becomes more urgent to savor the good times and to acknowledge happy moments. Some have credited reorienting their lives with the attainment of remission.

Context

With increasing numbers of survivors of cancer and other chronic illnesses, society will have to consider how to enhance their opportunities to continue living productively, provide financial assistance for medical care, and prevent families from becoming destitute. While insurance is meant to spread risk among policyholders, making a profit has increasingly meant excluding or offering limited coverage to people who are already ill or who are considered vulnerable. Approximately 37 million people in the United States have no health insurance, and another 50 million have inadequate medical coverage. Some people with cancer and their families must face the consequences of the illness totally on their own until they are bankrupt. This callous societal attitude is opposed to all existing evidence on survival, which highlights the benefits to the patient and community when ill people can live as normally as possible.

A growing number of survivor advocacy groups are helping to educate the public. They urge the enactment of such policies as hiring people despite their history of illness if they are competent to do the work; allowing time off for treatment, without fear of job loss; and having adequate medical and life insurance coverage. They are helping people with cancer to enjoy as full a life as possible by emphasizing positive qualities and endeavoring to reduce job discrimination. Bringing survivorship issues into the open is an important factual way to counter the myths equating cancer with death and to obtain figures which will provide a better actuarial base for insurance companies. The individual also benefits as more information about the range of survival time becomes available and the atmosphere for sharing experiences becomes more open.

The contributing role of environmental factors in causing cancer has gained media and research attention. While catastrophes such as the bombing of Hiroshima and the nuclear accident at Chernobyl illustrate the disastrous effects of massive radiation, it has become increasingly clear that pesticides, passive inhalation of tobacco smoke, and other components of modern life can increase the likelihood of cancer both at work and at home. Improved techniques for identifying hazards and limiting their effects are necessary to reduce external causes. Ultimately, educational bases for changing behavior and public health policies aimed at prevention are the most effective ways of coping with environmentally caused cancer.

Bibliography

Gould, Stephen Jay. "The Median Isn't the Message." *Discover* 6 (June, 1985): 40-42. A brief critique of cancer survival statistics, written for a general audience. Gould points out that a "median mortality of eight months," which many would read as a death sentence, also means that half the people will live longer, and some much longer.

Kubler-Ross, Elisabeth. *On Death and Dying.* New York: Macmillan, 1969. The first in an inspiring series of books helpful to patients, their families and friends, and health care professionals. Five stages of reaction to death are described—denial, anger, bargaining, depression, acceptance. The book suggests ways to assist people to live each day to the fullest and come to terms with mortality.

Kushner, Harold S. *When Bad Things Happen to Good People.* New York: Avon,

1983. A helpful attempt to make sense of personal tragedy and go beyond the initial question of "Why me?" to make renewed connections with meaningful living.

National Coalition for Cancer Survivorship. *Charting the Journey: An Almanac of Practical Resources for Cancer Survivors.* Mount Vernon, N.Y.: Consumers Union, 1990. Well-written and thorough presentation of advice and resources for people with cancer and their families. The focus is on survival techniques. Includes sections on treatment options, ways of mobilizing strength, and how to deal with employment and insurance discrimination.

Nessim, Susan, and Judith Ellis. *Cancervive: The Challenge of Life After Cancer.* Boston: Houghton Mifflin, 1991. An excellent reference on all aspects of coping with cancer, including dealing with the diagnosis, treatment, fears of recurrence, and job discrimination. Particularly useful for people who have had active treatment.

Robbins, Lillian, Barbara Goff, and Lynn Miller. *Cancer and the Workplace: Strategies for Support and Survival.* Newark, N.J.: Rutgers University Press, 1987. An overview of work-related issues that makes suggestions about how colleagues can give constructive support. Discusses the safeguards for which to strive in terms of job security, sick leave, and insurance protection. Reducing the stress of caring for sick family members while working is also considered.

Siegel, Bernie. *Love, Medicine, and Miracles.* New York: Harper & Row, 1986. Bestseller by a surgeon describing the importance of psychological factors in cancer recovery and the ability to deal with loss. Emphasizes the impact of love and courage as influences on the course of illness and the healing potential that can help patients become survivors.

Simonton, Carl, Stephanie Matthews-Simonton, and James Creighton. *Getting Well Again.* New York: Bantam, 1980. An important contribution on imagery and visualization as aids in coping with cancer. The book describes techniques that have been successful in helping people use their imagination to conquer serious illness. Critics are concerned that the focus on attitudes may cause those who do not improve or have recurrences to blame themselves.

Sontag, Susan. *Illness as Metaphor.* Garden City, N.Y.: Doubleday, 1978. A classic work on the stigma of cancer, as contrasted with other illnesses, and how the vocabulary and attitudes of society contaminate treatment. The 1990 paperback reissue adds an informative section on the parallels between AIDS and cancer.

Tsongas, Paul. *Heading Home.* New York: Random House, 1985. A former senator discusses the impact of lymphoma on his life choices. He describes how the illness served as a catalyst for redefining his goals and increasing his appreciation of family and the need to share.

Lillian Cukier Robbins
Edwin S. Robbins

Cross-References

Coping: Social Support, 700; Coping Strategies: An Overview, 706; Death and Dying: Theoretical Perspectives, 763; Group Therapy, 1120; Health Psychology, 1139; Meditation and Relaxation, 1499; Pain, 1727.

COUPLES THERAPY

Type of psychology: Psychotherapy
Field of study: Group and family therapies

Relationship distress represents one of the most common reasons that individuals seek psychological help in the United States. As a result, there is an increasing demand for treatment services which are both effective in altering destructive marital interactions and efficient in the use of the therapist's and client's time.

Principal terms

CROSS-COMPLAINING LOOP: an interactional sequence wherein both individuals describe areas of dissatisfaction within the relationship yet fail to attend to the issues raised by their partner

DOMESTIC VIOLENCE: physical, emotional, psychological, or sexual abuse perpetrated by a family member toward another family member; typically the abuse follows a repetitive, predictable pattern

OPERANT CONDITIONING: a type of learning in which behaviors are altered primarily by the consequences that follow them (reinforcement or punishment)

PREVENTION PROGRAMS: intervention strategies designed to reduce or eliminate difficulties in the future by providing training in specific skills

PROSOCIAL BEHAVIOR: activities or behaviors performed by an individual which are intended to benefit others or society

PSYCHOPHYSIOLOGICAL: referring to the interaction between the psyche (mind) and the physiology (such as the regulatory processes of the nervous system) of the organism

VALIDATION LOOP: an interactional sequence in which one partner expresses dissatisfaction and the other partner expresses either agreement or support

Overview

Traditionally, marriage vows have represented pledges of mutual love and enduring commitment. Since the 1960's, however, marital relationships have changed dramatically. In fact, while more than 90 percent of the United States population will marry at least once in their lifetime, it is anticipated that approximately 50 percent of first marriages and 60 percent of second marriages will end in divorce. Moreover, while the average first marriage in the United States will last only five to seven years, second marriages typically endure only for five years. It appears that a repetitive pattern of marriage, distress, and divorce has become commonplace. Such a cycle often results in considerable pain and psychological turmoil for the couple, their family, and their friends. These statistics dramatically indicate the need for effective ways to help couples examine and reapproach their relationships before deciding whether to terminate them.

Research has found evidence that links divorce and relationship distress to a wide variety of emotional disorders in spouses and their children. Depressive syndromes are evident in approximately half of female spouses and nearly 15 percent of male partners in dysfunctional marriages. Almost half of all first admissions to state hospitals in the United States have relationship stress as a major factor. Evidence further reveals that suicide often follows marital discord, separation, and divorce. In fact, divorce and marital separation represent two of the most common yet significant stressors in adult life.

Partners who seek couples therapy or counseling frequently have problems in two areas: communication and conflict resolution. These are the two major difficulties that most often lead to divorce. It has been shown that communication skills differentiate satisfied and dissatisfied couples more powerfully than any other factor. Indeed, communication difficulties are the most frequently cited complaint among partners reporting relationship distress.

Psychologist John M. Gottman, in his books *Marital Interaction: Experimental Investigations* (1979) and *A Couple's Guide to Communication* (Gottman et al., 1976), as well as various other researchers, has highlighted the importance of communication problems within distressed relationships. Many characteristic differences between distressed and satisfied couples have been noted. Partners in distressed couples often misperceive "well-intended" statements from their partners, whereas satisfied couples are more likely to rate well-intended messages as positive; distressed partners also engage in fewer rewarding exchanges and more frequent punishing interactions than nondistressed couples. A partner in a distressed relationship is more immediately reactive to perceived negative behavior exhibited by his or her partner. There is generally a greater emphasis on negative communication strategies between distressed partners.

Distressed couples appear to be generally unskilled at generating positive change in their relationship. Gottman also reported that distressed couples are often ineffectual in their attempts to resolve conflicts. Whereas nondistressed couples employ "validation loops" during problem-solving exercises (one partner states the conflict and the other partner expresses agreement or support), distressed couples typically enter into repetitive, cross-complaining loops. Moreover, as one spouse initiates aversive control tactics, the other spouse will typically reciprocate with similar behavior.

Couples therapy attempts to alleviate distress, resolve conflicts, improve daily functioning, and prevent problems via an intensive focus on the couple as a unit and on each partner as an individual. Couples therapists are faced with a variety of choices regarding treatment format and therapeutic approach. Individual therapy focuses treatment on only one of the partners. Although generally discouraged by most practitioners, individual treatment of one partner can provide greater opportunities for the client to focus more on his or her own thoughts, feelings, problems, and behaviors. Clients may feel less hesitant in sharing some details they would not want a spouse to hear, and individual treatment may encourage the client to take greater personal responsibility for problems and successes. In general, these advantages are outweighed by the difficulties encountered when treating "relationship problems" without both partners being present. In particular, interpersonal interactions are complex phenomena that need to be evaluated and treated with both partners present.

Concurrent therapy involves both partners being seen in treatment separately, either by the same therapist or by two separate but collaborating therapists. Advantages of the concurrent format include greater individual attention and opportunities to develop strategies to improve relationship skills by teaching each partner those techniques separately. Concurrent treatment, however, does not allow the therapist(s) to evaluate and treat the nature of the interpersonal difficulties with both partners simultaneously present in the same room.

Conjoint format, on the other hand, involves both partners simultaneously in the therapy session. Conjoint treatment tends to be widely used and generally recommended because it focuses intensively on the quality of the relationship, promotes dialogue between the couple, and can attend to the needs and goals of each partner as well as the needs and goals of the couple. The history of conjoint marital therapy begins, ironically, with Sigmund Freud's failures in this area. He believed firmly that it was counterproductive and dangerous for a therapist ever to treat more than one member of the same family. In fact, after attempting to provide services simultaneously to a husband and wife, Freud (in 1912) concluded that he was at a complete loss in terms of understanding how to treat relationship problems within a couple. He also added that he had little faith in individual therapy for them.

As currently practiced, conjoint treatment is designed to focus intensively on the relationship in order to effect specific therapeutic change for that particular couple. Interventions can be "tailor-made" for the couple seeking treatment, regardless of the nature of the problem the couple describes (such as sexual relations, child rearing, household responsibilities). Moreover, couples are constantly engaged in a direct dialogue with each other, which can foster improved understanding and resolution or conflict. As compared with other approaches, conjoint marital therapy can focus on each of the specific needs and goals of the individual couple.

Group couples treatment programs have received increased attention and have shown very good to excellent treatment success. Advantages of group treatment for couples include opportunities for direct assessment and intervention of the relationship within a setting which promotes greater opportunity for feedback and suggestions from other couples experiencing similar difficulties. In fact, group therapy may promote positive expectations through witnessing improvements among other couples as well as fostering a sense of cohesiveness among couples within the group. In the group format, each partner has the opportunity to develop improved communication and conflict resolution approaches by learning relationship skills via interaction with the therapist(s), his or her spouse, and other group members. In addition, the cost of individual, concurrent, and conjoint therapy, in terms of time as well as dollars, has prompted several researchers and clinicians to recommend group couples therapy.

Applications

There are numerous approaches to the treatment of relationship problems currently practiced in the United States. Psychodynamic therapy focuses attention on the unconscious needs and issues raised during an individual's childhood. Phenomenological therapists focus on the here-and-now experiences of being in a relationship and have developed a variety of creative therapeutic techniques. Systems therapists view interpersonal problems as being maintained by the nature of the relationship structure, patterns of communication, and family roles and rules.

Behavioral marital therapy, however, is the most thoroughly investigated approach within the couples therapy field. Starting from a focus on operant conditioning, behavioral marital therapy includes a wide range of assessment and treatment strategies. The underlying assumption that best differentiates behavioral treatments for distressed couples from other approaches is that the two partners are viewed as ineffectual in their attempts to satisfy each other. Thus, the goal of therapy is to improve relationship satisfaction by creating a supportive environment in which the skills can be acquired. Behavioral marital therapy incorporates strategies designed to improve daily interactions, communication patterns, and problem-solving abilities, and to examine and modify unreasonable expectations and faulty thinking styles.

Psychologists Philip and Marcy Bornstein, in their book *Marital Therapy: A Behavioral-Communications Approach* (1986), have described a sequential five-step procedure in the treatment of relationship dysfunction. These steps include intake interviewing, behavioral exchange strategies, communication skills acquisition, training in problem solving, and maintenance and generalization of treatment gains.

Intake interviewing is designed to accomplish three primary goals: development of a working relationship with the therapist, collection of assessment information, and implementation of initial therapeutic regiments. Because spouses entering treatment have often spent months, if not years, in conflict and distress, the intake procedure attempts to provide a unique opportunity to impact and assess the couple's relationship immediately. Since distressed couples often devote a considerable amount of time thinking about and engaging in discordant interpersonal interactions with each other, it naturally follows that they will attempt to engage in unpleasant interactions during initial sessions. Information about current difficulties and concerns is clearly valuable, but improved communication skills and positive interactions appear to be of even greater merit early in treatment. Thus, couples are discouraged from engaging in cross-complaining loops and are encouraged to develop skills and implement homework procedures designed to enhance the relationship.

Building a positive working relationship between partners is viewed as essential in couples treatment programs. During training in behavioral exchange strategies, couples are aided in specifying and pinpointing behaviors that tend to promote increased harmony in their relationship. Couples engage in contracting and compromise activities in order to disrupt the downward spiral of their distressed relationship.

Training in communication skills focuses on teaching and practicing the basics of communication (such as respect, understanding, and sensitivity), positive principles of communication (timeliness, marital manners, specification, and "mind reading"), improving nonverbal behaviors, and learning "molecular" verbal behaviors (such as assertiveness and constructive agreement). Improved communication styles are fostered via a direct, active approach designed to identify, reinforce, and rehearse desirable patterns of interactions. Clients are generally provided with specific instructions and "practice periods" during sessions in which partners are encouraged to begin improving their interactional styles. It is common that these sessions are audiotaped or videotaped to give couples specific feedback regarding their communication style.

Training in problem solving is intended to teach clients to negotiate and resolve conflicts in a mutually beneficial manner. Conflict resolution training focuses on teaching, practicing, and experiencing effective problem-solving approaches. Couples receive specific instruction on systematic problem-solving approaches and are given homework assignments designed to improve problem-solving skills. Because the value of couples therapy lies in the improvement, maintenance, and use of positive interaction styles over time and across situations, treatment often aims to promote constructive procedures after the termination of active treatment. Thus, people are taught that it is generally easier to change oneself than one's partner, that positive interaction styles may be forgotten or unlearned if these strategies are not regularly practiced, and that new positive interactions can continue to develop in a variety of settings even as treatment ends.

To highlight further the utility and effectiveness of behavioral-communications relationship therapy, Philip Bornstein, Laurie Wilson, and Gregory L. Wilson (1988) conducted an empirical investigation comparing conjoint behavioral-communications therapy and group behavioral-communications therapy to a waiting-list control group (the waiting-list control group included couples who were asked to wait two months prior to beginning treatment). Fifteen distressed couples were randomly assigned to experimental conditions and offered eight sessions of couples therapy. At the conclusion of treatment (as well as six months later), the couples in active treatment revealed significant alleviation of relationship distress. The conjoint and group couples revealed similar levels of improvement in communication skills, problem-solving abilities, and general relationship satisfaction. The waiting-list couples, on the other hand, revealed no improvement while they waited for treatment, indicating that relationship distress does not tend to improve simply as the result of the passage of time.

Another line of couples research has focused on the utility of premarital intervention, or distress and divorce prevention programs. Unlike treatment programs, prevention programs intervene prior to the development of relationship distress. Prevention efforts are focused on the future and typically involve the training of specific skills which are viewed as useful in preventing relationship distress. Three major approaches to premarital intervention include the Minnesota Couples Communication Program, Bernard Guerney's relationship enhancement approach, and the Premarital Relationship Enhancement Program. Research is generally supportive of the effectiveness of these programs in helping partners learn useful skills which translate into improved relationships for at least three to eight years following the program. In addition, some evidence indicates that the alarming divorce rate in the United States can be decreased if partners participate in prevention programs prior to marriage; prevention programs that emphasize communication and conflict-resolution skills seem most advantageous.

There has also been considerable interest in the utility of couples-based treatment for various psychological disorders, including depression, anxiety disorders, and alcoholism. For example, the rationale for couples intervention as a viable treatment for depressed clients rests on the assumption that marital dysfunction is either causative or related to the maintenance of the depressed state. Whereas more than 50 percent of married couples seeking relationship therapy have at least one spouse who is depressed, and nearly 50 percent of women seeking depression treatment report marital discord, it appears that depression and marital dysfunction are not necessarily distinct problems. Thus, a primary advantage of marital therapy strategies in the resolution of depression is the simultaneous emphasis and demonstrated effectiveness of such interventions in reducing relationship discord as well as depression.

Context

Since 1970, researchers and clinicians have witnessed large increases in the numbers of couples seeking treatment from therapists. As the demand for couples treatment has increased, more time and effort has been devoted to improving treatment methods. The behavioral approach has been shown to be highly effective in reducing relationship distress and preventing divorce; however, several investigations have demonstrated that cognitive components such as causal attributions and expectations are strongly related to satisfaction in the relationship. Moreover, it has been argued that dysfunctional cognitions may interfere with both the establishment and maintenance of positive behavior change. Evidence has prompted several researchers and practitioners alike to advocate a more systematic inclusion of strategies of cognitive behavior therapy within the behavioral marital therapy framework. Specifically, it is possible that the combination of cognitive and behavioral approaches will demonstrate increased utility if the two treatments are presented together in a singular, integrated treatment intervention. Such treatment would afford couples the opportunity to benefit from either one or both of the complementary approaches, depending on their own unique needs, at any time during the course of treatment. Moreover, such an integration of cognitive and behavioral tactics would parallel effective approaches already employed with depressed and anxious clients.

Interpersonal relationships are a highly complex yet important area of study and investigation. The decision to marry (or at least to commit to a serious intimate relationship) is clearly one of the most significant choices people make in their lives. Unfortunately, it is rare to find school curricula that offer any assistance, training, or education to help young people understand interpersonal relationships or make the decision to marry. Fortunately, advances in couples therapy have led to increased knowledge about interpersonal relationships and methods for improving relationship satisfaction. These advances have been documented in the scientific literature, and they extend to the treatment of cohabitating partners, premarital couples, remarried partners, gay or lesbian couples, separating or divorced couples, and stepfamilies. Moreover, couples-based treatment programs have shown effectiveness in the treatment of depression, anxiety disorders, domestic violence, sexual dysfunction, and a host of other problems.

Bibliography

Beck, Aaron T. *Love Is Never Enough.* New York: Harper & Row, 1988. Written for couples everywhere, this text presents a review of cognitive therapy and includes many suggestions for couples wishing to improve their relationship. Through many clinical examples and dialogues with various couples in treatment, Beck highlights some of the key strategies for avoiding difficulties associated with misperceptions and miscommunication.

Bornstein, Philip H., and Marcy T. Bornstein. *Marital Therapy: A Behavioral-Communications Approach.* New York: Pergamon Press, 1986. Highlights some of the key research findings that differentiate distressed and satisfied partners in the areas of communication and conflict resolution. Also presents a clinical guide for counselors and therapists who work with couples to alleviate relationship dysfunction.

Gottman, John M., et al. *A Couple's Guide to Communication.* Champaign, Ill.: Research Press, 1976. A very useful guidebook for couples wishing to improve their communication and conflict-resolution skills. Suggestions for practicing improved interactions and increasing daily happiness are included.

Gurman, A. S. *Casebook of Marital Therapy.* New York: Guilford Press, 1985. Reviews some of the various treatment strategies available for dealing with some of the most challenging difficulties in interpersonal relationships (including jealousy, sexual problems, and in-laws). Leaders from a variety of treatment approaches describe various aspects of their therapy approach.

Gurman, A. S., and D. P. Kniskern. *Handbook of Family Therapy.* Vol. 2. New York: Brunner/Mazel, 1991. A significant resource on the various models of treatment for couples and families. Presents a historical overview of marital and family therapy, describes various models and conceptualizations of treatment, and highlights special topics such as sex therapy and divorce interventions.

Jacobson, Neil S., and A. S. Gurman. *Clinical Handbook of Marital Therapy.* New York: Guilford Press, 1986. Provides an overview and numerous clinical sections on the major models of relationship therapy and treatment suggestions for selected psychiatric disorders. Designed for clinicians and researchers alike, this edited text presents the views of most of the major figures in marital therapy.

Jacobson, Neil S., and Gayla Margolin. *Marital Therapy: Strategies Based on Social*

Learning and Behavior Exchange Principles. New York: Brunner/Mazel, 1979. Presents a description of social learning theory and the methods typically employed in behavioral marital therapy. A landmark book in terms of the history of marital therapy which still offers much candid clinical insight into the most effective methods for alleviating relationship distress.

Gregory L. Wilson

Cross-References

Behavioral Family Therapy, 394; Cognitive Behavior Therapy, 546; Group Therapy, 1120; Midlife Crises, 1575; Psychotherapeutic Effectiveness, 1989; Separation, Divorce, and Family Life: Adult Issues, 2220; Separation, Divorce, and Family Life: Children's Issues, 2227; Strategic Family Therapy, 2382.

CREATIVITY: ASSESSING SPECIAL TALENTS

Type of psychology: Intelligence and intelligence testing
Fields of study: Ability tests; cognitive processes

Creativity and the assessment of creativity are crucial to society; creativity is the ability to create something new that goes beyond ordinary modes of thought. Various methods have been developed to assess creativity.

Principal terms

CONVERGENT THINKING: the type of ordinary thinking in which the majority of people generally engage

DIVERGENT THINKING: thinking that results in new, different responses that most people cannot, or do not, offer; it is the type of thinking most clearly involved in creativity

FLEXIBILITY: the ability to generate different kinds of ideas

FLUENCY: the ability to produce a number of ideas in response to a problem or scenario

ORIGINALITY: the production of ideas that are uncommon or rare and are often surprising

Overview

The study of creativity has undergone many changes and developments, particularly since the early 1960's, and it has received recognition as a field in its own right. Creativity has traditionally been assessed via the finished products of the artisan, musician, writer, poet, or inventor. The general consensus of the public has usually served as the final criterion of creativity. Any distinction between creativity and "talent" could be difficult to ascertain. The assessment of talent has usually been the province of people within a particular field. Musicians, artists, writers, and others in specific fields have assessed the skills of their students or protégés, either formally or informally; in some fields, specific tests do exist.

One generally accepted construct regarding creativity is divergent thinking. People who are considered creative seem to think in a more divergent mode. They see possibilities and options that are not perceived by most other people. If most people were to ask themselves the possible uses for a brick, they would probably list a few: to build a house, for example, or perhaps to use as a doorstop. Divergent thinkers may indicate that it could be used as a weapon, a hammer, a paperweight, a bookend, or a supportive device.

John A. Glover, in his book *Becoming a More Creative Person* (1980), described certain aspects or components of creativity: fluency, flexibility, elaboration, and originality. Fluency refers to the number of ideas a person can generate to solve a given problem or produce a certain result. Flexibility is the ability to generate a number of different kinds of ideas. The amount of detail that one can supply for one's ideas is known as the amount of elaboration. Originality refers to the novelty or statistical infrequency of an idea. This last concept has often been used as a synonym for creativity. If one person out of a hundred people has an idea that no one else has, for example, his or her idea may be termed original. It might be strange, even bizarre, but it might also be positive.

Some theorists view creativity as a process or a series of stages. Procuring an idea might be one stage, working on the idea would be another, and completing a final product would be another. Things may go wrong in any stage along the way. When difficulties are encountered, it is often effective to allow an "incubation" period to occur—to defer an idea for a period of time; often, this enables one to achieve a new insight into a problem. If one becomes fatigued, it is often best to "sleep on it" and return to the problem when one is refreshed.

Some researchers have described different types of creativity. One type has been termed expressive creativity; the drawings of children, doodling, scribbling, and the like are manifestations of this form of creativity. In productive creativity, the emphasis is on an artistic or scientific product—on doing something that will produce a definite finished product. In the domain of inventive creativity, ingenuity is displayed with techniques, tactics, methods, and strategies. Innovative creativity involves modifications that produce improvement through the use of conceptual skills. In emergentive creativity, an entirely new approach, paradigm, or assumption is founded; an entire community or group may flourish. When the Impressionists gathered in Paris, they developed a novel, divergent approach to painting, for example; this is one example of emergentive creativity.

Another aspect of creativity is validation. After one has created or invented something, one attempts to ascertain whether the idea, music, poem, or other creative endeavor truly has merit. The "test of time" is perhaps the ultimate element of validation. Sometimes an invention or creation is valued only for a time, then discarded; sometimes it is changed or improved upon. On the other hand, works such as the symphonies of Wolfgang Amadeus Mozart, the plays of William Shakespeare, and the artwork of Leonardo da Vinci have stood the test of time and are still held in high esteem.

Intelligence has been thought to be an important aspect of creativity; a certain minimal amount of intelligence is certainly necessary. Mentally retarded people are, in general, not very creative. On the other hand, and more surprising, there are few people with a very high intelligence quotient (IQ) score who are creative. They appear to be preoccupied with finding the "right" answer; perhaps they naturally think more convergently, or perhaps they have been trained to think more convergently. As previously noted, divergent thinking is a crucial aspect of creativity. If one is extremely intelligent, one may therefore need to "shift gears" radically in order to think in alternative ways.

Personality has also been examined in terms of creativity. Research indicates that creative people seem to have a greater range of knowledge and interests than noncreative people. They seem to have an openness to new experience and have a willingness to try new types of things. They appear to value independence, as well as complexity. A good sense of humor is also noted. The creative personality is persistent and is willing to take risks. Many creative people are seen to have high energy and activity levels. Organization and abstraction skills are well developed. Creative people are able to tolerate ambiguity better than less-creative people; they seem to function well in ill-defined settings or situations and employ fairly unusual problem-solving strategies.

Applications

A number of tests have been developed that attempt to measure creativity. E. Paul Torrance has been a leading figure in the field of creativity since the 1950's. His tests of creativity have been used and researched extensively, and much published research has resulted. There are two parts to the Torrance Tests of Creative Thinking (published by Scholastic Testing Service), a verbal section and a "figural" section. There are several subtests in each area. In the verbal test, seven activities must be performed. These include asking, guessing causes, guessing consequences, product improvement, unusual uses, unusual questions, and "just suppose." In the figural realm, there are three activities: picture construction, picture completion, and circles. There are complete manuals for administrative, scoring, and illustrative purposes. A number of organizations offer computerized scoring services. Teachers or others who have not had special training are able to score the tests fairly reliably if they have invested the time to study the scoring guides carefully.

A test developed by Frank Williams, another researcher in the field of creativity, is the Exercises in Divergent Thinking and Divergent Feeling. The creative thinking part of the test offers a total score as well as subscores in fluency, flexibility, originality, and elaboration. On the creative feeling test, scores are offered on curiosity, imagination, complexity, and risk taking; again, a total score is also offered. These tests represent the variables thought by Williams to be most important in creativity.

The parts of this test, in conjunction with the Williams Scale, can help to identify children with creative potential. The Williams Scale asks parents and teachers to rate children on a three-point scale in terms of their fluency, flexibility, originality, elaboration, curiosity, complexity, imagination, and risk taking. There are also four open-ended questions that allow parents and teachers to express specific concerns and offer salient information about the child. There is considerable specificity to the Williams Scale, but there is also a ceiling effect in that some students can only earn a certain number of points; this may therefore give a limited vision of the test taker's skills and creative potential.

The Group Inventory for Finding Talent (GIFT) is also available. This test is computer-scored by the company rather than by the examiner or teacher. This test was developed by Gary Davis and Sylvia Rimm, two well-known experts in the field of gifted education. A major cross-cultural effort was undertaken by Hans Jellen and Klaus Urban. Their test, the Test for Creative Thinking and Drawing Production (TCT-DP), has been administered to subjects in eleven countries.

All these tests can help to discover creative potential in children. It is hoped that, after creative potential is recognized, it can be nurtured and encouraged. Many teachers almost intuitively recognize creative abilities, and encourage and prompt the creative child in their classrooms. Yet high scores on tests such as the Torrance test do not necessarily mean that a person will continue to be creative or will be able to make significant contributions to society. Economic conditions may force a person to work at a job that provides no avenues or extra time to maximize creativity; some people never find an outlet for their talents and skills.

Context

Everyone has some creative potential, but it remains difficult to discern exactly how much potential one has or in what field or domain it may lie. Creativity remains an elusive concept, but one of great interest to many researchers; there are journals, conferences, and organizations devoted to the subject. There has also been much debate over the nature and assessment of creativity. Researchers have tried to differentiate between creativity and intelligence.

Some psychologists and educators have been concerned with ways of enhancing creativity; one method is the idea of "brainstorming." In this strategy, people offer ideas and suggestions regarding the clarification of or solution to a problem. All options are accepted, and no negativism is allowed; this enhances the climate of the group. Only later do the group members focus on which ideas are reasonable or possible. Some researchers have attempted to use behavioral reinforcement principles and procedures to promulgate creative responses; others have examined the effectiveness of creativity training. Methods have either focused on short-term or long-term programs.

Creativity in the classroom is another area that has been of concern. Some educators have worried in particular that educational reform movements may ultimately stifle creativity in the classroom. Psychologists John Glover and Roger Bruning have offered suggestions for enhancing classroom creativity. Teachers, they suggest, should "try to find something positive in all ideas." Strange or unusual questions from students should not be discounted. Creativity should systematically be rewarded; it should also be expected. Creativity should be rewarded as an "extra" when grades are given, and creative behaviors should be modeled by teachers. E. Paul Torrance has also emphasized rewarding creative behavior in the classroom. He has noted that most teachers seem to emphasize conformity to an inordinate extent and that education must be careful not to squelch creativity. Because creative people must ultimately provide answers to environmental and technological problems, creativity must be investigated, assessed, and nurtured.

Bibliography

Glover, John A. *Becoming a More Creative Person.* Englewood Cliffs, N.J.: Prentice-Hall, 1980. An excellent book on enhancing creativity. Glover's work is among the most understandable, clear, and concise representations of the field available today.

Glover, John A., and Roger H. Bruning. *Educational Psychology: Principles and Applications.* Boston: Little, Brown, 1987. The chapter on creativity in this book is a succinct and concise review of various aspects of creativity, creative behavior, and creative potential.

Glover, John A., Royce R. Ronning, and Cecil R. Reynolds, eds. *Handbook of Creativity.* New York: Plenum Press, 1989. A comprehensive book on creativity. Excellent source, with chapters by leading authorities in the field. Offers in-depth investigation of salient directions for creativity and creativity research.

Mansfield, Richard S., Thomas V. Busse, and Ernest J. Krepelka. "The Effectiveness of Creativity Training." *Review of Educational Research* 48, no. 4 (1978): 517-536. An excellent global review of some of the history and the older theories of creativity as well as an examination of the efficacy of the various creativity training programs. An example of scholarly research in the field.

Runco, Mark A., and Robert S. Albert, eds. *Theories of Creativity.* Newbury Park, Calif.: Sage, 1990. Runco and Albert have edited a text with chapters by the leading figures in the field. These twelve chapters are a gold mine for those interested in doing in-depth research in the field of creativity. Runco is also the editor of a major journal on the empirical study of creativity.

Torrance, Ellis Paul. *Creativity in the Classroom.* Washington, D.C.: National Education Association, 1977. This small monograph is one of Torrance's best works and is a frequently cited reference. It describes creativity at different levels, including what teachers can do to foster creativity and the goals that teachers should have in enhancing creativity.

_____. *Rewarding Creative Behavior: Experiments in Classroom Creativity.* Englewood Cliffs, N.J.: Prentice-Hall, 1965. Although somewhat dated, Torrance's ideas still influence many teachers and researchers today. This book "covers the waterfront" in terms of the issues relative to creativity and creative thinking.

Michael F. Shaughnessy

Cross-References

Ability Testing: Individual and Group, 1; Ability Tests: Uses and Misuses, 27; Intelligence: Definition and Theoretical Models, 1328; Intelligence: Giftedness and Retardation, 1334; Intelligence Tests, 1341.

CREATIVITY AND INTELLIGENCE

Type of psychology: Intelligence and intelligence testing
Field of study: General issues in intelligence

Creativity and intelligence are two aspects of cognitive performance in humans. Creativity refers to having inventive, productive, and imaginative qualities; intelligence refers to having mental acuteness, the ability to understand, and the ability to act effectively to solve problems within one's environment. The areas of creativity and intelligence have provided insights into what it means to be gifted and talented.

Principal terms

ANALOGICAL PROBLEM SOLVING: a process in which a person attempts to determine relationships between two terms, concepts, or situations and to correlate the relationship to two other terms, concepts, or situations

ANALOGY: a statement of a relationship between words, concepts, or situations

COGNITIVE ABILITIES: the effectiveness of a person's thinking processes

CREATIVITY: a person's cognitive abilities in areas such as fluency, flexibility, originality, elaboration, visualization, metaphorical thinking, problem definition, and evaluation

EMINENCE: recognition and ranking of one's talents by others who are experienced in appreciating and judging particular performance and results

GIFTEDNESS: consistent cognitive performance, usually based on a score on a standardized intelligence test, beyond the level normally expected for a given age; this may refer to people who are talented and creative

INTELLIGENCE: the ability to perform various mental tasks which include reasoning, knowledge, comprehension, memory, applying concepts, and manipulating figures

PROBLEM SOLVING: the way people seek to answer or respond to a situation that is unknown to them

Overview

Creativity and intelligence are two areas of cognitive functioning and performance which have been examined by researchers, educators, and others. Creativity refers to the process of being imaginative and innovative. A creative person is able to link existing information with new information in productive ways. Students who are creative may often be referred to as being gifted and/or talented. Charles F. Wetherall has listed many characteristics of gifted, talented, and/or creative students. Creative students, for example, have a keen sense of observation and a desire to improve their abilities, produce a variety of possible solutions to problems, are curious, are original, have the characteristic of persistence, are comfortable with ambiguity, are able to work independently, are able to analyze and synthesize information, demonstrate compulsivity and an urgency to complete a task or execute an idea, and have multiple latent abilities. Thus, when one's existing knowledge and information combine in a unique way, a creative product or idea is formed.

Many others have also sought to describe creativity. Characteristics of creative persons and creativity according to Gary A. Davis and Sylvia Rimm include valuing creative thinking, appreciating novel and far-fetched ideas, being open-minded and receptive to zany ideas, and being mentally set to produce creative ideas. Robert Sternberg describes creative people as those who have the ability and willingness to go beyond the ordinary limitations of themselves and their environment and think and act in unconventional and perhaps dreamlike ways. Further, he states that creative people go beyond the unwritten canons of society, have aesthetic taste, and are inquisitive and intuitive. Contributions of a major nature have been made to many fields of endeavor as a result of creative enterprise.

Creativity has been studied by research that sought to examine personality and family issues related to creativity, the ecology of creativity, musical creativity, and creative ability in women. Research by Robert Albert which examined relationships between creativity, identity formation, and career choice caused him to make six suggestions for parents and teachers to help students achieve maximally. This information would be beneficial both to students who are gifted and to those who are not. His suggestions include helping students experience emotions such as anger, joy, fear, and passion; teaching involvement rather than techniques to students; seeking to discover what people can do; allowing students to experience some novelty and flexibility; encouraging the students to ask the questions What do I think? How do I think? What can I do? and How do I feel about it now that I have tried?; and enhancing learning by being actively engaged with and taking chances with one another.

Intelligence, according to Paul Kline, refers to a person's ability to learn, understand, and deal with novel situations. The intelligent person may be viewed as quick-witted, acute, keen, sharp, canny, astute, bright, and brilliant. Robert Sternberg, in *Intelligence Applied: Understanding and Increasing Your Intellectual Skills* (1986), described intelligence as comprising a very wide array of cognitive and other skills; he does not see intelligence as a single ability.

After examining many theories of intelligence, Sternberg developed the triarchic (three-part) theory of intelligence. In the componential subtheory, the first part of the theory, intelligence is related to the external world of the individual. For example, a person who is intelligent in this area obtains high scores on standardized tests and is excellent in analytical thinking. The second part of the theory, the experiential subtheory, specifies intelligence in situations. A person who is intelligent in handling novel tasks with creativity, but who may not have the best standardized test scores, is demonstrating intelligence in this area. In the third part of the theory, the contextual subtheory, intelligence is related to the external world of the individual. For example, a person who is able to achieve success when interacting on the job or when influencing other people is demonstrating contextual intelligence.

Characteristics of intelligent persons include greater preference for, more attention to, and highly developed abilities for dealing with novelty; an ability to process information rapidly; an ability to ignore irrelevant information; and an ability to solve problems accurately. Problem-solving ability in intelligence may be observed in a person's ability to complete many tasks successfully. Among these tasks would be a person's ability to solve analogies.

Analogies are statements of a relationship between words, concepts, or situations. Problem solving by analogy occurs when students attempt to use the conditions and solution to one problem to assist them in understanding the conditions and solutions of another problem. Put another way, students use the relationships they see in one context or situation to assist them in understanding relationships in another context or situation. Many educators believe that solving analogies helps students to concretize their thinking, gauge how they understand information, tap and develop a facility for visual thinking, exercise and nurture creative and critical thinking, clarify and organize unfamiliar subject matter, and synthesize instructional material. Past research has pointed to an ability to solve analogies as one of the best predictors of intellectual ability. Intelligence has also been studied by examining the way that students who have been identified as gifted (based on high intelligence test scores) solve problems. It was found that highly intelligent people are better able to separate relevant and irrelevant information.

Applications

Both creativity and intelligence can be assessed by specialized tests designed for that purpose. E. Paul Torrance developed the Torrance Tests of Creative Thinking; these tests seek to assess creativity as it relates to fluency, flexibility, originality, and elaboration. Each of these areas can be understood in the context of examples. Fluency in creativity is the ability one has to produce numerous original ideas that solve problems. For example, persons may demonstrate fluency when they can give multiple uses for a ballpoint pen. Flexibility in creativity is the ability to produce ideas that show a variety of approaches that may be used. Originality is the ability to create uncommon or unusual responses; for example, a unique or unconventional use of the ballpoint pen would be classified as original. Elaboration refers to a person's ability to add details to a basic idea. For example, if a common item such as a ballpoint pen is discussed in extreme and minute details that do not focus on obvious aspects of the pen, elaboration is being demonstrated.

Intelligence tests consist of standardized questions and tasks which seek to determine the mental age of a person or the person's relative capacity to solve problems and absorb new information. Intelligence tests try to measure students' capacity to learn separate from their actual academic achievement.

Intelligence tests are either group administered or individually administered; in group testings, large numbers of students can be assessed at the same time. According to Miles Storfer, individual intelligence tests such as the Stanford-Binet and the Wechsler series provide a good approximation of most people's abilities in the cognitive skills that the tests are designed to measure. These cognitive skills include being able to solve problems well, reasoning clearly, thinking logically, having a good vocabulary, and knowing an abundance of information in many areas.

Creative discovery has led to many technological breakthroughs and innovations in science and industry. Technological breakthroughs and success in science and industry have been evident in the extensive research into creative activity conducted by W. J. Gordon. He provides some source material that points to the relationship between invention, discovery, and learning. There are a wide variety of technological fields wherein creativity and analogies have led to breakthroughs.

One example of the many technological breakthroughs and innovations in science and industry presented by Gordon occurred in 1865. A man named Dunlop was trying to think of a way to help his son be more comfortable when riding his bicycle over cobblestone streets. While watering his garden, he noticed how the hose resisted his fingers when he pressed his hand more firmly around it. He made the connections between the elastic resistance of the hose and how this type of elasticity would make his son more comfortable when biking. His first successful tire was made from a piece of garden hose.

Context

One of the first people to examine the concept of intelligence in the United States was James McKeen Cattell (1860-1944). He is credited with the introduction of the use of the phrase "mental tests." After studying in Europe, Cattell developed and sought to refine tests which focused on the cognitive skills that he believed indicated intellectual ability: strength, reaction time, and sensory discrimination.

The first test to examine individual differences in intelligence was devised and published in France by Alfred Binet and Theodore Simon in 1905; it was called the Binet-Simon test. The Binet-Simon test was translated into English and went through a series of revisions by various people. The version of the Binet-Simon test most used in the United States was the Stanford-Binet, which was first published in 1916.

Certain issues related to creativity and intelligence have evolved from discrepancies that have been found in obtaining relationships between creativity and intelligence. It is a mistake to lump creative and intelligent people together: Creative ability is not synonymous with intellectual ability. Many students who are very high in intelligence, as measured by a test, are not high in other intellectual functions, such as creativity. Many students who are high in creativity are not also high in intelligence.

The study of creativity and intelligence has developed based on studies in cognitive, developmental, and educational psychology. Given that psychology as a discipline may be defined as "the systematic study of the mind and behavior," when one studies creativity and intelligence, one learns how to improve performance and lead those persons who are creative, gifted, and talented to new heights. Specifically, when one studies creativity, one gains information about students' abilities in imagination, discovery, and ability to invent. When one studies intelligence, one gains information about students' abilities in logic, memory, and organization.

Creativity and intelligence have played a significant role in the history of psychology and an even greater role in the history of humankind. Progress in education is evident by at least three occurrences. First, interest in measuring individual differences led to the development of tests to quantify creative and intellectual abilities. Second, attention to persons who have been identified as creative, gifted, talented or highly intelligent has led to the development of special programs, learning experiences, and scholarships for these students. Third, the needs of these students have led to research on the students themselves. The results of numerous empirical students have been published to aid parents, educators, and even the gifted or creative individual in understanding the needs of those with special abilities.

The study of creativity and intelligence will continue to play a role in the study of psychology. The need to assess individual differences will continue, as will the need to gain information about how people solve problems. The development of more refined tests will lead to more efficient testing and to more accurate and informative results. They will provide better information to parents, educators, and psychologists about how to encourage and understand creative, gifted, talented, and intelligent students and will help identify persons with special needs. As technology continues to advance, there is a growing need for persons with a high capacity for understanding information as well as persons with the ability to approach old problems with new solutions to be placed in key positions that involve problem solving. Such persons may help address issues related to space exploration as well as maintaining and preserving natural resources.

Bibliography

Albert, Robert S. "Identity, Experiences, and Career Choice Among the Exceptionally Gifted and Eminent." In *Theories of Creativity*, edited by Mark A. Runco and Robert S. Albert. Newbury Park, Calif.: Sage, 1990. This twelve-chapter book on creativity is a compilation of the expertise of persons who have studied creativity in areas such as anthropology, behavior, cognition, development, and ecology. Topics are varied and include creativity in adolescents, creativity in women, relationships between emotional difficulties and creativity, and social factors that influence creativity.

Davis, Gary A., and Sylvia B. Rimm. *Education of the Gifted and Talented.* Englewood Cliffs, N.J.: Prentice-Hall, 1985. Presents various skills, behaviors, and characteristics of students who are gifted, talented, and/or creative. The abilities and skills involved in creative problem solving are explained in clear language. An excellent source to gain information on the educational needs of gifted, talented, or creative students.

Gordon, W. J. "Some Source Material in Discovery-by-Analogy." *Journal of Creative Behavior* 8, no. 4 (1974): 239-257. Focusing on an associative view of invention, discovery, and learning, Gordon cites thirty-eight examples of associative analogical connections which have triggered famous innovations and breakthroughs. A wide variety of technological fields are included. Interesting reading; gives the foundations of many items used in everyday life.

Kline, Paul. *Intelligence: The Psychometric View.* New York: Routledge, 1991. Provides a summary of studies focusing on the nature of intelligence and other human abilities. Topics include the history of the concept of intelligence, and ways to measure intelligence. The definitions of statistical and technical terms are presented in a clear and readable fashion.

Sternberg, Robert J. *Intelligence Applied: Understanding and Increasing Your Intellectual Skills.* Orlando, Fla.: Harcourt Brace Jovanovich, 1986. A training program based on the triarchic theory of intelligence that Sternberg has developed. Details effective strategies for solving various types of problems, including science insight problems and analogies. Exercises for practice are included.

Storfer, Miles D. *Intelligence and Giftedness: The Contributions of Heredity and Early Environment.* San Francisco: Jossey-Bass, 1990. Storfer presents information on the effects of nurture on intelligence, focusing on the nature and development of intellectual giftedness and the characteristics of intellectually gifted people. The concept of intelligence in different socioeconomic conditions, in enrichment programs, and in its varying types are highlighted in separate chapters. The factors that influence intelligence and giftedness are examined in detail.

Torrance, Ellis Paul. *Education and the Creative Potential.* Minneapolis: University of Minnesota Press, 1963. A compilation of seven papers and six experimental studies conducted by Torrance, who developed a test to measure creative thinking and conducted longitudinal studies on creativity. Information on topics such as developing creative potential in schoolchildren and factors that facilitate or inhibit creativity in children.

Weisberg, Robert W. *Creativity: Genius and Other Myths.* New York: W. H. Freeman, 1986. Weisberg discusses the behaviors, activities, and finished products of individuals who have been described as creative. Defines creativity by giving real-life examples and discusses the role that intense knowledge or expertise plays in creative problem solving.

Debra A. King-Johnson

Cross-References

Ability Testing: Individual and Group, 1; Ability Tests: Uses and Misuses, 27; Creativity: Assessing Special Talents, 726; Intelligence: Definition and Theoretical Models, 1328; Intelligence: Giftedness and Retardation, 1334; Intelligence Tests, 1341.

CROWD BEHAVIOR

Type of psychology: Social psychology
Field of study: Group processes

Crowd behavior is a form of group behavior that is characterized by a heightened sense of personal and/or physical anonymity. It results from the reciprocal influence of a temporary, often organized collective of individuals. Studies of the dynamics of crowd behavior have been valuable in understanding the nature of collective behavior, both prosocial (for example, heroic interventions) and antisocial (for example, rioting) in nature.

Principal terms
> COACTOR: a person who interacts, even on a temporary basis, with a crowd
> CROWD: a temporary collection of anonymous coactors that interact with and influence one another
> DEINDIVIDUATION: the loss of self-awareness and evaluation apprehension that accompanies situations that foster personal and physical anonymity
> DIFFUSION OF RESPONSIBILITY: the reduction of one's personal responsibility commonly experienced in group situations; diffusion of responsibility increases as the size of the crowd increases
> EVALUATION APPREHENSION: the awareness that others are observing and evaluating one's behavior; it is associated with a concern for following situational norms and maintaining others' approval
> MERE EXPOSURE EFFECT: the heightening of physiological arousal and an amplification of emotional responses as a result of one's spatial proximity to others
> SOCIAL FACILITATION: the enhancement of a person's most dominant response as a result of the presence of others; for some tasks, such as simple ones, performance is enhanced, while for others, such as novel tasks, performance is impaired
> SOCIAL LOAFING: the tendency to expend less effort while in the presence of others; this phenomenon is most likely to occur on additive tasks in which one's individual effort is obscured as a result of the collective efforts of the group

Overview

One of the first observations made by early psychologists involved the differences between individual and group behavior. A crowd is a collective of individuals who are temporarily engaged in social interaction that may involve a collective task (for example, participating in a demonstration march) or a common focus of attention (for example, listening to a speaker's address). Typically, members of a crowd are interacting in close spatial proximity, and people become influenced by their interactions with their immediate neighbors. Crowd behavior is a particular form of group behavior that is characterized by a heightened sense of personal and/or physical anonymity. Individual members of large crowds, in particular, are unlikely to be personally identifiable. Hence, people in a crowd respond as a collective rather than an aggregate of independent agents.

Crowd behavior is characterized by coactors' decreased sense of self-awareness and an increased sensitivity to situational cues. In particular, three psychological phenomena play important roles in the genesis and maintenance of crowd behavior. Individuals who become members of a crowd experience heightened levels of physiological arousal, diffusion of personal responsibility, and deindividuation.

One of the first systematic observations of the effect of the crowd on individual behavior was the influence of the crowd on physiological arousal. Norman Triplett noticed that cyclists who were pitted against other cyclists raced faster than when they were racing alone against the clock. He tested his notion about the energizing effect of the crowd in 1898 by conducting a laboratory study in which children were timed as they wound fishing reels, both in groups and alone. He found that children worked harder and reeled in their lines faster when they were in the presence of others. The results of this classic study were repeated by other investigators, who reported similar findings. A number of studies support the general rule that the presence of others is associated with enhanced performance in both human samples (for example, people perform simple problem-solving tasks more quickly in a group) and animal samples (for example, chickens eat more feed in a group). The evidence from these early studies suggests that individual levels of physiological arousal are heightened by the presence of coactors. In turn, heightened levels of physiological arousal facilitate the performance of well-learned tasks (that is, a person's dominant response). This phenomenon, the social facilitation effect, has been used to explain the energizing influence of the crowd on individual behavior.

The energizing nature of the crowd on people's levels of physiological arousal also is manifested in other ways. Robert Zajonc has argued that close proximity to others is reliably associated with elevations in subjects' blood pressure and heart rate. This phenomenon, the mere exposure effect, can help to explain the often extremely emotional reactions of crowds. Physiological arousal plays an important role in the experience of emotion. Thus, individual experiences of various emotional states can be intensified by increases in physiological arousal. Hence, in addition to its influence on task performance, the presence of a crowd can heighten the emotional reactions experienced by coactors.

The second phenomenon experienced by members of a crowd is diffusion of responsibility. Diffusion of responsibility refers to the reduction of a coactor's perception of individual responsibility for the consequences of the crowd's behavior. When a person acts alone, for example, he or she is fully responsible for the consequences of his or her behavior. Thus, if a person commits an antisocial act, such as throwing a brick through a windowpane, that person alone is responsible for that action. On the other hand, individual responsibility is diffused as the number of coactors increases. For example, a woman might be one of many members of a large crowd that is "baiting" a police officer. Alone, she may never scream obscenities at police officers. As a member of a crowd, however, she is not the only person responsible for the officer's harassment. She shares responsibility for the incident with other members of the crowd, thus lowering her sense of personal responsibility for the incident. In most people's perceptions, the crowd itself, rather than individual members, is responsible for its behavior.

Diffusion of responsibility is related to another psychological change in addition to decreased perceptions of personal responsibility. As members of a crowd, coactors are often relieved of any evaluation apprehension they might ordinarily experience. Evaluation apprehension involves the awareness that others are observing and evaluating one's behavior. People who experience evaluation apprehension are concerned with maintaining a positive impression and conforming to social norms. In a crowd, the focus of coactors is often away from the individual; thus, the individual may not be as concerned with maintaining a positive appearance for others' sake. Further, if a crowd is involved in a common task that involves a pooling of effort, studies show that diffusion of responsibility has been associated not only with reduced evaluation apprehension, but also with reduced effort. Coactors expend less effort in a common group task, such as a tug-of-war game, than when they are acting alone. The resultant behavior, social loafing, has been proposed as an explanation for the tendency of coactors to expend less effort in situations that encourage the diffusion of responsibility among the members of a crowd.

The final phenomenon, deindividuation, results from both the heightened levels of physiological arousal and the diffusion of responsibility experienced by members of a crowd. Deindividuation is a psychological state of reduced self-awareness that is particularly acute when crowd conditions foster physical and personal anonymity. Anonymity is heightened in very large crowds, crowds that form at night, and crowds that engage in ritualistic, rhythmic behaviors such as chanting, singing, or clapping. The individual experience of deindividuation involves a complete loss of evaluation apprehension, diminished attention to oneself and one's behavior, and a loss of self-restraint. When individuals experience deindividuation as a result of being part of a crowd, they become particularly responsive to the social cues of the situation. Hence, participants in a large religious ceremony may become extremely emotional, cry out, and become carried away by the ecstasy of their communal religious experience. Conversely, members of an angry mob may become increasingly angry, restless, and hostile, and ultimately cause a riot.

Applications

Over the last hundred years, a number of laboratory and field studies concerning the influence of others on the individual have been conducted by social psychologists. These studies are designed to identify and describe the situational factors that are critical in the elicitation and maintenance of crowd behavior.

One important finding is that the energizing effect of the crowd increases with the number of coactors and, thus, the density of the crowd. Jonathan Freedman and his colleagues investigated the effects of density on an audience's reactions to two films. In the low-density condition, subjects were instructed to spread out in a theater in order to ensure that they were comfortable. In the high-density condition, subjects were instructed to sit in the center of a theater. In each condition, a confederate of the experimenter was instructed to applaud loudly at the conclusion of only the second film. The results of this study suggested that the positive emotional response generated by the confederate was enhanced in the high-density condition. The experimenters' ratings of the audience responses to the second film indicated that there was much more applause in the high-density than in the low-density condition.

The proximity of others can explain the social facilitation effort observed in this study. Two factors are particularly important in explaining the response of the audience to the confederate's cued applause. First, high density is associated with increased arousal in both animals and humans. Second, coactors' responses are a valuable source of information when individuals assess a social situation. Subjects in this study reported how much they enjoyed each film, and although the audience as a whole responded more positively to the second film than the first, individual ratings of enjoyment did not differ between films. On the other hand, subjects reported that others in the audience had enjoyed the second film much more than the first. Thus, the social feedback one gathers from the responses of others in a crowd may play an important role in assessing and responding to the situation.

The presence of others, however, does not always produce a positive social facilitation effect. Psychologist Alan Ingham and his colleagues investigated the influence of the diffusion of responsibility on coactors' performance. In particular, these researchers were interested in identifying the factors that produce social loafing in a group that is charged with completing a task for which everyone is responsible but no one is individually accountable. An apparatus was designed for this experiment that simulated a tug-of-war game. Subjects were led, blindfolded, to an apparatus that had positions for six participants. They were then told to pull on a rope with all their strength.

In the alone condition, subjects were told that they were pulling on the rope by themselves. In the diffusion-of-responsibility conditions, subjects were told that they were pulling with two to five other persons. The results of the study indicated that subjects pulled 18 percent harder when they knew they were alone than when they believed they were working as a member of a group. As predicted, since subjects' individual performances could not be evaluated by others, the social-loafing effect was observed. Further, it is possible that the blindfolds eliminated any evaluation apprehension that subjects might have felt in this experiment.

These studies were concerned with fairly innocuous social behaviors performed in the safety of the laboratory. Other studies of crowd behavior are concerned with the antisocial nature of crowds. Social psychologist Brian Mullen was interested in studying the influence of crowd density on a particularly antisocial and virulent form of crowd behavior, the lynch mob. He collected sixty newspaper accounts of lynchings and analyzed them to determine the degree of violence and atrocity expressed by the mobs. Mullen assessed the density of the mob by comparing the number of victims with the total number of participants in each situation. He also recorded the occurrence of five acts of violence (hanging, shooting, burning, stabbing, and mutilation of the victim) and evaluated the duration of the lynching (relatively quick, moderate, or tortuous).

First, Mullen predicted that the lynchers would exhibit decreased self-awareness and increased deindividuation as the size of the mob increased relative to the number of victims. Then he predicted that the savagery of the attack directed toward the victim would increase as deindividuation increased. These predictions were upheld. As the size of the mob increased, behavioral self-restraint declined. The larger mobs were found to have committed the most savage acts of atrocity against the victims.

Context

Many historical events appear to have resulted from the collective behavior of the crowd. As such, the crowd has long been the focus of study in the humanities and social sciences. The psychology of crowd behavior began as a European phenomenon. Gustave Le Bon published the first systematic study, *Psychologie de foules* (1895; *The Crowd: A Study of the Popular Mind*, 1896). In Le Bon's view, individual logic and rationality are lost in the emotional contagion generated by the crowd. The group mind is presumed to take over, and the crowd becomes a homogeneous social organism, a spontaneous and violent entity that eschews rationality and responds to primeval, unconscious motivation. While Sigmund Freud agreed with Le Bon concerning inherent antisocial crowd behavior, he did not accept the concept of a group mind. Freud posited that membership in a crowd allowed the ego to relax its repression of the id impulse. As a result, when a person becomes a member of a crowd, he or she regresses and exhibits the free expression of the primitive libidinal energy of the id.

Le Bon's seminal work was further elaborated upon by his contemporary Gabriel Tarde, who described various types of crowds and crowd behaviors. In particular, his description of organized crowds, or masses, provided a means of analyzing the social effects of institutions such as the military and the church. His work described the process of suggestibility and imitation that characterizes crowds that have been mobilized by a charismatic leader. Tarde also provided early insights into the interactive roles of the media, public-opinion leaders, and mass communication.

These early theoretical formulations provided an important cornerstone for the European and American social psychological studies of crowd behavior that emerged after World War II. The orientation of social psychology moved the study of crowds away from the group mind and suggestibility to the identification of situational factors that encourage the expression of crowd behavior. Experimental and field studies of crowd behavior flourished within the context of the political unrest of the 1960's and public concerns over the dehumanizing consequences of urbanization. It is important to note that not all social psychological research has addressed the antisocial nature of the crowd. Perhaps as a result of cultural events such as the surprisingly peaceful Woodstock music festival of 1969, which had a crowd of 300,000 people, and the encounter movement of the late 1960's, a number of studies have investigated the prosocial consequences of crowd behavior.

Bibliography

Brown, Hedy. *People, Groups, and Society.* Philadelphia: Open University Press, 1985. An extremely accessible introduction to group influence and crowd behavior that includes an introduction to general principles of social influence and intergroup relations. The similarities and differences between crowds and other social groups are also discussed.

Galanter, Marc. *Cults: Faith, Healing, and Coercion.* New York: Oxford University Press, 1989. A fascinating study of charismatic groups that is particularly appropriate for the general reader. Discusses the unique social factors that characterize such groups and provides three famous case histories (Jonestown, the Unification Church, and Alcoholics Anonymous). A detailed explanation of the social forces that are experienced by members of cults and other extremely cohesive social groups.

Gaskell, George, and Robert Benewick, eds. *The Crowd in Contemporary Britain.* London: Sage, 1987. This edited volume is an excellent collection of studies and observations of crowd behavior. Theories of crowd behavior are introduced, then historical and contemporary examples of crowd behavior are presented. The chapters in this volume are concerned with a range of crowd behaviors, from peaceful to violent actions.

Hogg, Michael A., and Dominic Abrams. *Social Identifications: A Social Psychology of Intergroup Relations and Group Processes.* London: Routledge, 1988. This volume adopts a social-identity perspective on group influence. Two chapters are particularly relevant to the effects of crowd membership on personal identity and behavior. The authors present an excellent summary of the effects of the presence of others on social performance. Another excellent chapter addresses the nature of collective behavior and deindividuation. An accessible review of complex issues.

Milgram, Stanley. *The Individual in a Social World: Essays and Experiments.* Reading, Mass.: Addison-Wesley, 1977. An excellent introduction to group influence and crowd behavior. Milgram, a prominent researcher in the field, describes a number of classic experiments on social influence and crowd behavior. The articles in part 1 ("The Individual in the City") and part 2 ("The Individual and the Group") of this work are particularly relevant to crowd behavior.

Paulus, Paul B., ed. *Psychology of Group Influence.* 2d ed. Hillsdale, N.J.: Lawrence Erlbaum, 1989. This edited volume contains a selection of articles on many aspects of crowd behavior. Specific topics include the social facilitation effect, deindividuation, and environmental influences on crowds. An excellent source of theoretical perspectives and empirical data relevant to crowd behavior for the college-level reader.

Perry, Joseph B., Jr., and Meredith David Pugh. *Collective Behavior: Response to Social Stress.* St. Paul, Minn.: West, 1978. A general discussion of the crowd and its social influence. The authors first present a theoretical discussion of the crowd, rumor, contagion, and deindividuation, then provide many examples of crowd violence, control, mobilization, and social movements. A very accessible introduction to the topic with specific focus on collective behavior.

Zimbardo, Philip G. "The Human Choice: Individuation, Reason, and Order Versus Deindividuation, Impulse, and Chaos." In *Nebraska Symposium on Motivation: 1969*, edited by William J. Arnold and D. Levine. Lincoln: University of Nebraska Press, 1970. An accessible and authoritative discussion of the factors that elicit deindividuation. Presents a number of experiments, anecdotes, and everyday examples of the prosocial and antisocial behavioral effects of increased urbanization and other sociocultural factors that increase anonymity and reduce individual self-awareness and behavioral inhibitions.

Cheryl A. Rickabaugh

Cross-References

Affiliation and Friendship, 142; Aggression: Reduction and Control, 169; Altruism, Cooperation, and Empathy, 228; Cooperation, Competition, and Negotiation, 689; Crowding, 744; Group Decision Making, 1114; Groups: Nature and Function, 1125; Helping: Bystander Intervention, 1163.

CROWDING

Type of psychology: Stress
Field of study: Critical issues in stress

Crowding refers to feelings people have when they view their space as insufficient for their activities or their comfort. The study of crowding examines the relationship between high-density environments and stress reactions; stress reactions could include psychological or physical breakdown in an individual.

Principal terms

INSIDE DENSITY: the number of individuals per dwelling or per room
OUTSIDE DENSITY: the number of individuals (or sometimes the number of dwellings) per acre of land area
PERSONAL SPACE: the area around one's body which others may not enter without causing discomfort
SOCIAL DENSITY: the number of others with whom one shares an area
SPATIAL DENSITY: the amount of physical space available per individual
STRESS: a reaction with psychological and physiological components caused by having to adjust to the environment; at high levels, it can cause a breakdown of the organism
TERRITORY: an area of fixed boundaries over which one claims control

Overview

Crowding is a psychological response to a combination of environmental conditions. The feeling of being crowded is caused by the way one perceives the surrounding environment. Researchers have found it useful to distinguish between the actual physical characteristics of the environment and the way a person perceives it. In this overview, the major causes and the major effects of crowding will be described, as well as some of the factors that can reduce the negative effects of crowding.

One of the environmental conditions that can lead to the feeling of crowding is social density. Social density is determined by the number of people who share space with a person. Social density can be independent of spatial density. If there are ten people in a 93-square-meter space and twenty people in a 185-square-meter space, the social density is doubled in the second space, while the spatial density is equal for the two spaces. Increasing social density can cause the perception of crowding even though the physical space per person remains the same. An increase in spatial density (the number of people in a given area) can also cause a perception of crowding.

Another environmental condition that can cause the feeling of crowding to occur is the invasion of one's personal space. Robert Sommer, in his book *Personal Space: The Behavioral Basis of Design* (1969), defined personal space as "the area around one's body into which others may not come." It is proposed that each person has a space around his or her body that is considered personal. If another person comes into this area, the first person feels stressed and will try to reestablish a comfortable distance, either physically, by moving away, or psychologically, perhaps by ignoring the invader. The shape and the size of one's personal space varies with the individual's cultural customs, gender, and temperament, as well with the type of social situation and social relationship of the moment. The need for personal space will vary depending on whether one is male or female, at a party or a business meeting, with strangers or with friends. Personal space invasions can occur when only a single other person is present, but they are more likely when social and/or spatial density is high.

A fourth cause of crowding can be an encroachment upon one's territory. A territory is a fixed physical space that a person feels a right to control. This feeling may derive from legal ownership, as with a home or car, or it may depend upon repeated usage, as in the case of a seat in a classroom or other public area. When other people enter or use one's territory without permission, the individual will often feel a need to defend the territory in some way. The demand on the individual for adjustment to territorial encroachment can cause stress.

A fifth cause of the feeling of crowding is interference with goal-directed behavior. When the presence of others interferes with activities so that a person cannot accomplish his or her goals, a feeling of crowding may often result. The interference with one's ability to pursue goals may be an underlying reason that some of the other conditions lead to crowding. For example, when social and spatial density are high, the feeling of crowding that results may be largely caused by the interference with goal-directed behavior by the other people.

The three major categories of effects of crowding are affective reactions, physiological reactions, and changes in social behavior. Generally, crowding causes people to feel less happy, less comfortable, and more anxious. Physiological responses to crowding include increased heart rate, higher blood pressure, and higher arousal as measured by skin conductance, palmar sweat, and cortisol levels. These responses are each consistent with higher stress, which can cause a variety of physical illnesses. The increased stress level caused by crowding can reduce the effectiveness of a person's immune system so that the ability to resist infection and disease is reduced. Studies have found that students in high-density dormitories visited the student health center more than those in low-density dorms, and that those on high-density naval vessels had more illness complaints than those in low-density conditions.

Changes in social behavior have been observed as a result of crowding. Several studies have shown that males tend to dislike other males under conditions of high social and spatial density. Females, on the other hand, seem to like other females more under high-density conditions. It may be that the males' need for a larger personal space and their more competitive orientation lead to this difference between the sexes in the effect of density on interpersonal attraction. Another general response to high density is social withdrawal. People show a reduced tendency to give eye contact, are less willing to discuss intimate topics, and are less likely to interact in high-density settings. There is less helping behavior under high density, and aggression increases in some people.

Since crowding is a feeling based on a person's perception of the environment, the physical factors that sometimes cause the feeling of crowding do not always do so. Sometimes other circumstances can act to prevent the environmental conditions from causing the feeling of crowding which would then lead to the effects of crowding described above. For example, high social density does not always lead to stress, because some other conditions may prevent the feeling of crowding from occurring. These other conditions could be called mediators of crowding. Major mediators of the effects of crowding are feelings of control, privacy, and safety.

The feeling of having control can reduce the likelihood of a stress reaction in situations of high density, spatial invasions, and interference. A person who feels he or she has the ability to change the situation can tolerate it better even when no change is actually made. People in stressful situations who feel they could escape or remove the stress if they wanted to do not experience the negative effects experienced by those who have no such control. In high-density situations, the ability to maintain some feeling of privacy can mediate the effects of crowding. Sometimes the use of screens or partitions between people in high-density areas can reduce the perception of crowding.

In some instances of high density and spatial invasions, there is a threat to the individual which increases the stress reactions to crowding. When the safety of the individual can be assured, this aspect of the effect of crowding can be eliminated.

Applications

The notion of crowding as a concept explaining the relationship between the environmental conditions that cause it and the effects it has on people's lives has been used to understand how people act in numerous settings. Social and health problems in cities, neighborhoods, housing projects, dormitories, mental health facilities, prisons, offices, submarines, and individual residences have been examined and explained in terms of the concepts of crowding research.

Michael Saks and Edward Krupat, in their book *Social Psychology and Its Applications* (1988), describe an example of the application of the knowledge of crowding to the improvement of student life in dormitory living. Andrew Baum and Stuart Valins employed the notion of social density and spatial density as well as knowledge of some of the causes and effects of crowding in designing a study to compare the feelings of college students in two different types of dormitories. In one type of dormitory, there was a long corridor with sixteen or seventeen double-occupancy rooms. In the middle of the hall, there was a large bathroom. There was a lounge at one end of the hall. The other design employed a suite arrangement with three bedrooms, a bathroom, and a small lounge in each suite. Each of the designs had about the same closet space, the same number of students per dormitory floor, and the same amount of space per student.

The spatial density is the same in each design, but the social density of the long-corridor dorms is about four times that of the suites. At the end of the first year, 58 percent of the students in the long-corridor dorms reported feeling "crowded," while only 10 percent of the suite residents reported such feelings. Further, only 12 percent of the students in the long-corridor dorms believed that they could control what happened to them in their hallways, while 40 percent of the students in the suites believed they had control. These results led Baum and Glenn Davis to investigate the effects of making a change in the long-corridor design which is so common in many colleges. They simply divided the long corridors in half by installing a wall with a door in the middle of the hall, creating two sections of twenty students rather than one group of forty. Students were randomly assigned either to this modified short-corridor arrangement or to the long-corridor style. They found that stress-related and control-related problems were fewer in the shorter-corridor design. By seven weeks into the term, the short-corridor residents had more local group interest and interaction, more use of shared space for social purposes, and less withdrawal.

These studies illustrate how the knowledge of crowding not only can lead to designing improvements for future construction but also can enable the use of simple modifications to existing structures that improve the lives of those who inhabit them.

Another illustration of the application of the crowding concept has been the subject of federal court law suits in more than half the states in the United States. This is the issue of prison crowding. Between 1975 and 1980, the population of the nation's prisons increased 94 percent. The prison population increases of the 1970's and 1980's required many of the prisons in the United States to house far more prisoners than they were designed to hold. In numerous court cases throughout the country, prisoners sued on the basis that the crowded conditions violated their constitutional rights by constituting "cruel and unusual punishment." The reasoning behind these suits was that since crowding causes stress, which has negative effects on physical and psychological health, the extreme crowding in some of the prisons created a serious and unreasonable threat to the well-being of the inmates.

Since this was a national social, scientific, and legal issue which could affect the spending of hundreds of millions of dollars, as well as the lives of hundreds of thousands of prisoners, dozens of studies were conducted in prisons and jails to measure the effects of social and spatial density on the health and behavior of the inmates. Verne Cox, Paul Paulus, and Garvin McCain have published more than half a dozen studies done in prison settings. In an article that appeared in *American Psychologist* (1984), they reviewed more than forty articles published by others on the subject of prison crowding. Studies have shown an increase in death rates as the population increases. Disciplinary infractions are higher in higher density. Illness complaints increase as social density increases. Suicide rates increase by three times the increase in population. Cox, Paulus, and McCain believe that these effects of crowding are not necessarily restricted to a prison setting. The study of crowding and its effects will continue to have important applications as cities and institutions continue to grow in population.

Context

In 1962, John Calhoun published the results of several years of research in his article "Population Density and Social Pathology" in *Scientific American*. In his studies, he built mouse and rat cities and observed the effects of population growth over a period of many months. These rodents were always furnished with adequate food and water. The major change that occurred as their populations grew was the increase in social and spatial density that they experienced. In one case, eight mice founded a colony that grew to a population of twenty-two hundred in about one and one-half year's time. At this point, the population growth stopped and mice began to die faster than they were born. Even when the population dropped to what might be said to be normal levels, the dying continued, until the last mouse died, 1,553 days after the experiment began.

In other studies as well, the rats and mice responded to increases in population with a general breakdown of normal functioning. Some became aggressive; others were unusually withdrawn. Mothers did not care properly for their young and showed an unusually high rate of cannibalism. There were even increases in frequency in the rat equivalents of crime, delinquency, and sexual deviations. Other animal studies supported the notion that high population levels seemed to cause a stress-related breakdown in the functioning of the animals, sometimes to the point of the population dying out completely. All scientists are aware of the vast differences between the functioning and social behavior of rats and that of humans; however, they are also aware that there are often parallels between the functioning of lower animals and of humans. This awareness made the results of the rat studies extremely provocative for social psychologists and others interested in the environment-behavior relationship. It was apparent in the 1960's and early 1970's that there were problems in large population centers which were intriguingly similar to those shown in the rat populations.

Social and environmental psychologists began to study the effects of crowding on humans. By the 1970's, a body of research literature on the issue had accumulated. Another source of interest in this research was the environmental movement of the 1960's. Books such as Paul R. Ehrlich's *The Population Bomb* (1968) raised the specter of a population growing at an ever-increasing rate so that tremendous over-crowding was inevitable. This threat had to be assessed. Scientific data about the potential effects of this population growth were sought. These early prophecies of the danger resulting from a growing population were probably overly pessimistic, but data were needed to address the issues; still more data are needed to answer questions about the effects of the various aspects of crowding, as well as to provide methods for dealing with any undesirable effects.

Bibliography

Altman, I. *The Environment and Social Behavior: Privacy, Personal Space, Territory, and Crowding.* Monterey, Calif.: Brooks/Cole, 1975. Provides an overview of the social psychological theories of phenomena related to crowding as well as crowding itself. Stresses the relationship of crowding and related phenomena to social behavior rather than individual behavior. Provides a good introduction to the theoretical issues of crowding; the reader may see how more recent data fit into these conceptualizations.

Bell, P. A., J. D. Fisher, A. Baum, and T. E. Greene. "High Density and Crowding." In *Environmental Psychology.* Fort Worth, Tex.: Holt, Rinehart and Winston, 1990. This textbook chapter covers the entire field of environmental psychology. Other chapters in this book are useful for coverage of phenomena closely related to crowding such as "Personal Space and Territoriality" and "Architecture, Design, and Behavior." A comprehensive book which gives detailed coverage of crowding as well as related topics.

Fischer, Claude S. "The Individual in the City: States of Mind." In *The Urban Experience.* New York: Harcourt Brace Jovanovich, 1976. Focuses on crowding as viewed by city dwellers. First reviews the studies of crowding, then focuses on the relationship between urbanism and psychological stress and disorder. Goes on to consider "urban alienation" and, finally, provides evidence and conclusions about whether living in cities makes people unhappy.

Freedman, J. L. *Crowding and Behavior.* New York: Viking Press, 1975. Describes several of Freedman's studies on the effects of density on human performance and attitudes in a variety of settings. Proposes an original theory to explain these effects. Freedman's density-intensity theory explains how density may have negative effects in some situations and positive effects in others.

Insel, Paul, and Henry Clay Lindgren. *Too Close for Comfort: The Psychology of Crowding.* Englewood Cliffs, N.J.: Prentice-Hall, 1978. These authors have a background in personality and social psychology, cross-cultural psychology, and social ecology (the study of the relationship between the physical and social aspects of the environment). They bring this relevant experience to bear on the question of the effects of crowding on attitudes, personality, solving problems, and mental and physical health. A very readable paperback that covers the issues in an interesting way.

Saks, M. J., and Edward Krupat. "Environment and Behavior." In *Social Psychology and Its Applications.* New York: Harper & Row, 1988. An abbreviated overview of environmental psychology which places crowding in context. Deals with crowding and related issues concisely, so that it provides a good way to cover most of the issues quickly.

Gary T. Long

Cross-References

Aggression: Definitions and Theoretical Explanations, 162; Crowd Behavior, 737; Environmental Psychology, 978; Health Psychology, 1139; Stress Prediction and Control, 2458; Stress-Related Diseases, 2464, Stressors, 2471.

DATA DESCRIPTION: DESCRIPTIVE STATISTICS

Type of psychology: Psychological methodologies
Field of study: Descriptive methodologies

*Descriptive statistics are procedures by which data can be summarized and or-
ganized. These procedures provide a picture of the whole group and can be used in
more advanced statistical approaches.*

Principal terms
AVERAGE: also referred to as central tendency; a measure (mean,
median, or mode) that provides information about the typical score
CORRELATION: the relationship between two variables
DESCRIPTIVE STATISTICS: procedures that summarize and organize data
DISPERSION: also referred to as variability; a measure (range, semi-
interquartile range, standard deviation, or variance) that provides
information about the difference among the scores
FREQUENCY DISTRIBUTION: the pairing of a measurement with the
number of people obtaining that measurement
INFERENTIAL STATISTICS: procedures by which generalizations about
a large group can be made on the basis of a smaller group

Overview

Psychologists utilize descriptive statistics to organize and summarize the data they
collect from a research project. While these procedures provide information about
the group as a whole, the individual nature of the scores may be lost. Two of the
more common procedures to organize and summarize data are frequency distributions and graphs.

To create a frequency distribution, a psychologist counts the number of people
who obtain a particular score on some measure. This number becomes the frequency
of that particular score. For example, a psychologist may give a group of people a
scale that assesses depression—for example, the twenty-one-item Beck Depression
Inventory. Scores on this scale range from 0 to 63. If ten people obtain a score of 35,
then ten is the frequency of that score. From the frequency distribution, the psychologist can tell whether the group is depressed (high scores occur most frequently) or
not depressed (low scores occur most frequently), or some combination of the two (a
mix of low and high scores). When teachers communicate the number of As, Bs, Cs,
Ds, and Es made on a test, they are using a frequency distribution of test scores to
summarize class performance. From such a distribution, a student can tell his or her
relative standing on the test.

A frequency distribution is presented in tabular form. This distribution of scores
may also be presented as a graph that is composed of a horizontal (x-axis) and
vertical (y-axis) line. There are many ways to graph frequency distributions; however, all these graphs have frequency on the y-axis and measurement on the x-axis.

A graph may be preferred because "a picture is worth a thousand words." A bell-shaped curve is one example of a graph of a frequency distribution.

The data may be summarized further by calculating measures of average (central tendency). A psychologist may want to know the score the largest number of students got on the depression scale, that is, the mode of the depression scores. The most popular song, the most common college major, and the grade received most often on the test all are examples of modes. A psychologist may also want to know the score that splits the distribution in half, with half the scores falling above that score and half below. In this case, the psychologist wants to know the median of the depression scores. Knowing the median allows the researcher to do a median split, creating low and high depressed groups of subjects. The median score splits the data in half, just as the median strip of a highway splits the highway in half.

The mode and the median are both measures of central tendency; however, neither measure depends on every score in the distribution. If the psychologist wants the average of all scores, he or she calculates the mean of the data, sometimes referred to as the arithmetic average. The mean is obtained by adding all the scores and dividing by the number of scores. This measure of central tendency is often used in many types of inferential statistics. An overall grade point average, a baseball player's batting average, and the average grade received by the class on a test all are examples of means.

A measure of central tendency provides information about the typical score, but this is only one special aspect of a distribution. Further information that helps describe the distribution involves measures of how spread out the scores are. For this information, psychologists calculate measures of dispersion, or variability. These measures include the range, the semi-interquartile range, the variance, and the standard deviation. These dispersion scores are often paired with a particular measure of central tendency so that the psychologist knows the typical score and the difference among the scores in the distribution. This allows the psychologist to know how representative the typical scores really are. The median and the semi-interquartile range are paired, as are the mean and variance or standard deviation.

Once the psychologist has calculated the measures of central tendency and variability, he or she can ascertain the shape of the distribution of scores. The shape will, in turn, provide information that allows the psychologist to choose the appropriate measure of central tendency and variability to use to describe the data. If the data show a normal bell-shaped curve, the psychologist typically selects the mean and variance or standard deviation to represent the data. If there are some extremely high or low scores, however, the data may not show a normal bell-shaped pattern (a skewed distribution). In this case, the psychologist typically selects the median and semi-interquartile range to represent the data.

In the above examples, the psychologist is examining scores on one variable, such as depression. The psychologist could also examine the frequency of scores on two variables, such as depression and intelligence. The psychologist would then count the number of people who obtained both a particular depression score and a particular score on an intelligence test. Because the scores on two variables were considered, this would be called a bivariate frequency distribution.

From this distribution, the psychologist could establish the degree of relationship between the two variables by correlating them. One common type of correlation is the Pearson product moment correlation. This correlation indicates the extent to which the two variables are related in a linear way. For example, in the case of depression and intelligence, a correlation could indicate that more intelligent people are more depressed, or that less intelligent people are more depressed, or that there is no relationship between depression and intelligence. Once the correlation between two variables is known, the psychologist can then use one score to make predictions about the other. People who work in college admissions use this technique to predict how well a graduating senior will perform in college by using known correlations between high school and college grade point average.

Applications

Descriptive statistics are often used by researchers describing the subjects or methods involved in a research project. Such descriptions are useful for knowing what generalizations can be made from the results of that project. For example, researchers studying dating couples often utilize college students as subjects. The researchers usually provide information about whether the dating couples in the study are freshmen, sophomores, juniors, or seniors. The researchers typically also report the average length of time the couples have been dating. In research projects, it may be important to report the average age or educational level of the subjects. This information is useful in determining to whom the results of the research project may be realistically applied (generalized). For example, the results of a study using freshmen dating couples might not provide information about all dating couples.

It also may be important to describe the task utilized in a research study. As Ellen Lenney notes, one research area in which the task is an important issue is in gender research. In such studies, differences between the behavior of men and women are examined. It is important for the researcher to determine whether the differences found in such studies reflect the difference between men and women or result from the gender nature of the task. Answers to such questions become helpful in making judgments about the types of tasks and methodologies to which the results of the study generalize.

In addition to addressing questions about generalizability, descriptive statistics may be used to help manipulate a variable in a study. For example, a research interest of some psychologists is to examine behavioral differences between people who possess different levels of a personality trait. Such a researcher, for example, may want to know whether depressed people behave differently from nondepressed people, or whether people with high self-esteem behave differently from people with low self-esteem. One way this research is conducted is by giving subjects a personality test. Subjects may then be split into a high or a low group on the basis of the median score on the test.

In each of the above examples, the calculations of descriptive statistics would be a preliminary step in the data analysis. After the research study is conducted, the chances are good that the researcher will then take the descriptive statistics and use them in inferential statistics. In inferential statistics, the researcher uses the descriptive statistics to make some general statements about the population being studied (for example, depressed people, or people with high self-esteem).

Although psychologists are generally interested in individual behavior, some psychologists are concerned with information about the communities in which these individuals live. Psychologists who study how the environment affects behavior might find the descriptive statistics in a *County and City Data Book* issued by the United States Bureau of the Census very helpful. This book reports the median value of occupied housing units, not the mean or the mode. The median is reported here because data on the value of housing usually does not show a normal distribution as a result of the inclusion of very high-priced or very low-priced housing, which skews the distribution.

Similarly, in a book entitled *Crowding and Behavior* (1975), Jonathan Freedman is interested in the relationship between population density and other variables such as criminality. The researcher may define population density as the number of people per square mile, and include communities that vary along this dimension. This variable may then be correlated with a measure of criminality. Such information may influence where one wants to live and work.

A correlational study such as this may be criticized for two reasons. First, the two variables may be related because each is related to a third variable. Thus, population density and criminality may be related because each is related to socioeconomic status. Crime rate may be higher in more densely populated communities because of conditions of poverty, which affect both variables. This criticism can be handled with advanced statistical techniques which require that socioeconomic status be measured. Second, the existence of a correlation does not indicate which variable was the cause and which was the effect. Density may cause crime rate, or crime rate may cause density. This criticism can be handled with a more complex design that requires that the two variables be measured at two points in time. These two criticisms notwithstanding, the existence of a correlation between density and any second variable can help researchers make predictions about an overpopulated world.

Correlation can also be used to assess the reliability and validity of a test, such as the test of depression mentioned earlier. When assessing reliability, the psychologist is interested in knowing whether people obtain relatively the same test score on different testing occasions. One way the test's reliability can be established is by correlating people's scores on the same test across time. When assessing validity, the psychologist is interested in determining whether the test measures what it is supposed to measure. Psychologists can establish the test's validity in part by correlating test scores with some external measure. Psychologists generally use tests that are reliable and valid.

In many of the previous examples, descriptive statistics have been a means to an end, the end being their use in inferential statistics. Descriptive statistics may also be an end in themselves, such as when students learn the percentile ranks of their scores on college board tests. A psychologist may also want to know the average length of time a client is in therapy, or the violent crime rate of a given population. Thus, descriptive statistics are often used alone, and as a preliminary step to inferential statistics.

Context

Most textbooks on the history of psychology establish 1879 as the date of the founding of psychology as a discipline. At that time, Wilhelm Wundt founded the first psychological laboratory. Thus, from its inception, psychology has had strong scientific roots. From this perspective, then, psychologists have long believed that concepts have to be measured to be scientifically acceptable. Their adoption of the scientific method also meant that psychologists had to make carefully controlled observations of the phenomena they were studying.

During the nineteenth century, measurement became more sophisticated and many descriptive statistical concepts were being named, though many of them had been known and used in other disciplines for years. According to Edwin G. Boring in *A History of Experimental Psychology* (1950), statistical methods in psychology began in 1896; it was then that Karl Pearson established the correlational procedures that bear his name and are used today. Correlation was first reported in 1888 by Sir Francis Galton, who studied individual differences among people. Galton is credited with naming the median, whereas Pearson is credited with naming the mode.

As psychology has developed as a science, descriptive statistics have often been useful for inferential statistics. Indeed, textbooks on statistics for the behavioral and social sciences concentrate most heavily on inferential statistics, as do most articles in psychological journals, although the descriptive statistics are included. Over the years, the inferential statistics used by psychologists have become more complex because of the computer, software packages, and the types of questions psychologists are asking. Psychologists appear much less interested in new techniques for data summary, although recent textbooks in statistics for the social and behavioral sciences have included alternatives to frequency distributions. The inclination to use inferential statistics for hypothesis-testing purposes is unlikely to change in the foreseeable future.

Descriptive statistics will also continue to play a part in everyday life. People in many walks of life collect data that need to be organized and summarized. Many examples of descriptive statistics can be found in a daily newspaper. In the sports section, one may read about the number of gold, silver, or bronze medals won by the United States during the Olympics. The entertainment section may report the most popular motion picture, whereas the business section may report on the earnings of the major retail stores.

Descriptive statistics are used in other social sciences, such as political science and sociology, as well as in psychology. Descriptive statistics will increasingly be utilized as more and more data are collected on more and more phenomena. The ability to take large amounts of data and summarize them has helped and will continue to help people understand themselves and the world in which they live.

Bibliography

Beck, Aaron T., Robert A. Steer, and Margery G. Garbin. "Psychometric Properties of the Beck Depression Inventory: Twenty-five Years of Evaluation." *Clinical Psychology Review* 8, no. 1 (1988): 77-100. Discusses the Beck Depression Inventory and its history, as well as several types of reliability and validity. An excellent example of the research needed to demonstrate the reliability and validity of a psychological test.

Boring, Edwin Garrigues. *A History of Experimental Psychology.* 2d ed. New York: Appleton-Century-Crofts, 1950. A classic text on the history of experimental psychology. Provides an excellent account of the early days of psychology and the people who started and advanced the discipline.

Dudycha, Arthur L., and Linda W. Dudycha. "Behavioral Statistics: An Historical Perspective." In *Statistical Issues: A Reader for the Behavioral Sciences*, edited by Roger E. Kirk. Monterey, Calif.: Brooks/Cole, 1972. This highly readable article relates the history of descriptive and inferential statistics and their use by psychologists. Most textbooks on statistics for the social and behavioral neglect this important topic.

Freedman, Jonathan L. *Crowding and Behavior.* San Francisco: W. H. Freeman, 1975. Provides an in-depth analysis of research on population density. Both correlational and experimental work are presented here. Although Freedman's theory about the impact of population density is not the only approach taken by environmental psychologists, the book includes all the early research on this topic.

Lenney, Ellen. "Women's Self-Confidence in Achievement Settings." *Psychological Bulletin* 84, no. 1 (1977): 1-13. Reviews the psychological literature demonstrating that women have lower self-confidence than men, and delineates a number of variables on which this gender difference may depend.

Runyon, Richard P., and Audrey Haber. *Fundamentals of Behavioral Statistics.* 7th ed. New York: McGraw-Hill, 1991. Typical of the many textbooks written for the student studying statistics in the social and behavioral sciences. The formulas for the various descriptive statistics are presented, as are explanations of their utility. The authors do an excellent job of presenting the material clearly and as simply as possible.

George I. Whitehead III

Cross-References

Archival Data, 293; Behavioral Assessment and Personality Rating Scales, 387; Data Description: Inferential Statistics, 757; The Scientific Method in Psychology, 2148; Survey Research: Questionnaires and Interviews, 2507.

DATA DESCRIPTION: INFERENTIAL STATISTICS

Type of psychology: Psychological methodologies
Fields of study: Descriptive methodologies; methodological issues

Inferential statistics is a branch of mathematics that enables researchers to judge whether their findings about people in a sample are likely to be true of the larger group or population from which the sample is drawn, and whether a behavior difference between two experimental groups results from some condition imposed by the research design or simply occurs by chance.

Principal terms

DATA: a collection of observations from an experiment or survey
HYPOTHESIS: a scientific prediction about the outcome of a research study
MEAN: the arithmetic average of all the data measuring one characteristic; it can be used as a descriptive or inferential statistic
PARAMETER: a numerical characteristic or fact about a population
POPULATION: all members of a specified group that a researcher is interested in studying
PROBABILITY: the proportion of times a particular event will occur; also, the study of uncertainty that is the foundation of inferential statistics
SAMPLE: any subset or smaller part of a population which, for practical reasons, is studied in place of the entire population
STATISTIC: a numerical characteristic or fact about a sample
STATISTICS: summary measures of data; also, the science of analyzing data using mathematical tools and models

Overview

Statistics are numerical summary measures; that is, they are numbers that summarize larger groups of numbers. They are used to make sense of data collected as part of a research project. The field of statistics is divided into two major areas: descriptive statistics and inferential statistics. Descriptive statistics uses graphic tools such as tables, charts, and statistics such as averages to organize, summarize, and interpret data. A stock market report and the average score on the most recent history test for a fifth-grade class are both attempts to use statistical tools to summarize data in order to make the data more meaningful. No attempt is made to go beyond the actual observations. The fifth-grade teacher computing the mean, or average, grade is not going to use the result to make statements about all fifth-graders in the school district or about fifth-graders in general. He or she is simply concerned with the performance of the thirty students in the class.

The field of inferential statistics, however, goes beyond the actual data collected and thus forms the foundation of behavioral science research. Research psychologists want to reach conclusions about behavior that apply to a target group or population that is much bigger than the sample actually studied in the experiment or survey. Several factors prevent research psychologists from being more accurate and collecting data on the population or group in which they are really interested.

Most often, it is not possible or practical to study an entire population. A researcher may be interested in studying loneliness among college students. The population for this study is all college students, but this population is too large to study in its entirety. Such a population is also unobtainable; should an attempt be made to survey all college students, the researcher would find that many of the students would have been graduated or left college, and more would have entered college before the study was finished. Many populations of interest to psychologists are constantly changing. Even if these populations were not changing, they would still not be the true population in which the researcher was interested. A researcher hopes that his or her results will be accurate for some future, potential members of the population, such as college students five years from now. Thus, he or she obtains a sample for the research study and uses statistics computed with sample observations to make inferences and decisions about the population parameters.

While researchers use the results of their studies (sample statistics) to infer characteristics of the population, they are never completely sure that they are correct. If a study were to be run again with a different random sample, the results would not be exactly the same as those of the first study. If the study were conducted a third time, and a fourth, and so on, each time the results would be different from each other time, and some would be different from the true characteristics of the population (parameters). Researchers do not know how far their results are from the parameters, but they can estimate the level of uncertainty of their decision by obtaining probabilities when they compute the inferential statistics. Typically, psychological researchers make the decision that their sample mean, or average, is a good estimate of the population mean when they are at least 95 percent confident that the sample mean and population mean are reasonably close. Looking at the results from an error perspective, there is a 5 percent chance that the researcher is in error by saying that the population parameter is close to his or her reported sample statistic. This uncertainty and potential for error are always present in the use of inferential statistics. The probability of being correct or being in error is always presented with the value of the inferential statistic in published reports. It is important for researchers to tell the likelihood of error in their results.

Decision making in the inferential process is structured around hypotheses and the testing of hypotheses. After researchers have collected their observations or subject responses, they do not analyze the data searching for any results with a low probability of error; rather, they conduct the analysis as directed by the study's initial prediction or hypothesis. In psychological experiments, scientists are looking for more than an estimate of a population parameter. Experiments are designed with two or more groups that are given different treatments. For example, in an experiment designed to examine helping behavior, people in one group may have the opportunity to help with someone else present, while those in the other group have the same opportunity to help but with no one else present. The presence or absence of another person is an experimental condition or treatment.

Inferential statistics are used to test whether the difference in end behavior—in the example above, "helping"—was influenced by the experimental condition of having someone present or not. Specifically, inferential statistics test hypotheses such as "People are more helpful when another person is present and will know that they have helped." In this application of inferential statistics, making a decision about the difference between two groups, uncertainty is a problem just as it is when estimating a parameter. Probability theory is applied to get a probability value (p) indicating how likely it is that the researcher reached a correct decision (and, therefore, how likely it is that the researcher reached an incorrect decision). At the end of the experiment, the scientist decides whether the difference between the two or more experimental groups occurred by chance or was a real difference and reflects support for the initial hypothesis.

Applications

Inferential statistics are used to make decisions about the findings from a research study, to see whether the results can be extended and applied to people not in the study, and to see whether the difference between groups in an experiment are real differences or occurred by chance. Thus, inferential statistics are used to judge the success of almost all psychological research. The values of the inferential statistics computed are reported for every published behavioral study and are critical for doing research.

In most applications of inferential statistics, whether surveys or experiments, sample size is very small compared to the population size. The United States Bureau of Labor Statistics surveys less than 1 percent of the population of all United States households for computing the monthly unemployment rates. An experiment on factors influencing helping behavior may have employed four groups of fifteen each, a total of sixty volunteers, to be able to generalize a conclusion about the effects of anonymity and room temperature on rates of helping for all adults.

To meet the mathematical requirements of inferential statistics, randomness has to be a part of the sampling procedure. Random sampling is not haphazard selection, but rather the careful choosing of each member of the sample in a manner that ensures that everyone has the same chance of getting picked. The people to participate in the study are selected randomly from some master listing of all members of the population. Random sampling is a method to be used when the population is definable and it is practical to sample it. With a carefully done random sample, researchers can come to conclusions such as "11 percent of U.S. households have an unemployed member" or "25 percent of women in college have been the victims of rape or attempted rape." Estimation of the population percentage from the sample percentage is the goal of such research.

Most psychological research is focused not on population estimation but on finding differences between experimental groups. Small differences will always be present in the summary measures from two groups; inferential statistics are used to separate chance results from significant or nonchance differences. In these cases, researchers use samples of convenience or judgment samples, instead of random sampling. Human subjects volunteer to be part of the experiment, and the researcher judges how close the sample is to a hypothetical random sample. Randomness is accomplished in an experiment by random assignment to the experimental groups. The concept of randomness here is similar to that of random sampling: All subjects have the same chance of being assigned to group A or group B.

A real research example of using inferential statistics to make decisions about the differences between experimental groups is the investigation by Shelly Chaiken and Patricia Pliner (1987) on the effect of meal size and gender on perceived femininity and masculinity. Chaiken and Pliner instructed 254 college men and women to read a food diary supposedly written by either a male or female student who ate either a small breakfast and lunch (orange juice, toast and butter; green salad, oil and vinegar dressing, coffee with cream) or a large breakfast and lunch (pancakes and syrup, three slices of bacon, grapefruit with sugar, milk; bowl of vegetable soup, spaghetti with meat sauce, green salad, French dressing, chocolate brownie, banana, large Coke). They randomly assigned the 254 subjects to read the food diary of one of the four experimental groups: male who ate small meals, male who ate large meals, female who ate small meals, and female who ate large meals. Then all subjects had to rate the (fictional) male or female student who wrote the diary on several traits, including masculinity and femininity.

The results were as follows, with the higher mean averages indicating a greater tendency to perceive the diary writer as feminine or masculine. The ratings of femininity were: male/small meal = 2.02, male/large meal = 2.05, female/small meal = 3.90, female/large meal = 2.82. By calculating an inferential statistic on this data, Chaiken and Pliner concluded that the difference between the two female groups was a real difference, rather than one that occurred by chance, and women who ate small meals were rated as more feminine than those who ate large meals. The probability that this finding happened by chance was < .001, or less than one chance in a thousand. While the researchers are still not completely certain that the results reflect what happens in the larger population, they are reasonably certain (99.9 percent).

In the same study, the ratings of masculinity were: male/small meal = 3.19, male/large meal = 3.29, female/small meal = 2.08, female/large meal = 2.78. The differences found between the two male means, 3.19 and 3.29, were shown by inferential statistics to be merely chance variations. Inferential statistics indicated that the differences between the female means, 2.08 and 2.78, were most likely real differences. Thus, the researchers were able come to a second conclusion, that women who ate large meals were more likely to be rated masculine than those who ate smaller meals (p < .001). A third conclusion was that meal size had no impact on subjects' ratings of male eaters' masculinity or femininity.

Without inferential statistics, Chaiken and Pliner would have been able to make conclusions only about the 254 college students in their sample. With the application of inferential statistics, these researchers were able to make decisions about their data that extend their findings to many college students. The results of this study can be generalized to college students at schools similar to the research site and probably to other, similar adults. Inferential statistics allow psychological research to have the maximum benefit. The work of one set of researchers can provide a way for psychologists everywhere to increase their knowledge about behavior.

Context

Beginning several hundred years ago, the use of statistics as tools evolved from many sources—probability and games of chance, mortality rates of the plague periods, errors of measurements in astronomy, and agricultural studies, to name a few. Descriptive statistics were the first to be understood, with the development of inferential statistics occurring mainly in the twentieth century—although, in the seventeenth century, a sample of birth and death records in London was used to estimate the total number of people living in the city.

The most basic challenges in statistics came to full recognition in the twentieth century: the problems of how to obtain reliable samples from larger populations and of how to estimate values of parameters that would describe the parent population. Several scientists began to develop ways of addressing these sampling problems with mathematically precise methods. For example, in 1875 and 1900, Friedrich Helmert and Karl Pearson, respectively, worked out the mathematical basis for the chi-square, one of the inferential statistics that is the most frequently used for data that is of the "yes/no" kind and not suitable for calculating mean averages.

R. A. Fisher developed a wide range of formulas over a thirty-year period beginning in 1913, including the one for analysis of variance, an inferential statistic used in analyzing mean averages from experimental groups. William Gossett, a student of Pearson, developed the foundation for an inferential statistic for dealing with small samples (less than twenty), which occur commonly in psychology because of the high time and resource costs of many studies. The two areas of inferential statistics emerged between 1925 and 1935, with Fisher directing the development of estimation of parameters, and Egon Pearson and Jerzy Neyman responsible for the theory of hypothesis testing. Both these approaches are now standard practice.

After World War II, the number of statistical scientists increased, and many engaged in applying statistical inference to more experimental situations. Earlier starts on multivariate statistics, tools to apply when more than one experimental treatment or condition was being studied at one time, were refined. High-speed computers were introduced, and by the 1960's were proving to be invaluable both to researchers applying inferential statistics and to statisticians developing new statistical tools. Also, by the 1960's, techniques for minimizing errors in selecting samples for surveys had been developed. There are inferential tools for many different kinds of data and research situations. The future is likely to see investigations into a wide variety of methods of analyzing data than now exist.

Bibliography

Gigerenzer, Gerd, et al. *The Empire of Chance: How Probability Changed Science and Everyday Life.* Cambridge, England: Cambridge University Press, 1989. A narrative history of the ideas of chance in the nineteenth and twentieth centuries, including the influence of probability on the brain's cognitive processing. Especially relevant are the chapters "The Inference Experts" and "Statistics of the Mind." Formulas are mostly absent. Excellent conclusions are provided for each of the lengthy chapters.

Hayslett, H. T., Jr. *Statistics Made Simple.* Garden City, N.Y.: Doubleday, 1968. Chapters 5 to 12 provide a standard approach to understanding and calculating basic inferential statistics. Exercises and answers are provided for each chapter.

Phillips, John L., Jr. *How to Think About Statistics.* 3d ed. New York: W. H. Freeman, 1988. A very readable presentation of statistics that emphasizes the role of error in inference. Figures are interesting and elucidate the concepts. Sample research applications are provided for education, political science, social work, sociology, and psychology, as are answers designed to help readers think critically.

Rowntree, Derek. *Statistics Without Tears: A Primer for Non-Mathematicians.* New York: Charles Scribner's Sons, 1981. Explains the essential concepts in statistics without having the reader perform calculations. Sections on inferential statistics always specify which mean is being referenced, the sample mean or the population mean.

Witte, Robert S. "Inferential Statistics: Generalizing Beyond Data." In *Statistics.* 3d ed. New York: Holt, Rinehart and Winston, 1989. A text designed for "mathematically unsophisticated" students who may have some fear of statistics.

Jane A. Jegerski

Cross-References

Data Description: Descriptive Statistics, 751; Hypothesis Development and Testing, 1248; Psychological Experimentation: Independent, Dependent, and Control Variables, 1932; Sampling, 2122; The Scientific Method in Psychology, 2148; Statistical Significance Tests, 2375.

DEATH AND DYING: THEORETICAL PERSPECTIVES

Type of psychology: Developmental psychology
Fields of study: Aging; classic analytic themes and issues; stress and illness

Death is a universal human experience that, for most of history, has been primarily the province of religion and philosophy. It has, however, increasingly been a concern of social scientists; perhaps, more than has been previously realized, death has important things to teach both scientists and laypersons about human existence.

Principal terms

CHRONIC ILLNESSES: generally long-term illnesses, such as heart disease and cancer, which are the major cause of death in older Americans

DEATH ANXIETY: emotional apprehension or vague fear caused by thinking about or facing the fact of death

DEFENSE MECHANISMS: psychological strategies, generally unconscious, which the personality uses as a defense against anxiety

DENIAL: a common defense mechanism, in which one simply denies the reality of a situation

EMPIRICAL: the type of knowledge that relies on information which comes through the senses, as opposed to relying on logical or rational processes

GRIEF: the emotion associated with most experiences of loss, including death

STAGE THEORY: a type of psychological theory which suggests that many aspects of human development occur in a series of similar, and often invariable, stages

SYNDROME: a combination of behaviors or symptoms which together may be signs of illness or pathology

Overview

Although death is a universal phenomenon, it is a topic which has come late to psychology and the other social sciences. Authors, scholars, theologians, and ordinary people have dealt with death back to the beginning of recorded history—and certainly before that. Dealing with death in a scientific way is, to a large extent, a product of the twentieth century.

The reasons for the scientific neglect of death are manifold. It is a complex idea, and one against which most people build defense mechanisms. The scientist might argue that death is not an empirical fact, in the sense that no one can experience death firsthand in order to study it or write about it. Sigmund Freud said that no one can imagine his or her own death, and that does seem to be true; if one tries to imagine oneself dead, one still seems to be around, in some sense, doing the imagining.

Some scholars have distinguished between the death state and the death event.

The death state (what it is like to be dead) is essentially a religious or philosophical issue. It would seem not to be amenable to empirical study, although the impact of death on other people and the impact of thoughts about death while one is still alive can be studied. The death event, on the other hand, is, to some degree at least, a part of life. It is possible to study how, why, and where people die. It is possible to study the process of dying and to study grief and bereavement.

It has also become necessary, particularly in recent years, to ask difficult questions about death: questions about when physical death actually occurs, about humane treatment for the dying patient, about the "right to die," about children and the best way to answer their concerns about death, and about how best to help people deal with their grief. Most of these questions generally cannot be answered by science alone. Almost all deal with ethical, religious, and social issues as well as with scientific information.

It has been argued that America is a "death-denying" culture. Even though aspects of death are around all the time, Americans live most of the time as if death were not a reality. Ernest Becker argued in his classic book *The Denial of Death* (1973) that American lives are organized around the fear and denial of death. His often convincing, although primarily philosophical, argument is augmented by research such as that of psychologists at Princeton University who studied undergraduates, most of whom did not admit having much conscious death anxiety. Yet by a word-association test, measures of galvanic skin response (a biological electrical current in the skin assumed to be related to levels of psychological anxiety), and response latency (the time between the presentation of a stimulus word and the response from the subject), researchers collected data that clearly showed that these college students responded to words related to death with greater emotional intensity than to equivalent words drawn from other topic areas.

If the United States is a death-denying society, it is nevertheless apparent that in the latter part of the twentieth century some people became willing to look at death more clearly; this is demonstrated in the behavioral and social sciences. In research, books, articles, and in many other ways, interest in death and dying, and topics closely related, have multiplied enormously.

In 1944, Eric Lindemann did a systematic study of the grief reactions of individuals who had lost a close relative; many of his subjects were relatives of those who died in the tragic Coconut Grove nightclub fire in Boston. He was particularly interested in studying the differences between what he called "normal" grief and the "abnormal" reactions he saw in some of the survivors. He concluded from his study that acute grief is a definite syndrome, with psychological and somatic symptomatology. In his description of normal grief, he says: "Common to all is the following syndrome—sensations of somatic distress occurring in waves lasting from 20 minutes to an hour, a feeling of tightness in the throat, choking with shortness of breath, need for sighing, an empty feeling in the abdomen, lack of muscular power, and an intense subjective distress described as tension or mental pain." Lindemann then pointed out the pathologies of grief, many of which are the intensification, elongation, or absence of the symptoms of normal grief.

Lindemann was a pioneer in the attempt to bring death into the arena of science, and since his time there have been thousands of studies, the creation of several organizations (such as the Association for Death Education and Counseling) and journals (such as *Omega*), and the publishing of dozens of books (including textbooks) in the area of death and dying.

As an example of how science grows by building on the work of others, it was soon found that Lindemann had not contacted his bereaved subjects soon enough. Therefore, he had missed a stage of grief which seems to be almost universal—a period of shock, numbness, and denial in which the bereaved person acts as if nothing had happened for a few hours or even days—sometimes even longer in abnormal grief.

Applications

One of the major pieces of evidence that many people were indeed interested in the subject of death was the remarkable popularity of a book published in 1969. It was entitled *On Death and Dying* and was written by Elisabeth Kubler-Ross, a physician who had come to the United States from Switzerland. Perhaps the best-known aspect of Kubler-Ross' book, based on her informal research, was her outline of a series of stages which she had found that many dying patients go through. She had become convinced that modern medicine, in its efforts to keep the patient alive, treated dying patients in ways that were often inhumane. She found that very little was known about the psychology of the dying person; she pointed out that there were no courses on death and dying in medical schools or, for all practical purposes, anywhere else at the time.

Kubler-Ross interviewed several hundred persons who were dying of chronic illnesses. She found that dying patients, for the most part, go through five stages in the terminal period of their lives. The first stage is one of denial: "This isn't really happening. Someone has made a mistake. I am not really going to die." In most people, the probable reality of the diagnosis eventually replaces the denial with a sense of anger: "Why me? Why now?" Generally the anger is displaced onto the most available candidate—a physician, a family member, a nurse, a clergyperson, God. The real object of the anger is death, but it is difficult to express anger toward what is really an abstract and ill-defined concept. The third stage is one of bargaining: "If only I don't die, or at least if my life is extended, then I will change my ways." It generally becomes clear that the bargaining is not going to work, and the fourth stage is depression. Kubler-Ross describes it as "a sense of great loss." Losses of most any kind are one of life's major difficulties, and death is the ultimate loss—the loss of everything. Finally, the fifth stage that Kubler-Ross observed is the stage of acceptance. This is not the same as saying that the patient now wants to die or is looking forward to death. Kubler-Ross describes this stage as "almost void of feelings." It is the acceptance of the inevitability of what is about to happen.

Kubler-Ross' stage theory has come under criticism, as most theories do. Edwin

Shneidman, one of the first professionals to be called "thanatologists" because they specialize in working with the dying and the grieving, states that in his experience he rarely sees the neat progression through the five stages that Kubler-Ross enumerates. Many other people in the field believe that the five-stage theory is too simplistic for the way things happen in the real world. (Actually, Kubler-Ross herself agrees that the stage theory does not apply to all dying people.) Undoubtedly, factors such as the length of the terminal illness, religious beliefs of the dying person, amount of support, and even the age of the patient may make a difference in the way people deal with their dying. Nevertheless, a framework such as the five stages, if not held too literally, seems to be a great aid for many who have to support or work with one who is dying.

Turning from the individual to the society, it is easy to see many places where death plays an important role in social life. Robert Kastenbaum has characterized this as the "death system." Just as society has many systems to deal with essential functions, such as the economic system, the educational system, and the transportation system, society must also deal with death on a daily basis. The death system would include, among other matters, all that is involved with the disposition of the dead body: the funeral arrangements, the cemetery, the church or other religious organization. A large number of people are involved, in one way or another, full-time or part-time, in this aspect of the death system. Although the funeral business has taken its share of criticism, some of it undoubtedly deserved, it fills a need that the majority of people in Western society seem to feel.

The death system also has other functions. Already noted is the care of the dying, which involves a large part of the health care system in the United States, as well as family and friends, and organizations such as Hospice. One might also include in the death system the many aspects of society which are involved in trying to prevent death, from police officers to the national Centers for Disease Control in Atlanta to the hurricane warning center to the manufacturer of railroad crossing signals. Actually, few people in the United States do not have at least a peripheral connection to the death system. Many florists, for example, say that half or more of their business is the provisions of flowers and wreaths for funerals and for cemetery plots.

Context

Richard Kalish, among others, has pointed out a number of reasons for the contemporary interest in the study of death and dying in the social sciences. It is fairly easy to identify a number of factors that have increased concern about this topic. For example, more lives have been lost in the twentieth century in warfare than in any other period of history. The presence of thermonuclear weapons continues to be a realistic concern for the peoples of the world. The increase in the number and influence of the elderly is also undoubtedly a factor. Most of the elderly die of heart disease, cancer, or other chronic illnesses in which death takes place over a period of time. This has led to a different kind of acquaintance with death on the part of many people in our time, in comparison to times not so long ago when death came more commonly as the result of a short acute illness.

Closely related to the previous point are the advances in medical technology which allow some people with chronic illnesses to be kept alive on life-support systems when their brain, and thus their personality, is no longer functioning. Because of scientific advances such as this, serious questions arise as to when death really occurs and as to what decisions ought to be made about that situation—legally, morally, and psychologically.

Undoubtedly, the impact of television has profoundly influenced society in its attitudes toward death and dying. For several decades, television has brought death "up close and personal," in both real-life and fictional situations. The effect of all this death on television (as well as in motion pictures) has yet to be fully studied or understood by psychologists or other social scientists.

A more sanguine reason for the increased interest in death and dying is that, perhaps, society is becoming more humane in its attempt to deal with these issues. There is a concern for "dying with dignity" and for a "good death" (the original meaning of the term euthanasia). The Hospice movement mentioned earlier has grown rapidly in the past several decades in the attempt to give the dying (particularly those dying from chronic illnesses) more choices about their own dying and the opportunity to live out their final days in a way not so different from the way they lived the rest of their lives. Social scientists may be coming to realize that death has something important to teach humankind about human existence.

Bibliography

Becker, Ernest. *The Denial of Death*. New York: Free Press, 1973. A strong book on the power of death both for the individual and within a culture. Written, to a large extent, from a psychoanalytic standpoint. Not easy to read unless the reader has some background in psychology or anthropology.

Feifel, Herman, ed. *The Meaning of Death*. New York: McGraw-Hill, 1959. One of the original books which stimulated the current interest in death and dying. Contains essays by people such as Carl Jung, Paul Tillich, and Robert Kastenbaum, as well as articles reporting empirical studies. Generally reads well and contains myriad interesting and thoughtful ideas.

_____. *New Meanings of Death*. New York: McGraw-Hill, 1977. This is as interesting as the Feifel book listed above, and it is perhaps less oriented toward academicians. There is an article on Hospice and several articles on death and young people. As in the previous book, some of the articles may be of more interest to readers than others.

Kubler-Ross, Elisabeth. *On Death and Dying*. New York: Macmillan, 1969. A popular book which had a major impact on the general public. It reads well and is not only interesting but also of practical help to many who are personally dealing with the issue of dying.

Lifton, Robert Jay, and Eric Olson. *Living and Dying*. New York: Praeger, 1974. A short, readable volume which looks at death from a broader perspective than

merely as the end of life. The first author, Lifton, is one of the pioneers in studying and writing about death; all of his many books are worth reading.

Mitford, Jessica. *The American Way of Death.* New York: Simon & Schuster, 1963.
A polemical look at the funeral business. The book made many Americans aware
of excesses and shoddy practices, which eventually led to a number of changes—
some because of government regulation; however, the reader needs to be aware
that it is a quite one-sided book.

Stoddard, Sandol. *The Hospice Movement.* New York: Vintage Books, 1978. Written
by a layperson for the general public, this is a fascinating account of the author's
experiences at St. Christopher's Hospice in London and is one of the major sources
in introducing the American public to the idea of Hospice.

Wass, Hannelore, Felix Berardo, and Robert A. Neimeyer, eds. *Dying: Facing the
Facts.* 2d ed. Washington, D.C.: Hemisphere, 1988. Contains chapters on all the
issues talked about in this essay and a number of others not specifically discussed.
The reading level of the chapters is uneven; some read quite well, others were
written with the academic audience primarily in mind.

James Taylor Henderson

Cross-References

Aging: Physical Changes, 192; Theories of Aging, 198; Coping with Cancer, 711;
Emotion and Health, 928; Integrity: Erikson, 1321; Stress-Related Diseases, 2464;
Sudden Infant Death Syndrome, 2495; Suicide, 2501; Teenage Suicide, 2527.

DECISION MAKING AS A COGNITIVE PROCESS

Type of psychology: Cognition
Field of study: Cognitive processes

Because decision making is such a common and important human activity, it appears in theories of behavior in nearly every area of psychology. Behavioral decision researchers have been able to explain a variety of behaviors in terms of the cognitive processes involved in making decisions.

Principal terms

CONFIDENCE: a belief about the quality of a given alternative
DESCRIPTIVE THEORY: a detailed explanation of what one actually does in making a decision
HEURISTIC: a simple decision-making rule that is efficient but uses limited information
NORMATIVE THEORY: a prescriptive statement of what one should do when deciding
PREFERENCE: an alternative with relatively greater value to an individual
RATIONALITY: the ability to choose the alternative that maximizes self-interest
UNCERTAINTY: an inability to determine what has occurred or will occur
UTILITY: the subjective value of an outcome to an individual

Overview

Much of what people do—with the exceptions of reflexive and habitual behavior—results from the cognitive processes of deciding. Even a minor decision, such as whether to drive the car, take the bus, or walk to work, involves the coordination of many complex processes. In making this choice, one might take into consideration one's perception of the weather, guilt about contributing to smog, feeling of physical energy, goal of obtaining more exercise, memory of a recent bus trip, desire for company, or judged likelihood of working late. Even such a relatively minor decision can be difficult to make because there are numerous considerations, and some favor one alternative while remaining considerations favor other alternatives. In addition, the decision maker cannot know all relevant information, so there is uncertainty about the outcomes of important events.

A major goal of decision research is to understand the rules that people use in choosing an alternative. This often means gaining insight into the decision processes that are used when no alternative is clearly preferred. In order to accomplish this, it is necessary to understand what is meant by a rule and to identify different potential rules for selecting one of a set of alternative courses of action. Some rules are "heuristics," or strategies for simplifying choice that limit the evaluation of alternatives. Heuristics can be very efficient. In the above example about choosing the mode of transportation to work, if one used a heuristic, one might consider only the amount of time available for getting to work. Such a simplistic analysis of the decision problem can, however, lead to a poor decision. In other words, the employee might have more regrets after using this heuristic than would be the case if he or she had made a more careful analysis of the alternatives.

Decision theory has a long history of identifying normative procedures for decision making. These tell people what rules they should follow in making decisions. A standard rule is to take into account two dimensions for each decision alternative: likelihood and utility. This principle, which is embodied in subjective expected utility theory, is intended to maximize the personal value of one's anticipated outcomes. Suppose that one is given a choice between a 50 percent chance of winning $100 and a certain $2. The first alternative has an expected outcome of $50 (calculated by 50 percent of $100 = $50), since that is what one would expect to win on average if one played this game many times. The other alternative has an expected outcome of $2 (calculated by 100 percent of $2 = $2). Subjective expected utility theory indicates that one should choose the first alternative, the 50 percent chance of $100, because it has a higher expected outcome. This choice is called "rational" in the sense that it is the choice that is likely to maximize earnings.

The cognitive approach to decision making emphasizes an understanding of the ways in which various factors influence the choices that people make in reality—regardless of whether they follow normative principles. In contrast to the normative approach, the cognitive approach is focused on description of the actual processes that people use. To illustrate this, consider the following choice: a 30 percent chance of $100 or a certain $20. Calculations based on likelihood and value dictate that one should choose the first alternative, since its anticipated outcome of $30 (30 percent of $100 = $30) is more than $20. Many people, however, simply do not want to take the risk of receiving nothing with the first alternative. They prefer the security of knowing that they will receive $20 to the uncertainty of getting $100 or nothing. The possibility of an additional $10 is not worth the risk. This is not necessarily "irrational." As this example shows, normative decision theory cannot predict what many or even most people will choose. For this reason, psychologists have become increasingly interested in examining the processes that people actually use to make decisions.

Of particular interest in the cognitive approach to decision making are those factors that lead to miscalculations of likelihood or utility, since they will ultimately contribute to undesirable outcomes. Psychologists Amos Tversky and Daniel Kahneman have revolutionized the field of decision making by identifying factors that contribute to poor decision making. Some of these may be called "cognitive illusions," because they lead a decision maker to a judgment that is in fact a distortion of reality. One type of judgment that is often affected by such illusions concerns likelihood estimation, the chance of an event leading to a particular outcome.

Another type of judgment that is susceptible to illusionary distortion is the estimation of quantity or frequency. In making these estimations, people often use rules of thumb or heuristics. One heuristic for estimating quantity is called "anchoring and adjustment." When using this, one takes any available number as an initial starting point or anchor and then adjusts it to arrive at an estimate. For example, one might predict tomorrow's temperature by taking today's temperature and adjusting downward for forthcoming rainfall. Although heuristics can be more efficient than the careful and comprehensive analysis of relevant information, they can also be misleading.

Illusions and heuristics can be detrimental to good decision making, because they lead the decision maker to a distorted view of the problem and alternatives. It is often possible to develop procedures for improving the decision-making process. Elaborate technologies have been developed to assist people in making decisions in nearly every area. Sometimes it is instructive, however, merely to understand the processes that people use and know their limitations. It must be kept in mind that evaluating the quality of decisions is very difficult. One reason is that some decisions that are made with great care, thought, and objectivity can still have very disappointing outcomes. On other occasions, luck can operate to bring favorable outcomes despite poor decision processes. The ultimate key to improving human judgment and decision making is research that integrates normative and descriptive theories.

Applications

The principles of subjective expected utility theory have been applied in a wide variety of problem areas. A distinction between expectancy and utility can be quite useful. For example, two people who choose to continue to smoke may do so for different reasons. One may truly believe that he has a high chance of developing a serious disease such as lung cancer. He may anticipate great medical advances, however, and expect that lung cancer will be only a mild problem by the time he gets it. Though the expectation of a negative outcome is high, the outcome is not particularly negative to this individual. Another person may be convinced that lung cancer is—and will continue to be—a painful, expensive, deadly disease. Despite the fact that this outcome has great negative utility for this person, she may continue to smoke because her expectation is that she will not get lung cancer. Each of these individuals is influenced by different factors. Understanding how the decision to smoke or to quit is made can assist health advocates—and tobacco advertisers—to influence these decisions.

One of the areas in which subjective expected utility principles have been highly influential is that of motivation. While early theories of motivation viewed behavior as the result of basic drives or personality traits, subsequent theories emphasized the way in which people thought about their options. From this perspective, it is meaningless to label someone "unmotivated." Everyone is motivated, in the sense that all people have time and effort to give to activities. People choose how much time and effort to give to each of the various options open to them: work, leisure, and family activities. Employees who do little or no work do not necessarily lack "drive" or have flawed personalities. They have simply decided to spend their time and effort on other things. This does not excuse or overlook the workers' lack of productivity, but it does suggest methods to alter their lack of performance. The key is to understand their judgments of the utilities of outcomes from working and their perceived likelihood of obtaining these outcomes by choosing to put time and effort into work activities. Thus, the study of decision making is important to organizational efforts to enhance productivity.

In one sense, it is easy to observe instances of illusions and heuristics that lead to biases in decision making in real life. Bad decisions seem to be everywhere. As noted above, however, decisions that turn out badly may sometimes result from badly made decisions. People are accustomed to judging the actions of others and will label them irrational if it appears that they are choosing alternatives with inferior outcomes for themselves. During the Persian Gulf War of 1991, the American media frequently concluded that Saddam Hussein was "irrational" because he chose not to withdraw from Kuwait by the United Nations deadline. Though it is tempting to label an enemy "irrational," it is wise to keep in mind a serious problem in determining irrationality in a decision maker. It is exceedingly difficult to assess the utility of any alternative for the decision maker. By American standards, it would have been better for the Iraqis to withdraw from Kuwait before suffering enormous loss of life—and eventual forced withdrawal from Kuwait—so it seemed that Hussein could not possibly be evaluating the alternatives realistically. Either he did not understand the magnitude of his human and economic losses from a failure to withdraw or he did not understand the virtual certainty of losing the war. Hussein may, however, have understood both perfectly and simply have attached different utilities to the outcomes anticipated from withdrawal versus war. Perhaps from Saddam Hussein's perspective the loss of life could be offset easily by the opportunity to show himself to the Arab world as someone who "stood up" to the international community, if only briefly.

Scientific investigations of biases in decision making require that the investigator prove that a given alternative is superior to the one that is chosen by most people. This is often done by means of mathematics or statistics. In one demonstration of the representativeness bias, people are given a brief personality sketch of "Linda" and asked to determine how likely it is that Linda is a member of various categories. Most people tend to judge Linda as more likely to be a bank teller and a feminist than merely a bank teller. In fact, however, there must be at least as many bank tellers as there are feminist bank tellers, since the category "bank teller" will contain all feminist bank tellers as well as all nonfeminist bank tellers. The illusion comes from the erroneous conclusion that because Linda's personality traits represent both the occupation of a bank teller and the political perspective of a feminist, she is more likely to be both than either. Research such as this helps to determine how people can "jump to conclusions" and misjudge someone. Overestimating the likelihood that a person belongs to two categories diminishes one's ability to estimate appropriately the expected utilities of alternatives for decisions about that person.

The reader may wish to see how the use of a heuristic can bias judgment by conducting a demonstration with a few friends. Ask each one privately to write down the last three digits of his or her telephone number. Then ask each one to estimate the number of nations in the world. A typical finding is that each person tends to use the number written down from the phone number as a starting point and then adjust slightly away from it. Many people are quite unaware of the process that they used to estimate the number of nations. They may even insist that they merely guessed. As a consequence, many estimates will be closer to the phone numbers than to the actual answer.

Context

Numerous forces have come together to fuel the study of human decision making as a cognitive process. One of those is the coming of the "information age." With the transition from a production economy to a service economy, workers are no longer seen as people who engage in only physical work. Workers at all levels deal with information and decisions. It is no longer possible to attribute all the difficulty of making decisions to insufficient information. Decision makers are often over-loaded and overwhelmed by information. The real problem they face is knowing which information to select and how to integrate it into the decision-making process.

Within psychology, two areas of study that have had a great impact on behavioral decision making are perception and quantitative psychology. Both Kahneman and Tversky did extensive work in the area of perception before becoming interested in studying the cognitive processes in human judgment and decision making. Many other behavioral decision researchers began their studies in quantitative psychology or statistics. The primary objective in this area is to learn how to make decisions under uncertainty using the laws of probability. Since this is what people are routinely faced with in the course of their work and daily lives, there are many intriguing parallels between statistics and behavioral decision making.

Advances in understanding the rationality of human decision making were furthered, ironically, by economic theories that assumed rationality on the part of human decision makers. Psychologists who conducted empirical studies of people had data to show that many choices that people make do not follow rational economic models. For example, standard economic theory predicts that people will choose the option that maximizes their own payoff. Yet people often prefer a plan that they deem fair to everyone over one that is financially superior for themselves. Behavioral decision theory attempts to understand the way in which people actually make decisions—not the way that formal models say that they should.

Bibliography

Anderson, Barry F., et al. *Concepts in Judgment and Decision Research.* New York: Praeger, 1981. A reference guide to the language of judgment and decision making. Many terms are formally defined and cross-referenced. Examples are generally clear and useful.

Dawes, Robyn M. *Rational Choice in an Uncertain World.* San Diego: Harcourt Brace Jovanovich, 1988. A social-psychological perspective on judgment and decision processes. Highly interesting content and style for all audiences. Includes thoughtful discussions of controversial applications. Nontechnical and concise. Chapters can be read individually or out of order.

Russo, J. Edward, and Paul J. H. Shoemaker. *Decision Traps.* New York: Doubleday, 1989. Superb and colorful coverage of cognitive processes in decision making. Balance of research and applications. Examples are well-chosen, memorable illustrations of major concepts. Particularly relevant to the businessperson but will appeal to all.

Slovic, Paul, Sarah Lichtenstein, and Baruch Fischhoff. "Decision Making." In *Steven's Handboook of Experimental Psychology,* edited by Richard C. Atkinson et al. 2d ed. New York: John Wiley & Sons, 1988. A comprehensive review of the field of decision making. Traces the origins of subjective expected utility theory as well as other decision theories. Brief and well-written explanations of different perspectives in the field. Ties decision making to other areas of experimental psychology.

Tversky, Amos, and Daniel Kahneman. "Judgment Under Uncertainty: Heuristics and Biases." *Science* 185 (1974): 1124-1131. A classic paper written for the general scientific and lay community. The authors illustrate various judgment heuristics in thought-provoking fashion. This article is not intended to be a balanced view of human "rationality"; it emphasizes the cognitive limitations of human decision makers.

Yates, J. Frank. *Judgment and Decision Making.* Englewood Cliffs, N.J.: Prentice-Hall, 1990. A careful and detailed explanation of procedures for examining human judgment and decision making. Includes numerous examples and thoughtful discussion, with special appeal to students. The casual reader will find many graphs to be too technical. Extensive references to original journal articles.

Janet A. Sniezek

Cross-References

Artificial Intelligence, 299; Cognitive Development Theory: Piaget, 553; Cognitive Maps, 566; Computer Models of Cognition, 631; Consumer Psychology: Decisions, 669; Group Decision Making, 1114; Logic and Reasoning, 1471; Problem-Solving Stages, 1873; Problem-Solving Strategies and Obstacles, 1879.

DEFENSE REACTIONS: SPECIES-SPECIFIC

Type of psychology: Learning
Fields of study: Aggression; biological influences on learning; nervous system

All animal species employ maneuvers and deceptive tactics to protect themselves from conspecific competitors, predators, and parasites. These defensive reactions include alarm calls, flocking or herding, mimicry, bluffing, displays, and aggressive counterattacks. Defensive mechanisms vary from species to species, but some defensive tactics are common throughout the animal kingdom.

Principal terms

ALARM: a vocal, visual, or pheromonal communication given off by an individual to warn other members of the same species that danger is present

COMPETITION: the struggle for the acquisition of territory, mates, and food; a phenomenon of animal behavior that usually occurs among individuals and groups of the same species

DISPLAY: a visual dance or series of movements or gestures by an individual to communicate such things as dominance, aggression, and courtship to other individuals

DOMINANCE HIERARCHY: a pecking order; an ordered arrangement of dominant to subordinate individuals in an animal population that serves numerous social functions, including protection

FLOCKING: a defensive maneuver in many mammal and bird species in which a scattered group of individuals implodes into a compact cluster at the approach of a predator

MIMICRY: an inherited or behavioral defense phenomenon in which an individual of a species either looks dangerous to its predators or can exaggerate its appearance to fool a predator

PHEROMONE: a hormone that is released from the body of one individual to affect the behavior of other individuals nearby

PREDATION: an interspecific interaction in which the individuals of one animal species hunt and kill members of another species for food

PREY DENSITY: the concentration of individuals of an animal population in a given area; the higher the density, the greater the net protection to any one member of the population

SATURATION: an unusual defensive mechanism in some animal species in which a prey animal population synchronizes its growth so that it becomes too large for predators to consume any significant fraction of the population

Overview

All living organisms live within complicated food/energy webs in which energy is transferred from organism to organism through consumption. Plants convert energy from sunlight to manufacture organic nutrients. Herbivorous animals eat plants to obtain this energy, and carnivorous animals eat herbivores and other carnivores to obtain the same energy. Within an animal species, individuals compete with one another for available food and natural resources in order to survive; in the process, they establish dominance hierarchies in which dominant individuals overpower subordinates. Among different species, interactions occur that lead to predation, disease, and parasitism; in each case, one species is feeding on another species.

Intraspecific competition and interspecific predation and parasitism represent two principal animal behaviors important to the evolution of life. Each species possesses an innate (instinctive) drive to survive and to continue the transmission of its deoxyribonucleic acid (DNA) in space and time. Within the food webs of the living environment, each species evolves specific adaptations for survival that enable it to carve out a particular habitat, or place to live, and niche, or occupation, in the environment. Since the food webs of life on Earth are circular, the evolution of competition and predation are necessary for life to continue. All species will become predators (hunters) of certain other species and will simultaneously be prey (the hunted) for certain different species.

In order to survive, each species possesses specific adaptations for hunting its prey and for defending itself from predators. Defensive mechanisms come in many different varieties. There are some very effective defense mechanisms which are highly conserved between different species; other defenses are unique for only one or a few species. Of these defenses, some are instinctive, occurring automatically because of biochemical changes within individual animals, whereas others are learned from environmental experiences. Learned defensive mechanisms are prevalent in highly social mammal and bird species.

Intraspecific competition occurs among individuals of a given population or group and among different populations or groups. Within a population, the social structure is either genetically or behaviorally conditioned to construct castes or dominance hierarchies in which dominant individuals are superior to more subordinate individuals. The social insects (such as ants, termites, bees, and wasps), whose behavior is almost exclusively genetic in nature, construct their societies, or hives, around castes which have specific jobs to perform. Such societies revolve around a central, fertile queen, sterile female workers, and male drones. Workers are subdivided into several specializations, such as hunting for food and defending the hive. Soldier workers have specialized body structures for attacking intruders; furthermore, they release pheromones (chemical attractants) from their bodies at the sign of danger to attract other soldier workers to the region of intrusion.

Within the highly social and intelligent mammal and bird species, populations either migrate in bands or groups or set up individual adjacent territories that are heavily defended by the owner. In either of these situations, learned dominance hierarchies are established in which stronger individuals outcompete weaker individuals, thereby establishing a "pecking order" (as it is called for chickens) of precisely ranked dominant individuals to progressively more subordinate individuals. The dominant individuals possess the best territory, the most food, and the most mates. The most dominant individuals also have the best protection from predators, because their territories are central and therefore are shielded by the territories of more subordinate individuals. Consequently, the most subordinate individuals have the worst territories, poor food, few if any mates, and poor protection from predators, which usually attack outskirt territories. These territories are maintained by constant fighting between males, especially during the breeding season. Males vocalize and present visual displays to force their opponents to submit; submission is routine, and few encounters are fatal.

In interspecific predator-prey interactions, the prey utilize a variety of quick-response defenses. One of the most common defenses is the flocking, or herding, defense. When a predator approaches a group of prey and is identified, the discovering prey individual announces danger by a vocalization (an alarm call), specific movement, and/or the release of chemical pheromones to warn the other members of a group. The prey group response is instantaneous with all members collapsing into a dense mass. A predator is less likely to succeed in capturing a prey individual during an attack on a compact group than when the prey individuals are scattered. Furthermore, the predator may sustain personal physical damage in an attack on a compact group, which easily could turn upon the predator. Most predators are far more successful at capturing very young, old, or sickly individuals that are isolated or located at the poorly defended outskirts of a prey group. Some predators, such as hawks, falcons, and wolves, do make repeated passes at compact groups in sometimes successful attempts at panicking individuals and thereby scattering the group. Flocking behavior is a very effective defense that is utilized by bee swarms, fish schools, amphibian tadpoles, most bird species, and most mammal species. Prey species usually utilize excellent vision, hearing, and the sense of smell.

Other species-specific defense mechanisms include camouflage, mimicry, predator saturation, and long-term incubation. Most species have adaptations in skin and fur coloration in order to blend in with their particular environment. For example, albino hares and squirrels predominate in areas which have snow for a good portion of the year, whereas the same species in more temperate climates usually have a grayish-brown coloration. Zebras have a striped pattern that enables them to blend with tall grass; many mammalian predators (lions, wild dogs) are color-blind. Some species (the chameleon, for example) can alter their body color to their background by biochemical changes in their skin. Some lizard species simply discard body parts, such as their tails, when captured by predators.

Mullerian mimicry is a phenomenon used by moths and butterflies to defend themselves from bird predators. A few butterfly species with bright orange-black wings are poisonous; several dozen nonpoisonous species have coevolved bright black and orange or yellow wings and are therefore less likely to be eaten, since birds learn very quickly from only a few encounters with the poisonous varieties. Some species of fish, birds, and mammals have short, rapid bursts of reproduction, so that their predators are overwhelmed, or saturated, by the high prey densities. In both of these instances, some prey are eaten. The thirteen- and seventeen-year periodic locust species of North America greatly avoid predation by burrowing underground for many years before surfacing and reproducing within only a few weeks.

Applications

The study of species-specific defensive reactions is of intense interest to animal behavior researchers. Research into such behavior enables them to understand how highly adaptive and elaborate defenses have evolved in animal species over the past 500 million years. These studies also have potential impact upon the psychology of human behavior. Humans are very territorial animals and exhibit considerable competitive behavior, including interpersonal conflicts and aggression. Consequently, defense mechanism studies are strongly applicable to the study of human conflict, social tensions, and warfare. Furthermore, species-specific defense mechanisms are also of interest to medicine, since humans, while being the apparently dominant species on Earth, are subject to predation, particularly from parasitic bacterial, fungal, and viral diseases.

The dynamics of predator-prey interactions can be complicated, although numerous mathematical models of such relationships have been developed that are accurate and enable researchers to make predictions concerning future interactions in natural populations. Predator-prey interactions are important for the stability and survival of both the predator and prey populations. Without prey, predators would die; however, without predators, prey populations would grow unchecked until they exceeded the available resources in the environment, ending in a massive population crash in which many individuals would die. Such occurrences have been thoroughly documented in many species, including moose, deer, rabbit, and even human populations. Defensive mechanisms are important to all species in order to ensure the survival of enough members of each species population to reproduce and continue the transmission of the species' genetic information. Perfect defense, however, could be as detrimental to the population as no defense. Numerous mathematical ecologists have developed impressive models of animal population growth based upon predator-prey interactions. Among the most famous models are those that were developed by Alfred Lotka and Vito Volterra, and they still are in use. Such models are of critical importance to the study of human overpopulation.

The explosion of human technological growth during the past century has included medical advances that have eradicated many diseases which once were major killers of humans. Medicine has been a tremendous artificial defense mechanism that has been developed by the intelligence of the human species. It has defeated dozens of bacterial, fungal, and viral predators and parasites of humans. Because of these advances, humans live longer and better lives, human birth rates have soared, and human death rates have declined; however, the elimination of human predators has produced some very serious problems. One such problem is overpopulation. The explosive human population growth is approaching the planet's carrying capacity (the available food and resources). Some areas of the world, most notably Asia and Africa, have already seen human overpopulation far above the carrying capacity; the result has been devastating famines and millions of deaths. Furthermore, medical science is taxed by the appearance of new mutated viral and bacterial predators to replace the eradicated ones. The human immunodeficiency virus (HIV), which causes acquired immune deficiency syndrome (AIDS), is an example. Furthermore, certain diseases, such as cholera, are on the rise worldwide. Life on Earth is very homeostatic (i.e., self-regulatory); it contains mechanisms for keeping populations of all species in check.

Leaving the microscopic scale, humans and other primates defend themselves from competitors and very large predators in much the same fashion. Humans have territories that each territory-holder defends. Furthermore, several dominant males may group to attack intruders and other predators. There can be no doubt that such behavior has evolved into the large armies that different countries have amassed to defend their territorial borders. The structures of many such armies is somewhat reminiscent of mammalian dominance hierarchies. The front-line soldiers who face the brunt of an opponent's attack usually are individuals who are poorly equipped and trained. They are sometimes called "cannon fodder." Better-trained, more dominant individuals follow; they are more likely to survive hostile encounters with the enemy.

Species-specific defensive behaviors are also applicable to human behavior in terms of social and personal relationships. Complex human societies are rigidly structured along territorial lines, with laws to regulate the behaviors of individuals. Cross-sections through American cities reveal the segregation of the poor from the middle-class from the rich, the segregation of black from white from Hispanic. Individuals in each of these groups construct physical, social, and legal barriers to defend themselves from competition from outsiders. With overpopulation and competition for resources, individuals and countries resort to mechanical weapons ranging from handguns to semiautomatic rifles to atomic bombs. Stress, inequality, and mistrust of others involve biological reactions that have evolved over hundreds of millions of years.

Each of the approximately one million animal species on Earth has evolved through the endurance of predator-prey interactions. Understanding how species defend themselves can be of great importance in helping endangered species to survive and in controlling the overpopulations of species and the spread of disease. It also can help humankind to alleviate many of its own species' social problems.

Context

The study of species-specific defense mechanisms is of considerable interest to animal behaviorists and psychologists because of their implications for human behavior. All animal behaviors can be influenced by endogenous (instinctive) or exogenous (environmental) factors. Endogenous behaviors include imprinting and biochemical changes within the body of the individual that enable one to recognize events or situations instantaneously for survival. Such behaviors as recognizing danger are critical for survival and therefore must be instinctive. Within the intelligent and highly social mammals and birds, a period of learning during infancy enables the development of exogenous behaviors from experiences in one's immediate environment. Such learned behaviors are of equal importance in such species.

Competition and predator-prey interactions are real-life problems for all species, including humans. Such interactions, however undesirable they may sometimes seem, provide stable structures to animal populations and prevent the overpopulation or underpopulation of both predator and prey species. The human species, with its advanced technology and medicine, has somewhat overcome its own susceptibility to predation and has, in the process, created overpopulation and the stressful problems associated with overpopulation. Studies of many overpopulated animal societies uncover several recurring themes. These stress-associated factors include the breakdown of social structure, psychological disorders, increased acts of violence, antisocial behavior, and cannibalism. Associated with these stressful, overpopulated societies are increased aggressiveness and mistrust between individuals, phenomena which easily are seen in large, crowded human cities. Studies of other social animal societies and their offensive/defensive interactions with other species and with one another provide much insight into the psychology and sociality of the human species.

The study of species-specific defensive reactions allows scientists to uncover the intricacies of species interactions within the environment. In any given ecosystem (such as a forest, grassland, ocean, or desert) populations of thousands of different species are linked by intricate food webs. The destruction of the environment or the extinction of any one species can have irreparable effects upon all the other species within the ecosystem. The defensive mechanisms of most species can work only so well.

Species-specific defense mechanisms include flocking/herding, camouflage, mimicry, exaggerations of body size, saturation of predators, and specializations in life cycles. With respect to mimicry, several moth species have evolved "eyes" on their wings that presumably fool their bird predators into thinking that the moths are owls, predators of many bird species. Other species symbiose, or live cooperatively, with another species for protection. "Cleaner fish" species can actually enter the mouths of large fish without danger. Certain other species of fish safely inhabit the poisonous tentacles of the sea anemone. A classic example of symbiosis occurs in Africa, where *Crematogaster* ants live in and staunchly defend *Acacia* trees. The numbers of such defensive adaptations are many and illustrate the tremendous diversity of life on Earth, a diversity which humans must learn to defend from themselves.

Bibliography

Andrewartha, Herbert George. *Introduction to the Study of Animal Populations.* London: Methuen, 1961. This tremendous resource book for ecologists and animal behaviorists was written by one of the foremost authorities in animal behavior research. Andrewartha defines the parameters of animal population growth, including predator-prey interactions and species defense mechanisms, in the first part of the book. He devotes the second portion of the book to experimental methods and set-ups for gathering research data on animal populations. Describes all concepts with great clarity, even the mathematics and graphing of data.

Klopfer, Peter H., and Jack P. Hailman. *An Introduction to Animal Behavior: Ethology's First Century.* Englewood Cliffs, N.J.: Prentice-Hall, 1967. Klopfer and Hailman provide an excellent presentation of animal behavior research and the major theories describing the evolution of species' behaviors. Chapter 7, "The Social Life of Animals," explores social behavior in mammals and birds, including descriptions of competition and dominance hierarchies. Chapter 11, "How Is Behavior Controlled?", describes specific adaptations of various species to environmental stimuli, including danger. Extremely well written and referenced.

Krebs, Charles J. *Ecology: The Experimental Analysis of Distribution and Abundance.* 2d ed. New York: Harper & Row, 1978. This well-organized, information-packed introduction to ecology was written by a leading ecologist and represents an outstanding reference for both scientist and layperson. Numerous factors that influence animal and plant populations are described, including predator-prey interactions and defense mechanisms. Hundreds of species interactions are cited with clearly explained mathematical models. Chapters 5, "Factors Limiting Distributions: Interrelations with Other Organisms," 12, "Species Interactions: Competition," and 13, "Species Interactions: Predation," exhaustively cover offensive and defensive behaviors.

Lorenz, Konrad. *On Aggression.* Translated by Marjorie Kerr Wilson. New York: Harcourt, Brace & World, 1966. This excellent survey of aggressive animal behavior, written by a Nobel laureate and pioneer in behavior research, is aimed at the layperson. Lorenz clearly outlines the evolution of animal behavior and the adaptiveness of aggressive behavior. He cites several species interactions, illustrating both offensive and defensive animal behaviors. Also addresses aggression within the context of human behavior, stressing the need for human control of aggressive behaviors for our own survival.

Manning, Aubrey. *An Introduction to Animal Behavior.* 3d ed. Reading, Mass.: Addison-Wesley, 1979. A concise presentation of theory and experimentation in animal behavior research. Describes major behavior theories and relevant experimental work from the biological research. Chapter 3, "Stimuli and Communication," describes animal species' responses and adaptations to environmental stimuli, including displays, mimicry, and other responses to danger. Chapter 5, "Conflict Behavior," describes various offensive and defensive mechanisms used by different species in both competition and predator-prey interactions.

Marler, Peter Robert, and William J. Hamilton III. *Mechanisms of Animal Behavior.* New York: John Wiley & Sons, 1966. Marler and Hamilton's book is a thorough presentation of animal behavior theory and research. Clearly written and diagrammed, with extensive reference lists. Chapter 10, "Behavioral Functions of

Vision," describes visual defense mechanisms of various species, including forms of mimicry in moths and butterflies. Chapter 11, "Responsiveness to Mechanical Disturbance: Audition," discusses hearing adaptations for defense and other behaviors in various species. An outstanding reference.

Wilson, Edward O. *Sociobiology: The New Synthesis.* Cambridge, Mass.: The Belknap Press of Harvard University Press, 1975. This mammoth work, written by one of the world's leading entomologists and animal behaviorists, is a revival of an important theory in animal behavior and evolutionary research. Sociobiology maintains that the behavioral adaptations of a species constitute a driving force in the evolution of the species. Wilson clearly and exhaustively cites hundreds of detailed studies of various social animal species to drive home key points. Describes offensive and defensive behavioral mechanisms plus other behaviors.

David Wason Hollar, Jr.

Cross-References

Animal Experimentation, 252; Ethology, 992; Imprinting and Learning, 1262; Instinct Theory, 1309; Preparedness and Learning, 1866.

DEMENTIA, ALZHEIMER'S DISEASE, AND PARKINSON'S DISEASE

Type of psychology: Psychopathology
Field of study: Organic disorders

Dementia is the loss of memory. Alzheimer's disease is one of the most common causes of premature memory loss (presenile dementia); its effects on the patient, and often on the patient's family, are devastating. Parkinson's disease, another disorder of the central nervous system, can also cause memory loss.

Principal terms

CEREBELLUM: a part of the hindbrain; it is involved with controlling posture and body movement

EXTRAPYRAMIDAL MOTOR SYSTEM: one of the two parts of the nervous system involved in performing voluntary movement (the other is the pyramidal system); the cerebellum directs its functioning

NEURON: an individual nerve cell, the basic unit of the nervous system

NEUROTRANSMITTER: a chemical substance that enables a neuron to "communicate" with another neuron or a muscle cell

PATHOGENIC: relating to the causing of a disease; capable of causing a disease

PYRAMIDAL MOTOR SYSTEM: one of the two parts of the nervous system involved in performing voluntary movement (the other is the extrapyramidal system)

Overview

Aging has traditionally been blamed for a loss of intellectual abilities and is widely accepted to be the cause of memory failure. The word "senility" has therefore come to be equated with forgetfulness and loss of intellect; correctly, however, senility simply means old age, not those other characteristics that have come to be associated with it. Many studies have shown that cognitive abilities only slightly decrease with age and have suggested strongly that environmental and situational factors have greater impact on memory or cognitive loss than physiological factors do.

The accurate term for age-associated forgetfulness is "dementia." If dementia occurs in old age, it is called senile dementia; if its onset occurs prior to the conventional age of sixty-five or so, it is referred to as presenile dementia. Dementia as a clinical syndrome is a progressive cognitive deterioration that eventually causes functional impairment. It develops over time and causes deficits in intelligence, memory, affect (emotion), judgment, orientation, and visuo-spatial skills. Dementia may be caused or affected by many variables. Injury to the brain, as from an automobile accident, is one example. The most frequently noted cause is Alzheimer's disease.

The cause of Alzheimer's disease is not known. Therefore, neither preventive nor demonstrably effective curative treatments are available. It is estimated that there are more than 4 million people in the United States suffering from Alzheimer's disease. Even though age per se does not cause the disease, it is among the variables involved. For example, nearly 10 percent of the elderly between the ages of sixty-five and seventy-five suffer from Alzheimer's disease, whereas 35 to 45 percent of the elderly eighty years of age and older suffer from the disease.

Alzheimer's disease is the primary cause of dementia. Its symptoms, progressing from the earliest to the final stages, may involve the loss of recent memory, disorientation, drastic changes in judgment and personality, and loss of long-term memory, including the names of close relatives. It is considered primarily a cognitive disorder, but it also influences one's social behavior, increases agitation and anger, and disrupts patterns of family relationships.

There are many theories of the cause of Alzheimer's disease, all of which have mustered some degree of support from experimental evidence. Neuronal losses, changes in neurotransmitters, aluminum toxicity, and genetic factors are among the most probable causes being researched. Alois Alzheimer originally indicated that there is a loss of cortical neurons associated with the disease; quantitative documentation of his hypothesis was provided later. In general, at autopsy, a clear loss of brain tissues in comparison with the same age group without Alzheimer's disease can be seen. Perhaps of equal importance is the dramatic cognitive dysfunction that is caused by the disruption in the flow of neurotransmitters because of the loss of tissue.

Studies of neurotransmitters, their receptors, and the enzymes responsible for their synthesis and degeneration have demonstrated a vast amount of alteration. The major changes are observed to occur in a specialized group of neurons that are known as the cholinergic system. The cholinergic system is involved in the functioning of the cerebral cortex as well as other vital parts of the brain. Changes in neurotransmitters such as acetylcholine and somatostatin lead to interruptions of the cortical function of the brain, researcher Paul Newhouse has noted. It has been established that there is a correlation between the loss of cholinergic markers in the brain and the degree of cognitive dysfunction that occurs in the latter stages of Alzheimer's disease.

Evidence of genetic factors in Alzheimer's disease has also been found. In investigating large groups of patients with both presenile and senile dementia, 5 to 15 percent of the affected individuals have shown familial patterns; in most instances, the disease follows a dominant pattern of inheritance. In a study of a family of Alzheimer's disease patients in the northeastern New York area, Taher Zandi and Linda Morreale found a dominant pattern of familial Alzheimer's disease that can be traced up to four generations. Among the group of individuals with familial type Alzheimer's disease, it is common to find other disorders that may have been transferred genetically. For example, leukemia is reported to be a frequently observed disorder in correlation with both Alzheimer's disease and Down syndrome. All patients who live beyond the age of thirty-five with Down syndrome (Trisomy 21) develop pathological changes in the brain that are the same as the changes used to diagnose Alzheimer's disease (Karen Bick, 1987). Scientists are searching for a connection between chromosome number 21 and Alzheimer's disease.

Investigators of patients who are on renal (kidney) dialysis have shown that a small number of patients develop a progressive dementia that seems to be associated with an accumulation of aluminum in the brain. Animal studies have found that rabbits that were injected with an aluminum solution showed damage within the neurons that is similar to that of Alzheimer's disease. This possible connection to aluminum deposits is among the most controversial of the suggested causes of the disease.

The effects of Parkinson's disease, or parkinsonism, consist of an expressionless face, slowness (and minimization) of voluntary movement, tremors (mainly when at rest), a stooped posture, rigidity, and a festinating gait (that is, a gait that is abnormally affected by "chasing" the person's center of gravity). The onset of parkinsonism usually occurs between the ages of forty and seventy. It affects both sexes equally; past age fifty, the rate of incidence is 1 percent.

Parkinson's disease has been tied to a degeneration of certain neurons (dopaminergic neurons) in the midbrain. These neurons are crucial in the regulation of the parts of the nervous system that control voluntary movements—the pyramidal and extrapyramidal motor systems. In the pyramidal system, the motor cortex of the brain transmits commands from the cortex via the pyramidal tracts; the motor cortex of the right side of the brain stimulates the left side of the body, and vice versa. Technically, the remainder of the motor nervous system is called the extrapyramidal system, but the term most frequently is applied to the area of the basal ganglia and the cerebellum. It modulates the activities of the pyramidal motor system. Disease in this system causes rigidity, tremor, and lack of coordination (especially if the cerebellum itself is diseased). Furthermore, cranial motor neurons and spinal-cord motor neurons are also affected.

The extrapyramidal motor system sets the timing and pattern of action of the skeletal muscles in any projected action. Disease of the system may cause paresis (weakness of the muscle, but with some function remaining) or paralysis (complete loss of a muscle's function). Any of these conditions may be incapacitating. Fine tuning of the pyramidal and extrapyramidal networks requires a proper balance of certain neurotransmitters, specifically acetylcholine (the excitatory neurotransmitter) and dopamine (the inhibitor). In Alzheimer's disease, too little acetylcholine (ACh) occurs in certain localities of the brain. In Parkinson's disease, there is too little dopamine. Too little acetylcholine in the body results in myasthenia, a muscle weakness disease; too much acetylcholine in the body causes convulsions. As people age, the cells in the substantia nigra area of the brain's motor cortex become fewer, decreasing from some 425,000 cells in young adults to 200,000 cells at the age of eighty. In most cases of parkinsonism, there are fewer than 100,000 cells left. The enzyme for forming dopamine also decreases with age. These changes make elderly people more vulnerable to parkinsonism.

Applications

Although there are many theories seeking to explain the causes of Alzheimer's and Parkinson's diseases, none is yet exclusive or completely convincing. The major problem for those investigating the diseases has to do with the difficulty in distinguishing among the primary symptoms of the disorders, their manifestations, and the secondary reaction of individuals toward these symptoms.

Alzheimer's disease is defined by certain pathologies that are found in the nervous systems (specifically, in the brains) of people with the condition. These pathologies are found in the frontal, parietal, and temporal cortex areas of the brain as well as in the hippocampus, a primary memory storage area. They consist of what are called "neurofibrillary tangles" and "neuritic plaques." The neurofibrillary tangles have been found to be protein filaments. Neuritic plaques are accumulated dead neurons. The number of these looplike neurofibrillary tangles observed has been linked to the degree of dementia that existed in the patient. (The actual diagnosis based on these brain abnormalities can only practically be made in postmortem examination during an autopsy.) Another significant finding has been that both the neurotransmitter acetylcholine and the enzyme choline acetyltransferase are found in smaller amounts in the brains of patients with Alzheimer's disease. Again, there is a correlation with the severity of the disease's symptoms; the smaller the amounts of both chemicals, the worse the symptoms of the disease.

Unlike some other neurological disorders, there has been an absence of animal models for Alzheimer's disease, which has contributed to the mysteriousness of the disease. The characteristic neurofibrillary tangles have never been seen in old animals. In some very limited circumstances Alzheimer's disease has been induced in animals, but the induction procedure is based on a theory that may explain the disease partially at best, according to A. M. Clarfield.

Parkinson's disease is commonly treated through administration of L-dopa. L-dopa is a form of dopamine (the "levorotatory" form, essentially a chemical mirror-image of dopamine) that has been found most effective. It acts by binding to the dopamine receptors and producing almost the same effects as dopamine itself does. Side effects include nausea, hypertension, depression (which can be severe enough to result in suicide), and a heightening of the sex drive. Elevated mood and activity can result in fractures or even in heart attacks (myocardial infarctions). Amantadine, an antiviral drug also used in treating influenza, acts by releasing dopamine from striatal neurons.

Important in the attempt to understand the causes of these disorders—and thus to develop curative treatments for them—is their early recognition. Diagnosing Alzheimer's disease is complicated by the fact that the definitive indications of the disease can be found only upon autopsy. Since true cures do not yet exist, the efficient management of primary and secondary symptoms of the illnesses is of great importance. For example, memory loss, a primary behavioral symptom of Alzheimer's disease, results in communication difficulty between patient and care giver, which often increases the patient's frustration and the care provider's stress. Behavioral management strategies can provide the care giver with the proper skills, thus reducing the unneeded tension that is created in family life. Another important type of management strategy is medication management, which may improve the patient's sleeping pattern and therefore make life more manageable for the family members as well as for the patient.

Context

Alzheimer's disease is named for Alois Alzheimer, the German neurologist who first identified the disease in 1907. For most of the twentieth century, the disease remained extremely mysterious. It was not frequently recognized or diagnosed, and older people with severe memory and disorientation problems were considered to be suffering from extreme cases of the "normal" problems of growing old. Since the 1970's, however, investigations into both Alzheimer's and Parkinson's diseases have increased considerably, and much has been learned about the fundamental aspects of the diseases. Many advances have been related to technological improvements, such as the development and refinement of microchips for neurological imaging, as well as the availability of other instruments. It remains for scholars and researchers entering the fields of geriatrics, neurology, psychiatry, psychology, and other relevant disciplines to continue the search for cures for these diseases until preventive measures can become a reality.

Alzheimer's disease has a profound and disturbing impact on the spouse and family of the person affected by the disease. Emotionally, they must watch a person they know and love gradually lose memory and the ability to function and care for himself or herself. In the earlier stages of the disease, the patient is usually disturbed by the losses. Ironically, as the disease progresses and worsens, the patient is less aware of the problems, but the burden on the family increases as family members must care for the patient or decide to put the person in a nursing home or other care facility. The financial burden becomes immense, and it is unfortunately not uncommon for Alzheimer's patients and their spouses to lose all their savings as well as their homes in the frustrating attempt to pay the bills for a condition that can only get worse. Health insurance frequently is designed to cover hospital expenses but not long-term care in a nursing home. Medicaid, a federal program, will pay for "custodial" care, but only for people who cannot pay themselves—in other words, a person must first lose everything he or she has.

There is hope that research will develop ways to prevent, cure, or at least delay such degenerative diseases. New techniques for imaging the brain in detail are aiding research efforts. Positron emission tomography (PET scanning) and magnetic resonance imaging (MRI) technologies, for example, show promise in researching and diagnosing neurological disease. MRI is based on the unique magnetic properties of certain atoms within the body, and it applies a powerful magnetic field to the body, then, with computers, evaluates the results.

Bibliography

Bradley, W. "Alzheimer's Disease: Theories of Causation." In *New Directions in*

Understanding Dementia and Alzheimer's Disease, edited by Taher Zandi and Richard J. Ham. New York: Plenum Press, 1990. Bradley has investigated the role of genetics in the development of Alzheimer's disease. In this article he discusses the role of chromosome 21 and its possible linkage to Alzheimer's disease.

Clarfield, A. M. "The Reversible Dementias: Do They Reverse?" *Annals of Internal Medicine* 109 (1988): 476-486. Clarfield reviews a very important question of dementia. His analysis of more than twenty investigations of dementia suggests that the number of reversible dementias may be less than 2 percent.

Miner, Gary D., et al., eds. *Caring for Alzheimer's Patients: A Guide for Family and Healthcare Providers.* New York: Plenum Press, 1989. Presents a considerable amount of useful information in its 292 pages. Includes sections on the biology of the disease and on dealing with the disease (including legal information, caring for the patient, and public policy issues). Good references and helpful appendices.

Oliver, Rose, and Frances A. Bock. *Coping with Alzheimer's: A Caregiver's Emotional Survival Guide.* New York: Dodd, Mead, 1987. The emphasis is on advice for those taking care of a patient with Alzheimer's disease on how to handle the stresses they themselves will experience. Covers common emotional responses such as denial, anger, shame, and self-pity.

Zandi, Taher, and Richard J. Ham, eds. *New Directions in Understanding Dementia and Alzheimer's Disease.* New York: Plenum Press, 1990. Zandi and Ham provide a multidisciplinary look at this disorder. Discusses the fact that Alzheimer's disease, even though a neuropsychiatric disorder, has profound social and political implications that affect family members.

Taher Zandi

Cross-References

Aging: Cognitive Changes, 180; Aging: Institutional Care, 186; Aging: Physical Changes, 192; Theories of Aging, 198; Brain Injuries: Concussions, Contusions, and Strokes, 448; The Central and Peripheral Nervous Systems, 494; Death and Dying: Theoretical Perspectives, 763; Forgetting and Forgetfulness, 1049; Neural Damage and Plasticity, 1655; Neurotransmitters, 1673.

DEPRESSION: THEORETICAL EXPLANATIONS

Type of psychology: Psychopathology
Field of study: Depression

Depression is seen in all social classes, races, and ethnic groups; it is so pervasive that it has been called the "common cold of mental illness." The study of depression has focused on biological underpinnings, cognitive concomitants, stress and coping style precursors, and interpersonal context.

Principal terms

BIPOLAR DISORDER: a disorder characterized by the occurrence of one or more manic episodes, usually interspersed with one or more major depressive episodes

MAJOR DEPRESSIVE EPISODE: a disorder of mood and functioning, meeting clearly specified criteria and present for at least two weeks, which is characterized by dysphoric mood or apathy

MANIC EPISODE: a distinct period of mood disturbance, meeting clearly specified criteria, which is characterized by abnormally and persistently elevated, expansive, or irritable mood

UNIPOLAR DEPRESSION: a disorder characterized by the occurrence of one or more major depressive episodes but no manic episodes

Overview

Almost everyone gets "down in the dumps" or has "the blues" sometimes. Feeling sad or dejected is clearly a normal part of the spectrum of human emotion. This situation is so common that a very important issue is how to separate a normal "blue" or "down" mood or emotion from an abnormal clinical state. Most clinicians use measures of intensity, severity, and duration of these emotions to separate the almost unavoidable human experience of sadness and dejection from clinical depression.

Depression is seen in all social classes, races, and ethnic groups. It is so pervasive that it has been called "the common cold of mental illness" in the popular press. It is approximately twice as common among women as it is among men. Depression is seen among all occupations, but it is most common among people in the arts and humanities. Famous individuals such as Abraham Lincoln and Winston Churchill had to cope with depression; Churchill called the affliction "the black dog." More recently, United States senator Thomas Eagleton and astronaut Edwin Aldrin were known to have bouts of serious depression.

Of all problems that are mentioned by patients at psychological and psychiatric clinics, some form of depression is most common. It is estimated that approximately 25 percent of women in the United States will experience at least one significant depression during their lives. Contrary to a popular misconception that depression is most common among the elderly, it is actually most common in twenty-five- to forty-four-year-olds. About 10 percent of the college population report moderate depression, and 5 percent report severe depression. Suicidal thoughts are common in depressive clients. In long-term follow-up, it has been found that approximately 15 percent of depressed individuals eventually kill themselves. Alternatively viewed, approximately 60 percent of suicides are believed to be caused by depression or by depression in association with alcohol abuse. As has been vividly portrayed in the media, teenage suicide in the United States has increased in recent years at an alarming rate.

The role of family or genetic factors in depression was addressed long ago by Robert Burton in *The Anatomy of Melancholy* (1621), in which he noted that the "inbred cause of melancholy is our temperature, in whole or part, which we receive from our parents" and "such as the temperature of the father is, such is the son's, and look what disease the father had when he begot him, his son will have after him." More than 350 years later, the role of family factors in depression was addressed in a major collaborative study in the United States. In what was called the National Institute of Mental Health Collaborative Study of the Psychobiology of Depression, a large number of standardized instruments were developed to assess prevalence and incidence of depression, life histories, psychosocial stressors, and outcome of depression. The family members of depressed persons were assessed along with the depressed individual. It was found that bipolar depression was largely confined to relatives of individuals with bipolar disorder. Unipolar depression, however, was common among relatives of both unipolar and bipolar-depressed individuals. The different patterns of familial transmission for bipolar and unipolar disorders strengthen the general conviction that these two disorders should be kept distinct from each other.

One explanation for increased vulnerability to depression in close relatives of depressed individuals is an inherited deficiency in two key components of brain chemistry: norepinephrine and serotonin, both of which are neurotransmitters. If depressions could be reliably subtyped according to the primary neurotransmitter deficiency, the choice of antidepressant medication would logically follow. Research is conflicting, however, on whether there is one group of depressed individuals who are low in norephinephrine and normal in serotonin, and another group of depressives who are low in serotonin and normal in norepinephrine. Future developments in the study of neurotransmitters may have practical implications for the matching of particular pharmacotherapy interventions with particular types of depression. Evidence does indicate that for many depressed patients, substantial alteration in neurotransmitter activity occurs during their depression. This altered activity may directly mediate many of the disturbing symptoms of depression.

A different approach to understanding depression has been put forward by cognitive theorists. According to Aaron Beck, in *Cognitive Therapy and the Emotional Disorders* (1976), cognitive distortions cause many if not most of a person's depressed states. Three of the most important cognitive distortions are arbitrary inference, overgeneralization, and magnification and minimization. Arbitrary inference refers to the process of drawing a conclusion from a situation, event, or experience when there is no evidence to support the conclusion or when the conclusion is contrary to the evidence. For example, an individual concludes that his boss hates him because he seldom says positive things to him. Overgeneralization refers to an individual's pattern of drawing conclusions about his or her ability, performance, or worth based on a single incident. An example of overgeneralization is an individual concluding that she is worthless because she is unable to find her way to a particular address (even though she has numerous other exemplary skills). Magnification and minimization refer to errors in evaluation that are so gross as to constitute distortions. Magnification refers to the exaggeration of negative events; minimization refers to the underemphasis of positive events.

According to Beck, there are three important aspects of these distortions or depressive cognitions. First, they are automatic—that is, they occur without reflection or forethought. Second, they appear to be involuntary. Some patients indicate that these thoughts occur even though they have resolved not to have them. Third (interestingly), the depressed person accepts these thoughts as plausible, even though others would clearly not view them in the same manner.

While there is ample empirical support for the association of depression and negative cognitive factors such as cognitive distortions, irrational beliefs, and negative statements about oneself, only now is there beginning to be research that demonstrates the ability of cognitive variables to predict subsequent depression. It appears that a cognitive vulnerability plays a role in symptom formation for at least some individuals and in the maintenance of ongoing episodes of depression for many, if not all, depressed persons.

Yet another approach to understanding depression focuses on stress and coping. James Coyne (in a 1991 article) suggests that depression may be understood as a failure to cope with ongoing life problems or stressors. It has been hypothesized that coping effectively with problems and stressors can lessen the impact of these problems and help prevent them from becoming chronic. Depressed patients show slower recovery if they display poor coping skills. Avoidance coping strategies appear to be particularly likely in depression and are one example of poor coping. Depressed persons also show elevated levels of emotion-focused coping strategies, such as wishful thinking, distancing, self-blame, and isolation. These strategies also tend to be ineffective. While most forms of coping are impaired during an episode of depression, only self-isolation, an interpersonal avoidance strategy, appears to be an enduring coping style of persons vulnerable to depression. Thus, coping processes appear to change for the worse during an episode of depression, and poor coping helps to maintain the episode. In particular, depressed persons appear likely to avoid problem situations and to engage in strategies with a low likelihood of resulting in problem resolution or an enhanced sense of personal control.

Interpersonal approaches to understanding depression are related to stress and coping models but highlight the interpersonal environment as particularly important in depression. There is considerable evidence that low levels of social support are related to depression. Perhaps the relationship between social support and depression results from the fact that depressed persons do not seek social support; however, there is also evidence that poor social support leads to or maintains depressive symptomatology. In particular, evidence links the absence of close relationships with the development of depressive symptomatology. Accordingly, the work on general social support and depression can be seen as pointing in the direction of direct consideration of intimate relationships and their role in depression. Since the strongest family ties are usually in the marital relationship, it is natural to look to the marital relationship for particularly powerful opportunities to provide social support. Indeed, there is considerable evidence of an association between marital discord and depression. It had been expected by some that the association between marital discord and depression would be greater for women than men; however, it is generally equivalent between sexes when one looks across studies. Indeed, the risk of having a major depressive episode is approximately twenty-five times higher for both males and females if they are in a discordant marital relationship than if they are in a nondiscordant marital relationship.

Applications

There are a number of ways to understand depression, and each approach appears to have something to offer. Given the distressing nature of depression, it is not surprising that these differing approaches to understanding depression have led in turn to several different effective ways of treating depression.

Pharmacological interventions for unipolar depression have sometimes been held to normalize a genetically determined biochemical defect; the evidence, however, does not support this extreme biological characterization of unipolar depression. Yet neurotransmitters may directly mediate many of the behaviors affected in depression (for example, sleep, appetite, and pleasure), and neurotransmitter level and activity are disturbed as a concomitant of many episodes of depression; hence, the use of antidepressant agents that influence neurotransmitter level or activity should be helpful in reducing or eliminating symptoms of depression even if the disturbance in neurotransmitter level or activity is itself the result of environmental or cognitive changes. In addition, there is considerable direct evidence that antidepressants can be useful in the treatment of depression in many cases. In controlled trials, both more recently developed and older forms of antidepressants provided improvement rates of 66 to 75 percent, in contrast to placebos, which showed improvement rates of 30 to 60 percent. Exactly for whom they will work, however, and exactly how or why they work are still not entirely clear.

A second effective approach to the treatment of depression can be found in cognitive therapy. It has become clear that altering cognitions and behavior in a cognitive behavioral format can work to relieve an ongoing episode of depression and may reduce the likelihood of relapse more than the use of psychopharmacology alone.

Thus, cognitive processes are, at a minimum, reasonable targets of intervention in the treatment of many depressed patients. In addition, cognitive therapy appears to work well at decreasing depressive symptomatology even in the context of ongoing marital discord. Thus, for many depressed patients, interventions targeted at altering dysfunctional, negative automatic thoughts are likely to be useful.

Finally, interpersonal psychotherapy (IPT) has been developed by Gerald Klerman. This successful approach emphasizes abnormal grief, interpersonal disputes, role transitions, loss, and interpersonal deficits, as well as social and familial factors. Results of a large, multicenter collaborative study conducted by the National Institute of Mental Health indicated that IPT can work as well as antidepressant medication for many depressed patients. In addition, earlier research indicated that IPT can improve the social functioning of depressed patients in a manner not typically produced by antidepressant medications alone. Given the interpersonal problems which are often part of a depressive episode, these improvements in social functioning and interpersonal environment appear to be particularly important for depressed persons. In a related development, marital therapy has been tested as a treatment for depressed persons who are maritally discordant, and it appears to be successful.

Context

The identification of depression as a recognizable state has a very long history. Clinical depression was described as early as the eighth century B.C., in the biblical descriptions of Saul. During the fourth century B.C., Hippocrates coined the term "melancholy" to describe one of the three forms of mental illness he recognized. Later, Galen attempted to provide a biochemical explanation of melancholy based on the theory of "humors." Indeed, repeated descriptions and discussions of depression are present from classical times through the Middle Ages and into modern times.

The first comprehensive treatment of depression in English was provided by Timothy Bright's *Treatise of Melancholia* (1586). In 1624, Robert Burton provided his own major work on depression, *The Anatomy of Melancholy*. Most of the credit for developing the modern understanding of affective disorders, however, is given to Emil Kraepelin, a German psychiatrist. It was in Kraepelin's system that the term "depression" first assumed importance.

Since classical times, there have been debate and controversy over whether depression is best considered an illness or a response to an unhappy situation. Indeed, it is obvious to the most casual observer that sadness is a normal response to unhappy events. Even now, there is less than complete agreement on when fluctuations in mood should be considered pathological and when they are within normal limits. To help resolve this problem, diagnostic criteria have been developed, and structured interview procedures are often used to determine whether a particular individual should be considered depressed.

While many attempts have been made to divide the depressive disorders into subtypes, only the bipolar versus unipolar distinction has been widely accepted around the world. Unipolar depression is much more common than bipolar depression and so will continue to attract a larger share of research attention in the future. In most articles, the term "depression" refers to unipolar depression only. Models of depression have become increasingly sophisticated, progressing from Hippocrates' theory that depression was produced by an excess of black bile to modern biochemical, cognitive, coping, stress, and interpersonal models. It seems likely that even more sophisticated models of depression may provide guidance for the next great challenge facing clinical psychology: reversing the trend in Western societies toward ever-increasing rates of depression.

Bibliography

Beach, Stephen R. H., E. E. Sandeen, and K. D. O'Leary. *Depression in Marriage.* New York: Guilford Press, 1990. Summarizes the literature on basic models of depression. Provides the basis for understanding the important role of marriage in the etiology, maintenance, and treatment of depression.

Beck, Aaron T. *Cognitive Therapy and the Emotional Disorders.* New York: International Universities Press, 1976. Clearly lays out the basics of the cognitive model of depression. An important start for those who wish to understand the cognitive approach more thoroughly.

Burns, David D. *Feeling Good: The New Mood Therapy.* New York: William Morrow, 1980. Provides a very entertaining and accessible presentation of the cognitive approach to depression. Presents basic results and the basics of cognitive theory, as well as a practical set of suggestions for getting out of a depression.

Coyne, James C., ed. *Essential Papers on Depression.* New York: New York University Press, 1985. Includes representatives of every major theoretical position advanced between 1900 and 1985. Each selection is a classic presentation of an important perspective. This source will acquaint the reader with the opinions of major theorists in their own words.

Coyne, James C., and G. Downey. "Social Factors and Psychopathology: Stress, Social Support, and Coping Processes." *Annual Review of Psychology* 42 (1991): 401-426. This influential chapter ties together stress and coping with interpersonal processes to provide a deeper understanding of the nature of depression. Also provides an account of advances in the way both depression and interpersonal processes related to depression may be studied.

Kleinman, Arthur, and Byron Good. *Culture and Depression.* Berkeley: University of California Press, 1985. This exceptional volume examines the cross-cultural research on depression. Authors from anthropology, psychiatry, and psychology attempt to address the diversity that exists across cultures in the experience and expression of depression. The persevering reader will be rewarded with a journey through time and across many societies.

Paykel, Eugene S. *Handbook of Affective Disorders.* New York: Guilford Press, 1982. Provides comprehensive coverage of depression, mania, and anxiety in relation to depression. Includes detailed descriptions of symptoms, assessment procedures, epidemiology, and treatment procedures.

Stephen R. H. Beach

Cross-References

Abnormality: Biomedical Models, 39; Abnormality: Cognitive Models, 46; Bipolar Disorder, 422; Clinical Depression, 521; Cognitive Behavior Therapy, 546; Cognitive Therapy, 586; Coping: Social Support, 700; Psychoactive Drug Therapy, 1891; Seasonal Affective Disorder, 2155; Suicide, 2501.

DEPTH PERCEPTION

Type of psychology: Sensation and perception
Field of study: Vision

Depth perception describes the way people integrate visual cues to form a three-dimensional image of their surroundings. An understanding of the basic processes underlying this phenomenon is necessary for anyone, from artists to engineers, concerned with producing more realistic graphic representations of the visual world.

Principal terms
BINOCULAR CUE: a cue which is only available to both eyes working together, including convergence and retinal disparity cues
MONOCULAR CUE: a cue available to each eye separately; often used by artists to portray depth
RETINAL DISPARITY CUES: slight differences between the images of each eye caused by the distance between the eyes
STEREOGRAM: a two-dimensional image that appears three-dimensional when viewed binocularly; typically consists of two images of the same scene as viewed from slightly disparate viewpoints; when special glasses are worn, the images are fused into one image with the full three-dimensional effect
STEREOPSIS: the process whereby retinal disparity cues are translated into the subjective impression of depth

Overview

Visual depth perception describes the way a person can infer a three-dimensional representation of the world from a two-dimensional projection on the retina of the eye. People often take this amazing process for granted and only find it remarkable when it is made rather obvious—say, when they are watching a three-dimensional ("3-D") motion picture or gazing through a stereoscope. Such technical applications have grown out of an understanding of the basic processes which underly depth perception.

The evolutionary importance of depth perception may be understood through comparison of various mammalian species and the peculiar demands for their survival. Animals which are preyed upon tend to have lateral-facing eyes, which allow them to survey the visual surroundings in total or near panorama. Such animals include rodents (for example, mice) and ungulates (for example, cattle and horses), among others. For them, vision provides a means of long-range detection of predators. Predator species, on the other hand, make their living by precisely gauging distance to permit quick and accurate leaps toward prey. The eyes of these species, such as cats, are forward facing and work consensually, or in unison. This category of species with forward-facing eyes also includes the primates, who rely on precise distance estimation when brachiating, or swinging from trees through the forest canopy. For these animals, the forward placement of the eyes permits substantial overlap of the visual fields of each eye, which the brain "fuses" to form a unified image of the world. Since humans belong in the primate family, they benefit from this evolutionary history.

The various cues for depth perception may be divided into two categories: binocular cues, which rely on both eyes working together, and monocular cues, which may be derived from a single eye. Monocular cues are also those which artists have come to rely on for portraying depth in a two-dimensional image. A brief description of each of these cues follows. One binocular cue is known as convergence. As objects approach the viewer, the eyeballs converge (move closer together). This permits a form of distance estimation somewhat akin to triangulation. As the muscles surrounding the eyes bring them to focus on approaching objects, the increasing muscular tension provides a cue to the observer, particularly at close distances.

A second binocular cue is retinal disparity, the fundamental process underlying the so-called 3-D phenomenon used as a special effect in films and stereo viewers. Since the eyes are separated, they produce images that are slightly different. This disparity or difference increases as objects become increasingly close, within about 6 meters of the observer. Beyond 6 meters (20 feet) or so, the disparity information is no longer available, since the image seen by each eye is nearly identical. The visual processing centers of the brain fuse these separate images into one picture of the world, a process called binocular vision. Even animals with laterally placed eyes (for example, rabbits, chameleons) have been shown to possess this ability. The further ability to utilize disparity cues to form the subjective perception of depth is called stereopsis. This capability appears to be shared among a smaller subset of animals, and has been demonstrated in various primate species (as well as cats) and raptors (for example, hawks). Neuroscientists have shown that species capable of stereopsis possess cells in the visual cortex which respond to a specific range of retinal disparities.

The power of retinal disparity cues acting in isolation was demonstrated by Bela Julesz of the Bell Telephone Laboratories. He produced what are now referred to as Julesz stereograms, typically consisting of apparently random dots of two colors, usually red and green. When the dots are viewed through glasses with one red and one green lens, suddenly a shape materializes where one was not apparent before. For example, a central square composed of dots appears to "rise" above the background. The different colored lenses serve to eliminate the input from the same-colored dots, thereby separating the colors, with only one color going to each eye. In the example given above, the dots corresponding to the central square shape are slightly displaced laterally, thereby producing retinal disparity. The remaining or background dots all project to corresponding points on opposite retinas, thereby producing no disparity. The same effect is achieved in cinematography by filming scenes with one green and one red lens set somewhat apart (like human eyes). The viewers of the 3-D motion picture must wear similar glasses (with one green and one red lens) to derive the stereoptic effect.

Overlapping images are a monocular cue. When two objects are seen as overlapping, they provide a very compelling cue for relative distance, such that the object that is occluded is seen as farther away. This cue can be manipulated to produce powerful impressions of relative distance which are capable of overpowering other cues, such as expectations of size.

Another monocular cue is motion parallax. When someone is moving, objects at varying distances from the person appear to move at varying speeds, with closer objects sweeping past more quickly (for example, telephone poles along a highway). Even in the absence of binocular vision, motion parallax may be relied upon to convey relative distance. For example, tennis players who have lost sight in one eye can learn to compensate for the loss of binocular vision by moving back and forth when the ball is returned to them, which allows them to judge the speed of its approach.

Familiar size is also a monocular cue. If one were to view a picture showing a lamp post and a building of equal height, one would perceive the lamp post to be much closer to one. Through interacting with their world, people develop expectations of the relative sizes of familiar objects at various distances. Shadows are monocular cues. The shading of a rounded or angular surface has long been used by artists as a means of portraying objects displaced in depth. A circle with shadowing at the bottom, for example, is seen as a depression, whereas the reverse is perceived as a convex surface or bump. Aerial perspective is another monocular cue. Artists also take advantage of the fact that very distant objects typically appear hazy and indistinct, whereas near objects appear sharp and clear. Particles of dust and water in the air cause this effect.

Linear perspective is a monocular cue. Much of the human world is composed of straight lines and edges, such as roads and buildings. As one gazes down a highway, for example, these edges appear to converge at a vanishing point on the horizon. These linear cues are also used in graphic art to convey a three-dimensional world. Texture gradients are yet another type of monocular cue. James J. Gibson's *The Perception of the Visual World* (1950) describes the importance of the graded texture cues of surfaces such as those seen on floors and on the ground. The elements of texture of a carpet recede in size in a uniform manner as one gazes across it, as do the blades of grass of a lawn. Virtually every conceivable surface affords a viewer some form of textural cue.

Applications

Normally, all the above cues are available to varying extents; rarely does the visual world present one in isolation. The importance of each, however, may be demonstrated experimentally by singling out a given cue of interest or by juxtaposing two of these cues to determine which is more powerful. In the latter case, providing such contradictory information to the eye typically produces very compelling illusions.

An example of such an illusion occurs when someone is asked to peer into an experimental room through a small hole. The viewer sees what appears to be a small room with rectangular, windowlike shapes along the walls, ordinary in every respect except that there appears to be a giant child standing next to a very small adult. At the experimenter's request, the adult walks forward and the child walks backward, and the relative sizes are reversed. When the subjects move, the viewer realizes that things are not as they seem. The experimental room is called the Ames distorted room, and its ordinary appearance is deceptive. The room itself is not rectangular, but is trapezoidal, with one of its apparent "far" corners considerably farther away than the other. The fact that one corner is farther away from the observer than the other is disguised by the rectangular shapes along the walls and the edges of the walls themselves, which are constructed to appear identical on both the short and long sides of the room to a stationary observer. Perceptually, this produces a juxtaposition of familiar size cues (child versus adult) against those of linear perspective, and the latter appears to "win out."

Illusions amount to interesting demonstrations of the workings of depth cues, but perceptual scientists have generally been more interested in addressing issues such as people's sensitivity to differences in depth, both monocularly and binocularly, as well as whether the reliance on these cues is learned or innate. The issue of sensory sensitivity is typically addressed using what are called psychophysical experiments. Psychophysics has historically been interested in determining the ability to detect the presence of a given stimulus (for example, a spot of light), called an absolute threshold, as well as the ability to detect differences in intensity or amount (for example, comparing the weight of two objects), called a difference threshold. Determining the depth discrimination threshold has traditionally required comparison of the distance of two objects, thus making it more of a difference threshold. One method of doing this, called the Howard-Dolman apparatus, involves the subject's viewing two thin rods, and the experimenter varying the distance between them until the subject is able to determine reliably which is closer. Experiments involving the use of this device with human subjects typically show remarkable sensitivity to differences in depth. Additionally, estimates derived from binocular viewing are usually considerably better than those derived from monocular viewing, thus implying the relative importance of retinal disparity cues to human perception.

The nature-nurture issue of whether people learn to use these cues through experience or whether they are built in from birth has been more difficult to address. A comprehensive treatment of this subject was published in 1961 by Richard Walk and Eleanor Gibson in an article entitled "A Comparative and Analytical Study of Visual Depth Perception," published in *Psychological Monographs: General and Applied.* The authors compared the responses of a total of eleven different species, including human infants, on variations of a "visual cliff" apparatus. The apparatus generally consisted of an elevated platform divided into a shallow side, where the animals could comfortably walk, and a deep side with a substantial drop. The latter was actually covered by transparent glass and thus posed no threat. The floors of both sides were covered by square linoleum tiles of identical dimensions, which afforded texture gradient cues for depth. The variable of interest was whether very young animals, sometimes less than one day old, once placed on a neutral center area, would show a consistent preference for the shallow side. Nearly all the species tested (including human infants as young as six months) showed a clear preference for the shallow side and, when placed on the deep side, showed behavior strongly suggestive of fear or distress at the apparent lack of support. When texture cues were controlled for, by adjusting the size of the linoleum tiles so that those on the deep side appeared to be the same size as those on the shallow side, the animal subjects were still able to avoid the deep side. The latter suggested to the authors that the subjects were relying on motion parallax cues obtained when they moved.

The testing of extremely young animals (less than one day old) on the visual cliff device was limited to those capable of locomotion at an early age, including chicks, lambs, and kids. These species all showed clear discrimination of depth. The importance of learning was tested in other species by rearing them in the dark (thus obviating the possibility of experience with visual depth cues). Dark-reared cats and monkeys, however, showed maturational effects in which the shallow-side preference was not clearly evident for at least three or four days following exposure to light. The authors considered the latter evidence to be more indicative of a requirement of neural maturation than of learning. Thus, the overall evidence reported by Walk and Gibson is strongly suggestive that the utilization of visual depth cues is innate, at least in some species.

Nonexperimental applications of depth perception principles have focused primarily on attempts to make two-dimensional replications of the world more "real." For example, the sophistication and appeal of video games are increased substantially when linear perspective and motion parallax cues are included. The video operator can now pilot a jet or drive a race car with nearly all the visual authenticity of the real event, with only the kinesthetic feelings of motion absent. An even more impressive application has been made possible by the increased accessibility of high-capacity computers running programs designed to produce "virtual reality" (VR). In a typical VR application, the subject interacts with a visual image produced by the computer. The subject wears a helmet that projects televised images to each eye; this process affords the possibility of stereoscopic images using retinal disparity cues. The subject may wear sensors at different points along his or her body to detect movement, which causes a corresponding movement in the VR world. Many believe that VR represents the future of high-technology entertainment.

Stereoscopic cues have also permitted more effective interfacing between human operators and remote systems. The remote devices (similar to robots) tested thus far have been primarily designed for operations at extreme ocean depths, but they have obvious applications in space exploration as well. Similar to the VR operator, the remote operator wears a helmet with televised images projected to each eye. Each eye receives input from a corresponding television camera mounted on the remote unit. As the remote unit crawls along the sea floor, it sends back stereoscopic images of what it "sees," which allows the human operator to manipulate objects via robotic arms. If greater apparent separation in depth is required for close detail work, the television cameras may be separated even more, to produce what is called hyper-stereopsis.

Context

Experimental understanding of the importance of visual cues is relatively recent, having occurred mostly during the twentieth century. Historically, the principles of visual depth perception were mainly the concern of painters and graphic artists.

The use of perspective in paintings did not appear until the Italian Renaissance in the fourteenth century. Prior to this time, images were painted as flat and two-dimensional. Ancient Egyptian figures, for example, appear to assume impossible contortions, showing both legs in the same plane of depth. Early Chinese artists similarly had no technique for portraying distance other than to note more distant objects higher up on the painted surface.

When Leonardo da Vinci provided in his notebooks the first detailed description of the principles of perspective, artists finally had the means for more compelling representations of the three-dimensional world. Leonardo realized that perspective was nothing more than a branch of geometry, and he provided several techniques for capturing it, including the use of a pane of glass covered with translucent paper, which permitted artists to trace the outlines of objects directly onto the paper. Leonardo also discussed the importance of other monocular cues of direct relevance to painting, including increasing aerial haze with increasing distance and the use of shadows.

Among the earliest documented descriptions of the importance of binocular cues was that of the British philosopher George Berkeley, who in 1709 first described the possible use of kinesthetic cues produced by the eye muscles in accommodation (muscular contraction and relaxation of the lens) and convergence. Berkeley inferred these mechanisms without confirmation through experimentation. Later, the physicist Charles Wheatstone discovered the phenomenon of stereoscopic vision and the importance of retinal disparity cues; he invented the first stereoscope, which quickly became a standard European parlor feature.

The late 1800's marked the advent of psychophysics, which was concerned with the quantification of the limits and discrimination power of human perception. Experiments by Hermann von Helmholtz in the nineteenth century using a technique called the three-needle experiment demonstrated the smallest amount of retinal disparity which could be perceived as a difference in depth, referred to in psychophysics as a depth threshold. A slightly more sophisticated device called the Howard-Dolman apparatus was devised in 1919; it provided another source of such acuity or threshold estimates using wooden rods which could be adjusted in depth. It was used as a means of screening aviation candidates for adequate depth perception. Later improvements of the device, such as the use of illuminated slits rather than wooden rods, still produced acuity estimates that were similar to those derived earlier. Thus, today these early best-acuity estimates are accepted as accurate.

The next major development in the scientific study of visual depth perception came in 1961, with the development of random dot stereograms by Bela Julesz of the Bell Telephone Laboratories. Such stereograms typically consist of two panels of random dots which are presented side by side. Inspection of each reveals no apparent pattern. When the two are viewed stereoscopically (with 3-D glasses), however, a pattern—such as a word—emerges. The stereograms are designed with great precision by a computer, which prints the dots so that they either fall perfectly on converging points of the retina or are displaced laterally somewhat. The greater the lateral displacement or retinal disparity, the greater the perception of depth. These stereograms have proved invaluable in the study of stereoptic cues presented in total isolation—that is, without any other monocular or binocular cues for depth—and have permitted more detailed study of human stereopsis as well as the demonstration of stereopsis in a number of animal species, including macaque monkeys, hawks, and owls.

Bibliography

Graham, Clarence Henry. "Visual Space Perception." In *Vision and Visual Perception,* edited by Clarence Henry Graham. New York: John Wiley & Sons, 1965. Primarily a summary of all the possible monocular and binocular cues for depth perception, and of experimental understanding of their relative importance. Since the vast majority of psychophysical experiments on visual depth acuity were performed prior to this publication, it may be relied upon as an accurate summary of how such experiments were performed and their findings, the results of which are still cited in more current publications.

Gregory, Richard L. *Eye and Brain.* 4th ed. Princeton, N.J.: Princeton University Press, 1990. A very accessible description of the visual system, from eye to brain. Includes numerous illustrations and photographs which make for an extremely intelligible presentation. Topics include perception of brightness, movement, color, illusions, art and reality, and nature-nurture issues in perception. A good "primer" of human vision.

_____. *The Intelligent Eye.* New York: McGraw-Hill, 1970. Deals mainly with the issues involved in representing a three-dimensional world using two-dimensional images. Includes 3-D stereo illustrations (including 3-D glasses) and numerous examples of "impossible figures" and illusions. Often used as a supplementary text in college art courses.

Julesz, Bela. *The Foundations of Cyclopean Perception.* Chicago: University of Chicago Press, 1971. Detailed and somewhat technical review of investigations of stereopsis, or what the author refers to as cyclopean perception, using random-dot stereograms. The stereograms represent a tremendous advance in experimental technique in that they permit the study of retinal disparity cues in total isolation. The text is supplemented with numerous examples of random dot stereograms (includes 3-D glasses).

Pettigrew, John D. "The Neurophysiology of Binocular Vision." *Scientific American*

227 (August, 1972): 84-95. Review of the understanding of how information from two eyes is "fused" in the brain and retinal disparity cues extracted. Describes experiments performed by David Hubel and Torsten Wiesel, and other neuroscientists, which revealed cortical neurons that only respond to binocular input.

Walk, Richard D., and Eleanor J. Gibson. "A Comparative and Analytical Study of Visual Depth Perception." *Psychological Monographs* 75, no. 15 (1961): 1-44. A very accessible description of experimental investigations with eleven different animal species (including human infants as young as six months) using the visual-cliff apparatus. Authors discuss the possible visual depth cues upon which the subjects appeared to rely, as well as nature-nurture issues of depth perception.

Joseph R. Mobley, Jr.

Cross-References

Gestalt Laws of Organization, 1082; Motion Perception, 1600; Pattern Vision, 1752; Perceptual Constancies, 1771; Visual Illusions, 2622; Visual Neural Processing, 2629.

DEVELOPMENT: THEORETICAL ISSUES

Type of psychology: Developmental psychology
Fields of study: Adolescence; behavioral and cognitive models; infancy and
childhood

Developmental theories allow psychologists to manage and understand the enor-
mous body of data on behavioral development from infancy through old age. Theo-
ries of development focus on many different issues and derive from many perspec-
tives and periods in history. All, however, are concerned with explaining stability
and change in human behavior as individuals progress through their lives.

Principal terms

BEHAVIORISM: a theoretical perspective which holds that the proper
subject matter of psychology is behavior without reference to
consciousness or mentalistic issues

DEVELOPMENT: the progressive, systematic changes that occur in
organisms as they proceed through their life cycles

EMERGENT PROCESS: any process of behavior or development that was
not necessarily inherent in or predictable from its original
constituents

HEURISTIC: having the property of generating further research and
theory

"ORGANIC LAMP" THEORY: a term coined by Jonas Langer to denote a
theory that emphasizes the constructive role of the organism in its
own development

PSYCHODYNAMIC THEORY: a theoretical perspective which holds that
development involves the dynamic interplay of conscious and
unconscious processes

THEORY: a general principle that explains a group of related phenomena

Overview

Theoretical perspectives on development derive from a wide variety of viewpoints.
Although there are numerous important theoretical issues in development, three
questions are central for most theories. The first of these is the so-called nature-
nurture question, concerning whether most behavioral development derives from
"nature" (genetic or other inherited sources) or from "nurture" (learning and other
resources received from the parents, world, and society). The second of these issues
is the role of children in their own development: Are children active contributors to
their own development, or do they simply and passively react to the stimuli they
encounter? Finally, there is the question of whether development is continuous or
discontinuous: Does development proceed by a smooth accretion of knowledge and
skills, or by stepwise, discrete developmental stages? Current perspectives within
developmental psychology represent very different views on these issues.

Useful developmental theories must possess three properties. They must be parsimonious—as simple as possible to fit the available facts. They must be heuristically useful, generating new research and new knowledge. Finally, they must be falsifiable, or testable: A theory that cannot be tested can never be shown to be right or wrong. Developmental theories can be evaluated in terms of these three criteria.

Arguably, the oldest developmental theoretical formulation in use is the psychodynamic model, which gave rise to the work of Erik Erikson, Carl G. Jung, and, as its seminal example, the theory of Sigmund Freud. Freud's theory holds that all human behavior is energized by dynamic forces, many of which are consciously inaccessible to the individual. There are three parts to the personality in Freud's formulation: the id, which emerges first and consists of basic, primal drives; the ego, which finds realistic ways to gratify the desires of the id; and the superego, the individual's moral conscience, which develops from the ego. A primary energizing force for development is the libido, a psychosexual energy that invests itself in different aspects of life during the course of development. In the first year of life (Freud's "oral stage"), the libido is invested in gratification through oral behavior, including chewing and sucking. Between one and three years of age (the "anal stage"), the libido is invested in the anus, and the primary source of gratification has to do with toilet training. From three to six years, the libido becomes invested in the genitals; it is during this "phallic stage" that the child begins to achieve sexual identity. At about six years of age, the child enters "latency," a period of relative psychosexual quiet, until the age of twelve years, when the "genital stage" emerges and normal sexual love becomes possible.

Freud's theory is a discontinuous theory, emphasizing stage-by-stage development. The theory also relies mainly on nature, as opposed to nurture; the various stages are held to occur across societies and with little reference to individual experience. The theory holds that children are active in their own development, meeting and resolving the conflicts that occur at each stage.

How successful has psychodynamic theory been? Its parsimony is open to question: There are clearly simpler explanations of children's behavior. The falsifiability of these ideas is also highly questionable because the theories are quite self-contained and difficult to test. Psychodynamic theory, however, has proven enormously heuristic. Hundreds of studies have set out to test these ideas, and these studies have significantly contributed to developmental knowledge.

In contrast to psychodynamic theories, the behaviorist theories pioneered by John B. Watson and B. F. Skinner hold that development is a continuous process, without discrete stages, and that the developing child passively acquires and reflects knowledge. For behaviorists, development results from nurture, from experience and learning, rather than from nature. The most important extant behaviorist theory is the social learning theory of Albert Bandura, which holds that children learn by watching others around them and imitating others' actions. For example, Bandura demonstrated that children were far more inclined to commit violent acts (toward a toy) if someone else, particularly an adult, committed the acts first. The children were especially disposed to imitate if they perceived the acting individual as powerful or as rewarded for his or her violent actions.

The behaviorist theories are relatively parsimonious and heuristic. They are also testable, and it has been shown that, although many of the findings of the behaviorists have stood the test of time, there are developmental findings that do not fit this framework. To understand these findings, one must turn to the so-called organic lamp theories. This term comes from the fact that within these theories, children are seen as active contributors to their own development, and certain developmental processes are held to be "emergent": As fuel combusts to produce heat and light in a lamp, hereditary and environmental factors combine in development to produce new kinds of behavior. This framework was pioneered by Kurt Goldstein and Heinz Werner, but the most significant extant organic lamp theory is the cognitive developmental theory of Jean Piaget.

Piaget's theory involves a discontinuous process of development in four major stages. The sensorimotor stage (birth to two years) is followed by the preoperational stage (two to seven years), the concrete operational stage (seven years to adolescence), and the formal operational stage (adolescence to adulthood). During the sensorimotor stage, the child's behavior is largely reflexive, lacking coherent conscious thought; the child learns that self and world are actually different, and that objects exist even when they are not visible. During the preoperational stage, the child learns to infer the perspectives of other people, learns language, and discovers various concepts for dealing with the physical world. In the concrete operational stage, the ability to reason increases, but children still cannot deal with abstract issues. Finally, in formal operations, abstract reasoning abilities develop. The differences between the four stages are qualitative differences, reflecting significant, discrete kinds of behavioral change.

Piaget's theory is not entirely accurate; it does not apply cross-culturally in many instances, and children may, under some experimental circumstances, function at a higher cognitive level than would be predicted by the theory. In addition, some aspects of development have been shown to be more continuous in their nature than Piaget's ideas would indicate. Yet Piaget's formulation is relatively parsimonious. The various aspects of the theory are readily testable and falsifiable, and the heuristic utility of these ideas has been enormous. This theory has probably been the most successful of the several extant perspectives, and it has contributed significantly to more recent advances in developmental theory. This progress includes the work of James J. Gibson, which emphasizes the active role of the organism, embedded in its environment, in the development of perceptual processes; the information processing theories, which emphasize cognitive change; and the ethological or evolutionary model, which emphasizes the interplay of developmental processes, changing ecologies, and the course of organic evolution.

Applications

Developmental theory has been important in virtually every branch of medicine and education. The psychoanalytic theories of Sigmund Freud were the foundation of psychiatry and still form a central core for much of modern psychiatric practice. These theories are less emphasized in modern clinical psychology, but the work of Freud, Erikson, Jung, and later psychodynamicists is still employed in many areas of psychotherapy.

The behavioristic theories have proved useful in the study of children's learning for educational purposes, and they have considerable relevance for social development. An example is seen in the area of media violence. Bandura's work, and other research stemming from social learning theory, has repeatedly demonstrated that children tend to imitate violent acts that they see in real life or depicted on television and in the media, particularly if the individuals who commit these acts are perceived as powerful or as rewarded for their actions. Although this is disputed, especially by the media, most authorities are in agreement that excessive exposure to televised violence leads to real-world violence, largely through the mechanisms described by social learning theorists. Social learning theory has contributed significantly to an understanding of such topics as school violence, gang violence, and violent crime.

The organic lamp views have provided developmentalists with useful frameworks against which to understand the vast body of developmental data. Work within the Piagetian framework, for example, has shown that both nature and nurture contribute to successful development. One cannot, for example, create "super children" by providing preschoolers with college-level material. In general, they are simply not ready as organisms to cope with the abstract thinking required. On the other hand, the work of researchers on various Piagetian problems has shown that even very young children are capable of complex learning.

Organic lamp theory has demonstrated the powerful interplay between biological factors and the way in which children are reared. An example is seen in the treatment of Down syndrome, a chromosomal condition that results in mental retardation. The condition occurs when there are three chromosomes, rather than two, at the twenty-first locus. Clearly, this is a biological condition, and it was believed to be relatively impervious to interventions that come from the environment. It has now been shown, however, that children afflicted with Down syndrome develop much higher intelligence when reared in an intellectually stimulating environment, as opposed to the more sterile clinical environments typically employed in the past. The child's intellect is not entirely determined by biology; it is possible to ameliorate the biological effects of the syndrome by means of an environmental intervention. This type of complex interplay of hereditary and environmental factors is the hallmark of applied organic lamp theory.

The most important application of developmental theory generally, however, lies in its contribution to the improved understanding of human nature. Such an understanding has considerable real-world importance. For example, among other factors, an extreme faith in the nature side of the nature-nurture controversy led Adolf Hitler to the assumption that entire races were, by their nature, inferior, and should therefore be exterminated. His actions, based on this belief, led to millions of human deaths during World War II. Thus, one can see that developmental theories, especially if inadequately understood, may have sweeping applications in the real world.

Context

Developmental theory has changed greatly over time. The theories of different societies at various times in history have emphasized different aspects of development. The Puritans of the sixteenth and seventeenth centuries, for example, focused on the moral development of the child; they believed that Original Sin was inherent in children and that children had to be sternly disciplined in order to make them morally acceptable. In contrast to this view was the developmental theory of the eighteenth-century French philosopher Jean-Jacques Rousseau, who held that children are born good and are then morally corrupted by society. Sigmund Freud was interested in psychosexual development and in mental illness; his work therefore focused on these areas. John B. Watson, B. F. Skinner, and Albert Bandura worked during a period when the major impetus in psychology was the study of learning; not surprisingly, this was the focus of their work.

Historically, as developmental theorists worked intently within given areas, they often arrived at extreme positions, philosophically and scientifically. For example, some theorists have focused upon the biology of behavior; impressed by the importance of nature in development, they may have neglected nurture. Others focused upon societal and social learning effects, and decided that nurture was the root of behavior; nature has often been relegated to subsidiary theoretical roles in physiological and anatomical development. Similar conflicts have arisen concerning developmental continuity or discontinuity, the relative activity or passivity of children in contributing to their own development, and a host of other issues in the field. These extreme positions would at first appear to be damaging to the understanding of development; however, psychologists are now in a position to evaluate the extensive bodies of research conducted by adherents of the various theoretical positions. It has become evident that the truth, in general, lies somewhere in between. Some developmental functions proceed in a relatively stepwise fashion, as Piaget or Freud would hold; others are much smoother and more continuous. Some development results largely from the child's rearing and learning; other behavior in the developing organism appears to be largely biological. Some developmental phenomena are emergent processes of the way in which the developing individual is organized, resulting both from nature and nurture in intricate, interactive patterns that are only beginning to be understood. These findings, and the therapeutic and educational applications that derive from them, are only comprehensible when viewed against the existing corpus of developmental theory. This corpus in turn owes its existence to the gradual construction and modification of developmental theories of the past. Thus, the real value of any given theory of development lies less in its perspective on any specific issue than in its contribution to the overall, constantly growing body of developmental knowledge and understanding.

Bibliography

Gollin, Eugene S., ed. *Developmental Plasticity: Behavioral and Biological Aspects of Variations in Development.* New York: Academic Press, 1981. Excellent coverage of important theoretical issues in modern developmental psychology. Accessible to college or graduate students with some background in psychology and/or biology.

Langer, Jonas. *Theories of Development.* New York: Holt, Rinehart and Winston, 1969. Although somewhat dated, this is an excellent account of theories in development and of their construction and history. Particularly recommended for the treatment of psychodynamic theory. Available in most libraries, and accessible to college students.

Lerner, Richard M. *On the Nature of Human Plasticity.* New York: Cambridge University Press, 1984. Insightful discussion of modern theory in developmental psychology and some historic antecedents. Emphasis on biological issues. Accessible to advanced students, graduate students, or professionals.

Miller, Patricia H. *Theories of Developmental Psychology.* 2d ed. New York: W. H. Freeman, 1989. Excellent, comprehensive treatment of developmental theory. Describes extant theories in detail and discusses commonalities and dissimilarities. Accessible to the layperson with some background in psychology.

Piaget, Jean. *Biology and Knowledge.* Chicago: University of Chicago Press, 1971. This is a seminal summary of Piagetian theory that contains more general information and information concerning theory construction than do Piaget's other, more specific works. Readily accessible to the college student or the advanced high school student.

Shaffer, David Reed. *Developmental Psychology: Childhood and Adolescence.* 2d ed. Pacific Grove, Calif.: Brooks/Cole, 1989. Good general textbook on developmental psychology, with an excellent basic treatment of theoretical issues in development. Accessible to the college or high school student.

Siegler, Robert S. *Children's Thinking.* 2d ed. Englewood Cliffs, N.J.: Prentice-Hall, 1991. Although this book is primarily a technical treatise on a specific area in development, the author discusses modern theory in cognitive development in terms of both Piagetian and information processing perspectives and introduces issues of current theoretical interest in a clear, readable manner.

Matthew J. Sharps

Cross-References

Adolescence: Cognitive Skills, 118; Aging: Cognitive Changes, 180; Attachment and Bonding in Infancy and Childhood, 307; Behaviorism: An Overview, 401; Cognitive Development Theory: Piaget, 553; Developmental Methodologies, 817; Ego Psychology: Erik Erikson, 867; Gender-Identity Formation, 1062; Physical Development: Environmental versus Genetic Determinants, 1823; Psychosexual Development, 1969.

DEVELOPMENT OF EMOTION

Type of psychology: Emotion
Field of study: Infancy and childhood

The development of emotions is intertwined with all aspects of human development; understanding how and when to express emotions, for example, is an essential component of personality and normal developmental processes.

Principal terms
EMOTIONAL ELICITOR: a stimulus event that is necessary for an emotion to occur
EMOTIONAL EXPERIENCE: the background needed for the interpretation and evaluation of an emotional state and expression
EMOTIONAL EXPRESSIONS: the observable behaviors, such as facial expressions, changes in heart rate, and vocalizations, that often accompany emotional states
EMOTIONAL RECEPTORS: certain cells or structures in the brain that detect and respond to events
EMOTIONAL STATE: a set of changes in somatic and/or neurophysiological activity that occur when emotional receptors are activated
STRANGER ANXIETY: a common phenomenon that generally occurs during the end of the first year of life in which the elicitor of a stranger tends to produce the emotion of anxiety
TEMPERAMENT: an inborn set of moods and patterns of reacting

Overview

In their book entitled *Children's Emotions and Moods: Developmental Theory and Measurement* (1983), Michael Lewis and Linda Michalson outline a model of the development of emotion. According to Lewis and Michalson, emotion consists of five components: elicitors, receptors, states, expressions, and experiences.

An elicitor is a stimulus event that is necessary for an emotion to occur. The stimulus may be either external or internal to the individual. Some elicitors are assumed to produce emotion almost automatically. In other words, little experience is needed for emotion to result once the elicitor is presented. Other types of elicitors produce different results as the individual develops. For example, the elicitor of a stranger tends to produce the emotion of fear in most infants. This phenomenon, which generally occurs during the end of the first year of life, is called "stranger anxiety." As children get older, this fear tends to decrease. The influence of an elicitor may change over time for several reasons. For example, as children develop, their cognitive capacities increase. Thus, in order for a child to be afraid of a stranger, he or she must first gain the ability to tell the difference between a stranger and a parent. Therefore, some elicitors change in their relation to emotion as children develop.

Receptors are cells or structures in the brain that detect and respond to events.

There is debate as to the specificity of these receptors—that is, whether there are specific receptors for specific emotions or more general receptors that activate over-all arousal. There is limited information available about how development relates to these receptors. It is possible that the receptors can change in sensitivity over time through either biological development, social experiences, or a complex interaction between biological growth and learning experiences.

In the third component of Lewis and Michalson's model, emotional states involve a set of changes in somatic and/or neurophysiological activity that occur when emo-tional receptors are activated. These emotional states have been conceptualized in two ways. In one view, emotional states are thought to be inborn and development does not play a particularly important role. An alternative view is that the newborn infant has two general emotional states: negative and positive. As the child develops, these states become more differentiated. That is, whereas an infant of three months may experience a limited number of emotional states, including distress, excitement, and delight, a two-year-old child can experience a wider (more differentiated) vari-ety of emotions, including fear, anger, jealousy, joy, and affection.

The fourth component of this developmental model concerns the expression of emotion. Emotional expressions differ from emotional states in that they are the observable behaviors (such as facial expressions, posturing, and vocalizations) that often accompany emotional states. Some researchers have examined facial expres-sion in infants to provide evidence of discrete emotional expressions at a very young age. For example, psychologists have been able to distinguish eight different emo-tions in the facial expression of twelve-month-old children. It is unknown, however, whether these observed expressions in infants truly represent separate internal emo-tional states.

The fifth component of emotion, emotional experience, involves the interpreta-tion and evaluation by the child of an emotional state. As the child develops, he or she gradually gains the ability to experience a broad range of emotions. Whereas a newborn is capable of experiencing distress, the older child has the ability to evalu-ate his or her own behavior and emotional state as well as the situational context in order to experience an emotion such as embarrassment.

It should be clear from the above discussion that the child's experience and expres-sion of emotion change considerably as the child develops. As early as three to four months, infants display patterns of behaviors that suggest emotional states of dis-tress, gratification, and excitement. An infant who displays increased motor move-ment and heart rate, closes the eyes, and cries in response to pain, cold, or hunger is showing distress. When an infant experiences gratification, he or she displays be-haviors such as decreased muscle tension and closing of the eyes after feeding.

At around six months of age, infants appear to experience new emotions, includ-ing fear and anger. When infants of this age are confronted with a new or unfamiliar situation, they often respond by retracting their mouths, widening their eyes, and raising their brows; they may also cry. Prior to this time, infants may attend to unfamiliar events but do not appear to be frightened by them. Six-month-old infants also seem to experience anger in response to frustrating situations, such as the removal of an interesting toy. As early as the first year, infants are able to respond to certain emotions displayed by other people. For example, one-year-old children tend to become upset when they witness someone being angry.

The sequence of the development of emotions and their universality has led psychologists to postulate that emotions may develop because they serve an adaptive purpose for survival. Children early display emotions that tend to keep the caretaker nearby, such as crying at separation. Children's fearfulness of the unfamiliar may protect them from approaching situations that they are as yet unable to handle.

Childrens' inferences about others' emotions also develop over time. Preschool children can correctly interpret facial expressions of emotions in others and can make accurate predictions about how other people will feel in certain situations. While young children are able to infer whether someone feels "good" or "bad," older children are able to make more refined evaluations of others' emotions, differentiating "bad" feelings into "mad," "scared," or "sad." With maturation, children become able to tell when people are hiding their feelings or are pretending to feel a certain way.

Finally, unlike very young children, older children learn to use labels to describe their internal states. As children become more verbal and reflective, they learn from others how to label their own emotional states in a variety of situations. With age, children are also better able to monitor and modify the expression of their own emotional experience.

Applications

The role of emotional states, expressions, and experiences is pertinent to many aspects of psychology, particularly the study of personality and psychopathology. Emotional expression is a fundamental aspect in the way one relates to and communicates with others. Thus, psychologists who are interested in almost any aspect of normal or abnormal development find an understanding of emotional development essential.

Stella Chess and Alexander Thomas conducted pioneering studies in the area of infant temperament. The term "temperament" describes infants' inborn moods and activity levels. For example, some babies are easily soothed, while others are irritable and cry much more. Individual differences in temperament play a role in the way an infant's emotional state is related to the environment (elicitors). Based on their observations of infants, Thomas and Chess described a child with a difficult temperament as one who shows intense irritability and withdrawal regarding new situations. Infants with difficult temperaments are more likely than infants with easy temperaments to react negatively to certain elicitors. For example, an infant with an easy temperament may be pleasantly surprised when opening a jack-in-the-box, whereas an infant with a difficult temperament may be startled and upset. Chess and Thomas' research, as well as the research of many other psychologists who have built on their work, suggests that early temperament is predictive of later social competence—children with difficult temperaments are more likely to have problems with peers later in life.

Differences among children in their emotional expression and their ability to regulate their own emotions have an effect on later emotional and social development. For example, children who are extremely fearful of new situations are less likely to approach unfamiliar situations or people, and thus are less likely to explore and gain new information about the world. In addition, the ways in which children express themselves and regulate their emotions can have enormous impact on the reactions and behaviors of significant others. When a father and infant interact, they communicate with each other through facial expressions and bodily movements. Although a father cannot know for certain what his child is feeling, he makes inferences based on the baby's expressions. Fathers are delighted by their child's smiles and cooing noises. These behaviors keep the father engaged and encourage him to continue these satisfying interactions with the child. Thus, the child who smiles and coos will be more likely to receive the father's attention than a child who is more subdued and withdrawn. Given the countless interactions that a father and infant have, the temperament style of the child can have a powerful influence on the social environment experienced by the child.

One area in the field of emotional development is "attachment." John Bowlby, a British psychiatrist, proposed that infants are born with the capacity for certain behaviors (such as crying, smiling, and cooing) that help keep adults close. According to Bowlby, being able to keep adults in close proximity is adaptive in that it ensures the infant will be cared for and will be more likely to survive. Through repeated interactions between parent and child, an attachment is formed. Bowlby, as well as Mary Ainsworth, who expanded on Bowlby's ideas and tested them empirically, proposed that all normal infants form attachments. These attachments are thought to provide the basis for healthy emotional and social development. It is within the context of a healthy attachment with a caregiver that the infant is able to feel safe in exploring his or her surroundings. If a child develops unhealthy or insecure emotional attachments, social and emotional development suffers.

Mothers who form "anxious attachments" with their children are unable to evaluate and react to their children's needs and behaviors effectively. For example, a mother may misinterpret her child's reaction to seeing a large dog as fear (as opposed to interest). When the mother communicates to the child her own anxiety about the child's safety, the child is likely to reinterpret his or her own emotional state as fearful. The child might then learn that all dogs are dangerous. Psychologists are studying the relation between the quality of early parent/child attachments and the child's later ability to form healthy relationships in adulthood.

As it becomes increasingly clear that the ability to regulate one's emotions plays an important role in development, clinical psychologists have incorporated this information into various aspects of therapy. Children, as do adults, experience different emotions in part because of their interpretations and explanations of their own and other people's behavior. For example, if a child thinks that another child bumped into her by accident, she is less likely to be mad or upset than if she made the interpretation that the child bumped her intentionally. Children who are aggressive may lack basic skills in understanding the behavior of others and in dealing with interpersonal relations. Thus, a clinical psychologist might help aggressive children by teaching them to be aware of others' feelings and reactions. When children are able to interpret nonhostile behavior appropriately, they are less likely to become angry and retaliate.

Similarly, overly anxious and fearful children can be taught to make more reasonable evaluations about their environment and the consequences of certain behaviors. For example, a child who has an abnormal fear of new situations can learn to confront new situations with the help of a trusted person. By confronting these fearful situations, and learning that there are no negative consequences, the child develops self-confidence and can become less fearful.

Context

Although the study of emotion dates back to Plato and Aristotle, a comprehensive formulation of how emotions develop is far from complete. In fact, compared to the study of other areas of development, such as cognition, language, and memory, the development of emotion has received limited attention.

The study of most aspects of psychology has been subject to debates about the relative importance of biological factors versus learning or socialization. The study of emotional development is no exception. At the extremes, there are two interpretations of the development of emotion. The biological model of the development of emotion is based on Charles Darwin's ideas that emotional expressions are biologically determined and have adaptive value. According to this model, the components of emotion (elicitors, receptors, states, and expressions) are biologically determined and are relatively unaffected by learning.

The socialization or interactive model of emotion focuses on the ways in which emotions are learned. This model does not disregard the role of biological factors in the development of emotions; rather, it emphasizes the importance of the environmental influences of emotional development. In this model, the connections between elicitors, emotional states, and experiences are based on one's experiences with parents and peers. This model provides an understanding of the ways children learn how and when to express their emotions.

Most psychologists today recognize that the biological model and the socialization model provide information about different aspects of emotional development. As in other areas of child development, emotional development is understood to be the result of the interaction of biological and socialization factors; although the complex interaction between biological and social influences on emotional development is poorly understood. Today, emotional development is viewed in the context of the child's social, psychological, and physical development. Psychologists are interested in understanding how infants begin to make sense of the world around them and how infants experience early emotions. It has been found that infants have enormous capacities very early in life. They are able to perceive differences in the world around them, act upon the external world, and experience a wide variety of emotions and sensations.

Understanding the intricacies of emotional development is a challenging task. One difficulty in this area of research is that infants are unable to talk about (and indeed, even to know) what they are feeling. Therefore, researchers must rely on external signs such as crying and smiling as indicators of emotion as well as on physiological changes that can be reliably measured. As psychologists become more creative in their research and continue to develop more sophisticated tools for investigating emotions, they will continue to piece together the puzzle of emotional development.

Bibliography

Bower, T. G. R. *A Primer of Infant Development.* San Francisco: W. H. Freeman, 1977. Describes the process and features of development during the first two years of life. Presents basic information regarding infant emotional, social, motor, language, perceptual, and cognitive development. Provides a basis for placing emotional development in the context of other areas of development.

Emde, Robert N., T. J. Gaensbauer, and R. J. Harmon. *Emotional Expression in Infancy: A Biobehavioral Study.* New York: International Universities Press, 1976. In this research monograph in the "Psychological Issues" series, Emde and his colleagues report on their study of normal infant development during the first year of life. Their research involves the longitudinal study of emotional expression in sixteen infants using a variety of investigative techniques.

Flavell, J. H. *Cognitive Development.* 2d ed. Englewood Cliffs, N.J.: Prentice-Hall, 1985. This classic book, in its second edition, provides a comprehensive overview of the contemporary field of cognitive development. The chapter on social cognition provides interesting examples and descriptions of research evidence on social-cognitive development during infancy.

Lewis, Michael, and Linda Michalson. *Children's Emotions and Moods: Developmental Theory and Measurement.* New York: Plenum Press, 1983. Examines emotional development from its theoretical perspective and, through a structural analysis of the meaning of emotion, outlines a theory of emotional development. Presents a measurement system for assessing emotional development in young children that is based on situation-specific assessments of children's emotional behaviors.

Lewis, Michael, and Leonard A. Rosenblum, eds. *The Development of Affect.* New York: Plenum Press, 1978. Presents the work of more than twenty-five contributors, including Harry Harlow, Jerome Kagan, L. Alan Sroufe, and Robert Emde. It is the first volume in a series edited by Michael Lewis and Leonard Rosenblum entitled "Genesis of Behavior." Surveys advances in methodology and theory which have promoted understanding of the meaning and development of affect.

Laurence Grimm
Laurie S. Miller

Cross-References

Attachment and Bonding in Infancy and Childhood, 307; Development: Theoretical Issues, 804; Emotion: Cognitive and Physiological Interaction, 881; Emotion: Definition and Assessment, 893; Functions of Emotion, 900; Emotion: Mind-Body Processes, 907; Emotion and Learning Theory, 934; Emotional Expression, 954.

DEVELOPMENTAL METHODOLOGIES

Type of psychology: Developmental psychology
Fields of study: Adulthood; infancy and childhood; methodological issues

Developmental methodologies describe how information about age-related changes in people's physical growth, thought, and behavior is collected and interpreted. Sound methodologies are essential for describing accurately the course of life-span development, comparing people with different environmental and biological backgrounds, predicting developmental patterns, and explaining the causes of positive and negative outcomes in development.

Principal terms
COHORT: an identifiable group of people; in developmental research, group members are commonly associated by their birth dates
CONTROL: the extent to which a researcher can regulate who participates in a study, what the participants experience, and how the participants respond
DEVELOPMENT: the continuous and cumulative process of age-related changes in physical growth, thought, and behavior of people; a result of both biological and environmental influences
GENERALIZABILITY: the extent to which research results are applicable to people beyond those who participated in the study
RESEARCH DESIGNS: frameworks within which research methods are applied, ensuring that data are collected at two or more points in developmental time
RESEARCH METHODS: a diverse category of procedures for gathering developmental information; include observational, self-report, and experimental types of studies, and their associated data collection techniques

Overview

Developmental methodologies have as their purpose the investigation of questions about age-related changes throughout the life span, and they include both a variety of research methods and the designs within which these methods are applied. The overarching framework for developmental methodologies is the scientific process. This process embodies systematic rules for testing hypotheses or ideas about human development under conditions in which the hypotheses may be supported or refuted. This process also requires that research be done in such a way that it can be observed, evaluated, and replicated by others.

Data collected through developmental methodologies can be characterized as descriptive, correlational, or experimental. Descriptive data simply describe a variable—for example, the average age of the adolescent growth spurt. Correlational data provide information on relationships between variables, such as the association between newborn size and the amount of smoking a mother did during pregnancy. Experimental data result from the careful manipulation of one variable to discover its effect on another, and only in experimental studies can cause-and-effect relationships among variables be inferred. For example, experimental studies demonstrate that training techniques can cause an improvement in the memory performance of persons in late adulthood.

Developmental research methods are commonly separated into three general categories. One of these categories is observational methods, in which researchers observe people as they go about their lives. The settings for such research can be homes, schools, playgrounds, nursing homes, and so on. Observational research may be quite subjective, as in diary studies in which the researcher writes down observations and impressions in a free-flowing manner. The extensive cognitive developmental model of Jean Piaget had its beginnings in hypotheses which emerged from diary studies of his children. On the other hand, observational research may be very rigorous and systematic; researchers carefully define what they will observe and record, how they will observe and record, and then train data collectors before any formal observations are made. Videotaping of children's language samples which are then carefully segmented and analyzed is an example of this systematic approach.

The second category, self-report methods, is generally more intrusive than observational research. It involves asking questions of participants and may take the form of interviews, questionnaires, or standardized tests. Interviews may be free-flowing or highly structured, with predetermined questions and sequence. The famous studies of sexual behavior by Alfred Kinsey, for example, utilized carefully planned interview techniques. Questionnaires and standardized tests are usually structured with both questions and response categories provided. Questionnaires are often used to gather descriptive information such as size of family or educational level, as well as opinions on a variety of social issues. Standardized tests are used to assess a great variety of information, including measured intelligence, vocational interests, and self-concept.

The third category of developmental methods involves experimentation. Experimentation can occur in natural settings where individuals may not be aware that they are participating in research, such as in situational studies of children's moral behavior. It can also occur in laboratories where individuals may be unaware of their participation or fully aware of the artificiality of the setting and even the study's intent. Research using a complex apparatus to study newborn perception is one example of the former, while research using nonsense syllables in memory tasks to assess age differences in free recall is an example of the latter.

Research methods can be compared according to their generalizability and their ability to control participants' selection, experiences, and responses. Generally, methods which are more intrusive and contrived provide the greatest opportunity for control. Thus, laboratory experimentation often is associated with high levels of control. For the same reasons, however, questions are raised regarding the applicability to the real world of data collected in the artificiality of a laboratory. Thus, observation in natural settings is often associated with high levels of generalizability. Both control and generalizability are desirable and are sought in developmental research regardless of method.

In order to assess whether age-related changes exist, developmental research methods are applied within larger frameworks of research designs which require that data be collected at two or more points in developmental time. These designs permit inquiry into whether behavior is the result of maturational changes associated with age changes, such as the emergence of language in infancy; the effect of the immediate social context, such as a nation at war; or the effect of historical events which affected everyone born at about the same time (a group known as a cohort), such as growing up during the Great Depression. Two of the most common designs are the cross-sectional and longitudinal designs. In cross-sectional designs, data are collected on different cohorts at the same time. These designs permit an examination of age differences in behavior; however, they cannot separate out the effects of different life experiences between cohorts. In longitudinal designs, data are collected on the same cohort a number of times. These designs permit an examination of developmental trends within individuals; however, they cannot separate out the effects of social change, since no comparison can be made to a group *not* experiencing the social context. An alternative to cross-sectional and longitudinal designs are the sequential designs, in which data are collected on a number of cohorts a number of times. These designs are able to reveal the effects of age, cohort, and social context. Because of the difficulties of administering these complex designs and their expense, sequential designs are least often applied, even though they provide the most useful developmental information.

Regardless of the research methods or designs utilized, developmental methodologies must account for the complexity of human development. They must control for multiple variables, such as age, cohort, social context, socioeconomic class, gender, educational level, and family structure. They must take into account the culture of the participants, and they must protect against bias in formulating the research hypothesis, applying the methods, and interpreting the data collected.

Applications

Developmental methodologies are applicable to literally any developmental question, from conception to death. Resultant data permit description of current status, comparison between groups, prediction of developmental patterns, and explanation of the causes of developmental outcomes. Description, comparison, prediction, and explanation all contribute to a better understanding of development, which in turn permits the fostering of social settings that promote healthy development, as well as intervention to prevent potential developmental problems or to counter developmental problems already in existence.

Research on the competencies of newborns provides one demonstration of the relationship between understanding and therapeutic intervention. Observational research of newborns and young infants indicates a cyclical relationship in infant attention when the infant is interfacing with a care giver. This cycle is one of activation, discharge, and then recovery when the infant withdraws its attention. Care givers who adjust their behavior to their infants' rhythms by entering into interaction when their infants are responsive, and slackening off when their infants withdraw attention, experience a greater amount of time in which the infant looks at them than do care givers who either attempt to force their own rhythms on their infants or continuously bombard their infants with stimulation. Psychologists are applying this understanding as part of an overall intervention program with premature infants who enter the world at risk for physical, social, and intellectual impairments. Premature newborns require greater stimulation than full-term newborns before they respond; however, they also are overwhelmed by a level of stimulation to which full-term newborns respond very positively. This narrow range of tolerance can disrupt the relationship between a parent and the premature infant. In experimental research, parents of premature newborns have been trained to imitate everything their infants do, and by so doing follow their infants' rhythms. This training helps parents remain within the narrow tolerance of their infants, and increases the amount of positive interaction both experience. This, in turn, contributes positively to healthy social development of this high-risk group of infants.

Research on the developmental effects of television provides a demonstration of the relationship between understanding and influences on social policy. Beginning in the middle 1950's with a series of inquiries and hearings sponsored by a Senate subcommittee on juvenile delinquency, followed by a Surgeon General's report and associated Senate hearings in the early 1970's, and a major National Institute of Mental Health report in the early 1980's, questions about the effect of violent programming on children have been raised in the public domain. Consequently, public efforts have emerged to control the amount and timing of violence on television and to regulate the number and content of television commercials targeted at children. Central to the national debate and social policies surrounding television content has been the application of developmental methodologies.

Significant research in this area emerged in the early 1960's with the now-classic "Bobo" doll studies of Stanford University psychologist Albert Bandura. In a series of experimental laboratory studies, nursery school children observed a variety of televised models behaving aggressively against an inflatable punching-bag clown. Later, when their play behavior was observed in a controlled setting, children clearly demonstrated imitation of specific aggressive behaviors they had viewed. Additional experimental laboratory studies have been conducted; however, they have been consistently criticized for their artificiality. Consequently, field experiments have emerged in which the experimental variables have been actual television programs, and the effects have been assessed on spontaneous behavior in natural settings, such as playgrounds. Since experimental studies require systematic manipulating of variables for their effects to be observed, and since the manipulations of levels and types of aggression and other relevant variables such as home violence are either unethical or impractical, numerous correlational studies have also been conducted. Most of these have assessed the relationship between the amount of violence viewed and subsequent violent behavior, violent attitudes, or perceptions of violence in the real world. Many of these studies have applied longitudinal or sequential designs covering many years, including one longitudinal study which covered a span of twenty-two years from childhood into adulthood. These studies have controlled multiple variables including age, educational level, and initial level of aggressive behavior. Although not all studies have supported a causal link between television violence and aggressive behavior and attitudes, the large majority of laboratory experimental, field experimental, and correlational studies indicate that children do learn antisocial and aggressive behavior from televised violence, and that some of them may directly imitate such behaviors. The effects depend on the characteristics of the viewers and the settings.

Not only have developmental methodologies been used after the fact to discover the effects of television programming; they have also been applied proactively to develop prosocial children's programming, and then to evaluate the effects of those prosocial programs on children's development. The program "Sesame Street," for example, has as its foundation research into child development, attention, and learning. In fact, one of its objectives has been to act as an experimental variable, intervening into homes in which children are economically and educationally disadvantaged. Although researchers have had limited access to those high-risk homes, both experimental research and correlational longitudinal research support the effectiveness of *Sesame Street* in developing early academic skills, school readiness, positive attitudes toward school, and positive attitudes toward people of other races.

Context

Today's developmental methodologies have their origins in the nineteenth century, with its advances in science and medicine, the emergence of the fields of psychology and psychoanalysis, and developments in measurement and statistics. Developmental psychological research and methodologies often emerged to deal with concrete social problems. With compulsory education bringing approximately three-quarters of all children into classrooms at the beginning of the twentieth century, social concerns were focused primarily on child health, education, and social welfare. Consequently, the first major research into child intellectual, social, and emotional development also occurred during this period, and developmental psychology began to consolidate as a distinct discipline of psychology. The universal draft of World War I required assessment of multitudes of older adolescent and young adult men with vast differences in education, health status, and social and emotional stability. Standardized testing became the tool to evaluate these men, and has since remained a major tool in developmental methodologies, as well as in other disciplines of psychology. Following the war, efforts to understand these individual differences led to the first major longitudinal studies, which were focused on descriptions of normative growth and predictions of developmental patterns; some of these studies have followed their participants and next generations for more than fifty years.

In the two decades following World War II, the baby boom and national anxiety over falling behind the Soviet Union in science and technology rekindled efforts dampened during the war years in the disciplines of developmental and educational psychology. Of particular interest were methodologies in applied settings such as school classrooms, focused on learning and academic achievement. Also during this period, greater accessibility to computers permitted increases in the complexity of developmental research methods and designs, and of resultant data analyses. Complex sequential designs, intricate correlational techniques, and multiple-variable techniques became much more frequently used in research.

Heightened awareness of economic and social inequalities in the United States following the Civil Rights movement has led to many carefully designed educational, health, social, and economic interventions into communities which are economically at risk. The interventions have been part of developmental methodologies in which experimental, correlational, and descriptive data have been collected longitudinally to assess their outcomes. Head Start educational programs have been one prominent example.

In more recent decades, with changes in family structure, developmental methodologies have been applied to questions about single parenting, day care, and "latch-key" children. With substance abuse, developmental methodologies have been applied to questions about prenatal development in wombs of addicted mothers, postnatal development of infants born drug-addicted, and developmental intervention for drug-related disabilities in many of these infants. With more adults living longer and healthier lives, developmental methodologies have been applied to questions about learning and memory, self-esteem, and life satisfaction among persons in late adulthood. This list goes on. Clearly, developmental methodologies will continue to be relevant as long as persons are motivated to understand and nurture healthy life-span development and to intervene into social problems.

Bibliography

Mussen, Paul Henry, ed. *Handbook of Research Methods in Child Development.* New York: John Wiley & Sons, 1960. Commissioned by the Committee on Child Development of the National Academy of Sciences, this handbook continues to be a classic. Although dated in its applications, it provides conceptual and theoretical underpinnings for a variety of developmental methodologies. Includes many chapters written by quite eminent developmental psychologists.

Nielsen, Joyce McCarl, ed. *Feminist Research Methods: Exemplary Readings in the Social Sciences.* Boulder, Colo.: Westview Press, 1990. Challenges the traditional scientific method, including traditional developmental methodologies. Argues that Western cultural and masculine biases are pervasive in research assumptions and process, and provides alternative methodologies. Hyde's critique of developmental research into cognitive sex differences is particularly relevant. Advanced reading level.

Sears, Robert R. "Your Ancients Revisited: A History of Child Development." In *Review of Child Development Research.* Vol. 5, edited by E. M. Hetherington. Chicago: University of Chicago Press, 1975. A well-respected developmental psychologist, himself a participant in a longitudinal study from childhood, reviews the founding of the field in a readable and interesting chapter. Places developmental research and methodologies in the context of changes in society's needs and priorities. Discusses influences from other fields of study including anthropology and psychoanalysis.

Siegel, Michael H., and H. Philip Zeigler, eds. *Psychological Research: The Inside Story.* New York: Harper & Row, 1976. Personal accounts of their research by prominent psychologists. Chapters provide a good overview of the variety of types of studies and designs used by developmental researchers and other psychologists. Includes insiders' insights into how hypotheses emerge and how research plans grow, change, and mature. Readable and at times humorous.

Sommer, Barbara B., and Robert Sommer. *A Practical Guide to Behavioral Research: Tools and Techniques.* 3d ed. New York: Oxford University Press, 1991. A jargon-free, understandable first introduction to behavioral research. Further describes observational, self-report, and experimental research methods, and descriptive, correlational, and experimental data analyses.

Triandis, H. C., and A. Heron, eds. *Basic Methods.* Vol. 4 in *Handbook of Cross-Cultural Psychology: Developmental Psychology.* Boston: Allyn & Bacon, 1981. Presents conceptual basis for cross-cultural developmental research and research methodologies. Clearly demonstrates the potentialities and limitations of adapting Western developmental methodologies to the study of non-Western peoples. Presents a variety of research areas including language, memory, Piagetian cognitive structures, and personality development.

Wolman, Benjamin B., ed. *Handbook of Developmental Psychology.* Englewood Cliffs, N.J.: Prentice-Hall, 1982. A comprehensive handbook, the first ten chapters of which focus on research methods and theories. Surveys a variety of developmental methodologies, and demonstrates the relationship between theoretical models and methodologies applied. Includes a chapter on ethics and regulation of research with children.

Michael D. Roe

Cross-References

Data Description: Descriptive Statistics, 751; Data Description: Inferential Statistics, 757; Development: Theoretical Issues, 804; Hypothesis Development and Testing, 1248; Observational Methods in Psychology, 1700; Psychological Experimentation: Independent, Dependent, and Control Variables, 1932; The Scientific Method in Psychology, 2148.

DISSOLUTION

Type of psychology: Social psychology
Field of study: Interpersonal relations

Dissolution is the process of relationship breakdown and termination. The ending of a relationship is usually difficult, even traumatic, although strategies for coping can be developed.

Principal terms

ACCOUNT: an explanatory narrative or story of relationship and loss
BREAKDOWN: the period when a close relationship weakens and approaches termination
CONFLICT: tension attributable to incompatibility of goals
DYADIC: pertaining to a couple
NEGATIVE AFFECT RECIPROCITY: the exchange of bad feelings during communication
SELF-SUMMARIZING: repeating one's complaints although they are not heard or understood

Overview

Relationship dissolution refers to the breakdown and termination of a personal relationship. While not all relationships are dissolved, those that are involve similar processes, causes, and themes. Dissolution is the last stage of the life cycle of relationships. George Levinger developed one life-cycle view of relationships, termed the ABCDE model. In this model, relationships progress in five possible stages: awareness, buildup, continuance, deterioration, and ending. Awareness is the first contact two people have, and from which they develop their relationship through buildup and continuance. Dissolution encompasses the last two stages of Levinger's model, deterioration and ending.

Early theories of dissolution suggested that relationships end at a rate of change similar to that of their beginning. Social penetration theory, developed by Irwin Altman and Dalmas Taylor, suggests that intimacy develops as communication between two people increases in both breadth and depth. Broader communication includes more topic areas in conversation; deeper communication moves from superficial exchange to deeper revelations of personal hopes and fears. Most successful relationships were thought to develop slowly—first in breadth, then in depth. Such relationships involve a large intersection of the partners' lives, and they are not easily or quickly dissolved. In contrast, Altman and Taylor claimed, unusually narrow and deep relationships were more easily ended. For example, two people may have an intense but short-lived encounter; their communication is not broad although it is deep. They are more likely to encounter conflict, because they have not established a common history or a basis of trust. Any conflict they encounter is more likely to be terminal—to cause the end of their relationship. Altman and Taylor suggest that, because the relationship formed so quickly, it can be ended equally quickly. Thus, life cycles are symmetrical: Slowly developing relationships are slow to end, while sudden intimacies can end suddenly.

Subsequent research, however, has failed to confirm any obvious symmetry between buildup and breakdown. Instead, relationship development seems to involve a series of changes, choices, and crises. Conflict is a common experience in relationships, a natural consequence of mixing goals and communication styles. Conflict itself is not necessarily a sign of impending dissolution; most conflict is not terminal.

Research on communication has provided some clues about the difference between terminal and nonterminal conflict. Couples who eventually break up do not differ from stable couples in the content of their conflict; most couples appear to experience conflict over the same issues. What leads to termination is not the issues in conflict but the way the partners express and deal with the conflict.

Researcher John Gottman has identified differences in the ways satisfied versus dissatisfied couples communicate. In dissatisfied relationships, partners engage in negative affect reciprocity: They exchange bad feeling for bad feeling. For example, one partner may complain that the other has failed to perform a chore. In response, instead of validating or apologizing, the other offers his or her own complaint to arouse bad feelings. Cross-complaining is a common form of negative affect reciprocity. Unhappy couples are more likely to make their complaints general and vague, so one partner finds it difficult to respond to the other's complaint. Finally, dissatisfied couples engage in self-summarizing—repetitiously arguing or complaining without recognizing the other's reasons for not responding.

In contrast, when satisfied couples argue, a complaint is validated instead of echoed. For example, if one partner complains, "You did not do the dishes," the other admits it and responds, rather than offering a cross-complaint such as "Well, you did not do the laundry." In satisfied couples, partners make their complaints specific, so that it is clear what needs to be corrected. Finally, satisfied couples listen to each other and communicate constructively, rather than repeating themselves in self-summary even though no one is listening.

Caryl Rusbult has proposed that four reactions most frequently occur during relationship dissatisfaction: exit (one person leaves the relationship); voice (one actively tries to improve the relationship); loyalty (one passively waits for the relationship to improve); and neglect (one passively allows the relationship to deteriorate). Which of these four a person chooses will depend on the role that person has played in the relationship and on what his or her skills are. Exit and voice are active responses, while loyalty and neglect are passive. Exit and neglect are both negative options, while loyalty and voice are positive and hopeful. The choice to exit is more likely if one has been active within the relationship and has negative feelings about continuing it.

When continuation is unlikely or conflict is unresolvable, partners may agree to separate. Theorist Steve Duck suggests that at first, the decision to terminate is not mutual. Duck proposes a four-phase theory of breakdown and dissolution, in which the first phase begins with one partner's secret dissatisfaction. In this, the intra-psychic phase, the dissatisfied partner considers the costs and benefits of leaving the relationship. If he or she concludes that leaving is justified, the other partner is told, beginning the second, dyadic phase. In the dyadic phase, both partners discuss their relationship and the possibility of dissolution. If attempts to repair or reconcile fail, they enter the third, social phase; they announce their impending breakup to their friends and family. Finally, when parting is inevitable, they enter the final, "grave-dressing" phase, when the relationship becomes a memory to be understood and left behind.

Applications

Research on dissolution suggests that ending a relationship can be a behavioral choice or strategy, not merely a passive loss or failure. This explains how exiting a relationship can be a response to one form of relationship dissatisfaction, inequity. Equity is fairness, achieved when the relationship between one partner's outcomes and inputs is equal to the other partner's. According to equity theory, if two part-ners' investments or inputs into a relationship are equal, then equal division of the relationship's outcomes is fair and equitable; however, if their inputs are unequal, then equal outcomes will be inequitable. For example, if one partner does most of the housework, and the other very little, it is inequitable for them to share equally in the comforts of a clean, well-ordered home. The one who has invested more is being underbenefited by that outcome, and will eventually feel cheated. The other is being overbenefited and may feel guilty.

Inequity is a common source of conflict in relationships. Equity researchers sug-gest that there are four responses an unhappy partner can make in reaction to ineq-uity: change outcomes, change inputs, change perceptions, or exit the relationship. First, the unhappy partner can change his or her outcomes: The harder-working partner can demand greater benefits in compensation for his or her extra work. Sec-ond, the dissatisfied partner can change his or her inputs; by doing less housework, he or she will be making contributions commensurate with the equal division of outcomes. Third, the dissatisfied partner can change his or her perceptions of the arrangement. By coming to believe that the arrangement is really fair, he or she may feel convinced that all is well, and stay. Finally, the dissatisfied partner can exit the relationship.

Research supports the view that dissolution results when a relationship is per-ceived as unfair. Exchange theorists note that a committed relationship shifts from an exchange basis to a communal basis. Exchange relationships are short-term, tit-for-tat interactions. While most relationships begin with such tentative exchanges, when friends or partners make a commitment, the relationship shifts to commu-nality: Both partners invest in the relationship as being jointly rewarding, with no expectation of short-term return. Observations of couples in dissolution show that, when partners part ways, they begin to shift back to an exchange basis of interaction.

They "keep score" in their dealings with each other, exacting repayment of favors, and separating property and possessions.

In the late 1970's, Charles Hill, Zick Rubin, and L. Anne Peplau conducted a longitudinal study (a study of a group of subjects over time) of more than two hundred heterosexual couples, identifying differences between those who had broken up and those who were still together two years later. They found that couples were more likely to have broken up if the partners had initially been less similar to each other in intelligence, attractiveness, and educational goals. The researchers also found that, although most respondents claimed that it had been their idea to end the relationship, it was more likely the women who had actually taken the first steps to end the relationship. Other researchers have suggested that, because women are identified more strongly with their relationships than men, women are more likely to remain sensitive to the success and satisfaction of their relationships than men are. Breakups may be the result of failed intimacy or of more serious problems in conflict and communication.

Other researchers concur that relationship loss is a serious trauma. As with other stressful experiences, there are ways to cope with it. Behavioral psychologist Debora Phillips recommends a series of exercises to assist in "falling out of love." The first step involves thought-stopping—reducing the number of obsessive thoughts one has about the former partner and replacing them with alternative thoughts that are unconnected with the relationship. The second step involves silent ridicule, imagining the former partner in a humorous, human situation. The last steps involve positive image building and self-congratulations—rewarding oneself for success and providing self-approval rather than depending on a partner for such reinforcement. Sociologist Robert Weiss has examined the emotional consequences of dissolution in his 1975 work, *Marital Separation.* Because one's spouse is one's most important attachment figure, Weiss observes, the initial response to separation is severe emotional distress, including depression, confusion, disorientation, and loneliness. Separated persons experience two kinds of loneliness: emotional loneliness, at the loss of an intimate partner; and social loneliness, at the loss of community and "belonging" that accompanies the end of a marriage. Separated persons engage in obsessive review, an incessant concern with what went wrong and why. In the course of trying to understand their experience, separated persons form an "account," an explanation in narrative form of the relationship and its ending. The account seeks to identify and impart meaning to the loss. In the wake of account-making and post-separation adjustments, the separated person undergoes an identity change. He or she will identify different personal qualities as important, may cultivate new interests and new friends, and may change in ways that are hard for others to understand but that can be personally satisfying and fulfilling.

Context

Interest in relationship dissolution is growing, and much work is yet to be done. There are strategic difficulties in studying relationship dissolution. Cross-sectional studies (studies conducted at one point in time) depend on retrospective information: Respondents must remember how they felt and behaved when their relationships ended. Longitudinal studies, however, by definition, are time-consuming and expensive. More studies have examined marital than nonmarital breakups, and they have focused on heterosexual relationships. Research samples must include different relationship forms and sexual orientations if conclusions are to be drawn about relationship processes rather than culture and gender differences.

More is known about coping with loss through death than about dealing with dissolution. To some extent, the models are comparable. In both experiences, one has sustained a significant loss and must understand and explain it in order to continue the business of living. An important distinction, however, is that after dissolution, one's former partner continues to live in a life chosen apart. There is an implication of continued rejection in the wake of dissolution, in addition to the bereavement and grief that one faces after a death.

One avenue of research focuses on the cognitive and emotional work done by survivors of dissolution. This includes attributions about oneself and one's former partner, the formation of accounts of loss, the identification of appropriate confidants, and the reworking of one's own sense of identity, purpose, and direction.

Dissolution is an important focus for researchers who wish to understand how people deal with the tragedies and losses that are part of intimacy. Few people ask for help when they begin close relationships, but few reject it when they experience the ending. Social scientists as well as laypersons require a better understanding of the tasks involved in addressing conflict, negotiating the end of a relationship, and coping with the loss. Responding to such crises can involve people's finest efforts as well as their most painful tragedies.

Bibliography

Duck, Steve, and Robin Gilmour, eds. *Personal Relationships Four: Dissolving Personal Relationships.* New York: Academic Press, 1982. This excellent volume (fourth in a series) by a leading relationships writer features ten chapters on processes of dissolution, different forms of termination, the roles of cognitive processes, attribution, communication, age factors, and family implications.

Harvey, John H., Ann L. Weber, and Terri L. Orbuch. *Interpersonal Accounts: Social Psychological Perspectives.* Cambridge, Mass.: Basil Blackwell, 1990. This work reviews the forms and functions of the accounts or stories that people compose about loss, proposing a theory of account-making as a response to stress, and applying the theory to person perception, grief, and literature.

Levinger, George, and Oliver C. Moles, eds. *Divorce and Separation: Context, Causes, and Consequences.* New York: Basic Books, 1979. This edited work includes chapters on five aspects of marital termination: historical and cultural perspectives, social and psychological determinants of breakup (including a chapter by Hill, Rubin, and Peplau about their longitudinal study), economic determinants, consequences for former spouses, and consequences for children and families.

Phillips, Debora, with Robert Judd. *How to Fall out of Love.* Boston: Houghton Mifflin, 1978. This book reviews a brief, practical, behavior modification approach to coping with terminated or unsatisfactory relationships.

Vaughan, Diane. *Uncoupling: Turning Points in Intimate Relationships.* New York: Oxford University Press, 1986. Vaughan reviews the noticeable changes and rituals involved in relationship dissolution, illustrating her analysis with real-life examples from survivors of broken relationships.

Weiss, Robert Stuart. *Marital Separation.* New York: Basic Books, 1975. Weiss recounts the experiences of participants in his series of seminars for the separated, reviewing emotional reactions to separation, practical and philosophical problems. Very readable and helpful to the professional and the layperson.

Ann L. Weber

Cross-References

Coping Strategies: An Overview, 706; Couples Therapy, 718; Emotion and Attribution Theory, 921; Intimacy in Adulthood: Erikson, 1363; Love, 1486; Separation, Divorce, and Family Life: Adult Issues, 2220; Separation, Divorce, and Family Life: Children's Issues, 2227; Stressors, 2471.

DREAM ANALYSIS

Type of psychology: Personality
Fields of study: Classic analytic themes and issues; personality theory; psychodynamic therapies

Dream analysis refers to efforts to understand the meaning of dreams by closely examining, or analyzing, their content. Freudian psychoanalysis and Carl Jung's analytic psychology present differing views on dream interpretation.

Principal terms

ANALYTIC PSYCHOLOGY: the depth psychology developed by Carl Jung

ARCHETYPES: as described in analytic psychology, universal themes that originate in the collective unconscious

COMPENSATION: the idea that dream events psychologically adjust (compensate) for waking imbalances

CONDENSATION: the collection in a single dream image of several different sources

DISPLACEMENT: the shifting of intense emotion away from its real source in the dream to a less important object

DREAM WORK: work with dreams in psychotherapy or for personal growth and understanding

FREE ASSOCIATION: the psychoanalytic method of talking without restriction

LATENT CONTENT: according to psychoanalytic theory, the hidden content of a dream, camouflaged by the manifest content

MANIFEST CONTENT: the content of a dream just as it is experienced

PSYCHOANALYSIS: the psychological theory and therapeutic method developed by Sigmund Freud and his followers

Overview

Today there are a variety of theories of the nature of dreams and dreaming. Sigmund Freud, however, was the first to investigate the meaning of dreams systematically and, in the broad sense, scientifically. The "analytic" approach to dreams began with Freud and was later modified, particularly by his younger colleague Carl G. Jung. Freud's early study *Die Traumdeutung* (1900; *The Interpretation of Dreams*, 1913) is considered by many to have been one of the most influential books in the history of Western thought. The importance of the book is attributable not solely to his theory of dreams and their interpretation but also to the implications his theory carried for human nature itself. It suggests that many of the most important themes in the human psyche (a term used to mean the entire psychological life of the individual) are unconsciousness and, moreover, represent desires that are unacceptable to traditional social value systems.

Freud considered the content of dreams to be symbolic. This was not a new idea in and of itself, as witnessed by Joseph's well-known biblical interpretation of the pharaoh's dreams. What was new was that the symbolic nature of the dream content concerned deep, taboo impulses within the unconscious mind. Such impulses were often of a forbidden sexual nature, dealing, for example, with incestuous impulses or homosexuality. They might also contain aggressive material unacceptable to the waking mind, such as a "death wish"—that is, a desire for the death of someone well known to the dreamer. In all events, Freud considered the dream enactment to be carried out in the service of wish fulfillment, though often such wishes were repressed and thus unconscious.

According to Freud, each dream must be understood on two distinct levels. First is the manifest content of the dream. This is the dream simply as it appears, and as it might be related to another person or written down. The manifest content, however, is not the true subject of the dream; it serves to camouflage a deeper meaning, while at the same time presenting it in a morally acceptable way. The true meaning of the dream is to be found only in its hidden, or latent content—for example, in the sexual or aggressive material that the manifest content symbolically hides.

In terms of Freud's theory of personality, the dream is a creation of the infantile unconscious, seeking fulfillment for desires or impulses too morally painful to be entertained consciously by the ego. The moral aspect of the personality censors the dream content, allowing it expression only in the symbolic or manifest form experienced by the dreamer. Rather than dreaming directly about sexual intercourse, for example, a woman might dream that she is riding bareback on a horse, because the rhythmic motion of the horse resembles that of intercourse. She might awaken surprised to find herself sexually aroused. Many such dreams were recorded by Freud and his followers.

Freud was a shrewd observer of dreams, and he noticed that the vast majority of objects seen in them represent things seen in waking life during the day or two immediately preceding the dream. For example, after dreaming of a train with a steam engine, one might recall that on the previous day he or she had parked near a toy store that displayed an electric train in the window—one that resembled in general form the train later seen in the dream. Subsequent investigations of this idea have confirmed that this is indeed true. Freud also noted that a single object in a dream—a person, for example—could represent several objects, a process that he called condensation. A man might see an attractive woman in a dream and on later reflection realize that she had the hair of one woman he had known in the past, the eyes of another, and so on, all in a perfectly natural alliance.

Other important dream processes include dramatization, by which dream content represents its basic themes involving wish fulfillment, in imagistic form, usually in concrete pictorial representations. In other words, dreams present their stories largely in picture form. Another important process in Freudian dream theory is displacement, the idea that some object or event of relatively little importance in terms of the actual latent meaning of the dream takes on intense emotional meaning, acting as a decoy, as it were, for the emotion connected with a far more sinister theme.

Carl G. Jung, Freud's younger contemporary, at first supported Freud's ideas with great enthusiasm but later developed a psychology of his own quite independent of Freud. This came to be termed analytic psychology, in contrast to Freudian psychoanalysis. Freud had stressed the importance of individual biographical material in the dreams of his patients, whereas Jung tended to stress the importance of universal themes. He believed that such themes, or archetypes, appear not only in dreams but also in mythic stories from all over the world, as well as in art and literature—and in the delusional symptoms of psychotic patients. Such themes include water (as symbolic of the spirit or the collective unconscious), the great mother, the hero, the king, and so on. Many are seen among the pantheon of ancient Greek gods. The most important archetype is the self, which represents the integration or unity of the psyche. It is symbolized by many round or symmetrical images, termed mandalas. Examples include the rose, the lotus flower, starbursts such as those seen in the stained glass windows of Gothic cathedrals, the solar disk, and so on.

While such images are taken in analytic psychology to be symbolic in the sense that they represent truths greater than themselves, they in no sense are thought to camouflage any kind of latent content in the dream. In other words, Jungians believe in the transparency of dreams, in the sense that they hide nothing, but make the most direct symbolic expression of the disposition of the unconscious. They function both as a communication from the deep collective unconscious and as compensation for events and dispositions of waking life. A lonely man may dream of women, for example, not simply as a sexual fulfillment, but as a compensation for the absence of the feminine in his waking life. Thus, from the Jungian perspective, dreams represent to the dreamer a side of life often overlooked during waking existence.

Applications

The term "dream work" refers to the use of dreams as an adjunct to psychotherapy; more recently, it has come into common use as any systematic effort to work with dreams as part of personal exploration or growth. Both Freud and Jung utilized dream interpretation in psychotherapy. Even today, psychoanalysis (Freudian therapy) as well as Jungian analysis rely heavily on it for providing insights into unconscious processes.

To begin with a simple example of a dream understood from a Freudian perspective, suppose that a man argues with his mother in the afternoon and that night dreams he is at a funeral. The atmosphere is unusual for a funeral, however, as no one seems unhappy. Indeed, the ambience is like that of a cocktail party. He does not know whom the funeral is for, so he asks one of the guests. The answer is, "your mother." He wakes up.

This dream thinly disguises a death wish toward the mother. This is not necessarily as bad as it may seem. It simply means that on some irrational level he "wishes she were dead." Notice, however, that the man himself appears in the dream only in the third person—that is, he does not actually attack and kill his mother. The superego, or moral aspect of the personality, would not allow such an act even in the dream. Rather, this individual simply arrives somehow at a funeral and discovers that it is his mother who has died. Thus, he has no sense of guilt to connect with the event, yet the death wish is satisfied.

To take a more complex example, suppose that a young woman preparing to enter college dreams that she is presented with a nurse's cap and a piece of chalk of the type used for writing on blackboards. After some consideration, she picks up the piece of chalk and holds it above her head. A crowd of students sitting in the background gives her a rousing cheer, and the chalk turns to gold in her hands.

From a Freudian point of view, the nurse's cap and the piece of chalk are both sexual symbols. The cap represents female genitalia (as do jewelry boxes, orchids, and many other symbols), while the stick of chalk is a standard phallic symbol, representing the penis. What one would seem to have, from this perspective, is a sexual struggle in which heterosexuality wins out over homosexuality. The analyst would not, however, proceed by simply interpreting the dream to the patient. Rather, he or she would encourage the patient to free associate on the events and objects of the dream. In free association, one is asked to let one's mind move freely and without inhibition or intentional direction across the material of the dream, voicing all thoughts that come to mind. If this process is continued for long enough, and over sufficient therapeutic sessions, the patient may come to the real meaning of the dream, bringing the latent content into consciousness. In the process of free associating, the analyst may make occasional interpretations to the patient, but only after sensing that the patient is prepared to accept and understand the nature of the threatening material at hand.

In thinking about and discussing a dream, certain aspects of the dream may become more important, while other parts may recede into the background of memory. These transformations are termed secondary revision or elaboration, and may themselves become the object of examination in the therapeutic session.

For an example of a Jungian approach to dream interpretation, one could return to the above dream of the nurse's cap and the chalk. To begin with, the Jungian analyst would not use free association, but would engage the patient in an active dialogue about the dream. Of particular importance, he or she would be less likely to stress sexual issues and more likely to look at the apparent career choice poised by the dream. Indeed, Jungian psychology views the psyche as drawn toward a purposeful future rather than being, as in the case of Freudian theory, driven inexorably from the past. The selection of the chalk, and particularly the fact that the chalk is transformed in the end to gold, a universal symbol for that which is of ultimate value, are key considerations. Notice that an interpretation of this type implies no hidden agenda for the dream beyond the full connotations of the content itself. In this sense, the Jungian interpretation views the meaning of the dream as transparent, though not necessarily obvious.

An example typical of the Jungian approach is a dream that was experienced by a middle-aged man shortly after entering analysis. It was a simple dream in which he found himself traveling to the ocean and preparing to go scuba diving, something he had never done in waking life. In this dream the ocean represents the spirit, or the collective unconscious, in which the rich variety of deep-sea life exemplifies the archetypal life of the unconscious. This is what the man hopes to be able to experience in his analysis. In the Jungian perspective, consciousness ultimately derives its life-giving energy from the collective unconsciousness. For this reason, dreams of such things as water and fish are often considered good, since they depict the active life of the unconscious. In the early years of Christianity, for example, Christ was frequently symbolized by a fish, the creature of the spirit, or water.

Context

Freud's approach to dreams was the first to place dream activity squarely in the context of a unified theory of the mind. Earlier efforts at understanding the meaning of dreams had derived from religious or mythological contexts, as was the case in much of the ancient world and in Europe during the Middle Ages. The ancient Greeks wrote at some length about dreams, usually insisting that they had some literal meaning. In the "dream incubation," conducted at special temples dedicated to that purpose, dreams were associated with healing.

Freud's early writing was unique in that it emphasized the biological roots of the mind, and thus of dreams, in concepts such as instincts, drives, and psychic energy (libido). He believed that the entire structure of dreams, with their manifest content produced by censorship of their latent content by the moral agency of the personality, was fundamentally biological. This stress on biological foundations eventually decreased in importance as psychoanalytic thinkers, including Freud, began to recognize the importance of social influences on the personality, especially during infancy. Freud, for example, came to recognize a class of dreams that did not seem to operate in the service of wish fulfillment at all, but seemed to be an attempt of the mind in fantasy to resolve pressing emotional issues. An example that was discussed in the 1920's dealt with "war neurosis," an emotionally distraught state brought about by traumatic events experienced on the battlefield or elsewhere during war. Victims are later prone to repetitious dreams that seem again and again to enact the terror of these traumatic events.

Ego psychology, a more recent school of psychoanalytic thought, especially practiced in the United States, tends to stress the autonomy of the ego rather than the instinctual unconscious. It emphasizes the importance of early childhood experiences. Object relations theory, on the other hand, stresses the importance of "objects" of attachment, especially the mother, during the first ten years of life. The basic agenda of dream analysis, however, remains central to psychoanalytic dream work in virtually all of its forms, namely the notion that latent dream content must be made manifest.

The basic notion of a division of dream content into latent and manifest meaning has come increasingly under attack by dream theorists and researchers of a variety of persuasions, including a number of neuroscientists working on the nature of dreaming as a natural activity of the brain. The latter tend to view dreaming as a fundamentally biological event that incidentally reflects the concerns of waking life. Such reflections represent a more or less straightforward chewing over of the individual's daily concerns. Thus, while not subscribing to Jung's ideas concerning archetypes and the collective unconscious, such an approach agrees that the real meaning of the dream is not actively hidden from view.

Bibliography

Foulkes, William David. *A Grammar of Dreams.* New York: Basic Books, 1978. While not a general introduction to dream analysis, this formally written book is a landmark study which argues that dream events are essentially grammatical in form.

Freud, Sigmund. *The Interpretation of Dreams.* Translated by James Strachey. New York: Avon Books, 1965. One of the most influential books in Western history, this book describes in detail Freud's original theory of dreams. Those who have not previously read Freud in the original will be delighted to discover that he was a superb writer. This book was first published in German in 1900.

Hillman, James. *The Dream and the Underworld.* New York: Harper & Row, 1979. The most prominent of the neo-Jungians, Hillman views the dream as an experience of the underworld of traditional mythology.

Hobson, J. Allan. *The Dreaming Brain.* New York: Basic Books, 1988. This highly readable book is an excellent general introduction to the study of dreams from a historical and scientific point of view, with special emphasis on Hobson's own area of study, the biological understanding of the dreaming brain.

Jung, Carl Gustav. *Dreams.* Translated by R. F. C. Hull. Princeton, N.J.: Princeton University Press, 1974. This is number 20 in the Bollingen Series; the volume contains papers taken from vols. 4, 8, 12, and 16 of *The Collected Works of C. G. Jung.* Jung discusses his views of dreams as communications of the unconsciousness, as well as the role of archetypes in dreams and dreams as compensation.

Allen L. Combs

Cross-References

Analytical Psychology: Carl G. Jung, 240; Analytical Psychotherapy, 246; Archetypes: Origins and Nature, 286; The Collective Unconscious, 592; Levels of Consciousness, 663; Dreams, 836; Psychoanalytic Psychology: An Overview, 1905; Psychoanalytic Psychology and Personality: Sigmund Freud, 1912; Sleep: Stages and Functions, 2277.

DREAMS

Type of psychology: Consciousness
Fields of study: Classic analytic themes and issues; sleep

Dreams provide a unique window into psychological life. The dream's presentation of a story, experienced as meaningful in its own right, is a real and original form of human existence; it also discloses unrealized possibilities in the dreamer's waking life.

Principal terms

ACTIVATION-SYNTHESIS HYPOTHESIS: a theory that dreams are the brain's attempt to make sense of random and meaningless nervous system activity

EXISTENCE: as a psychological term, refers to the uniquely human existence of a person; a person's own standing forth or involvement in a personal history

LATENT CONTENT: in Freudian theory, the unconscious meaning of the dream, which has been disguised

MANIFEST CONTENT: in Freudian theory, the actual events of the dream, which are taken as symbolic of other, unconscious meanings

PHENOMENOLOGY: a philosophical approach used by some psychologists to understand meanings as they appear in actual experience

PSYCHOANALYSIS: Freud's label for his psychology in general as well as its distinctive type of psychotherapy; psychoanalysis emphasizes the determining role of unconscious desires

RAPID EYE MOVEMENT (REM) SLEEP: a distinct phase of sleep characterized by rapid eye movements of the sleeper; it has been reliably correlated with occasions when dreaming is occurring

UNCONSCIOUS: in Freudian psychology, that part of psychological life unavailable to awareness, repressed because of the anxiety that the unconscious desires would arouse if known

Overview

Dreaming is a state of consciousness wherein a sleeping person experiences a real involvement with objects, events, or other people that are not objectively present in that location at that time. Dreams may also incorporate an item that is actually present, such as a ringing alarm clock, but it will not be the objective clock in the bedroom with which the dreaming person is involved. In the dream, for example, it might be experienced as a telephone. The allure of dreams is precisely their providing an experience of something beyond objective presences. Furthermore, this "beyond" is not usually something the dreamer can choose in advance. Even a person who goes to sleep seeking to have a specific question answered in a dream experiences it as arising from an unforeseen depth. Because dreams "take" the person, it is more accurate to describe the experience of dreaming, as Medard Boss does, in terms of "it dreamt me." The only exception is the rare experience in a lucid dream (that is, one in which the dreamer is aware that it is a dream) of deliberately choosing how to interact with events in the dream.

Two different approaches have dominated twentieth century psychology's understanding of dreams, both of which are rooted in much older assumptions about dreaming. One explains dreaming as a neurophysiological event, while the other understands dreaming as a meaningful expression of the dreamer's waking life. Neurophysiological psychology takes the position that the dream is not a reflection of waking life, but of nervous system activity within the brain: nonsensical "noise" unrelated to any personally lived meaning. In the 1970's, J. Alan Hobson and Robert W. McCarley proposed the activation-synthesis hypothesis, which theorized that dreams are merely the brain's attempt to make sense of random activity by neurons (nerve cells) in the brain stem (the most phylogenetically primitive brain structure). According to their view, this random neuronal discharge stimulated or "activated" the cortex part of the brain, which then formed a dream in order to synthesize, or make sense of, that stimulation. In 1991, their theory was updated with the more recently developed "connectionist" view of the brain's neuronal activity.

Such theories may provide an explanation of the brain structure and activity necessary for dreaming to occur; however, they do not offer a basis for comprehending the experienced meaning of dreams. Specifying what happens physiologically during dreaming is not the same as understanding the dream itself, any more than an analysis of ink, paper, and the printing process could account for the plot of a book. By dismissing in advance the meaningfulness of dreams, neurophysiological psychology cannot address the question of why a dream should form precisely the particular synthesis it does, rather than some other. The understanding of the dream itself requires a different level of psychological investigation.

It was this sort of study that Sigmund Freud pioneered with his psychoanalytic theory of dreams. In his key book *Die Traumdeutung* (1900; *The Interpretation of Dreams*, 1913), Freud interpreted the meaningfulness of dreams as fulfillments of repressed, unconscious wishes, usually originating in childhood and mostly of a sexual nature. His claim that the apparently unreal consciousness of dreams masked a real unconsciousness effected a major breakthrough. This theory required a split in the reality status of the dream, however, since what it interpreted as real (the dream's disclosure of an unconscious desire) was not part of the actually dreamed story. Because of this discrepancy, Freud viewed the plot of the dream, its "manifest content," as a disguise, as a merely symbolic substitution of something else that remained concealed (the "latent content" of the dream). He saw the dream as a compromise solution by which an unconscious desire could be expressed while still remaining protected from full disclosure. Similarly, the disguised dream also guards the dreamer's sleep from being disrupted by the anxiety of fully facing repressed desires.

A variety of subsequent psychoanalytic theorists modified Freud's original insight. Carl Jung developed the most richly elaborated view of dream symbolization. He considered dreams as originating not in one's individual unconscious but from a "collective unconscious," and understood them as compensations for imbalances within one's waking life. Other psychoanalysts departed from Freud on more basic grounds, influenced by the existential phenomenological philosophy of Martin Heidegger.

Ludwig Binswanger and Medard Boss, independently, were the first psychoanalysts to explore dreaming phenomenologically. In doing so, they established a decisive advance beyond the Freudian interpretation of dreams. Rather than searching behind or beneath the dream for a symbolized reality cut off from the dreamer's experience, Binswanger and Boss recognized the imaginative power of dreams as the dreamer's movement into the real. They understood how the dream itself is meaningful to the dreamer—not as a symbol for something else, but as an original mode of existing on its own terms. They saw dreams as a movement by which dreamers imaginatively project themselves toward the truth of their personal histories. In other words, a phenomenology of dreaming takes dreams as "allusions" pointing to reality, rather then as "illusions" pointing away from it. Any discussion of a latent content is seen as a shift away from the dream itself, to waking associations about it. Thus, no approach based on latent contents could ever more than hypothetically disclose the meaningfulness of a dream. Instead of interpreting dream phenomena as symbols, Boss recommended "explicating" them within their array of spontaneous references and relationships in the dream itself.

Applications

The possibility that dreams may provide knowledge of the dreamer's own existence makes them useful for psychotherapy and personal growth. This application has been especially characteristic of Freudian psychoanalysis, a form of therapy devoted to helping patients become conscious of previously unconscious material. Because Freud regarded dreams as the "royal road" to the unconscious, dream interpretation became a principal technique in psychoanalysis. The psychoanalyst strives, like a detective, to decode the dream's disguised symbols and bring to light the patient's unconscious desires.

Other types of therapy use dream interpretation differently, depending on their view of the role of the unconscious in the patient's illness. For example, in Gestalt therapy, developed by Fritz Perls, the patient might "act out" the role of a person (or even object) in the dream, based on the theory that each character in the dream represents some aspect of the dreamer's own self. If, for example, a man dreamed of being frightened by a viciously snarling dog, he may be asked to assume the position of the dog and to describe that perspective.

It is not only in psychotherapy that dream work can be valuably applied. A growing movement emphasizes how individuals, alone or in dream groups, can benefit from attending to their dreams. Psychologists such as Stanley Krippner, Henry Reed, Gayle Delaney, Montague Ullman, and Alvin Mahrer have devised methods of working with one's own dreams to achieve personal growth.

Phenomenological psychology's understanding of dreams as imaginative enactments of the real provides support for both therapeutic and personal applications. As Boss has noted, certain "possibilities to be" may address themselves to people for the first time in their lives through dreams. Erik Craig calls these "larval" possibilities, for they become realized first in dreaming. Craig points out that within the sanctuary of their dreaming mode of existence, people are often open to possibilities that are ignored while awake. In dreaming, these "disenfranchised possibilities" appear with striking clarity as the real and meaningful features of one's existence that they are. Dreaming anticipates the realization of one's possibilities by allowing them to emerge within the dream state. In working phenomenologically with a dream, one aims to clarify the imaginative, allusive power of the dream by making these emerging possibilities explicit.

As an imaginative arc toward the actual achievement or realization of one's possibilities, a dream can be a decisive point in the life of the dreamer. It may be the very point at which one can either embrace the authentic existence to which the dream alludes or shrink from it, psychopathologically alienating oneself from one's own possibilities. The dream faces the dreamer with the choice between freedom and inauthenticity. The following two illustrations (taken from research on transformative dream experiences) show this liberating value of the dream's imaginative capacity.

Ellen, a sixty-three-year-old woman, dreams of walking sturdily up a mountain, following a much younger man. She finds that she simply cannot keep up with his pace; she begins to walk slower, then stops and sits upon a rock outcropping. She looks up for the first time and is struck by the beauty of the view. She sees an eagle fly and observes the younger man reassuringly continuing his walk over the next mountain. At that time in her waking life, Ellen was struggling to realize that it was time to slow down the very busy pace of her professional work. She had been unable, however, to resist the temptations of taking on additional commitments, until the dream presented her with another possibility. Afterward, she realized that sitting, reflecting, and observing was the new way for her to be. She saw that the work would get done: The journey would be continued by other, younger people. Through her dream, Ellen was able to make the difficult passage from the productive, generative stage of middle age to the reflective, integrative stage of old age.

At other times, a dream may finally resolve a long-standing constriction from an earlier stage of life. For example, in her early forties, Betty dreamed of being confronted in a tunnel by hideous monsters, the most terrifying of which appeared as "the evil one." He came right up to her, threatening to contaminate her with his evil, yet she could not face him. Finally, sensing a fate worse than death if she continued to avoid this monstrous other, she looked him in the eye and told him he was evil. She demanded that he respect her, and he did, backing off and letting her pass. In waking life, Betty had been living with the conviction of her own evilness ever since she had been told she was a devil by a relative who had repeatedly sexually abused her as a child. She was afraid of virtually everything. After the dream, she felt released from this fear and no longer believed that her own powers were evil. She began doing things, such as walking alone at night, that would have been impossible before. Taking hold of her new possibilities, Betty could live an expanded existence, made real for her for the first time in her dream.

Context

Ancient peoples understood their dreams as portraits of a meaningful reality—not as something made up by their minds, but as actual experiences of their souls' communication with the divine. Already in A.D. 140, however, the Greek philosopher Artemidorus of Daldi had proposed that dreams revealed not divine nature but the human nature of the dreamer.

Scientific psychology, limited by its model of the experiment as its research methodology, was slow to study dreaming. Indeed, Edwin Boring's highly regarded *A History of Experimental Psychology* (1929, rev. 1950) did not even mention dreaming in its expansive review of psychology. This began to change in the 1950's, with studies at the University of Chicago by Nathaniel Kleitman and Eugene Aserinsky, who discovered a phase of sleep characterized by rapid eye movement (REM). Using recording equipment to detect the onset of this phase of sleep, they were able to discover its correlation to dreaming. By waking subjects in REM sleep, they found that the vast majority could remember a dream, even those who had been unable previously to recall dreams. Since normal sleep patterns involve REM phases every ninety minutes or so, it was concluded that people dream several times each night, despite their wide variations in ability to remember dreams.

This ability to detect the apparent occurrence of dreaming scientifically has inspired, in the decades since then, many laboratory studies of sleep and dreaming. Two unsettled issues cloud much of this research. One is the unknown representativeness of dreams in laboratory conditions as compared with those dreamed in one's own home. Calvin Hall, who has collected thousands of dreams from ordinary life, notes that laboratory dreams tend to be more mundane, home dreams more dramatic. A second problem is that the precise relation of REM sleep to dreams remains unsettled. Unable to specify whether REM sleep caused dreaming or dreaming caused REM sleep, early researchers had simply stated that REM signaled the occurrence of dreaming. Recent research shows, however, that dreaming can also occur apart from REM sleep. Other research shows that REM sleep is present even in those considered unable to dream. These include anencephalic infants (who lack most of their brain, except for the brain stem), and cats that have had the brain structures deemed essential for dreaming surgically disconnected.

Despite these theoretical problems, the scientific study of dreaming is now a flourishing subdiscipline in theoretical and research psychology. The trend to approach dreams as meaningful is also thriving, not only within theoretical and research psychology, but also in psychotherapeutic applications. The many books, journals, and conferences devoted to dreaming indicate it will continue to be one of psychology's growing edges in the near future. Additionally, dream work has overflowed the discipline of psychology altogether and is gathering momentum among the general public. This movement is supported by a number of thoughtful how-to books and by an enduring interest in the personal transformation afforded by plumbing the depths of one's psychological life.

Bibliography

Boss, Medard. *I Dreamt Last Night. . . .* New York: Gardner Press, 1977. Boss forcefully argues for his phenomenological approach to understanding dreams. He describes dreaming as a mode of existing that can be understood as such directly on its own terms, without the need to interpret it symbolically. He clearly demonstrates that position by his analysis of many dreams.

Craig, P. Erik. "Dreaming, Reality, and Allusion: An Existential-Phenomenological Inquiry." In *Advances in Qualitative Psychology*, edited by Florence Van Zuuren, Frederick J. Wertz, and Bep Mook. Berwyn, Pa.: Swets North America, 1987. Craig provides a masterfully stated argument for the appreciation of the real experience of the dreamer. His careful example also shows the relevance of dreaming to waking life.

Delaney, Gayle. *Living Your Dreams.* New York: Harper & Row, 1979. Delaney has developed and popularized a means of dream interpretation for personal growth, in which dreams are used as sources of insight for solving personal life problems. This book offers an easily accessible manual for applying her approach.

Freud, Sigmund. *The Interpretation of Dreams.* Translated by James Strachey. New York: Avon Books, 1965. This challenging book is an English translation of Freud's pioneering study of dreams, which was first published in German in 1900. It revolutionized psychological thought and contains, by Freud's own acknowledgment, his most valuable discoveries.

Hall, Calvin Springer, and Robert L. Van de Castle. *The Content Analysis of Dreams.* New York: Appleton-Century-Crofts, 1966. An extremely comprehensive collection of dreams. It features more than a thousand, collected from college students and sorted for the statistical frequency of contents such as setting, character traits, mood, and relationships.

Jung, Carl. *Dreams.* Translated by R. F. C. Hull. Princeton, N.J.: Princeton University Press, 1974. This book assembles some of Jung's basic writings on dreams published earlier (from volumes 4, 8, 12, and 16 in his collected works). It offers a sampling of his views on the relation of dreams and psychoanalysis, psychic energy, alchemy, and the practical use of dream symbols.

LaBerge, Stephen. *Lucid Dreaming.* Los Angeles: J. P. Tarcher, 1985. By experimentally demonstrating lucid dreaming (the awareness, while dreaming, that one is dreaming), LaBerge's research has opened a new wave of theory, research, and applications.

Mahrer, Alvin. *Dream Work in Psychotherapy and Self-Change.* New York: W. W. Norton, 1989. This book is directed both to psychotherapists and laypersons. To the first group, it offers a new experiential approach to dream work. To the second, it offers a complete instructional guide to using dreams to promote self-change.

Christopher M. Aanstoos

Cross-References

Altered States of Consciousness, 220; Levels of Consciousness, 663; Dream Analysis, 830; Psychoanalytic Psychology: An Overview, 1905; Psychoanalytic Psychology and Personality: Sigmund Freud, 1912; Sleep: Stages and Functions, 2277.

DRIVE THEORY

Type of psychology: Motivation
Field of study: Motivation theory

A drive is a state influenced by an animal's need; the animal is motivated to reduce tension or to seek a goal. Drive theory is concerned with the nature of the internal forces that compel an animal to behave.

Principal terms

BEHAVIOR: responses and activities of an animal that usually lead to a changed relationship between it and its environment

DRIVE: an intervening process referring to the behavioral energy originating from a need; a drive is directly related to behavior

DRIVE REDUCTION: behaviors that result in the animal encountering certain environmental resources; such behaviors will be repeated when the drive state recurs

LAW OF EFFECT: a term describing the concept that responses which are followed by a reward will tend to be repeated

NEED: a state of an organism attributable to deprivation of a biological or psychological requirement; it is related to a disturbance in the homeostatic state

REINFORCEMENT: a situation that occurs when a stimulus closely following a behavior makes the behavior likely to recur

Overview

One goal of science is to understand, predict, or manipulate natural events. A scientist may start by observing an event of interest and measuring it as precisely as possible to detect any changes. In experimental research, scientists systematically manipulate various other events to see whether the event of interest also varies. In survey research, various events are measured to see whether they vary with the event of interest. Understanding is achieved when the relationship between the event of interest (the dependent variable) and other events (independent variables) is established. One can then predict and/or manipulate the event of interest. A theory provides a guideline to organize the variables into a system based upon some common properties that they share. To a psychologist, the dependent variable is the behavior of all animals and humans. The independent variable (also called a determinant) may be any other variable related to behaviors. Psychological research aims to discover the determinants of certain behavior; some of them are motivational variables. The field of motivation examines why particular behavior occurs, why it is so strong, and why it is so persistent.

A drive is a process related to the source of behavioral energy originating from within the body that is created by disturbances in homeostasis. A homeostatic imbalance creates a state of need for certain stimuli from the environment which can restore the balance. For example, abnormal body temperature and hyperosmolality of the body fluid (electrolyte concentration outside cells that is higher than that of the intracellular fluid, resulting in cell dehydration) are disturbances in homeostasis. The homeostatic balance can be restored through two means. Physiological means such as vasodilation, sweating, and panting serve to reduce body temperature; concentration of electrolytes in the urine by the kidneys reduces hyperosmolality. Second, behavioral means such as taking off clothes, turning on an air conditioner, and drinking cold liquid lower body temperature; drinking water would also result in reducing the hyperosmolality. One may examine a case of homeostatic imbalance in detail to illustrate how the two means function to restore the balance.

When the body fluid volume is reduced (hypovolemia) because of loss of blood or body fluid from intense sweating, the body responds immediately by vasoconstriction, reducing urine volume (through vasopressin release), and conserving sodium (through aldosterone release). Those are physiological means that will restore the blood pressure and prevent circulatory failure. Eventually, however, the body must get back the lost fluid from the environment via behavior (water seeking and drinking) to achieve long-lasting homeostasis. The physiological means are immediate and effective, but they are only stopgap measures. Behavior is the means with which the animal interacts with its environment to get back the lost resource.

The concept of drives is very important to the theories of Clark L. Hull, a neo-behaviorist. According to Hull, a drive has at least two distinct functions as far as behavioral activation is concerned. Without drives there could be no reinforcement and thus no learning, because drive reduction is the reinforcement. Without drives there could be no response, for a drive activates behavioral potentials into performance. Drive theory maintains that a state named "drive" (or D) is a necessary condition for behavior to occur; however, D is not the same as the bodily need. D determines how strongly and persistently a behavior is to occur; it connects the need and behavior. This distinction between need and drive is necessary, because while the state of need serves as the source of behavior, the intensity of behavior is not always related to the intensity of need. There are cases in which the need increases but behavior does not, or in which the need is still there but behavior is no longer manifested. Prolonged deprivation, for example, may not result in a linear or proportional increase in behavior. A water-deprived animal may stop drinking even before cellular dehydration is restored to the normal state; the behavior is changing independent of homeostatic imbalance. Cessation of behavior is seen as being attributable to drive reduction.

Hull uses D to symbolize drive and sHr (H is commonly used to denote this, for convenience) to symbolize a habit which consists of an acquired relationship between stimulus (S) and response (R). It represents a memory of experience in which certain environmental stimuli and responses were followed by a reward. An effective reward establishes an S-R relationship; the effect is termed reinforcement. One example of an H would be an experience of maze stimuli and running that led to food. H is a behavioral potential, not a behavior. Food deprivation induces a need state that can be physiologically defined; then D will energize H into behavior. The need increases monotonically with hours of deprivation, but D increases only up to three days without food. A simplified version of the Hullian formula for a behavior would be "behavior $= H \times D$," or "performance $=$ behavioral potential $\times$ energizer." The formula indicates that learning, via establishing behavioral potential, and D, via energizing the potential, are both necessary for performance to occur. This is a multiplicative relationship; that is, when either H or D is zero, a specific performance cannot occur.

Sigmund Freud proposed, in his psychoanalytical approach to behavioral energy, that psychic energy is the source of human behaviors. The id is the reservoir of instinctual energy presumed to be directly from the somatic processes. This energy is unorganized, illogical, timeless, knowing "no values, no good or evil, no morality" (according to Freud in 1933). The id operates according to the pleasure principle, using the primary process to discharge its energy as soon as possible, with no regard for reality. When the discharge is hindered by reality, however, the ego handles the situation according to the reality principle, using a secondary process to pursue realistic gratification. The ego mediates the id on the one hand and reality on the other.

Freud thus conceptualized the id to be the energy source, and the ego to manage behavior in terms of reality. Learning is manifested in the way the ego manages behavior for gratification under restriction of the environment and the superego. In this model, the drive is seen as the energizer of behavior. The similarity between the Freudian and Hullian concepts of drive is obvious. Food deprivation would generate homeostatic imbalance, which is the somatic process, and the need, which is similar to the energy of the id. The organism cannot obtain immediate gratification because of the environmental constraints to obtain food, so behavior is generated to negotiate with the environment. Drive is much like the ego, since it energizes the behavioral potentials into behaviors to seek reality gratification, which is equivalent to drive reduction. The concept of pleasure and behavioral changes commonly appears in various theories that incorporate a subtle influence of Freudian thought.

Applications

In one classic experiment, Carl J. Warden studied the persistence of behavior as a function of various sources, including the strength of a drive, using an apparatus called a Columbia obstruction box. He demonstrated that a rat without food would cross an electrified grid to reach a goal box that held food. When the rat was immediately brought back from the goal box to the start box, it would cross the grid again and again. The number of grid crossings was positively related to the number of days without food for up to three days. From the fourth day without food, however, the number of crossings slowly decreased. When baby rats were placed in the goal box, a mother rat would cross the grid repeatedly. When a male or female rat was placed in the goal box, a rat of the opposite sex would cross repeatedly. The number of crossings by the male rat was positively related to the duration it spent without a female companion.

These animals were all manifesting the effect of different drives: hunger, maternal instinct, or sex. It was shown that the maternal drive was associated with the greatest number of crossings (twenty-two times in twenty minutes), followed by thirst (twenty times), hunger (seventeen), female sex drive (fourteen), male sex drive (thirteen), and exploration (six). Warden demonstrated that various internal forces, created by deprivation and hormonal state, and external forces, created by different goal objects, together determine the grid-crossing behavior. The level of deprivation induces drive motivation; the reward in the goal box induces incentive motivation. In this example, the focus is on drive motivation.

If one were to place a well-trained rat into a maze, it might or might not run to the goal box. Whether it would run, how fast it would run, and how well (in terms of errors) it would run would depend upon whether the subject were food-deprived. With food deprivation, the well-trained rat would run to the goal box with few errors. If it had just been fed, it would not run; it would simply wander, sniff at the corner, and go to sleep. The environmental stimuli (the maze) are the same; the rat's behavior is different because the internal force—the drive created by food deprivation—is different. A need state produces D, and D then triggers behavior. The behavior that will occur is determined jointly by the past experience of learning, which is termed H, as well as stimuli, S, from the environment. An inexperienced rat, without the H of maze running, will behave differently from a well-trained rat in a maze. D is an intervening variable: It connects need and behavior, so one must consider both the source (need) and the consequence (behavior) to define D. When D is zero, there will be no maze running, no matter how well-trained the rat is. On the other hand, if there is no H (training), the proper maze-running behavior will not occur, no matter how hungry the rat is. An animal must be exposed to a maze when hungry to learn to negotiate the various turns on the way to the goal box containing food. Without food deprivation (and the resultant D), the animal would not perform even if it could; one cannot tell whether an animal has the knowledge to run the maze until one introduces a D variable. H is a potential of behavior, and D makes the potential into the observable reality of performance. Motivation turns a behavior on.

These ideas can be applied to countless real-life examples. If a person is not very good at playing tennis (has a low H), for example, no matter how motivated (high D) he is, he will not be able to beat a friend who is an expert at the game. If a person is very good at tennis (high H) but does not feel like playing (low D), perhaps because of a lack of sleep, she will not perform well. The same situation would apply for taking a test, delivering a speech, or running a marathon.

In another experiment involving drive, Edward L. Thorndike put a cat into a puzzle box. The cat attempted to get out via various behaviors (mewing, scratching, and so on). By chance, it stepped on a plate that resulted in the door opening, allowing the cat to escape. The cat was repeatedly returned to the box, and soon it would escape right away by stepping on the plate; other, useless behaviors were no longer manifested. The source of D in this case was the anxiety induced by confinement in the box, which could be measured by various physiological changes, such as heart rate and hormonal levels. Escaping would make the anxiety disappear; D is reduced. D reduction results in an increase in the probability that the behavior immediately preceding it (stepping on the plate) will recur. Thorndike describes this puzzle-box learning as trial and error, implying a blind attempt at various means of escape until one happens to work. He states that a "satisfying effect" will create repetition, calling this the law of effect; the essence of the satisfying effect appears to be drive reduction. A five-stage learning cycle is then complete: It consists of need, drive, behavior, drive reduction, and behavior repetition.

Context

Research on how a habit (H) is formed and how it is stored in the brain is a lively research topic in the field of psychobiology of learning, memory, and cognition, as well as in neuropsychology, which deals with learning deficit and loss of memory. Drive and reinforcement are important variables that determine whether learning will succeed and whether past learning will be manifested as behaviors. Research on hunger and thirst forms one subfield of psychobiology.

If D is the common energizer of various behaviors, then all sources of D— hunger, thirst, sex, mothering, exploration—should have something in common physiologically. The so-called central motive state is hypothesized to be such a state. It is known that arousal is common to the sources of D. Research involves biological delineation of the sources of D; researchers are studying the mechanisms of hunger, for example. There has been insufficient attention paid to the physiological processes by which hunger may motivate various behaviors and by which drive reduction would serve as a reinforcement in learning. Extreme lack of motivation can be seen in some depressed and psychotic patients, which results both in a lack of new learning and in a lack of manifesting what is already known. The neuronal substrates of this "lack of energy" represent one problem under investigation in the area of drive and motivation.

Bibliography

Bolles, Robert C. *Theory of Motivation.* 2d ed. New York: Harper & Row, 1975. This standard text in motivation reviews the concepts of motivation and drive and present pros and cons of the drive concept. The author is a contemporary psychological theoretician.

Freud, Sigmund. *New Introductory Lectures on Psychoanalysis.* New York: W. W. Norton, 1933. Freud explains his theory of the workings of the id, ego, and superego. His concept of behavioral energy is described in this book.

Hull, Clark Leonard. *Principles of Behavior.* New York: Appleton-Century, 1943. This bible of the Hullian neobehavioristic theory delineates the concepts of D and H and the philosophical bases of behavioral study. The theory has excited many students into studying psychology; it has gone through many revisions and additions.

Logan, Frank A., and Douglas P. Ferraro. *Systematic Analyses of Learning and Motivation.* New York: John Wiley & Sons, 1978. Logan, who was a student of Hull, describes how motivation is involved in learning.

Pfaff, Donald W., ed. *The Physiological Mechanisms of Motivation.* New York: Springer-Verlag, 1982. Various authors describe the physiological substrates of different sources of drive and motivation in terms of the nervous system, hormones, and body fluid parameters.

Stellar, James R., and Eliot Stellar. *The Neurobiology of Motivation and Reward.* New York: Springer-Verlag, 1985. Eliot Stellar, one of the best known theorists in biopsychology of motivation, along with his son, describes how biological antecedents of motivation can be found to explain various behavior.

Warden, Carl John. *Animal Motivation: Experimental Studies on the Albino Rat.* New York: Columbia University Press, 1931. This was the first research attempting to compare different sources of drive using various reward substances.

Sigmund Hsiao

Cross-References

Hunger: Biological Bases, 1217; Hunger Regulation, 1229; Incentive Motivation, 1269; Instinct Theory, 1309; Sex Hormones and Motivation, 2234; Thirst, 2547.

DYSLEXIA

Type of psychology: Language
Field of study: Childhood and adolescent disorders

Dyslexia is often defined as severe reading disability in children of otherwise average or above-average intelligence; it is thought to be caused by neuropsychological problems. Dyslexia frustrates afflicted children, damages their self-image, produces grave maladjustment in many cases, and decreases their adult contributions to society.

Principal terms

AUDITORY DYSLEXIA: the inability to perceive individual sounds associated with written language (for example, certain vowels or consonants)

BRAIN DYSFUNCTION: disordered or impaired brain function resulting from damage too minor to be observed by existing biomedical technology

COGNITIVE: relating to the mental process or faculty by which knowledge is acquired

COMPUTERIZED AXIAL TOMOGRAPHY (CAT) SCAN: a detailed X-ray picture, obtained by a complex method using a computer, that allows examination of organ structures for abnormalities

DYSGRAPHIA: the inability to write legibly, resulting from badly impaired hand-eye coordination

ELECTROENCEPHALOGRAM (EEG): a graphic record of the electrical activity of the brain, recorded by an electroencephalograph and used for diagnostic purposes

IMPRINTING: a method of training a dyslexic person to overcome reading problems by use of often-repeated, exaggerated language drills

KINESTHETIC: related to the sensation of body position, presence, or movement, resulting mostly from the stimulation of sensory nerves in muscles, tendons, and joints

PHONOLOGY: the science of speech sounds, especially phonetics and phonemics

SELF-IMAGE: the self as a person pictures or imagines it

VISUAL DYSLEXIA: the lack of ability to translate observed written or printed language into meaningful terms

Overview

The ability to read quickly and well is essential for success in modern industrialized societies. Several researchers, including Robert E. Valett, have pointed out that an individual must acquire considerable basic cognitive and perceptual-linguistic skills in order to learn to read. First, it is necessary to learn to focus one's attention, to concentrate, to follow directions, and to understand the language spoken in daily life. Next, it is essential to develop the following: auditory and visual memory with sequencing ability; word-decoding skills; a facility for structural-contextual language analysis; the ability to interpret the written language; a useful vocabulary that expands as needed; and speed in scanning and interpreting written language. Valett has noted that these skills are taught in all good developmental reading programs.

Yet 20 to 25 percent of the population of the United States and many other industrialized societies, people who otherwise possess at least average intelligence, cannot develop good reading skills. Many such people are viewed as suffering from a neurological disorder called dyslexia, a term that was first introduced by a German ophthalmologist, Rudolph Berlin, more than one hundred years ago. Berlin meant it to designate all those individuals who possessed an average or above-average performance intelligence quotient (IQ) but who could not read adequately because of an inability to process language symbols.

Others reported children who could see perfectly well but who acted as if they were blind to the written language. For example, they could see a bird flying but were unable to identify the word bird written in a sentence. In essence, though the problem has been redefined many times over the ensuing years, the modern definition of dyslexia is still fairly close to Berlin's definition.

Two basic explanations have evolved for dyslexia. Many physicians propose that it is caused by either brain damage or brain dysfunction. Evolution of the problem is attributed to accident, to disease, or to faults in body chemistry. Diagnosis is made by the use of electroencephalograms (EEGs), computerized axial tomography (CAT) scans, and other related technology. After such evaluation, medication is often used to diminish hyperactivity and nervousness, and a group of physical training procedures called patterning are used as tools to counter the neurological defects.

In contrast, many special educators and other related researchers believe that the problem is one of dormant, immature, or undeveloped learning centers in the brain. The proponents of this concept encourage the correction of dyslexic problems by emphasized teaching of specific reading skills to appropriate individuals. While such experts also agree that use of appropriate medication can be of value, they lend most of their efforts to curing the problem by a process called imprinting, which essentially trains the dyslexic patient through use of often-repeated, exaggerated language drills.

Another interesting point of view is the idea that dyslexia may at least partly be the fault of the written languages of the Western world. Rudolph F. Wagner has pointed out that children in Japan exhibit an incidence of dyslexia that is less than 1 percent. One explanation for this, say Wagner and others, is that the languages of the Western world require reading from left to right. This characteristic is absent in Japanese—possibly, they suggest, making it easier to learn.

A number of experts, among them Dale R. Jordan, recognize three types of dyslexia. The most common type—and the one most often identified as dyslexia—is visual dyslexia: the lack of ability to translate observed written or printed language into meaningful terms. The major difficulty here is that the afflicted people see certain letters backward or upside down. The result is that, to them, a written sentence is a jumble of letters whose accurate translation may require five times as much time as would be needed by an unafflicted person.

The other two problems viewed as dyslexia are auditory dyslexia and dysgraphia. Auditory dyslexia is the inability to perceive individual sounds of spoken language. Despite having normal hearing, auditory dyslexics are deaf to the differences between certain vowel or consonant sounds; what they cannot hear, they cannot write. Dysgraphia is the inability to write legibly. The basis for this problem is a lack of the hand-eye coordination required to write legibly.

Usually, a child who suffers from visual dyslexia also exhibits elements of auditory dyslexia. This complicates the issue of teaching such a student, because only one type of dyslexic symptom can be treated at a time. Also, dyslexia appears to be a sex-linked disorder; three to four times as many boys have it as do girls. In all cases, early diagnosis and treatment of dyslexia are essential to its eventual correction. For example, if treatment begins before the third grade, there is an 80 percent probability that dyslexia can be corrected. When dyslexia remains undiscovered until the fifth grade, this probability is halved. If treatment does not begin until the seventh grade, the probability of successful treatment is only 3 to 5 percent.

Applications

Preliminary identification of the dyslexic child often can be made from symptoms that include poor written schoolwork, easy distractibility, clumsiness, poor coordination and spatial orientation, confused writing and/or spelling, and poor left-right orientation. Because nondyslexic children can also show many of these symptoms, the second step of such identification is the use of written tests designed to pick out dyslexic children. These include the Peabody Individual Achievement Test, the Halstead-Reitan Neuropsychological Test Battery, and the SOYBAR Criterion Tests. Many more personalized tests are also available.

Once conclusive identification of a dyslexic child has been made, it becomes possible to begin a corrective treatment program. Most such programs are carried out by special-education teachers in school resource rooms, in special classes limited to children with reading disabilities, and in schools that specialize in treating the disorder.

One often-cited method is that of Grace Fernald, which utilizes kinesthetic imprinting, based on a combination of "language experience" and tactile stimulation. In this popular method, a given child learns to read as follows. First, the child relates a spontaneous story to the teacher, who transcribes it. Next, each word unknown to the child is written down by the teacher, and the child traces its letters over and over until he or she can write that word without using the model. Each word learned becomes part of the child's word file. A large number of stories are handled this way. Many variants of the method are in use. Though it is quite slow, many anecdotal reports praise its results. (Despite this, Donald K. Routh pointed out in

1987 that the method had never been subjected to a rigorous, controlled study of its efficacy.)

A second common method utilized by special educators is the Orton-Gillingham-Stillman method, developed in a collaboration by teachers Anna Gillingham and Essie Stillman and the pediatric neurologist Samuel T. Orton. The method evolved from Orton's conceptualization of language as developing from a sequence of processes in the nervous system that end in unilateral control by the left cerebral hemisphere. He proposed that dyslexia arises from conflicts, which need to be corrected, between this hemisphere and the right cerebral hemisphere, usually involved in the handling of nonverbal, pictorial, and spatial stimuli.

Consequently, the method used is multisensory and kinesthetic, like Fernald's; however, it begins with the teaching of individual letters and phonemes, and progresses to dealing with syllables, words, and sentences. Children taught by this method are drilled systematically to imprint a mastery of phonics and the sounding out of unknown written words. They are encouraged to learn how the elements of written language look, how they sound, how it feels to pronounce them, and how it feels to write them down. Donald Routh has pointed out that the Orton-Gillingham-Stillman method is equally laborious as that of Fernald. It is widely used and appreciated, however, and believed to work well.

Another method that merits brief discussion is the use of therapeutic drugs in the treatment of dyslexia. Most physicians and educators propose the use of these drugs as a useful adjunct to the training of dyslexic children who are easily distracted and restless or who have low morale because of embarrassment resulting from peer pressure. The drugs used most often are the amphetamine Dexedrine and methylphenidate (Ritalin).

These stimulants, taken in appropriate doses, lengthen the time period during which some dyslexic children function well in the classroom and also produce feelings of self-confidence. Side effects of overdose, however, include lost appetite, nausea, nervousness, and sleeplessness. Furthermore, there is the potential problem of drug abuse. Despite this, numerous sources (including both Valett and Jordan) indicate that stimulant benefits far outweigh any possible risks when the drugs are utilized carefully and under close medical supervision. Other, less dependable therapies sometimes attempted include special diets and the use of vitamins and minerals.

One other important aspect of the treatment of dyslexia is good parental emotional support, which helps children cope with their problems and with peer pressure. Useful aspects of this support include a positive attitude toward the afflicted child; appropriate home help for the child that complements efforts undertaken at school; encouragement and praise for achievements, without recrimination when repeated mistakes are made; and good interaction with special-education teachers assigned to a child.

Context

The identification of dyslexia more than one hundred years ago, which resulted from the endeavors of the German physician Rudolf Berlin and of W. A. Morgan, in England, launched efforts to find a cure for this unfortunate disorder. In 1917, the Scottish eye surgeon James Hinshelwood published a book on dyslexia, which he viewed as being a hereditary problem, and the phenomenon became better known to physicians. Attempts at educating dyslexics, as recommended by Hinshelwood and other physicians, were highly individualized until the endeavors of Orton and co-workers and of Fernald led to more standardized and soon widely used methods.

Furthermore, with the development of a more complete understanding of the brain and its many functions, better counseling facilities, and the conceptualization and actualization of both parent-child and parent-counselor interactions, the prognosis for successful dyslexic training has improved significantly. Also, a number of extensive studies of dyslexic children have been carried out and have identified dyslexia as a complex syndrome composed of numerous associated behavioral dysfunctions related to visual-motor brain immaturity. These include poor memory for details, easy distractibility, poor motor skills, letter and word reversal, and the inability to distinguish between important elements of the spoken language.

A particularly extensive and useful study was carried out by Edith Klasen and described in her book *The Syndrome of Specific Dyslexia: With Special Consideration of Its Physiological, Psychological, Testpsychological, and Social Correlates* (1972). The Klasen study identified the role of psychoanalytical interventions in the treatment of some dyslexic subjects, and it pointed out that environmental and socioeconomic factors contribute relatively little to occurrence of dyslexia but affect the outcomes of its treatment.

It is the endeavors of special education that have made the greatest inroads into treatment of dyslexia. Further advances in the area will undoubtedly be made, as the science of the mind grows and diversifies and as the contributions of the psychologist, physician, physiologist, and special educator mesh together more effectively.

Bibliography

Hartstein, Jack, ed. *Current Concepts in Dyslexia.* St. Louis: C. V. Mosby, 1971. Introduces the reader to the terms, specialists, and available treatments of dyslexia. Topical coverage includes dyslexia diagnosis and treatment; roles of reading teachers in educating dyslexics; dimensions of reading and reading disability; the use of therapeutic drugs; and functions of neurologists.

Jordan, Dale R. *Dyslexia in the Classroom.* 2d ed. Columbus, Ohio: Charles E. Merrill, 1977. An interesting book aimed at providing useful information to "grassroots professionals" who work with the group of problems the author sees as composing dyslexia. Includes definitions of the three types of dyslexia, their classroom characteristics, methodology for correcting them, methods for distinguishing dyslexia from other learning disabilities, and several useful screening tests.

Klasen, Edith. *The Syndrome of Specific Dyslexia: With Special Consideration of Its Physiological, Psychological, Testpsychological, and Social Correlates.* Baltimore: University Park Press, 1972. Klasen's study of five hundred dyslexic students—

containing 153 references—provides much useful information. Covers many aspects of dyslexia etiology, associated speech disorders, related organic-sensory and neuropsychological symptoms, psychopathology, therapy, psychological test results, socioeconomic and family backgrounds, intersibling relationships, and parental attitudes.

Routh, Donald K. "Disorders of Learning." In *The Practical Assessment and Management of Children with Disorders of Development and Learning*, edited by Mark L. Wolraich. Chicago: Year Book Medical Publishers, 1987. Succinctly summarizes many salient facts about learning disorders, including their etiology, their assessment, their management, and their outcome. The interested reader will also find many useful references to more detailed works.

Snowling, Margaret J. *Dyslexia: A Cognitive Developmental Perspective*. New York: Basil Blackwell, 1987. Covers many aspects of dyslexia, including its identification, associated cognitive defects, the basis for development of language skills, and the importance of phonology. Also contains many references.

Valett, Robert E. *Dyslexia: A Neuropsychological Approach to Educating Children with Severe Reading Disorders*. Belmont, Calif.: Fearon Pitman, 1980. Contains hundreds of references. Of interest to readers wishing detailed information on dyslexia and on educating dyslexics. There are two main divisions: The first, covering neuropsychological foundations of reading, includes topics such as critical neuropsychological factors, language acquisition, and diagnosis; the second describes a wide variety of special-education topics.

Wagner, Rudolf F. *Dyslexia and Your Child: A Guide for Teachers and Parents*. Rev. ed. New York: Harper & Row, 1979. A clear, useful, and simply written book "for teachers and parents concerned with children . . . referred to as dyslexic." Includes careful exposition of dyslexic symptoms, commentary on the problem, ways to treat dyslexia and associated problems, other useful topics, an appendix of recommended reading, and a glossary.

Sanford S. Singer

Cross-References

Attention, 313; Brain Injuries: Concussions, Contusions, and Strokes, 448; Brain Specialization, 455; The Cerebral Cortex, 500; Language Acquisition Theories, 1394; Language and Cognition, 1401.

EDUCATIONAL PSYCHOLOGY

Type of psychology: Learning
Field of study: Cognitive learning

Educational psychology is a diverse and dynamic discipline aimed at facilitating human learning through effective instruction.

Principal terms

EDUCATIONAL TASK: an intended learning experience designed to foster competencies

INTERACTIVE MODELS: learning as affected by compounded variables— variables that work together

LEARNING: the processes of acquiring, storing, and retrieving information

LEARNING STYLE: a predisposition to approach learning tasks in a consistent way

PROCESS: the ongoing activities of learning

PRODUCT: the outcome or manifestation of learning

THEORY: a network of principles that is testable and allows for generalization

VARIABLE: nonuniform characteristics of persons and environments that are observed and measured to determine their relationship to learning; variables may be fairly stable, such as personality, or unstable, such as the level of anxiety in a particular situation

Overview

Teaching is a complex undertaking involving decision making at many levels as well as a diversity of skills. From kindergarten to college, teachers are involved in designing curricula, planning lessons, selecting texts, evaluating the products of learning, and monitoring a full range of action within the classroom. The choices are many, and effective teaching demands additional expertise in terms of the delivery of instruction. Indeed, the teacher functions both as a theorist, objectively analyzing the situation of learning and methods of instruction, and as a practitioner, in the more spontaneous delivery of instruction in an attempt to inspire young minds.

Teaching is the deliberate facilitation of learning; learning is a relatively permanent change in behavior or gaining of a new perspective on or insight into a problem. Learning may take place without teaching. For example, children seem to acquire language without specific instruction. Teaching, on the other hand, may or may not be effective in stimulating learning. It is the goal of educational psychology to facilitate effective instruction to foster human learning.

Educational psychology, a diverse scientific discipline, attempts to apply psychological principles to classroom learning. Just as teaching and learning are ongoing processes, so is educational psychology an evolving enterprise. Researchers search for dependable answers to many practical educational questions. They ask which teaching methods are most effective, as well as which methods work best for particular students. They examine whether grades are effective motivators (and again, for which students they are effective). They look at whether holding a student back a grade has positive or negative effects on subsequent performance. Research in educational psychology is often inconclusive, because of the complexity of the questions, discrepancies in terminology, and/or faulty methodologies. For this reason, research is replicated; sound educational practice is based on well-supported trends. Educational psychology is a continually developing discipline, integrating theoretical perspectives with practical concerns.

James Jenkins (1979) devised an interactive model for learning researchers that can be used as a guide to understanding classroom learning in terms of both personal and environmental (outside the person) factors. This tetrahedral model posits that learning is influenced by four types of variables: characteristics of the learner (beliefs, skills, energy level, and so on), characteristics of the teacher (voice, gender, attitude), criterion of evaluation (for example, whether the work is for a grade), and characteristics of the task (such as whether it is written or verbal, and whether it is timed). The interplay of these four types of variables affects the quality of learning. In helping a child who apparently has difficulty with mathematics, a teacher familiar with the principles of the tetrahedral model might consider interventions such as changing the type of tests (timed tests might not be fair to some learners), changing the grading system, or even changing the lessons to include visual or diagrammatic materials to explain math principles. Often the solution focuses on changing the learner who is perhaps the hardest to change. Jenkins' model also serves as a framework for understanding how educational psychology is applied to classroom learning situations.

Student learning is complex, as are the variables that affect it. Learner and teacher characteristics, for example, include a variety of attributes. Some are stable, or constant (sex, race, or ability). Others are consistent or generally stable, changing little over time or situation, such as attitudes, beliefs, and learning styles. Some learner and teacher attributes are unstable and likely to change, such as the level of arousal, anxiety, or mood. It is the more consistent variables that affect learning in general, are more easily measured, and are investigated more frequently. Research on learning styles, in particular, has spurred the individualization of instruction to suit a wider range of learner needs, thus increasing instructional efficiency. Educational psychology functions as a tool for teachers and administrators in terms of planning, implementing, and evaluating educational programs or lessons.

In addition to fostering understanding for teachers and researchers, educational psychology serves students by helping them understand their own learning. This results in increased personal responsibility for learning and often creates higher levels of competence and a more positive self-image for the student as a manager of knowledge rather than as a passive recipient. Classes such as study-skills training and remedial workshops often emphasize these principles.

Applications

In investigating how college students learn, Gordon Pask and others (1972) differentiated holist and serialist learning styles. Using a "teach-back" procedure, Pask had students create ficticious zoological taxonomies and then teach those classifications back to the experimenter. Serialists were characterized as remembering information in terms of lengthy "strings" of data. That is, bits of information were related sequentially and in a linear, step-by-step fashion. The serial style relies on memorization. Holists, on the other hand, remembered in terms of hierarchical relations, imaging the entire system of facts or principles in a more general manner; they focused on the big picture and fit details in later. The holist strategy was related to what Pask called "comprehension learning," with the serialist orientation reflective of "operational learning" (focusing on details and procedures). Pask also found that teaching materials could be structured in either a holist (meaningful) or serialist (memorization) fashion and were most effective when matched to the student's corresponding learning style.

In addition to investigating learner characteristics, researchers in educational psychology have explored how it is that teacher characteristics affect student learning. In particular, teachers' motivational beliefs, a fairly consistent variable, have been linked to teaching behaviors. Carole Ames and Russell Ames (1984) have identified three systems of teacher motivation based on specific values held by teachers that result in different perceptions, motivations, and teaching strategies. In the "ability evaluative" system, teachers tend to maintain their notions of self-worth by protecting their own positive notions of their ability. That is, teachers see their personal value as contingent on students' success. This results in blaming the student for failure and crediting themselves when students are successful. In the second system, the "moral responsibility" system, teachers primarily are concerned with the pupil. The resulting behaviors are the opposite of those associated with the ability evaluative orientation—blaming self for failures and crediting the student for success. In the "task mastery" condition, the task is of primary importance rather than a teacher's self-image. The focus is on accomplishing educational goals and fostering competence. Thus, from an interactionist perspective, teachers' beliefs about learning and about themselves are an integral part of the learning process.

The characteristics of the task are the third major type of variable affecting classroom learning and are a primary area of concern for researchers. Attributes of the task might include the type of task: aural or visual, motor or verbal, comprehension or memorization, self-instructional or teacher-assisted. A major development in the area of self-instruction as related to learning tasks has been computer-aided instruction. Educational psychologists James Kulik, Robert Bangert, and George Williams (1983) have reviewed numerous studies regarding the use of computers for instructional purposes in sixth- to twelfth-grade classrooms. They found that there were moderate benefits in terms of improvement on examinations and in reducing the amount of time needed for learning. Also, children taught with computers developed more positive attitudes toward computers than those who were taught in the traditional manner.

Finally, the type of evaluation has an effect on classroom learning. Perhaps the most common type of student evaluation is grading, assigning letter or number ratings to reflect the quality of student work. Although grades may be intended to function as incentives or motivators to encourage students to perform, it is unlikely that they do so. Robert Slavin (1991) has found that grades are used for three primary functions: evaluation, feedback, and incentives. As a result, grades function as less than ideal motivators. Also, grades are given too infrequently for young children to see any relationship between their daily work and a grade received weeks later. Grades may be effective incentives for older students, however; studies comparing college students in graded versus ungraded classes have found that grades do function as an incentive.

Context

Educational psychology draws on many resources to form well-grounded models. The philosophical roots of educational psychology lie in the early twentieth century work of William James and John Dewey. Both were scholars who shared a concern for the application of psychological principles in the classroom. James described the teacher's role as that of developing good habits and productive thinking in the student. Dewey, on the other hand, called for the transformation of education in terms of expanding the curriculum to include the needs of an increasingly industrial society. Dewey saw schools as agents of social change.

As the twentieth century progressed, psychology developed as a social science, and two major conceptions of learning were spawned: the Gestalt model and behaviorism. In the Gestalt view, learning is defined as a change in the perceptual process, or as understanding a problem in a new way—insight. In contrast, the behavioral view rests on the assumption of stimulus substitution: existing responses became associated with new stimuli through the process of conditioning. The emphasis is on observed relationships—behaviors. Behaviorism had a profound influence on American education, in terms of both instruction and classroom management. For example, "time-out," or removing a child from the stimuli of the existing environment to a quiet and boring place, has been used as a form of punishment.

Since 1975, cognitive psychology, with its emphasis on the processes of learning, has dominated the instructional scene. The advent of computer technology offered a model of information processing, and advances in military technology demanded that researchers consider how it is that humans carry out decision-making processes. More specifically, it was wondered how learners attend to, organize, store, and retrieve information. Margaret Bell-Gredler (1986) cites three reasons for increased emphasis on cognitive processes: Behaviorism was too limited in explaining human activity, learners had come to be viewed as active manipulators rather than as passive recipients of knowledge, and learners were viewed as interacting with environments. Prominent instructional models based on cognitive theory include Jerome Bruner's discovery learning, emphasizing the teacher's role in creating situations in which students can learn on their own, and, in contrast, David Ausubel's reception learning, which focuses on teacher-structured learning in the form of well-organized lessons. From an interactive perspective, discovery learning empowers the learner by positing the teacher as a facilitator, whereas reception learning empowers the teacher in controlling the learning situation. Finally, Robert Gagné's "events of learning" model includes eight phases of learning: expectancy, attention, coding, memory, retrieval, transfer, responding, and reinforcement. The critical phases are paired with corresponding instructional events to offer a practical model for classroom instruction.

Bibliography

Bell-Gredler, Margaret E. *Learning and Instruction.* New York: Macmillan, 1986. Bell-Gredler discusses the functions of learning theory as it applies to instruction, the history of the development of educational psychology, and six contemporary views on learning and instruction. The presentation is concise, informative, and appropriate for secondary and college students.

Biehler, Robert Frederick, and Jack Snowman. *Psychology Applied to Teaching.* 6th ed. Boston: Houghton Mifflin, 1990. A well-researched and timely look at classroom learning, this text emphasizes practical applications with real classroom situations. Especially useful for future teachers in secondary or college levels.

Gagné, Robert Mills, and Marcy Perkins Driscoll. *Essentials of Learning for Instruction.* Englewood Cliffs, N.J.: Prentice-Hall, 1988. Offers an in-depth look at Gagné's conditions for learning and the outcomes of learning as well as instructional applications. Written at the undergraduate/graduate level, the book is important reading for future professionals.

Schmeck, Ronald R., ed. *Learning Strategies and Learning Styles.* New York: Plenum Press, 1988. Offers a timely selection of current thinking on student learning styles based on a variety of methodologies. Included are neuropsychological, cognitive, and affective perspectives. Well-suited for college students as well as professionals.

Slavin, Robert E. *Educational Psychology.* 3d ed. Englewood Cliffs, N.J.: Prentice-Hall, 1991. Slavin offers a practical look at effective classroom practice based on recent research findings. The college-level text, which includes references to the author's own research, illustrates how research may directly affect classroom practice.

Ellen Lavelle

Cross-References

Cognitive Development Theory: Piaget, 553; Cognitive Maps, 566; Concept Formation, 637; Cooperative Learning, 695; Learning: Concept, Expectancy, and Insight, 1431; Reduction of Prejudice, 1855.

EGO DEFENSE MECHANISMS

Type of psychology: Personality
Fields of study: Personality theory; classic analytic themes and issues

Ego defense mechanisms are a central feature of Sigmund Freud's psychoanalytic theory; they help explain many everyday behaviors as well as how psychological symptoms develop. They also help explain why some people resist psychotherapy and why people sometimes distort or deny their experiences.

Principal terms
ANXIETY: an unpleasant emotional state accompanied by physiological arousal that signals impending danger
CONSCIOUS: one of Freud's levels of mental life; includes thoughts in one's immediate awareness
EGO: the decision-making part of the personality; it is in contact with reality
FRUSTRATION: an unpleasant emotional reaction to being unable to reach a goal
ID: the part of the psyche, in Freudian theory, that contains and seeks to gratify instinctual drives
INSTINCTS: internal and inborn impulses that propel one's thoughts and behaviors; the two most powerful instincts are sex and aggression
SUPEREGO: the part of the psyche that contains parental and societal standards of morality; acts to prohibit expression of instinctual drives
UNCONSCIOUS: the level of mental life that includes all thoughts, feelings, and images which are beyond one's awareness and are not easily accessible
UNCONSCIOUS MOTIVATION: the idea that much of human behavior is influenced by factors and forces that are not in one's awareness

Overview

The concept of defense mechanisms is an integral part of Sigmund Freud's psychoanalytic theory. According to Freud, the purpose of defense mechanisms is to protect the ego from anxiety. Much of this anxiety is attributable to internal conflicts. A conflict is caused when two or more equally powerful influences cannot be satisfied at the same time. It is resolved when one of the influences prevails, but this often leads to frustration because one (or more) of the other goals is thwarted. Most internal conflicts involve the interactions of the id, ego, and superego. For example, one may have a strong id impulse to overeat, but one's superego may exert an equally powerful influence to remain thin. Thus, the sight of food may cause one to feel anxious without knowing why, because this conflict may be buried in the unconscious.

Conflicts may be either conscious or unconscious; according to Freud, all conflicts are accompanied by anxiety. Anxiety is an unpleasant emotional response that signals impending danger. It is anticipation of danger to be experienced in the future. Only the ego can feel anxiety, and this anxiety can be unbearable. It can occur in the absence of any objective external threat; even when a real threat exists, the emotional reaction is often much greater than warranted. For example, speaking in front of an audience is, in the real sense, not dangerous, but it can cause extreme anxiety in some people. Frequently, the threat that causes anxiety is unconscious, and the person may not be aware of the source.

Anxiety is a signal to take action, so it is both adaptive and self-regulating. That is, when faced with anxiety, the ego automatically attempts to reduce it, which at the same time should reduce the potential danger. In this regard, fear and anxiety are similar. For example, if a person is attacked, the person can fight the attacker or can run away. In both cases, the danger will be removed and the fear will subside. Since one of the main functions of the ego is to maintain survival, its typical response is to take actions which will protect itself and the organism. The ego responds in a defensive manner to all types of anxiety, no matter what their source. In the example above, the mode of reducing fear is overt—that is, it easily observable (the person fights or runs away). In other situations, the actions taken by the ego to protect itself are said to be covert, which means they are not directly observable. These covert actions of protecting the ego from anxiety are called ego defense mechanisms. According to Freud, they operate at an unconscious level.

The first defense mechanism identified by Freud, and the most important one, is called repression. Freud's daughter Anna, who was a famous psychoanalyst in her own right, suggested that perhaps the purpose of the other defense mechanisms is to complete the job that repression has left undone. The process of repression begins when the ego fully separates itself from the id, but it probably does not fully operate until the phallic psychosexual stage of development. In repression, the ego blocks or diverts any ideas, thoughts, feelings, or urges that it finds unacceptable or anxiety producing. For example, a person might have a desire to have sex with his or her boss or teacher, but this wish might be totally unacceptable to the superego; it is then repressed into the unconscious. Allowing this wish to become conscious would result in punishment from the person's superego in the form of guilt or shame. In order to avoid this psychological response, the ego prevents the idea from ever becoming conscious. Although there is no memory of this impulse, it is never destroyed; in fact, it maintains all of its energy. It remains immediately under the level of awareness but has the potential to surface at any time. Because of this, the person may feel ill at ease or anxious but has no awareness concerning the origin of this distress. Furthermore, the repressed energy continues to seek expression, and it often escapes in a disguised form.

The most important disguised forms of repressed material are neurotic symptoms. According to Freud, repressed energy must be released if the organism is to remain healthy. As the ego puts more and more effort into repressing unacceptable drives, it becomes weaker; sooner or later, something has to give in. Symptoms serve as a compromise, because they allow the repressed ideas to be expressed indirectly in a disguised form, thus without arousing anxiety. The symptoms may be either psychological or physical. Physical symptoms are sometimes called conversion reactions, because the energy associated with the original repressed idea is converted into symptoms such as paralysis or even blindness; however, these symptoms are attributable to psychological causes, and there is no real organic impairment.

Although Freud wrote about various defense mechanisms in a number of his works, his daughter Anna Freud is credited with bringing them all together in a book called *Das Ich und die Abwehrmechanismen* (1936; *The Ego and the Mechanisms of Defense*, 1937). In it, she describes the original nine defense mechanisms of repression, regression, undoing, isolation, turning against self, reaction formation, reversal, projection, and introjection. She also adds sublimation or displacement to these. Over the years, other defense mechanisms, such as denial, rationalization, identification, intellectualization, and idealization have been added.

Regression involves reducing anxiety by attempting to return to an earlier and less stressful stage of development, and engaging in immature behavior or thinking characteristic of that stage. The most basic type of regression is sleep, which occupies most of the time of infants. For example, in response to an anxiety-producing test, a person might sleep through the alarm and thus miss the test (and avoid anxiety). Another example of regression is engaging in behaviors such as thumb sucking, or the adult behavior of smoking, which has its roots in the oral stage of infancy. Regression is one of the first defense mechanisms to emerge: It begins in the first year of life.

Undoing is an attempt by the ego to reconstruct previous behaviors so that they are less anxiety producing. For example, the catch that a person failed to make at an important football game may be recalled as an opposing player tipping the ball just before it reached the person. In this case, reality is distorted, and at the conscious level the person may not have any memory of engaging in inappropriate actions or behaviors.

Isolation is the process that separates unpleasant memories with emotions that were once connected to them. In this case, the ideas remain, but only in isolated form. For example, one might vividly remember a childhood situation of being spanked by one's father but not recall the intense negative feelings one had toward him at that time, because such feelings would be anxiety producing. This defense mechanism probably begins to emerge in the anal psychosexual stage, but it fully develops between ages three and five.

Introjection is also called identification. It involves modeling or incorporating the qualities of another person, such as one's parents or teachers. Sometimes people do this with people that they fear; by doing so, the fear associated with them is reduced. Anna Freud calls this "identification with the aggressor." An example of this is when little boys identify with their fathers in order to reduce the castration anxiety associated with the Oedipus complex. As a result, boys adopt the social, moral, and cultural values of the father, all of which become incorporated into the superego.

Reaction formation occurs when a person expresses a repressed unconscious impulse by its direct opposite behavior. Hate may be replaced by love, or attraction by repulsion. The original feeling is not lost, but it does not become conscious. For example, a reaction formation to strong sexual impulses may be celibacy, or a parent who unconsciously hates her child may "smother" it by being overly protective. Reaction formation is another defense mechanism that is closely related to repression.

Projection is when one first represses, then assigns one's own unacceptable or dangerous impulses, attitudes, or behaviors to other persons. For example, one blames others for one's failures. Freud believed that this occurs unconsciously, but some modern psychoanalysts believe that it can occur consciously as well. Another example would be when a married man with an unconscious desire to have an affair accuses his wife of having done so.

Denial occurs when the ego does not acknowledge anxiety-producing reality. For example, a person may not "see" that his marriage is falling apart and may behave as if nothing is wrong; a good student may "forget" that he failed a test in school. An extreme form of denial is the example of a woman who continued to sleep with her husband for several days after he had died. Rationalization is when the ego tries to excuse itself logically from blame for unacceptable behaviors. For example, a student declares that she failed a test because her roommate kept her up the night before, or a man gets drunk because he had such a "tough day" at the office.

The only defense mechanisms that may lead to adaptive or useful behaviors are displacement and sublimation. According to Freud, the energy of the id impulses must be discharged in some way in order to avoid unbearable frustration. Since people often cannot discharge their sexual and aggressive energy directly, they need to do it indirectly. Displacement occurs when this energy is shifted to some other related form of gratification. For example, if the boss makes a man angry, he might go home and kick the dog. When the displacement occurs in socially acceptable ways, it is called sublimation. Freud believed that people's strong sexual desires are often sublimated into scientific or artistic behaviors and that culture and society are built in this way. That is, the power of instincts is rechanneled into writing books, building cities, doing research, or landing a person on the moon.

Applications

Freud believed that many psychological symptoms are associated with the sex drive. For example, a man with an unusually strong superego may repress all sexual impulses. Through the process of reaction formation, these impulses may be converted into compulsive handwashing. According to psychoanalytic theory, the symptoms serve as a substitute for sexual gratification for this person, which he is not allowed to obtain in real life. This is an unconscious process, and the man has no idea of the connection between the symptoms and his sex drive. When a person's behavior is dominated by defense mechanisms, or symptoms become severe, there may be a need for psychotherapy. The goal of therapy is not to eliminate defense mechanisms, but rather to strengthen the ego so that it becomes less dependent on them and can respond to conflicts in a more adaptive and productive manner.

One of the objectives of psychoanalytic therapy is to uncover repressed material that is responsible for the unconscious conflicts or symptoms. In a sense, people relive their lives in the therapy room so the conflict can be traced to its origin. In order to help the patient do this, two major techniques are used. The first is called free association. This involves having the person talk about anything and everything that enters his or her mind no matter how trivial or embarrassing it may be. This is based on the idea that thoughts and ideas do not enter one's mind accidentally. There is usually an important reason for their appearance, and eventually thoughts that are related to the conflict are revealed. The second technique is dream interpretation. Freud called dreams the "royal road" to the unconscious. During sleep, ego defense mechanisms are weakened; therefore, many unconscious conflicts or desires may emerge—although still in a disguised form that needs to be interpreted by the therapist.

Therapy usually takes a long time, because once material is repressed, the ego sets up a counterforce that prevents it from becoming conscious in the future. This counterforce is called resistance. It is responsible for a person unconsciously resisting treatment, because removing the symptoms only serves to return the ego to the original anxiety-producing conflict.

In the example above, once the resistance is overcome, the therapist may determine that the compulsive handwashing behavior is rooted in an unresolved Oedipus complex. In this case, the man's sexual attraction to his mother was repressed, and eventually all sexual impulses were treated in the same way. With careful consideration of timing, the therapist voices an interpretation, which is the method by which the unconscious meaning of a person's thoughts, behaviors, or symptoms is divulged. One interpretation is not enough to cure the patient, but a slow process of "working through," which involves many interpretations and reinterpretations, finally leads to insight. This last step occurs when a person fully understands and accepts the unconscious meaning of his or her thoughts and behaviors; at this point, the symptoms often disappear.

Context

In Freud's own words, "the doctrine of repression is the foundation stone on which the whole structure of psychoanalysis rests." Freud hit upon the notion of repression when he first noticed that his patients were resisting his attempts to help them. In this sense, repression is intimately linked to resistance. According to Freud, when he was using hypnosis to treat his patients, this resistance was hidden; however, as soon as the technique of free assocation replaced hypnosis, resistance was clearly evident, and psychoanalysis was born.

Freud's concept of repression (which he first called "defense") appeared in print in 1894. At that time, most of his patients were women who were suffering from an emotional disorder that was then called hysteria. Freud believed that hysteria was caused primarily by the repression of sexual impulses, and that it could be cured by means of a "talking" therapy. At the time, it was a giant leap for psychology, because the prevailing viewpoint of the nineteenth century was that emotional disorders were caused by organic or physical factors. Freud's theory emphasized a psychological cause and cure for emotional disorders, and thus opened a new area of exploration and set the stage for clinical psychology and psychiatry.

One could speculate that Freud's notion of repression (and thus the other defense mechanisms as well) was rooted in the highly sexually restrictive mores of the Victorian era. In other words, had Freud lived in a more sexually liberated society, he may not have had a need for the concept of repression. It is impossible to know whether this is true. Whatever factors were responsible for Freud's conceptualization of defense mechanisms, it is clear that they led directly to his formulation of psychoanalysis, which was the first major personality theory and treatment method in psychology. Virtually all personality theories and treatment methods since then have been directly or indirectly influenced by the notions of defense and resistance.

It is difficult to predict what role ego defense mechanisms will play in the future. Some psychological theorists have discounted their importance for therapy and for psychology as a whole. Others believe that the study of defense mechanisms will find a new home in the emerging fields of cognitive psychology and the neurosciences. Whatever the future brings, it is clear that the concept of defense mechanisms has become an important part of Western language and culture.

Bibliography

Appignanesi, Richard. *Freud for Beginners.* Illustrated by Oscar Zarate. New York: Pantheon Press, 1979. The authors describe this book as a "documentary comic book" about the world of Freud. Brief and easy to follow, it very simply reviews the major aspects of Freud's theory, such as the unconscious, sex drives, and dreams, in a picture format. It caricatures Freud's family, friends, and some of his patients. Although it is light and enjoyable, it must be supplemented by other works.

Bettelheim, Bruno. *Freud and Man's Soul.* New York: Alfred A. Knopf, 1983. A brief book written by a man who, like Freud, grew up in Vienna. Bettelheim, who read Freud's books in the original German, maintains that the English translations of Freud's works distort much of what he actually said. He sees this as resulting in a theory of psychoanalysis that is artificial and inhuman. Although Bettelheim attempts to explain what Freud really said, it is not clear that he succeeds. For the serious student of psychoanalysis.

Freud, Anna. *The Ego and the Mechanisms of Defense.* Rev. ed. New York: International Universities Press, 1966. A short and relatively easy-to-read book written by Freud's daughter. She begins with a brief introduction to psychoanalysis and continues with a comprehensive review of all the ego defense mechanisms, which includes clear examples. Includes a short bibliography. Throughout the book, she notes original sources from her father's writing.

Freud, Sigmund. *A General Introduction to Psychoanalysis.* Translated by Joan Riviere. New York: Garden City Books, 1952. This is a collection of twenty-eight lectures written by Freud for the general public that covers the complete theory of psychoanalysis. It is easy to read and includes extensive material on the psychology of errors (parapraxes), dream interpretation, and the development of symptoms. It is an excellent starting point for those who know very little about psychoanalysis.

_____. *The Standard Edition of the Complete Psychological Works of Sigmund Freud.* 24 vols. Edited by James Strachey. London: Hogarth Press, 1953-1974. Starting in 1953, all of Freud's written material was published in English in twenty-four volumes. Although these works are more appropriate for advanced readers, all the volumes include an extensive bibliography and comprehensive footnotes which clarify the material very well. The volumes with subject matter related to ego defense mechanisms include *The Interpretation of Dreams* (vols. 4-5), *The Psychopathology of Everyday Life* (vol. 6), and *Inhibitions, Symptoms, and Anxiety* (vol. 20).

Salvatore Cullari

Cross-References

Abnormality: Psychodynamic Models, 74; Anxiety Disorders: Theoretical Explanations, 272; Levels of Consciousness, 663; Dream Analysis, 830; Psychoanalysis: Classical versus Modern, 1898; Psychoanalytic Psychology: An Overview, 1905; Psychoanalytic Psychology and Personality: Sigmund Freud, 1912; Psychosexual Development, 1969.

EGO PSYCHOLOGY: ERIK ERIKSON

Type of psychology: Personality
Fields of study: Personality theory; psychodynamic and neoanalytic models

Erik Erikson emphasized the importance of social, rather than sexual, factors in the development of personality; he also expanded the number of stages of development to eight in order to cover the entire life span. It was Erikson who introduced the notion of the identity crisis.

Principal terms
BASIC ANTIPATHY/CORE PATHOLOGY: the negative personality characteristic developed when the individual experiences mostly the dystonic (disruptive) element of a psychosocial crisis; the antithesis of a basic strength
BASIC STRENGTH: the positive personality characteristic developed when the individual experiences mostly the syntonic (harmonious) element of a psychosocial crisis
PLAY CONSTRUCTION: a projective personality test technique developed by Erikson to reveal unconscious memories and concerns of patients who are too young to express themselves in other ways
PSYCHOHISTORY: a technique of analysis in which the actions of the subject are examined in the light of the social and historical forces that affect the psychological makeup and personality of the subject
PSYCHOSOCIAL CRISIS: a turning point in the process of development precipitated by the individual having to face a new set of social demands and new social relationships
PSYCHOSOCIAL STAGES OF DEVELOPMENT: sequential and specific periods of life during which crises precipitated by changing social demands and relationships necessitate personality changes and new attitudes in the individual

Overview

Erik Erikson was born in 1902. Some reports suggest that he was born out of wedlock; others suggest that his mother was married but that his father had abandoned her. Still other reports suggest that Erikson's father died shortly before or immediately after his birth. Whatever the exact circumstances of his conception and birth, it is known that his mother married young Erik's pediatrician three years after his birth. Erik grew up in comfortable surroundings as Erik Homburger in southern Germany and was expected to become a doctor like his stepfather. Both his mother and his stepfather were from Jewish families, but Erik was considered an outsider when he attended temple because of his blond hair and blue eyes. Ironically, at school he was also considered an outsider despite his Aryan features and was referred to by his classmates as a Jew. It is generally believed that his unknown paternal lineage and his religious heritage were underlying causes of his later focus on the concept that he is most famous for developing: the identity crisis typically experienced in adolescence.

Erik Homburger, in his late teens, abandoned his family's plans for him to become a doctor; he opted for traveling throughout southern Germany and northern Italy and exercising his talent for sketching, both in his travels and in art school. Erikson himself has described those years as a time of discontent, rebellion, and confusion, the same feelings experienced by many teenagers as they try to come to grips with the necd to establish their own sense of identity.

During his late twenties, he worked for, and was psychoanalyzed by, Anna Freud, another of the leaders of the ego psychology movement and the daughter of Sigmund Freud. He was graduated from the Vienna Psychoanalytic Institute in 1933 and emigrated to the United States a year later. He became a United States citizen and changed his name to Erik Homburger Erikson. He never fully explained why he chose Erikson for his last name, but the most interesting suggestion is that his sons wanted to be known as "Erik's son."

In the 1940's, Erikson began to develop his own theory of personality development. He always believed that his theory, while separate and different from Freud's psychoanalysis, was not incompatible with Freud's. He had become acquainted with Freud, and had come to admire him greatly, while undergoing personal analysis by Anna Freud in Vienna. From the beginning of his theorizing, Erikson identified himself as a post-Freudian rather than as anti-Freudian or neo-Freudian. In 1950, Erikson published *Childhood and Society*, the first major book that explained the theory he was in the process of developing. Erikson subsequently authored several books, as well as chapters in books edited by others, elaborating his theory and applying his concepts.

Erikson's theory differs from Freud's psychoanalytic theory in many respects. While Freud viewed the ego as a relatively weak portion of the personality, barely able to control the much stronger id, Erikson viewed it as a more positive, powerful, and adaptive force. Erikson's theory therefore exemplifies a branch of personality theories classified as ego psychology. Further, Erikson emphasized the importance of social interactions in the development of the individual's personality, while Freud emphasized unconscious sexual factors.

Erikson's theory provides a much more positive, hopeful perspective on the human condition than is found in traditional psychoanalytic theory. Freud believed that either overindulgence or excessive conflict during any of the early psychosexual stages of development could cause the individual either to fixate in that stage or to regress back to an earlier stage. Erikson believed that the individual would adopt a negative characteristic, but would also move on to the next psychosocial stage of development. Freud also believed that, without therapy, the person who fixated or regressed would be unable to develop further, because he or she would not have the opportunity to work through the psychosexual tasks of the remaining stages. Erikson, however, believed that since each psychosocial stage of development demands a different pattern of social relationships, the person has a chance to begin anew in each stage. In addition, he believed that a particularly good situation in a later stage could result in the reversal of the negative characteristic adopted in an earlier stage.

Erikson concluded that personality develops over the entire life of the individual. He postulated the existence of eight psychosocial stages of development, the last of which encompasses the period of old age. Freud, on the other hand, proposed five psychosexual stages of development and focused on only the periods of infancy and early childhood. In Freud's theory, all the important parts of the personality are in place, and all the most significant events have been experienced, by the time the individual is six years of age.

In addition to those theoretical differences with Freud, Erikson emphasized the need to develop in either a positive or a negative direction during each of the psychosocial stages of development. In his view, each new set of social demands sets up a new crisis for the individual to resolve. The best known of these crises occurs in adolescence, when the individual must either develop a positive sense of identity or experience role confusion. Today it is widely recognized that "crisis" was probably a bad choice of terminology, because common use of that term implies negative connotations Erikson never intended. He meant for the term to denote an important, even essential, turning point, but not necessarily one that was traumatic or difficult. Later researchers, in fact, have found that most teenagers are able to establish their identity without undue difficulties; only about 20 to 25 percent of teenagers experience the degree of difficulty that would be implied by the common usage of the term "crisis."

Applications

In describing the development of personality, Erikson identified eight stages of psychosocial development, each of which covers a specific period of time and is biologically based. At each stage, the individual encounters a different kind of social situation, is expected to meet different social demands, and experiences different social relationships. Different opportunities for personality development are offered, and new elements are added to the individual's personality at each stage. One element is syntonic (harmonious or positive), while the other is dystonic (disruptive or negative); together they constitute the psychosocial crisis faced by the individual. The conflict between the two elements produces either a basic strength or its basic antipathy or core pathology.

During the first year of life, the infant experiences the psychosocial conflict Erikson identified as trust versus mistrust. The infant is essentially helpless and is dependent upon others for satisfaction of its basic needs. The degree to which its needs are met will determine whether the infant develops the basic strength of hope, or its antipathy and core pathology, withdrawal. Both the syntonic and dystonic elements of trust and mistrust must be experienced by the infant in order for optimum development to occur. If the infant's needs were so well anticipated and perfectly met that the infant never experienced frustration, the result would be an extreme form of trust, and the infant would become too gullible. On the other hand, if the infant's needs were rarely or never met, the result would be an extreme form of mistrust, and the infant would become excessively suspicious and cynical. Optimum development requires a favorable balance of trust and mistrust, which leads to the development of hope. The same principle holds true for optimum development at each of the remaining stages, and the balance must favor the syntonic elements.

During early childhood, the second and third years of life, the child experiences the psychosocial conflict of autonomy versus shame and doubt. As his or her body continues to develop, the child is able to do things he or she was incapable of doing before, and his or her relationships with others change. The cognitive development of the child allows him or her to begin to differentiate between himself or herself and the rest of the world. The negativism of the period, known as the "terrible twos," results from this cognitive development. Now the child can say "No" to mother without denying himself or herself. Many parents perceive the negativism of this period as evidence of disrespect and willfulness, and try to teach the child "proper respect" for elders. Such parents might teach a child to be ashamed of his or her natural desire to be a separate, independent, autonomous person. Parents who understand the cognitive development that is going on can understand that the child is simply becoming his or her own person, and allow the child the freedom necessary to begin to become an effective, self-sufficient individual. If the child is allowed to express freely his or her efforts at developing independence of action, he or she is able to develop a sense of autonomy and will develop the basic strength of will. If, on the other hand, the child is punished or made to feel ashamed of these efforts to express independence, the child will experience shame and doubt and develop the basic antipathy of compulsion.

Early childhood is followed by a period Erikson called the play age. Between the ages of three and six, the child faces the psychosocial crisis of initiative versus guilt. After developing the capacity for autonomous activity, the child can now develop the capacity to initiate purposefully that autonomous behavior in an effort to attain his or her own goals. If the child is able to initiate successfully purposeful activities that lead to the attainment of his or her desired goals, he or she will develop purpose, the basic strength of the play age. If the child's goals are forbidden, or if he or she must delay seeking those goals on a regular basis, the child can experience guilt for desiring those goals and develop inhibition, the core pathology of the play age.

School age extends from about the age of six to about the time of puberty, usually at twelve or thirteen. The psychosocial task of the school age is to confront the issue of industry versus inferiority. Industry refers to the willingness of the child to stick with a task and finish it. If he or she is unable to complete tasks successfully or to reach goals, the dystonic attitude of inferiority results. While industry leads to the development of the basic strength of competence, inferiority leads to the basic antipathy of inertia, and the child may give up and regress to the more infantile, nonproductive play characteristic of the play age.

During adolescence, from puberty to the late teens or early twenties, the individual is faced with the need to develop a stable, secure sense of identity and the basic strength of fidelity. The alternative is to experience role confusion and the core pathology of repudiation. Adolescence is a time for the individual to try different roles and ideologies in the search for meaning in his or her own life. The intense concern for fitting in with an in-group, copying the clothing styles that are popular, and using the currently popular vocabulary are all the result of the effort to find one's place in the world. It seems that in every successive generation, teenagers must go through this trial-and-error method of finding out who they are, what they want to do, and how best to accomplish their goals.

Young adulthood is the stage that has the greatest variability in length. Traditionally, it has been described as the middle to late twenties, but some individuals may not complete this stage until they are in their thirties, or even later. The young adult must face the psychosocial conflict Erikson identified as intimacy versus isolation. To develop intimacy and the basic strength of love, the young adult must be able to merge his or her identity with the identity of another without fear of losing his or her own identity. If the young adult is unable to take a chance risking his or her identity by sharing intimacy, he or she will experience isolation and develop the core pathology known as exclusivity.

Adulthood, which encompasses the fourth, fifth, and part of the sixth decade of life, is the time for the individual to generate or produce. The desire to produce and rear children, to produce works that will last beyond one's own lifetime, to help the next generation to develop, and to build a better world all result from the psychosocial crisis Erikson called generativity versus stagnation. Generativity leads to the basic strength of care. If the adult is unable to become generative, the alternative is to stagnate, become self-absorbed, and develop the core pathology of adulthood, rejectivity. According to Erikson, rejectivity leads to some of the worst aspects of what others call human nature: hatred of individuals and groups, wars, and the resulting destruction and atrocities.

Old age is the time for the individual to experience the psychosocial conflict of ego integrity versus despair. This final stage of development lasts from the sixties until the individual's death. For the individual who has mostly experienced the syntonic developments of trust, autonomy, initiative, industry, identity, intimacy, and generativity, the characteristic of integrity will predominate. That person will develop the basic strength Erikson called wisdom. Wisdom enables the person to maintain an informed and detached concern with life while facing the inevitability of death. The individual who has mostly experienced the dystonic developments of mistrust, shame and doubt, guilt, inferiority, ego confusion, isolation, and stagnation will develop the basic antipathy Erikson called disdain.

Context

Erik Erikson made a number of significant contributions to the field of psychology and to the ways in which the lay public both views and describes the world. Many people, in fact, use ideas advanced by Erikson without being aware of whose ideas they are.

Erikson moved the focus of attention in developmental theories from the sexual domain into the social domain. He introduced the notion of identity crisis into the common vocabulary. He also expanded the time span of personality development to cover the entire life of the individual. Like many other psychologists, he added to the repertoire of clinical techniques available for both investigation and therapy. His theory also offers a more positive, hopeful view of the human condition than did Sigmund Freud's psychoanalysis.

Finally, one must include among Erikson's contributions to the field of psychology play construction and psychohistorical analysis. Play construction is a projective technique Erikson developed to explore the unconscious processes of children. A child is given a random selection of toys and is asked to construct a scenario using those toys. The scenario that is constructed is, according to Erikson, an unconscious expression of the child's life history that reveals hidden needs and motives.

Psychohistorical analysis refers to an approach pioneered by Erikson in which the investigator examines the role that historical factors and personal experiences play in the personality development of the individual. While Freud argued that "anatomy is destiny," Erikson countered that "anatomy, history, and personality are our combined destiny." A psychohistory is similar to a case history, except that psychohistories usually involve individuals who are essentially emotionally stable, while case histories are developed for persons who experience emotional difficulties. Erikson published psychohistorical biographies of Mahatma Gandhi and Martin Luther.

Bibliography

Coles, Robert. *Erik H. Erikson: The Growth of His Work.* Boston: Little, Brown, 1970. A well-written biography, though Coles has been criticized by some as too friendly toward his subject; some reviewers have gone so far as to accuse him of hero worship.

Erikson, Erik Homburger. *Childhood and Society.* New York: W. W. Norton, 1950. The first major book that explained the theory Erikson was in the process of developing. Republished in 1963 and again in 1985, this remains one of the most popular, and most frequently recommended, psychology books ever published.

_____. *Gandhi's Truth: On the Origins of Militant Nonviolence.* New York: W. W. Norton, 1969. The better of Erikson's psychohistorical biographies. Erikson examines in detail the historical period in which Gandhi grew up, and the personal experiences that eventually led Gandhi to become one of the world's most influential religious and spiritual leaders. Erikson believes that the writer of a psychohistory should become emotionally involved with the subject; his emotional attachment to Gandhi is apparent. Erikson attributes that attachment to his own lifelong search for the father he had never known.

Evans, Richard Isadore. *The Making of Psychology: Discussions with Creative Contributors.* New York: Alfred A. Knopf, 1976. An excellent compilation of interviews with many of the major forces in the history of psychology. The chapter on Erikson includes not only a discussion of the eight psychosocial stages but also a psychohistorical discussion comparing Adolf Hitler's and Mahatma Gandhi's lives and contributions to the world (Hitler does not fare well in the comparison).

Roazen, Paul. *Erik H. Erikson: The Power and Limits of a Vision.* New York: Free Press, 1976. Although Roazen is more critical of Erikson than Coles is, he finds Erikson's approach more likely than Freud's to be helpful in therapeutic encounters. This biography, coupled with Coles's, is likely to produce a more balanced view of Erikson's place in the history of psychology than if either book is read alone.

John W. Nichols

Cross-References

Development: Theoretical Issues, 804; Generativity in Adulthood: Erikson, 1075; Identity Crises: Erikson, 1255; Integrity: Erikson, 1321; Intimacy in Adulthood: Erikson, 1363; Personality Theory: Major Issues, 1804; Psychoanalytic Psychology: An Overview, 1905; Psychoanalytic Psychology and Personality: Sigmund Freud, 1912; Trust, Autonomy, Initiative, and Industry: Erikson, 2591.

ELECTROCONVULSIVE THERAPY

Type of psychology: Psychotherapy
Field of study: Biological treatments

Electroconvulsive therapy (ECT), or "shock" therapy, is the controlled application of an electric current to the brain to induce a seizure. This treatment is used primarily for severe and debilitating mental disorders, such as major depression. It is a controversial treatment that has both proponents and opponents.

Principal terms

ANTEROGRADE AMNESIA: the inability to remember new material

BRAIN HEMISPHERES: the two halves of the brain, which have both common and unique functions and components

DEPRESSION: a mental disorder marked by loss of interest or pleasure in nearly all activities and a sad mood

GRAND MAL SEIZURE: a seizure characterized by intense stiffening of the body followed by sharp, jerky movements and unconsciousness

MANIA: a mental disorder marked by extreme hyperactivity, agitation, racing thoughts, and distractibility

NEUROTRANSMITTERS: chemical substances that transmit information from one cell in the brain to another

PSYCHOTROPIC MEDICATION: medication that is used in the treatment of mental disorders

RETROGRADE AMNESIA: the inability to remember things from the past

SCHIZOPHRENIA: a mental disorder marked by disorganized and odd thinking, hearing or seeing things that are not there, and flattened or blunt affect

SOMATIC THERAPY: a treatment for a mental disorder that involves a physical component, such as medications or ECT

Overview

Electroconvulsive therapy (ECT), sometimes known as shock therapy, is a somatic, or physical, form of therapy that is used for some individuals who suffer from severe mental disorders. It involves the direct application of an electric current to the brain. Typically, this current lasts for up to one second at a rate of 140 to 170 volts. The purpose of this electrical charge is to induce a grand mal seizure that will usually last for thirty to sixty seconds. The seizure that is induced is similar to those experienced in some types of epilepsy. It is through this grand mal seizure that ECT has its beneficial effect in reducing the symptoms of the patient.

The use of electrical charges as a medical treatment has been reported for centuries. As early as A.D. 47, Scribonius Largus used an electric eel to treat headaches. During the sixteenth century, Ethiopians were reported to have used electric catfish to expel evil spirits from the bodies of the mentally ill. Direct electric charges for the treatment of nervous complaints was also reported during the eighteenth century in Europe.

The modern application of electric current for the treatment of individuals with mental disorders began in 1938. It was at this time that two Italians, Ugo Cerletti, a psychiatrist, and Lucino Bini, a neuropathologist, invented the first ECT machine for use on humans. Cerletti and Bini first used their newly developed ECT machine to induce convulsions for the treatment of schizophrenic patients, and they reported that the treatment was a success.

ECT was introduced into the United States in 1940, at which time it quickly became the major somatic treatment for all severely disturbed individuals, regardless of mental disorder. By the mid-1950's, its use began to decline rapidly for several reasons, including the introduction of psychotropic medications, increasing demands for civil rights for the mentally ill, and concerns about potential adverse effects of ECT. Subsequently, however, a growing body of research has indicated that ECT is an effective treatment for some severe mental disorders. This research has led to a gradual increase in the acceptance of its use, particularly in the treatment of severely depressed individuals.

When ECT was first used for the treatment of mental disorders, the patient would be strapped to a table and, without any medications or other medical safeguards, would be administered the electrical current and sent into a convulsion. During this convulsion, the patient would thrash around on the table, often being left with broken limbs and other physical complications. In its current use, prior to administration of the ECT, the patient is given a muscle relaxant, which completely immobilizes the body, and anesthesia, which makes the patient completely unconscious. The result of these safeguards has been a much safer treatment of the patient.

Although ECT has been demonstrated to be an effective treatment, it is not known how and why ECT works. The theoretical basis of the original use of ECT had to do with the observation that schizophrenia and epilepsy rarely occur together, suggesting that the two are mutually exclusive. Based on this observation, it was hypothesized that, if a seizure could be induced in a schizophrenic, the schizophrenic symptoms could be eliminated. Physicians had tried previously to induce such seizures by means of injections of insulin, camphor, and other chemicals, but these approaches proved to be too dangerous for the patients.

Although this early theory of the mechanics of ECT has been refuted, there still is little knowledge of how and why ECT actually works. The only fact that has been firmly established is that it is the seizure that ECT induces that creates any positive changes in the patient's symptoms. There is no clear-cut explanation, however, of how the seizure creates the changes. Several theories have been developed to explain the process, most of which center on ECT's effect on neurotransmitters.

Neurotransmitters are chemicals that are used in the brain to transmit messages from one cell to another. One well-accepted theory holds that abnormalities in the level and utilization of certain neurotransmitters lead to the development of mental disorders such as depression, schizophrenia, and mania. Consequently, it is thought that ECT, through the creation of a seizure, somehow affects the level and utilization of some of these neurotransmitters, and that it is this process that reduces the patient's symptoms of mental disorder. While research to investigate how ECT works continues, it is important to remember that, as with all somatic treatments, ECT does not cure the disorder; it provides only temporary relief from the symptoms.

Despite its reported effectiveness, ECT remains a controversial treatment for mental disorders. Opponents point to potential adverse effects that ECT can cause, particularly the possibility of permanent brain damage resulting from the induced seizure. These opponents, who highlight the negative effects that ECT can have on a patient's memory, prefer the use of alternative treatment methods. The public media have served to exacerbate negative perceptions of ECT by depicting it as an inhumane treatment that is used only to control and punish malcontents, not to help the severely disturbed. There is perhaps no better example of the media's distorted depiction of ECT than that found in the film *One Flew over the Cuckoo's Nest* (1975), in which ECT was used as a brutal method to control and manage the main character. As a result of these misunderstandings and distorted perceptions, ECT is often not used when it might be helpful.

Applications

It has been estimated that each year 60,000 to 100,000 people in the United States receive electroconvulsive therapy. This form of treatment has been used to treat a variety of mental disorders, including severe major depression, schizophrenia, and mania. Several surveys have indicated that more than three-fourths of individuals who receive ECT have been diagnosed as suffering from severe major depression. The second-largest group of individuals receiving ECT consists of those who have been diagnosed as schizophrenic. While there is substantial evidence that ECT is effective in the treatment of severe major depression, the evidence supporting the use of ECT to treat other disorders is not as strong.

Generally speaking, ECT is not seen as a treatment of choice. That is, it will most likely not be the first treatment given to someone suffering from a severe mental disorder. Instead, it is typically viewed as the treatment of last resort and is used primarily to treat individuals who do not respond to any other treatments. For example, a typical course of treatment for an individual suffering from debilitating severe major depression would be first to try talking therapy and to use one of the many antidepressant medications. For most people, it takes two to four weeks to respond to such medications. If the patient does not respond to the medication, another antidepressant medication may be tried. If, after several trials of medication, the patient still does not respond and continues to be severely depressed, ECT might be considered a viable option.

There are a few individuals for whom ECT might be considered the treatment of choice. These individuals include those who are in a life-threatening situation, such as those who show symptoms of severe anorexia or strong suicidal tendencies, or those for whom medications would be damaging. ECT might be used to treat pregnant women, for example, since it presents fewer risks for a fetus than medication does, or individuals with heart disease, for whom medications can cause severe complications.

Because of the stigma attached to ECT as a result of its historical misuse and its characterization in the popular media, many physicians believe that ECT is not used as widely as it could and should be. Often, ECT is suggested as the treatment of choice, but because of its stigma, other approaches are tried first. The effect of this decision is to deprive the patient of an effective treatment and delay or prevent remission.

When ECT is indicated for the treatment of a mental disorder, it usually involves five to ten applications of ECT administered at a rate of two or three per week. The number of ECT treatments given, however, will vary depending on the individual's medical history and the severity of the presenting symptoms. ECT is always administered by a physician; it cannot be ordered by a psychologist. When ECT is applied, many medical safeguards are used to prevent or minimize adverse effects. These include the use of a muscle relaxant, anesthesia, and oxygen. These medical procedures have made the use of ECT much safer than it was during the days when the patient would thrash about the table, breaking bones.

There have been additional refinements in the use of ECT that have made it even safer. One such refinement is the application of unilateral, rather than bilateral, ECT. In unilateral ECT, the electric shock is sent through only one of the brain's two hemispheres. Usually, the shock is sent through the right hemisphere, which controls abstract thinking and creativity, rather than the left hemisphere, which controls language and rational thinking. While usually as effective as bilateral ECT, in which the shock goes through the entire brain, unilateral ECT has been shown to cause fewer adverse side effects.

Despite the refinements in ECT and the caution exercised in its use, there are several documented potential adverse side effects. Although most research indicates that these effects are temporary, some researchers suggest that ECT can cause permanent brain damage. The major adverse effects of ECT relate to how well the patient's brain functions after the treatment. The most common effect is extreme confusion and disorientation in the patient upon awakening after an ECT treatment. Generally, this confusion will last for only a few minutes to a few hours.

Another serious concern about ECT's effects on the cognitive functioning of the patient has to do with the patient's memory. ECT can cause retrograde amnesia, the inability to remember things from the past, and anterograde amnesia, the inability to memorize new material. Both forms of amnesia are most noticeable in the first days and weeks after the ECT treatments have stopped. With the passage of time, the patient will slowly remember more from the past and will regain or strengthen the ability to remember new material. In most patients, this recovery of memory will take no more than two to six months. The patient may, however, permanently lose memories of events that occurred immediately prior to the ECT treatments or while the patient was hospitalized for the treatments. The degree of memory loss appears to be related to the number of ECT treatments the patient received.

Research investigating permanent brain damage from the use of ECT has been mixed. Some research has indicated that any application of ECT will cause brain damage and that more brain damage will occur as more treatments are applied. Long-term impairment in the patient's memory is one effect that has thus been identified as permanent. Other researchers, however, have reported that ECT does not cause permanent brain damage. In the meantime, ECT is used cautiously, and research continues into its potential adverse effects.

Context

Prior to the advent of psychotropic medications, there were few effective treatments for the severely mentally ill. Numerous treatment methods were attempted to help relieve the symptoms of mental illness. Among these methods were bloodletting, the use of leeches, and immersion in water. Perhaps the most common approach was the permanent institutionalization of severely mentally ill individuals. This was done not only to control patients but also to protect others, since patients were viewed as a threat to others and themselves.

As a result of the ineffectiveness of the treatments described above and the growing concern about the institutionalization of the mentally ill, a number of new treatment approaches were developed and applied. Among these new approaches was electroconvulsive therapy. Electroconvulsive shock therapy was first used on schizophrenic patients, and the treatment met with some success. It was also tried on depressed and manic patients with even greater success. As a result of these successes and the lack of other effective treatment approaches, ECT quickly came to be a commonly used treatment for individuals who suffered from a variety of mental disorders.

There were many factors that led to ECT's falling out of favor during the late 1950's. First, the earlier applications of ECT held significant dangers for the patient. The risk of death was approximately one in one thousand, and the risk of physical damage, such as broken bones, was even greater—in fact, such damage was noted in up to 40 percent of the patients. Concerns about complications caused by the use of ECT continue today, and their focus is ECT's impact on cognitive functioning.

Another factor that led to the decline in the use of ECT was the development and introduction of psychotropic medications. These medications revolutionized the treatment of the mentally ill and led to thousands of patients being deinstitutionalized. In terms of both effectiveness and safety, it soon became evident that the use of these medications was substantially preferable to the use of ECT.

A third major influence on the decline of ECT's use was the growing civil rights movement for the mentally ill. Many community and religious leaders began to advocate the fair and humane treatment of the seriously mentally ill. These individuals saw ECT as an undesirable treatment method, used as an instrument for controlling and punishing individuals who could not defend themselves. This view of ECT as inhumane soon came to be widely held. ECT was perceived as a method to control, rather than help, patients—as a punishment rather than a therapy.

These and other factors led to the substantially decreased use of ECT. Subsequently, however, well-designed research has begun to define ECT as a relatively safe treatment method that may be the best therapy in certain situations. Additionally, refinements in the application of ECT have increased its effectiveness and reduced its complications. As a result of not only the ambiguity about its potential adverse effects but also the emotional issues related to its use, the controversy about ECT and its relative risks and benefits is likely to continue for many years.

Bibliography

American Psychiatric Association. *Electroconvulsive Therapy: Report of the Task Force on Electroconvulsive Therapy of the American Psychiatric Association.* Washington, D.C.: Author, 1978. This report provides the results of a major task force charged with examining the clinical use of ECT. It thoroughly reviews the issues in a very readable format. Extensive recommendations for the use of ECT are provided.

Breggin, Peter R. *Electroshock: Its Brain-Disabling Effects.* New York: Springer, 1979. This book describes many adverse effects of ECT, but severe mental dysfunction in particular. Citing research from both animal and human research, this author makes a strong argument against the use of ECT, stating that it is no more effective than a placebo, but considerably more dangerous.

Endler, N. S., and E. Persad. *Electroconvulsive Therapy: The Myths and the Realities.* Toronto: Hans Huber, 1988. This book is written for a wide audience, from psychiatrists to patients, and therefore it provides a very readable review of the topic. Much space is devoted to exploring nontechnical issues, including the myths about using ECT, the stigma attached to it, and legal and ethical concerns. An extensive bibliography is included.

Fink, Max. *Convulsive Therapy: Theory and Practice.* New York: Raven Press, 1979. Provides a thorough review of numerous issues surrounding the use of ECT. Includes a study of its effectiveness, risks, and legal, economic, and ethical concerns, as well as a comparison of ECT with other treatment methods. Several chapters are committed to a technical review of the mechanisms of ECT.

Friedberg, John. *Shock Treatment Is Not Good for Your Brain.* San Francisco: Glide, 1976. Provides a strong condemnation of ECT. The author believes that mental illness is a myth and that the use of ECT is unnecessary as well as inhumane. This book, which is written in a personal, nontechnical manner, includes interviews with seven individuals who have received ECT and are opposed to its further use.

Peck, Robert E. *The Miracle of Shock Treatment.* Jericho, N.Y.: Exposition Press, 1974. This short book provides a nontechnical introduction to ECT. It is written in a very readable style and is intended for the layperson who has little knowledge of the topic. The book includes brief case examples that highlight the usefulness of ECT in certain situations.

Mark E. Johnson

Cross-References

Abnormality: Biomedical Models, 39; Clinical Depression, 521; Depression: Theoretical Explanations, 789; Madness: Historical Concepts, 1492; Neuropsychology, 1667; Neurotransmitters, 1673; Psychoactive Drug Therapy, 1891; Schizophrenia: Theoretical Explanations, 2141; Synaptic Transmission, 2514.

EMOTION: COGNITIVE AND PHYSIOLOGICAL INTERACTION

Type of psychology: Emotion
Fields of study: Cognitive processes; cognitive therapies; coping

Research suggests there are two ingredients that combine to create emotions: thoughts and physiological responses. Research into the ingredients of emotions has provided researchers and therapists with a better understanding of how to help individuals who want to change undesirable emotions.

Principal terms
> AFFECT: a term commonly used by psychologists to refer to emotional feelings
> COGNITIONS: thoughts; some psychologists use the term only for conscious thoughts, while others use it for conscious, unconscious, and preconscious thoughts
> COGNITIVE: related to thinking
> COGNITIVE THERAPY: therapy that helps an individual question and change specific thoughts or ways of thinking
> EMOTIONS: feelings or moods; psychologists also use the term "affect" as a synonym for emotions
> PHYSIOLOGICAL RESPONSES: involuntary responses of the body; these include such responses as increased heart rate, respiration, and blood pressure, as well as the release of chemicals in the brain or bloodstream

Overview

Many people, including psychologists, find that defining "emotion" is difficult, much like trying to describe the taste of a potato. For both emotion and the taste of a potato, the easiest way to define the experience is to describe the elements that make up the experience.

When discussing the elements that define emotion, psychologists often begin by stating what an emotion is not. First, emotions are not actions. In other words, jumping up and down may be an action that expresses a person's joy, but jumping up and down is not the joy itself. Second, emotions are not thoughts. The thoughts one has about a car accident might be considered sad thoughts, but they are not the actual sadness.

The sadness, and also the joy, are feelings—something one experiences, not something one does or thinks. These experiences are typically either desirable, as is joy, or undesirable, as is sadness. Experiences also vary in intensity. Joy can range from happiness to euphoria, for example. Thus, some elements of emotions are that they are something one experiences, they vary in intensity, they are either good or bad, and they are not actions or thoughts.

If affect, or emotion, is neither an action i·or a thought, then what is it? Psychologists assert that affect is a mixture of emotionally laden thoughts and bodily symptoms, such as a change in heart rate or breathing. In other words, emotions are a combination of emotional thoughts and physiological symptoms. Experiencing joy is not the same as experiencing a rapid heart beat, nor is it the same as thinking a joyful thought, but the rapid heart beat and other symptoms combine with the joyful thoughts to create the joyful feeling, the joyful mood, the emotion called "joy."

There are several ways that thoughts and bodily symptoms combine to produce moods. One way is that thoughts can affect the physiological responses that one has. For example, Richard Lazarus and Susan Folkman showed that when individuals watched a stressful motion picture, the thoughts they held during the film influenced their bodily responses. Individuals watched a film of a man having a bloody accident with a power saw. Some individuals were instructed to think about how they would feel if they were having the accident, and others were asked to remember that it was only a fictional script. Compared to individuals who focused on the fictional nature of the film, individuals who identified with the main character showed more arousal of their sympathetic nervous system, the part of the nervous system that increases physiological symptoms, such as heart rate, blood pressure, and breathing, and releases adrenaline. Furthermore, individuals who identified with the main character were more likely than the other individuals to report feeling stressed.

This research clearly shows that thoughts can affect physiological symptoms, and it thus demonstrates one way that thoughts and physiological symptoms work together to create emotions. Yet from this study, one cannot conclude that the thoughts and bodily symptoms actually combined to create the emotion; perhaps the physiological symptoms alone were enough to produce the stressed mood.

To know if physiological symptoms alone are enough to produce affect, one must examine a study that produces symptoms both with and without emotional thoughts. Dolf Zillmann and other researchers have conducted several such studies, all with similar results: Those individuals who are somehow made aroused but do not have emotional thoughts tend to show less emotion than do individuals who both have physiological symptoms and emotional thoughts.

In one such study, individuals either exercised or did not exercise. In each of these two groups, some individuals had been insulted earlier by a research assistant, and some had not. All four groups later were given the opportunity to give electric shock to the research assistant, under the guise of a learning assignment. The researchers then examined the levels of electric shock administered by each of the four groups. In this study, those who had exercised and who had been insulted gave more intense shocks than did those individuals who had exercised but were not initially insulted. Although this research study measured actions rather than actual anger, these results strongly suggest that bodily arousal is not enough to produce anger. Arousal is much more likely to show up as anger if arousal is combined with angry thoughts. This study and many others also suggest another way that emotional thoughts and physiological symptoms can act together to affect moods: Emotional experience can be made more intense by increasing physiological arousal by using outside means, such as exercise.

Finally, researcher Robert Baron has shown yet another way that thoughts and physiological symptoms combine to produce emotions. At low levels of arousal, existing anger can be turned into happiness by changing one's thoughts from angry to happy thoughts.

Applications

Since it is known that thoughts (cognitions) and physiological symptoms combine to produce moods, it is also known how to exert some control over those moods. Cognitions and physiological responses combine to produce affect, therefore, it follows that one can change emotional responses by changing either one's cognitions or physiological symptoms, or both. An important application of these techniques is in the area of stress management.

Research clearly shows that the way one thinks about a situation will affect the emotions one feels in that situation. For example, individuals who view a situation as a threat will feel more stress than will individuals who view the same situation as a challenge. Furthermore, individuals who view situations as a challenge rather than a threat are less likely to become ill. The same sympathetic nervous system symptoms that are involved in many of one's unpleasant intense emotions also are implicated in one's physical health. It is no surprise then that individuals who often are depressed or anxious also tend to get sick more often; the two are closely related physiologically.

How, then, do psychologists help individuals who are at risk for unpleasant emotions and for physical illnesses? What can be done for those individuals who view situations as threats? There are four answers to these questions. The first step a person can take is to look for something in the situation that is pleasant, and the second step is to try and bring that good aspect to mind often. Thinking positive thoughts can help counteract mild, unpleasant emotions. Unfortunately, this is not often true with stronger unpleasant emotions. To deal with these, a person will need to take additional steps.

The third step is for the person to try to discover what it is about the situation that he or she finds threatening. This is not always easy, since many people are hesitant to acknowledge threatening thoughts. Although according to Lazarus and Folkman, to eliminate the problem, one must acknowledge one's threatening thoughts. Once those thoughts are clear, the fourth step often is necessary.

The fourth step is to take some action to eliminate the threat. This could mean learning some new skills, or it could mean questioning and changing certain beliefs. For example, consider a person who feels anxious taking tests. This person might find tests a threat rather than a challenge because the person knows that one needs good grades to get into college and does not believe that he or she possesses the skills to do well.

One action this person can take is to learn some different study skills. Another action would be to get involved in some extracurricular activities that would increase the chances of a college being interested in him or her. These would be examples of learning skills to reduce the threat.

If, however, a person finds tests a threat because he or she believes, "I have to get A's to prove I am worthwhile," this person would be wise to question that belief. The belief is problematic for several reasons. First, if it is leading to unpleasant emotions during the test, it could interfere with the person's ability to take the test. Second, most psychologists would not consider it useful to base one's whole sense of self-worth on one's school performance (or any other performance). A cognitive therapist might encourage this person to think, "I am a worthwhile person regardless of my performances." Thinking this way will not only boost self-esteem, it will eliminate the stressful emotions; it may also eliminate the thoughts that are interfering with achieving good grades. To reiterate, people who view a situation as a threat might need to develop some skills to cope with the threat. They might also need to change some of the perceptions that make the situation appear threatening.

It is not always easy to change one's unpleasant thoughts. Many thoughts are deeply ingrained and take time to change. In such cases, a person would also be wise to pay attention to the causes of his or her physiological arousal. In other words, one should recognize that exercise, caffeine, sugar, roller coasters, and, for women, menstruation can cause sympathetic nervous system symptoms. If people find themselves having stronger than usual emotional experiences, they should consider that part of the strong emotion might be attributable to extra arousal from caffeine or some other source, not from the situation about which they are upset. The opposite might be true as well: Roller coasters or exercise might increase anger, but they might also increase the excitement of a first date.

During strong unpleasant emotions, a useful technique is to take some deep, slow, relaxed breaths. This is a well-accepted way of reducing sympathetic nervous system symptoms, and thus reducing the intensity of the emotion. On the other hand, slow, sad emotions sometimes can be helped by becoming aroused from outside sources, such as exercise. Exercise can also help to calm a person, taking a person's mind off whatever is bothering him or her. All these facts are so because emotions derive from a combination of thoughts and physiological symptoms.

Context
In the late 1800's, psychologists William James and Carl Lange asserted that anger results from one set of physiological symptoms, jealousy from another set, spite from another, and so forth. Their theory, called the James-Lange theory, is only partially accepted because research shows that the different patterns of bodily responses are not as clear-cut as the James-Lange theory would suggest. In addition, individuals who have spinal cord injuries, and thus have no sensations from the neck down, still experience emotions, something that would not be predicted from the James-Lange theory.

In 1962, Stanley Schachter and Jerome Singer showed that a person's specific thoughts, not specific patterns of bodily arousal, influence emotions. In their study, individuals were led to believe that they were participating in a study on how drugs can improve memory, although it actually was a study on how physiological arousal and thoughts influence emotions. Some individuals received a drug that produced arousal, and other individuals received no such drug. Furthermore, some individuals knew the drug would arouse them, and others did not. All individuals were then asked to complete a questionnaire, which was written to be offensive. Schachter and Singer wanted to know which group of individuals would experience the most anger over the questionnaire. In this study, those individuals who received the stimulant and who did not know it was a stimulant were angrier than individuals in the other groups. They were angrier than those who received no stimulant and angrier than those who received a stimulant but who knew it would cause arousal. Schachter and Singer thus concluded that the arousal and the angry thoughts worked together to produce the high levels of arousal.

Although Schachter and Singer's study has been criticized for various reasons, many studies followed it with similar results. The idea that thoughts play a strong role in emotions took hold, and therapists such as Aaron T. Beck and Albert Ellis began creating techniques to help clients change the irrational thoughts that can lead to unnecessary and unpleasant emotions. This type of therapy, cognitive therapy, is accepted by many as the main type of therapy for depression, for example.

Many researchers, however, wanted to know why changing irrational thoughts is often slow, so research on emotions continued. One important finding is that it takes approximately two years to change completely an old, deeply ingrained, irrational belief. A second, perhaps more disturbing, finding is that some emotional symptoms come before conscious thoughts, which is contrary to Schachter and Singer's theory. Perhaps this explains why it often takes more than two years to change old ways of thinking and feeling.

Bibliography

Beck, Aaron T. *Cognitive Therapy and the Emotional Disorders.* New York: International Universities Press, 1976. Valuable source on how irrational thoughts can create serious problems. Gives hints on how to become more aware of things one says to oneself. Also describes cognitive therapy. Informative chapters on depression, anxiety, and phobias.

Bernstein, Douglas A., E. Roy, T. Srull, and C. Wickens. *Psychology.* 2d ed. Boston: Houghton Mifflin, 1991. Well-organized text written for college students. Defines emotions, tracing research history and integrating different theories. Discusses the sympathetic nervous system and the brain. Also presents a section on the disadvantages of not talking about emotions.

Brehm, Sharon S., and Saul M. Kassin. *Social Psychology.* Boston: Houghton Mifflin, 1989. Chapter on aggression addresses the negative affect theory, the model of incompatible responses, and the arousal-affect theory—theories that address how thoughts and bodily arousal affect anger and aggressive actions. Chapter on interpersonal attraction addresses the excitation transfer hypothesis, showing how arousal from one source can affect unrelated emotions.

Burns, David D. *Feeling Good.* New York: William Morrow, 1980. Self-help book, accepted by the psychological community, that shows how irrational thoughts can lead to unnecessary feelings and gives suggestions for changing. Chapters on perfectionism, self-esteem, guilt, depression, suicide, and love.

Plotnik, Rod. *Introduction to Psychology.* 2d ed. New York: Random House, 1989. Useful chapter on stress and stress management that shows how thoughts and physiological symptoms influence stress response. Chapter also discusses coping strategies and personality factors that put one at risk for stress and stress-related illnesses.

Schneider, David J., Albert H. Hastorf, and Phoebe C. Ellsworth. *Person Perception.* 2d ed. Reading, Mass.: Addison-Wesley, 1979. Interesting chapter on self-attributions. Discusses several relevant attributional theories, including one that explains how a person can come to enjoy a task less after receiving a reward for engaging in the task.

Julie A. Felender

Cross-References

Abnormality: Cognitive Models, 46; Cognitive Behavior Therapy, 546; Coping Strategies: An Overview, 706; Depression: Theoretical Explanations, 789; Emotion: Definition and Assessment, 893; Emotion: Mind-Body Processes, 907; Emotion: Neurophysiology and Neuroanatomy, 914; Emotion and Attribution Theory, 921; Emotion and Stress, 941; Rational-Emotive Therapy, 2052.

EMOTION: CULTURAL VARIATIONS

Type of psychology: Emotion
Fields of study: Cognitive processes; personality theory; thought

Emotions are an important part of a person's way of perceiving, thinking, and feeling. Some aspects of emotion appear to be universal; the expression of smiling, for example, is associated with positive emotions around the world. Other aspects are more culturally specific. Cultural expectations have a major impact on an individual's self-regulation, evaluation, and expression of emotions.

Principal terms

ATTRIBUTION: the process by which people explain emotions; people's judgments about why they behave the way they do

CULTURE: the deposit of knowledge, experience, beliefs, values, attitudes, meanings, religion, notions of time, roles, concepts of the universe, and material objects and possessions acquired by a group of people

DISPLAY RULES: rules taught by culture through socialization regarding appropriate expressions of emotions

FEELING RULES: patterns of interpretation that determine what is to be felt in various situations

NORMS: learned socioculturally based rules that prescribe how people should behave in various situations; they are transmitted through various agents of cultures, such as teachers, parents, peers, and television

SELF-REGULATION: an individual's sensitivity and responsivity to situational and cultural cues for what is appropriate

Overview

Emotions contribute to a rich and variable existence; they determine happiness, sadness, anger, and fear. Without them life would seem meaningless and dull. Culture affects emotional expression by establishing values, beliefs, and rules regarding appropriate expression. Expressed emotions are generally those deemed acceptable by a specific culture or collective and will vary from culture to culture and situation to situation. For example, crying at weddings is considered normal in some cultures and abnormal in others. At any point in time, a person's emotions are a product of history, physiological makeup, gender, age, and personality, as well as situational evaluations.

Some psychologists believe that there are only a certain number of basic or primary emotions and that other emotions are a combination of these. Carroll Izard (1977) believes that there are ten basic emotions: joy, interest-excitement, surprise, sadness, anger, disgust, contempt, fear, shame, and guilt. Most of these basic emotions are then interpreted through culture, which in turn determines values, feelings, beliefs, and rules for behavioral expression.

Emotions may be considered to be the result of three interacting variables: events within the individual's sociocultural environment, internal cognitive processes, and physiological responses. When a person is emotionally aroused, there is an accompanying physiological arousal. This arousal may affect the entire body, including perspiration, breathing, and heart rate. The sympathetic nervous system activates certain responses; the adrenal glands release the hormones epinephrine (adrenaline) and norepinephrine (noradrenaline), which trigger increased heart rate, blood pressure, and blood-sugar levels. To the extent that emotions are physiologically based, they should be understood universally with minimal cultural variations.

Theodore D. Kemper (1987) proposed cross-cultural universality of six emotions, including four he considers primary (fear, anger, depression, and satisfaction). According to Kemper, primary emotions are those that are neurologically structured in all people and so are not likely to be a product of culture. Other emotions are products of the sociocultural environment. Examples of these include signs of love, objects of pride and shame, and guilt. These emotions are dependent on the differentiation of one or more of the primary emotions into new ones.

Norms regarding the expression or concealment of emotions will vary from culture to culture. For example in China, women are encouraged to conceal happiness and exaggerate grief; in the United States, this is somewhat reversed.

Both the feelings or evaluation associated with specific emotions and the expression of those emotions will be influenced by a combination of cultural norms, individual dispositions, and the situation. In any particular situation, a person's emotional state will be affected by a variety of factors. For example, in a doctor's waiting room, a person's emotional state will be determined by personality factors such as patience, past learning, and experiences with physicians, as well as the factors surrounding the present visit. Cultural display rules will control how emotions will be expressed in this situation.

Perceived and expressed emotions depend on the current appraisal of the situation, and they take on the unique qualities derived from the interplay of self and culture. Individual reactions are affected by how external situations are addressed and labeled. Such labels are closely related to the causes attributed to physiological arousal or people's interpretation of what is going on with them and their environment. Specific labels for feelings are a result of feeling rules regarding the appropriateness of certain reactions. These rules dictate what people ought to feel. For example, a bride on her wedding day is obliged to feel happy. Culture provides labels for symptoms and actions determining the interpretations on which individuals will rely. Conscious awareness about how things work, including sensitivity and responsivity to situational and cultural cues for appropriate expression, are referred to as the cognitive component of emotion. This internal process (thoughts, images, and perceptions) is heavily influenced by past learning and experiences. Individuals selectively internalize values and meanings while cultures help define the conditions of appraisal. Cognitive processes operate between internal emotional states and expression. Effective evaluation and self-regulation necessitate a balance between inner thoughts and beliefs and outer expression.

An important component in the understanding of emotion focuses on the ways in which a person controls or regulates emotional expression. This includes verbal expression through words and language chosen to convey thoughts and feelings; body language, such as posture, tone of voice, and eye contact; and methods of demonstrating affection, such as hugging, kissing, and shaking hands. Also important are the diverse ways in which emotions such as anger and fear are expressed.

The process of evaluation is not always a conscious one. Emotional reactions are often quicker than a person's understanding and interpretation of them. Richard Lazarus (1984) states that some of one's emotional responses, such as simple likes, dislikes, and fears, do not require deliberate conscious evaluation. Often, a quick "gut reaction" is all that is required.

In addressing the connection between physiological reactions and cognitive appraisal, Stanley Schachter proposed a two-factor theory which states that one's understanding or interpretation of emotional experiences grows out of the awareness of the physical arousal of one's body. In other words, a specific emotion will be experienced depending on how the physiological arousal is labeled and interpreted. Culture determines the values, feelings, beliefs, and expression of meanings. Individuals learn this expression through the process of socialization.

Some aspects of emotional expression would appear to be universal. The expression of smiling, for example, is associated with positive emotions around the world. Blind children who have never seen a face will smile when happy and cry when distressed. Other aspects of emotion are more culturally specific. For example, when greeting someone in the United States, it is proper to shake hands or kiss; in Japan, people generally bow, and they seldom kiss in public. Otto Klineber, in 1938, noted that in Chinese literature people clapped their hands to express worry and disappointment, whereas in the West the clapping of hands signifies a positive response such as appreciation. In the United States, controlled, rational expression of emotion is considered desirable. Individuals are taught to moderate impulses, desires, and wishes.

Applications

Practical implications concerning emotional expressions are an important consideration in the changing national and international arena. As the world becomes more interdependent, an understanding of cultural variations in emotional interpretation and expression is important in helping people understand one another. Differences in expression may be associated with problems in intercultural communication. Relationships as well as professional situations are increasingly impacted by cultural diversity. The deep structure of a culture often determines a person's reactions to situations and to people. If racism and ethnocentrism are to decrease, it becomes necessary to understand the diverse ways in which people express their thoughts and feelings.

The rules of a specific culture will influence how emotions are developed and expressed. In some cultures, especially those that encourage individuality and the importance of a person's sense of self, emotional displays are often more intense and of longer duration. On the other hand, in some cultures where interdependence and the importance of the group is stressed over the individual, negative emotions, such as anger, are rarely expressed. Emotions such as concern, sympathy, respect, and shame, however, are more common in these cultures than in the United States. Interpretations of emotions will also coincide with a person's concept of self. Studies have shown that while all cultures appear to provide their members with some concept of self, there is considerable variation in the form and structure of this concept. A person's sense of self is not self-contained, but rather a product of social and cultural interactions and individual experiences.

Gestures and their meanings will also vary from culture to culture. For example, Tongans sit down in the presence of superiors, whereas in the United States, standing up is expected. The ways in which people use language will also vary culturally. In Arab cultures, language that emphasizes rhetorical devices such as repetition, metaphor, and simile are valued. The Japanese tradition emphasizes minimum expression. In the United States, people believe in the importance of discussing problems, though in Asia, the Buddhist tradition supports the belief that wisdom can be obtained only during silence. Culture-specific rules that are learned early in life will govern and manage emotional expression. The differences in expression and methods for controlling emotions vary from culture to culture as well.

Primary emotions, such as fear and anger, are generally said to be physiologically based and expressed in similar ways across cultures. Secondary emotions, such as pride, guilt, and shame, are developed through participation in the sociocultural environment and from individual experiences. The effects of culture are evident in the different ways people express some emotions. From a psychological point of view, emotions are considered healthy unless they take an extreme or inappropriate form. If the assumption is made that individuals are in conscious control of their emotions and actions, then these can be altered based on changing feedback from the environment. In the process of development, individuals learn the rules that govern appropriate expression. These display rules will not only vary from culture to culture but may vary in one culture over time.

Emotion is of central importance in the process of understanding human behavior. Culture has been defined as the most influential dimension in accounting for emotional differences.

Context

The study of emotions has a long history, beginning with the writings of Plato. Charles Darwin studied emotions through facial expressions. He found that some facial expressions seem to be universal in their expression of emotion. He therefore proposed that these emotions are biologically determined and inherited from generation to generation. Psychoanalytic approaches rely on the ideas of Sigmund Freud in their views on emotion. Freud gave considerable attention to emotions of shame and guilt that are reactions to a person's violation of what is considered acceptable. More recent psychoanalytic approaches view emotion as an attempt on the part of a person to integrate internal pressures with external demands.

William James and Carl Lange introduced the James-Lange theory of emotion in 1893. This theory states that the brain interprets a situation and then physiological responses, such as a palpitating heart, perspiration, and so forth, occur. From an awareness of these responses, feelings are interpreted. Walter B. Cannon was an American physiologist who believed that physiological reactions were not easily differentiated and labeled as specific emotions, such as love, fear, or anger, and that the process proposed by the James-Lange theory was too slow. Cannon, with another physiologist, Phillip Bard, suggested an alternative to the James-Lange theory. They proposed that the experience of emotion originates in the central nervous system. Cannon and Bard believed that peripheral responses occur independently of the central experience. The brain is aware of fear before the feedback from the autonomic nervous system reaches the brain.

The most widely accepted theory explaining emotion is the previously mentioned cognitive-physiological theory developed by Stanley Schachter. He believes emotion involves two states, a physiological arousal and the way the person interprets this. The theories described each focus on the complex relationship between physiological responses, cognitive awareness, and emotional experience.

There are two major areas of emphasis in the study of emotion. One focuses on biological universals: From a biological perspective, emotions are viewed as unlearned reactions that help assure survival. The other is a sociocultural perspective that focuses on meanings acquired through social and individual experiences. The interaction of cultural influences on emotions are addressed from this perspective. Culture will directly affect the shaping of emotions as a result of cultural norms of appropriate feelings and appropriate expression of those feelings.

Bibliography

Collins, W. Andrew, and S. A. Kuczaj II. *Developmental Psychology: Childhood and Adolescence.* New York: Macmillan, 1991. Discusses developmental psychology and addresses emotional experiences from a theoretical and practical perspective.

Izard, Carroll E. "Emotions in Personality and Culture." *Ethos* 11, no. 4 (1983): 305-312. Discusses contemporary research on emotions and socialization. Also addresses cultural differences in standards for emotional expression.

Kemper, Theodore D. "How Many Emotions Are There? Wedding the Social and the Autonomic Components." *American Journal of Sociology* 93, no. 2 (1987): 263-289. Discusses physiological similarities and cultural variations in emotion. Reviews primary and secondary emotions.

Markus, Hazel R., and Shinobu Kitayama. "Culture and the Self: Implications for Cognition, Emotion, and Motivation." *Psychological Review* 98, no. 2 (1991): 224-253. Focuses on cultural differences between people's sense of self and others, and how this impacts on personal experiences such as emotions. Addresses emotions as a product of social life.

Myers, David G. *Psychology.* 3d ed. New York: Worth, 1992. Good, readable introduction to psychology. The chapter on emotion is comprehensive and includes an emphasis on multiculturalism and the changing world situation.

Samovar, Larry A., and Richard E. Porter. *Communication Between Cultures.* Belmont, Calif.: Wadsworth, 1991. Summary of intercultural communication. Presents information on international cultures and co-cultures within the United States, and translates communication principles and concepts into practical situations.

Thompson, Jack George. *The Psychobiology of Emotions.* New York: Plenum Press, 1988. Reviews the topic of psychobiology, the relationships between mind and body during emotions, discussing physiological activity during emotional states. Also covers major materialistic, mentalistic, and interactionist models.

Jasmin T. McConatha

Cross-References

Development of Emotion, 810; Emotion: Definition and Assessment, 893; Functions of Emotion, 900; Emotion and Attribution Theory, 921; Emotion in Primates, 947; Emotional Expression, 954.

EMOTION: DEFINITION AND ASSESSMENT

Type of psychology: Emotion
Field of study: Motivation theory

Emotion is a basic aspect of human functioning. Emotions are personal experiences that arise from a complex interplay among physiological, cognitive, and situational variables. Theories and measurement of emotion allow psychologists to understand diverse expressions of behavior, and they form the cornerstone of many approaches to the treatment of psychological problems.

Principal terms

COGNITIVE APPRAISAL: a person's interpretation of a situation; cognitive appraisal influences what emotion the person experiences

EMOTIONAL INTENSITY: the strength with which a person experiences positive and negative emotions

PRIMARY EMOTIONS: basic, innate emotions

PSYCHOSOMATIC DISORDERS: physical disorders that are a result of chronic, negative emotions

SECONDARY EMOTIONS: emotions that derive from the combination of primary emotions

STATE EMOTION: the momentary experience of an emotion

TRAIT EMOTION: the frequency that a person experiences a given emotional state; a person that exhibits the trait of hostile emotion is one who frequently shows hostility

VISCERAL RESPONSES: internal, physiological responses such as heart rate and blood pressure

Overview

An emotion is a valenced experience that is felt with some degree of intensity, involves a person's interpretation of the immediate situation, and is accompanied by learned and unlearned physical responses. Emotions are transitory states, and they have five characteristics. First, emotions are experiences, not specific behaviors or thoughts. Although thoughts can sometimes lead to emotions, and behaviors can sometimes be caused by emotions, an emotion is a personal experience. Second, an emotional experience has "valence," meaning that the emotion has a positive or negative quality. Because emotions have valence, they often motivate people toward action. People tend to seek activities, situations, and people that enhance their experience of positive emotional states, and they tend to avoid situations that are connected with the experience of negative emotions.

Third, emotions involve cognitive appraisals. That is, one's interpretation of the immediate situation influences which emotion is experienced. For example, a child may experience either joy or fear when being chased, depending on whether the child interprets the chase as playful or dangerous. Fourth, emotions involve physical responses. Physical responses may be internal, such as changes in heart rate, blood pressure, or respiration (called visceral responses); physical responses can also be external, such as facial expressions. In addition, the bodily responses that characterize emotions are partly reflexive (unlearned) and partly learned. An increase in heart rate is a reflexive response that accompanies intense fear. That which a person fears, however, and his or her accompanying bodily response, may be the product of learning; crying when afraid is an emotional expression that is subject to learning experiences. Fifth, emotions can vary in intensity: Anger can become rage, amusement can become joy, and fear can be heightened to a state of terror.

Psychologist Robert Plutchik contends that there are eight innate, primary emotions: joy, anticipation, anger, disgust, sadness, surprise, fear, and acceptance. Like the colors of a color wheel, primary emotions can combine to produce secondary emotions. For example, surprise plus sadness can produce disappointment; anger plus disgust can produce contempt; and fear plus surprise can produce awe. Since each primary emotion can vary in intensity, and each level of intensity for one emotion can combine with some other level of intensity of another emotion, the total number of possible emotions runs to the hundreds. Although many psychologists agree that there exist primary emotions, there is no way that a person could distinguish such a large number of personal emotional experiences. Moreover, psychologists have not even attempted to measure such an unwieldy array of secondary emotions.

Nevertheless, psychologists have developed numerous assessment instruments to study common emotions. (An assessment instrument is simply a method used to measure something.) Since there are several different emotions, the study of emotion requires the development of specific methods that can accurately measure each of the common emotions. The most popular method of measuring an emotion is a self-report questionnaire in which a person answers questions relevant to a particular emotion. When measuring emotions, researchers make a distinction between "state" and "trait" emotion. An emotional state refers to what a person is experiencing at the moment. If one were interested in assessing how anxious someone currently is, one might use a questionnaire that asks the person to respond to several anxiety-related statements, using a scale from 1 ("not at all") to 5 ("very much"). Some examples of relevant statements are "I feel tense," "I feel nervous and shaky inside," "My heart is beating rapidly," and "I feel a sense of foreboding." The higher the total score on the questionnaire, the more anxiety the person is experiencing at the moment.

Trait emotion refers to how often an emotion is experienced. An "anxious person" is someone who frequently experiences the state of anxiety. Moreover, one would call someone a "hostile person" if one determined that he or she frequently exhibits states of anger. Examples of statements that assess trait anxiety are "I frequently become tense," "I often feel afraid for no apparent reason," "I am bothered by dizzy spells," and "I tend to worry a lot."

Psychologists have developed numerous questionnaires to assess emotions. There are self-report measures to assess anxiety, anger, guilt, happiness, and hopelessness, to name a few. In addition to measures of specific emotions, researchers have developed methods for assessing emotional intensity. Emotional intensity refers to the strength with which a person experiences both positive and negative emotions. It has been found that people who are emotionally intense report a feeling of well-being as "exuberance, animated joyfulness, and zestful enthusiasm." On the other hand, people who score low on a measure of emotional intensity experience a state of well-being as "serenity, contentment, tranquil calmness, and easygoing composure."

In addition to the use of self-report measures of emotion, psychologists often use physiological measures. Using sophisticated biological measuring instruments, psychologists are able to assess emotional arousal by measuring, for example, heart rate, skin sweating, respiration, blood pressure, and muscle tension. By examining the amount these measures change in response to a stimulus, researchers are able to infer emotional arousal. For example, it has been found that people who have the type of personality that puts them at risk for heart attacks show greater increases in blood pressure when trapped in a traffic jam, in comparison to those people who have personality characteristics that do not predispose them to heart attacks. In this instance, the psychologist uses the measure of blood pressure to infer a negative emotion, such as anger or frustration.

One question that arises when using physiological measures to assess emotions is whether each emotion has a specific pattern of physiological responses. For example, blood pressure appears to be particularly responsive to anger-inducing situations. People's heart rates, however, increase during emotional states of excitement, anxiety, anger, and sexual arousal. For this reason, researchers may use multiple measures of emotion, assessing self-reports of emotion while physiological responses are being recorded. Another way of assessing emotions is by direct observation of overt behavior. Approach behavior can indicate acceptance, and avoidance behavior can reflect fear or disgust. In addition, facial expressions have been used to assess various emotional states.

The experience of emotion involves psychological, physiological, and behavioral components. Different emotions are assessed using a variety of questionnaires, physiological indices, and observational methods. The study of emotion has far-reaching implications for the understanding of human functioning and has important applications in many fields of psychology.

Applications
When researchers developed means for measuring visceral responses and discovered that these responses are associated with emotions, it was not long before the question arose, "Is it possible to detect when someone is lying?" The use of a polygraph to detect lying is based on the assumption that people will feel anxious or guilty when asked a question that has personal, emotional significance to past deeds. The polygraph tester measures and compares physiological responses to both control questions and relevant questions to infer lying. For example, suppose someone is

suspected of murdering John Smith on May 16. The tester may ask the following control question: "Have you ever hurt someone?" Since everyone has hurt someone at one time or another, and probably feels guilty about it, some level of emotional response will be registered as changes in heart rate and respiration. The relevant question is "Did you kill John Smith on May sixteenth?" Supposedly, the innocent person will show a greater emotional response to the control question than the relevant question. The perpetrator of the crime should show a greater emotional response to the relevant question because of its extreme emotional significance.

The use of polygraph testing is surrounded by controversy. Although some liars can be detected, what if a perpetrator does not feel guilty about the crime—or does not believe that the polygraph can measure lying? These people will not show the expected response to the critical questions about the crime. In addition, research has shown that some innocent people will become so anxious when asked "relevant" questions that they are mistakenly viewed as guilty. The American Psychological Association has expressed grave concern over the validity of polygraph testing. The United States Congress has outlawed the use of pre-employment testing to predict who might, for example, steal inventory. Despite the reservations of the American Psychological Association, however, security agencies and defense industries are allowed to use polygraph testing.

The development of theories of emotion and of methods for measuring emotions has wide application in the field of clinical psychology. Many psychological disorders are defined by emotional problems. People with phobias exhibit excessive anxiety in situations that offer little or no possibility of harm. Strong fears of water, heights, insects, closed spaces, flying, and social situations are common examples of phobias. Theories of emotion provide a framework within which clinicians can understand the development of phobias. Measures of anxiety can be used to help diagnose those people who suffer from phobias.

Depression is another example of a psychological disorder that has a strong emotional component. Twenty percent of females and 10 percent of males will experience a major depression at some time in their lives. This complex disorder is manifested by distorted thinking (such as self-critical thinking), physical difficulties (such as fatigue), and an array of emotions. Some of the emotional symptoms of depression include sadness, anxiety, and guilt. Thus, when psychologists assess the emotional aspects of depression, they use questionnaires that include items that address several different emotions.

Not only does the study of emotion help psychologists to understand psychological disorders, but also methods of treatment have been developed based on the understanding of emotion. For example, psychological research has shown that emotional responses, such as anxiety, can be learned. Consequently, treatment strategies have been developed to help people "unlearn" their anxiety reactions. As a result, many people who suffer from simple phobias can be effectively treated in a short period of time. Theories of emotion that examine the relation between thinking and emotion have led to therapies to alleviate depression. Aaron Beck has shown that the sadness, anxiety, and guilt that accompany depression can be treated by helping people change their styles of thinking.

Another topic area within clinical psychology that has benefited by the increasing understanding of emotion is psychosomatic disorders. A psychosomatic disorder (also called a psychophysiological disorder) is an abnormal physical condition brought about by chronic negative emotions. Ulcers, hypertension, headaches, and arthritis are examples of conditions that can be brought about or worsened by negative emotions. The emotions that are most often implicated in the development of psychosomatic disorders are anger and anxiety. For example, researchers have discovered that prolonged anxiety induced by internal conflict can cause ulcers in susceptible people. In addition, researchers now have evidence that chronic hostility is a risk factor for the development of heart disease.

Social psychologists study the influence of social factors on behavior. Theories of emotion have been a focus of social psychologists because one's experience of emotion is in part determined by the immediate situation, and the immediate situation often includes the behavior of others. Indeed, Stanley Schachter, a social psychologist, is responsible for the development of a theory of emotion that underscores the importance of one's cognitive appraisal of the social context in determining what emotion one experiences. For example, when people experience physiological arousal, their own emotional experience will most likely be consistent with their interpretation of the social context. If they are with a happy person they will experience happiness; if they are in the presence of an angry person, they will experience anger. Theories of emotion have increased understanding of many social phenomena, such as aggression and interpersonal attraction.

Context

Emotions and their expression have been of interest to philosophers and theologists for more than two thousand years. In the fifth century B.C., the Greek physician Hippocrates classified people on the basis of emotional temperament. The view that people differ in temperament remains today. Arnold Buss and Robert Plomin have hypothesized that newborns differ in their susceptibility to distress, fear, and anger. Everyday descriptions of people as "happy-go-lucky," "stoic," and "volatile" represent the tendency to group people according to characteristic styles of emotional expression. Clinical psychologists speak of the "hysterical personality" as exhibiting excessive emotional lability and the "schizoid personality" as showing emotional indifference toward others. Thus, for centuries, philosophers and psychologists have recognized the importance of understanding personality differences based on the type and degree of emotional expression.

Theologians have traditionally approached emotion as representing the dark side of human nature. What elevates humans above other animals has been thought to be the capacity to overcome passion with reason. Even this seemingly archaic view of emotion has its counterpart in modern psychology. Psychoanalysts help people gain control of their feelings through understanding the unconscious roots of their emotions. Cognitive therapists attempt to alleviate emotional dysfunctions by teaching clients to "think more rationally."

The modern era of research on emotion can be traced to Charles Darwin's 1872 book, *The Expression of the Emotions in Man and Animals*. Darwin believed that emotional displays evolved as a means of communication and had adaptive significance for the survival of the species. Indeed, there is some scientific support for the assertion that emotional expressions are basic biological responses: Newborn infants show expressions of emotions that closely match the expressions of adults; all infants, including those born deaf and blind, exhibit similar facial expressions in similar situations; very young babies can tell the difference between different emotional expressions; and there is considerable similarity in the expression of emotions across diverse cultures.

In the last half of the twentieth century, psychologists have made important advances in formulating theories of emotions and devising assessment instruments to measure emotions. Scientists have arrived at the point where they recognize many of the fundamental aspects of emotion: the nervous system, thought, behavior, and the immediate situation. The challenge for the future is to map the intricate interplay among these variables and achieve a thorough understanding of this basic facet of human functioning.

Bibliography

Arnold, Madga B., ed. *The Nature of Emotion*. Harmondsworth, Middlesex, England: Penguin Books, 1968. Reprints a number of classic articles published before 1960. Valuable for gaining insight into the historical sweep of the topic of emotion. Some chapters are largely philosophical or theoretical, yet not too difficult to understand. Other chapters require some knowledge of physiology. This volume is not an introductory treatment of theories of emotion, and thus should be consulted only after gaining a knowledge base of the field.

Barlow, David H. *Anxiety and Its Disorders*. New York: Guilford Press, 1988. In the early part of the book, the author reviews basic aspects of emotion. The remainder is devoted to the emotion of anxiety, and how anxiety forms the basis of many clinical disorders. Some of the disorders addressed are panic disorder, obsessive-compulsive disorder, phobias, and post-traumatic stress disorder. A very comprehensive treatment of anxiety disorders. Barlow takes a strong research orientation and presents the material at a college level.

Bernstein, Douglas A., E. F. Roy, Thomas K. Srull, and D. C. Wickens. *Psychology*. 2d ed. New York: Houghton Mifflin, 1991. Chapter 12 presents an introduction to the topic of emotion. Covers a wide range of areas: definition of emotion, physiology of emotion, major theories, social aspects of emotion, and facial expressions. The authors do not assume that the reader has any background in psychology, and they write in a clear, concise manner, providing interesting examples and graphics. Indeed, most college textbooks that cover an introduction to psychology have a chapter on emotion.

Corcoran, Kevin J., and Joel Fischer. *Measures for Clinical Practice: A Sourcebook.* New York: Free Press, 1987. Reprints more than one hundred self-report assessment instruments. Among them are numerous measures of various emotions and psychological problems in which emotional dysfunction is prominent; there are instruments to measure anxiety, guilt, anger, hostility, depression, stress, and mood. An excellent source for learning how researchers measure emotions, and can be used should one want to conduct a study. Bear in mind, however, that this book does not include some of the most commonly used questionnaires for measuring emotions.

Laurence Grimm

Cross-References

Behavioral Assessment and Personality Rating Scales, 387; Clinical Depression, 521; Development of Emotion, 810; Emotion: Cognitive and Physiological Interaction, 881; Functions of Emotion, 900; Emotion and Attribution Theory, 921; Emotion and Learning Theory, 934; Emotional Expression, 954; Personality: Psychophysiological Measures, 1790; Phobias, 1816.

FUNCTIONS OF EMOTION

Type of psychology: Emotion
Field of study: Motivation theory

Scientists have explored the possibility that emotion has an adaptive purpose; that is, it may increase the ability of a species to survive. Various theorists have suggested that emotion may serve important functions in social communication, the warding off of aggression, the exercise of power and maintenance of status, and the direction of attention to important events.

Principal terms

ADAPTATION: the process of adjusting to certain relatively constant conditions in the environment; certain traits may allow the organism to fit the demands and opportunities presented by the environment better, and these tend to be preserved in the species

EMOTION: a state often associated with goal-directed behavior and often marked by peripheral physiological arousal, such as increased heart rate; expressive behaviors, such as facial expression; and subjective experience, such as feelings of pleasure or displeasure

ETHOLOGY: a branch of zoology that studies animals in their natural environments; it is often concerned with investigating the adaptive significance and innate basis of behaviors

EXPRESSION OF EMOTION: the use of any channels or means for communicating emotion, such as facial expression, voice, and body position

FUNCTION: something that serves a purpose, especially the purpose of enhancing the ability of the species to survive; an action that is part of or contributes to a larger action

MOTIVATION: processes that energize, maintain, and direct behavior; the potential for energizing behavior built into a behavioral regulation system

NATURAL SELECTION: the process by which those characteristics of a species that help it to survive or adapt to its environment tend to be passed along by members that live long enough to have offspring

Overview

Two primary meanings of the word "function" have concerned emotion theorists in search of the functions of emotion. The first and most important has concerned finding the possible purposes served by emotion or emotions, especially those functions that might enhance the ability of the organism to adapt to its environment and hence to survive. This notion of emotions as serving an adaptive function was first introduced and investigated by Charles Darwin, the great English naturalist of the nineteenth century. A second, more recent sense of the word "function" used by emotion theorists concerns the question of how emotion fits or works within the larger behavioral control system—that is, the function of emotion as a component of a behavioral regulation system.

In 1872, Darwin published *The Expression of the Emotions in Man and Animals.* In this work Darwin provided many examples of how the expressions of both animals and humans serve to signal their intentions. Darwin provides an example of a dog approaching another dog or human in a hostile or aggressive manner. The dog approaches stiffly, with its head held erect or slightly lowered, the hair on its back bristling, its eyes in a fixed stare, its ears flattened against its head, and its teeth bared in a snarl. Darwin argued that it is not difficult to infer the intentions of the animal—it is ready to attack; furthermore, he argued that this signals the hostile frame of mind of the animal. Darwin contended that some of these patterns of expression and the muscle movement patterns are habits that developed to serve a purpose through learning; however, most of the movements of expression are innate or inherited. Another of Darwin's examples illustrates this. A hungry baby does not need to learn how to cry and move its facial muscles in an expression of distress. Rather, the behavior has been inherited. The baby's expression of distress functions for the welfare of the baby by communicating to its mother its need for food.

This expression is an adaptive response that will make it more likely that the baby will get what it needs to survive. According to Darwin's notion of natural selection, infants or young that cannot get their own food but can signal their need state in this way would be more likely to receive adequate nutrition and would therefore be more likely to live long enough to pass this trait or behavioral disposition to their own offspring. In other words, infants who cried to communicate their distress from hunger would have a selective advantage over infants who did not or could not show this expression of their motivational state.

In spite of Darwin's great contribution to understanding the functions of motives, emotions, and expressive tendencies, the preceding arguments can be criticized on two counts. First, as with most arguments using natural selection and evolutionary theory, the reasoning proceeds backward from the fact to the occurrence. In other words, the argument proceeds in the following manner: Since many surviving and apparently prospering animals have the ability to cry in distress from what humans suppose to be a hungry state, this behavior must have been adaptive for the organism. It is difficult to do experiments to test the assumption of natural selection with higher organisms, because the time between generations is too long to detect much effect of pressures from the environment.

A second criticism concerns the quality of the inferences made about animals' motivational and emotional states. From the evidence that Darwin provided on the expression of motivation and emotion in humans and other animals, it has been argued that there is continuity between humans and other animals in the inheritance of certain expressions that signal similar internal states in both humans and animals. For example, although humans less often bare their teeth in anger than dogs, they often have a similar fixed stare as the dog cited in the previous example. The assumption is that the dog is also experiencing anger. This is an error called anthropomorphism, which is the act of attributing characteristics of humans to animals. Unlike humans, other animals cannot say what it is that they are feeling. Many researchers in emotion forgive Darwin for this error, since there is converging evidence to support the notion that there are similarities in the underlying states that correspond to similar expressions for at least some expressions.

If there is continuity between the species in the expression of internal motivated states, then, according to Darwin's theory, it would be expected that humans would likely show more similarities in expression of emotions with nearer relatives (for example, other primates, such as monkeys and chimpanzees) than with organisms that are not as closely related to humans, such as dogs. William Redikan in 1982 reviewed research on the evolution of human facial expressions or displays, discussing the possible functions of those displays. For example, he argues that a sadness display in the chimpanzee may be signaled by a low-intensity silent pout, while laughter may be signaled by what is termed the "play face" of the chimpanzee. The tense-mouth display is found in several species of primates, including humans, and is thought to signal anger or imminent attack. In it, the lips are compressed tightly together and the eyes are fixed and staring. In some species, the ears are flattened against the head. Parts of this display are similar to that of Darwin's example of the dog.

What is the function of these expressive displays? The tense-mouth display may function as protective movements prior to attack, especially one that might involve biting. The ears pressed against the head would serve to protect them from injury.

Nico Frijda has suggested that all expressive movements may have a functional explanation in terms of the organism's relationship to some aspect of its environment. For Frijda, emotions are tendencies toward specific modes of interaction with others, objects, and the environment. The expression of these tendencies is the embodiment of the emotion. For example, the hiding and crouching movements associated with fear serve to reduce the chances of being seen or hurt; the pattern of movement of the mouth in the display of disgust serves to eject distasteful substances from the mouth. According to Frijda, these expressive movements that embody the emotion are ways of contacting the environment.

In general, a primary function of the expression of emotion is to communicate to others the motivational-emotional state or situation of the organism. These can serve important social functions that enhance the survivability of individuals and members of the group. The ethologist Irenaus Eibl-Eibesfeldt has argued that several expressions may serve to diffuse possible aggression in potentially aggressive encounters for both humans and other animals. Smiles in humans and perhaps smilelike displays for some other primates may help control aggression. Also, facial displays that signal potential aggression or threat may serve to warn other individuals so they can adopt some strategy to avoid aggressive confrontation, thus preserving the individuals. As Robert Plutchik has noted, however, if the prediction process of an organism leads it to conclude that another individual is threatening, then the appropriate feeling may be anger, with an appropriate behavior being attack for the purpose of injuring or destroying the other individual. According to Plutchik, emotions function as bodily reactions to survival-related problems.

The sociologist Theodore Kemper has further argued that emotions are adaptive for group survival. He describes social structure as depending on power and status. For him, emotions result from outcomes of power and status relations. Religion, for example, can use emotions such as guilt and joy to maintain a particular pattern of power and status relations within the society and thus preserve the social order and the individuals that depend on it for survival.

Other emotion theorists have examined the function of emotion in terms of how emotion operates within systems for the regulation of behavior. For example, Klaus Scherer has noted that often emotion theorists view the function of emotion as a disruption of behavioral sequences that allows the organism to redirect its attention to some important or survival-related event in the environment. He further argues that emotions are adaptive motivating mechanisms and that mild emotional states can be present without disrupting ongoing behavior. In this view, emotions are a part of the behavioral regulation system, and they allow organisms to adapt more flexibly to their environments.

Applications

One of the many possible applications of the research on the functions of emotion is the possibility of improving the nonverbal communication of emotion in both clinical and nonclinical settings. Another is improving communication and understanding between humans and other animal species by better comprehending the motives and emotions of animals.

Plutchik has pointed out that while people often think they understand much about emotions at an implicit or intuitive level, there are gaps in this knowledge—concerning questions about the functions of emotions, for example. In fact, there is no formal instruction on the purposes behind emotional expression. Attention to this kind of knowledge could be useful in contributing to what Ross Buck has termed "emotional education." In addition, a better understanding of the adaptive functions of particular emotional displays could help clinicians, such as psychiatrists and clinical psychologists, to understand the meaning and purposes of expressions of emotion in their clients.

The evidence for continuity in the expressions of emotion in humans and other animals has definite implications for those who work with animals, such as animal trainers, police, pet owners, and researchers. Understanding the purposes behind particular motivated behaviors can be very important for success in attempts to train animals. Research on animal learning contains many examples of failures to train certain behaviors because the animals were motivated for some other purpose; sometimes these other motives are revealed in their expressions.

Much of the interest in examining the functions of emotion, especially the role of expressive behaviors, came directly from Darwin's own work on the expression of emotion in humans and animals. Darwin's careful research was seminal in developing many lines of research concerning the biological basis of expressive behaviors, especially facial expression. For example, considerable research has been done by Paul Ekman, Carroll Izard, and others that shows that the same facial expressions for a small set of primary emotions such as joy, sadness, anger, disgust, and fear can be found universally in the human species. These "core" facial expressions are essentially unlearned (innate) and can be elicited almost reflexively and automatically under the appropriate stimulus conditions. Since the facial expression for each of the primary emotions has a unique pattern of facial muscle activity that can be discriminated and perceived, this can provide the basis for communicating specific emotions. Furthermore, many theorists (such as Frijda) have argued that each emotion has a specific function that relates the organism to the environment in a particular way. According to Frijda, each emotion corresponds to a particular action-readiness tendency. In other words, the emotion prepares the organism to contact the environment in a specific, often adaptive, manner.

Darwin's notions of the natural selection of behaviors and the continuity of mental and behavioral processes among species have been instrumental in unifying constructs within a single theoretical framework. These should continue to be important to behavioral scientists in explaining the functions of emotion.

Context

The modern study of the functions of emotion began with the evolutionary theory of Charles Darwin. He argued that, just as some physical traits might be adaptive, some behaviors, behavioral patterns, or their dispositions might enhance the ability of organisms to live long enough to pass along the behaviors to their offspring. In other words, those behaviors that would enhance the ability of a species' members to survive would be preserved in their offspring through natural selection. On the other hand, behaviors that would reduce an individual's ability to survive would probably be selected against.

Darwin's evolutionary theory had important implications for areas of science other than biology, especially psychology. First of all, the theory emphasized the continuity among species. According to Darwin's view, the differences between humans and other animals are not so much differences of kind as differences of degree. This contradicted the teachings of the Judeo-Christian tradition, which argued that humans are a special part of creation and are to have dominion over the other animals or lesser creatures.

A second implication of the theory related to both the passing along of adaptive behaviors and the continuity of humans and other animals is the notion that mental abilities could develop through natural selection. Darwin argued that perhaps human intellectual abilities increased through natural selection. According to this view, other behaviors and psychological states and dispositions, such as motives and emotions, might change through natural selection and would be expected to show some similarities when closely related species were compared. In other words, as Lewis Petrinovich has noted, Darwin suggested a "mental continuity" among species.

This assumption of continuity had a profound influence on the development of behavioral science. In biology, the field of ethology came to rely heavily on Darwin's evolutionary theory to explain patterns of animal behavior, especially innately based behaviors, reviving the idea of instincts. In psychology, the assumption of continuity legitimized interest in animal behavior at the end of the nineteenth century. Moreover, early influential psychologists such as William James and other functionalists assumed that mental processes are useful to an organism in helping it adapt to its environment. Petrinovich has further argued that, in general, the James-Lange theory of emotion views the organism within its total situation or environment. William McDougall, also influenced by Darwinian theory, argued that instincts are associated with specific emotions. As Robert Franken has noted, McDougall thought the instinct of flight corresponded to the emotion of fear; repulsion to disgust; and curiosity to wonder. So, according to McDougall, an adaptive response such as fleeing from a threatening situation was associated with an emotional state.

Bibliography

Atkinson, Rita, Richard Atkinson, Edward Smith, and Daryl Bem. "Emotion." In *Introduction to Psychology*. 10th ed. San Diego: Harcourt Brace Jovanovich, 1990. This general psychology text provides a sophisticated and detailed treatment of various issues and phenomena in the study of emotion, including the function of particular displays in the aggressive behavior of animals.

Buck, Ross. *Human Motivation and Emotion*. 2d ed. New York: John Wiley & Sons, 1988. This is a comprehensive textbook on emotion that places emotion within a model including motivation and cognition, while thoroughly exploring biological aspects as well.

Darwin, Charles. "The Expression of the Emotions in Man and Animals." In *What Is an Emotion? Classic Readings in Philosophical Psychology*, edited by Cheshire Calhoun and Robert Solomon. New York: Oxford University Press, 1984. The authors include excerpts from the writings of some of the most important thinkers in the development of emotion theory, such as René Descartes, Charles Darwin, William James, Sigmund Freud, and Walter B. Cannon. Also included are introductory and summary comments about the passages.

Eibl-Eibesfeldt, Irenaus. "Strategies of Social Interaction." In *Emotion: Theory, Research, and Experience*, edited by Robert Plutchik and Henry Kellerman. Vol. 1. New York: Academic Press, 1980. The famous ethologist examines the function of expressions in the development of basic social strategies involved in sharing, giving, taking, friendly encounters, and so on.

Franken, Robert E. *Human Motivation*. 2d ed. Pacific Grove, Calif.: Brooks/Cole, 1988. This text on motivation offers a good historical introduction to the field of motivation, summarizing the major theories and influences.

Frijda, Nico. *The Emotions*. Cambridge, England: Cambridge University Press, 1986. Frijda discusses emotion in terms of expressive behaviors, physiology, experience, regulation, and so on in a detailed yet readable account. At the same time, he develops a model of motivation and emotion, emphasizing their function.

Kemper, Theodore D. "Power, Status, and Emotions: A Sociological Contribution to a Psychophysiological Domain." In *Approaches to Emotion*, edited by Klaus R. Scherer and Paul Ekman. Hillsdale, N.J.: Lawrence Erlbaum, 1984. Kemper takes a sociological approach to what is often thought to be a psychological domain. He argues that strong emotions often arise when there are changes in a group or in a group member's power and status as compared to the larger social surround.

Petrinovich, Lewis. "Darwin and the Representative Expression of Reality." In *Darwin and Facial Expression: A Century of Research in Review*, edited by Paul Ekman. New York: Academic Press, 1973. The author traces the far-reaching influence of Darwin's theory of evolution on the development of various psychological theories and approaches including animal psychology, structuralism, functionalism, learning theory, social psychology, and ethology.

Plutchik, Robert. "A General Psychoevolutionary Theory of Emotion." In *Emotion: Theory, Research, and Experience*, edited by Robert Plutchik and Henry Kellerman. Vol. 1. New York: Academic Press, 1980. Plutchik summarizes his theory of emotion, placing it within evolutionary theory and discussing various theoretical and methodological problems encountered in the study of emotion.

Redikan, William K. "An Evolutionary Perspective on Human Facial Displays." In *Emotions in the Human Face*, edited by Paul Ekman. 2d ed. Cambridge, England: Cambridge University Press, 1982. Redikan reviews the evidence for the functions of various emotional displays in humans and other animals.

Scherer, Klaus R. "On the Nature and Function of Emotion: A Component Process Approach." In *Approaches to Emotions*, edited by Klaus R. Scherer and Paul Ekman. Hillsdale, N.J.: Lawrence Erlbaum, 1984. Scherer proposes a theory of emotion that examines the function of emotion as a component in a behavioral regulation process.

D. Alan Bensley

Cross-References

Development of Emotion, 810; Emotion: Cultural Variations, 887; Emotion: Definition and Assessment, 893; Emotion: Mind-Body Processes, 907; Emotion and Health, 928; Emotion in Primates, 947; Emotional Expression, 954; Ethology, 992.

EMOTION: MIND-BODY PROCESSES

Type of psychology: Emotion
Fields of study: Cognitive processes; motivation theory

The mind-body processes of emotion include how people perceive, know about, and are affected by bodily aspects of emotion, such as facial expression, changes in heart rate, and other physiological changes. The way in which the relationship between mind and body in emotion is viewed has important implications for theories of emotion and clinical practice.

Principal terms

AUTONOMIC NERVOUS SYSTEM: a part of the nervous system that operates automatically to activate various bodily functions; one part of it, the sympathetic nervous system, prepares the body for emergencies

COGNITION: those mental activities or thought processes that are involved in the acquisition, storage, retrieval, and use of knowledge

EXPRESSION OF EMOTION: the use of any of a number of means for communicating emotion, such as facial expression, voice, and body position

LIMBIC SYSTEM: a group of structures located in the center of the brain that are involved in motivation and emotion

MIND-BODY PROBLEM: a psychological question originating from philosophy and religion that concerns how to understand the relationship between a physical body or brain and a nonphysical mind or subjective experience

PERIPHERAL PHYSIOLOGICAL CHANGES: changes relating to the functions of organs—such as the changes in heart rate, blood pressure, and skin temperature—that occur in aroused states and emotions

SOMATIC PERCEPTION: the awareness of bodily changes; often this refers to the degree of accuracy of an individual in perceiving the physiological changes that accompany emotion, especially those that are related to the autonomic nervous system

Overview

Understanding the relationship between the mind and body in emotion has been a central question in the development of psychological theories of emotion. Philosophers first addressed this mind-body question centuries ago, trying to explain the seemingly dual aspects of existence: the physical and the mental. People live their lives in physical bodies that are subject to physical effects—such as birth, growth, damage, and death—yet their thoughts and feelings extend beyond the confines of immediate physical reality.

The emotions, too, seem to exhibit these dual aspects. When people are afraid, they tend to show peripheral physiological changes, such as increases in heart rate, blood pressure, and perspiration. In addition to these somatic or bodily changes, other bodily expressive changes may occur in emotion. There may also be changes in facial expression, tone of voice, and movement or body position. An important purpose of these external signs of emotion is to communicate the emotional state. In addition to these somatic or physical aspects, there is a third important aspect of an emotion: the subjective experience of the emotion. For example, there may be an awareness that the heart is racing, that the mouth has dropped open, and that the eyes are wide open in fear. Moreover, there is usually an awareness of some stimulus event that initiated the fear in the first place, such as the sudden stopping of a car in the lane in which one is driving. This often involves a cognitive evaluation of the event; in other words, thought processes are used to decide the relevance of the stimulus to a person. For example, if a car stopped abruptly in front of one's car, one would probably decide that this situation was threatening, while if the car were a half of a mile ahead, one would probably not view this as immediately threatening.

These three aspects have been combined to form a definition of emotion. In 1988, Ross Buck defined emotion in terms of peripheral physiological response, expressive behavior, and subjective feeling. This definition encompasses both the physical aspects and the mental or subjective experiential aspects of emotion.

There is strong evidence that these peripheral physiological changes and other emotional responses are generally controlled in the brain. In particular, the limbic system, a ring of brain structures roughly in the middle of the brain, has been implicated. Damage to various areas in this region may result in aggressive behaviors, uncontrollable laughter, fear responses, or even a pronounced lack of emotion, depending on the area.

Other research has investigated whether specific emotions show specific peripheral physiological response patterns. For example, does an angry person show greater increases in heart rate and skin temperature than a happy person, a disgusted person, or a surprised person? Early research failed to reveal much evidence for the differentiation of emotion by specific peripheral response patterns, but in 1983, Paul Ekman, Robert Levenson, and Wallace Friesen were successful in demonstrating the foregoing pattern of response as well as other patterns. The differentiation of emotion remains a controversial issue.

Expressive changes, especially changes in facial expression, have also been shown to be different for specific emotions. By the early 1970's, evidence from research by Paul Ekman, Carroll Izard, and their colleagues began to suggest that specific patterns of facial muscles are activated in the expression of specific emotions. Moreover, people appear to use these same facial expressions to express the appropriate emotions across cultures, so the facial expression of primary emotions may be universal.

Much other research, often using subjective, self-reporting measures, has shown that people within the same culture have at least some agreement on the use of emotional terms and language. There is also some agreement in people's evaluations of situations in terms of the emotions that those situations would cause. Although there is much evidence suggesting that thought, evaluation of situations, verbal labeling of emotions, and other cognitions are part of the subjective experience of emotion, people show many individual differences in their subjective experiences.

The research that suggests that peripheral physiological response, expression, and subjective experience are parts of emotional experience does not explain, however, how mental and physical aspects of emotion are related. One approach to answering this question has been to find out to what extent people are aware of the physical aspects of their emotions. Research on somatic or bodily perception in emotion assesses whether people's awareness of their autonomic nervous system-related functioning during emotional arousal is accurate or not. In general, people are not very accurate in detecting the amount of change in their heart rate and other peripheral physiological changes that occur during an emotion. This does not mean that people do not know at some level that physical or bodily changes do occur during emotional experiences; rather, they are not accurate in their perception of these changes.

A related question is: What kinds of details do people remember from their emotional experiences? Do they remember more details related to bodily and expressive aspects of their experience or more details about their thoughts, evaluations, and other cognitive aspects of the experience? A study by Alan Bensley in 1990 has shown that people recall and report many more references to cognitive, evaluative aspects than to bodily and expressive aspects of angry and sad experiences. In fact, unless subjects were given cues about the bodily and expressive aspects, they recalled very few details about them, although they recalled much cognitive, evaluative material. This suggests that human awareness and/or knowledge of the cognitive, evaluative aspects and the somatic, expressive aspects may be at different levels.

Traditional theories of emotion have also had much to say about the relationship between peripheral physiological changes and cognitive and subjective experience in emotional states. An early theory of emotion proposed by William James in 1891, later called the James-Lange theory, has suggested that the awareness of an emotional state (subjective experience) depends on feedback from peripheral physiological changes. For example, according to this theory, an individual knows because his heart is racing that he is afraid of a bear that he sees.

Others, such as Walter Cannon in 1927, objected that peripheral physiological changes were too slow and diffuse or undifferentiated to account for the feeling or subjective experience of emotion. He argued that one first becomes aware of the emotion through more rapid central arousal (involving the brain) and that the function of these peripheral physiological changes is to help the person to adapt to his or her environment. For example, activation of the sympathetic nervous system would increase the heart rate and the blood flow to the muscles that would enable a person to run away from a bear.

Finally, cognitive theories have emphasized the importance of a cognitive evaluation of a stimulus event as being the first step in the elicitation of an emotion. A variation on this type of theory, the Schachter-Singer attribution theory of emotion, was proposed by Stanley Schachter and Jerome Singer in 1962. They argued that both peripheral physiological arousal (which they see as undifferentiated) and a cognitive evaluation that labels the arousal and attributes it to one emotion or another must be present for an emotion to be aroused.

At this point, the bulk of the research evidence does not support any one of these theories. In response to the challenges from Cannon's theory, some supporters of the James-Lange theory have argued that feedback from the face is specific enough to differentiate emotional experience, but this claim, too, has not always been supported by the results of research.

Applications

The way in which the relationship between mental and physical experience is viewed has implications not only for theories of emotion but also for applications in clinical and other settings. Three applications will illustrate the importance of the relationships between mental and bodily processes in emotion. The first involves the detection of deception versus true emotion by examining the facial expressions of patients or clients; the second involves the modification of emotional and mood states by manipulating mental and physical experience and contexts; and the third involves the use of peripheral physiological changes to detect lying with a polygraph.

First, it is generally important for clinicians to know what a client or patient is feeling. Sometimes, however, people seeking help from a psychotherapist, psychiatrist, or other helping professional will either deny that they are experiencing an emotion or will not be aware of that emotion. For example, a patient thinks that she must not reveal her true emotions and so disguises her actual feelings. In 1985, Paul Ekman presented an interesting example of this kind of deception. He described the case of a depressed patient who had been admitted to a hospital following her third, quite serious suicide attempt. Although therapy seemed to help her and her appearance seemed to brighten, she was actually hiding her true feelings. She was able to convince her doctors that she was well enough to leave the hospital, but shortly after she left the hospital she appeared to become depressed again. Ekman later discovered that she had been deceiving her doctors about her persisting depression. This was discovered when he analyzed the micromovements of her facial muscles as seen in videotaped interviews with her before she left the hospital. Although she was able to disguise her actual emotion (depression) most of the time, careful observation of her facial expression revealed that for a brief moment before she was able to pose a happy facial expression her face showed a depressed facial expression. The significance of this clinical example is that it provides evidence for two systems of facial expression operating in emotion, an involuntary one that may show true emotions and a voluntary one that may be susceptible to control by voluntary mental processes, and it reveals a glimpse of the potential of technologically sophisticated equipment and methods that may be used to detect deception in emotional presentation or to make patients aware of their emotions.

A second type of application is the modification of emotional and mood states by using the connections between the mind and body in emotion. Some methods use somatic and expressive components to modify emotion. For example, one method has subjects pose their facial muscles in a facial expression of a particular emotion; in so doing, they experience the emotion that goes with that facial expression. Other methods use cognitions—thoughts, beliefs, and evaluations of the subjects—to induce emotions. For example, a subject may be asked to recall and think about an event that made him or her feel very sad in order to induce sadness, or a subject may be asked to repeat negative, self-devaluative statements concerning his or her competence in order to induce depression. Other methods are hybrids that use both the mental and the physical approach, such as the method in which a person is asked to think about and reexperience somatic aspects of being depressed, such as feelings of tiredness, heaviness, and lack of energy. These approaches to inducing emotional states have been used both to study how psychological disorders of emotion, such as depression, develop and are maintained and to help individuals to regulate their emotions and moods when these feelings become problematic.

A third important application is the use of the polygraph for lie detection. The basic assumptions underlying the use of the polygraph are that a person who lies will show some negative emotion such as anxiety or guilt and that this emotion will be indicated by physiological changes. A polygraph measures multiple physiological changes, such as changes in heart rate, breathing, skin conductance or resistance (depending on amount of perspiration), and blood pressure. Usually, these changes are written, or graphed, with a pen recorder. These changes are interpreted as indicating lies when, for example, the subject's heart rate increases relative to a baseline rate after he or she is asked a possibly incriminating question. In general, the standard polygraph test has not been shown to be reliable in identifying lying. Ekman has suggested that the method might be improved if other methods for differentiating emotions by means of physiological response patterns were also improved.

Context

As Robert Lundin suggested in 1991, early Christian theology contributed much to the distinctions between mind and body. Primarily, the mind-body question was phrased in terms of a separation between the body, which was physical and a part of the world of nature, and the spirit or soul, which was a nonphysical entity with a very different essence from that of the body.

This position was not challenged seriously until the 1600's, when René Descartes and other philosophers offered different explanations of how the mind and body might be related. Descartes argued that the body and soul interact at the level of the pineal gland in the brain. He believed that the body, which was extended matter, was like a machine and that its activities, such as the heart beating and breathing, were automatic and reflexive. Although the soul, which manifests the desires, was unextended matter, it could still have a willful effect on the physical body through interaction with the body at the level of the pineal gland in the brain. Against Descartes' theory of the interaction of mind and body, Gottfried Leibniz argued that the activities of the mind and body are parallel and do not interact. Baruch Spinoza proposed that mind and body are only apparently different and are really two aspects of the same substance. Finally, some have argued that only mind or only body exists. The behaviorist John B. Watson, for example, denied the existence of mind.

It remained for psychologists to test these theories that specified how the mind and body are related, and this was an important part of the study of emotion. Some theories have emphasized the importance or priority of bodily or physical aspects of emotion, while others have emphasized the mental (subjective and cognitive) aspects. Two of these theories have suggested that the mental and physical aspects or components of emotion are connected or interact. The James-Lange theory gives priority to peripheral physiological changes and assumes that the experience of emotion depends on feedback from these sources. Cognitive theories of emotion, however, assume that a stimulus situation must be evaluated before an emotion can occur and that the physiological changes are part of the reaction that follows. The Schachter-Singer attribution theory suggests that both physiological arousal and a cognitive evaluation must be present for an emotion to be experienced. Cannon's theory takes a somewhat parallelist position, at least with respect to emotion, by asserting that peripheral physiological response is not necessary for the subjective experience of emotion, but rather is a part of the organism's adaptive reaction to a stimulus, often a part of its preparation to respond to an emergency situation.

Investigation of the relationships between mental and bodily processes of emotion has also had a major influence on the development of psychology. It has forced the collaboration of psychologists and the merging of theories across different subject areas. For example, clinical psychologists have developed cognitive theories of anxiety, depression, and other emotions. Cognitive psychologists have had to learn about physiological arousal, facial expression, and other emotion-related issues in order to understand the effects of emotion on memory and decision making.

This collaboration and thinking across subfields in psychology has revealed new relationships between mind and body in emotion and encourages the development of new technologies for detecting emotional states. Understanding the relationships between mind and body in emotion has had important implications for understanding what it means to be human. Humans should now be understood not only as "thinking" but also as "feeling" and "wanting" beings that exist by means of a biological system (the body).

Bibliography

Atkinson, Rita L., et al. "Emotion." In *Introduction to Psychology*, edited by Rita L. Atkinson and Richard C. Smith. 10th ed. San Diego: Harcourt Brace Jovanovich, 1990. This general psychology text provides a sophisticated and detailed treatment of various issues and phenomena in the study of emotion.

Bensley, D. Alan. *Cueing and Organization in the Autobiographical Memory of Emotional Incidents.* Ann Arbor, Mich.: University Microfilms, 1990. This dissertation reviews the literature on what kinds of information people remember and report from their emotional experiences and presents research on the effects of cues and mood-induction procedures on the memory of those incidents.

Buck, Ross. *Human Motivation and Emotion.* 2d ed. New York: John Wiley & Sons, 1988. This is a comprehensive textbook on emotion that places emotion within a model that also includes motivation and cognition.

Ekman, Paul. *Telling Lies: Clues to Deceit in the Marketplace, Politics, and Marriage.* New York: W. W. Norton, 1985. A highly readable treatment of some of Ekman's research on the expression and physiology of emotion that explains the practical significance of this research.

Frijda, Nico H. *The Emotions.* Cambridge, England: Cambridge University Press, 1986. Frijda discusses emotion in terms of expressive behaviors, physiology, experience, regulation, and other things in a detailed yet readable account. At the same time, he develops a model of motivation and emotion, emphasizing their function.

James, William. "William James on Emotion." In *Emotion: Bodily Change*, edited by Douglas K. Candland. Princeton, N.J.: Van Nostrand, 1962. This book provides a reprinting of some of the original statements by James defining emotion as well as several other seminal articles on bodily aspects of emotion.

Kalat, James W. *Biological Psychology.* 2d ed. Belmont, Calif.: Wadsworth, 1984. In this introductory textbook, Kalat reviews the biological basis of emotion-related issues such as pleasure centers in the brain, aggression, and drugs that mediate emotion.

Lundin, Robert William. *Theories and Systems of Psychology.* 4th ed. Lexington, Mass.: D. C. Heath, 1991. Lundin handles the mind-body problem in detail, showing both the philosophical origins and relevant psychological perspectives in this textbook on the intellectual history of psychology.

D. Alan Bensley

Cross-References

The Autonomic Nervous System, 362; Emotion: Cognitive and Physiological Interaction, 881; Emotion: Definition and Assessment, 893; Functions of Emotion, 900; Emotion and Attribution Theory, 921; Emotion and Stress, 941; Emotional Expression, 954; The Facial Feedback Theory of Emotion, 1019.

EMOTION: NEUROPHYSIOLOGY AND NEUROANATOMY

Type of psychology: Emotion
Field of study: Nervous system

Subjective feelings of emotion are accompanied by a number of physiological changes. Researchers have made great progress in discovering what physiological processes occur with emotion and what parts of the brain are responsible for these changes, leading to improvements in measuring emotion and treating emotional disorders.

Principal terms
AUTONOMIC NERVOUS SYSTEM: the division of the peripheral nervous system that controls the organs and glands of the body
BIOFEEDBACK: a method of providing information about the state of the body so that a person can learn to control physiological arousal
BRAIN STEM: the lowest part of the brain, just above the spinal cord; it alerts the rest of the brain to the presence of an emotionally important event
CEREBRAL CORTEX: the outside layer of the brain; it provides conscious awareness of emotion and regulation of limbic system activity
LIMBIC SYSTEM: the middle part of the brain, lying under the cerebral cortex and surrounding the brain stem; it produces the basic emotions, particularly those associated with motivational states
PHYSIOLOGICAL AROUSAL: the body's state of readiness for action; symptoms include increases in heart rate, blood pressure, and breathing rate
POLYGRAPH TEST: a test involving measurement of physiological arousal in order to determine the presence of emotion; also known as a lie detector test
PSYCHOSURGERY: brain surgery done to alter a person's behavior even though there may be no evidence of a physical disorder

Overview

Physiological changes accompany emotion. A pounding heart, sweaty palms, or stomach "butterflies" are familiar occurrences in emotional situations. Other bodily changes that accompany emotion are no less important. This physiological arousal is a sign of activity in the sympathetic nervous system, a subdivision of the part of the nervous system that controls the organs and glands, called the autonomic nervous system. The word "sympathetic" comes from the Greek words meaning "with emotion," and activity in the sympathetic nervous system is responsible for what Walter Cannon referred to in 1929 as the body's "fight-or-flight" response to emotional situations. During emotion-arousing situations, the blood is diverted away from other organs to the brain and muscles; the heart rate, blood pressure, and breathing rate are increased; and stored sugars and fats are released. The neurons of the sympathetic nervous system act on the organs of the body through the release of the neurotransmitter norepinephrine. The sympathetic neurons also cause the adrenal gland to release the hormone epinephrine (also known as adrenaline) into the bloodstream. These two substances cause most of the physiological changes that are associated with emotional arousal. Finally, in addition to the sympathetic nervous system activity, a number of other substances are released into the bloodstream that help prepare the body for action: substances that promote blood clotting, fight infection, and relieve pain in case of injury. Each emotion appears to be associated with a different pattern of autonomic arousal, although the differences are difficult to measure. In addition, people differ in their degree of arousal to emotional events; some respond greatly, while others show little responsivity.

While people have always been aware of the visceral changes that accompany emotion, it was only in the nineteenth century that it was learned that these changes are commanded by the brain. Incoming information flows from peripheral sensory receptors to the brain stem region at the base of the brain. One part of the brain stem region, the recticular activating system, acts as a filter, alerting the rest of the brain to the presence of potentially important stimuli in the environment. The primary neurotransmitter of the neurons that project from the recticular activating system to the rest of the brain is norepinephrine. Norepinephrine, however, is not the only neurotransmitter involved with emotional arousal; dopamine and serotonin from brain stem structures such as the locus coeruleus, substantia nigra, and the raphe nucleus all are known to contribute to emotional arousal.

The information then flows upward through a collection of brain areas encircling the brain stem and lying immediately under the cerebral cortex: the limbic system. While the brain stem arouses the organism, it is in the limbic system that emotions occur. The role of the limbic system in emotion was first described by the neuroanatomist James W. Papez in 1937. According to Papez, it is in the limbic system that sensory excitation receives its emotional flavor. The boundaries of this system are not clearly defined, but most researchers include the hypothalamus, septum, hippocampus, amygdala, anterior thalamus, parts of the surrounding cortex, and their interconnections as the major structures of the limbic system. Through the hypothalamus, the limbic system influences both the autonomic and the neuroendocrine changes associated with emotion. Damage to the various structures of the limbic system can lead to profound changes in a person's emotional and motivational state. While the exact nature of the emotional changes may depend upon which structures are damaged, in general, all the limbic system structures appear to contribute to all emotional states.

Finally, the cerebral cortex is also known to be important for emotion. The cortex is responsible for identifying the exact nature of emotion-arousing stimuli and for formulating the appropriate response. Several different parts of the cortex appear to contribute to emotion. The temporal lobes of the cortex, for example, are important for thought and emotion. In humans, tumors, epilepsy, and other abnormalities of the temporal lobe can result in severe emotional outbursts, violent behavior, uncontrollable laughter, ecstatic pleasure, or feelings of oneness with the universe. The disease rabies, for example, is caused by a virus that primarily attacks the temporal lobes. The frontal lobes of the cortex, especially the prefrontal cortex, have also been linked with emotion and temperament. The famous 1848 case of Phineas P. Gage illustrates the role of the frontal lobes. Gage, a foreman on a railroad gang, was injured when a gunpowder explosion shot a 1-meter rod up through his cheek and out the top of his head. Miraculously, Gage survived, but his left frontal lobe was severely damaged and his behavior was very much changed. The formerly responsible Gage became impulsive, uninhibited, and subject to extreme mood changes. He was no longer able to control the emotions welling up from the limbic system. Gage's case demonstrates that while emotions originate in the limbic system, the cortex is important for inhibiting and controlling these emotions. Researchers have suggested that the left and right sides of the brain may differ in their role in emotion. For example, the right side of the brain is primarily responsible for producing and interpreting facial expressions of emotion. In addition, the right hemisphere has been associated with negative emotions, while positive emotions have been associated with the left.

The important point to remember is that emotion is a product of brain activity. A person feels afraid or sad or elated because of neural events and processes that take place in the systems of the brain that regulate emotion. In general, the brain receives and interprets emotion-inducing information from the environment, controls automatic and voluntary responses, and monitors feedback from these actions. Thus, while physiological arousal is linked to the autonomic nervous system, this activity is triggered by actions of the brain.

Applications

Research into the physiology and anatomy of emotion has led to several practical applications of this knowledge. One application has involved the development of techniques for measuring the presence of emotion. The best-known method is the polygraph, or lie detector, test. In this test, several physiological measures are taken, such as heart rate, breathing rate, and the electrical conduction of the skin (which changes as a function of sweating). The polygraph test, then, is essentially a measure of sympathetic nervous system activity. The assumption of the lie detector test is that lying leads to emotional arousal, and that the resulting physiological arousal can be detected by the polygraph. The major problem with this is that there are many reasons that a person might be emotionally aroused by a question. Simply being accused of a crime, for example, can cause emotions to run high. Typically, a polygraph test will mistakenly identify about one-third of honest people as liars and about one-fourth of liars as honest. For these reasons, the results of lie detector tests have rarely been accepted by the courts, and in 1988, the U.S. Congress passed a law prohibiting most uses of polygraph tests by private employers.

One assumption in the use of the polygraph test is that individuals are not able to control their autonomic arousal in emotional situations. For a long time, psychologists did believe that it is impossible to exert voluntary control over autonomic nervous system processes. In the early 1960's, however, Neal Miller, Leo DiCara, and their colleagues reported that animals could learn to control their "involuntary" responses through instrumental conditioning. When rats were rewarded for increases or decreases in heart rate, for example, they soon learned to produce the rewarded response. Unfortunately, subsequent studies failed to replicate these findings. In the meantime, however, this animal research led to the development of biofeedback, a human application that does work.

In this procedure, people are given continuous information about the internal state which they are trying to learn to control. For example, a light might get brighter as the heart rate increases and dimmer as the heart rate decreases. By watching the light, one can learn to control the rate of one's heart or other "involuntary" behaviors. The biofeedback technique has been particularly useful in helping people deal with stress, because reducing physiological arousal serves to decrease emotional arousal as well. The effect of biofeedback, however, usually does not persist after the machine is disconnected. For this reason, most biofeedback programs aimed at alleviating stress achieve more long-lasting effects by training people to relax their voluntary, skeletal muscles.

More direct control over emotion has been obtained through surgery or drugs. The use of brain surgery for the treatment of emotional disorders, termed psychosurgery, has had a long and somewhat sordid history. Inspired by a report that removal of the frontal lobes successfully quieted an agitated chimpanzee, the Portuguese neurologist António Egas Moniz performed the first prefrontal lobotomy in 1936. Subsequently, some forty thousand people in the United States were subjected to frontal-lobe operations to alter behavior without evidence of physical disorders of the brain. Prefrontal lobotomies were so highly regarded as a way to treat mental disorders that Egas Moniz was awarded the Nobel Prize in Physiology or Medicine in 1949. By the end of the 1950's, however, the number of surgeries dwindled, and now they are only rarely performed in the United States.

One of the major reasons for the decline of psychosurgery was the development of drugs to treat emotional disorders. In 1952, the French surgeon Henri Laborit developed a drug, chlorpromazine, that successfully treated emotional disorders that had previously been treatable only with electroconvulsive shock therapy or psychosurgery. This antischizophrenic drug and other related compounds work by blocking the activity of the neurotransmitter dopamine. Thus, the effectiveness of these drugs indicated that schizophrenia may be related to a disturbance in dopamine activity in the brain. Soon after the discovery of the antischizophrenic drugs, a host of other therapeutic drugs were developed to treat emotional disorders. Most of them were found to work by acting on the neurotransmitter systems in the emotion circuits of the brain. Antidepressants, for example, increase emotional arousal by enhancing activity in the neural pathways that use norepinephrine. Antianxiety compounds act on gamma-aminobutyric acid (GABA) receptors located throughout the limbic system. Aggression has been treated with drugs that increase serotonin activity. The pharmacological treatment of emotional disorders is in its infancy, but it promises not only to lead to better therapies but also to provide insight into the possible causes of these disorders. Drugs such as alcohol and opium have been used for centuries by people to alter mood. Because of research on the neurophysiology and neuroanatomy of emotion, it is now known that most of the rewarding aspects of these drugs are caused by their action on the brain stem and limbic system structures responsible for emotion.

Context

In the late 1800's, the American psychologist William James created one of the first theories of emotion that attempted to relate the experience of emotion to physiological functioning. Drawing upon the ideas of the Danish psychologist Carl Lange, James proposed that emotion occurs when individuals perceive the internal physiological changes that occur in an emotion-arousing situation. By this account, it is the physiological arousal that is the emotion. An example of this principle is the feeling one experiences after a close call in one's car. Upon perceiving the danger, one takes immediate evasive action, but it is only several moments later that one feels weak-kneed and queasy. According to the James-Lange theory, it is as a result of these feelings that a person feels frightened by a near accident.

The physiologists Walter Cannon, Phillip Bard, and others argued against the James-Lange theory. In 1929, Cannon wrote that the perception of the emotion-arousing situation causes simultaneous feelings of emotion by the cortex as well as physiological arousal. He believed that the experience of emotion is separate from the physiological arousal. He argued against the James-Lange theory for several reasons. First, the James-Lange theory requires that each emotion be caused by a different pattern of physiological arousal. At the time, measurement techniques failed to indicate any difference between different emotional states. Since 1955, however, a number of physiological differences have been found between the different emotions. Therefore, it is theoretically possible that different emotions can be caused by the perception of the different physiological states. A second criticism of the James-Lange theory is that people who cannot perceive their state of autonomic arousal because of damage to the spinal cord still experience emotion. Yet George Hohmann has found that while people who are paralyzed report emotional feelings, the intensity of their emotions is diminished because of the lack of autonomic arousal.

In 1962, social psychologists Stanley Schachter and Jerome Singer proposed a theory that contains elements of both the James-Lange and the Cannon-Bard theories of emotion. They proposed that emotion is a result of both the body's physiological arousal and the brain's cognitive appraisal of the situation. They injected epinephrine into their subjects, which produced autonomic arousal but had no effect on emotion. When the drug-injected subjects were placed in an emotion-arousing situation, however, they reacted much more strongly than noninjected subjects. These results were obtained when the emotional situation was either a positive, happy situation or a negative, angry situation. Thus, the autonomic arousal and the specific situation were both necessary. The cognitive appraisal indicated the nature of the appropriate emotional state, and the autonomic arousal influenced its intensity.

There continues to be considerable interest in the study of human emotion, particularly in the relationship between emotional stress and physiological changes in the body. One approach by psychobiologists has been to emphasize the dynamic relationships among the processes of the brain, behavior, and the environment. Research into the neurophysiology and neuroanatomy of emotion has contributed much to the understanding of these interactions and of how they contribute to both normal and abnormal emotional functioning.

Bibliography

Andreasen, Nancy C. *The Broken Brain.* New York: Harper & Row, 1984. A wonderful discussion of the biological revolution in psychiatry, by an English professor turned psychiatrist. Written for the general public, it describes how emotional disorders can be linked to disorders of the brain. The focus is mainly on schizophrenia and depression.

Bloom, Floyd E., and Arlyne Lazerson. *Brain, Mind, and Behavior.* 2d ed. New York: W. H. Freeman, 1988. The chapter entitled "Emotions: The Highs and Lows of the Brain" has several wonderful diagrams of the brain structures involved in emotion. The first edition of this beautifully illustrated and readable text was written to accompany the excellent eight-part television series *The Brain* (1985), produced by WNET in New York and seen on the Public Broadcasting Service. That, and a later series, *The Mind* (1988), are highly recommended.

Kalat, James W. *Biological Psychology.* 3d ed. Belmont, Calif.: Wadsworth, 1988. The chapter entitled "Emotional Behavior" contains a readable discussion of both the neuroanatomy and neurophysiology of emotion and the biological theories of emotion. Also included is a discussion of the biological basis of aggression and anxiety disorders. A highly recommended textbook.

Valenstein, Elliot S. *Great and Desperate Cures: The Rise and Decline of Psychosurgery and Other Radical Treatments for Mental Illness.* New York: Basic Books, 1986. This book, along with other works by this experimental psychologist, including *Brain Control* (1973), chronicles the sometimes horrifying history of research and treatment of mental disorders. Although much has been learned about the physiological and anatomical bases of emotion, this book is a good example of the limitations of human understanding and of an all-too-common practice: seeking cures based on weak theories. A careful and well-documented book.

Valzelli, Luigi. *Psychobiology of Aggression and Violence.* New York: Raven Press, 1981. This thorough and scholarly work contains a good review of emotional behavior in general and aggressive behavior in particular. A good book to consult in order to understand the logic of trying to relate physiological processes and anatomical structures to behavioral functions. Most of the basic research on the role of the limbic system in emotion has been based on the aggression research reviewed in this book.

C. Robin Timmons

Cross-References

The Autonomic Nervous System, 362; Emotion: Cognitive and Physiological Interaction, 881; Emotion: Mind-Body Processes, 907; Emotion and Health, 928; Emotion and Stress, 941; Forebrain Structures, 1043; Neural and Hormonal Interaction, 1648; Stress: Physiological Responses, 2425; Stress and the Endocrine System, 2445; Stress and the Nervous System, 2452.

EMOTION AND ATTRIBUTION THEORY

Type of psychology: Social psychology
Field of study: Social perception and cognition

The relationship between emotion and attribution theory concerns physiological arousal and the individual's interpretation of that arousal as emotion. Work on this topic has provided insights into the nature of emotional experience and the role of emotions in a variety of types of social behavior.

Principal terms
ATTRIBUTION: a causal explanation for an event
EMOTION: a subjectively experienced strong feeling
MISATTRIBUTION: attributing an event to any factor other than the true cause
PHYSIOLOGICAL AROUSAL: an activation of the sympathetic nervous system that results in increased heart rate and blood pressure
PLACEBO: a substance or treatment (such as a pill or an injection) that has no intrinsic effect but is presented as having some effect
RESIDUAL EXCITATION: arousal from an event that remains after the individual is no longer aware that he or she is aroused

Overview

Attribution theory is not a theory in the formal sense, but rather a perspective that emphasizes the importance of the individual's causal explanations for behavior in various psychological phenomena. In 1962, psychologists Stanley Schachter and Jerome Singer used this perspective in what has become known as Schachter's theory of emotions. Schachter proposed that emotions consist of two factors. The first factor is general physiological arousal, which is assumed to be roughly equivalent regardless of the type of emotion. The greater the physiological arousal, the more intense the emotion that the individual experiences.

The second factor is a cognitive label for the arousal, which is based on the individual's inference concerning the source of the arousal. This inference, in turn, depends on cues in the individual's environment and learning experiences that have linked certain situations with particular emotions. Thus, if a person is aroused in the presence of a rattlesnake, the person is likely to attribute that arousal to fear of the snake; if a person is aroused in the presence of an attractive member of the appropriate gender, the person may attribute the arousal to love.

According to Schachter, both the arousal and the label are necessary for the individual to experience an emotion. In the first investigation of the theory, Schachter and Singer created physiological arousal in subjects and assessed whether their emotional experience would be determined by situational cues as to the appropriate label for the arousal. In this study, subjects were given an injection under the guise of a study of a vitamin's effect on vision.

Four groups of subjects were in the euphoria condition of the study. For one group of subjects, the injection was a saline solution that had no detectable effects (the placebo group). For three other groups, the injection was epinephrine (adrenaline), which creates physiological arousal involving an increase in systolic blood pressure and heart rate. Within three to five minutes after injection, these subjects would begin experiencing symptoms of arousal, such as a pounding heart and hand tremors. One group of aroused subjects was accurately told that the injection would cause these symptoms (epinephrine-informed). The second group was told they would experience symptoms other than the actual ones, such as numbness, itching, and a slight headache (epinephrine-misinformed). The third aroused group was told that they would not feel any effects of the injection (epinephrine-ignorant).

In this way, the researchers created a placebo group with no arousal; an informed group that would have an appropriate label for its symptoms of arousal; and two groups, the misinformed and the ignorant, that would have symptoms of arousal but no ready explanation for them. These latter two groups would therefore have unlabeled arousal that could be labeled subsequently as an emotion if the appropriate situational cues were present. To test this hypothesis, ostensibly while waiting for the vitamin to take effect, all four groups were exposed to a person who posed as another subject and behaved in a euphoric manner. For example, this confederate of the experimenter doodled, crumpled paper, attempted fancy basketball shots into a wastebasket, and joyously explained that he "felt like a kid again."

The theoretical prediction was that the groups with unlabeled arousal would use the confederate's behavior as a cue to their own feelings and therefore label their arousal as euphoria. Both observations of the subjects' behavior in the presence of the confederate and the subjects' subsequent ratings of their own mood supported the prediction that the unlabeled arousal groups would experience more euphoria than the informed and placebo groups. The researchers also found an analogous tendency for unlabeled arousal subjects to experience anger when the confederate was instructed to display anger rather than euphoria.

Schachter's work on emotions has been criticized on both conceptual and empirical grounds. Although the theory explains what happens once physiological arousal occurs, it offers no explanation for the onset of arousal in naturally occurring emotional experiences. While it may be true that the emotion is not felt until arousal is present, there must be some cognitive appraisal of a situation as one that warrants an emotional reaction for initial activation of the sympathetic nervous system to occur. For example, if one stumbles upon a rattlesnake, there must be some recognition of danger and that a fear response is appropriate for the initial arousal to be triggered. Thus, in most instances, an emotion label is probably available prior to experience of the arousal.

A second conceptual criticism is that all emotions do not involve the same pattern of physiological arousal (for example, fear and anger). If emotions consist simply of general arousal and a cognitive label, why are there different patterns of arousal associated with different emotions? Schachter's theory cannot answer this question and is therefore an incomplete account of emotion, at best. Schachter attempted to minimize this criticism, however, by arguing that people are poor at differentiating different patterns of physiological activation. Thus the individual's perception of arousal is posited to be the same across many emotional experiences regardless of any subtle differences in the physiological components of various emotions. Research has generally supported this notion.

Psychologist Stuart Valins took this reasoning a step further by proposing that the extent of perceived arousal, rather than the extent of actual arousal, determines emotional experience. In support of this view, Valins and his colleagues have shown that when subjects are given false biofeedback about their heart rate in the presence of potentially emotion-producing stimuli, the extent to which they experience emotion depends on this false heart rate information rather than on their actual level of arousal. In addition to limited ability to differentiate patterns of physiological activation, people also seem to lack accurate knowledge of their levels of psychological arousal.

On empirical grounds, the original study supporting the theory was criticized because the placebo groups seemed to experience emotion in the presence of the confederate even though they were not psychologically aroused by the injection. The evidence, however, seems to suggest that this occurred because the placebo subjects generated their own arousal, probably as a result of the extreme behavior of the confederates.

More recently, there have been a few failures to replicate the original findings, with researchers concluding that subjects generally experience unlabeled arousal as negative emotion. In rebuttal, Schachter pointed to a number of procedural factors that may have accounted for the discrepant results in the more recent studies. Despite these conceptual and empirical concerns, the basic tenets of Schachter's theory of emotions have gained strong support, particularly from studies showing that people can be led to misattribute emotion-related arousal to placebo pills.

The first of these studies of misattribution of arousal was reported by psychologist Richard Nisbett and Schachter in 1966. In that study, subjects were asked to take a series of electric shocks of steadily increasing intensity. For half of the subjects, the shocks were described by the experimenter as extremely painful (high fear); for the other half, the shocks were described as mild, although somewhat painful (low fear). Prior to the shock, half of each group of subjects were given a placebo pill that was purported to cause arousal. In the high-fear condition, it was expected that the source of the subjects' arousal would so clearly be the shock that there would be no misattribution to the pill. In contrast, in the low-fear condition, it was expected that subjects given the placebo pill would attribute their arousal to the pill; therefore these latter subjects were expected to find the shocks less unpleasant and actually be willing to tolerate more shock.

These expectations were confirmed, supporting the notion that, at least when the source of a person's arousal is not completely clear, arousal from one source can be misattributed to a plausible alternative source. Similar results have been found for a wide variety of emotions and situations. Thus research has clearly shown that the experience of emotion involves labeling of arousal based on an imperfect inference process influenced by situational cues rather than based on direct internal access to the causes of one's arousal.

Applications

Schachter's theory of emotions has led to two lines of research with particularly important implications. The first is the research on misattribution of arousal, which has demonstrated that bogus sources of arousal can be used to alter the individual's emotional experiences. The second line of research has been guided largely by Dolf Zillmann's excitation transfer theory, which specifies how arousal caused by an initial event can, a short time later, be misattributed to a second event and thereby can intensify the emotional reaction to that second event.

Overly intense emotions, such as excessive anxiety or anger, can contribute to a variety of physical and psychological problems. The notion that emotion-related arousal can be misattributed to a placebo suggests a way in which such maladaptive emotional reactions could be modified. Nisbett and psychologist Michael Storms applied this idea to insomnia. They reasoned that if insomniacs have trouble falling asleep because they experience anxiety at bedtime, misattribution of their arousal at bedtime to a placebo could reduce their anxiety and thereby help them fall asleep faster. To test this idea, the researchers asked insomniac subjects to report what time they went to bed and what time they actually fell asleep on two consecutive nights. Then, for the following two nights, the subjects were asked to take a placebo pill fifteen minutes before going to bed. Control subjects were told that the pill would have no detectable effects. Arousal subjects were told that the pill would cause symptoms of arousal such as rapid heart rate and alertness. Relaxation subjects were told that the pill would cause reduced heart rate and reduced alertness.

Arousal subjects were expected to be aroused as usual but to attribute that arousal to the pill rather than to anxiety; inferring less anxiety than usual, they should fall asleep very quickly. In contrast, relaxation subjects would be aroused as usual despite having taken a pill that was supposed to relax them and so should infer an especially high level of anxiety; thus these subjects were expected to have extra difficulty falling asleep. Strong support for these predictions was found. Similar emotion-reducing effects have been found for other placebo sources of arousal, such as loud noise or uncomfortable surroundings, and for other feelings, such as anger, social anxiety, fear, empathy, disgust, pain, and guilt.

These findings run counter to the commonly held belief that people will experience whatever effect a placebo is purported to cause. There is substantial evidence supporting such a direct suggestion effect of placebos, and yet the misattribution research demonstrates a reverse placebo effect. This anomaly has been resolved by recent research showing that the effect of a placebo depends on the type of person to whom it is given.

Misattribution of arousal depends on the person having an awareness that he or she is aroused, although no more so than is typical in the given context. The person can then be led to attribute that arousal to a placebo rather than to an emotion. Thus, reverse placebo effects occur in people with relatively accurate knowledge of their internal states. Alternatively, people who are not very aware of their internal states tend to exhibit a suggestion effect, experiencing whatever effect that a placebo is purported to have. These people believe they are aroused if they expect a placebo to be arousing, and they believe they are relaxed if they expect a placebo to be relaxing. To use placebos effectively, then, one needs to know the type of person one is trying to help; otherwise they may have effects opposite to those intended.

The above research demonstrates misattribution with the use of placebos, but does not explain how it might happen in everyday life. Zillmann's excitation transfer theory explains how misattribution can happen in the natural course of events and suggests that it may, in fact, happen quite often. Zillmann has found that physiological arousal decays slowly until the heart rate returns to an unaroused baseline level. People's awareness of arousal, however, dissipates more quickly than the arousal actually does. For example, after one minute of exercise on a stationary bike, people, on average, perceive that their heart rate is back to normal five minutes later, whereas their heart rate does not actually return to baseline until nine minutes after the exercise. Thus at the five-minute point, there is leftover arousal that Zillmann refers to as residual excitation.

Because the person is no longer aware that there is still arousal from the prior event, this residual excitation is unlabeled arousal that can subsequently be misattributed to a new event, and thereby intensify an emotional reaction to that second event. Zillman therefore hypothesized that the emotional reaction to a second event will be stronger five minutes after such exercise (when there is residual excitation) than it would be one minute after (when arousal is high but attributed to the exercise) or nine minutes after (when the arousal is gone).

Research by Zillmann and others has supported this hypothesis with many types of emotional reactions. When there is residual excitation, whether caused by exercise or emotion-evoking stimuli, people have been shown to be more angered and aggressive following frustration, more aroused and attracted by erotica, more moved by music and films, more amused by comics, and more disgusted by unpleasant images. Thus, when people are physiologically aroused from one event and exposed to a second emotion-evoking event, if the timing is right for excitation transfer, an inappropriately intense emotional reaction is likely to occur. Although excitation transfer theory has been useful in understanding many types of behavior, it has probably been most helpful in the study of aggression and the complex relationships among sexual arousal, hostility, and aggression.

Context
Schachter's theory of emotions originally developed out of psychologist Leon Festinger's 1954 theory of social comparison processes. Festinger argued that people have a need to evaluate the quality and appropriateness of their beliefs and behavior,

which often leads people to compare with others. In 1959, Schachter conducted studies of affiliation, showing that subjects anticipating electric shocks seek out others in the same situation, presumably because they want to assess the appropriateness of their own apprehensions. This led Schachter to consider the possibility that when people are aroused, they seek social cues to determine the causes of their arousal.

The theory was also influenced by the 1890 James-Lange theory of emotions, which posited that emotional experience results from an inference process. According to that theory, however, the individual infers the emotion based solely on his or her own bodily changes (encompassing both overt behavior and visceral feelings) rather than based on arousal and situational cues. Psychophysiologist Walter Cannon's well-known critique of this theory included the argument that the same visceral changes occur in very different emotional states and in nonemotional states as well. This argument led Schachter to posit that arousal is general, and external cues must determine the particular type of emotion experienced.

Schachter's theory of emotions has played a highly significant role in social psychology. Schachter's theory anticipated psychologist Daryl Bem's self-perception theory and a large body of evidence demonstrating that individuals infer specific internal states based on external cues rather than on introspective knowledge. In addition, the use of placebos and excitation transfer to create misattribution of arousal has become a standard strategy for assessing the roles of motivation and emotion in a wide variety of types of behavior, including helping, interpersonal attraction, aggression, attitude change, and self-esteem defense.

Bibliography

Schachter, Stanley. "The Interaction of Cognitive and Physiological Determinants of Emotional State." In *Advances in Experimental Social Psychology*, edited by Leonard Berkowitz. Vol. 1. New York: Academic Press, 1964. Reviews author's previous work on emotions and provides a detailed presentation of his theory of emotions and the research it had generated by 1964. Should be the starting point for any further investigation of emotion and attribution theory.

Storms, Michael D., and Kevin D. McCaul. "Attribution Processes and Emotional Exacerbation of Dysfunctional Behavior." In *New Directions in Attribution Research*, edited by John H. Harvey, William John Ickes, and Robert F. Kidd. Vol. 1. Hillsdale, N.J.: Lawrence Erlbaum, 1976. Summary of early research on the use of placebos to study misattribution of arousal. Chapter focuses on how misattribution may be applied to the understanding and treatment of dysfunctional behaviors such as insomnia.

Valins, Stuart, and Richard E. Nisbett. "Attribution Processes in the Development and Treatment of Emotional Disorders." In *Attribution: Perceiving the Causes of Behavior*, edited by Edward E. Jones et al. Morristown, N.J.: General Learning Press, 1972. This chapter concerns the role of causal attributions in both the development and the treatment of emotional disorders such as phobias. Also includes a review of research on the effects of both misattribution of arousal and false biofeedback of arousal. Clinical applications of the author's suggestions for treatment have not been particularly successful.

Zillmann, Dolf. *Connections Between Sex and Aggression.* Hillsdale, N.J.: Lawrence Erlbaum, 1984. Reviews considerable evidence concerning the relationship between sex and aggression, with a particular emphasis on sexual violence and pornography. Describes excitation transfer theory and relevant research, and discusses implications of this work for understanding the relationship between sex and aggression.

_____. *Hostility and Aggression.* Hillsdale, N.J.: Lawrence Erlbaum, 1979. Thorough examination of the role of negative emotions in aggressive behavior. Reviews a wide range of research on emotion and aggression, and presents the author's excitation transfer theory. Discusses theoretical and practical implications of the theory for understanding and controlling aggression.

_____. "Transfer of Excitation in Emotional Behavior." In *Social Psychophysiology: A Sourcebook*, edited by John T. Cacioppo and Richard E. Petty. New York: Guilford Press, 1983. Presentation of Zillmann's excitation transfer theory and the existing research relevant to the theory. Chapter is an excellent source for understanding Zillmann's theory and the research generated by the theory.

Jeff Greenberg

Cross-References

Aggression: Reduction and Control, 169; Attributional Biases, 338; Causal Attribution, 487; Emotion: Cognitive and Physiological Interaction, 881; Emotion: Mind-Body Processes, 907; Love, 1486; Self-Perception Theory, 2193; Violence and Sexuality in the Mass Media, 2603.

EMOTION AND HEALTH

Type of psychology: Emotion
Fields of study: Depression; endocrine system; nervous system

Health is a multidetermined state: It depends on biological, psychological, and social factors. Emotions are important for maintaining wellness and for recovering from illness; emotional states may contribute to the development of illness or be changed as a consequence of illness.

Principal terms

BIOPSYCHOSOCIAL MODEL: the model for health which stipulates that health is the interaction of biology, psychology, and social environment

EMOTIONAL EXPRESSION: the outward display of emotions

ENDOCRINE SYSTEM: a system of glands in the body which release hormones to facilitate organ functioning

FUNCTIONAL DISORDER: a symptomatology with no known physiological or neurological basis

NERVOUS SYSTEM: the system of cells, called neurons, which governs all behaviors and bodily functions

ORGANIC DISORDER: a symptomatology with a known physiological or neurological basis

PSYCHOIMMUNOLOGY: the field which studies the impact of thoughts and emotions on the functioning of the immune system

Overview

Health is best understood as a continuum from maximum wellness to maximum illness with a large area in between. Most people spend the majority of their lives somewhere between the two extremes. Emotions can influence how close to the two endpoints a person is at any point in time. In the past, the health care industry practiced under what was called the medical model, which was biologically based and focused on curing illness. It is now recognized that wellness is not merely the absence of illness but is a positive construct. As medical science has mastered many of the former killers, such as smallpox, tuberculosis, and pneumonia, it has become apparent that microscopic organisms are not the only threats to life. Heart attacks, cancer, and accidents each individually kill many more people than do infectious diseases in developed countries. Life-style contributes to approximately half of the deaths beyond infancy in the United States. Unrealistic beliefs, preferences, social norms, and values thus contribute to mortality and morbidity alongside such biological factors as genetics and infectious agents. Research has shown that many people think they are invincible, enjoy eating the wrong foods, and prefer watching television to exercising. The biopsychosocial model, which focuses on the interaction of biology, psychological factors (beliefs, emotions, and motives), and social factors (family, friends, culture), has, to some extent, replaced the medical model for understanding health.

Emotion is one of the major components in the biopsychosocial model. "Emotion" is a general term which can be used to refer to intense experiences such as joy, sadness, fear, or anger. It is also used to describe various feelings associated with blends of the primary emotions. Some theorists suggest that emotions are innate and universal; others suggest that they are culturally bound and based on cognitive interpretation of stimuli in the environment. Both interpretations have been supported in research. While the extent to which emotions are caused by nature (biology) or nurture (environment) or by the interaction of the two has not been clarified definitely, it is clear that emotions are associated with physiological changes.

Emotional reactions begin in the central nervous system, primarily in a group of subcortical areas called the limbic system. The hypothalamus is one of the most important structures in the limbic system for initiating emotional responses. The cortex of the brain, however, can override the subcortical areas and suppress the outward expression of the emotion. For example, when people believe that their boss is treating them unfairly and get angry, the cortex of the brain—the primary location for higher-level cognitive functions—tells them to temper the anger and not strike out at the unreasonable boss.

The central nervous system communicates with the peripheral nervous system and causes changes to occur there also. For example, one subdivision of the peripheral nervous system which is activated by emotional arousal is the autonomic nervous system, which is responsible for changes in heartbeat, blood pressure, respiration, and many similar bodily functions. The other division of the peripheral nervous system is called the somatic nervous system; it is responsible for skeletal muscle reactions, such as muscle tension, which may accompany emotions. These nervous systems bring about chemical changes in the body through the action of substances called neurotransmitters, which are released when the cells in the nervous systems are activated.

In addition to marked nervous system responses to emotion, there are also responses of the endocrine system to emotion. At the base of the hypothalamus, in the central nervous system, is the pituitary gland. The pituitary is considered the master gland because it controls the functioning of other glands. The hypothalamus communicates with the pituitary gland, and through it exerts an influence on the functioning of the entire endocrine system. These endocrine glands release chemicals called hormones which dissipate and travel to target sites throughout the body. Thus, emotional responses involve diffuse changes throughout the body. Within this context, it is easy to understand the relationship between emotion and health.

It is important to make the distinction between hypochondriasis and psychosomatic disorders. Someone who suffers from hypochondria is looking for physical symptoms on which to focus, but he or she (this affects women more than men) does not have any known biological or neurological basis for physical symptoms. A hypochondriac is suffering from a functional disorder, which is likely to have been triggered by an underlying emotional crisis. A hypochondriac is mentally, not physically, ill. On the other hand, emotions can cause or contribute to physiological changes which exhibit themselves as physical symptoms. These are organic disorders, and because the psychological state influences their development and prognosis, they are called psychosomatic disorders: "psycho" from the psychological component, and "somatic" from the body symptoms. In this case, the individual has a physical illness which is caused or made worse, at least in part, by emotional reactions.

Applications

An ulcer is one well-known example of a psychosomatic disorder. It was once believed that only middle-aged adults developed ulcers. It is now known that even a child can develop an ulcer. Peptic ulcers are open sores in the lining of the stomach or duodenum which occur when the enzyme pepsin actually digests a portion of the stomach or duodenal wall. Ulcers have been shown to be created by stress. Some research has implicated feelings of anger and anxiety in the face of stress as the trigger for the overproduction of gastric acids, which leads to the open wounds. In this example, the emotional response precedes the physical symptoms. This timing sequence is not the case with all forms of psychosomatic disorders.

Asthma is another common example of a psychosomatic disorder. In this case, the physical symptoms are likely to precede the emotional response. Asthma is a disorder which afflicts children even more than adults. The attack is most likely to have been initiated by exposure to something to which the individual is allergic or by a respiratory infection. Fear is the normal emotional response to the inability to breathe. Fear can contribute to further constriction of the respiratory tract, and it can also make attempts at breathing more rapid and shallower. Thus, fear makes recovery from the asthma attack more difficult. In some cases, anger, fear, and stress can trigger an asthma attack, even in the absence of a known allergen or infection. Whatever the cause, the physiological course of the disorder is the same, and keeping the sufferer as calm as possible is essential to alleviating the deadly symptoms.

Emotions have been shown to play a role in a wide variety of disorders which are not commonly thought of as psychosomatic (perhaps because people tend to confuse psychosomatic disorders with hypochondriasis). Heart attacks are recognized as being caused by diet, lack of exercise, and having a "Type A" personality. Type A personality really refers to a behavior pattern in which someone is always in a hurry, is overly competitive, and is angry or hostile in his dealings with others (in contrast to hypochondriasis, more men than women exhibit the Type A behavior syndrome). Research indicates that it is the emotional component, the anger and hostility, which is the best predictor of coronary disease. Type A people can be said to be highly reactive emotionally, especially highly reactive with negative emotions. Frequent episodes of this high arousal seem to produce an excessive amount of wear and tear on the cardiovascular system and thus leave the individual prone to heart disease.

Just as people were once surprised to hear that heart attacks may be psychosomatic, people are similarly surprised to learn of research which links cancer with emotions. In contrast to coronary disease's association with emotional reactivity, many studies have shown that the opposite is true for cancer: It appears to be an inability to express emotions that would make one prone to cancer. While accepting that cancer is a group of disorders, some of which seem to have a genetic basis and some an environmental basis, researchers have associated the inability to express emotions with an increase in incidence of cancerous growths and with rapid spread of cancerous tumors. It appears here that emotions and physiology interact to produce this health threat.

The field of psychoimmunology has helped to explain this correlation between emotional expressiveness and cancer. Cancers appear to be a disorder of the immune system. The stress exerted on the body when emotions are suppressed lowers the number of killer T cells circulating in the body. It is the job of the killer T cells to seek out and destroy foreign invaders, such as the cancerous tissue. It appears that when one suppresses emotions, one may be suppressing the immune system as well, and consequently suppressing one's ability to fight cancer and other disorders of the immune system.

Although heart disease-prone and cancer-prone personalities are related to emotional expression in opposite ways, both types of people would benefit from similar psychological interventions aimed at developing more appropriate ways to deal with emotions. The cancer-prone personality might benefit from assertiveness training, which highly encourages individuals to express themselves. The Type A individual needs to learn to react less when faced with adversity; the focus here is not to suppress emotions but to redefine the adversity and express one's feelings without the hostility. Emotional expression is not synonymous with confrontation, which implies some challenge being put forth. The hostility exhibited by the Type A individual results largely from focusing on what others are doing to the individual rather than on what he or she is feeling. What assertiveness training does for both cancer-prone and Type A personalities is to teach them to focus on what they are feeling and to share those feelings with others in a nonthreatening way. Appropriate expression of emotions is essential for good health.

Context

People have been interested in the relationship between emotions and health since ancient times. Anthropologists have found evidence suggesting that early cultures considered the mind and body to be one system, and evil spirits to cause the body to get sick. This mystical explanation of illness, however, did not sit well with the more scientifically minded. Hippocrates, an ancient Greek and the father of modern medicine, tried to amend the way of thinking about health to a focus on biology. He believed that the body was governed by four circulating "humors"—blood, black bile, yellow bile, and phlegm—and that illness was caused by an imbalance of the humors. In the Middle Ages, health and illness were understood in terms of religion, and evil spirits again predominated. With the Renaissance, the separation of mind and body (called mind-body dualism) again predominated, and it was once again believed that thoughts and emotions played no role in illness. The biomedical model for disease flourished. Thus, medicine until very recently has focused more on restoring balance in the biological system than it has on the psychological or social components of illness.

Social factors were first addressed seriously by modern medicine as a result of the impact of a very limited set of social factors, such as crowded living conditions, on the spread of germs. This attention led to the development of inoculations and better sanitation, which has led to the elimination of many previously feared infections as major causes of mortality and morbidity in the developed world. Psychosocial factors in health have been slower to gain widespread recognition.

When Sigmund Freud reported his case histories in the early twentieth century suggesting that repressed emotions can trigger physical symptoms, his work was met with mixed reactions. Gradually, however, it became accepted that thoughts and emotions can influence health. The focus was on functional, or, as Freud termed them, "hysterical" disorders rather than on the interaction between psychosocial and biological factors in producing organic disorders.

Only in the latter half of the twentieth century was there widespread recognition that social factors such as the quality of interpersonal interactions play important roles in both wellness and illness. The role of thought processes and emotions in health is still not understood nearly as well as the role of the biological mechanisms in disease, but progress is being made daily in understanding the linkage. As neuroscience and medicine advance, it will be easier to document the biological consequences of emotional responses.

Interest in the relationship between emotions and health has been more accepted as a legitimate subject for scientific inquiry as the field of health psychology has developed. Health psychology is a relatively new subdivision of psychology. It has roots in both social and clinical psychology and subscribes to the interactive biopsychosocial model for health rather than the unidimensional biomedical model for disease. Practitioners now take a "systems" approach to understanding health. The systems approach does not separate mind and body, and takes what is sometimes referred to as a holistic (meaning "whole") approach to health care. As the relationship between emotion and health is elucidated through scientific study in the future, it is likely that interventions aimed at emotional reactions will become a larger part of the field of medicine.

Bibliography

Cousins, Norman. *Anatomy of an Illness.* New York: W. W. Norton, 1979. This popular book was written for the layperson and discusses the role of cognitions and emotions in illness. Emphasis is on the protective properties of having a sense of humor, a positive outlook, and a strong will to live.

Friedman, Meyer, and Diane Ulmer. *Treating Type A Behavior.* New York: Fawcett

Crest, 1984. The thesis is that emotional overreactivity is not innate, but is learned and can be changed. The authors describe successful interventions to alter Type A behavior.

Hughes, Jennifer. *Cancer and Emotion.* New York: John Wiley & Sons, 1987. A sensitive account of the relationship between cancer and emotions. Addresses the predisposing factors, responses to the diagnosis, and the terminal phases. Concludes with patients' accounts of their experiences with breast cancer.

Lazarus, Richard S. "The Trivialization of Distress." In *Psychology and Health,* edited by Barbara L. Hammonds and C. James Scheirer. Washington, D.C.: American Psychological Association, 1984. Addresses a much-neglected area of emotional responses to illness. Focuses on how, by telling patients that the distress they feel when something bad happens to them is inappropriate, doctors undermine its legitimacy and indirectly tell them it is wrong to be upset at losing one of life's most precious possessions, health—or even life itself. Trivialization is neither realistic nor in the best interest of the patient.

McNaughton, Neil. *Biology and Emotion.* New York: Cambridge University Press, 1989. Part of the Problems in the Behavioral Sciences series, this book provides an excellent, comprehensive overview of the physiological components of emotions. Covers early theorists such as Charles Darwin, Walter B. Cannon, and William James through the more modern discoveries of neuroscientists.

Barbara A. Bremer

Cross-References

Emotion: Cognitive and Physiological Interaction, 881; Functions of Emotion, 900; Emotion: Mind-Body Processes, 907; Emotion: Neurophysiology and Neuroanatomy, 914; Emotion and Stress, 941; Emotional Expression, 954; Health Psychology, 1139; Effects of Stress, 2417; Stress-Related Diseases, 2464; Type A Behavior Pattern, 2597.

EMOTION AND LEARNING THEORY

Type of psychology: Emotion
Fields of study: Cognitive learning; instrumental conditioning; Pavlovian
 conditioning

*Emotions are a fundamental aspect of human functioning; everyone is born with
the capacity to experience emotions. All emotions are reactions to events, and it is
assumed by learning theorists that emotional responses are often learned through
experience. A learning theory approach to emotion attempts to specify the conditions under which events come to elicit emotions.*

Principal terms

CLASSICAL CONDITIONING (PAVLOVIAN CONDITIONING): a process of
 learning whereby a neutral stimulus is paired with an unconditioned
 stimulus; after enough pairings, the neutral stimulus (conditioned
 stimulus) comes to elicit a conditioned response similar to the
 unconditioned response

CONDITIONED RESPONSE: a learned response elicited by a conditioned
 stimulus

CONDITIONED STIMULUS: a stimulus that has gained the ability to elicit a
 response because of its association with an unconditioned stimulus

EXTINCTION: the weakening of a conditioned response as a result of
 repeated presentation of the conditioned stimulus in the absence of
 the unconditioned stimulus

OPERANT CONDITIONING: the modification of a response because of its
 history of reinforcement (consequences)

POSITIVE REINFORCER: a consequence that increases the likelihood of a
 response

STIMULUS GENERALIZATION: in classical conditioning, the process
 whereby a stimulus that is similar to the conditioned stimulus used
 during training will also elicit a conditioned response

UNCONDITIONED RESPONSE: an unlearned response elicited by an
 unconditioned stimulus

UNCONDITIONED STIMULUS: a stimulus that elicits an unconditioned
 response; the relationships between unconditioned stimuli and
 unconditioned responses are unlearned

VICARIOUS CONDITIONING: the acquisition of a response through
 observation

Overview

Learning involves any relatively permanent change that results from experience.
Learning theories are used to account for the acquisition, maintenance, and weaken-

ing of emotional responses. These theories focus on emotional responses as they occur in a context. In other words, learning theorists study the acquisition of emotions as reactions to various stimuli. Psychologists have identified three specific types of learning that explain how people develop emotional reactions: classical conditioning, vicarious conditioning, and operant conditioning.

Classical (Pavlovian) conditioning involves learning by association—the association or pairing of two stimulus events. This model accounts for how the emotion-producing properties of one stimulus can cause a second stimulus to elicit the same emotion. An electric shock is a stimulus that produces the emotion of fear. One does not need to learn a fear response to electric shock; the response is an unlearned reflex reaction. Because no learning is involved, the electric shock is called an unconditioned stimulus, and the fear response is called an unconditioned response. A tone, on the other hand, does not cause a fear response, so a tone is a neutral stimulus with respect to fear. Through the learning process of classical conditioning, however, the tone can be made to elicit a fear response. Repeatedly pairing (associating) the tone with the shock by sounding the tone immediately before the shock is delivered will cause the tone to take on the fear-producing properties of the electric shock. Consequently, the tone becomes a conditioned stimulus and can, by itself, elicit fear. Learning has now taken place, and the fear produced by the tone is referred to as a conditioned response.

An interesting phenomenon, known as stimulus generalization, occurs during classical conditioning. Using the above example, psychologists have observed that a person will also respond with fear to tones that have pitches similar to the pitch of the tone used during conditioning. In other words, the fear response has "generalized" to other stimuli that bear a resemblance to the original conditioned stimulus.

Classical conditioning describes not only the conditions under which emotional responses are acquired but also the way in which conditioned stimuli lose the ability to elicit emotions. If the conditioned stimulus is presented repeatedly without further pairings with the unconditioned stimulus, the conditioned emotional response will gradually disappear. This process is called extinction. For example, if the tone is presented numerous times without being associated with electric shock, the tone will eventually lose its fear-producing properties.

Classical conditioning is used to account for the development of emotions other than fear. For example, one can become disgusted by the smell of food that has previously been associated with nausea. Most of the research on the classical conditioning of emotional responses involves negative emotions; however, psychologists believe that other emotions, such as joy, excitement, and sexual arousal, can be learned through classical conditioning.

If humans could learn to associate emotions with stimuli only by direct experience, the survival rate of the species would be much less than it is. For example, if a person had to be hit by a car to learn not to step into the street before looking, had to be attacked by wild animals to learn to avoid dangerous animals, or had to be beaten and robbed to learn not to walk alone at night in crime-ridden neighborhoods, his or her chances of survival would be greatly diminished. Fortunately, humans (as well as other species) are capable of learning through indirect experience. Vicarious conditioning is the process whereby emotional responses are learned through observation or instruction. A child who observes a parent's fear of dogs will be likely to learn the same emotional response to dogs. Many people report being afraid of or repulsed by snakes, even though they have not had any direct experience with snakes. Snakes are portrayed on television and in books as dangerous and repulsive. Positive emotions can also be learned vicariously. A culture that defines beauty as "blonde hair and blue eyes" will portray this physical type in a positive manner. Thus, without necessarily having any direct positive experiences with someone having these physical attributes, a positive emotional response can be conditioned to these physical characteristics.

A third learning theory that addresses the development of emotional responses is called operant conditioning. Operant conditioning emphasizes the role of the consequences of responses in shaping and maintaining behavior. Positive consequences, called positive reinforcers, strengthen and maintain responses. Negative consequences, called punishers, suppress responding. Suppose a child shows fear and runs to a parent when a stranger enters the room. If the parent comforts the child and takes him or her into another room, the child's fear is being positively reinforced by the attention and affection provided by the parent. Consequently, the child's fear of strangers is strengthened. In addition, a child who is punished for exhibiting joy and laughter when a playmate is hurt is less likely to experience that emotion in the future when witnessing the misfortune of others.

Operant conditioning as a model for the development of emotional responses is controversial. First, note that in classical and vicarious conditioning, one can clearly show that a stimulus can begin as neutral and become a conditioned stimulus for eliciting emotional responses. An emotional response has developed in reaction to the stimulus. In operant conditioning, the emotional response is already present, and a social consequence of the emotional display is assumed to either strengthen or suppress the response. Thus, this is a model that focuses more on the maintenance rather than the development or acquisition of emotional responses. Second, an emotion involves more than the observable expression of the emotion. There is an internal, physiological component to emotions. In operant conditioning, what is reinforced is the outward display of the emotion. It is unclear whether the physiological aspect of an emotion is modifiable by positive or negative consequences.

Applications

The learning approach to emotions has considerable generality and has application to many fields of psychology. Social psychologists study how people influence one another, especially in groups. Since human behavior is strongly affected by emotions, social psychologists are interested in how social contexts influence emotions. For example, classical and vicarious conditioning models are used by learning theorists to account for the development of prejudice.

Classical conditioning would be used to explain why a person who has had a bad experience with someone of a particular ethnic group shows a generalized negative emotional reaction to all members of the group (stimulus generalization). Since prejudices are more commonly formed in the absence of direct negative experiences with members of an ethnic group, however, vicarious conditioning is a model with greater applicability to understanding prejudice. Children can develop the negative emotions associated with prejudicial attitudes by exposure to the racist attitudes of parents and friends. Moreover, literature and television frequently depict certain ethnic groups in a stereotypic, negative manner. Since vicarious conditioning is a model that accounts for the development of positive emotions as well as negative emotions, learning theorists would predict that stories and films that portray an ethnic group in a positive light could weaken negative emotions (extinction) and perhaps condition positive emotions toward that group.

Clinical psychology studies the development and treatment of behavioral disorders. Behavioral disorders are frequently accompanied by undesirable emotional responses. Phobias are often found to be rooted in traumatic experiences. The person who will not ride in a car after a serious accident, the child who will not go outside because he or she has been stung by a bee, and the person who avoids speaking in front of a group because of an embarrassing incident during a previous public speaking engagement are all examples of anxiety responses and behavioral avoidance that result from classical conditioning.

Post-traumatic stress disorder (PTSD) is an excellent example of the consequences of classical conditioning. One of the symptoms of PTSD is the re-experience of a traumatic event. The Vietnam War veteran who hears firecrackers and a helicopter overhead during a Fourth of July celebration may relive an emotionally charged experience from the war. This is an example of the stimulus generalization of a classically conditioned emotional response. That is, his reaction is to auditory stimuli that are similar to stimuli that once were associated with extreme trauma.

Learning theories can not only help psychologists understand the development of clinical disorders but also suggest treatment techniques. Recall that learning theories address both the development and the weakening of emotional responses. If emotional responses can be learned, then they can be unlearned. Here unlearning does not mean forgetting, but rather it means that the emotional reaction to a stimulus will be weakened or deconditioned. For example, the vicarious conditioning model has been used to help children overcome fears. Consider a child who is afraid of dogs. By having the fearful child observe another child calmly playing with a dog, the fearful child learns that all dogs need not be feared. Another treatment approach combines operant and classical conditioning. Here the child would be positively reinforced with praise for approaching a friendly dog (operant conditioning). As the child spends time with the dog, nothing bad happens, and the child's fear weakens (extinction).

Another approach to eliminating anxiety is by associating a feared stimulus with a response opposite to anxiety. This procedure is called counterconditioning (it is also called systematic desensitization). Suppose a student experiences strong anxiety when taking class examinations. The therapist and student would construct a list of situations arranged in order of increasingly anxiety-provoking situations. At the bottom of the list might be "studying for the exam one day before the test." At the top of the list might be "having the exam handed to me by the teacher." The intervening items on the list would represent events approaching the time of the exam (reviewing notes the morning of the exam, walking to class, waiting for the exam to begin, and so on). The student would first be taught how to achieve a deep state of relaxation. Using counter-conditioning, the student would be asked to imagine the least anxiety-provoking item on the list while in a state of relaxation. Over sessions, increasingly difficult situations are presented from the list while the student remains in a state of relaxation. The student is thus experiencing, in an imaginal way, the feared situation while relaxed instead of anxious. This procedure has been shown to reduce anxiety to tests, even though the feared situation is only imagined. The treatment is even more effective when the student is taught to use the relaxation method during the examination.

Learning theories of emotion can be used to understand social psychological phenomena as well as the etiology of many psychological disorders, and they have led to the development of treatment techniques for emotional problems.

Context

The philosophical roots of conditioning run deep, extending back two thousand years. Aristotle, in the fourth century B.C., formulated his "Laws of Association" in which sensory experiences give rise to ideas. These ideas give rise to other ideas according to the law of contiguity. For example, a child associates seeing and feeling a table with hearing the word "table." Later, hearing the spoken word "table" causes the child to imagine seeing and feeling a table. As a theory of human behavior, Aristotle's notions were simplistic; however, all modern learning theories, in one way or another, make use of the concept of "association."

The modern impetus for the study of emotion began with Charles Darwin's book *The Expression of the Emotions in Man and Animals*, published in 1872. By the beginning of the twentieth century, most philosophers of human behavior, such as William James and William McDougall, emphasized the importance of heredity and instincts in explaining emotional behavior. During this period, Ivan Pavlov, a Russian physiologist, was conducting systematic research on what became known as classical conditioning (also called Pavlovian conditioning). In the United States, John B. Watson argued vehemently (and convincingly) against the prevailing notion that much of human behavior, including emotions, is instinctual. His view, known as behaviorism, is reflected in his oft-quoted statement, "Give me a dozen healthy infants, well formed, and my own specified world to bring them up in and I'll guarantee to take any one at random and train him to become any type of specialist I might select." Borrowing from Pavlov's work with animals, Watson performed many classical conditioning experiments with infants, many involving the classical conditioning of fear responses. There is no debate today about whether emotional responses can be learned. What is at issue, however, is how learning occurs. For example, cognitive psychologists reject the behavioristic view that conditioning occurs without awareness. Most modern learning theorists reject Watson's narrow view of all emotions being the product of classical conditioning, as well as the philosophical position that it is possible to mold "anyone into anything."

Many psychologists who acknowledge the importance of classical conditioning in the development of emotions, especially fear reactions, question whether all fears can be conditioned with equal ease. For example, why is it that so many people fear snakes, yet so few people fear electrical outlets? Surely the number of people who have experienced an electric shock when plugging in a lamp is greater than those who have been bitten by a snake. Some psychologists have postulated that humans, as well as other species, are "physiologically prepared" to react negatively to certain things. Perhaps a biological readiness to learned negative emotions to poisons, fires, neights, snakes, animals, and insects has survival value. Since these stimuli were indeed dangerous to humankind's prehistoric ancestors, those individuals who quickly developed fear responses to them were most likely to survive and reproduce. This is not to say that a fear of insects, for example, is instinctual. Rather, people are "built" in such a way that the laws of conditioning must take into consideration biological predispositions in the acquisition of emotional responses. This notion of physiological preparedness in learning can be traced directly to Darwin's theory of evolution: Those individuals most adapted to the environment are favored to survive.

The learning approach to emotions has a long history, and it has been influenced by the biological writings of Darwin, the philosophical approach of Watson, and the experimental work of Pavlov. Although no single theory can account for the full range of emotional expression, learning theorists have provided convincing demonstrations of the importance of experience in the development of emotion, and their work has led to many successful treatment techniques for the amelioration of emotional problems.

Bibliography

Barlow, David H. *Anxiety and Its Disorders.* New York: Guilford Press, 1988. In the early part of the book, the author reviews basic aspects of emotion. His theorizing relies heavily on the work of learning theorists, particularly with respect to the development of negative emotions. The latter chapters explain the development of anxiety disorders from the perspective of learning theories. Written at an advanced level; may be difficult for the reader who has not mastered basic concepts of learning theories.

Bernstein, D. A., E. F. Roy, T. K. Srull, and D. C. Wickens. *Psychology.* 2d ed. New York: Houghton Mifflin, 1991. Chapter 7 provides basic coverage of classical, vicarious, and operant conditioning. Chapter 12 discusses the topic of emotion and makes reference to the role of learning in the development of emotional behavior. Most college textbooks that provide an introduction to psychology have chapters on learning theories and emotion; introductory psychology texts are a good source for learning basic concepts.

Hergenhahn, B. R. *An Introduction to Theories of Learning.* 3d ed. Englewood Cliffs, N.J.: Prentice-Hall, 1988. Provides an easily understood overview of the major learning theories of the twentieth century. No prior knowledge of psychology is assumed. The chapter on Pavlov's work is an excellent summary of his theoretical position and experimental work. This book does not emphasize learning theories of emotion, but to understand learning theories of emotion it is helpful to gain knowledge of learning theories.

Staats, A. W. *Social Behaviorism.* Homewood, Ill.: Dorsey Press, 1975. The author proposes a behavioristic theory to explain a broad range of behavioral phenomena, including social behavior, language, abnormal behavior, attitudes, and personality development. Chapter 4 offers Staats's behavioral theory of emotion, which relies heavily on Pavlov's work as well as other learning theorists. Written at an intermediate level and should be consulted after one has studied the rudiments of learning theory. This source would be a good follow-up to the Hergenhahn text cited above.

Watson, John B. *Behaviorism.* Chicago: University of Chicago Press, 1959. This is a reprint of the book that "initiated a revolution in its attempt to make psychology an objective science." Watson provides a very readable account of the early work in the conditioning of emotional responses in infants (chapters 7 and 8). Unlike most psychology books written in the 1920's, this gem can be easily understood by the beginning student.

Laurence Grimm
Julie Nelson

Cross-References

Development of Emotion, 810; Emotion: Definition and Assessment, 893; Functions of Emotion, 900; Emotion and Attribution Theory, 921; Learning Defined, 1443; Radical Behaviorism: B. F. Skinner, 2045; Social Learning: Albert Bandura, 2304.

EMOTION AND STRESS

Type of psychology: Stress
Fields of study: Coping; critical issues in stress; depression

Studies of emotion in stressful situations have demonstrated the importance of physiological responses as both a source of information and a product of the emotion. The ability to predict and control the stressor is more critical than the physical nature of the stimuli.

Principal terms

AUTONOMIC NERVOUS SYSTEM: a peripheral division of the nervous system that controls involuntary responses of glands, visceral organs, and smooth muscles

CLASSICAL CONDITIONING: the process of learning the relationships between environmental stimuli that are associated; also called Pavlovian conditioning

HORMONE: a naturally occurring chemical released into the bloodstream by an endocrine gland to promote some general response in other organ systems

INTROSPECTION: the self-report of internal feelings and thoughts

PARASYMPATHETIC NERVOUS SYSTEM: a division of the autonomic nervous system that controls energy restoration processes

SYMPATHETIC NERVOUS SYSTEM: a division of the autonomic nervous system that prepares the organism for energy expenditure

Overview

Emotions flavor all human experiences, both positive and negative, but they seem most poignant during times of adversity and turmoil—the conditions of stress. When Hans Selye defined the modern concept of stress in 1956, one of his central points was that all types of injury, illness, and other forms of trauma share a common foundation. Despite the differences in individual symptoms, all types of trauma have the ability to trigger similar physiological defenses and similar emotional responses. The study of emotions has aided in the understanding of the effects of stress.

Emotions have presented psychologists with a difficult problem: How can one objectively study the personal and introspective feelings of another individual? One way to sidestep the problem of introspection is to recognize that not all aspects of emotions are private events. Many psychologists have distinguished between the emotional experience (a private event) and the emotional expression (a more or less public event). The expression of emotion can be directly studied by measuring either external expressions (such as aggressive behavior, interpersonal contact, facial expressions, and postural changes) or internal expressions (such as heart rate, blood pressure, brain activity, and hormonal changes).

Another way to study emotions objectively is to manipulate the environment in which the emotions occur. Humans come equipped to experience and express a wide range of emotions, but only a handful of these (perhaps the response to certain facial expressions) appear to be innate. The vast majority of one's emotional responses is acquired through the laws of learning, especially through classical conditioning. Stimuli that are associated with pain come to elicit fear; those associated with comfort come to elicit attraction; those associated with thwarting of goals come to elicit anger.

The cornerstone for understanding the emotional responses to stress was set in place by physiologist Walter B. Cannon. During the 1920's, Cannon (and later, Phillip Bard) studied the physiological responses to stressful events, with particular emphasis on the hormones released by the adrenal gland. Adrenaline and other hormones produce a chorus of bodily changes: Heart rate and blood pressure increase, blood is redistributed from the viscera and skin to the muscles, blood sugar increases, the skin of the palms becomes moist and supple, breathing becomes deeper and more rapid; all prepare the organism for flight or fight. According to the Cannon-Bard theory, these physiological changes are strictly in the service of the emotion.

Psychologists William James and Carl Lange had already proposed a more complicated role for these physiological changes. According to the James-Lange theory, the environmental situation elicits the physiological changes first. Then these physiological changes are monitored and interpreted to determine the emotional feeling. (Opponents of this theory suggested, wryly, that one might be scared as a result of fleeing from a bear or be angry as a result of having hit someone.) Cannon presented formal arguments against this theory, proposing that the physiological responses occurred too slowly to be a cause of emotion and that they were too nonspecific to allow a discrimination between fear and physical exercise.

The James-Lange theory fell into disrepute for several decades, but over the years, the results of numerous experiments began to provide support for this theory. Finally, in the early 1960's, Stanley Schachter and Jerome Singer resurrected this theory as a part of a new formulation for emotion. According to the Schachter-Singer theory, there are two requirements for the development of an emotional response: physiological arousal and cognitive appraisal. They demonstrated that adrenaline administration alone produced the expected physiological changes, but the subjects did report emotional feelings. (Cannon had used this same observation in his early arguments against James.) Similarly, mild environmental situations did not result in emotional responses. In one of their experiments, a confederate pretending to be a subject displayed anger over the conditions of the experiment. Normal subjects noted this response but did not feel angry themselves. By contrast, subjects who had unknowingly received adrenaline beforehand fell into line and became angry along with the confederate. In the words of Schachter and Singer, the adrenaline injections had produced a physiological change in search of a cognition.

The idea that bodily responses play a role in the formation of emotional feelings has also received support from other sources. Feedback from the muscles of the face can contribute to emotional feelings that are appropriate to the expression. In a more general sense, muscle tension can contribute to feelings of anxiety, while relaxation of these muscles is therapeutic in relieving anxiety. It would appear then that James was correct in his assertion that bodily responses contribute to emotional feelings. The James-Lange theory and its more recent extensions propose that an emotional feeling is based upon a melding of information from the external environment, the internal environment, and the behavioral history of the individual.

Applications

The study of emotion has gone hand in hand with the development of better treatment procedures for human patients. Several separate lines of research have reached parallel conclusions about the importance of the behavioral history of the subject.

In the 1940's, French surgeon Henri Laborit sought to reduce the number of deaths that followed surgery. Despite modern surgical procedures, many patients died without obvious cause. Laborit recognized that the patient's fear of dying was an important factor. He tried many drugs to combat this stress, but drugs that blocked these responses also tended to block the beneficial effects of the body's responses.

Laborit wanted to combat stress at its origin—the fear of surgery. He was looking for a drug that would dissolve these fears—in his words, a "Pavlovian deconditioner." He finally developed the compound, chlorpromazine, that had exactly the effect that he was seeking. It reduced presurgical fears and dramatically increased survival.

Meanwhile, psychologist Curt Richter made a discovery while designing a test to determine the vigor of the albino laboratory rat relative to its wild, ancestral stock. Laboratory rats swam several hours in a water tank before exhaustion, but to Richter's surprise, wild rats swam for only a few minutes before sinking. He reasoned that wild rats found the situation to be more stressful than did the more docile laboratory rats.

According to Cannon's view of emotion, these wild rats should have been releasing large amounts of adrenaline as a result of sympathetic nervous system activity. Richter, however, linked their disability to excessive activity of the parasympathetic nervous system. He recalled other instances of "sudden death." In one case, a rabbit, confronted by a ferret, fell motionless and died. In another, Richter had clipped the whiskers of rats to prevent food spillage and, mysteriously, several of the rats died.

Richter hypothesized that the sudden-death phenomenon was not the result of the flight-or-fight response but was rather the product of hopeless fear. Laboratory rats without whiskers also failed the swimming test, presumably because the lack of this important sensory information rendered the situation more perilous. Drugs that blocked parasympathetic activity restored the swimming. Chlorpromazine, a drug that blocks fear, also blocked the sudden-death phenomenon. Furthermore, if Richter "rescued" the wild rats a few times, they began to swim vigorously, showing two to three times more endurance than the laboratory rats. Richter concluded that hopelessness was an important contributor to sudden death and suggested that this phenomenon might be involved in voodoo deaths, in increasing the success of suicide attempts, and in various forms of "unexplained" deaths in perilous situations.

In the 1960's, Richard Solomon and Robert A. Rescorla found that Pavlovian conditioning with electric shock retarded the later ability to learn an instrumental response. They suggested that during the Pavlovian conditioning, in which the subject had no control over the presentation of the shock, the subjects had learned that their behavior was ineffective. They called this learned helplessness.

Other investigators soon expanded these findings into related areas. Martin E. P. Seligman developed a comprehensive account of learned helplessness as a contributor to depression. Jay Weiss improved the methodology of these experiments, developing the triad design. In this design, three groups are compared: a group that is able to predict and control the occurrence of an aversive stimulus; a group that receives exactly the same presentations of the aversive stimulus, but with no ability to predict or control; and a group that receives no treatment. The rats that could not predict or control aversive events developed ulcers, whereas the group that had this ability remained healthy and did not differ from the untreated subjects. These results point to a remarkable conclusion: Aversive events are not inherently damaging. The potential for harm lies in the inability to control their duration once they do.

Julian B. Rotter developed a similar concept in the 1960's termed the "locus of control." Individuals vary in the degree to which they see themselves as being in control of their environment (internal control) or as being controlled by chance events or by others (external control). Albert Bandura showed that these perceptions had far-reaching consequences in terms of motivation to achieve, feelings of self-efficacy, and various social interactions. Individuals who ascribe control to external forces tend to have low self-esteem and low motivation to achieve.

An important question remained: Do individuals suffer from the symptoms of depression because of exposure to unfavorable environments, or because they have misjudged the locus of control in a normal environment? Lauren Alloy, while working in Solomon's laboratory, provided an intriguing insight. She administered a survey to measure depression in college students, then compared those students with high depression scores to those students with low scores. The students participated in a computer game that had varying degrees of actual control, then were asked to estimate how much control they had. Surprisingly, depressed subjects showed nearly perfect estimates. Even more surprising was the fact that the nondepressed subjects tended to exaggerate the degree of control. It would appear, then, that the normal condition is to overestimate one's abilities to interact with the environment.

Context

The study of emotion and stress represents one of the success stories of psychology. Early approaches to these areas presented emotions as private events that could only be accessed through introspection. The concept of stress hardly existed, and aversive events were viewed simply in terms of their direct physical effects on the individual. The late twentieth century view of these concepts presents a much more dynamic and interactive view.

The role of the physiological responses to aversive stimuli began with Cannon, who showed that the body responded in a consistent and adaptive manner to these stimuli. James saw the relationship between emotions and physiology as a two-way street. He viewed the body's physiological response not only as a means of preparing to deal with adversity but also as a source of information. This insight that the human body represents an important part of the environment is a thread that has continued to run through various theories of behavior. Emotions and other behaviors are determined through an assessment of information from the external world, the internal world, and past experience.

Hans Selye's concept of stress provides another crucial insight into the way humans respond to adversity. Certainly, many others before Selye had observed the deleterious effects of disease, injury, and hostile environments. Selye's contribution was to see that widely different types of events have important elements in common. The marriage of this concept with the more sophisticated views of emotion set the stage for numerous applications.

The application of this information has revolved around the concepts of prediction and control. With these concepts, it has been determined that stress cannot be determined simply by knowing how noisy, how hot, or how intense the aversive stimuli might be. On the contrary, the level of stress seems almost entirely determined by the ability to predict or control these stimuli.

The therapeutic potential of this knowledge can hardly be overestimated. Some of the most common clinical disorders—ulcers, depression, pain disorders, immune disorders—can be viewed as errors in the prediction and control of aversive stimuli. Patients suffering from all these disorders have benefited from the manipulation of their perceptions of prediction and control in their day-to-day interactions with the environment.

Bibliography

Cannon, Walter B. *The Wisdom of the Body.* New York: Raven, 1932. This is a classic presentation of the body's physiological adjustments to stress and other situations by one of the most important physiologists of the century. Although parts are technical, the book is worth perusing for its historical interest.

Feuerstein, Michael, Elise E. Labbe, and Andrezej R. Kuczmiercsyk. *Health Psychology: A Psychobiological Perspective.* New York: Plenum Press, 1986. This textbook provides a thorough background and discussion of the effects of stress on health, and it includes discussion of stress management techniques.

Girdano, D. A., and G. S. Everly, Jr. *Controlling Stress and Tension: A Holistic Approach.* 2d ed. Englewood Cliffs, N.J.: Prentice-Hall, 1986. This book provides theoretical background along with many self-tests and practical guides to stress management. It is an excellent source for readers who are looking for applications.

Schachter, Stanley. *Emotion, Obesity, and Crime.* New York: Academic Press, 1971. This book provides an excellent account of Schachter's extension of the James-Lange theory of emotion. It includes the results of numerous experiments in support of his arguments.

Seligman, Martin E. P. *Helplessness: On Depression, Development, and Death.* San Francisco: W. H. Freeman, 1975. A readable and convincing argument for the importance of prediction and control in stressful environments.

Selye, Hans. *The Stress of Life.* New York: McGraw-Hill, 1956. This classic introduction to the concept of stress remains as relevant today as when it was first written. Selye's book represents one of the most important contributions to the area.

Leonard W. Hamilton

Cross-References

Depression: Theoretical Explanations, 789; Emotion: Cognitive and Physiological Interaction, 881; Emotion: Mind-Body Processes, 907; Emotion and Health, 928; Health Psychology, 1139; The Concept of Stress, 2411; Theories of Stress, 2432; Stress and the Endocrine System, 2445; Stress-Related Diseases, 2464; Stressors, 2471.

SURVEY
OF
SOCIAL
SCIENCE

ALPHABETICAL LIST

Ability Testing: Individual and Group, 1

Ability Tests, Bias in, 7

Ability Tests: Design and Construction, 13

Ability Tests: Reliability, Validity, and Standardization, 21

Ability Tests: Uses and Misuses, 27

Abnormality: Behavioral Models, 33

Abnormality: Biomedical Models, 39

Abnormality: Cognitive Models, 46

Abnormality: Family Models, 53

Abnormality: Humanistic-Existential Models, 60

Abnormality: Legal Models, 67

Abnormality: Psychodynamic Models, 74

Abnormality: Sociocultural Models, 82

Abnormality Defined, 89

Achievement Motivation, 96

Addictive Personality and Behaviors, 102

Adlerian Psychotherapy, 110

Adolescence: Cognitive Skills, 118

Adolescence: Cross-Cultural Patterns, 124

Adolescence: Sexuality, 130

Adrenal Gland, The, 136

Affiliation and Friendship, 142

Affiliation Motive, The, 148

Ageism, 156

Aggression: Definitions and Theoretical Explanations, 162

Aggression: Reduction and Control, 169

Aggression Motive, The, 174

Aging: Cognitive Changes, 180

Aging: Institutional Care, 186

Aging: Physical Changes, 192

Aging, Theories of, 198

Agoraphobia and Panic Disorders, 206

Alcoholism, 213

Altered States of Consciousness, 220

Altruism, Cooperation, and Empathy, 228

Amnesia, Fugue, and Multiple Personality, 234

Analytical Psychology: Carl G. Jung, 240

Analytical Psychotherapy, 246

Animal Experimentation, 252

Anorexia Nervosa and Bulimia Nervosa, 259

Antisocial Personality, 265

Anxiety Disorders: Theoretical Explanations, 272

Aphasias, 279

Archetypes: Origins and Nature, 286

Archival Data, 293

Artificial Intelligence, 299

Attachment and Bonding in Infancy and Childhood, 307

Attention, 313

Attitude-Behavior Consistency, 320

Attitude Formation and Change, 326

Attraction Theories, 332

Attributional Biases, 338

Auditory System, The, 344

Autism, 350

Automaticity, 356

Autonomic Nervous System, The, 362

Aversion, Implosion, and Systematic Desensitization Therapies, 368

Avoidance Learning, 375

Bed-Wetting, 381

Behavioral Assessment and Personality Rating Scales, 387

Behavioral Family Therapy, 394

Behaviorism: An Overview, 401

Bilingualism: Acquisition, Storage, and Processing, 408

Biofeedback and Relaxation, 416

Bipolar Disorder, 422

Birth: Effects on Physical Development, 429

Birth Order and Personality, 436

Borderline, Histrionic, and Narcissistic Personalities, 441

Brain Injuries: Concussions, Contusions, and Strokes, 448

Brain Specialization, 455

Brain-Stem Structures, 461

Career and Personnel Testing, 467

Career Selection, Development, and Change, 474

Case-Study Methodologies, 481

Causal Attribution, 487

Central and Peripheral Nervous Systems, The, 494

Cerebral Cortex, The, 500

Child Abuse, 507

Circadian Rhythms, 514

Clinical Depression, 521

Clinical Interviewing, Testing, and Observation, 527

Codependent Personality, The, 534

Cognitive Ability: Gender Differences, 540

Cognitive Behavior Therapy, 546

Cognitive Development Theory: Piaget, 553

Cognitive Dissonance Theory, 560

Cognitive Maps, 566

Cognitive Psychology: An Overview, 572

Cognitive Social Learning: Walter Mischel, 580

Cognitive Therapy, 586

Collective Unconscious, The, 592

College Entrance Examinations, 598

Color Blindness, 606

Color Vision, 611

Community Psychology, 618

Complex Experimental Designs: Interactions, 625

Computer Models of Cognition, 631

Concept Formation, 637

Conditioning: Higher-Order, 643

Conditioning: Pavlovian versus Instrumental, 649

Consciousness, Functions of, 656

Consciousness, Levels of, 663

Consumer Psychology: Decisions, 669

Contact Hypothesis, The, 675

Conversion, Hypochondriasis, Somatization, and Somatoform Pain, 682

Cooperation, Competition, and Negotiation, 689

Cooperative Learning, 695

Coping: Social Support, 700

Coping Strategies: An Overview, 706

Coping with Cancer, 711

Couples Therapy, 718

Creativity: Assessing Special Talents, 726

Creativity and Intelligence, 731

Crowd Behavior, 737

Crowding, 744

Data Description: Descriptive Statistics, 751

Data Description: Inferential Statistics, 757

Death and Dying: Theoretical Perspectives, 763

Decision Making as a Cognitive Process, 769

Defense Reactions: Species-Specific, 775

Dementia, Alzheimer's Disease, and Parkinson's Disease, 783
Depression: Theoretical Explanations, 789
Depth Perception, 796
Development: Theoretical Issues, 804
Development of Emotion, 810
Developmental Methodologies, 817
Dissolution, 824
Dream Analysis, 830
Dreams, 836
Drive Theory, 843
Dyslexia, 849

Educational Psychology, 855
Ego Defense Mechanisms, 860
Ego Psychology: Erik Erikson, 867
Electroconvulsive Therapy, 874
Emotion: Cognitive and Physiological Interaction, 881
Emotion: Cultural Variations, 887
Emotion: Definition and Assessment, 893
Emotion, Functions of, 900
Emotion: Mind-Body Processes, 907
Emotion: Neurophysiology and Neuroanatomy, 914
Emotion and Attribution Theory, 921
Emotion and Health, 928
Emotion and Learning Theory, 934
Emotion and Stress, 941
Emotion in Primates, 947
Emotional Expression, 954
Encoding Strategies and Encoding Specificity, 960
Endocrine System, The, 966
Endorphins, 973
Environmental Psychology, 978
Escape Conditioning, 985
Ethology, 992
Existential Analysis and Therapy, 999
Experimental Bias, Sources of, 1006

Experimentation: Ethics and Subject Rights, 1013

Facial Feedback Theory of Emotion, The, 1019
Feminist Psychotherapy, 1025
Field Experimentation, 1031
Field Theory: Kurt Lewin, 1038
Forebrain Structures, 1043
Forgetting and Forgetfulness, 1049
Functionalism, 1055

Gender-Identity Formation, 1062
General Adaptation Syndrome, 1068
Generativity in Adulthood: Erikson, 1075
Gestalt Laws of Organization, 1082
Gestalt Therapy, 1088
Gonads, 1094
Grammar and Speech, 1100
Grandparenthood, 1107
Group Decision Making, 1114
Group Therapy, 1120
Groups: Nature and Function, 1125

Habituation and Sensitization, 1132
Health Psychology, 1139
Hearing: Loudness, Pitch, and Frequency, 1146
Hearing and Sound Waves, 1151
Hearing Loss, 1157
Helping: Bystander Intervention, 1163
Helping: Theoretical Perspectives, 1169
Hindbrain Structures, 1175
Homosexuality, 1182
Hormones and Behavior, 1189
Human Resource Training and Development, 1197
Humanism: An Overview, 1203
Humanistic Trait Models: Gordon Allport, 1210
Hunger: Biological Bases, 1217

Hunger: Psychological Bases, 1223
Hunger Regulation, 1229
Hyperactivity, 1235
Hypnosis, 1241
Hypothesis Development and
    Testing, 1248

Identity Crises: Erikson, 1255
Imprinting and Learning, 1262
Incentive Motivation, 1269
Individual Psychology: Alfred
    Adler, 1275
Industrial and Organizational
    Psychology, 1283
Infant Perceptual Systems, 1290
Inhibitory and Excitatory
    Impulses, 1296
Insomnia, 1303
Instinct Theory, 1309
Instrumental Conditioning:
    Acquisition and Extinction, 1315
Integrity: Erikson, 1321
Intelligence: Definition and
    Theoretical Models, 1328
Intelligence: Giftedness and
    Retardation, 1334
Intelligence Tests, 1341
Interest Inventories, 1349
Intergroup Relations, Theories of, 1356
Intimacy in Adulthood: Erikson, 1363

Jealousy, 1370
Juvenile Delinquency, 1375

Kinesthesis and Vestibular
    Sensitivity, 1381

Language: The Developmental
    Sequence, 1387
Language Acquisition Theories, 1394
Language and Cognition, 1401
Language in Primates, 1407

Law and Psychology, 1413
Leadership, 1419
Learned Helplessness, 1425
Learning: Concept, Expectancy, and
    Insight, 1431
Learning: Generalization and
    Discrimination, 1437
Learning Defined, 1443
Linguistic Relativity Theory, 1450
Linguistic Structure: Phonemes and
    Morphemes, 1457
Lobotomy, 1464
Logic and Reasoning, 1471
Long-Term Memory, 1479
Love, 1486

Madness: Historical Concepts, 1492
Meditation and Relaxation, 1499
Memory: Animal Research, 1505
Memory: Empirical Studies, 1511
Memory: Long-Term versus Short-
    Term, 1517
Memory: Physiology, 1523
Memory: Sensory, 1531
Memory, Theories of, 1537
Memory and Eyewitness
    Testimony, 1544
Memory and Schemata, 1549
Memory Enhancement, 1556
Memory Storage: Episodic versus
    Semantic, 1562
Mental Health Practitioners, 1569
Midlife Crises, 1575
Misbehavior and Learning, 1581
Modeling Therapies, 1588
Moral Development, 1594
Motion Perception, 1600
Motivation: Cognitive Theories, 1606
Motivation: Opponent Process
    Theory, 1611
Motivational Constructs, 1616
Motor Development, 1623

Music, Dance, and Theater
Therapy, 1629

Nearsightedness and
Farsightedness, 1634
Neural Anatomy and Cognition, 1640
Neural and Hormonal
Interaction, 1648
Neural Damage and Plasticity, 1655
Neurons, 1661
Neuropsychology, 1667
Neurotransmitters, 1673
Nonverbal Communication, 1681

Obesity, 1688
Observational Learning, 1694
Observational Methods in
Psychology, 1700
Obsessions and Compulsions, 1707
Operant Conditioning Therapies, 1714
Optimal Arousal Theory, 1721

Pain, 1727
Pain Management, 1734
Parenting Styles, 1740
Pattern Recognition as a Cognitive
Process, 1747
Pattern Vision, 1752
Pavlovian Conditioning: Acquisition,
Extinction, and Inhibition, 1757
Pavlovian Conditioning: Theoretical
Foundations, 1764
Perceptual Constancies, 1771
Person-Centered Therapy, 1777
Personal Constructs: George A.
Kelly, 1784
Personality: Psychophysiological
Measures, 1790
Personality Interviewing
Strategies, 1797
Personality Theory: Major Issues, 1804
Personology: Henry A. Murray, 1810

Phobias, 1816
Physical Development: Environmental
versus Genetic Determinants, 1823
Pituitary Gland, The, 1829
Play Therapy, 1835
Post-traumatic Stress, 1841
Prejudice, Effects of, 1848
Prejudice, Reduction of, 1855
Prenatal Physical Development, 1861
Preparedness and Learning, 1866
Problem-Solving Stages, 1873
Problem-Solving Strategies and
Obstacles, 1879
Projective Personality Traits, 1885
Psychoactive Drug Therapy, 1891
Psychoanalysis: Classical versus
Modern, 1898
Psychoanalytic Psychology: An
Overview, 1905
Psychoanalytic Psychology and
Personality: Sigmund Freud, 1912
Psycholinguistics, 1918
Psychological Diagnosis and
Classification: DSM-III-R, 1925
Psychological Experimentation:
Independent, Dependent, and
Control Variables, 1932
Psychology: Fields of
Specialization, 1939
Psychology Defined, 1945
Psychology of Women: Karen
Horney, 1950
Psychology of Women: Sigmund
Freud, 1956
Psychophysical Scaling, 1963
Psychosexual Development, 1969
Psychosomatic Disorders, 1975
Psychosurgery, 1983
Psychotherapeutic
Effectiveness, 1989
Psychotherapeutic Goals and
Techniques, 1996

Psychotherapy: Historical Approaches to Treatment, 2002
Psychotherapy with Children, 2009
Punishment, 2016

Quasi-Experimental Designs, 2024

Race and Intelligence, 2031
Racism, 2037
Radical Behaviorism: B. F. Skinner, 2045
Rational-Emotive Therapy, 2052
Reality Therapy, 2059
Reflexes, 2066
Reflexes in Newborns, 2072
Reinforcement Schedules, 2077
Reinforcers and Reinforcement, 2084
Religion and Psychology, 2090
Religiosity: Measurement, 2096
Reticular Formation, 2103
Retirement, 2109
Rule-Governed Behavior, 2115

Sampling, 2122
Schizophrenia: Background, Types, and Symptoms, 2129
Schizophrenia: High-Risk Children, 2135
Schizophrenia: Theoretical Explanations, 2141
Scientific Method in Psychology, The, 2148
Seasonal Affective Disorder, 2155
Self: Definition and Assessment, 2162
Self-Actualization, 2168
Self-Concept Origins, 2175
Self-Disclosure, 2182
Self-Esteem, 2188
Self-Perception Theory, 2193
Self-Presentation, 2200
Sensation and Perception Defined, 2207

Sensory Modalities and Stimuli, 2214
Separation, Divorce, and Family Life: Adult Issues, 2220
Separation, Divorce, and Family Life: Children's Issues, 2227
Sex Hormones and Motivation, 2234
Sexism, 2240
Sexual Behavior Patterns, 2246
Sexual Dysfunction, 2253
Sexual Variants and Paraphilias, 2259
Short-Term Memory, 2265
Signal Detection Theory, 2271
Sleep: Stages and Functions, 2277
Sleep Apnea Syndromes and Narcolepsy, 2284
Smell and Taste, 2290
Social Identity Theory, 2297
Social Learning: Albert Bandura, 2304
Social Perception: Others, 2311
Social Psychological Models: Erich Fromm, 2318
Social Psychological Models: Karen Horney, 2324
Social Schemata, 2329
Sound Localization, 2335
Speech Disorders, 2342
Speech Perception, 2348
Split-Brain Studies, 2355
Sport Psychology, 2363
S-R Theory: Miller and Dollard, 2369
Statistical Significance Tests, 2375
Strategic Family Therapy, 2382
Stress, Adaptation to, 2390
Stress: Behavioral and Psychological Responses, 2397
Stress: Cognitive Appraisals, 2404
Stress, The Concept of, 2411
Stress, Effects of, 2417
Stress: Physiological Responses, 2425
Stress, Theories of, 2432
Stress and Reappraisal, 2438

Stress and the Endocrine
    System, 2445
Stress and the Nervous System, 2452
Stress Prediction and Control, 2458
Stress-Related Diseases, 2464
Stressors, 2471
Structuralism, 2477
Stuttering, 2483
Substance Abuse: An Overview, 2489
Sudden Infant Death Syndrome, 2495
Suicide, 2501
Survey Research: Questionnaires and
    Interviews, 2507
Synaptic Transmission, 2514

Taste Aversion and Learning
    Theory, 2520
Teenage Suicide, 2527
Temperature, 2533
Testing: Historical Perspectives, 2540
Thirst, 2547
Thought: Inferential, 2552

Thought: Study and
    Measurement, 2558
Thought Structures, 2565
Thyroid Gland, The, 2571
Touch and Pressure, 2578
Transactional Analysis, 2584
Trust, Autonomy, Initiative, and
    Industry: Erikson, 2591
Type A Behavior Pattern, The, 2597

Violence and Sexuality in the Mass
    Media, 2603
Vision: Brightness and Contrast, 2610
Visual Development, 2616
Visual Illusions, 2622
Visual Neural Processing, 2629
Visual Spectrum, The, 2635
Visual System Anatomy, 2640

Within-Subject Experimental
    Designs, 2647
Work Motivation, 2654

CATEGORY LIST

BIOLOGICAL BASES OF BEHAVIOR

Endocrine System
The Adrenal Gland, 136
The Endocrine System, 966
Gonads, 1094
Hormones and Behavior, 1189
Neural and Hormonal Interaction, 1648
The Pituitary Gland, 1829
The Thyroid Gland, 2571

Nervous System
The Autonomic Nervous System, 362
Brain Injuries: Concussions, Contusions, and Strokes, 448
Brain Specialization, 455
Brain-Stem Structures, 461
The Central and Peripheral Nervous Systems, 494
The Cerebral Cortex, 500
Endorphins, 973
Forebrain Structures, 1043
Hindbrain Structures, 1175
Inhibitory and Excitatory Impulses, 1296
Neural Damage and Plasticity, 1655
Neurons, 1661
Neurotransmitters, 1673
Reflexes, 2066
Reticular Formation, 2103
Split-Brain Studies, 2355
Synaptic Transmission, 2514

COGNITION
Artificial Intelligence, 299
Computer Models of Cognition, 631
Language and Cognition, 1401
Neural Anatomy and Cognition, 1640

Cognitive Processes
Decision Making as a Cognitive Process, 769
Logic and Reasoning, 1471
Pattern Recognition as a Cognitive Process, 1747

Problem Solving
Problem-Solving Stages, 1873
Problem-Solving Strategies and Obstacles, 1879

Thought
Concept Formation, 637
Consumer Psychology: Decisions, 669
Thought: Inferential, 2552
Thought: Study and Measurement, 2558
Thought Structures, 2565

CONSCIOUSNESS
Altered States of Consciousness, 220
Attention, 313
Automaticity, 356
Functions of Consciousness, 656
Levels of Consciousness, 663
Dreams, 836
Hypnosis, 1241
Meditation and Relaxation, 1499

Sleep
Circadian Rhythms, 514
Insomnia, 1303
Sleep: Stages and Functions, 2277
Sleep Apnea Syndromes and Narcolepsy, 2284

DEVELOPMENTAL PSYCHOLOGY

Development: Theoretical Issues, 804
Developmental Methodologies, 817

Infancy and Childhood: Cognitive Development

Cognitive Ability: Gender Differences, 540
Cognitive Development Theory: Piaget, 553
Moral Development, 1594

Infancy and Childhood: Physical Development

Birth: Effects on Physical Development, 429
Infant Perceptual Systems, 1290
Motor Development, 1623
Physical Development: Environmental versus Genetic Determinants, 1823
Prenatal Physical Development, 1861
Reflexes in Newborns, 2072
Sudden Infant Death Syndrome, 2495

Infancy and Childhood: Social and Personality Development

Attachment and Bonding in Infancy and Childhood, 307
Birth Order and Personality, 436
Child Abuse, 507
Gender-Identity Formation, 1062
Parenting Styles, 1740
Separation, Divorce, and Family Life: Children's Issues, 2227
Trust, Autonomy, Initiative, and Industry: Erikson, 2591

Adolescence

Adolescence: Cognitive Skills, 118
Adolescence: Cross-Cultural Patterns, 124
Adolescence: Sexuality, 130
Identity Crises: Erikson, 1255
Juvenile Delinquency, 1375
Teenage Suicide, 2527

Adulthood

Career Selection, Development, and Change, 474
Generativity in Adulthood: Erikson, 1075
Intimacy in Adulthood: Erikson, 1363
Midlife Crises, 1575
Separation, Divorce, and Family Life: Adult Issues, 2220

Aging

Ageism, 156
Aging: Cognitive Changes, 180
Aging: Institutional Care, 186
Aging: Physical Changes, 192
Theories of Aging, 198
Death and Dying: Theoretical Perspectives, 763
Grandparenthood, 1107
Integrity: Erikson, 1321
Retirement, 2109

EMOTION

Development of Emotion, 810
Emotion: Cognitive and Physiological Interaction, 881
Emotion: Cultural Variations, 887
Emotion: Definition and Assessment, 893
Functions of Emotion, 900
Emotion: Mind-Body Processes, 907
Emotion: Neurophysiology and Neuroanatomy, 914
Emotion and Attribution Theory, 921
Emotion and Health, 928

Emotion and Learning Theory, 934
Emotion in Primates, 947
Emotional Expression, 954
The Facial Feedback Theory of
    Emotion, 1019

**INTELLIGENCE AND
    INTELLIGENCE TESTING**
General Issues in Intelligence
Creativity and Intelligence, 731
Intelligence: Definition and
    Theoretical Models, 1328
Intelligence: Giftedness and
    Retardation, 1334

Ability Tests
Ability Testing: Individual
    and Group, 1
College Entrance Examinations, 598
Creativity: Assessing Special
    Talents, 726
Intelligence Tests, 1341

Intelligence Assessment
Bias in Ability Tests, 7
Ability Tests: Design and
    Construction, 13
Ability Tests: Reliability, Validity, and
    Standardization, 21
Ability Tests: Uses and Misuses, 27
Race and Intelligence, 2031
Testing: Historical Perspectives,
    2540

LANGUAGE
Aphasias, 279
Bilingualism: Acquisition, Storage,
    and Processing, 408
Dyslexia, 849
Grammar and Speech, 1100
Language: The Developmental
    Sequence, 1387

Language Acquisition Theories, 1394
Language in Primates, 1407
Linguistic Relativity Theory, 1450
Linguistic Structure: Phonemes and
    Morphemes, 1457
Nonverbal Communication, 1681
Psycholinguistics, 1918
Speech Disorders, 2342

LEARNING
Educational Psychology, 855
Habituation and Sensitization,
    1132
Learning: Generalization and
    Discrimination, 1437
Learning Defined, 1443

Aversive Conditioning
Avoidance Learning, 375
Escape Conditioning, 985
Punishment, 2016

Biological Influences on Learning
Defense Reactions:
    Species-Specific, 775
Imprinting and Learning, 1262
Misbehavior and Learning, 1581
Preparedness and Learning, 1866
Taste Aversion and Learning
    Theory, 2520

Cognitive Learning
Cognitive Maps, 566
Learned Helplessness, 1425
Learning; Concept, Expectancy,
    and Insight, 1431
Observational Learning, 1694

Instrumental Conditioning
Instrumental Conditioning:
    Acquisition and Extinction,
    1315

Reinforcement Schedules, 2077
Reinforcers and Reinforcement, 2084
Rule-Governed Behavior, 2115

Pavlovian Conditioning
Conditioning: Higher-Order, 643
Conditioning: Pavlovian versus Instrumental, 649
Pavlovian Conditioning: Acquisition, Extinction, and Inhibition, 1757
Pavlovian Conditioning: Theoretical Foundations, 1764

MEMORY
Encoding Strategies and Encoding Specificity, 960
Forgetting and Forgetfulness, 1049
Long-Term Memory, 1479
Memory: Animal Research, 1505
Memory: Empirical Studies, 1511
Memory: Long-Term versus Short-Term, 1517
Memory: Physiology, 1523
Memory: Sensory, 1531
Theories of Memory, 1537
Memory and Eyewitness Testimony, 1544
Memory and Schemata, 1549
Memory Enhancement, 1556
Memory Storage: Episodic versus Semantic, 1562
Short-Term Memory, 2265

MOTIVATION
Motivational Constructs, 1616

Motivation Theory
Drive Theory, 843
Incentive Motivation, 1269
Instinct Theory, 1309

Motivation: Cognitive Theories, 1606
Motivation: Opponent Process Theory, 1611
Optimal Arousal Theory, 1721

Social Motives
Achievement Motivation, 96
The Affiliation Motive, 148
The Aggression Motive, 174
Human Resource Training and Development, 1197
Sport Psychology, 2363
Work Motivation, 2654

Physical Motives
Homosexuality, 1182
Hunger: Biological Bases, 1217
Hunger: Psychological Bases, 1223
Hunger Regulation, 1229
Obesity, 1688
Sex Hormones and Motivation, 2234
Sexual Behavior Patterns, 2246
Thirst, 2547

ORIGIN AND DEFINITION OF PSYCHOLOGY
Behaviorism: An Overview, 401
Cognitive Psychology: An Overview, 572
Ethology, 992
Functionalism, 1055
Humanism: An Overview, 1203
Neuropsychology, 1667
Psychoanalytic Psychology: An Overview, 1905
Psychology: Fields of Specialization, 1939
Psychology Defined, 1945
Structuralism, 2477

PERSONALITY

Personality Theory
Field Theory: Kurt Lewin, 1038
Personality Theory: Major Issues, 1804

Personality Assessment
Behavioral Assessment and
  Personality Rating Scales, 387
Career and Personnel Testing, 467
Interest Inventories, 1349
Personality: Psychophysiological
  Measures, 1790
Personality Interviewing
  Strategies, 1797
Projective Personality Traits, 1885

Behavioral and Cognitive Models
Cognitive Social Learning: Walter
  Mischel, 580
Personal Constructs: George A.
  Kelly, 1784
Radical Behaviorism: B. F. Skinner,
  2045
Social Learning: Albert
  Bandura, 2304
S-R Theory: Miller and Dollard, 2369

Classic Analytic Themes and Issues
Archetypes: Origins and Nature, 286
The Collective Unconscious, 592
Dream Analysis, 830
Ego Defense Mechanisms, 860
Psychology of Women: Karen
  Horney, 1950
Psychology of Women: Sigmund
  Freud, 1956
Psychosexual Development, 1969

Humanistic-Phenomenological Models
Existential Analysis and
  Therapy, 999
Humanistic Trait Models: Gordon
  Allport, 1210
Personology: Henry A. Murray,
  1810
Self-Actualization, 2168

Psychodynamic and Neoanalytic Models
Analytical Psychology: Carl G.
  Jung, 240
Ego Psychology: Erik Erikson, 867
Individual Psychology: Alfred
  Adler, 1275
Psychoanalytic Psychology and
  Personality: Sigmund Freud, 1912
Social Psychological Models: Erich
  Fromm, 2318
Social Psychological Models: Karen
  Horney, 2324

PSYCHOLOGICAL METHODOLOGIES

Descriptive Methodologies
Archival Data, 293
Case-Study Methodologies, 481
Data Description: Descriptive
  Statistics, 751
Data Description: Inferential
  Statistics, 757
Field Experimentation, 1031
Observational Methods in
  Psychology, 1700
Survey Research: Questionnaires and
  Interviews, 2507

Experimental Methodologies
Complex Experimental Designs:
  Interactions, 625
Quasi-Experimental Designs,
  2024
Within-Subject Experimental
  Designs, 2647

Methodological Issues
Animal Experimentation, 252
Sources of Experimental Bias, 1006
Experimentation: Ethics and Subject
  Rights, 1013
Hypothesis Development and
  Testing, 1248
Psychological Experimentation:
  Independent, Dependent, and
  Control Variables, 1932
Sampling, 2122
The Scientific Method in
  Psychology, 2148
Statistical Significance Tests, 2375

PSYCHOPATHOLOGY
Models of Abnormality
Abnormality: Behavioral Models, 33
Abnormality: Biomedical Models, 39
Abnormality: Cognitive Models, 46
Abnormality: Family Models, 53
Abnormality: Humanistic-Existential
  Models, 60
Abnormality: Legal Models, 67
Abnormality: Psychodynamic
  Models, 74
Abnormality: Sociocultural
  Models, 82
Abnormality Defined, 89
Madness: Historical
  Concepts, 1492

Anxiety Disorders
Agoraphobia and Panic Disorders, 206
Amnesia, Fugue, and Multiple
  Personality, 234
Anxiety Disorders: Theoretical
  Explanations, 272
Conversion, Hypochondriasis,
  Somatization, and Somatoform
  Pain, 682
Obsessions and Compulsions, 1707

Phobias, 1816
Post-traumatic Stress, 1841

Childhood and Adolescent
  Disorders
Anorexia Nervosa and Bulimia
  Nervosa, 259
Autism, 350
Bed-Wetting, 381
Hyperactivity, 1235
Stuttering, 2483

Depression
Bipolar Disorder, 422
Clinical Depression, 521
Depression: Theoretical
  Explanations, 789
Seasonal Affective Disorder,
  2155
Suicide, 2501

Organic Disorders
Dementia, Alzheimer's Disease, and
  Parkinson's Disease, 783
Psychosomatic Disorders, 1975

Personality Assessment
Clinical Interviewing, Testing, and
  Observation, 527
Psychological Diagnosis and
  Classification: DSM-III-R, 1925

Personality Disorders
Antisocial Personality, 265
Borderline, Histrionic, and Narcissistic
  Personalities, 441

Schizophrenias
Schizophrenia: Background, Types,
  and Symptoms, 2129
Schizophrenia: High-Risk
  Children, 2135

Schizophrenia: Theoretical
    Explanations, 2141

Sexual Disorders
Sexual Dysfunction, 2253
Sexual Variants and Paraphilias, 2259

Substance Abuse
Addictive Personality and
    Behaviors, 102
Alcoholism, 213
The Codependent Personality, 534
Substance Abuse: An Overview, 2489

PSYCHOTHERAPY
Mental Health Practitioners, 1569
Psychotherapy: Historical Approaches
    to Treatment, 2002

Behavioral Therapies
Aversion, Implosion, and Systematic
    Desensitization Therapies, 368
Cognitive Behavior Therapy, 546
Modeling Therapies, 1588
Operant Conditioning
    Therapies, 1714

Biological Treatments
Electroconvulsive Therapy, 874
Lobotomy, 1464
Psychoactive Drug Therapy, 1891
Psychosurgery, 1983

Cognitive Therapies
Cognitive Therapy, 586
Community Psychology, 618
Rational-Emotive Therapy, 2052
Reality Therapy, 2059
Transactional Analysis, 2584

Evaluating Psychotherapy
Psychotherapeutic Effectiveness, 1989

Psychotherapeutic Goals and
    Techniques, 1996

Group and Family Therapies
Behavioral Family Therapy, 394
Couples Therapy, 718
Group Therapy, 1120
Strategic Family Therapy, 2382

Humanistic Therapies
Gestalt Therapy, 1088
Person-Centered Therapy, 1777
Play Therapy, 1835

Psychodynamic Therapies
Adlerian Psychotherapy, 110
Analytical Psychotherapy, 246
Feminist Psychotherapy, 1025
Music, Dance, and Theater
    Therapy, 1629
Psychoanalysis: Classical versus
    Modern, 1898
Psychotherapy with Children, 2009

SENSATION AND PERCEPTION
General Constructs and Issues
Psychophysical Scaling, 1963
Sensation and Perception
    Defined, 2207
Sensory Modalities and Stimuli, 2214
Signal Detection Theory, 2271

Auditory, Chemical, Cutaneous,
    and Body Senses
The Auditory System, 344
Hearing: Loudness, Pitch, and
    Frequency, 1146
Hearing and Sound Waves, 1151
Hearing Loss, 1157
Kinesthesis and Vestibular
    Sensitivity, 1381
Pain, 1727

Smell and Taste, 2290
Sound Localization, 2335
Speech Perception, 2348
Temperature, 2533
Touch and Pressure, 2578

Vision
Color Blindness, 606
Color Vision, 611
Depth Perception, 796
Gestalt Laws of Organization, 1082
Motion Perception, 1600
Nearsightedness and
    Farsightedness, 1634
Pattern Vision, 1752
Perceptual Constancies, 1771
Vision: Brightness and Contrast, 2610
Visual Development, 2616
Visual Illusions, 2622
Visual Neural Processing, 2629
The Visual Spectrum, 2635
Visual System Anatomy, 2640

SOCIAL PSYCHOLOGY
Aggression
Aggression: Definitions and
    Theoretical Explanations, 162
Aggression: Reduction and
    Control, 169
Violence and Sexuality in the Mass
    Media, 2603

Attitudes and Behavior
Attitude-Behavior Consistency, 320
Attitude Formation and Change, 326
Cognitive Dissonance Theory, 560
Community Psychology, 618

Group Processes
Cooperation, Competition, and
    Negotiation, 689
Crowd Behavior, 737

Group Decision Making, 1114
Groups: Nature and Function, 1125
Leadership, 1419

Interpersonal Relations
Affiliation and Friendship, 142
Attraction Theories, 332
Dissolution, 824
Jealousy, 1370
Love, 1486
Self-Disclosure, 2182

Prejudice and Discrimination
The Contact Hypothesis, 675
Cooperative Learning, 695
Theories of Intergroup
    Relations, 1356
Effects of Prejudice, 1848
Reduction of Prejudice, 1855
Racism, 2037
Sexism, 2240
Social Identity Theory, 2297

Prosocial Behavior
Altruism, Cooperation, and
    Empathy, 228
Helping: Bystander Intervention, 1163
Helping: Theoretical Perspectives, 1169

Social Perception and Cognition
Attributional Biases, 338
Causal Attribution, 487
Industrial and Organizational
    Psychology, 1283
Law and Psychology, 1413
Religion and Psychology, 2090
Religiosity: Measurement, 2096
Self: Definition and Assessment, 2162
Self-Concept Origins, 2175
Self-Esteem, 2188
Self-Perception Theory, 2193
Self-Presentation, 2200

Social Perception: Others, 2311
Social Schemata, 2329

STRESS
Biology of Stress
Stress and the Endocrine System, 2445
Stress and the Nervous System, 2452

Coping
Biofeedback and Relaxation, 416
Coping: Social Support, 700
Coping Strategies: An Overview, 706
Coping with Cancer, 711
Pain Management, 1734
Adaptation to Stress, 2390
Stress and Reappraisal, 2438
Stress Prediction and Control,
    2458

Critical Issues in Stress
Crowding, 744
Emotion and Stress, 941
General Adaptation Syndrome, 1068
Stress: Behavioral and Psychological
    Responses, 2397
Stress: Cognitive Appraisals, 2404
The Concept of Stress, 2411
Effects of Stress, 2417
Stress: Physiological Responses, 2425
Theories of Stress, 2432
Stressors, 2471

Stress and Illness
Environmental Psychology, 978
Health Psychology, 1139
Stress-Related Diseases, 2464
The Type A Behavior Pattern, 2597